Lecture Notes in Computer Science 3255

Commenced Publication in 1973
Founding and Former Series Editors:
Gerhard Goos, Juris Hartmanis, and Jan van Leeuwen

András Benczúr   János Demetrovics
Georg Gottlob (Eds.)

Advances in Databases and Information Systems

8th East European Conference, ADBIS 2004
Budapest, Hungary, September 22-25, 2004
Proceedings

 Springer

Volume Editors

András Benczúr
Hungarian Academy of Sciences
Computer and Automation Institute, Informatics Laboratory
Lagymanyosi ut 11, 1111, Budapest, Hungary
E-mail: benczur@sztaki.hu

János Demetrovics
Hungarian Academy of Sciences
Computer and Automation Institute
Lagymanyosi ut 11, 1111 Budapest, Hungary
E-mail: demetrovics@sztaki.hu

Georg Gottlob
Technische Universität Wien, Institut für Informationssysteme
Favoritenstraße 9-11, 1040 Wien, Austria
E-mail: gottlob@dbai.tuwien.ac.at

Library of Congress Control Number: 2004112841

CR Subject Classification (1998): H.2, H.3, H.4, H.5, J.1

ISSN 0302-9743
ISBN 3-540-23243-5 Springer Berlin Heidelberg New York

Springer is a part of Springer Science+Business Media

springeronline.com

© Springer-Verlag Berlin Heidelberg 2004
Printed in Germany

Typesetting: Camera-ready by author, data conversion by PTP-Berlin, Protago-TeX-Production GmbH
Printed on acid-free paper   SPIN: 11320166   06/3142   5 4 3 2 1 0

Preface

This volume continues the series of proceedings of the annual ADBIS conferences in the field of advances in databases and information systems.

ADBIS, founded by the Moscow ACM SIGMOD Chapter, was extended into a regular East-European conference in 1996 to establish a forum for promoting interaction and collaboration between the database research communities of Eastern and Central Europe and the rest of the world, and thus the ADBIS conferences provide an international platform for the presentation of research on database theory, development of advanced DBMS technologies, and their advanced applications.

The fact that this year eight of the countries that have representatives in the ADBIS Steering Committee became member countries of the European Union gives a new perspective on the role and mission of the ADBIS community.

Following Dresden (Germany, 2003), Bratislava (Slovakia, 2002), Vilnius (Lithuania, 2001), Prague (Czech Republic, as a joint ADBIS-DASFAA conference in 2000), Maribor (Slovenia, 1999), Poznan (Poland, 1998), and the starting place St. Petersburg (Russia, 1997), and preceding Tallin (Estonia, 2005), the next venue, the "tour of Eastern and Central Europe" of ADBIS conferences arrived at Budapest (Hungary, 2004).

The series of East-European Conferences on Advances in Databases and Information Systems continues, with a growing interest that is demonstrated in the number of submitted contributions. This year the international Program Committee had an intensive load in evaluating the 130 submitted papers.

As a tradition since 1998, the best 25–30 contributions were selected to be published in the Springer LNCS series. This year's volume contains 27 submitted papers and one invited paper.

In response to the high activity in paper submission and to fulfil the main objective of the ADBIS conferences, the organizers decided to give more room for presentation, and accepted from the PC ranking the next 25 papers for presentation. Thanks to the support from one of the organizing institutions, the Computer and Automation Research Institute of the Hungarian Academy of Sciences, these contributions will also be published, in a local volume of the proceedings in the series of publications of CARI.

Many individuals and institutions supported the organization of this conference and made this year's publication possible. Our special thanks go first to the authors and invited speaker for their outstanding and strenuous work and contributions. Also, the work of the Program Committee members who accepted the unexpectedly heavy load in reviewing a large number of contributions so that we were able to meet the deadline is gratefully acknowledged.

We received important financial support for the publication of the proceedings from the Faculty of Informatics of the Eötvös Loránd University.

Finally, we should express our thanks to Springer for supporting the publication of the proceedings in their LNCS series.

We do hope that the papers included in the present publication serve as a useful tool for becoming more familiar with recent research results in the field of databases and information systems.

July 2004

András Benczúr
János Demetrovics
Georg Gottlob

Organizing Committee

The 8th East-European Conference on Advances of Databases and Information Systems (ADBIS) was organized by the members of the Department of Information Systems of the Eötvös Loránd University, Budapest and of the Informatics Laboratory and Conference Department of the Computer and Automation Research Institute of the Hungarian Academy of Sciences, in cooperation with the Moscow ACM SIGMOD Chapter.

General Chair

András Benczúr, Head of the Department of Information Systems, Eötvös Loránd University, Budapest

General Co-chair

Georg Gottlob, Vienna University of Technology (TU Wien), Vienna

Local Program Committee Co-chair

János Demetrovics, Computer and Automation Research Institute of the Hungarian Academy of Sciences

Program Committee Chair

András Benczúr, Head of the Department of Information Systems, Eötvös Loránd University, Budapest

Program Committee Co-chairs

Georg Gottlob, Vienna University of Technology (TU Wien), Vienna
János Demetrovics, Computer and Automation Research Institute of the Hungarian Academy of Sciences

Program Committee

Albertas Caplinskas	Heinz Schweppe	Julius Stuller
Béla Uhrin	Hele-Mai Haav	Kjetil Norvag
Bogdan Czejdo	Jacek Plodzien	Klaus Meyer-Wegener
Boris Novikov	Jaroslav Pokorny	Leonid Kalinichenko
Gunter Saake	Johann Eder	Leopoldo Bertossi

Mihhail Matskin

Mikhail Kogalovsky

Nikolay Nikitchenko

Oscar Pastor

Peri Loucopoulos

Rainer Manthey

Remigijus Gustas

Robert Wrembel

Silvio Salza

Theo Härder

Tomas Hruska

Toni Urpí

Vladimir Zadorozhny

Yannis Manolopoulos

Vu Duc Thi

Peter Spyns

Luciano Baresi

Elyar Gasanov

Nghia Vu

V.B. Kudryavtsev

Pavol Navrat

Christelle Vangenot

Torben Bach Pedersen

Local Organizing Committee

Chairman: Gusztáv Hencsey (Computer and Automation Research Institute, Budapest, Hungary)

Secretary: Magdolna Zsivnovszki (Computer and Automation Research Institute, Budapest)

Tibor Márkus, Attila Kiss, Zsolt Hernáth, Zoltán Vinczellér, Balázs Kósa, András Molnár (Eötvös Loránd University, Budapest)

András Lukács, Béla Uhrin, Károly Móczár (Computer and Automation Research Institute, Budapest)

ADBIS Steering Committee Chair

Leonid Kalinichenko, Russian Academy of Sciences

ADBIS Steering Committee

András Benczúr (Hungary)

Radu Bercaru (Romania)

Albertas Caplinskas (Lithuania)

Johann Eder (Austria)

Janis Eiduks (Latvia)

Hele-Mai Haav (Estonia)

Mirjana Ivanovic (Yugoslavia)

Mikhail Kogalovsky (Russia)

Yannis Manolopoulos (Greece)

Rainer Manthey (Germany)

Tadeusz Morzy (Poland)

Pavol Navrat (Slovakia)

Boris Novikov (Russia)

Jaroslav Pokorny (Czech Republic)

Boris Rachev (Bulgaria)

Anatoly Stogny (Ukraine)

Bernhard Thalheim (Germany)

Tatjana Welzer (Slovenia)

Viacheslav Wolfengagen (Russia)

Sponsoring Institutions

Faculty of Informatics of the Eötvös Loránd University

Table of Contents

Query Processing and Data Streams

Spatial Databases

Agents and Mobile Systems

Quantifier-Elimination for the First-Order Theory of Boolean Algebras with Linear Cardinality Constraints[*]

Peter Revesz

Department of Computer Science and Engineering
University of Nebraska-Lincoln, Lincoln, NE 68588, USA
revesz@cse.unl.edu

Abstract. We present for the first-order theory of atomic Boolean algebras of sets with linear cardinality constraints a quantifier elimination algorithm. In the case of atomic Boolean algebras of sets, this is a new generalization of Boole's well-known variable elimination method for conjunctions of Boolean equality constraints. We also explain the connection of this new logical result with the evaluation of relational calculus queries on constraint databases that contain Boolean linear cardinality constraints.

1 Introduction

Constraint relations, usually in the form of semi-algebraic or semi-linear sets, provide a natural description of data in many problems. What programming language could be designed to incorporate such constraint relations? Jaffar and Lassez [27] proposed in a landmark paper *constraint logic programming*, with the idea of extending Prolog, and its usual top-down evaluation style, with constraint solving (which replaces unification in Prolog). That is, in each rule application after the substitution of subgoals by constraint tuples, the evaluation needs to test the satisfiability of the constraints, and proceed forward or backtrack according to the result.

As an alternative way of incorporating constraint relations, in a database framework, Kanellakis, Kuper, and Revesz [29,30] proposed *constraint query languages* as an extension of relational calculus with the basic insight that the evaluation of relational calculus queries on X-type constraint relations reduces to a quantifier elimination [15,16] in the first-order theory of X.[1] As an example from [29,30], if the constraint relations are semi-algebraic relations, then

---

[*] This work was supported in part by USA National Science Foundation grant EIA-0091530.

[1] They also considered various bottom-up methods of evaluating Datalog queries and the computational complexity and expressive power of constraint queries. Since relational calculus is closely tied with practical query languages like SQL, it has captured the most attention in the database area.

A. Benczúr, J. Demetrovics, G. Gottlob (Eds.): ADBIS 2004, LNCS 3255, pp. 1–21, 2004.

the quantifier elimination for real closed fields [2,3,12,13,40,54] can be used to evaluate queries.

There are advantages and disadvantages of both styles of program/query evaluations. Constraint logic programs have the advantage that their implementation can be based on only constraint satisfiability testing, which is usually easier and faster than quantifier elimination required by constraint relational calculus. On the other hand, the termination of constraint logic programs is not guaranteed, except in cases with a limited expressive power. For example, for negation-free Datalog queries with integer (gap)-order constraints the termination of both the tuple-recognition problem [14] and the least fixed point query evaluation [41, 42] can be guaranteed. When either negation or addition constraints are also allowed, then termination cannot be guaranteed. In contrast, the evaluation of constraint relational calculus queries have a guaranteed termination, provided there is a suitable effective quantifier elimination method.

While many other comparisons can be made (see the surveys [28,43] and the books [31,33,47]), these seem to be the most important. Their importance becomes clear when we consider the expected users. Professional programmers can write any software in any programming language and everything could be neatly hidden (usually under some kind of options menu) from the users. In contrast, database systems provide for the users *not ready-made programs but a easy-to-use high-level programming language*, in which they can write their own simple programs. It is unthinkable that this programming language not terminate, and, in fact, run efficiently. Therefore constraint database research focused on the efficient evaluation of simple non-recursive query languages.[2]

The constraint database field made initially a rapid progress by taking off-the-shelf some quantifier elimination methods. Semi-linear sets as constraint relations are allowed in several prototype constraint database systems [8,21,24,25, 48,49] that use Fourier-Motzkin quantifier elimination for linear inequality constraints [18]. The latest version of the DISCO system [9,50] implements Boolean equality constraints using Boole's existential quantifier elimination method for conjunctions of Boolean equality constraints.

Relational algebra queries were considered in [20,42,46]. As in relational databases, the algebraic operators are essential for the efficient evaluation of queries. In fact, in the above systems logical expressions in the form of relational calculus, SQL, and Datalog rules are translated into relational algebra.

There were also deep and interesting questions about the relative expressive power and computational complexity of relational versus constraint query languages. Some results in this area include [4,23,37,45] and a nice survey of these can be found in Chapters 3 and 4 of [31].

---

[2] Of course, many database-based products also provide menus to the users. However, the users of database-based products are only indirect users of database systems. The direct users of database systems are application developers, who routinely embed SQL expressions into their programs. Thanks to today's database systems, they need to worry less about termination, efficiency, and many other issues than yesterday's programmers needed while developing software products.

After these initial successes, it became clear that further progress may be possible only by extending the quantifier elimination methods. Hence researchers who happily got their hands dirty doing implementations found themselves back at the mathematical drawing table.

The limitations of quantifier elimination seemed to be most poignant for Boolean algebras. It turns out that for conjunctions of Boolean equality *and inequality* constraints (which seems to require just a slight extension of Boole's method) no quantifier elimination is possible. Let us see an example, phrased as a lemma.

Lemma 1. *There is no quantifier-free formula of Boolean equality and inequality constraints that is equivalent in every Boolean algebra to the following formula:*

$$\exists d \ (d \sqcap g \neq \perp) \wedge (\overline{d} \sqcap g \neq \perp)$$

where d and g are variables and $\perp$ is the zero element of the Boolean algebra.   □

Consider the Boolean algebra of sets, with the one element being the names of all persons, the zero element being the empty set, the domain being the powerset (set of all subset of the one element).

In the formula variable d may be the set of students who took a database systems class, variable g may be the set of students who graduate this semester. Then the formula expresses the statement that "some graduating student took a database systems class, and some graduating student did not take a database systems class." This formula implies that g has at least two elements, that is, the cardinality of g is at least two, denoted as:

$$|g| \geq 2$$

But this fact can not be expressed by any quantifier-free formula with Boolean equality and inequality constraints and g as the only variable.

Lemma 1 implies that there is no general quantifier elimination method for formulas of Boolean equality and inequality constraints. This negative result was noted by several researchers, who then advocated approximations. For example, Helm et al. [26] approximate the result by a formula of Boolean equality and inequality constraints. Can we do better than just an approximation?

The only hopeful development in the quantifier elimination area was by Marriott and Odersky [32] who showed that formulas with equality and inequality constraints admit quantifier elimination for the special case of *atomless* Boolean algebras. However, many Boolean algebras are not atomless but atomic. How can we deal with those Boolean algebras? Could any subset of atomic Boolean algebras also admit quantifier elimination? In this paper we show that the atomic Boolean algebras of sets, i.e., Boolean algebras where the Boolean algebra operators are interpreted as the usual set operators of union, intersection and complement with respect to the one element, also admit quantifier elimination, in spite of the pessimistic looking result of Lemma 1.

Let us take a closer look at the Lemma. Surprisingly, the condition $|g| \geq 2$ is not only necessary, but it is also sufficient. That is, for any Boolean algebra of sets if G is any set with at least two elements, then we can find a set D such that the above formula holds. Therefore, $|g| \geq 2$ is exactly the quantifier-free formula that we would like to have as a result of the quantifier elimination. However, quantifier elimination techniques are normally required to give back equivalent quantifier-free formulas with the same type of constraints as the input. This condition is commonly called being *closed* under the set of constraints. This raises the interesting question of what happens if we allow cardinality constraints in our formulas.

While cardinality constraints on sets are considered by many authors, and interesting algorithms are developed for testing the satisfiability of a conjunction of cardinality constraints, there were, to our knowledge, no algorithms given for quantifier elimination for atomic Boolean algebras of sets with cardinality constraints.

Calvanese and Lenzerini [11,10] study cardinality constraints that occur in ER-diagrams and ISA hierarchies. They give a method to test the satisfiability of a schema. This is a special case of cardinality constraints, because the ER-diagrams do not contain inequality constraints.

Ohlbach and Koehler [35,36] consider a simple description logic with cardinality constraints. They give methods to test subsumption and satisfiability of their formulas, but they do not consider quantifier elimination.

Seipel and Geske [51] use constraint logic programming to solve conjunctions of cardinality constraints. Their set of constraint logic programming [27] rules is sound but incomplete.

Surprisingly, in this paper, we show that the augmented formulas, called *Boolean linear cardinality constraint formulas*, admit quantifier elimination. It is surprising that by adding to the set of atomic constraints, the problem of quantifier elimination becomes easier, not harder. Indeed, the end result, which is our quantifier elimination method described in this paper, may strike the reader as simple. But the finding of the trick of adding cardinality constraints for the sake of performing quantifier elimination is not obvious as shown by the following history summarized in Figure 1. In the figure the arrows point from less to more expressive Boolean constraint theories, but the labels on them indicate that the Boolean algebra needs to be of a certain type. Let's describe Figure 1 in some detail (please see Section 2 for definitions of unfamiliar terms).

Precedence between variables: A naive elimination of variables from a set of Boolean precedence constraints between variables or constants (in the case of algebras of sets set containment constraints between sets) occurs in syllogistic reasoning. Namely, the syllogistic rule *if all x are y, and all y are z, then all x are z* yields a simple elimination of the y variable. Such syllogisms were described already by Aristotle and developed further in medieval times and can be used as the basis of eliminating variables. Srivastava, Ramakrishnan, and Revesz [52] gave an existential quantifier elimination method for a special subset of the Boolean algebra of sets. They considered existentially quantified formulas with

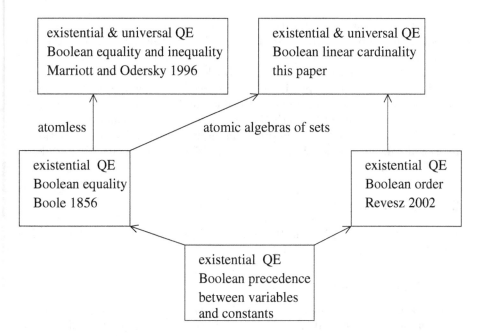

Fig. 1. Quantifier elimination methods for Boolean theories.

the quantifier-free part being only a conjunction of atomic constraints of the form $v \subseteq w$, where v and w are constants or variables ranging over the elements of a Boolean algebra of sets. Gervet [19] independently derived a similar method about the same time. This shows that the problem of quantifier elimination for sets arises naturally in different contexts.

Boolean equality: The quantifier elimination procedure for Boolean formulas with equality constraints was given by George Boole in 1856. His method allows the elimination of only existentially quantified variables.

Boolean order: Revesz [44,47] shows that Boolean order constraints allow existential quantifier elimination. Boolean order constraints (see Section 2.2) are equality constraints of the form $x \sqcap t'_{mon} = \bot$ and inequality constraints of the form $t_{mon} \neq \bot$ where x is a variable and t is a *monotone Boolean term*, that is, a term that contains only the $\sqcap$ and $\sqcup$ operators. In Boolean algebras of sets, the first of these constraints can be written as $t_{mon} \supseteq x$. This is clearly a generalization of precedence constraints between variables. However, it is incomparable with Boolean equalities. This theory contains some inequality constraints (which cannot be expressed by equality constraints), namely when the left hand side is a monotone term, but it cannot express all kinds of equality constraints, but only those that have the form $t'_{mon} \wedge x = \bot$.

Boolean equality and inequality: Marriott and Odersky [32] show that atomless Boolean algebras admit both existential and universal quantifier elimination. Clearly, their method is a generalization of Boole's method in the case of atomless Boolean algebras.

Boolean linear cardinality: The quantifier elimination for this is introduced in this paper. In the case of atomic Boolean algebras of sets, the new linear cardinality constraints quantifier elimination is another generalization of the quantifier elimination considered by Boole as shown by Lemma 3.

The outline of this paper is as follows. Section 2 gives some basic definitions regarding Boolean algebras, constraints, and theories. Section 3 describes a new quantifier elimination method for conjunctions of Boolean cardinality constraints. Section 4 uses the quantifier elimination method for the evaluation of relational calculus queries. Finally, Section 5 gives some conclusions and directions for further research.

2   Basic Definitions

We define Boolean algebras in Section 2.1, Boolean constraints in Section 2.2, and Boolean theories in Section 2.3.

2.1   Boolean Algebras

Definition 1. *A* Boolean algebra *B is a tuple $\langle \delta, \sqcap, \sqcup,', \perp, \top \rangle$, where δ is a non-empty set called the* domain; *$\sqcap$, $\sqcup$ are binary functions from $\delta \times \delta$ to δ;' is a unary function from δ to δ; and $\perp$, $\top$ are two specific elements of δ (called the* zero *element and the* one *element, respectively) such that for any elements x, y, and z in δ the following axioms hold:*

$$x \sqcup y = y \sqcup x \qquad\qquad x \sqcap y = y \sqcap x$$
$$x \sqcup (y \sqcap z) = (x \sqcup y) \sqcap (x \sqcup z) \quad x \sqcap (y \sqcup z) = (x \sqcap y) \sqcup (x \sqcap z)$$
$$x \sqcup x' = \top \qquad\qquad\qquad x \sqcap x' = \perp$$
$$x \sqcup \perp = x \qquad\qquad\qquad x \sqcap \top = x$$
$$\perp \neq \top$$

For Boolean algebras we define the *precedence* relation, denoted as $\sqsupseteq$, by the following identity:

$$x \sqsupseteq y \text{ means } x' \wedge y = \perp$$

We also write the above as $y \sqsubseteq x$ and say that y precedes x.

The above gives a formal definition of a Boolean algebra. It can be considered its syntax. The semantics of a Boolean algebra is given through *interpretations* for the elements of its structure. Without going into deep details about the numerous possible interpretations, we give one common interpretation of the domain and operators.

Definition 2. *A* Boolean algebra of sets *is any Boolean algebra, where:*
δ is a set of sets,
$\sqcup$ is interpreted as set union, denoted as $\cup$,
$\sqcap$ is interpreted as set intersection, denoted as $\cap$,
' is interpreted as set complement with respect to $\top$, denoted as $^-$, and
$\sqsubseteq$ (or $\sqsupseteq$) is interpreted as set containment, denoted as $\subseteq$ (or $\supseteq$).

Note: We call two Boolean algebras *isomorphic* if there is between them a bijection which preserves their respective Boolean operations. By Stone's representation theorem, any Boolean algebra is isomorphic to a Boolean algebra of sets [53]. Hence restricting our attention in this paper to Boolean algebras of sets is without any significant loss of generality.

An *atom* of a Boolean algebra is an element $x \neq \perp$ such that there is no other element $y \neq \perp$ with $y \sqsubseteq x$. It can happen that there are no atoms at all in a Boolean algebra. In that case, we call the Boolean algebra *atomless*; otherwise we call it *atomic*.

Let $\mathcal{N}$ denote the set of non-negative integer, $\mathcal{Z}$ denote the set of integer, and $\mathcal{Q}$ denote the set of rational numbers.

Example 1.

$$B_Z = \langle \mathcal{P}owerset(\mathcal{Z}), \cap, \cup, ^-, \emptyset, \mathcal{Z} \rangle$$

is a Boolean algebra of sets. In this algebra for each $i \in \mathcal{Z}$ the singleton set $\{i\}$ is an atom. This algebra is atomic.   □

Example 2. Let H be the set of all finite unions of half-open intervals of the form $[a, b)$ over the rational numbers, where $[a, b)$ means all rational numbers that are greater than or equal to a and less than b, where a is a rational number or $-\infty$ and b is a rational number. Then:

$$B_H = \langle H, \cap, \cup, ^-, \emptyset, \mathcal{Q} \rangle$$

is another Boolean algebra of sets. This algebra is atomless.   □

2.2   Boolean Constraints

In the following we consider only atomic Boolean algebras of sets with either a finite or a countably infinite number of atoms. For example, the Boolean algebra B_Z has a countably infinite number of atoms. We also assume that we can take the union or the intersection of an infinite number of elements of the Boolean algebra, i.e., our Boolean algebras are *complete*.

Cardinality can be defined as follows.

Definition 3. *Let x be any element of an atomic Boolean algebra of sets with a finite or countably infinite number of atoms. If x can be written as the finite union of $n \in \mathcal{N}$ number of distinct atoms, then the cardinality of x, denoted $|x|$, is n. Otherwise the cardinality of x is infinite, which is denoted as $+\infty$.*

The following lemma shows that the cardinality is a well-defined function from elements of an atomic Boolean algebra to $\mathcal{N} \cup \{+\infty\}$.

Lemma 2. *Let x be any element of an atomic Boolean algebra of sets with a finite or countably infinite number of atoms. Then x can be written as the union of some $n \in \mathcal{N}$ or $+\infty$ number of distinct atoms in the Boolean algebra. Moreover, there is no other set of atoms whose union is equivalent to x.*   □

For example, in the Boolean algebra B_Z we can write $\{1,2\}$ as $\{1\} \cup \{2\}$ or as $\{2\} \cup \{1\}$. In either way, we use the same two distinct atoms, i.e., $\{1\}$ and $\{2\}$. It follows from Lemma 2 that it is enough to allow only atomic constant symbols in *Boolean terms* and *Boolean constraints*, which we define as follows.

Definition 4. Let $B = \langle \delta, \cap, \cup, ^-, \perp, \top \rangle$ be an atomic Boolean algebra of sets. A *Boolean term* over B is an expression built from variables ranging over δ, atomic constants denoting particular atoms of B, $\perp$ denoting the zero element, $\top$ denoting the one element, and the operators for intersection, union, and complement.

A Boolean term is *monotone* if it is built without the use of the complement operator.

Definition 5. Boolean constraints have the form:

Equality :	$t = \perp$
Inequality :	$t \neq \perp$
Order :	$t_{mon} \neq \perp$ or $t_{mon} \sqsupseteq x$
Linear Cardinality :	$c_1\|t_1\| + \ldots + c_k\|t_k\| \; \theta \; b$

where t and each t_i for $1 \leq i \leq k$ is a Boolean term, t_{mon} is a monotone Boolean term, x is a Boolean variable, each c_i for $1 \leq i \leq k$ and b is an integer constant and θ is:

$=$ for the equality relation,
$\geq$ for the greater than or equal comparison operator,
$\leq$ for the less than or equal comparison operator, or
$\equiv_n$ for the congruence relation modulus some positive integer constant n.

2.3 Boolean Theories

A *formula* of Boolean algebras of sets is a formula that is built in the usual way from the existential quantifier $\exists$, the universal quantifier $\forall$, the logical connectives $\wedge$ for *and* $\vee$ for *or*, the apostrophe $'$ for *negation*, and one of the above types of Boolean algebra constraints.

A solution or *model* of a Boolean algebra constraint (or formula) is an assignment of the (free) variables by elements of the Boolean algebra such that the constraint (or formula) is satisfied. A constraint (or formula) is *true* if every possible assignment is a solution.

Example 3. Consider the Boolean algebra B_Z of Example 1. Then the Boolean linear cardinality constraint:

$$3|x \cap y| - 2|z| = 4$$

has many solutions. For example $x = \{3,6,9\}$ and $y = \{3,4,5,6\}$ and $z = \{1\}$ is a solution. The Boolean linear cardinality constraint:

$$|x \cup \{1\} \cup \{2\}| \geq 2$$

is true, because every assignment to x is a solution.   □

Example 4. Suppose that we know the following facts about a company:

1. The number of salespersons is a multiple of 6.
2. The number of engineers is a multiple of 9.
3. There are seven employees who are both salespersons and engineers but not managers.
4. There are twice as many managers who are salespersons than managers who are engineers.
5. Each manager is either a salesperson or an engineer but not both.

Using variables x for managers, y for salespersons, and z for engineers, we can express the above using the following Boolean cardinality formula S:

$$|y| \equiv_6 0 \, \wedge$$
$$|z| \equiv_9 0 \, \wedge$$
$$|\overline{x} \cap y \cap z| \; = \; 7 \, \wedge$$
$$|x \cap y| - 2|x \cap z| \; = \; 0 \, \wedge$$
$$|x \cap y \cap z| + |x \cap \overline{y} \cap \overline{z}| \; = \; 0$$

□

Example 5. Suppose that we know the following additional fact about the company in Example 4:

6. Person a is both a manager and an engineer but not a salesperson.

Here a is a constant symbol that denotes a particular atom of the Boolean algebra. We can express this by the following Boolean constraint:

$$|x \cap \overline{y} \cap z \cap a| = 1$$

□

In any given Boolean algebra two formulas are *equivalent* if they have the same set of models. The purpose of *quantifier elimination* is to rewrite a given formula with quantifiers into an equivalent quantifier-free formula [16]. A quantifier elimination method is *closed* or has a *closed-form* if the type of constraints in the formula with quantifiers and the quantifier-free formula are the same. (It is sometimes possible to eliminate quantifiers at the expense of introducing more powerful constraints, but then the quantifier elimination will not be closed-form.)

In arithmetic theories quantifier elimination is a well-studied problem. A well-known theorem due to Presburger ([38] and improvements in [6,7,17,55,56]) is that a closed-form quantifier elimination is possible for formulas with linear equations (including congruence equations modulo some fixed set of integers). We will use this powerful theorem in this paper.

The following lemma shows in the case of atomic Boolean algebras of sets a simple translation from formulas with only equality and inequality constraints into formulas with only linear cardinality constraints.

Lemma 3. *In any atomic Boolean algebra of sets, for every term t we have the following:*

$$t = \bot \quad \text{if and only if} \quad |t| = 0$$
$$t \neq \bot \quad \text{if and only if} \quad |t| \geq 1$$

Moreover, using the above identities, any formula with only equality and inequality constraints can be written as a formula with only linear cardinality constraints. □

Finally, we introduce some useful technical definitions related to Boolean theories and formulas.

Let F be a formula that contains the variable and atomic constant symbols $z_1, \ldots, z_n$. Then the *minterms* of F, denoted $Minterm(F)$, are the set of expressions of the form $\zeta_1 \sqcap \ldots \sqcap \zeta_n$ where each ζ_i is either z_i or $\overline{z_i}$, that is, each minterm must contain each variable and atomic constant symbol either positively or negatively. Note that there are exactly 2^n minterms of F. We can order the minterms in a lexicographic order assuming that positive literals precede negative literals.

Example 6. Suppose that we use only the following variables and no constant symbols in a formula: x, y, z. Then we can form from these variables the following eight minterms in order:

$$x \cap y \cap z, \quad x \cap y \cap \overline{z}, \quad x \cap \overline{y} \cap z, \quad x \cap \overline{y} \cap \overline{z},$$
$$\overline{x} \cap y \cap z, \quad \overline{x} \cap y \cap \overline{z}, \quad \overline{x} \cap \overline{y} \cap z, \quad \overline{x} \cap \overline{y} \cap \overline{z}$$

If we also use the atomic constant symbol a, then we can form the following minterms:

$$x \cap y \cap z \cap a, \quad x \cap y \cap z \cap \overline{a}, \quad x \cap y \cap \overline{z} \cap a, \quad x \cap y \cap \overline{z} \cap \overline{a},$$
$$x \cap \overline{y} \cap z \cap a, \quad x \cap \overline{y} \cap z \cap \overline{a}, \quad x \cap \overline{y} \cap \overline{z} \cap a, \quad x \cap \overline{y} \cap \overline{z} \cap \overline{a},$$
$$\overline{x} \cap y \cap z \cap a, \quad \overline{x} \cap y \cap z \cap \overline{a}, \quad \overline{x} \cap y \cap \overline{z} \cap a, \quad \overline{x} \cap y \cap \overline{z} \cap \overline{a},$$
$$\overline{x} \cap \overline{y} \cap z \cap a, \quad \overline{x} \cap \overline{y} \cap z \cap \overline{a}, \quad \overline{x} \cap \overline{y} \cap \overline{z} \cap a, \quad \overline{x} \cap \overline{y} \cap \overline{z} \cap \overline{a}$$

□

Note that any minterm that contains two or more atoms positively is equivalent to $\bot$. This allows some simplifications in certain cases.

Each Boolean cardinality constraint with n variables and atomic constants can be put into the *normal form*:

$$c_1 |m_1| + \ldots + c_{2^n} |m_{2^n}| \ \theta \ b \tag{1}$$

where b and each c_i is an integer constant and each m_i is a minterm of the Boolean algebra for $1 \leq i \leq 2^n$, and θ is as in Definition 5.

Example 7. We rewrite S of Example 4 into the following normal form (omitting minterms with zero coefficients and the $\wedge$ symbol at the end of lines):

$$|x \cap y \cap z| + |x \cap y \cap \bar{z}| + |\bar{x} \cap y \cap z| + |\bar{x} \cap y \cap \bar{z}| \equiv_6 0$$
$$|x \cap y \cap z| + |x \cap \bar{y} \cap z| + |\bar{x} \cap y \cap z| + |\bar{x} \cap \bar{y} \cap z| \equiv_9 0$$
$$|x \cap y \cap z| + |\bar{x} \cap y \cap z| \qquad\qquad = 7$$
$$|x \cap y \cap z| - |x \cap y \cap \bar{z}| + 2|x \cap \bar{y} \cap z| \qquad = 0$$
$$|x \cap y \cap z| + |x \cap \bar{y} \cap \bar{z}| \qquad\qquad = 0$$

The constraint in Example 5 is already in normal form.

3 Quantifier Elimination Method

We give below a quantifier elimination algorithm for Boolean linear cardinality constraint formulas in atomic Boolean algebras of sets.

Theorem 1. [constant-free case] *Existentially quantified variables can be eliminated from Boolean linear cardinality constraint formulas. The quantifier elimination is closed, that is, yields a quantifier-free Boolean linear cardinality constraint formula.*   □

Example 8. Let S be the Boolean cardinality formula in Example 4. A quantifier elimination problem would be to find a quantifier-free formula that is logically equivalent to the following:

$$\exists x \, S$$

First we put S into a normal form as shown in Example 7. Then let S^* be the conjunction of the normal form and the following:

$$|y \cap z| - |x \cap y \cap z| - |\bar{x} \cap y \cap z| = 0$$
$$|y \cap \bar{z}| - |x \cap y \cap \bar{z}| - |\bar{x} \cap y \cap \bar{z}| = 0$$
$$|\bar{y} \cap z| - |x \cap \bar{y} \cap z| - |\bar{x} \cap \bar{y} \cap z| = 0$$
$$|\bar{y} \cap \bar{z}| - |x \cap \bar{y} \cap \bar{z}| - |\bar{x} \cap \bar{y} \cap \bar{z}| = 0$$

Second, we consider each expression that is the cardinality of a minterm (over x, y, z or over y, z) as an integer variable. Then by integer linear constraint variable elimination we get:

$$|y \cap z| + |y \cap \bar{z}| \equiv_6 0$$
$$|y \cap z| + |\bar{y} \cap z| \equiv_9 0$$
$$|y \cap z| \qquad\quad = 7$$

By Theorem 1, the above is equivalent to $\exists x \, S$. For instance, the following is one solution for the above:

$$|y \cap z| = 7$$
$$|y \cap \bar{z}| = 5$$
$$|\bar{y} \cap z| = 2$$
$$|\bar{y} \cap \bar{z}| = 0$$

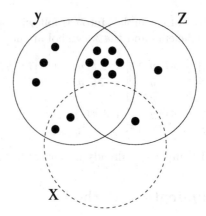

Fig. 2. Venn diagram for the employee example.

Corresponding to this we can find the solution:

$$|x \cap y \cap z| = 0 \qquad |\overline{x} \cap y \cap z| = 7$$
$$|x \cap y \cap \overline{z}| = 2 \qquad |\overline{x} \cap y \cap \overline{z}| = 3$$
$$|x \cap \overline{y} \cap z| = 1 \qquad |\overline{x} \cap \overline{y} \cap z| = 1$$
$$|x \cap \overline{y} \cap \overline{z}| = 0 \qquad |\overline{x} \cap \overline{y} \cap \overline{z}| = 0$$

Finally, given any assignment of sets to y and z such that the first group of equalities holds, then we can find an assignment to x such that the second set of equalities also holds. While this cannot be illustrated for all possible assignments, consider just one assignment shown in Figure 2 where each dot represents a distinct person. Given the sets y and z (shown with solid lines), we can find a set x (shown in Figure 2 with a dashed line) that satisfies the required constraints.
□

In the constant-free case, once we know the cardinality of each minterm, any assignment of the required number of arbitrary distinct atoms to the minterms yields an assignment to the variables that satisfies the Boolean formula.

Of course, when the minterms contain atoms, we cannot assign arbitrary atoms. We have to assign to a minterm that contains an atom a positively either the atom that a denotes or the bottom element $\perp$. There is no other choice that can be allowed.

We handle atomic constants as follows. We consider them as additional Boolean algebra variables that have cardinality one and the cardinality of their intersection is zero. That is, if we have atomic constants $a_1, \ldots, a_c$ in a formula, then we add to system (3) the following for each $1 \le i \le c$:

$$|a_i| = 1$$

and also for each $1 \le i, j \le c$ and $i \ne j$:

$$|a_i \cap a_j| = 0$$

Of course, both of the above conditions have to be put into a normal form before adding them to system (3). Then we solve these as in Theorem 1. Now we can prove the following.

Theorem 2. [with atomic constants] *Existentially quantified variables can be eliminated from Boolean linear cardinality constraint formulas. The quantifier elimination is closed, that is, yields a quantifier-free Boolean linear cardinality constraint formula.*   □

Example 9. Let S be the Boolean cardinality formula that is the conjunction of the formula in Example 4 and the constraint in Example 5. A quantifier elimination problem would be to find a quantifier-free formula that is logically equivalent to the following:

$$\exists x\, S$$

First we put S into a normal form. Then let S^* be the conjunction of the normal form and the following:

$$|y \cap z \cap a| - |x \cap y \cap z \cap a| - |\overline{x} \cap y \cap z \cap a| = 0$$
$$|y \cap z \cap \overline{a}| - |x \cap y \cap z \cap \overline{a}| - |\overline{x} \cap y \cap z \cap \overline{a}| = 0$$
$$|y \cap \overline{z} \cap a| - |x \cap y \cap \overline{z} \cap a| - |\overline{x} \cap y \cap \overline{z} \cap a| = 0$$
$$|y \cap \overline{z} \cap \overline{a}| - |x \cap y \cap \overline{z} \cap \overline{a}| - |\overline{x} \cap y \cap \overline{z} \cap \overline{a}| = 0$$
$$|\overline{y} \cap z \cap a| - |x \cap \overline{y} \cap z \cap a| - |\overline{x} \cap \overline{y} \cap z \cap a| = 0$$
$$|\overline{y} \cap z \cap \overline{a}| - |x \cap \overline{y} \cap z \cap \overline{a}| - |\overline{x} \cap \overline{y} \cap z \cap \overline{a}| = 0$$
$$|\overline{y} \cap \overline{z} \cap a| - |x \cap \overline{y} \cap \overline{z} \cap a| - |\overline{x} \cap \overline{y} \cap \overline{z} \cap a| = 0$$
$$|\overline{y} \cap \overline{z} \cap \overline{a}| - |x \cap \overline{y} \cap \overline{z} \cap \overline{a}| - |\overline{x} \cap \overline{y} \cap \overline{z} \cap \overline{a}| = 0$$

We also add the constraint $|a| = 1$ expressed using minterms as:

$$|x \cap y \cap z \cap a| + |x \cap y \cap \overline{z} \cap a| + |x \cap \overline{y} \cap z \cap a| + |x \cap \overline{y} \cap \overline{z} \cap a|$$
$$+ |\overline{x} \cap y \cap z \cap a| + |\overline{x} \cap y \cap \overline{z} \cap a| + |\overline{x} \cap \overline{y} \cap z \cap a| + |\overline{x} \cap \overline{y} \cap \overline{z} \cap a| = 1$$

Second, we consider each expression that is the cardinality of a minterm (over x, y, z, a or over y, z, a) as an integer variable. Then by integer linear constraint variable elimination we get:

$$|y \cap z \cap a| + |y \cap z \cap \overline{a}| + |y \cap \overline{z} \cap a| + |y \cap \overline{z} \cap \overline{a}| \equiv_6 0$$
$$|y \cap z \cap a| + |y \cap z \cap \overline{a}| + |\overline{y} \cap z \cap a| + |\overline{y} \cap z \cap \overline{a}| \equiv_9 0$$
$$|y \cap z \cap a| + |y \cap z \cap \overline{a}| \qquad\qquad\qquad\quad = 7$$
$$|\overline{y} \cap z \cap a| \qquad\qquad\qquad\qquad\qquad\qquad = 1$$

The last linear cardinality constraint comes from the constraint in Example 5 and the constraint that $|a| = 1$. By Theorem 2, the above is equivalent to $\exists x\, S$.

For instance, the following is one solution for the above:

$$|y \cap z \cap a| = 0$$
$$|y \cap z \cap \overline{a}| = 7$$
$$|y \cap \overline{z} \cap a| = 0$$
$$|y \cap \overline{z} \cap \overline{a}| = 5$$
$$|\overline{y} \cap z \cap a| = 1$$
$$|\overline{y} \cap z \cap \overline{a}| = 1$$
$$|\overline{y} \cap \overline{z} \cap a| = 0$$
$$|\overline{y} \cap \overline{z} \cap \overline{a}| = 0$$

Corresponding to this we can find the solution:

$$|x \cap y \cap z \cap a| = 0 \qquad |\overline{x} \cap y \cap z \cap a| = 0$$
$$|x \cap y \cap z \cap \overline{a}| = 0 \qquad |\overline{x} \cap y \cap z \cap \overline{a}| = 7$$
$$|x \cap y \cap \overline{z} \cap a| = 0 \qquad |\overline{x} \cap y \cap \overline{z} \cap a| = 0$$
$$|x \cap y \cap \overline{z} \cap \overline{a}| = 2 \qquad |\overline{x} \cap y \cap \overline{z} \cap \overline{a}| = 3$$
$$|x \cap \overline{y} \cap z \cap a| = 1 \qquad |\overline{x} \cap \overline{y} \cap z \cap a| = 0$$
$$|x \cap \overline{y} \cap z \cap \overline{a}| = 0 \qquad |\overline{x} \cap \overline{y} \cap z \cap \overline{a}| = 1$$
$$|x \cap \overline{y} \cap \overline{z} \cap a| = 0 \qquad |\overline{x} \cap \overline{y} \cap \overline{z} \cap a| = 0$$
$$|x \cap \overline{y} \cap \overline{z} \cap \overline{a}| = 0 \qquad |\overline{x} \cap \overline{y} \cap \overline{z} \cap \overline{a}| = 0$$

Finally, given any assignment of sets to y, z, and a such that the first group of equalities holds and the correct atom is assigned to a, then we can find an assignment to x such that the second set of equalities also holds. Again, consider just one assignment shown in Figure 3 where each dot represents a distinct person. Given the sets y, z, and a (shown with solid lines), we can find a set x (shown in Figure 3 with a dashed line) that satisfies the required constraints.

It is interesting to compare the above with Example 8. There we could choose for x an arbitrary atom of the set $\overline{y} \cap z$, but here we must choose the atom a. More precisely, we can choose an arbitrary atom of the set $\overline{y} \cap z \cap a$, which, of course, is the same.   □

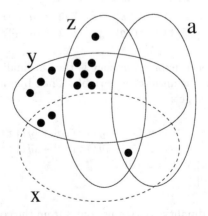

Fig. 3. Venn diagram for Example 9.

Theorem 3. *Universally quantified variables can be eliminated from Boolean linear cardinality constraint formulas. The quantifier elimination is closed, that is, yields a quantifier-free Boolean linear cardinality constraint formula.*   □

Given any formula, it can be decided whether it is true by successively eliminating all variables from it. Then it becomes easy to test whether the variable-free formula is true or false. Hence, this also shows that:

Corollary 1. *It can be decided whether a Boolean linear cardinality constraint formula is true or false.*   □

4 Query Evaluation

It is well-known that several practical query languages, such as SQL without aggregation operators, can be translated into relational calculus [1,39]. Hence while relational calculus is not used directly in major database systems, many theoretical results are stated in terms of it with clear implications for the more practical query languages. Hence we will do the same here.

A relational calculus formula is built from relation symbols R_i with variable and constant symbol arguments, the connectives $\wedge$ for *and*, $\vee$ for *or*, $\rightarrow$ for *implication*, and overline for *negation*, and the quantifiers $\exists$ and $\forall$ in the usual way. Each relation has a fixed *arity* or number of arguments. If R_i is a k-arity relation, then it always occurs in the formula in the form $R_i(z_1, \ldots, z_k)$, where each z_j for $1 \leq j \leq k$ is a variable or constant symbol.

A general framework for using constraint databases is presented in [29,30]. The following three definitions are from that paper.

1. A *generalized k-tuple* is a quantifier-free conjunction of constraints on k ordered variables ranging over a domain δ. Each generalized k tuple represents in a finite way a possibly infinite set of regular k-tuples.
2. A *generalized relation of arity k* is a finite set of generalized k-tuples, with each k-tuple over the same variables.
3. A *generalized database* is a finite set of generalized relations.

Let r_i be the generalized relation assigned to R_i. We associate with each r_i a formula F_{r_i} that is the disjunction of the set of generalized k-tuples of r_i. According to the above definition, F_{r_i} is a quantifier-free *disjunctive normal form* (DNF) formula. This is not absolutely necessary, and other researchers allow non-DNF formulas too. The above the generalization is from finite relations found in relational database systems to *finitely representable* (via constraints) but possibly infinite relations.

Let ϕ be any relational calculus formula. Satisfaction with respect to a domain δ and database d, denoted $< \delta, d > \models$, is defined recursively as follows:

$$< \delta, d > \models R_i(a_1, \ldots, a_k) \text{ iff } F_{r_i}(a_1, \ldots, a_k) \text{ is true} \tag{2}$$
$$< \delta, d > \models \phi \wedge \psi \text{ iff } < \delta, d > \models \phi \text{ and } < \delta, d > \models \psi \tag{3}$$
$$< \delta, d > \models \phi \vee \psi \text{ iff } < \delta, d > \models \phi \text{ or } < \delta, d > \models \psi \tag{4}$$

$$< \delta, d > \models \phi \rightarrow \psi \text{ iff not } < \delta, d > \models \phi \text{ or } < \delta, d > \models \psi \qquad (5)$$
$$< \delta, d > \models \phi \leftrightarrow \psi \text{ iff } < \delta, d > \models \phi \rightarrow \psi \text{ and } < \delta, d > \models \psi \rightarrow \phi \quad (6)$$
$$< \delta, d > \models \overline{\phi} \text{ iff not } < \delta, d > \models \phi \qquad (7)$$
$$< \delta, d > \models \exists x_i \phi \text{ iff } < \delta, d > \models \phi[x_i/a_j] \text{ for some } a_j \in \delta \qquad (8)$$
$$< \delta, d > \models \forall x_i \phi \text{ iff } < \delta, d > \models \phi[x_i/a_j] \text{ for each } a_j \in \delta \qquad (9)$$

where $[x_i/a_j]$ means the instantiation of the free variable x_i by a_j.

The above semantics does not immediately suggest a query evaluation method.[3] In relational databases, the above would suggest a query evaluation, because in the last two rules we clearly need to consider a finite number of cases, but we cannot rely on this finiteness in constraint databases. However, the following alternative semantics, that is equivalent to the above, is discussed in [29, 30]:

Let $\phi(x_1, \ldots, x_m)$ be a relational calculus formula with free variables $x_1, \ldots, x_m$. Let relation symbols $R_1, \ldots, R_n$ in ϕ be assigned the generalized relations $r_1, \ldots, r_n$ respectively. Let $\phi_1 = \phi[R_1/F_{r_1}, \ldots, R_n/F_{r_n}]$ be the formula that is obtained by replacing in ϕ each relation symbol $R_i(z_1, \ldots, z_k)$ by the formula

$$F_{r_i}[x_1/z_1, \ldots, x_k/z_k]$$

where $F_{r_i}(x_1, \ldots, x_k)$ is the formula associated with r_i. Note that ϕ_1 is a simple first order formula of constraints, that is, it does not have any of the relation symbols R_i in it, hence d is no longer relevant in checking the satisfaction of ϕ_1. The output database of ϕ on input database $r_1, \ldots, r_n$ is the relation

$$r_{out} = \{(a_1, \ldots, a_m) : < \delta > \models \phi_1(a_1, \ldots, a_m)\}.$$

The above is a possibly infinite relation that needs to be also finitely represented.

Such a finite representation can be found by quantifier elimination. For the goal of quantifier elimination is to find a quantifier-free formula F_1 that has the same models as ϕ_1 has [16]. That is,

$$r_{out} = \{(a_1, \ldots, a_m) : < \delta > \models F_1(a_1, \ldots, a_m)\}.$$

Hence the alternative semantic definition yields an effective method for query evaluation based on quantifier elimination. Moreover, F_1 can be put into a DNF to preserve the representation of constraint relations.

The above general approach to query evaluation also applies when the input relations are described by linear cardinality constraints in atomic Boolean algebras of sets. In particular, the existential quantifier elimination in Theorem 2 and the universal quantifier elimination in Theorem 3 can be used to evaluate relational calculus queries.

---

[3] This semantic definition closely follows the usual definition of the semantics of relational calculus queries on relational databases. Indeed, the only difference is that in rule (4) the usual statement is that $(a_1, \ldots, a_k)$ is a tuple in the relation or "a row in the table" instead of the tuple satisfying a formula.

Theorem 4. *Relational calculus queries on constraint relations that are described using quantifier-free Boolean linear cardinality constraint formulas can be evaluated in closed-form.*   □

Example 10. Each strand of a DNA can be considered as a string of four letters: A, C, G, and T. In bioinformatics, we often have a set of probes, which are small already sequenced fragments from different already known parts of a long DNA string. For example, one probe may be located from the first to the tenth location on the long DNA strand and be the following:

$$C \, A \, T \, C \, G \, A \, T \, C \, T \, C$$

Another may be located between the eighth and 20th and be the following:

$$C \, T \, C \, G \, G \, G \, A \, G \, G \, G \, A \, T \, C$$

and so on.

Each of these probes can be represented in B_Z as a tuple of sets (x_A, x_C, x_G, x_T), where x_A, x_C, x_G, and x_T are the positions where A, C, G, and T occur, respectively. Hence the first probe can be represented by:

$$(\{2, 6\}, \{1, 4, 8, 10\}, \{5\}, \{3, 7, 9\})$$

while the second probe can be represented by:

$$(\{14, 18\}, \{8, 10, 20\}, \{11, 12, 13, 15, 16, 17\}, \{9, 19\})$$

Suppose we have a large number of probe data in a relation $Probe(x_A, x_C, x_G, x_T)$, and we'd like to reconstruct the long DNA strand using the probe data. There may be some errors in the sequencing information, for example, a letter A on the DNA may be incorrectly indicated as C in the probe data. Suppose we are satisfied with a 95 percent accuracy regarding the probe data. Suppose also, that we know that the long DNA sequence contains between 5000 and 6000 letters. The following relational calculus query finds possible long DNA sequences (y_A, y_C, y_G, y_T) that contain each probe with at least a 95 percent accuracy.

$$(|y_A \cup y_C \cup y_G \cup y_T| - |y_A| - |y_C| - |y_G| - |y_T| = 0) \wedge$$
$$(|y_A \cup y_C \cup y_G \cup y_T| \geq 5000) \wedge$$
$$(|y_A \cup y_C \cup y_G \cup y_T| \leq 6000) \wedge$$
$$(\forall x_A, x_C, x_G, x_T \quad (Probe(x_A, x_C, x_G, x_T) \rightarrow$$
$$|x_A \cap y_A| + |x_C \cap y_C| + |x_G \cap y_G| + |x_T \cap y_T| \geq 0.95 \, |x_A \cup x_C \cup x_G \cup x_T|))$$

In the above the solution is (y_A, y_C, y_G, y_T), which we can get by eliminating the universally quantified variables x_A, x_C, x_G, x_T. The first line ensures that the four sets y_A, y_C, y_G, y_T are disjoint. If they are disjoint, then the length of the solution is: $|y_A \cup y_C \cup y_G \cup y_T|$, which is restricted to be between 5000 and 6000 letters in the second and third lines of the relational calculus query. The fourth and fifth lines express that for each probe its overlap with the solution (left hand side of the cardinality constraint) must be greater than or equal to 95 percent of the length of the probe (right hand side).

We also need to check that the solution is a continuous sequence, that is, there are no gaps. We can do that by defining an input relation $Order(x, z)$, which will contain all tuples of the form $(\{i\}, \{j\})$ such that $1 \leq i \leq j \leq 6000$ and $i, j \in \mathcal{N}$. Then the following relational calculus formula tests whether the solution is a continuous sequence:

$$\exists z \, \forall x \;\; Order(x, z) \;\leftrightarrow\; |x \cap (y_A \cup y_C \cup y_G \; y_T)| \;=\; 1$$

The formula says that there must be a last element z in the solution, such that any x is an element of the solution, if and only if it is less than or equal to z.   □

5   Conclusions and Future Work

Quantifier elimination from Boolean linear cardinality constraint formulas by reduction to quantifier elimination in Presburger arithmetic is a new approach. The complexity of the quantifier elimination needs to be investigated. Especially the handling of (atomic) constants may be simplified.

It is also interesting to look at more complex cardinality constraints. For example, one cannot express using only linear cardinality constraints that the cardinality of set A is always the square of the cardinality of set B. We avoided such constraints, because even existential quantifier elimination from integer polynomial equations is unsolvable in general [34]. However, with restrictions on the number of variables we may have an interesting solvable problem.

Example 10 shows that relational calculus with Boolean linear cardinality constraints can handle some string problems. It is interesting to compare this in expressive power and computation complexity with query languages for string databases. Grahne et al. [22] proposed an extension of relational calculus with alignment operators for string databases, but the evaluation of their query language is unsolvable in general [22]. Benedikt et al [5] proposed several other extensions of relational calculus with various string operators. They show that the language S_{len} with only the prefix, the concatenation of a single character of the alphabet (at the end of a string), and the test-of-equal-length operators on strings does not admit quantifier elimination, although some weaker logics have quantifier elimination.

Finally, there are many practical implementation questions, for example, defining algebraic operators for query evaluation, data structures for representing the Boolean linear cardinality constraints, indexing for fast retrieval, and other issues of query optimization.

Acknowledgment. I thank the conference organizers, especially András Benczúr, for encouraging submission of this paper.

References

1. S. Abiteboul, R. Hull, and V. Vianu. *Foundations of Databases.* Addison-Wesley, 1995.
2. D.S. Arnon, G.E. Collins, and S. McCallum. Cylindrical algebraic decomposition, I: The basic algorithm. *SIAM Journal on Computing*, 13:865–877, 1984.
3. S. Basu. New results on quantifier elimination over real closed fields and applications to constraint databases. *Journal of the ACM*, 46(4):537–55, 1999.
4. M. Benedikt, M. Grohe, L. Libkin, and L. Segoufin. Reachability and connectivity queries in constraint databases. In *Proc. ACM Symposium on Principles of Database Systems*, pages 104–15, 2000.
5. M. Benedikt, L. Libkin, T. Schwentick, and L. Segoufin. Definable relations and first-order query languages over strings. *Journal of the ACM*, 50:694–751, 2003.
6. L. Berman. Precise bounds for Presburger arithmetic and the reals with addition. In *Proc. 18th IEEE FOCS*, pages 95–99, 1977.
7. A. Boudet and H. Comon. Diophantine equations, Presburger arithmetic and finite automata. In *Proceedings of CAAP'96*, number 1059 in Lecture Notes in Computer Science, pages 30–43. Springer-Verlag, 1996.
8. A. Brodsky, V. Segal, J. Chen, and P. Exarkhopoulo. The CCUBE constraint object-oriented database system. *Constraints*, 2(3–4):245–77, 1997.
9. J.-H. Byon and P. Revesz. DISCO: A constraint database system with sets. In G. Kuper and M. Wallace, editors, *Proc. Workshop on Constraint Databases and Applications*, volume 1034 of *Lecture Notes in Computer Science*, pages 68–83. Springer-Verlag, 1995.
10. D. Calvanese and M. Lenzerini. On the interaction between ISA and cardinality constraints. In *Proceedings of the Tenth International Conference on Data Engineering*, pages 204–213. IEEE Computer Society Press, 1994.
11. D. Calvanese, M. Lenzerini, and D. Nardi. A unified framework for class based representation formalisms. In *Proceedings of the Fourth International Conference on Principles of Knowledge Representation and Reasoning*, pages 109–120. Morgan Kaufmann, 1994.
12. B. F. Caviness and J. R. Johnson, editors. *Quantifier Elimination and Cylindrical Algebraic Decomposition.* Springer-Verlag, 1998.
13. G. E. Collins. Quantifier elimination for real closed fields by cylindrical algebraic decomposition. In H. Brakhage, editor, *Automata Theory and Formal Languages*, volume 33 of *Lecture Notes in Computer Science*, pages 134–83. Springer-Verlag, 1975.
14. J. Cox and K. McAloon. Decision procedures for constraint based extensions of Datalog. In *Constraint Logic Programming*, pages 17–32. MIT Press, 1993.
15. H.-D. Ebbinghaus, J. Flum, and W. Thomas. *Mathematical Logic.* Undergraduate Texts in Mathematics. Springer-Verlag, 2nd edition, 1994.
16. H.B. Enderton. *A Mathematical Introduction to Logic.* Academic Press, 1972.
17. M.J. Fisher and M.O. Rabin. Super-exponential complexity of Presburger arithmetic. In *Proc. SIAM-AMS volume VII.* American Mathematical Society, 1974.
18. J. B. J. Fourier. Solution d'une question particliére du calcul des inégalités. *Nouveau Bulletin des Sciences par la Société philomathique de Paris*, pages 99–100, 1826.
19. C. Gervet. Conjunto: Constraint logic programming with finite set domains. In *Proc. International Logic Programming Symposium*, pages 339–58, 1994.

20. D. Goldin and P. C. Kanellakis. Constraint query algebras. *Constraints*, 1:45–83, 1996.
21. D. Goldin, A. Kutlu, M. Song, and F. Yang. The constraint database framework: Lessons learned from CQA/CDB. In *Proc. International Conference on Data Engineering*, pages 735–737, 2003.
22. G. Grahne, M. Nykänen, and E. Ukkonen. Reasoning about strings in databases. *Journal of Computer and System Sciences*, 59:116–162, 1999.
23. S. Grumbach and Z. Lacroix. Computing queries on linear constraint databases. In *5th International Workshop on Database Programming Languages*, Electronic Workshops in Computing. Springer-Verlag, 1995.
24. S. Grumbach, P. Rigaux, and L. Segoufin. The DEDALE system for complex spatial queries. In *Proc. ACM SIGMOD International Conference on Management of Data*, pages 213–24, 1998.
25. S. Grumbach, P. Rigaux, and L. Segoufin. Spatio-temporal data handling with constraints. In *ACM Symposium on Geographic Information Systems*, pages 106–11, 1998.
26. R. Helm, K. Marriott, and M. Odersky. Spatial query optimization: From Boolean constraints to range queries. *Journal of Computer and System Sciences*, 51(2):197–201, 1995.
27. J. Jaffar and J. L. Lassez. Constraint logic programming. In *Proc. 14th ACM Symposium on Principles of Programming Languages*, pages 111–9, 1987.
28. J. Jaffar and M. Maher. Constraint logic programming: A survey. *J. Logic Programming*, 19/20:503–581, 1994.
29. P. C. Kanellakis, G. M. Kuper, and P. Revesz. Constraint query languages. In *Proc. ACM Symposium on Principles of Database Systems*, pages 299–313, 1990.
30. P. C. Kanellakis, G. M. Kuper, and P. Revesz. Constraint query languages. *Journal of Computer and System Sciences*, 51(1):26–52, 1995.
31. G. M. Kuper, L. Libkin, and J. Paredaens, editors. *Constraint Databases*. Springer-Verlag, 2000.
32. K. Marriott and M. Odersky. Negative Boolean constraints. *Theoretical Computer Science*, 160(1–2):365–80, 1996.
33. K. Marriott and P. J. Stuckey. *Programming with Constraints: An Introduction*. MIT Press, 1998.
34. Y. Matiyasevich. *Hilbert's Tenth Problem*. MIT Press, 1993.
35. H. J. Ohlbach and J. Koehler. *How to extend a formal system with a Boolean algebra operator*, pages 57–75. Kluwer Academic Publisher, 1998.
36. H. J. Ohlbach and J. Koehler. Modal logics, description logics, and arithmetic reasoning. *Journal of Artificial Intelligence*, 109(1-2):1–31, 1999.
37. J. Paredaens, J. Van den Bussche, and D. Van Gucht. First-order queries on finite structures over the reals. *SIAM Journal of Computing*, 27(6):1747–63, 1998.
38. M. Presburger. Über die vollständigkeit eines gewissen systems der arithmetik ganzer zahlen, in welchem die addition als einzige operation hervortritt. In *Comptes Rendus, I. Congrès des Math. des Pays Slaves*, pages 192–201, 1929.
39. R. Ramakrishnan. *Database Management Systems*. McGraw-Hill, 1998.
40. J. Renegar. On the computational complexity and geometry of the first-order theory of the reals. *Journal of Symbolic Computation*, 13(3):255–352, 1992.
41. P. Revesz. A closed form for Datalog queries with integer order. In *International Conference on Database Theory*, volume 470 of *Lecture Notes in Computer Science*, pages 187–201. Springer-Verlag, 1990.
42. P. Revesz. A closed-form evaluation for Datalog queries with integer (gap)-order constraints. *Theoretical Computer Science*, 116(1):117–49, 1993.

43. P. Revesz. Constraint databases: A survey. In B. Thalheim and L. Libkin, editors, *Semantics in Databases*, volume 1358 of *Lecture Notes in Computer Science*, pages 209–46. Springer-Verlag, 1998.

44. P. Revesz. The evaluation and the computational complexity of Datalog queries of Boolean constraint databases. *International Journal of Algebra and Computation*, 8(5):472–98, 1998.

45. P. Revesz. Safe Datalog queries with linear constraints. In *Proc. 4th International Conference on Principles and Practice of Constraint Programming*, volume 1520 of *Lecture Notes in Computer Science*, pages 355–69. Springer-Verlag, 1998.

46. P. Revesz. Safe query languages for constraint databases. *ACM Transactions on Database Systems*, 23(1):58–99, 1998.

47. P. Revesz. *Introduction to Constraint Databases*. Springer-Verlag, New York, 2002.

48. P. Revesz and Y. Li. MLPQ: A linear constraint database system with aggregate operators. In *Proc. 1st International Database Engineering and Applications Symposium*, pages 132–7. IEEE Press, 1997.

49. P. Rigaux, M. Scholl, and A. Voisard. *Spatial Databases with Application to GIS*. Morgan Kaufmann, 2001.

50. A. Salamon. Implementation of a database system with Boolean algebra constraints. Master's thesis, University of Nebraska-Lincoln, May 1998.

51. D. Seipel and U. Geske. Solving cardinality constraints in (constraint) logic programming. In *Proceedings of the International Workshop on Functional and Logic Programming*, 2001.

52. D. Srivastava, R. Ramakrishnan, and P. Revesz. Constraint objects. In A. Borning, editor, *Proc. 2nd International Workshop on Principles and Practice of Constraint Programming*, volume 874 of *Lecture Notes in Computer Science*, pages 218–28. Springer-Verlag, 1994.

53. M. H. Stone. The theory of representations for Boolean algebras. *Transactions of the American Mathematical Society*, 40:37–111, 1936.

54. A. Tarski. *A Decision Method for Elementary Algebra and Geometry*. University of California Press, Berkeley, 1951.

55. H. P. Williams. Fourier-Motzkin elimination extension to integer programming problems. *Journal of Combinatorial Theory (A)*, 21:118–23, 1976.

56. P. Wolper and B. Boigelot. An automata-theoretic approach to Presburger arithmetic constraints. In *Proc. Static Analysis Symposium*, volume 983 of *Lecture Notes in Computer Science*, pages 21–32. Springer-Verlag, 1995.

Update Propagation in Deductive Databases Using Soft Stratification

Andreas Behrend and Rainer Manthey

University of Bonn, Institute of Computer Science III,
Römerstr. 164, D-53117 Bonn, Germany
{behrend,manthey}@cs.uni-bonn.de

Abstract. Update propagation in deductive databases can be implemented by combining rule rewriting and fixpoint computation, analogous to the way how query answering is performed via Magic Sets. For efficiency reasons, bottom-up propagation rules have to be subject to Magic rewriting, thus possibly loosing stratifiability. We propose to use the soft stratification approach for computing the well-founded model of the magic propagation rules (guaranteed to be two-valued) because of the simplicity and efficiency of this technique.

1 Introduction

In the field of deductive databases, a considerable amount of research has been devoted to the efficient computation of induced changes by means of update propagation (e.g. [5,6,10,12,17]). Update propagation has been mainly studied in order to provide methods for efficient incremental view maintenance and integrity checking in stratifiable databases. The results in this area are particularly relevant for systems which will implement the new SQL:1999 standard and hence will allow the definition of recursive views. In addition, update propagation methods based on bottom-up materialization seem to be particularly well suited for updating distributed databases or in the context of WWW applications for signaling changes of data sources to mediators.

The aim of update propagation is the computation of implicit changes of derived relations resulting from explicitly performed updates of the extensional fact base. As in most cases an update will affect only a small portion of the database, it is rarely reasonable to compute the induced changes by comparing the entire old and new database state. Instead, the implicit modifications should be iteratively computed by propagating the individual updates through the possibly affected rules and computing their consequences. Although most approaches essentially apply the same propagation techniques, they mainly differ in the way they are implemented and in the granularity of the computed induced updates. We will consider the smallest granularity of updates, so called true updates, only, in order to pose no restrictions to the range of applications of update propagation. Moreover, we will use deductive rules for an incremental description of induced updates.

A. Benczúr, J. Demetrovics, G. Gottlob (Eds.): ADBIS 2004, LNCS 3255, pp. 22–36, 2004.

Incremental methods for update propagation can be divided into bottom-up and top-down approaches. In the context of pure bottom-up materialization, the benefit of incremental propagation rules is that the evaluation of their rule bodies can be restricted to the values of the currently propagated update such that the entire propagation process is very naturally limited to the actually affected derived relations. However, similar bottom-up approaches require to materialize the simulated state of derived relations completely in order to determine true updates. By contrast, if update propagation were based on a pure top-down approach, as proposed in [10,17], the simulation of the opposite state can be easily restricted to the relevant part by querying the relevant portion of the database. The disadvantage is that the induced changes can only be determined by querying all existing derived relations, although most of them will probably not be affected by the update. Additionally, a more elaborated control is needed in order to implement the propagation of base updates to recursive views.

Therefore, we propose to combine the advantages of top-down and bottom-up propagation. To this end, known transformation-based methods to update propagation in stratifiable databases (eg. [6,17]) are extended by incorporating the Magic Sets rewriting for simulating top down query evaluation. The resulting approach can be improved by other relational optimization techniques, handles non-linear recursion and may also propagate updates at arbitrary granularity. We show that the transformed rules can be efficiently evaluated by the soft stratification approach [4], solving stratification problems occurring in other bottom-up methods. This simple set-oriented fixpoint process is well-suited for being transferred into the SQL context and its (partial) materialization avoids expensive recomputations occurring in related transformation-based approaches (e.g. [5,17]).

1.1   Related Work

Methods for update propagation have been mainly studied in the context of Datalog, relational algebra, and SQL. Methods in Datalog based on SLDNF resolution cannot guarantee termination for recursively defined predicates (e.g. [17]). In addition, a set-oriented evaluation technique is preferred in the database context. Bottom-up methods either provide no goal-directed rule evaluation with respect to induced updates (e.g. [10]) or suffer from stratification problems (cf. Section 2) arising when transforming an original stratifiable schema (e.g. [6,12]). Hence, for the latter approaches (for an overview cf. [6]) the costly application of more general evaluation techniques like the alternating fixpoint [20] is needed.

In general, approaches formulated in relational algebra or SQL are not capable of handling (non-linear) recursion, the latter usually based on transformed views or specialized triggers. Transformed SQL-views directly correspond to our proposed method in the non-recursive case. The application of triggers (e.g. production rules even for recursive relations in [5]), however, does not allow the reuse of intermediate results obtained by querying the derivability and effectiveness tests. In [7] an algebraic approach to view maintenance is presented which is capable of handling duplicates but cannot be applied to general recursive views. For recursive views, [9] proposes the "Delete and Rederive" method which avoids the costly test of alternative derivations when computing induced deletions. However, this approach needs to compute overestimations of the tuples to be deleted and additional pretests are necessary to check whether a view is affected by a given update [11].

The importance of integrating Magic Sets with traditional relational optimizations has been discussed already in [15]. The structured propagation method in [6] represents a bottom-up approach for computing Magic Sets transformed propagation rules. However, as these rules are potentially unstratifiable, this approach is based on the alternating fixpoint computation [20] leading to an inefficient evaluation because the specific reason for unstratifiability is not taken into account. Therefore, we propose a less complex magic updates transformation resulting in a set of rules which is not only smaller but may in addition be efficiently evaluated using the soft stratification approach. Thus, less joins have to be performed and less facts are generated.

2   Basic Concepts

We consider a first order language with a universe of constants $U = \{a, b, c, \ldots\}$, a set of variables $\{X, Y, Z, \ldots\}$ and a set of predicate symbols $\{p, q, r \ldots\}$. A *term* is a variable or a constant (i.e., we restrict ourselves to function-free terms). Let p be an n-ary predicate symbol and t_i ($i = 1, \ldots, n$ and $n \geq 0$) terms then $p(t_1, \ldots, t_n)$ (or simply $p(\boldsymbol{t})$) is denoted *atom*. An atom is *ground* if every t_i is a constant. If A is an atom, we use $\mathbf{pred}(A)$ to refer to the predicate symbol of A. A *fact* is a clause of the form $p(t_1, \ldots, t_n) \leftarrow true$ where $p(t_1, \ldots, t_n)$ is a ground atom. A *literal* is either an atom or a negated atom. A *rule* is a clause of the form $p(t_1, \ldots, t_n) \leftarrow L_1 \wedge \cdots \wedge L_m$ with $n \geq 0$ and $m \geq 1$ where $p(t_1, \ldots, t_n)$ is an atom denoting the rule's head, and $L_1, \ldots, L_m$ are literals representing its body. We assume all deductive rules to be *safe*, i.e., all variables occurring in the head or in any negated literal of a rule must be also present in a positive literal in its body. If A is the head of a given rule R, we use $\mathbf{pred}(R)$ to refer to the predicate symbol of A. For a set of rules $\mathcal{R}$, $\mathbf{pred}(\mathcal{R})$ is defined as $\cup_{r \in \mathcal{R}} \mathbf{pred}(r)$.

Definition 1. *A deductive database $\mathcal{D}$ is a tuple $\langle \mathcal{F}, \mathcal{R} \rangle$ where $\mathcal{F}$ is a finite set of facts and $\mathcal{R}$ a finite set of rules such that $\mathbf{pred}(\mathcal{F}) \cap \mathbf{pred}(\mathcal{R}) = \emptyset$. Within a deductive database $\mathcal{D} = \langle \mathcal{F}, \mathcal{R} \rangle$, a predicate symbol p is called derived (view predicate), if $p \in \mathbf{pred}(\mathcal{R})$. The predicate p is called extensional (or base predicate), if $p \in \mathbf{pred}(\mathcal{F})$.*

For simplicity of exposition, and without loss of generality, we assume that a predicate is either base or derived, but not both, and that constants do neither occur in rule heads nor in body literals referring to a derived relation. Both conditions can be easily achieved by rewriting a given database. Before defining the semantics of a deductive database, we briefly introduce the notions *stratification* and *soft stratification* for partitioning a given deductive rule set.

A stratification λ on $\mathcal{D}$ is a mapping from the set of all predicate symbols $Rel_{\mathcal{D}}$ in $\mathcal{D}$ to the set of positive integers $I\!N$ inducing a partition of the given rule set such that all positive derivations of relations can be determined before a negative literal with respect to one of those relations is evaluated (cf [1]). For every partition $\mathcal{P} = P_1 \uplus \ldots \uplus P_n$ induced by a stratification the condition $\mathtt{pred}(P_i) \cap \mathtt{pred}(P_j) = \emptyset$ with $i \neq j$ must necessarily hold.

In contrast to this, a soft stratification λ^s on $\mathcal{D}$ is a mapping from the set of all rules in $\mathcal{D}$ to the set of positive integers $I\!N$ inducing a partition of the given rule set for which the condition above does not necessarily hold (cf [4]). A soft stratification is solely defined for Magic Sets transformed rule sets (or Magic Updates rewritten ones as shown later on) which may be even unstratifiable.

Given a deductive database $\mathcal{D}$, the Herbrand base $\mathcal{H}_{\mathcal{D}}$ of $\mathcal{D}$ is the set of all ground atoms that can be constructed from the predicate symbols and constants occurring in $\mathcal{D}$. Any subset I of $\mathcal{H}_{\mathcal{D}}$ is a Herbrand interpretation of $\mathcal{D}$. Given a Herbrand interpretation I, its complement set with respect to the Herbrand base, i.e. $\mathcal{H}_{\mathcal{D}} \setminus I$, is denoted $\overline{I}$ while $\neg \cdot I$ represents the set that includes all atoms in I in negated form. Based on these notions, we define the soft consequence operator [4] which serves as the basic operator for determining the semantics of stratifiable or softly stratifiable deductive databases.

Definition 2. *Let* $\mathcal{D} = \langle \mathcal{F}, \mathcal{R} \rangle$ *be a deductive database and* $\mathcal{P} = P_1 \uplus \ldots \uplus P_n$ *a partition of* $\mathcal{R}$*. The soft consequence operator* $T_{\mathcal{P}}^s$ *is a mapping on sets of ground atoms and is defined for* $\mathcal{I} \subseteq \mathcal{H}_{\mathcal{D}}$ *as follows:*

$$T_{\mathcal{P}}^s(\mathcal{I}) := \begin{cases} \mathcal{I} & \text{if } T_{P_j}(\mathcal{I}) = \mathcal{I} \text{ for all } j \in \{1, \ldots, n\} \\ T_{P_i}(\mathcal{I}) & \text{with } i = \min\{j \mid T_{P_j}(\mathcal{I}) \supsetneq \mathcal{I}\}, \text{ otherwise.} \end{cases}$$

where $T_{\mathcal{R}}$ *denotes the immediate consequence operator by van Emden/Kowalski.*

As the soft consequence operator $T_{\mathcal{P}}^s$ is monotonic for stratifiable or softly stratifiable databases, its least fixpoint $\mathtt{lfp}\,(T_{\mathcal{P}}^s, \mathcal{F})$ exists, where $\mathtt{lfp}\,(T_{\mathcal{P}}^s, \mathcal{F})$ denotes the least fixpoint of operator $T_{\mathcal{P}}^s$ containing $\mathcal{F}$ with respect to a stratified or softly stratified partition of the rules in $\mathcal{D}$. Given an arbitrary deductive database $\mathcal{D}$, its semantics is defined by its well-founded model $\mathcal{M}_{\mathcal{D}}$ which is known to be two-valued for stratifiable or softly stratifiable databases.

Lemma 1. *Let* $\mathcal{D} = \langle \mathcal{F}, \mathcal{R} \rangle$ *be a (softly) stratifiable deductive database and* (λ^s) λ *a (soft) stratification of* $\mathcal{R}$ *inducing the partition* $\mathcal{P}$ *of* $\mathcal{R}$*. The well-founded model* $\mathcal{M}_{\mathcal{D}}$ *of* $\langle \mathcal{F}, \mathcal{R} \rangle$ *is identical with the least fixpoint model of* $T_{\mathcal{P}}^s$*, i.e.,*

$$\mathcal{M}_{\mathcal{D}} = \mathtt{lfp}(T_{\mathcal{P}}^s, \mathcal{F}) \uplus \neg \cdot \overline{\mathtt{lfp}(T_{\mathcal{P}}^s, \mathcal{F})}.$$

Proof. cf [4].

For illustrating the notations introduced above, consider the following example of a stratifiable deductive database $\mathcal{D} = \langle \mathcal{F}, \mathcal{R} \rangle$:

$\underline{\mathcal{R}:}$		$\underline{\mathcal{F}:}$	
$\mathtt{one\_way}(X)$	$\leftarrow \mathtt{path}(X, Y) \wedge \neg \mathtt{path}(Y, X)$	$\mathtt{edge}(1, 2)$	
$\mathtt{path}(X, Y)$	$\leftarrow \mathtt{edge}(X, Y)$	$\mathtt{edge}(2, 1)$	
$\mathtt{path}(X, Y)$	$\leftarrow \mathtt{edge}(X, Z) \wedge \mathtt{path}(Z, Y)$	$\mathtt{edge}(2, 3)$	

Relation `path` represents the transitive closure of relation `edge` while relation `one_way` selects all $path(X, Y)$-facts where Y is reachable from X but not vice versa. A stratification induces (in this case) the unique partition $\mathcal{P} = P_1 \uplus P_2$ with P_1 comprising the two `path`-rules while P_2 includes the `one_way`-rule. The computation of $\mathtt{lfp}(T_{\mathcal{P}}^s, \mathcal{F})$ then induces the following sequence of sets

$$F_1 := \mathcal{F}$$
$$F_2 := T_{P_1}(F_1) = \{\text{path}(1,2), \text{path}(2,1), \text{path}(2,3)\} \cup F_1$$
$$F_3 := T_{P_1}(F_2) = \{\text{path}(1,1), \text{path}(2,2), \text{path}(1,3)\} \cup F_2$$
$$F_4 := T_{P_2}(F_3) = \{\text{one\_way}(1), \text{one\_way}(2)\} \cup F_3$$
$$F_5 := F_4.$$

The fixpoint F_5 coincides with the positive portion of the well-founded model $\mathcal{M_D}$ of $\mathcal{D}$, i.e. $\mathcal{M_D} = F_5 \uplus \neg \cdot \overline{F_5}$.

3 Update Propagation

We refrain from presenting a concrete update language but rather concentrate on the resulting sets of update primitives specifying insertions and deletions of individual facts. In principle every set oriented update language can be used that allows the specification of modifications of this kind. We will use the notion *Base Update* to denote the 'true' changes caused by a transaction; that is, we restrict the set of facts to be updated to the minimal set of updates where compensation effects (given by an insertion and deletion of the same fact or the insertion of facts which already exist in the database) are already considered.

Definition 3. *Let* $\mathcal{D} = \langle \mathcal{F}, \mathcal{R} \rangle$ *be a stratifiable database. A base update* u_D *is a pair* $\langle u_D^+, u_D^- \rangle$ *where* u_D^+ *and* u_D^- *are sets of base facts with* $\mathtt{pred}(u_D^+ \cup u_D^-) \subseteq \mathtt{pred}(\mathcal{F})$, $u_D^+ \cap u_D^- = \emptyset$, $u_D^+ \cap \mathcal{F} = \emptyset$ *and* $u_D^- \subseteq \mathcal{F}$. *The atoms* u_D^+ *represent facts to be inserted into* $\mathcal{D}$, *whereas* u_D^- *contains the facts to be deleted from* $\mathcal{D}$.

We will use the notion *induced update* to refer to the entire set of facts in which the new state of the database differs from the former after an update of base tables has been applied.

Definition 4. *Let* $\mathcal{D}$ *be a stratifiable database,* $\mathcal{M_D}$ *the semantics of* $\mathcal{D}$ *and* u_D *an update. Then* u_D *leads to an induced update* $u_{D \to D'}$ *from D to D' which is a pair* $\langle u_{D \to D'}^+, u_{D \to D'}^- \rangle$ *of sets of ground atoms such that* $u_{D \to D'}^+ = \mathcal{M}_{D'} \backslash \mathcal{M}_D$ *and* $u_{D \to D'}^- = \mathcal{M}_D \backslash \mathcal{M}_{D'}$. *The atoms* $u_{D \to D'}^+$ *represent the induced insertions, whereas* $u_{D \to D'}^-$ *consists of the induced deletions.*

The task of update propagation is to provide a description of the overall occurred modifications in $u_{D \to D'}$. Technically, such a description is given by a set of delta facts for any affected relation which may be stored in corresponding delta relations. For each predicate symbol $p \in \mathtt{pred}(\mathcal{D})$, we will use a pair of delta relations $\langle \Delta^+ p, \Delta^- p \rangle$ representing the insertions and deletions induced on p by an update u_D. In the sequel, a literal L which references a delta relation is called *delta literal*. In order to abstract from negative and positive occurrences of atoms in rule bodies, we use the superscripts "+" and "−" for indicating what kind of delta relation is to be used. For a positive literal $A \equiv p(t_1, \ldots, t_n)$ we define $A^+ \equiv \Delta^+ p(t_1, \ldots, t_n)$ and $A^- \equiv \Delta^- p(t_1, \ldots, t_n)$. For a negative literal $L \equiv \neg A$, we use $L^+ := A^-$ and $L^- := A^+$.

In the following, we develop transition rules and propagation rules for defining such delta relations. First, quite similar to query seeds used in the Magic Sets method, we generate a set of delta facts called *propagation seeds*.

Definition 5. *Let $\mathcal{D}$ be a stratifiable deductive database and $u_D = \langle u_D^+, u_D^- \rangle$ a base update. The set of propagation seeds $\mathtt{prop\_seeds}(u_D)$ with respect to u_D is defined as follows:*

$$\mathtt{prop\_seeds}(u_D) := \{ \ \Delta^\pi p(c_1, \ldots, c_n) \mid p(c_1, \ldots, c_n) \in u_D^\pi \ and \ \pi \in \{+, -\}\}.$$

Propagation seeds form the starting point from which induced updates, represented by derived delta relations, are computed. An update propagation method can only be efficient if most derived facts eventually rely on at least one fact in an extensional delta relation.

Generally, for computing true updates references to both the old and new database state are necessary. We will now investigate the possibility of dropping the explicit references to one of the states by deriving it from the other one and the given updates. The benefit of such a state simulation is that the database system is not required to store both states explicitly but may work on one state only. The rules defining the simulated state will be called *transition rules* according to the naming in [17].

Although both directions are possible, we will concentrate on a somehow pessimistic approach, the simulation of the new state while the old one is actually given. The following discussion, however, can be easily transferred to the case of simulating the old state [6]. In principle, transition rules can be differentiated by the way how far induced updates are considered for simulating the other database state. We solely use so-called *naive transition rules* which derive the new state from the physically present old fact base and the explicitly given updates. The disadvantage of these transition rules is that each derivation with respect to the new state has to go back to the extensional delta relations and hence makes no use of the implicit updates already derived during the course of propagation. In the Internal Events Method [17] as well as in [12] it has been proposed to improve state simulation by employing not only the extensional delta relations but the derived ones as well. However, the union of the original, the propagation and this kind of transition rules is not always stratifiable, and may even not represent the true induced update anymore under the well-founded semantics [6].

Assuming that the base updates are not yet physically performed on the database, from Definition 4 follows that the new state can be computed from the old one and the true induced update $u_{D \to D'} = \langle u_{D \to D'}^+, u_{D \to D'}^- \rangle$:

$$\mathcal{M}_{\mathcal{D}'} \ = \ (\mathcal{M}_{\mathcal{D}} \setminus u_{D \to D'}^-) \cup u_{D \to D'}^+.$$

We will use the mapping **new** for referring to the new database state which syntactically transform the predicate symbols of the literals it is applied to. Using the equation above directly leads to an equivalence on the level of tuples

$$\text{new } A \iff (A \wedge \neg(A^-)) \vee A^+.$$

which holds if the referenced delta relations correctly describe the induced update $u_{D \to D'}$. Note that we assume the precedence of the superscripts "+" and "−" to be higher than the one of ¬. Thus, we can omit the brackets in $\neg(A^-)$ and simply write $\neg A^-$. Using Definition 5 and the equivalence above, the deductive rules for inferring the new state of extensional relations can be easily derived. For instance, for the extensional relation **edge** of our running example the new state is specified by the rules (in the sequel, all relation names are abbreviated)

$$\text{new } e(X, Y) \leftarrow e(X, Y) \wedge \neg \Delta^- e(X, Y)$$
$$\text{new } e(X, Y) \leftarrow \Delta^+ e(X, Y),$$

From the new states of extensional relations we can successively infer the new states of derived relations using the dependencies given by the original rule set. To this end, the original rules are duplicated and the **new** mapping is applied to all predicate symbols occurring in the new rules. For instance, the rules

$$\text{new } o(X) \quad \leftarrow \text{new } p(X, Y) \wedge \neg\text{new } p(Y, X)$$
$$\text{new } p(X, Y) \leftarrow \text{new } e(X, Y)$$
$$\text{new } p(X, Y) \leftarrow \text{new } e(X, Z) \wedge \text{new } p(Z, Y)$$

specify the new state of the relations **path** and **one_way**. Note that the application of ¬ and the mapping **new** is orthogonal, i.e. $\text{new}\neg A \equiv \neg\text{new } A$, such that the literal $\text{new}\neg p(Y, X)$ from the example above may be replaced by $\neg\text{new } p(Y, X)$.

Definition 6. *Let $\mathcal{D} = \langle \mathcal{F}, \mathcal{R} \rangle$ be a stratifiable deductive database. Then the set of naive transition rules for true updates and new state simulation with respect to $\mathcal{R}$ is denoted $\tau(\mathcal{R})$ and is defined as the smallest set satisfying the following conditions:*

1. *For each n-ary extensional predicate symbol $p \in pred(\mathcal{F})$, the direct transition rules*

$$\text{new } A \leftarrow A \wedge \neg A^- \qquad \text{new } A \leftarrow A^+$$

   are in $\tau(\mathcal{R})$ where $A \equiv p(x_1, \ldots, x_n)$, and the x_i are distinct variables.
2. *For each rule $A \leftarrow L_1 \wedge \ldots \wedge L_n \in \mathcal{R}$, an indirect transition rule of the form*

$$\text{new } A \leftarrow \text{new } (L_1 \wedge \ldots \wedge L_n)$$

   is in $\tau(\mathcal{R})$.

It is obvious that if $\mathcal{R}$ is stratifiable, the rule set $\mathcal{R} \cup \tau(\mathcal{R})$ must be stratifiable as well. The following proposition shows that if a stratifiable database $\mathcal{D} = \langle \mathcal{F}, \mathcal{R} \rangle$ is augmented with the naive transition rules $\tau(\mathcal{R})$ as well as the propagation seeds $\text{prop\_seeds}(u_D)$ with respect to a base update u_D, then $\tau(\mathcal{R})$ correctly defines the new database state.

Proposition 1. *Let $\mathcal{D} = \langle \mathcal{F}, \mathcal{R} \rangle$ be a stratifiable database, u_D an update and $u_{D \to D'} = \langle u_{D \to D'}^+, u_{D \to D'}^- \rangle$ the corresponding induced update from $\mathcal{D}$ to $\mathcal{D}'$. Let $\mathcal{D}^a = \langle \mathcal{F} \cup \text{prop\_seeds}(u_D), \mathcal{R} \cup \tau(\mathcal{R}) \rangle$ be the augmented deductive database of $\mathcal{D}$. Then $\mathcal{D}^a$ correctly represents the implicit state of $\mathcal{D}'$, i.e. for all atoms $A \in \mathcal{H}_{D'}$ holds $A \in \mathcal{M}_{D'} \iff \text{new } A \in \mathcal{M}_{\mathcal{D}^a}$.*

The proof of this proposition is omitted as it directly follows from Definition 5 and from the fact that the remaining transition rules are a copy of those in $\mathcal{R}$ with the predicate symbols correspondingly replaced. We will now introduce incremental propagation rules for true updates. Basically, an induced insertion or deletion can be represented by the difference between the two consecutive database states. However, for efficiency reasons we allow to reference delta relations in the body of propagation rules as well:

Definition 7. *Let $\mathcal{R}$ be a stratifiable deductive rule set. The set of propagation rules for true updates with respect to $\mathcal{R}$, denoted $\varphi(\mathcal{R})$, is defined as the smallest set satisfying the condition:*

For each rule $A \leftarrow L_1 \wedge \ldots \wedge L_n \in \mathcal{R}$ and each body literal L_i $(i = 1, \ldots, n)$ two propagation rules of the form

$$A^+ \leftarrow L_i^+ \wedge \ \mathbf{new}\ (L_1 \wedge \ldots \wedge L_{i-1} \wedge L_{i+1} \wedge \ldots \wedge L_n) \wedge \quad \neg A$$
$$A^- \leftarrow L_i^- \wedge \quad (L_1 \wedge \ldots \wedge L_{i-1} \wedge L_{i+1} \wedge \ldots \wedge L_n) \wedge \mathbf{new}\ \neg A$$

are in $\varphi(\mathcal{R})$. The literals $\mathbf{new}\ L_j$ *and* L_j $(j = 1, \ldots, i-1, i+1, \ldots, n)$ *are called side literals of L_i.*

The propagation rules perform a comparison of the **old** and **new** database state while providing a focus on individual updates by applying the delta literals L_i^{π} with $\pi \in \{+, -\}$. Each propagation rule body may be divided into the *derivability test* and the *effectiveness test*. The derivability test $(L_i^{\pi} \wedge \{\mathbf{new}\}$ $(L_1 \wedge \ldots \wedge L_{i-1} \wedge L_{i+1} \wedge \ldots \wedge L_n))$ checks whether A is derivable in the new respectively old state. The *effectiveness test* (called *derivability test* in [21] and *redundancy test* in [10]) $(\{\mathbf{new}\}(\neg A))$ checks whether the fact obtained by the derivability test is not derivable in the opposite state. In general, this test cannot be further specialized as it checks for alternative derivations caused by other rules defining $\mathrm{pred}(A)$.

The obtained propagation rules and seeds as well as transition rules can be added to the original database yielding a safe and stratifiable database. The safeness of propagation rules immediately follows from the safeness of the original rules. Furthermore, the propagation rules cannot jeopardize stratifiability, as delta relations are always positively referenced and thus cannot participate in any negative cycle. Consider again the rules from Section 2:

1. $o(X) \quad \leftarrow p(X, Y) \wedge \neg p(Y, X)$
2. $p(X, Y) \leftarrow e(X, Y)$
3. $p(X, Y) \leftarrow e(X, Z) \wedge p(Z, Y)$

The corresponding propagation rules would look as follows:

1. $\varDelta^+ o(X) \quad \leftarrow \varDelta^+ p(X, Y) \wedge \mathbf{new} \neg\, p(Y, X) \wedge \quad \neg o(X)$
   $\varDelta^+ o(X) \quad \leftarrow \varDelta^- p(Y, X) \wedge \mathbf{new}\ p(X, Y) \wedge \quad \neg o(X)$
   $\varDelta^- o(X) \quad \leftarrow \varDelta^- p(X, Y) \wedge \quad \neg\, p(Y, X) \wedge \mathbf{new} \neg o(X)$
   $\varDelta^- o(X) \quad \leftarrow \varDelta^+ p(Y, X) \wedge \quad\quad p(X, Y) \wedge \mathbf{new} \neg o(X)$

2. $\Delta^+p(X,Y) \leftarrow \Delta^+e(X,Y) \qquad\qquad \wedge \quad \neg p(X,Y)$
   $\Delta^-p(X,Y) \leftarrow \Delta^-e(X,Y) \qquad\qquad \wedge\ new\,\neg p(X,Y)$

3. $\Delta^+p(X,Y) \leftarrow \Delta^+e(X,Z) \wedge new\ \ p(Z,Y) \wedge \quad \neg p(X,Y)$
   $\Delta^+p(X,Y) \leftarrow \Delta^+p(Z,Y) \wedge new\ \ e(X,Z) \wedge \quad \neg p(X,Y)$
   $\Delta^-p(X,Y) \leftarrow \Delta^-e(X,Z) \wedge \qquad\ p(Z,Y) \wedge new\,\neg p(X,Y)$
   $\Delta^-p(X,Y) \leftarrow \Delta^-p(Z,Y) \wedge \qquad\ e(X,Z) \wedge new\,\neg p(X,Y)$

Note that the upper indices π of the delta literal $\Delta^\pi p(Y,X)$ in the propagation rules for defining $\Delta^{\overline{\pi}}o(X)$ are inverted as p is negatively referenced by the corresponding literal in the original rule. Each propagation rule includes one delta literal for restricting the evaluation to the changes induced by the respective body literal. Thus, for each possible update (i.e., insertion or deletion) and for each original rule $2n$ propagation rules are generated if n is the number of body literals. It is possible to substitute not only a single body literal but any subset of them by a corresponding delta literal. This provides a better focus on propagated updates but leads to an exponential number of propagation rules.

Proposition 2. *Let* $\mathcal{D} = \langle \mathcal{F}, \mathcal{R} \rangle$ *be a stratifiable database,* $u_\mathcal{D}$ *an update and* $u_{D \to D'} = \langle u^+_{D \to D'}, u^-_{D \to D'} \rangle$ *the corresponding induced update from* $\mathcal{D}$ *to* $\mathcal{D}'$. *Let* $\mathcal{D}^a = \langle \mathcal{F} \cup \mathtt{prop\_seeds}(u_\mathcal{D}), \mathcal{R} \cup \tau(\mathcal{R}) \cup \varphi(\mathcal{R}) \rangle$ *be the augmented deductive database of* $\mathcal{D}$. *Then the delta relations defined by the propagation rules* $\varphi(\mathcal{R})$ *correctly represent the induced update* $u_{D \to D'}$. *Hence, for each relation* $p \in \mathtt{pred}(\mathcal{D})$ *the following conditions hold:*

$$\Delta^+p(t\ ) \in \mathcal{M}_{\mathcal{D}^a} \iff p(t\ ) \in u^+_{D \to D'}$$
$$\Delta^-p(t\ ) \in \mathcal{M}_{\mathcal{D}^a} \iff p(t\ ) \in u^-_{D \to D'}\ .$$

Proof. cf. [6, p. 161-163].

Transition as well as propagation rules can be determined at schema definition time and don't have to be recompiled each time a new base update is applied. For propagating true updates the results from the derivability and effectiveness test are essential. However, the propagation rules can be further enhanced by dropping the effectiveness test or by either refining or even omitting the derivability test in some cases. As an example, consider a derived relation which is defined without an implicit union or projection. In this case no multiple derivations of facts are possible, and thus the effectiveness test in the corresponding propagation rules can be omitted. Additionally, the presented transformation-based approach solely specifies true updates, but can be extended to describe the induced modifications at an arbitrary granularity (cf. [6,14]) which allows for cutting down the cost of propagation as long as no accurate results are required. In the sequel, however, we will not consider these specialized propagation rules as these optimizations are orthogonal to the following discussion.

Although the application of delta literals indeed restricts the computation of induced updates, the side literals and effectiveness test within the propagation rules as well as the transition rules of this example require the entire new and old state of relation e, p and o to be derived within a bottom-up materialization. The reason is that the supposed evaluation over the two consecutive database states is performed using deductive rules which are not specialized with respect to the particular updates that are propagated. This weakness of propagation rules in view of a bottom-up materialization will be cured by incorporating Magic Sets.

4   Update Propagation via Soft Stratification

In Section 3 we already pointed to the obvious inefficiency of update propagation, if performed by a pure bottom-up materialization of the augmented database. In fact, simply applying iterated fixpoint computation [1] to an augmented database implies that all old and new state relations will be entirely computed. The only benefit of incremental propagation rules is that their evaluation can be avoided if delta relations are empty. In a pure top-down approach, however, the values of the propagated updates can be passed to the side literals and effectiveness tests automatically restricting their evaluation to relevant facts. The disadvantage is that all existing delta relations must be queried in order to check whether they are affected by an update, although for most of them this will not be the case.

In this section we develop an approach which combines the advantages of the two strategies discussed above. In this way, update propagation is automatically limited to the affected delta relations and the evaluation of side literals and effectiveness tests is restricted to the updates currently propagated. We will use the Magic Sets approach for incorporating a top-down evaluation strategy by considering the currently propagated updates in the dynamic body literals as abstract queries on the remainder of the respective propagation rule bodies. Evaluating these *propagation queries* has the advantage that the respective state relations will only be partially materialized. Moreover, later evaluations of propagation queries can re-use all state facts derived in previous iteration rounds.

4.1   Soft Update Propagation by Example

Before formally presenting the soft update propagation approach, we will illustrate the main ideas by means of an example. Let us consider the following stratifiable deductive database $\mathcal{D} = \langle \mathcal{F}, \mathcal{R} \rangle$ with

$\underline{\mathcal{R}:}$ $p(X, Y) \leftarrow e(X, Y)$
$\quad\quad p(X, Y) \leftarrow e(X, Z) \wedge p(Z, Y)$

$\underline{\mathcal{F}:}$ $e(1,2)$, $e(1,4)$, $e(3,4)$, $e(10,11)$, $e(11,12)$, $\ldots$, $e(99,100)$

The positive portion $\mathcal{M}_{\mathcal{D}}^{+}$ of the corresponding total well-founded model $\mathcal{M}_{\mathcal{D}} = \mathcal{M}_{\mathcal{D}}^{+} \cup \neg \cdot \overline{\mathcal{M}_{\mathcal{D}}^{+}}$ consists of 4098 p-facts, i.e. $|\mathcal{M}_{\mathcal{D}}^{+}| = 4098 + |e| = 4191$ facts. For maintaining readability we restrict our attention to the propagation of insertions. Let the mapping **new** for a literal $A \equiv r(x)$ be defined as **new** $A := r^{new}(x)$. The respective propagation rules $\varphi(\mathcal{R})$ are

$$\Delta^+p(X,Y) \leftarrow \Delta^+e(X,Y) \wedge \qquad\qquad \neg p(X,Y)$$
$$\Delta^+p(X,Y) \leftarrow \Delta^+e(X,Z) \wedge p^{new}(Z,Y) \wedge \neg p(X,Y)$$
$$\Delta^+p(X,Y) \leftarrow \Delta^+p(Z,Y) \wedge e^{new}(X,Z) \wedge \neg p(X,Y)$$

while the naive transition rules $\tau(\mathcal{R})$ are

$$p^{new}(X,Y) \leftarrow e^{new}(X,Y) \qquad\qquad e^{new}(X,Y) \leftarrow e(X,Y) \wedge \neg\Delta^- e(X,Y)$$
$$p^{new}(X,Y) \leftarrow e^{new}(X,Z) \wedge p^{new}(Z,Y) \qquad e^{new}(X,Y) \leftarrow \Delta^+ e(X,Y).$$

Let $u_\mathcal{D}$ be an update consisting of the new edge fact $e(2,3)$ to be inserted into $\mathcal{D}$, i.e. $u_\mathcal{D}^+ = \{e(2,3)\}$. The resulting augmented database $\mathcal{D}^a$ is then given by $\mathcal{D}^a = \langle \mathcal{F} \cup \{\Delta^+e(2,3)\}, \mathcal{R}^a \rangle$ with $\mathcal{R}^a = \mathcal{R} \cup \varphi(\mathcal{R}) \cup \tau(\mathcal{R})$. Evaluating the stratifiable database $\mathcal{D}^a$ leads to the generation of 8296 facts for computing the three induced insertions $\Delta^+p(1,3)$, $\Delta^+p(2,3)$, and $\Delta^+p(2,4)$ with respect to p.

We will now apply our *Magic Updates* rewriting to the rules above with respect to the propagation queries represented by the set $Q^u = \{\Delta^+e(X,Y), \Delta^+e(X,Z), \Delta^+p(Z,Y)\}$ of delta literals in the propagation rule bodies. Let $\mathcal{R}^a_{Q^u}$ be the adorned rule set of $\mathcal{R}^a$ with respect to the propagation queries Q^u. The rule set resulting from the Magic Updates rewriting will be denoted $mu(\mathcal{R}^a_{Q^u})$ and consists of the following answer rules for our example

$$\Delta^+p(X,Y) \leftarrow \Delta^+e(X,Y) \wedge \neg p_{bb}(X,Y)$$
$$\Delta^+p(X,Y) \leftarrow \Delta^+e(X,Z) \wedge p^{new}_{bf}(Z,Y) \wedge \neg p_{bb}(X,Y)$$
$$\Delta^+p(X,Y) \leftarrow \Delta^+p(Z,Y) \wedge e^{new}_{fb}(X,Z) \wedge \neg p_{bb}(X,Y)$$

$$p^{new}_{bf}(X,Y) \leftarrow m\_p^{new}_{bf}(X) \wedge e^{new}_{bf}(X,Z) \wedge p^{new}_{bf}(Z,Y) \qquad p^{new}_{bf}(X,Y) \leftarrow m\_p^{new}_{bf}(X) \wedge e^{new}_{bf}(X,Y)$$
$$p_{bb}(X,Y) \leftarrow m\_p_{bb}(X,Y) \wedge e(X,Z) \wedge p_{bb}(Z,Y) \qquad p_{bb}(X,Y) \leftarrow m\_p_{bb}(X,Y) \wedge e(X,Y)$$
$$e^{new}_{fb}(X,Y) \leftarrow m\_e^{new}_{fb}(Y) \wedge e(X,Y) \wedge \neg\Delta^- e(X,Y) \qquad e^{new}_{fb}(X,Y) \leftarrow m\_e^{new}_{fb}(Y) \wedge \Delta^+e(X,Y)$$
$$e^{new}_{bf}(X,Y) \leftarrow m\_e^{new}_{bf}(X) \wedge e(X,Y) \wedge \neg\Delta^- e(X,Y) \qquad e^{new}_{bf}(X,Y) \leftarrow m\_e^{new}_{bf}(X) \wedge \Delta^+e(X,Y)$$

as well as the following subquery rules

$$m\_p^{new}_{bf}(Z) \leftarrow m\_p^{new}_{bf}(X) \wedge e^{new}_{bf}(X,Z) \qquad\qquad m\_p^{new}_{bf}(Z) \leftarrow \Delta^+e(X,Z)$$
$$m\_e^{new}_{fb}(Z) \leftarrow \Delta^+p(Z,Y) \qquad\qquad m\_e^{new}_{bf}(X) \leftarrow m\_p^{new}_{bf}(X)$$
$$m\_p_{bb}(X,Y) \leftarrow \Delta^+p(Z,Y) \wedge e^{new}_{fb}(X,Z) \qquad\qquad m\_p_{bb}(X,Y) \leftarrow \Delta^+e(X,Y)$$
$$m\_p_{bb}(X,Y) \leftarrow \Delta^+e(X,Z) \wedge p^{new}_{bf}(Z,Y) \qquad\qquad m\_p_{bb}(Z,Y) \leftarrow m\_p_{bb}(X,Y) \wedge e(X,Z).$$

Quite similar to the Magic sets approach, the Magic Updates rewriting may result in an unstratifiable rule set. This is also the case for our example where the following negative cycle occurs in the respective dependency graph of $mu(\mathcal{R}^a_{Q^u})$:

$$\Delta^+p \xrightarrow{pos} m\_p_{bb} \xrightarrow{pos} p_{bb} \xrightarrow{neg} \Delta^+p$$

We will show, however, that the resulting rules must be at least softly stratifiable such that the soft consequence operator could be used for efficiently computing their well-founded model. Computing the induced update by evaluating $\mathcal{D}^{ma} = \langle \mathcal{F} \cup \{\Delta^+e(2,3)\}, mu(\mathcal{R}^a_{Q^u}) \rangle$ leads to the generation of two new state facts for e, one old state fact and one new state fact for p. The entire number of generated facts is 19 in contrast to 8296 for computing the three induced insertions with respect to p. The reason for the small number of facts is that only relevant state facts are derived which excludes all p facts derivable from $\{e(10, 11), e(11, 12), \ldots, e(99, 100)\}$ as they are not affected by $\Delta^+e(2, 3)$.

Although this example already shows the advantages of applying Magic Sets to the transformed rules from Section 3, the application of Magic Updates rules does not necessarily improve the performance of the update propagation process. This is due to cases where the relevant part of a database represented by Magic Sets transformed rules together with the necessary subqueries exceeds the amount of derivable facts using the original rule set. For such cases further rule optimizations have been proposed (e.g. [16]) which can be also applied to a Magic Updates transformed rule set, leading to a well-optimized evaluation.

4.2   The Soft Update Propagation Approach

In this section we formally introduce the soft update propagation approach. To this end, we define the Magic Updates rewriting and prove its correctness.

Definition 8 (Magic Predicates). *Let $A \equiv p_{ad}(x)$ be a positive literal with adornment* ad *and* bd(x) *the sequence of variables within x indicated as bound in the adornment* ad. *Then the magic predicate of A is defined as* magic$(A) :=$ $m\_p_{ad}(\text{bd}(x))$. *If $A \equiv \neg p_{ad}(x)$ is a negative literal, then the magic predicate of A is defined as* magic$(A) := m\_p_{ad}(\text{bd}(x))$.

Given a rule set $\mathcal{R}$ and an adorned query $Q \equiv p_{ad}(c)$ with $p \in \text{pred}(\mathcal{R})$, the adorned rule set of $\mathcal{R}$ with respect to Q shall be denoted $\mathcal{R}_Q$. Additionally, let ms$(\mathcal{R}_Q)$ be the set of Magic Sets transformed rules with respect to $\mathcal{R}_Q$.

Definition 9 (Magic Updates Rewriting). *Let $\mathcal{R}$ be a stratifiable rule set, $\mathcal{R}^a = \mathcal{R} \cup \varphi(\mathcal{R}) \cup \tau(\mathcal{R})$ an augmented rule set of $\mathcal{R}$, and Q^u the set of abstract propagation queries given by all delta literals occurring in rule bodies of propagation rules in $\varphi(\mathcal{R})$. The Magic Updates rewriting of $\mathcal{R}^a$ yields the magic rule set* mu$(\mathcal{R}^a_{Q^u}) := \mathcal{R}^u_P \cup \mathcal{R}^u_S \cup \mathcal{R}^u_M$ *where $\mathcal{R}^u_P$, $\mathcal{R}^u_S$ and $\mathcal{R}^u_M$ are defined as follows:*

1. *From $\varphi(\mathcal{R})$ we derive the two deductive rule sets $\mathcal{R}^u_P$ and $\mathcal{R}^u_S$: For each propagation rule $A^\pi \leftarrow \Delta^{\hat{\pi}}e \wedge L^1 \wedge \ldots \wedge L^n \in \varphi(\mathcal{R})$ with $\Delta^{\hat{\pi}}e \in Q^u$ is a dynamic literal and $\pi, \hat{\pi} \in \{+, -\}$, an adorned answer rule of the form*

$$A^\pi \leftarrow \Delta^{\hat{\pi}}e \wedge L^1_{ad_1} \wedge \ldots \wedge L^n_{ad_n}$$

is in $\mathcal{R}^u_P$ where each non-dynamic body literal L^i $(1 \leq i \leq n)$ is replaced by the corresponding adorned literal $L^i_{ad_i}$ while assuming the body literals $\Delta^{\hat{\pi}}e \wedge L^1 \wedge \ldots \wedge L^{i-1}$ have been evaluated in advance. Note that the adornment of each non-derived literal consists of the empty string. For each derived adorned body literal $L^i_{ad_i}$ $(1 \leq i \leq n)$ a subquery rule of the form

$$\text{magic}(L^i_{ad_i}) \leftarrow \Delta^{\hat{\pi}}e \wedge L^1_{ad_1} \wedge \ldots \wedge L^{i-1}_{ad_{i-1}}$$

is in $\mathcal{R}^u_S$. No other rules are in $\mathcal{R}^u_P$ and $\mathcal{R}^u_S$.

2. *From the set $\mathcal{R}^{state} := \mathcal{R} \uplus \tau(\mathcal{R})$ we derive the rule set $\mathcal{R}_M^u$: For each relation symbol $\mathtt{magic}(L_{ad}) \in \mathtt{pred}(\mathcal{R}_S^u)$ the corresponding Magic Set transformed rule set $\mathtt{ms}(\mathcal{R}_W^{state})$ is in $\mathcal{R}_M^u$ where $W \equiv L_{ad}$ represents an adorned query with $\mathtt{pred}(L) \in \mathtt{pred}(\mathcal{R}^{state})$ and $\mathcal{R}_W^{state}$ is the adorned rule set of $\mathcal{R}^{state}$ with respect to W. No other rules are in $\mathcal{R}_M^u$.*

Theorem 1. *Let $\mathcal{D} = \langle \mathcal{F}, \mathcal{R} \rangle$ be a stratifiable database, $u_\mathcal{D}$ an update, $u_{D \to D'} = \langle u_{D \to D'}^+, u_{D \to D'}^- \rangle$ the corresponding induced update from $\mathcal{D}$ to $\mathcal{D}'$, Q^u the set of all abstract queries in $\varphi(\mathcal{R})$, and $\mathcal{R}^a = \mathcal{R} \cup \varphi(\mathcal{R}) \cup \tau(\mathcal{R})$ an augmented rule set of $\mathcal{R}$. Let $\mathtt{mu}(\mathcal{R}_{Q^u}^a)$ be the result of applying Magic Updates rewriting to $\mathcal{R}^a$ and $\mathcal{D}^{ma} = \langle \mathcal{F} \cup \mathtt{prop\_seeds}(u_\mathcal{D}), \mathtt{mu}(\mathcal{R}_{Q^u}^a) \rangle$ the corresponding augmented deductive database of $\mathcal{D}$. Then $\mathcal{D}^{ma}$ is softly stratifiable and all delta relations in $\mathcal{D}^{ma}$ correctly represent the induced update $u_{D \to D'}$, i.e. for all atoms $A \in \mathcal{H}_{D'}$ with $A \equiv p(\boldsymbol{t})$:*

$$\Delta^+ p(\boldsymbol{t}) \in \mathcal{M}_{\mathcal{D}^{ma}} \iff p(\boldsymbol{t}) \in u_{D \to D'}^+$$
$$\Delta^- p(\boldsymbol{t}) \in \mathcal{M}_{\mathcal{D}^{ma}} \iff p(\boldsymbol{t}) \in u_{D \to D'}^- .$$

Proof (Sketch). The correctness of the Magic Updates rewriting with respect to an augmented rule set $\mathcal{R}^a$ is shown by proving it to be equivalent to a specific Magic Set transformation of $\mathcal{R}^a$ which is known to be sound and complete. A Magic Sets transformation starts with the adornment phase which basically depicts information flow between literals in a database according to a chosen sip strategy. In [2] it is shown that the Magic Sets approach is also sound for so-called *partial sip strategies* which may pass on only a certain subset of captured variable bindings or even no bindings at all. Let us assume we have chosen such a sip strategy which passes no bindings to dynamic literals such that their adornments are strings solely consisting of $'f'$ symbols representing unbounded attributes. Additionally, let $\mathcal{R}_{\acute{p}} = \mathcal{R}^a \uplus \{h \leftarrow \Delta^{\pi 1} p1(\boldsymbol{x}_1)\} \uplus \ldots \uplus \{h \leftarrow \Delta^{\pi n} pn(\boldsymbol{x}_n)\}$ be an extended augmented rule set with rules for defining an auxiliary 0-ary relation h with $h \notin \mathtt{pred}(\varphi(\mathcal{R}))$, $\{\Delta^{\pi 1} p1, \ldots, \Delta^{\pi n} pn\} = \mathtt{pred}(\varphi(\mathcal{R}))$ distinct predicates, and $\boldsymbol{x}_i$ $(i = 1, \ldots, n)$ vectors of pairwise distinct variables with a length according to the arity of the corresponding predicates $\Delta^{\pi i} pi$. Relation h references all derived delta relations in $\varphi(\mathcal{R})$ as they are potentially affected by a given base update. Note that since $\mathcal{R}^a$ is assumed to be stratifiable, $\mathcal{R}_{\acute{p}}$ must be stratifiable as well. The Magic Sets rewriting of $\mathcal{R}_{\acute{p}}$ with respect to the query $H \equiv h$ using a partial sip strategy as proposed above yields the rule set $\mathtt{ms}(\mathcal{R}_{\acute{p}})$ which is basically equivalent to the rule set $\mathtt{mu}(\mathcal{R}_{Q^u}^a)$ resulting from the Magic Updates rewriting. The set $\mathtt{ms}(\mathcal{R}_{\acute{p}}^H)$ differs from $\mathtt{mu}(\mathcal{R}_{Q^u}^a)$ by the answer rules of the form $h \leftarrow m\_h, \Delta^{\pi 1} p1_{ff\ldots}(\boldsymbol{x}_1), \ldots, h \leftarrow m\_h, \Delta^{\pi n} pn_{ff\ldots}(\boldsymbol{x}_n)$ for the additional relation h, by subquery rules of the form $m\_\Delta^{\pi 1} p1_{ff\ldots} \leftarrow m\_h, \ldots, m\_\Delta^{\pi n} pn_{ff\ldots} \leftarrow m\_h$, by subquery rules of the form $m\_\Delta^{\pi i} pi_{ff\ldots} \leftarrow m\_\Delta^{\pi j} pj_{ff\ldots}$ with $i, j \in \{1, \ldots, n\}$, and by the usage of $m\_\Delta^{\pi i} pi_{ff\ldots}$ literals in propagation rule bodies for defining a corresponding delta relation $\Delta^{\pi i} pi_{ff\ldots}$. Obviously, these rules and literals can be removed from $\mathtt{ms}(\mathcal{R}_{\acute{p}}^H)$ without changing the semantics of the remaining delta relations which themselves coincide with the magic updates rules $\mathtt{mu}(\mathcal{R}_{Q^u}^a)$. Using the Propositions 1 and 2, it can be followed that $\mathcal{R}_{\acute{p}}^H$ is stratifiable and all delta relations defined in it correctly represent the induced update $u_{D \to D'}$. Thus, the Magic Sets transformed rules $\mathtt{ms}(\mathcal{R}_p^H)$ must be sound and complete as well. As the magic updates rules $\mathtt{mu}(\mathcal{R}_{Qu}^a)$ can be derived from $\mathtt{ms}(\mathcal{R}_p^H)$ in the way described above, they must correctly represent the induced update $u_{D \to D'}$ as well. In addition, since $\mathtt{ms}(\mathcal{R}_p^H)$ is softly stratifiable, the magic updates rules $\mathtt{mu}(\mathcal{R}_{Qu}^a)$ must be softly stratifiable, too.

From Theorem 1 follows that the soft stratification approach can be used for computing the induced changes represented by the augmented database $\mathcal{D}^{ma}$. For instance, the partition $\mathcal{P} = P_1 \uplus P_2$ of the Magic Updates transformed rule set $\mathtt{mu}(\mathcal{R}_{Qu}^a)$ of our running example with P_1 consisting of

$$\mathtt{p_{bb}}(X, Y) \leftarrow \mathtt{m\_p_{bb}}(X, Y) \wedge \ \mathtt{e}(X, Z) \wedge \ \mathtt{p_{bb}}(Z, Y) \quad \mathtt{p_{bb}}(X, Y) \leftarrow \mathtt{m\_p_{bb}}(X, Y) \wedge \ \mathtt{e}(X, Y)$$

$$\mathtt{m\_p_{bb}}(X, Y) \leftarrow \Delta^+\mathtt{p}(Z, Y) \wedge \ \mathtt{e_{fb}^{new}}(X, Z) \qquad \mathtt{m\_p_{bb}}(X, Y) \leftarrow \Delta^+\mathtt{e}(X, Y)$$
$$\mathtt{m\_p_{bb}}(X, Y) \leftarrow \Delta^+\mathtt{e}(X, Z) \wedge \ \mathtt{p_{bf}^{new}}(Z, Y) \qquad \mathtt{m\_p_{bb}}(Z, Y) \leftarrow \mathtt{m\_p_{bb}}(X, Y) \wedge \ \mathtt{e}(X, Z).$$

and with partition P_2 consisting of all rules, i.e. $P_2 := \mathtt{mu}(\mathcal{R}_{Qu}^a) \setminus P_1$, satisfies the condition of soft stratification. Using the soft consequence operator for the determination of $\mathtt{lfp}(T_\mathcal{P}^s, \mathcal{F} \cup \{\Delta^+\mathtt{e}(2, 3)\})$ then yields their well-founded model.

5   Conclusion

We have presented a new bottom-up evaluation method for computing the implicit changes of derived relations resulting from explicitly performed updates of the extensional fact base. The proposed transformation-based approach derives propagation rules by means of range-restricted *Datalog*⁻ rules which can be automatically generated from a given database schema. We use the Magic Sets method to combine the advantages of top-down and bottom-up propagation approaches in order to restrict the computation of true updates to the affected part of the database only. The proposed propagation rules are restricted to the propagation of insertions and deletions of base facts in stratifiable databases. However, several methods have been proposed dealing with further kinds of updates or additional language concepts. As far as the latter are concerned, update propagation in the presence of built-ins and (numerical) constraints has been discussed in [22], while views possibly containing duplicates are considered in [5,7]. Aggregates and updates have been investigated in [3,9]. As for the various types of updates, methods have been introduced for dealing with the modification of individual tuples, e.g. [5,19], the insertion and deletion of views (respectively rules) and constraints, e.g. [13,18], and even changes of view and constraint definitions, e.g. [8]. All these techniques allow for enhancing our proposed framework.

References

1. KRZYSZTOF R. APT, HOWARD A. BLAIR, AND ADRIAN WALKER. *Towards a theory of declarative knowledge*. Foundations of Deductive Databases and Logic Programs, pages 89–148, M. Kaufmann, 1988.

2. ISAAC BALBIN, GRAEME S. PORT, KOTAGIRI RAMAMOHANARAO, AND KRISHNA-MURTHY MEENAKSHI. *Efficient bottom-up computation of queries.* JLP, 11(3&4): 295–344, October 1991.

3. ELENA BARALIS AND JENNIFER WIDOM. *A rewriting technique for using delta relations to improve condition evaluation in active databases.* Technical Report CS-93-1495, Stanford University, November 1993.

4. ANDREAS BEHREND. *Soft stratification for magic set based query evaluation in deductive databases.* PODS 2003, New York, June 9–12, pages 102-110.

5. STEFANO CERI AND JENNIFER WIDOM. *Deriving incremental production rules for deductive data.* Information Systems, 19(6):467-490, 1994.

6. ULRIKE GRIEFAHN. *Reactive Model Computation–A Uniform Approach to the Implementation of Deductive Databases.* PhD Thesis, University of Bonn, 1997.

7. TIMOTHY GRIFFIN AND LEONID LIBKIN. *Incremental maintenance of views with duplicates.* SIGMOD 1995, May 23–25, 1995, San Jose, pages 328–339.

8. ASHISH GUPTA, INDERPAL S. MUMICK, AND KENNETH A. ROSS. *Adapting materialized views after redefinitions.* SIGMOD 1995, 24(2):211–222, 1995.

9. ASHISH GUPTA, INDERPAL S. MUMICK, AND V. S. SUBRAHMANIAN. *Maintaining views incrementally.* SIGMOD 1993, volume 22(2), pages 157–166.

10. VOLKER KÜCHENHOFF. *On the efficient computation of the difference between consecutive database states.* DOOD 1991: 478–502, volume 566 of LNCS, Springer.

11. ALON Y. LEVY AND YEHOSHUA SAGIV. *Queries Independent of Updates.* VLDB 1993: 171–181, Morgan Kaufmann.

12. RAINER MANTHEY. *Reflections on some fundamental issues of rule-based incremental update propagation.* DAISD 1994: 255-276, September 19-21.

13. BERN MARTENS AND MAURICE BRUYNOOGHE. *Integrity constraint checking in deductive databases using a rule/goal graph.* EDS 1988: 567–601.

14. GUIDO MOERKOTTE AND STEFAN KARL. *Efficient consistency control in deductive databases.* ICDT 1988, volume 326 of LNCS, pages 118–128.

15. INDERPAL S. MUMICK AND HAMID PIRAHESH. *Implementation of magic-sets in a relational database system.* SIGMOD 1994, 23(2): 103–114.

16. JEFFREY F. NAUGHTON, RAGHU RAMAKRISHNAN, YEHOSHUA SAGIV, AND JEFFREY D. ULLMAN.: *Efficient Evaluation of Right-, Left-, and Multi-Linear Rules.* SIGMOD 1989: 235-242.

17. ANTONI OLIVÉ. *Integrity constraints checking in deductive databases.* VLDB 1991, pages 513–523.

18. FARIBA SADRI AND ROBERT A. KOWALSKI. *A theorem proving approach to database integrity.* Foundations of Deductive Databases and Logic Programs, pages 313–362, M. Kaufmann, 1988.

19. TONI URPÍ AND ANTONI OLIVÉ. *A method for change computation in deductive databases.* VLDB 1992, August 23–27, Vancouver, pages 225–237.

20. ALLEN VAN GELDER. *The alternating fixpoint of logic programs with negation.* Journal of Computer and System Sciences, 47(1):185–221, August 1993.

21. LAURENT VIEILLE, PETRA BAYER, AND VOLKER KÜCHENHOFF. *Integrity checking and materialized views handling by update propagation in the EKS-V1 system.* Technical Report TR-KB-35, ECRC, München, June, 1991.

22. BEAT WÜTHRICH. *Detecing inconsistencies in deductive databases.* Technical Report 1990TR-123, Swiss Federal Institute of Technology (ETH), 1990.

Query Rewriting Using Views in a Typed Mediator Environment

Leonid A. Kalinichenko, Dmitry O. Martynov, and Sergey A. Stupnikov

Institute of Informatics Problems, Russian Academy of Sciences,
Vavilov Street, 44 building 2, 119333, Moscow, Russian Fed.
{leonidk,domart,ssa}@synth.ipi.ac.ru

Abstract. Query rewriting method is proposed for the heterogeneous information integration infrastructure formed by the subject mediator environment. Local as View (LAV) approach treating schemas exported by sources as materialized views over virtual classes of the mediator is considered as the basis for the
subject mediation infrastructure. In spite of significant progress of query rewriting with views, it remains unclear how to rewrite queries in the typed, object-
oriented mediator environment. This paper embeds conjunctive views and queries into an advanced canonical object model of the mediator. The "selection-
projection-join" (SPJ) conjunctive query semantics based on type specification
calculus is introduced. The paper demonstrates how the existing query rewriting
approaches can be extended to be applicable in such typed environment. The
paper shows that refinement of the mediator class instance types by the source
class instance types is the basic relationship required for establishing query containment in the object environment.

1 Introduction

This work has been performed in frame of the project [12] aiming at building large
heterogeneous digital repositories interconnected and accessible through the global
information infrastructure[1]. In this infrastructure a middleware layer is formed by
subject mediators providing a uniform ontological, structural, behavioral and query
interface to the multiple data sources. In a specific domain the subject model is to be
defined by the experts in the field independently of relevant information sources. This
model may include specifications of data structures, terminologies (thesauri), concepts (ontologies), methods applicable to data, processes (workflows), characteristic
for the domain. These definitions constitute specification of a subject mediator. After
subject mediator had been specified, information providers can register their information at the mediator for integration in the subject domain. Users should know only
subject domain definitions that contain concepts, data structures, methods approved
by the subject domain community. Thus various information sources belonging to
different providers can be registered at a mediator. The subject mediation is applicable to various subject domains in science, cultural heritage, mass media, e-commerce, etc.

---

[1] This work has been partially supported by the grants of the Russian Foundations for Basic
Research N 03-01-00821 and N 04-07-90083.

A. Benczúr, J. Demetrovics, G. Gottlob (Eds.): ADBIS 2004, LNCS 3255, pp. 37–53, 2004.

Local as View (LAV) approach [8] treating schemas exported by sources as materialized views over virtual classes of the mediator is considered as the basis for the subject mediation infrastructure. This approach is intended to cope with dynamic, possibly incomplete set of sources. Sources may change their exported schemas, become unavailable from time to time. To disseminate the information sources, their providers register them (concurrently and at any time) at respective subject mediators. A method and tool supporting process of information sources registration at the mediator were presented in [1]. The method is applicable to wide class of source specification models representable *in hybrid semi-structured/object canonical mediator model*. Ontological specifications are used for identification of mediator classes semantically relevant to a source class. A subset of source information relevant to the *mediator classes* is discovered based on identification of maximal commonality between a source and mediated level class specification. Such commonality is established so that compositions of mediated class instance types could be *refined* by a source class instance type.

This paper (for the same infrastructure as in [1]) presents an approach for query rewriting in a typed mediator environment. The problem of rewriting queries using views has recently received significant attention. The data integration systems described in [2,13] follow an approach in which the contents of the sources are described as views over the mediated schema. Algorithms for answering queries using views that were developed specifically for the context of data integration include the Bucket algorithm [13], the inverse-rules algorithm [2,3,15], MiniCon algorithm [14], the resolution-based approach [7], the algorithm for rewriting unions of general conjunctive queries [17] and others.

Query rewriting algorithms evolved into conceptually simple and quite efficient constructs producing the maximally-contained rewriting. Most of them have been developed for conjunctive views and queries in the relational, actually typeless data models (Datalog). In spite of significant progress of query rewriting with views, it remains unclear how to rewrite queries in the typed, object-oriented mediator environment. This paper is an attempt to fill in this gap. The paper embeds conjunctive views and queries into an advanced canonical object model of the mediator [9,11]. The "selection-projection-join" (SPJ) conjunctive query semantics based on type specification calculus [10] is introduced. The paper shows how the existing query rewriting approaches can be extended to be applicable in such object framework. To be specific, the algorithm for rewriting unions of general conjunctive queries [17] has been chosen. The resulting algorithm for the typed environment proposed in the paper exploits the heterogeneous source registration facilities [1] that are based on the refining mapping of the specific source data models into the canonical model of the mediator, resolving ontological differences between mediated and local concepts as well as between structural, behavioral and value conflicts of local and mediated types and classes. Due to the space limit, this paper does not consider various aspects of query rewriting, e.g., such issues as complexity of rewriting, possibility of computing all certain answers to a union query are not discussed: these issues are built on a well known results in the area (e.g., it is known that the inverse-rules algorithm produces the maximally-contained rewriting in time that is polynomial in the size of the query and the views [8]).

The paper is structured as follows. After brief analysis of the related works, an overview of the basic features of the canonical object model of the subject mediator is given. This overview is focused mostly on the type specification operations of the model that constitute the basis for object query semantics. In Section 4 an object query language oriented on representation of union of conjunctive queries under SPJ set semantics is introduced. Section 5 and 6 provide source registration and query rewriting approach for such query language. Section 7 gives an example of query rewriting in the typed environment. Results are summarized in the conclusion.

2 Related Work

The state of the art in the area of answering queries using views ranging from theoretical foundations to algorithm design and implementation has been surveyed in [8]. Additional evaluations of the query rewriting algorithms can be found in the recent papers [7,17] that have not been included into the survey [8]. Inverse rules algorithms are recognized due to their conceptual simplicity, modularity and ability to produce the maximally-contained rewriting in time that is polynomial in the size of the query and the views. Rewriting unions of general conjunctive queries using views [17] compares favorably with existing algorithms, it generalizes the MiniCon [14] and U-join [15] algorithms and is more efficient than the Bucket algorithm. Finding contained rewritings of union queries using general conjunctive queries (when the query and the view constraints both may have built-in predicates) are important properties of the algorithm [17].

Studies of the problem of answering queries using views in the context of querying object-oriented databases [4,5] exploited some semantic information about the class hierarchy as well as syntactic peculiarities of OQL. No concern of object query semantics in typed environment has been reported.

In the paper [6] in different context (logic-based query optimization for object databases) it has been shown how the object schema can be represented in Datalog. Semantic knowledge about the object data model, e.g., class hierarchy information, relationship between objects, as well as semantic knowledge about a particular schema and application domain are expressed as integrity constraints. An OQL object query is represented as a logic query and query optimization is performed in the Datalog representation.

Main contribution of our work is providing an extension of the query rewriting approach using views for the typed subject mediation environment. In contrast with [17], we extend conjunctive queries with object SPJ semantics based on type refinement relationship and type calculus. The paper shows that refinement of the mediator class instance types by the source class instance types is the basic relationship required for establishing query containment in the object environment.

3 Overview of the Basic Features of the Canonical Model

In the project [12] for the canonical model of a mediator we choose the SYNTHESIS language [9] that is a hybrid semi-structured/object model [11]. Here only the very basic canonical language features are presented to make the examples demonstrating ideas of the query rewriting readable. It is important to note that the compositional specification calculus considered [10] does not depend on any specific notation or modeling facilities. The canonical model [9] provides support of wide range of data - from untyped data on one end of the range to strictly typed data on another.

Typed data should conform to *abstract data types* (ADT) prescribing behaviour of their instances by means of the type's operations. ADT describes interface of a type whose signature define names and types of its operations. Operation is defined by a predicative specification stating its mixed pre/post conditions. Object type is a sub-type of a non-object ADT with an additional operation *self* on its interface providing OIDs. In this paper only typed capabilities of the SYNTHESIS language are ex-ploited. Query rewriting with semi-structured (frame) data is planned to be discussed in the future works.

Sets in the language (alongside with bags, sequences) are considered to be a gen-eral mechanism of grouping of ADT values. A class is considered as a subtype of a set type. Due to that these generally different constructs can be used quite uniformly: a class can be used everywhere where a set can be used. For instance, for the query language formulae the starting and resulting data are represented as sets of ADT val-ues (collections) or of objects (classes).

3.1   Type Specification Operations

Semantics of operations over classes in the canonical model are explained in terms of the compositional specification calculus [10]. The manipulations of the calculus in-clude decomposition of type specifications into consistent fragments, identification of common fragments, composition of identified fragments into more complex type specifications conforming to the resulting types of the SPJ operations. The calculus uses the following concepts and operations.

A signature Σ_T of a type specification $T = <V_T, O_T, I_T>$ includes a set of operation symbols O_T indicating operations argument and result types and a set of predicate symbols I_T (for the type invariants) indicating predicate argument types. Conjunction of all invariants in I_T constitutes the type invariant. We model an extension V_T of each type T (a carrier of the type) by a set of proxies representing respective instances of the type.

Definition 1. *Type reduct* A signature reduct R_T of a type T is defined as a subsigna-ture Σ_T of type signature Σ_T that includes a carrier V_T, a set of symbols of operations $O'_T \subseteq O_T$, a set of symbols of invariants $I'_T \subseteq I_T$.

This definition from the signature level can be easily extended to the specification level so that a type reduct R_T can be considered a *subspecification* (with a signature Σ_T) of specification of the type T. The specification of R_T should be formed so that R_T becomes a supertype of T. We assume that only the states admissible for a type re-main to be admissible for a reduct of this type (no other reduct states are admissible). Therefore, the carrier of a reduct is assumed to be equal to the carrier of its type.

Definition 2. Type U is a *refinement* of type T iff

- there exists a one-to-one correspondence *Ops*: $O_T \leftrightarrow O_U$;
- there exists an abstraction function *Abs*: $V_U \rightarrow V_T$ that maps each admissible state of U into the respective state of T;

- $\forall x \in V_U (I_U(x) \rightarrow I_T (Abs(x)))$;
- for every operation $o \in O_T$ the operation $Ops(o) = o' \in O_U$ is a refinement of o. To establish an operation refinement it is required that operation precondition $pre(o)$ should imply the precondition $pre(o')$ and operation postcondition $post(o')$ should imply postcondition $post(o)$.

Based on the notions of reduct and type refinement, a measure of common information between types in the type lattice $\mathcal{T}$ can be established. *Subtyping* is defined similarly to the refinement, but *Ops* becomes an injective mapping.

Definition 3. *Type meet operation.* An operation $T_1 \cap T_2$ produces a type T as an 'intersection' of specifications of the operand types. Let $T_1 = <V_{T1}, O_{T1}, I_{T1}>$, $T_2 = <V_{T2}, O_{T2}, I_{T2}>$, then $T = <V_T, O_T, I_T>$ is determined as follows. O_T is produced as an intersection of O_{T1} and O_{T2} formed so that if two methods – one from O_{T1} and another one from O_{T2} – are in a refinement order, then the most abstract one is included in O_T, $I_T = I_{T1} \vee I_{T2}$. T is positioned in a type lattice as the most specific supertype of T_1 and T_2 and a direct subtype of all common direct supertypes of the meet argument types.

If one of the types T_1 or T_2 or both of them are non-object types then the result of meet is a non-object type[2]. Otherwise it is an object type. If T_2 (T_1) is a subtype of T_1 (T_2) then T_1 (T_2) is a result of the meet operation.

Definition 4. *Type join operation.* An operation $T_1 \cup T_2$ produces type T as 'join' of specifications of the operand types. Let $T_1 = <V_{T1}, O_{T1}, I_{T1}>$, $T_2 = <V_{T2}, O_{T2}, I_{T2}>$, then $T = <V_T, O_T, I_T>$ is determined as follows. O_T is produced as a union of O_{T1} and O_{T2} formed so that if two methods – one from O_{T1} and another one from O_{T2} – are in a refinement order, then the most refined one is included in O_T, $I_T = I_{T1}$ & I_{T2}. T is positioned in a type lattice as the least specific subtype of T_1 and T_2 and a direct supertype of all the common direct subtypes of the join argument types.

If one of the types T_1 or T_2 or both of them are object types then the result of join is an object type. Otherwise it is a non-object type. If T_2 (T_1) is a subtype of T_1 (T_2) then T_2 (T_1) is a result of a join operation.

Operations of the compositional calculus form a *type* lattice [10] on the basis of a subtype relation (as a partial order). In the SYNTHESIS language the type composition operations are used to form type expressions that in a simplified form look as follows:

```
<type expression>::= <type term>[<compositional operation><type expression>] |
      (<type expression>)
<compositional operation>::= ∩ | ∪
<type term>::= <type variable> | <type designator> | <function designator>
<type designator>::= <type name> | <attribute name> | <reduct>
<reduct>::= <type name>[<attribute name list>]
<attribute name>::= <identifier> [/<type name>] [:<attribute path expression>]
<attribute path expression>::= <identifier>[.<identifier>]...
```

---

[2] If a result of type meet or join operation is an object type then an instance of the resulting type includes a *self* value taken from a set of not used OID values.

Reduct *T[b/S]* where *b* is an attribute of type *T* and *S* is a supertype of a type of the attribute *b*, denotes a type with the attribute *b* of type *S*. Reduct *T[a:b.c]* where *a* is an identifier, *b* is an attribute of type *T*, type of the attribute *b* is *S*, *c* is an attribute of *S* and type of the attribute *c* is *U*, denotes a type with the only attribute *a* of type *U*. Type expressions are required to type variables in formulae:

<typed variable>::= <variable>/<type expression>

3.2 Mediator Schema Example

For the subject mediator example a Cultural Heritage domain is assumed and a respective mediated schema is provided (table 1, table 2). Attribute types that are not specified in the table should be string, text (*title, content, description, general_Info*) or time (various dates are of this type). Text type is an ADT providing predicates used for specifying basic textual relationships for text retrieval. Time type is an ADT providing temporal predicates. Mentioning text or time ADT in examples means their reducts that will be refined by respective types in the sources. These types require much more space to show how to treat them properly. Therefore in the examples we assume texts to be just strings and dates to be of integer type. In the schema *value* is a function giving an evaluation of a heritage entity cost (+/- marks input/output parameters of a function).

Table 1. Classes of the mediated schema

Class	Subclass of	Class inst. type/ Type	Subtype of
heritage_entity		*Heritage_Entity*	*Entity*
painting	*heritage_entity*	*Painting*	*Heritage_Entity*
sculpture	*heritage_entity*	*Sculpture*	*Heritage_Entity*
antiquities	*heritage_entity*	*Antiquities*	*Heritage_Entity*
museum		*Repository*	
creator		*Creator*	*Person*

Table 2. Types of the mediated schema

Type	Attributes
Entity	*title, date, created_by: Creator,*
	value:{in:function; params:{+e/Entity[title, n/created_by.name],-
Heri-	*v/real}}*
tage_Entity	*place_of_origin, date_of_origin, content, in_collection: Collection,*
	digital_form:Digital_Entity
Painting	*dimensions*
Sculpture	*material_medium, exposition_space:{sequence; type_of_element: inte-*
Antiquities	*ger}*
Repository	*type_specimen, archaeology*
Collection	*name, place, collections: {set-of: Collection}*
	name, location. description, in_repository: Repository,
Person	*contains:{set-of: Heritage_Entity}*
Creator	*name, nationality, date_of_birth, date_of_death, residence*
	culture, general_Info, works: {set-of: Heritage_Entity}

4 Subset of the SYNTHESIS Query Language

In the paper a limited subset of the SYNTHESIS query language oriented on representation of union of conjunctive queries under SPJ set semantics is experienced. To specify query formulae a variant of a typed (multisorted) first order predicate logic language is used. Predicates in formulae correspond to collections (such as sets and bags of non-object instances), classes treated as set subtypes with object-valued instances and functions. ADTs of instance types of collections and classes are assumed to be defined. Predicate-class (or predicate-collection) is always a unary predicate (a class or collection atom). In query formulae functional atoms[3] corresponding to functions F syntactically are represented as n-ary predicates $F(X,Y)$ where X is a sequence of terms corresponding to input parameters i_0, ..., i_r (i_0 is an input parameter typed by an ADT (or its reduct) that includes F as its functional attribute (method); i_1, ..., i_r – input parameters having arbitrary types ($r \geq 0$)) and Y is a sequence of typed variables having arbitrary types ($s \geq 1$) and corresponding to output parameters o_1, ...,o_s. For terms the expressions (in particular cases - variables, constants and function designators) can be used. Each term is typed.

Definition 5. *SYNTHESIS Conjunctive Query (SCQ, also referred as a rule)* is a query of the form $q(v/T_v):- C_1(v_1/T_{v1})$, ..., $C_n(v_n/T_{vn})$, $F_1(X_1,Y_1)$, ..., $F_m(X_m,Y_m)$, B where $q(v/T_v)$, $C_1(v_1/T_{v1})$, ..., $C_n(v_n/T_{vn})$ are collection (class) atoms, $F_1(X_1,Y_1)$, ..., $F_m(X_m,Y_m)$ are functional atoms, B, called constraint, is a conjunction of predicates over the variables v, v_1, ..., v_n, typed by T_v, T_{v1}, ..., T_{vn}, or output variables $Y_1 \cup Y_2 \cup ... \cup Y_m$ of functional atoms. Each atom $C_i(v_i/T_{vi})$ or $F_j(X_j,Y_j)$ ($i = 1$, ..., n; $j = 1$, ..., m) is called a subgoal. The value v structured according to T_v is called the output value of the query. A union query is a finite union of SCQs. Atoms $C_i(v_i/T_{vi})$ may correspond to intensional collections (classes) that should be defined by rules having the form of SCQ[4].

The SPJ set semantics of SCQ body is introduced further[5]. General schema of calculating a resulting collection for a body of SCQ $C_1(v_1/T_{v1})$, ..., $C_n(v_n/T_{vn})$, $F_1(X_1,Y_1)$, ..., $F_m(X_m,Y_m)$, B is as follows. First, Cartesian product of collections in the list is calculated. After that for each instance obtained functional predicates are executed. A method to be executed is determined by a type of the first argument of a functional predicate. A type of the resulting collection of a product is appended with the attributes of the output arguments for each function in SCQ. Each instance of the resulting collection of a product is appended with the values of the output arguments for each function in SCQ calculated for this particular instance. After that those instances of the resulting collections are selected that satisfy B. After that joins of product domains are undertaken. We assume that such joins are executed in the order of appearance of the respective collection predicates in the SCQ body, from the left to the right. The semantics of SCQ conjunctions $C_i(v_i/T_{vi})$, $C_j(v_j/T_{vj})$ are defined by the instance types

---

[3] State-based and functional attributes are distinguished in type definitions. Functional attributes are taken (similarly to [6]) out of the instance types involved into the formula to show explicitly and plan the required computations.

[4] To make presentation more focused, in the paper everywhere non-recursive SCQs and views are assumed.

[5] For the bag semantics additionally it is required to ensure that the multiplicity of answers to the query are not lost in the views (applying set semantics), and are not increased.

of the arguments resulting in a type defined by *join* operation of the specifications of the respective argument types. Formal semantics of SCQ are given in Appendix.

The semantics of disjunctions $C_i(v_i/T_{vi}) \vee C_j(v_j/T_{vj})$ requires that for T_{vi} and T_{vj} a resulting type of disjunction is defined by type operation *meet* and the disjunction means a union of C_i and C_j. If the result of *meet* is empty then the disjunction is undefined. Note that in atom $C_i(v_i/T_{vi})$ for T_{vi} any reduct of C_i instance type may be used. This leads to a "projection" semantics of $C_i(v_i/T_{vi})$.

Under such interpretation, SCQ (or a rule) is *safe* if the instance type of the SCQ (rule) head is a supertype of the resulting type of the SCQ (rule) body. Such resulting type may include also attributes equated (explicitly or implicitly) by B to a variable or to a constant. "Implicitly" may mean that such attribute is equated to output argument of a function.

Two SCQs $q_1(v_1/T_{v1})$ and $q_2(v_2/T_{v2})$ are said to be *comparable* if T_{v1} is a subtype of T_{v2}. Let q_1 and q_2 be two comparable queries. q_1 is said *to be contained* in q_2, denoted $q_1 \subseteq q_2$, if for any database instance, all of the answers to q_1 after their transformation to type T_{v2} are answers to q_2.

5   Sources Registration and Inverse Rules

During the registration a local source class is described as a view over virtual classes of the mediator having the following general form of SCQ.

$$V(h/T_h) \subseteq P_1(b_1/T_{b1}), \ ..., \ P_k(b_k/T_{bk}), \ F_1(X_1, Y_1), \ ..., \ F_r(X_r, Y_r), \ B$$

Here V is a source class, P_1, ..., P_k are classes of the mediator schema[6], F_{b1}, ..., F_{br} are functions of the mediator schema, B is a constraint imposed by the view body. This SCQ should be safe. The safety property is established during the registration process. Due to that one-to-one correspondence between attributes of a reduct of the resulting instance type of a view body (mediator) and the instance type of a view head (source) is established. On source registration [1] this is done so that a reduct of the view body instance type *is refined* by the concretizing type T_h designed above the source. Since the open world assumption is applied, each class instance in a view may contain only part of the answers computed to the corresponding query (view body) on the mediator level. To emphasize such incompleteness, a symbol $\subseteq$ is used to interconnect a head of the view with its body.

For the local sources of our Cultural Heritage domain example few schemas are assumed for Louvre and Uffizi museum Web sites. Several view definitions for these sources registered at the mediator follow. In the views it is assumed that reducts of their instance types refine reducts of the respective mediator classes instance types or their compositions. Details on that can be found in [1]. The same is assumed for attribute types having the same names in a view and in the mediator.

---

[6] These atoms may also correspond to intensional classes defined by rules in the mediator schema.

Uffizi Site Views

canvas(p/Canvas[title, name, culture, place_of_origin, r_name]) ⊆
painting(p/Painting[title, name: created_by.name, place_of_origin, date_of_origin, r_name:
in_collection.in_repository.name]), creator(c/Creator[name, culture]), r_name = 'Uffizi',
date_of_origin >= 1550, date_of_origin < 1700

artist (a/Artist[name, general_Info, works]) ⊆ *creator(a/Creator[name, general_Info,*
works/{set-of:Painting}])

Louvre Site Views

workP(p/Work[title, author, place_of_origin, date_of_origin, in_rep]) ⊆
painting(p/Painting[title, author: created_by.name, place_of_origin, date_of_origin, in_rep:
in_collection.in_repository.name]), in_rep = 'Louvre'

workS(p/Work[title, author, place_of_origin, date_of_origin, in_rep]) ⊆
sculpture(p/Sculpture[title, author: created_by.name, place_of_origin, date_of_origin, in_rep:
in_collection.in_repository.name]), in_rep = 'Louvre'

To produce inverse rules out of the mediator view definitions as above, first, replace in the view each not contained in T_h attribute from T_{b1}, ...,T_{bk} with a distinct Skolem function of h / T_h producing output value of the type of the respective attribute. Such replacing means substitution of the attribute *get* function in a type with a method defined as a Skolem function that can not be expressed in terms of a local source. In the text Skolemized attributes are marked with #. All Skolemized attributes are added to the type T_h. Such Skolemizing mapping of the view is denoted as ρ. After the Skolemizing mapping, inverse rules for the mediator classes in the view body are produced as $\rho(P_i(b_i/T_{bi}) \leftarrow V(h/T_h))$ (for $i = 1, ..., k$)[7]. It is assumed that types T_{bi} and T_h are defined as $T_{bi} [a_1 / T_1:t_1, ..., a_n / T_n:t_n]$ and $T_h[a_1 / S_1, ..., a_m / S_m]$ so that T_{bi} is a supertype of T_h and T_i is a supertype of S_i, $i = 1, ..., n$.

For the mediator functions being type methods the inverse rules look like $\rho[m/T_m]$ $F_{bj}(X_{bj},Y_{bj}) \leftarrow [s/T_s]F_{hl}(X_{hl},Y_{hl}))$, for $j = 1, ...,r$, here F_{bj} and F_{hl} are methods of T_m and T_s such that type of function of F_{hl} refines type of function of F_{bj}. Types T_m and T_s (defined for the mediator and a source respectively) may be given implicitly in the view definition and (or) deduced from the registration information. Functional inverse rules are obtained during the source registration at the mediator, not from the view body.

$\rho(B_b)$ will be called the *inferred constraint* of the view predicate $V(h/T_h)$. The inverse rules generated from different views must use different Skolem functions (indexing of # will denote this).

---

[7] If T_{bi} is an object type then common reduct of T_{bi} and T_h should be such that *self* attribute of T_{bi} has an interpretation in T_h, otherwise *self* is to be replaced with a Skolem function generating OIDs.

Inverse Rules for canvas View of Uffizi

painting(p/Painting[title, name: created_by.name, place_of_origin, #$_i$date_of_origin, r_name: in_collection.in_repository.name]) ← canvas(p/ Canvas[title, name, culture, place_of_origin, #$_i$date_of_origin, r_name])

creator(c/ Creator[name, culture]) ← canvas(p/ Canvas[title, name, culture, place_of_origin, r_name])

The inferred constraint for *canvas(p/Canvas[title, name, culture, place_of_origin, #$_i$date_of_origin, r_name]):*
r_name = 'Uffizi', #$_i$date_of_origin >= 1550, #$_i$date_of_origin < 1700

During Uffizi registration a functional inverse rule is registered as

value(h/Entity[title, name: created_by.name], v/real) ← amount(h/Entity[title, name: created_by.name], v/real)

Inverse Rules for workP and workS Views of Louvre

painting(p/Painting[title, author: created_by.name, place_of_origin, date_of_origin, in_rep: in_collection.in_repository.name]) ← workP(p/Work[title, author, place_of_origin, date_of_origin, in_rep])

The inferred constraint for *workP: in_rep = 'Louvre'*

To save space, similar rule for sculpture is not shown here. During Louvre registration a functional inverse rule is registered as

value(h/Entity[title, name: created_by.name], v/real) ← amount(h/Entity[title, name: created_by.name], v/real)

Given a union query Q_m defined over the mediator classes, collections and functions, our task is to find a query Q_v defined solely over the view classes, collections and functions such that, for any mediator database instance, all of the answers to Q_v computed using any view instance are correct answers to Q_m. Q_v should be a *contained rewriting* of Q_m. There may be many different rewritings of a query.

6 Query Rewriting

Let Q_u be a union mediator query to be rewritten. Without loss of generality, all the SCQs in Q_u are assumed to be comparable. Similarly to [17], the method for rewriting Q_u consists of two steps. In the first step, we generate a set of *candidate formulae* (candidates for short) which may or may not be rewritings. These candidates are generated separately for every SCQ in Q_u. In the second step, all these candidates are checked to see whether correct rewritings can be obtained. A set I of compact inverse rules is assumed to be obtained for various sources as a result of their registration at the mediator [1].

For each SCQ $q(v/T_v):- C_1(v_1/T_{v1}), ..., C_n(v_n/T_{vn}), F_1(X_1,Y_1), ..., F_m(X_m,Y_m), B$ in Q_u denoted as Q do the following.

For each subgoal $C_i(v_i/T_{vi})$ or $F_j(X_j,Y_j)$ of Q find inverse rule $r \in I$ with the head $P_i(b_i/T_{bi})$ or $F_{bo}(X_{bo},Y_{bo})$ such that $C_i = P_i$ (or P_i is a name of any transitive subclass of C_i) and T_{bi} is a subtype of T_{vi} (or $F_j = F_{bo}$ and F_{bo} function type is a refinement of F_j type). Further such discovery is called *subgoal unification*.

A *destination* of Q is a sequence D of atoms $P_1(b_1/T_{b1})$, ..., $P_n(b_n/T_{bn})$, $F_{b1}(X_{b1},Y_{b1})$, ..., $F_{bm}(X_{bm},Y_{bm})$ obtained as a result of the query subgoals unification with the heads of inverse rules from I. Several destinations can be produced as various combinations of SCQ subgoals unifications found. Additionally each destination should conform to the following constraints:

1. There is no j such that a constant in X_j of $F_j(X_j,Y_j)$ $(j=1, ...,m)$ of Q corresponds to a different constant in the same argument of the respective functional subgoal of destination $F_{bj}(X_{bj},Y_{bj})$.
2. No two occurrences of the same variable or of the same function in F_j $(j=1, ..., m)$ of Q correspond to two different constants in F_{bj} $(j=1, ..., m)$ of D, and no two occurrences of the same variable or of the same function in the same head of a rule correspond to two different constants in Q.

Once a destination D of Q is found, we can use it to construct a candidate formula as follows. For each atom $P_i(b_i/T_{bi})$ or $F_{bj}(X_{bj},Y_{bj})$ in D (supposing it is a head of the inverse rule $P_i(b_i/T_{bi}) \leftarrow V_i(h_i/T_{hi})$ resp. $F_{bj}(X_{bj},Y_{bj}) \leftarrow F_{hj}(X_{hj},Y_{hj})$) do the following (if there are rules that have the same head but different bodies, then choose one of them in turn to generate different candidates).

Establish a mapping ϕ_i of attributes and variables in the atom $P_i(b_i/T_{bi})$ of D and in the associated atom $V_i(h_i/T_{hi})$ to the attributes and variables of the respective atom $C_i(v_i/T_{vi})$ of Q. For each variable z in T_{hi} of $V_i(h_i/T_{hi})$ which does not appear in $P_i(b_i/T_{bi})$ as a free variable, let ϕ_i map z to a distinct new variable not occurring in Q or any other view atom $\phi_j(V_j(h_j/T_{hj}))$, $(i \neq j)$. Free variables in the atom $P_i(b_i/T_{bi})$ of D and its associated atom $V(h_i/T_{hi})$ are mapped to the respective atom of Q as follows. For the atom $P_i(b_i/T_{bi})$ of D and the associated atom $V(h_i/T_{hi})$ the mappings of b_i and h_i to v_i are added to ϕ_i. For all T_{hi} attributes do the following. If an attribute a does not belong to T_{vi} then add to ϕ_i the mapping of a to an empty attribute (i.e., remove the attribute). If an attribute a belongs to T_{vi} but it has the form a/R where R is a supertype of a type of the attribute a, then add to ϕ_i the mapping of a to a/R or to $a/R:\#a$ if a is a Skolem attribute. If an attribute a of the type T_{vi} contains an attribute of the form $b/R:t.s$ and the type T_{bi} contains an attribute of the form $a/T:t$ (where t and s are attribute path expressions, R is a supertype of T and T is a supertype of a type of a) then add to ϕ_i the mapping of a to $b/R:a.s$ or to $a/R:\#a$ if a is a Skolem attribute. Similarly we build a mapping ϕ_j of attributes and variables in the atom $F_{bj}(X_{bj},Y_{bj})$ of D and in the associated atom $F_{hj}(X_{hj},Y_{hj})$ to the attributes and variables of the respective atom $F_j(X_j,Y_j)$ of Q.

For each destination and variable mappings defined, construct a formula Φ.

$$\phi_1(P_1(b_1/T_{b1})), ..., \phi_n(P_n(b_n/T_{bn})), \phi_{n+1}(F_{b1}(X_{b1},Y_{b1})), ..., \phi_{n+m}(F_{bm}(X_{bm},Y_{bm})) \qquad (\Phi)$$

Construct the mapping δ of a constraint of Q to a constraint in Φ. Let $S_q = (a_1, a_2, ..., a_k)$ and $S_f = (c_1, c_2, ..., c_k)$ be the sequences of function arguments in Q and Φ respectively. The mapping δ is constructed as follows.

Initially, an associated equality of the constraint in Φ, $E_\delta = True$. For $i = 1$ to m:

1. If a_i is a constant α or a function that results in α, but c_i is a variable y, then let $E_\delta = E_\delta \wedge (y = \alpha)$. α should be of y type or any of its subtypes.
2. If a_i is a variable x, and x appears the first time in position i, then let δ map x to c_i. If x appears again in a later position $j > i$ of S_q, and $c_i \neq c_j$, then let $E_\delta = E_\delta \wedge (c_i = c_j)$. a_i, c_i types and a_j, c_j types are assumed to be the same or in a subtyping order. We shall get SCQ:

$$q(v/T_v)\text{:-} \ \phi_1(P_1(b_1/T_{b1})), \ ..., \ \phi_n(P_n(b_n/T_{bn})), \ \phi_{n+1}(F_{b1}(X_{b1},Y_{b1})), \ ..., \tag{Φ_1}$$
$$\phi_{n+m}(F_{bm}(X_{bm},Y_{bm})), \ \delta(B), \ E_\delta$$

Replace heads of the inverse rules in the above SCQ with the rules bodies to get the formula

$$q(v/T_v)\text{:-} \ \phi_1(V_1(h_1/T_{h1})), \ ..., \ \phi_n(V_n(h_n/T_{hn})), \ \phi_{n+1}(F_{h1}(X_{h1},Y_{h1})), \ ..., \tag{Φ_2}$$
$$\phi_{n+m}(F_{hm}(X_{hm},Y_{hm})), \ \delta(B), \ E_\delta$$

If the constraint $\delta(B) \wedge E_\delta$ and the inferred constraints of the view atoms in the candidate formula *are consistent* and there are no Skolem functions in the candidate of Q then the formula is a rewriting (remove duplicate atoms if necessary). If there are Skolem functions in $\delta(B) \wedge E_\delta$, then the candidate formula is not a rewriting because the values of Skolem functions in $\delta(B) \wedge E_\delta$ can not be determined. Note that $x=y$ in the constraint for terms x and y typed with ADTs T and S is recursively expanded as $x.a_1=y.a_1 \ \& \ ... \ \& \ x.a_n=y.a_n$ where $a_1, ..., a_n$ are common attributes of T and S.

Containment property of the candidate formulae. The candidate formula (Φ_2) has the following property. If we replace each view atom with the corresponding Skolemized view body and treat the Skolem functions as variables, then we will get a safe SCQ Q' (the expansion of the candidate formula (Φ_2)) which is contained in Q. This is because (Φ_1) is a safe SCQ which is equivalent to (Q), and all subgoals and built-in predicates of (Φ_1) are in the body of Q' (this is a containment mapping). We constructed Φ_2 so that for any collection (class) subgoal pair in Φ_2 and Q an instance type of a subgoal of Φ_2 is a refinement of the instance type of the respective subgoal of Q, for any functional subgoal pair in Φ_2 and Q a type of function of a subgoal of Φ_2 is a refinement of type of function of the respective subgoal of Q. In some cases it is possible to obtain rewritings from the candidate formulae eliminating Skolem functions [17]. If the inferred constraints of the view atoms imply the constraints involving Skolem functions in the candidate formula, then we can remove those constraints directly.

Consistency Checking

Main consistency check during the rewriting consists in testing that constraint $\delta(B) \wedge E_\delta$ together with the inferred constraints of the view atoms in a candidate formula are consistent. Here we define how it can be done for the arithmetic constraints following complete algorithm for checking implications of arithmetic predicates [16].

1. Assuming that in SCQ we can apply only arithmetic predicates, form $Arith = \delta(C)$ $\wedge E_\delta \wedge$ <inferred constraints of the view atoms in a candidate formula Φ>.

2. For a candidate formula Φ it is required to show that there exist correct substitutions of type attributes and function arguments[8] in Φ satisfying $Arith$.

7 Query Rewriting Example in a Subject Mediator

Rewrite the following query to the Cultural Heritage domain mediator:

valuable_Italian_heritage_entities(h/Heritage_Entity_Valued[title, c_name, r_name, v]) :-
heritage_entity(h/Heritage_Entity[title,   c_name:created_by.name,   place_of_origin,
date_of_origin, r_name: in_collection.in_repository.name]), value(h/ Heritage_Entity [title,
name: c_name], v/real), v >= 200000, date_of_origin >= 1500, date_of_origin < 1750,
place_of_origin = 'Italy'

Destinations Obtained

For Uffizi site *heritage_entity* subgoal of a query unifies with *painting* as a *heritage_entity* subclass. The first destination is obtained as:

painting(p/Painting[title, name: created_by.name, place_of_origin, #, date_of_origin, r_name:
in_collection.in_repository.name]), value(h/Entity[title,name:
created_by.name], v/real)

ϕ **Mapping for the Destination** (only different name mappings are shown):

ϕ_1 mapping	$p \rightarrow h$, $\#_1 date\_of\_origin \rightarrow date\_of\_origin:\#_1 date\_of\_origin$, $r\_name \rightarrow c\_name: r\_name$
ϕ_2 mapping	*name: created_by_name → name:c_name*

For the query constraint δ is an identity mapping and $E = true$. Applying

$\phi_1(canvas(p/Canvas[title, name, culture, place\_of\_origin, r\_name]))$,
$\phi_2(amount(h/Entity[title, name: created\_by.name], v/real))$, $v >= 200000$, $date\_of\_origin >=$ *1500, date_of_origin < 1750, place_of_origin = 'Italy'*

we get the candidate formula

valuable_Italian_heritage_entities(h/Heritage_Entity_Valued[title, c_name, r_name, v]) :-
canvas(h/Canvas[title, name, culture, place_of_origin, date_of_origin: #, date_of_origin,
c_name: r_name]), amount(h/Entity[title, name: c_name], v/real), v >= 200000,
date_of_origin >= 1500, date_of_origin < 1750, place_of_origin = 'Italy'

For Louvre the *heritage_entity* subgoal of a query unifies with *painting, sculpture* as *heritage_entity* subclasses. Only destination formed for *painting* is shown here. This second destiniation is obtained as:

---

[8] It follows that an ability to compute functions during the consistency check to form admissible combination of input – output argument values is required.

painting(p/Painting[title, author: created_by.name, place_of_origin, date_of_origin, in_rep: in_collection.in_repository.name]), value(h/Entity[title, name: created_by.name], v/real)

ϕ Mapping for the Destination:

ϕ_1 mapping	*author → c_name:author, in_rep → r_name:in_rep*
ϕ_2 mapping	*name:created_by.name → name:c_name*

Again, δ is an identity mapping and $E = true$. Finally we get the second candidate formula

valuable_Italian_heritage_entities(h/Heritage_Entity_Valued[title, c_name, r_name, v]) :- workP(h/Work[title, c_name: author, place_of_origin, date_of_origin, r_name: in_rep]), amount(h/[title, name: c_name], v/real), v >= 200000, date_of_origin >= 1500, date_of_origin < 1750, place_of_origin = 'Italy'

Obtaining Rewritings from Candidate Formulae

To retrieve a rewriting we eliminate Skolem functions from the first candidate formula.. Note that the inferred constraint for *canvas(h/Canvas[title, c_name: name, culture, place_of_origin, date_of_origin: #$_i$date_of_origin, r_name])* that looks as *r_name = 'Uffizi', #$_i$date_of_origin >= 1550, #$_i$date_of_origin < 1700* implies *date_of_origin >= 1500, date_of_origin < 1750* for Uffizi. Due to that Skolem functions can be eliminated from this candidate formula and after the consistency check we get the following rewriting:

valuable_Italian_heritage_entities(h/Heritage_Entity_Valued[title, c_name, r_name, v]) :- canvas(h/ Canvas[title, c_name: name, culture, place_of_origin, r_name]), amount(h/[title, name: c_name], v/real), v >= 200000, place_of_origin = 'Italy'

The second candidate formula is a correct rewriting without any transformation.

Conclusion

The paper presents a query rewriting method for the heterogeneous information integration infrastructure formed by a subject mediator environment. LAV approach treating schemas exported by sources as materialized views over virtual classes of the mediator is considered as the basis for the subject mediation infrastructure. Main contribution of this work consists in providing an extension of the query rewriting approach using views for the typed environment of subject mediators. Conjunctive views and queries are considered in frame of an advanced canonical object model of the mediator. The "selection-projection-join" (SPJ) conjunctive query semantics based on type specification calculus has been introduced. The paper shows how the existing query rewriting approaches can be extended to be applicable in such typed framework. The paper demonstrates that refinement of the mediator class instance types by the source class instance types is the basic relationship required for query containment in the typed environment to be established. The approach presented is under implementation for the subject mediator prototype [1]. This implementation creates also a platform for providing various object query languages (e.g., a suitable subset of OQL (ODMG) or SQL:1999) for the mediator interface. Such languages can be implemented by their mapping into the canonical model of the mediator.

In a separate paper it is planned to show how an optimized execution plan for the rewritten query is constructed under various limitations of the source capabilities. Future plans include also extension of the query rewriting algorithm for frame-based semi-structured (XML-oriented) queries as well as investigations for queries (views) with negation and recursion.

References

1. D.O. Briukhov, L.A. Kalinichenko, N.A. Skvortsov. Information sources registration at a subject mediator as compositional development. In Proc. of the East European Conference on "Advances in Databases and Information Systems", Lithuania, Vilnius, Springer, LNCS No. 2151, 2001
2. O.M. Duschka, M.R. Genesereth. Query planning in infomaster. In Proc. of the ACM Symposium on Applied Computing, San Jose, CA, 1997
3. O.Duschka, M. Genesereth, A. Levy. Recursive query plans for data integration. Journal of Logic Programming, special issue on Logic Based Heterogeneous Information Systems, 43(1): 49-73, 2000
4. D. Florescu, L. Raschid, P. Valduriez. Answering queries using OQL view expressions. In Workshop on Materialized Views, Montreal, Canada, 1996
5. D. Florescu. Search spaces for object-oriented query optimization. PhD thesis, University of Paris VI, France, 1996
6. J. Grant, J. Gryz, J. Minker, L. Raschid. Semantic query optimization for object databases. In Proc. of the 13th International Conference on Data Engineering (ICDE'97), p.p. 444 – 454, April 1997
7. J. Grant, J. Minker. A logic-based approach to data integration. Theory and Practice of Logic Programming, Vol 2(3), May 2002, 293-321
8. A.Y. Halevy. Answering queries using views: a survey. VLDB Journal, 10(4): 270 – 294, 2001
9. L. A. Kalinichenko. SYNTHESIS: the language for description, design and programming of the heterogeneous interoperable information resource environment. Institute of Informatics Problems, Russian Academy of Sciences, Moscow, 1995
10. L.A. Kalinichenko. Compositional Specification Calculus for Information Systems Development. In Proc. of the East European Conference on Advances in Databases and Information Systems, Maribor, Slovenia, September 1999, Springer Verlag, LNCS No 1691
11. L.A. Kalinichenko. Integration of heterogeneous semistructured data models in the canonical one. In Proc. of the First Russian National Conference on "Digital Libraries: Advanced Methods and Technologies, Digital Collections", Saint-Petersburg, October 1999
12. L.A. Kalinichenko, D.O. Briukhov, N.A. Skvortsov, V.N. Zakharov. Infrastructure of the subject mediating environment aiming at semantic interoperability of heterogeneous digital library collections In Proc. of the Second Russian National Conference on "Digital Libraries: Advanced Methods and Technologies, Digital Collections", Protvino, October 2000
13. A.Y. Levy, A. Rajaraman. J.J. Ordille. Querying Heterogeneous Information Sources Using Source Descriptions. In Proc. of the Int. Conf. on Very Large Data Bases (VLDB), Bombay, India, 1996
14. R.Pottinger, A.Levy. A scalable algorithm for answering queries using views. In Proc. of the Int. Conf. on Very Large Data Bases (VLDB), Cairo, Egypt, 2000

15. X. Qian. Query folding. In Proc. of Int. Conf. on Data Engineering (ICDE), p.p. 48 – 55, New Orleans, LA, 1996
16. M. Staudt, Kai von Thadden. Subsumption checking in knowledge bases. Technical report 95-11, Aachener Informatik – Berichte, RWTH Aachen
17. J. Wang, M. Maher, R. Topor. Rewriting Unions of General Conjunctive Queries Using Views. In Proc. of the 8th International Conference on Extending Database Technology, EDBT'02, Prague, Czech Republic, March 2002

Appendix. Formal Semantics of SYNTHESIS Conjunctive Query

Semantics of SCQ $(q(v/T_v):- C_1(v_1/T_{v1}), ..., C_n(v_n/T_{vn}), F_1(X_1,Y_1), ..., F_m(X_m,Y_m), B$ where $q(v/T_v), C_1(v_1/T_{v1}), ..., C_n(v_n/T_{vn})$ are collection (class) atoms, $F_1(X_1,Y_1), ..., F_m(X_m,Y_m)$ are functional atoms, B is a conjunction of predicates over the variables v, $v_1, ..., v_n)$ are given by a semantic function $s[\cdot]$ constructing a result set of SCQ body. $s[\cdot]$ is defined recursively starting with the semantics of collection atoms. Collection C_i is considered as a set of values of type T_{vi}. Any value of type T_{vi} is an element of the extent V_{Tvi} of type T_{vi}. Thus a result set $s[C_n(v_i/T_{vi})]$ of collection atom $C_n(v_i/T_{vi})$ is a subset of the extent V_{Tvi}.

The first stage of constructing of the result set of the SCQ body is as follows. Construct a Cartesian product of sets $c_i=s[C_n(v_i/T_{vi})]$, append elements corresponding to the values of output parameters of functions $F_i(X_i,Y_i)$ to the tuples of the product and select all the tuples satisfying predicate B. Semantic function $ccp[\cdot]$ (conditional Cartesian product) is provided for that:

$$ccp[C_1(v_1/T_{v1}), ..., C_n(v_n/T_{vn}), F_1(X_1,Y_1), ..., F_m(X_m,Y_m), B] =$$
$$\{ v_1,..., v_n, \zeta_1,..., \zeta_m |$$
$$(v_1,..., v_n) \in c_1 \times ... \times c_n \wedge$$
$$\zeta_1 \in V_{R1} \wedge \mathcal{F}1 \wedge ... \wedge \zeta_m \in V_{Rm} \wedge \mathcal{F}m \wedge$$
$$B\{y_1^1 \to \zeta_1.y_1^1,..., y_1^{\beta 1} \to \zeta_1.y_1^{\beta 1},..., y_m^1 \to \zeta_m.y_m^1,..., y_1^{\beta m} \to \zeta_m.y_m^{\beta m}\}$$
$$\}$$

$\mathcal{F}i$ is a formula defining values of output parameters of F_i in a tuple. To define formally what $\mathcal{F}i$ is, it is required to make the following assumptions. Let X_i and Y_i be

$$X_i = v_{ni}, x_i^1,..., x_i^{\alpha i}$$
$$Y_i = y_i^1,..., y_i^{\beta i}$$

Let R_i be a type of the structure of the output parameters of the method F_i.

```
{ R_i; in: type; y_i^1: W_i^1;... y_i^βi: W_i^βi; }
```

Let method F_i has input parameters $a_i^1/U_i^1,..., a_i^{\alpha i}/U_i^{\alpha i}$, output parameters $b_i^1/W_i^1,..., b_i^{\beta i}/W_i^{\beta i}$ and predicative specification f.

Let $Q_1,..., Q_i$ be all subtypes of the type of the variable v_{nyi} – type T_{vnyi}. Let $f_1,..., f_{ni}$ be predicative specifications of the method F_i for the types $Q_1,..., Q_i$ respectively.

Then formula $\mathcal{F}i$ (taking into consideration a polymorphism of the method F_i) looks as follows.

$\mathcal{F}_i =$

$v_{n\,i} \in V_{Q1} \in f_i\{this \rightarrow v_n\,, a_i^1 \rightarrow x_i^1,..., a_i^{\alpha i} \rightarrow x_i^{\alpha i}, b_i^1 \rightarrow \zeta_i.y_i^1,..., b_i^{\beta i} \rightarrow \zeta_i.y_i^{\beta i}\} \wedge ... \wedge$

$v_{n\,i} \in V_{Q\,i} \in f_{ni}\{this \rightarrow v_{ny_i}, a_i^1 \rightarrow x_i^1,..., a_i^{\alpha i} \rightarrow x_i^{\alpha i}, b_i^1 \rightarrow \zeta_i.y_i^1,..., b_i^{\beta i} \rightarrow \zeta_i.y_i^{\beta i}\}$

A notation $f\{a \rightarrow t\}$ where f is a formula, a is a variable of f, t is a term, means the formula f with a substituted by t.

The second stage of the construction of the result set is a calculation of joins of product domains. The calculation of a single join is performed by semantic function *sjoin*. It takes a set of r-tuples s with types of elements $T_1,..., T_r$ and produces a set of $(r-1)$- tuples with types of elements $T_1 \cup T_2, T_3,..., T_r$.

$$sjoin(t) = \{ \mu_1,..., \mu_{r-1} \mid \exists (\lambda_1,..., \lambda_r) \in t, v \in V_{T1 \cup T2} (v =_{T1} \lambda_1 \wedge v =_{T2} \lambda_2 \wedge \mu_1 = v \wedge$$
$$\mu_2 = \lambda_3 \wedge ... \wedge \mu_{r-1} = \lambda_r) \}$$

For every tuple from t the function *sjoin* "glues" first two elements $\lambda_1 \in V_{T1}, \lambda_2 \in V_{T2}$ of the tuple into one element $\mu_i \in V_{T1 \cup T2}$. As value of type T_1, μ_i has all the attributes of the type T_1 and values of these attributes are the same as values of respective attributes of λ_1. As value of type T_2, μ_i has all the attributes of the type T_2 and values of these attributes are the same as values of respective attributes of λ_2. Equality of values of attributes is expressed by the following notation.

$v =_T w \doteq v.d_1 =_{Q1} w. d_1 \wedge ... \wedge v.d_g =_{Qg} w. d_g$

Type T here has attributes $d_1,...,d_g$ of types $Q_1,...,Q_g$ respectively.

To perform all joins for the product

$ccp[C_1(v_1/T_{v1}), ..., C_n(v_n/T_{vn}), F_1(X_1,Y_1), ..., F_m(X_m,Y_m), B]$

it is required to apply *sjoin* function $n+m-1$ times.

In case when all types $T_{v1}, ..., T_{vn}$ are nonobject types, the type of the result set is nonobject and the semantic function s provided for producing the result set of SCQ right-hand part $C_1(v_1/T_{v1}), ..., C_n(v_n/T_{vn}), F_1(X_1,Y_1), ..., F_m(X_m,Y_m), B$ is defined as follows.

$s[C_1(v_1/T_{v1}),...,C_n(v_n/T_{vn}),F_1(X_1,Y_1),...,F_m(X_m,Y_{m1}),B] =$

$\underbrace{sjoin(sjoin(... sjoin}_{n+m-1 \text{ times}}(ccp[C_1(v_1/T_{v1}),...,C_n(v_n/T_{vn}),F_1(X_1,Y_1),...,F_m(X_m,Y_{m1}),B])...))$

In case when at least one type of $T_{v1}, ..., T_{vn}$ is an object type, the type of the result set is object and the semantic function s is defined as follows.

$s[C_1(v_1/T_{v1}), ...,C_n(v_n/T_{vn}),F_1(X_1,Y_1), ... ,F_m(X_m,Y_{m1}),B] =$

$objectify(\underbrace{sjoin(sjoin(... sjoin}_{n+m-1 \text{ times}}(ccp[C_1(v_1/T_{v1}), ...,C_n(v_n/T_{vn}),F_1(X_1,Y_1), ... ,F_m(X_m,Y_{m1}),B]) ...)))$

Semantic function *objectify* here converts a collection of nonobject values into a collection of objects. This is done by adding an attribute *self* obtaining some new unique identifier to each value of the nonobject collection.

Reasoning About Web Information Systems
Using Story Algebras

Klaus-Dieter Schewe[1] and Bernhard Thalheim[2]

[1] Massey University, Department of Information Systems &
Information Science Research Centre
Private Bag 11 222, Palmerston North, New Zealand
k.d.schewe@massey.ac.nz
[2] Christian Albrechts University Kiel
Department of Computer Science and Applied Mathematics
Olshausenstr. 40, D-24098 Kiel, Germany
thalheim@is.informatik.uni-kiel.de

Abstract. As web information systems (WIS) tend to become large, it becomes decisive that the underlying application story is well designed. Such stories can be expressed by a process algebra. In this paper we show that such WIS-oriented process algebras lead to many-sorted Kleene algebras with tests, where the sorts correspond to scenes in the story space. As Kleene algebras with tests subsume propositional Hoare logic, they are an ideal candidate for reasoning about the story space. We show two applications for this: (1) the personalisation of the story space to the preferences of a particular user, and (2) the satisfaction of particular information needs of a WIS user.

Keywords: Web information system, Kleene algebra, process algebra, personalisation, navigation

1   Introduction

A *web information system* (WIS) is a database-backed information system that is realized and distributed over the web with user access via web browsers. Information is made available via pages including a navigation structure between them and to sites outside the system. Furthermore, there should also be operations to retrieve data from the system or to update the underlying database(s).

Various approaches to develop design methods for WISs have been proposed so far. The ARANEUS framework [1] emphasises that conceptual modelling of web information systems should approach a problem triplet consisting of content, navigation and presentation. This leads to modelling databases, hypertext structures and page layout. Other authors refer to the ARANEUS framework. The work in [2] addresses the integrated design of hypermedia and operations, but remains on a very informal level. Similarly, the work in [4] presents a web modelling language WebML and starts to discuss personalisation of web information systems and adaptivity, but again is very informal.

A. Benczúr, J. Demetrovics, G. Gottlob (Eds.): ADBIS 2004, LNCS 3255, pp. 54–66, 2004.
© Springer-Verlag Berlin Heidelberg 2004

The OOHDM framework [14] emphasises an object layer, hypermedia components and an interface layer. This is more or less the same idea as in the work of the ARANEUS group except that OOHDM explicitly refers to an object oriented approach. The approach in [5] emphasises a multi-level architecture for the data-driven generation of WISs, personalisation, and structures, derivation and composition, i.e. it addresses almost the same problem triplet as the ARANEUS framework.

Our own work in [7,16] emphasises a methodology oriented at abstraction layers and the co-design of structure, operations and interfaces. Among others this comprises a theory of *media types*, which covers extended views, adaptivity, hierarchies and presentation style options. This theory is coupled with *storyboarding*, an activity that – roughly speaking – addresses the design of an underlying application story. As soon as WISs become large, it becomes decisive that such an underlying application story is well designed.

Application stories can be expressed by some form of process algebra. That is, we need atomic activities and constructors for sequencing, parallelism, choice, iteration, etc. to write stories. The language SiteLang [6] is in fact such a process algebra for the purpose of storyboarding. In addition to the mentioned constructors it emphasises the need for modelling *scenes* of the story, which can be expressed by indexing the atomic activities and using additional constructs for entering and leaving scenes.

In this paper we show that such WIS-oriented process algebras lead to many-sorted Kleene algebras with tests, where the sorts correspond to scenes in the story space. Kleene algebras (KAs) have been introduced in [10] and extended to Kleene algebras with tests (KATs) in [12]. In a nutshell, a KA is an algebra of regular expressions, but there are many different interpretations other than just regular sets. A KAT imposes an additional structure of a Boolean algebra on a subset of the carrier set of a Kleene algebra.

If we ignore assignments, KATs can be used to model abstract programs. Doing this, it has been shown in [13] that KATs subsume propositional Hoare logic [9]. This subsumption is even strict, as the theory of KATs is complete, whereas propositional Hoare logic is not. Therefore, we consider KATs an ideal candidate for reasoning about the story space. In this paper we show two applications for this:

- the personalisation of the story space to the preferences of a particular user, and
- the satisfaction of particular information needs of a WIS user.

We will use the on-line loan application example from [3,15] to illustrate these applications in the practically relevant area of electronic banking.

In Section 2 we briefly introduce storyboarding and discuss process algebra constructs that are needed to reason about storyboards. In Section 3 we explain KATs and our version of many-sorted KATs, as they arise from storyboarding. Then, in Section 4 we address the reasoning with KATs and demonstrate the two applications. We conclude with a short summary.

2   Storyboarding in Web Information Systems

As WISs are open in the sense that anyone who has access to the web could become a user, the design of such systems requires some anticipation of the users' behaviour. Storyboarding addresses this problem. Thus, a *storyboard* will describe the ways users may choose to navigate through the system.

2.1   Scenario Modelling

At a high level of abstraction we may think of a WIS as a set of abstract locations, which abstract from actual pages. A user navigates between these locations, and on this navigation path s/he executes a number of actions. We regard a location together with local actions, i.e. actions that do not change the location, as a unit called *scene*.

Then a WIS can be decribed by an edge-labelled directed multi-graph, in which the vertices represent the scenes, and the edges represent transitions between scenes. Each such transition may be labelled by an action executed by the user. If such a label is missing, the transition is due to a simple navigation link. The whole multi-graph is then called the *story space*.

Roughly speaking, a *story* is a path in the story space. It tells what a user of a particular type might do with the system.

The combination of different stories to a subgraph of the story space can be used to describe a "typical" use of the WIS for a particular task. Therefore, we call such a subgraph a *scenario*. Usually storyboarding starts with modelling scenarios instead of stories, coupled by the integration of stories to the story space.

At a finer level of details, we may add a triggering *event*, a *precondition* and a *postcondition* to each action, i.e. we specify exactly, under which conditions an action can be executed and which effects it will have. Further extensions to scenes such as adaptivity, presentation, tasks and roles have been discussed in [3] and [7], but these extensions are not relevant here.

Looking at scenarios or the whole story space from a different angle, we may concentrate on the flow of actions:

- For the purpose of storyboarding, actions can be treated as being atomic, i.e. we are not yet interested in how an underlying database might be updated. Then each action also belongs to a uniquely determined scene.
- Actions have pre- and postconditions, so we can use annotations to express conditions that must hold before or after an action is executed.
- Actions can be executed sequentially or parallel, and we must allow (demonic) choice between actions.
- Actions can be iterated.
- By adding an action `skip` we can then also express optionality and iteration with at least one execution.

These possibilities to combine actions lead to operators of an algebra, which we will call a *story algebra*. Thus, we can describe a story space by an element of a suitable story algebra. We should, however, note already that story algebras have to be defined as being many-sorted in order to capture the association of actions with scenes.

2.2   Story Algebras

Let us take now a closer look at the storyboarding language SiteLang [6], which in fact defines a story algebra. So, let $\mathcal{S} = \{s_1, \ldots, s_n\}$ be a set of scenes, and let $\mathcal{A} = \{\alpha_1, \ldots, \alpha_k\}$ be a set of (atomic) actions. Furthermore, assume a mapping $\sigma : \mathcal{A} \to \mathcal{S}$, i.e. with each action $\alpha \in \mathcal{A}$ we associate a scene $\sigma(\alpha)$.

This can be used to define inductively the set of *processes* $\mathcal{P} = \mathcal{P}(\mathcal{A}, \mathcal{S})$ determined by $\mathcal{A}$ and $\mathcal{S}$. Furthermore, we can extend σ to a partial mapping $\mathcal{P} \to \mathcal{S}$ as follows:

- Each action $\alpha \in \mathcal{A}$ is also a process, i.e. $\alpha \in \mathcal{P}$, and the associated scene $\sigma(\alpha)$ is already given.
- skip is a process, for which $\sigma(\text{skip})$ is undefined.
- If p_1 and p_2 are processes, then the *sequence* $p_1; p_2$ is also a process. Furthermore, if $\sigma(p_1) = \sigma(p_2) = s$ or one of the p_i is skip, then $\sigma(p_1; p_2)$ is also defined and equals s, otherwise it is undefined.
- If p_1 and p_2 are processes, then also the *parallel process* $p_1 \| p_2$ is a process. Furthermore, if $\sigma(p_1) = \sigma(p_2) = s$ or one of the p_i is skip, then $\sigma(p_1 \| p_2)$ is also defined and equals s, otherwise it is undefined.
- If p_1 and p_2 are processes, then also the *choice* $p_1 \square p_2$ is a process. Furthermore, if $\sigma(p_1) = \sigma(p_2) = s$ or one of the p_i is skip, then $\sigma(p_1 \square p_2)$ is also defined and equals s, otherwise it is undefined.
- If p is a process, then also the *iteration* p^* is a process with $\sigma(p^*) = \sigma(p)$, if $\sigma(p)$ is defined.
- If p is a process and φ is a boolean condition, then the *guarded process* $\{\varphi\}p$ and the *post-guarded process* $p\{\varphi\}$ are processes with $\sigma(\{\varphi\}p) = \sigma(p\{\varphi\}) = \sigma(p)$, if $\sigma(p)$ is defined.

Doing this, we have to assume tacitly that navigation between scenes is also represented by an activity in $\mathcal{A}$, and the assigned scene is the origin of the navigation. SiteLang provides some more constructs, which we have omitted here. Constructs such as non-empty iteration p^+ and optionality $[p]$ can be expressed by the constructs above, as we have $p^+ = p; p^*$ and $[p] = p\square\text{skip}$.

Furthermore, we deviated from the SiteLang syntax used in [6] and [3]. For instance, SiteLang provides constructors $\nearrow$ and $\searrow$ to enter or leave a scene, respectively. We simply use parentheses and make the associated scene explicit in the definition of σ.

Parallel execution is denoted by $\|$ and choice by $\oplus$ in SiteLang, whereas here we use the more traditional notation.

SiteLang also uses φ to mark a parallel execution with a synchronisation condition φ, which in our language here can be expressed by a post-guarded parallel process $(\ldots \| \ldots)\{\varphi\}$.

Example 2.1. Consider the loan application from [15]. A rough sketch of the story space can be described as follows:

enter_loan_system ;
$\quad$ ((($\{\varphi_0\}$ look_at_loans_at_a_glance $\square$
$\qquad$ ($\{\varphi_1\}$ request_home_loan_details ;
$\qquad\quad$ (look_at_home_loan_samples $\square$ **skip**) $\{\varphi_3\}$) $\square$
$\qquad$ ($\{\varphi_2\}$ request_mortgage_details ;
$\qquad\quad$ (look_at_mortgage_samples $\square$ **skip**) $\{\varphi_4\}$))* $\{\varphi_5\}$) ;
$\quad$ (select_home_loan $\{\varphi_6\}$ $\square$ select_mortgage $\{\varphi_7\}$) ;
$\quad$ (($\{\varphi_6\}$ (provide_applicant_details ;
$\qquad\quad$ (provide_applicant_details $\square$ **skip**) ;
$\qquad$ (describe_loan_purpose $\parallel$ enter_amount_requested $\parallel$
$\qquad\qquad$ enter_income_details) ;
$\qquad$ select_hl_terms_and_conditions) $\{\varphi_8\}$) $\square$
$\quad$ ($\{\varphi_7\}$ (provide_applicant_details ; provide_applicant_details* ;
$\qquad\quad$ (describe_object $\parallel$ enter_mortgage_amount $\parallel$
$\qquad\qquad$ describe_securities*) ;
$\qquad\quad$ (enter_income_details $\parallel$ enter_obligations*) ;
$\qquad\quad$ (($\{\neg\varphi_{12}\}$ select_m_terms_and_conditions ;
$\qquad\qquad$ calculate_payments)* ;
$\qquad\qquad$ $\{\varphi_{12}\}$ select_m_terms_and_conditions)) $\{\varphi_9\}$)) ;
$\quad$ confirm_application $\{\varphi_{10} \vee \varphi_{11}\}$

involving the conditions

$$\varphi_0 \equiv \text{information\_about\_loan\_types\_needed}$$
$$\varphi_1 \equiv \text{information\_about\_home\_loans\_needed}$$
$$\varphi_2 \equiv \text{information\_about\_mortgages\_needed}$$
$$\varphi_3 \equiv \text{home\_loans\_known}$$
$$\varphi_4 \equiv \text{mortgages\_known}$$
$$\varphi_5 \equiv \text{available\_loans\_known}$$
$$\varphi_6 \equiv \text{home\_loan\_selected}$$
$$\varphi_7 \equiv \text{mortgage\_selected}$$
$$\varphi_8 \equiv \text{home\_loan\_application\_completed}$$
$$\varphi_9 \equiv \text{mortgage\_application\_completed}$$
$$\varphi_{10} \equiv \text{applied\_for\_home\_loan}$$
$$\varphi_{11} \equiv \text{applied\_for\_mortgage}$$
$$\varphi_{12} \equiv \text{payment\_options\_clear}$$

The set of scenes is $\mathcal{S} = \{s_1, \ldots, s_9\}$ with

$$s_1 = \text{type\_of\_loan} \quad s_2 = \text{applicant\_details} \quad s_3 = \text{home\_loan\_details}$$
$$s_4 = \text{home\_loan\_budget} \quad s_5 = \text{mortgage\_details} \quad s_6 = \text{securities\_details}$$
$$s_7 = \text{mortgage\_budget} \quad s_8 = \text{confirmation} \quad s_9 = \text{income}$$

The set of actions is $\mathcal{A} = \{\alpha_1, \ldots, \alpha_{20}\}$ using

$$\alpha_1 = \text{enter\_loan\_system} \quad \alpha_2 = \text{look\_at\_loans\_at\_a\_glance}$$
$$\alpha_3 = \text{request\_home\_loan\_details} \quad \alpha_4 = \text{request\_mortgage\_details}$$
$$\alpha_5 = \text{look\_at\_home\_loan\_samples} \quad \alpha_6 = \text{look\_at\_mortgage\_samples}$$
$$\alpha_7 = \text{select\_home\_loan} \quad \alpha_8 = \text{provide\_applicant\_details}$$
$$\alpha_9 = \text{describe\_loan\_purpose} \quad \alpha_{10} = \text{enter\_amount\_requested}$$
$$\alpha_{11} = \text{enter\_income\_details} \quad \alpha_{12} = \text{select\_hl\_terms\_and\_conditions}$$
$$\alpha_{13} = \text{select\_mortgage} \quad \alpha_{14} = \text{describe\_object}$$
$$\alpha_{15} = \text{enter\_mortgage\_amount} \quad \alpha_{16} = \text{describe\_securities}$$
$$\alpha_{17} = \text{enter\_obligations} \quad \alpha_{18} = \text{select\_m\_terms\_and\_conditions}$$
$$\alpha_{19} = \text{calculate\_payments} \quad \alpha_{20} = \text{confirm\_application}$$

Finally, we get the scene assignment σ with

$$\sigma(\alpha_1) = s_1 \quad \sigma(\alpha_2) = s_1 \quad \sigma(\alpha_3) = s_1 \quad \sigma(\alpha_4) = s_1 \quad \sigma(\alpha_5) = s_1$$
$$\sigma(\alpha_6) = s_1 \quad \sigma(\alpha_7) = s_1 \quad \sigma(\alpha_8) = s_2 \quad \sigma(\alpha_9) = s_3 \quad \sigma(\alpha_{10}) = s_3$$
$$\sigma(\alpha_{11}) = s_9 \quad \sigma(\alpha_{12}) = s_4 \quad \sigma(\alpha_{13}) = s_1 \quad \sigma(\alpha_{14}) = s_5 \quad \sigma(\alpha_{15}) = s_5$$
$$\sigma(\alpha_{16}) = s_6 \quad \sigma(\alpha_{17}) = s_7 \quad \sigma(\alpha_{18}) = s_7 \quad \sigma(\alpha_{19}) = s_7 \quad \sigma(\alpha_{20}) = s_8$$

As a consequence, the scene associated with the sub-process

enter_loan_system ;
$\quad$ (($\{\varphi_0\}$ look_at_loans_at_a_glance $\square$
$\quad\quad\quad$ ($\{\varphi_1\}$ request_home_loan_details ;
$\quad\quad\quad\quad\quad$ (look_at_home_loan_samples $\square$ skip) $\{\varphi_3\}$) $\square$
$\quad\quad\quad$ ($\{\varphi_2\}$ request_mortgage_details ;
$\quad\quad\quad\quad\quad$ (look_at_mortgage_samples $\square$ skip) $\{\varphi_4\}$))* $\{\varphi_5\}$) ;
$\quad\quad$ (select_home_loan $\{\varphi_6\}$ $\square$ select_mortgage $\{\varphi_7\}$)

will also be s_1.

3 Many-Sorted Kleene Algebras with Tests

Let $\mathcal{A}$ be an alphabet. Then it is well known that the *set of regular expressions over $\mathcal{A}$* is inductively defined as the smallest set $\mathcal{R}$ with $\mathcal{A} \subseteq \mathcal{R}$ satisfying the following conditions:

- the special symbols 1 and 0 are regular expressions in $\mathcal{R}$;
- for $p, q \in \mathcal{R}$ we also have $p + q \in \mathcal{R}$ and $pq \in \mathcal{R}$;
- for $p \in \mathcal{R}$ we also have $p^* \in \mathcal{R}$.

The usual interpretation is by regular subsets of $\mathcal{A}^*$, where 1 corresponds to the regular language $\{\epsilon\}$ containing only the empty word, 0 corresponds to $\emptyset$, any $a \in \mathcal{A}$ corresponds to $\{a\}$, + corresponds to union, concatenation to the product of regular sets, and * corresponds to the Kleene hull.

3.1   Kleene Algebras

Abstracting from this example of regular expressions we obtain the notion of a Kleene algebra as follows.

Definition 3.1. A *Kleene algebra* (KA) $\mathcal{K}$ consists of

- a carrier-set K containing at least two different elements 0 and 1, and
- a unary operation * and two binary operations $+$ and $\cdot$ on K

such that the following axioms are satisfied:

- $+$ and $\cdot$ are associative, i.e. for all $p, q, r \in K$ we must have $p + (q + r) = (p + q) + r$ and $p(qr) = (pq)r$;
- $+$ is commutative and idempotent with 0 as neutral element, i.e. for all $p, q \in K$ we must have $p + q = q + p$, $p + p = p$ and $p + 0 = p$;
- 1 is a neutral element for $\cdot$, i.e. for all $p \in K$ we must have $p1 = 1p = p$;
- for all $p \in K$ we have $p0 = 0p = 0$;
- $\cdot$ is distributive over $+$, i.e. for all $p, q, r \in K$ we must have $p(q+r) = pq+pr$ and $(p+q)r = pr + qr$;
- p^*q ist the least solution x of $q + px \leq x$ and qp^* is the least solution of $q + xp \leq x$, using the partial order $x \leq y \equiv x + y = y$.

We adopted the convention to write pq for $p \cdot q$, and to assume that $\cdot$ binds stronger than $+$, which allows us to dispense with some parentheses. In the sequel we will write $\mathcal{K} = (K, +, \cdot, ^*, 0, 1)$ to denote a Kleene algebra.

Of course, the standard example is regular sets. For other non-standard examples refer to [10] and [11].

Here, we want to use Kleene algebras to represent story algebras as discussed in the previous section. Obviously, $+$ will correspond to the choice-operator, $\cdot$ to the sequence-operator, and * to the iteration operator. Furthermore, 1 will correspond to skip and 0 to the undefined process fail. However, we will need an extension to capture guards and post-guards, we have to think about the parallel-operator, and we have to handle associated scenes. Capturing guards and post-guards leads to Kleene algebras with tests, which were introduced in [12].

Definition 3.2. A *Kleene algebra with tests* (KAT) $\mathcal{K}$ consists of

- a Kleene algebra $(K, +, \cdot, ^*, 0, 1)$;
- a subset $B \subseteq K$ containing 0 and 1 and closed under $+$ and $\cdot$;
- and a unary operation $^-$ on B, such that $(B, +, \cdot, ^-, 0, 1)$ forms a Boolean algebra.

We write $\mathcal{K} = (K, B, +, \cdot, ^*, ^-, 0, 1)$.

3.2 Representing Story Algebras by Kleene Algebras with Tests

Now obviously the conditions appearing as guards and post-guards in a story algebra, form the set B of tests. So, if we ignore the parallel-constructor $\|$ for the moment, a story algebra gives rise to a KAT. However, we have to be aware that in such a KAT the operators $+$ and $\cdot$ and the constants 0 and 1 play a double role:

- The operator $+$ applied to two tests $\varphi, \psi \in B$ represents the logical OR, whereas in general it refers to the choice between two processes. As we have $(\varphi + \psi)p = \varphi p + \psi p$ this does not cause any problems.
- The operator $\cdot$ applied to two tests $\varphi, \psi \in B$ represents the logical AND, whereas in general it refers to the sequencing of two processes. As we have $(\varphi\psi)p = \varphi(\psi p)$ this also does not cause any problems.
- The constant 1 represents both TRUE and `skip`, whereas 0 represents both FALSE and `fail`, which both do not cause problems, as can easily be seen from the axioms of Kleene algebras.

Furthermore, we may define a *scene assignment* to a KAT by simply following the rules for the scene assignment in story algebras. That is, we obtain a partial mapping $\sigma : K \to S$ with a set $S = \{s_1, \ldots, s_n\}$ of scenes as follows:

- For $p_1, p_2 \in K$ with $\sigma(p_1) = \sigma(p_2) = s$ or one of the p_i is 1 or 0 or a test in B, then $\sigma(p_1 p_2) = s$.
- For $p_1, p_2 \in K$ with $\sigma(p_1) = \sigma(p_2) = s$ or one of the p_i is 1 or 0 or a test in B, then $\sigma(p_1 + p_2) = s$.
- For $p \in K$ with $\sigma(p) = s$ we obtain $\sigma(p^*) = s$.

Finally, let us look at parallel processes. From the intuition of scenes as abstract locations, we should assume that atomic actions from different scenes can be executed in parallel, which could be rephrased in a way that the order does not matter. Obviously, this extends to processes that are associated with different scenes. Therefore, the operator $\|$ is not needed for processes that belong to different scenes – any order will do. More formally, this means the following:

- If we have $p_1 \| p_2$ with $\sigma(p_i)$ both defined, but different, then this will be represented by $p_1 p_2$ (or $p_2 p_1$) in the KAT.
- In the KAT we then need $p_1 p_2 = p_2 p_1$, whenever $\sigma(p_1) \neq \sigma(p_2)$.

This leads to our definition of a many-sorted Kleene algebra with tests.

Definition 3.3. A *many-sorted Kleene algebra with tests* (MKAT) is a KAT $\mathcal{K} = (K, B, +, \cdot, ^*, ^-, 0, 1)$ together with a set $S = \{s_1, \ldots, s_n\}$ of scenes and a scene assignment $\sigma : K \to S$ such that $p_1 p_2 = p_2 p_1$ holds for all $p_1, p_2 \in K$ with $\sigma(p_1) \neq \sigma(p_2)$.

From our discussion above it is clear that we can represent a story space by an element of the MKAT that is defined by the atomic actions, the tests and the scenes.

Example 3.1. If we rewrite the story space from Example 2.1 we obtain the following KAT expression:

$$\alpha_1((\varphi_0\alpha_2 + \varphi_1\alpha_3(\alpha_5 + 1)\varphi_3 + \varphi_2\alpha_4(\alpha_6 + 1)\varphi_4)^*\varphi_5)(\alpha_7\varphi_6 + \alpha_{13}\varphi_7)$$
$$(\varphi_6\alpha_8(\alpha_8 + 1)\alpha_9\alpha_{10}\alpha_{11}\alpha_{12}\varphi_8 + \varphi_7\alpha_8\alpha_8^*\alpha_{14}\alpha_{15}\alpha_{16}^*\alpha_{11}\alpha_{17}(\overline{\varphi_{12}}\alpha_{18}\alpha_{19})^*\varphi_{12}\alpha_{18}\varphi_9)$$
$$\alpha_{20}(\varphi_{10} + \varphi_{11})$$

4   Applying Many-Sorted Kleene Algebras with Tests

In order to reason about story spaces, we may now exploit the fact that they can be described by many-sorted KATs.

4.1   Equational Reasoning with KATs

Hoare logic [9] is the oldest formal system for reasoning about abstract programs. Its basic idea is to use partial correctness assertions – also called *Hoare triplets* – of the form $\{\varphi\}p\{\psi\}$. Here p is a program, and φ and ψ are its pre- and postcondition, respectively, i.e. logical formulae that can be evaluated in a program state.

The informal meaning of these triplets is that "whenever the program p is started in a state satisfying φ and terminates, then it will do so in a state satisfying ψ".

Using KATs, such a Hoare triplet corresponds to a simple equation $\varphi p \bar{\psi} = 0$. Equivalently, this can be formulated by $\varphi p \leq p\psi$ or $p\bar{\psi} \leq \bar{\varphi}p$ or $\varphi p = \varphi p\psi$.

In [13] it has been shown that KATs subsume propositional Hoare logic (PHL), i.e. all derivation rules of Hoare logic can be proven to be theorems for KATs. However, the theory of KATs is complete, whereas PHL is not.

In order to use KATs to reason about story spaces, the general approach is as follows. First we consider the atomic actions and scene and the many-sorted KAT defined by them. In this KAT we can express the story space or parts of it by some process expression p. We then formulate a problem by using equations or conditional equations in this KAT. Furthermore, we obtain (conditional) equations, which represent application knowledge. This application knowledge arises from events, postconditions and knowledge about the use of the WIS for a particular purpose. We then apply all equations to solve the particular problem at hand.

The application knowledge contains at least the following equations:

1. If an action p has a precondition φ, then we obtain the equation $\bar{\varphi}p = 0$.
2. If an action p has a postcondition ψ, we obtain the equation $p = p\psi$.
3. If an action p is triggered by a condition φ, we obtain the equation $\varphi = \varphi p$.
4. In addition we obtain exclusion conditions $\varphi\psi = 0$ and tautologies $\varphi + \psi = 1$.

4.2 Personalisation of Story Spaces

The problem of story space personalisation according to the preferences of a particular WIS user can be formalised as follows. Assume that $p \in K$ represents the story space. Then we may formulate the *preferences* of a user by a set Σ of (conditional) equations. Let χ be the conjunction of the conditions in Σ. Then the problem is to find a minimal process $p' \in K$ such that $\chi \Rightarrow px = p'x$ holds for all $x \in K$.

Preference equations can arise as follows:

1. An equation $p_1 + p_2 = p_1$ expresses an unconditional preference of activity (or process) p_1 over p_2.
2. An equation $\varphi(p_1 + p_2) = \varphi p_1$ expresses a conditional preference of activity (or process) p_1 over p_2 in case that the condition φ is satisfied.
3. Similarly, an equation $p(p_1 + p_2) = pp_1$ expresses another conditional preference of activity (or process) p_1 over p_2 after the activity (or process) p.
4. An equation $p_1 p_2 + p_2 p_1 = p_1 p_2$ expresses a preference of order.
5. An equation $p^* = pp^*$ expresses that in case of an iteration it will be executed at least once.

For instance, assume that the story space is $p = p_1(\varphi(p_2 + p_3) + \bar{\varphi} p_4^* p_5)$ and that we have the conditional preference rules $\varphi(p_2 + p_3) = \varphi p_2$ and $p_1 \bar{\varphi} p_4^* = p_1 \bar{\varphi} p_4 p_4^*$. Then we get

$$px = p_1(\varphi(p_2 + p_3) + \bar{\varphi} p_4^* p_5)x = p_1 \varphi p_2 x + p_1 \bar{\varphi} p_4^* p_5 x =$$
$$p_1 \varphi p_2 x + p_1 \bar{\varphi} p_4 p_4^* p_5 x = p_1(\varphi p_2 + \bar{\varphi} p_4 p_4^* p_5)x.$$

That is, we can simplify p by $p' = p_1(\varphi p_2 + \bar{\varphi} p_4 p_4^* p_5)$. Obviously, we have $p' \leq p$, but further equations in our application knowledge may give rise to an even smaller solution. Let us finally illustrate this application with a non-artificial example.

Example 4.1. Let us continue Example 3.1. Assume that we have to deal with a user who already knows everything about loans. This can be expressed by the application knowledge equation $\varphi_5 x = x$ for all $x \in K$. Furthermore, as knowledge about loans implies that there is no need for information about loans, we obtain three additional exclusion conditions:

$$\varphi_5 \varphi_0 = 0 \qquad \varphi_5 \varphi_1 = 0 \qquad \varphi_5 \varphi_2 = 0$$

Taking these equations to the first part of the expression in Example 3.1 we obtain

$$\alpha_1((\varphi_0 \alpha_2 + \varphi_1 \alpha_3(\alpha_5 + 1)\varphi_3 + \varphi_2 \alpha_4(\alpha_6 + 1)\varphi_4)^* \varphi_5)x =$$
$$\alpha_1((\varphi_0 \varphi_5 \alpha_2 + \varphi_1 \varphi_5 \alpha_3(\alpha_5 + 1)\varphi_3 + \varphi_2 \varphi_5 \alpha_4(\alpha_6 + 1)\varphi_4)^* \varphi_5)x =$$
$$\alpha_1((0\alpha_2 + 0\alpha_3(\alpha_5 + 1)\varphi_3 + 0\alpha_4(\alpha_6 + 1)\varphi_4)^* \varphi_5)x =$$
$$\alpha_1 1 \varphi_5 x =$$
$$\alpha_1 x$$

That is, the whole story space can be simplified to

$$\alpha_1(\alpha_7\varphi_6 + \alpha_{13}\varphi_7)$$
$$(\varphi_6\alpha_8(\alpha_8+1)\alpha_9\alpha_{10}\alpha_{11}\alpha_{12}\varphi_8 + \varphi_7\alpha_8\alpha_8^*\alpha_{14}\alpha_{15}\alpha_{16}^*\alpha_{11}\alpha_{17}(\overline{\varphi_{12}}\alpha_{18}\alpha_{19})^*\varphi_{12}\alpha_{18}\varphi_9)$$
$$\alpha_{20}(\varphi_{10} + \varphi_{11})$$

This means that for a user who knows about loans the part of the story space that deals with information about loans including sample applications will be cut out.

4.3   Satisfaction of Information Needs

The problem of satifying the information needs of a particular WIS user can be formalised by assuming that there is a *goal* that can be represented by some formula ψ. Thus, we can take $\psi \in B$. Furthermore, assume that our story space is represented by some process expression $p \in K$. Then the problem is to find a minimal process $p' \in K$ such that $p\psi = p'\psi$.

In order to find such a p' we have to use the application knowledge. In this case, however, we only obtain the general application knowledge that we already described above, unless we combine the application with personalisation.

For instance, assume we can write the story space p as a choice process $p_1 + p_2$. Let equations $\varphi\psi = 0$ and $p_2 = p_2\varphi$ (postcondition) be part of our application knowledge. If the goal is ψ, we get

$$p\psi = (p_1 + p_2)\psi = p_1\psi + p_2\psi = p_1\psi + p_2\varphi\psi = p_1\psi.$$

This means we can offer the simplified story space p_1 to satisfy the goal ψ. Let us finally illustrate this application with a non-artificial example.

Example 4.2. Let us continue Example 3.1 and look at a user who is going to apply for a home loan. This can be expressed by the goal φ_{10}. Then we express application knowledge by the equations $\varphi_{10}\varphi_{11} = 0$ (a user either applies for a home loan or a mortgage, not for both), $\varphi_{10}\varphi_9 = 0$ (a user applying for a home loan does not complete a mortgage application) and $\varphi_6\varphi_7 = 0$ (a user either selects a home loan or a mortgage, but not both).

Then we can simplify $p\varphi_{10}$ with the expression p from Example 3.1 step by step. First we get $(\varphi_{10} + \varphi_{11})\varphi_{10} = \varphi_{10}$, which can then be used for

$$(\varphi_6\alpha_8(\alpha_8+1)\alpha_9\alpha_{10}\alpha_{11}\alpha_{12}\varphi_8$$
$$+ \varphi_7\alpha_8\alpha_8^*\alpha_{14}\alpha_{15}\alpha_{16}^*\alpha_{11}\alpha_{17}(\overline{\varphi_{12}}\alpha_{18}\alpha_{19})^*\varphi_{12}\alpha_{18}\varphi_9)\varphi_{10} =$$
$$\varphi_6\alpha_8(\alpha_8+1)\alpha_9\alpha_{10}\alpha_{11}\alpha_{12}\varphi_8\varphi_{10}$$
$$+ \varphi_7\alpha_8\alpha_8^*\alpha_{14}\alpha_{15}\alpha_{16}^*\alpha_{11}\alpha_{17}(\overline{\varphi_{12}}\alpha_{18}\alpha_{19})^*\varphi_{12}\alpha_{18}\varphi_9\varphi_{10} =$$
$$\varphi_6\alpha_8(\alpha_8+1)\alpha_9\alpha_{10}\alpha_{11}\alpha_{12}\varphi_8\varphi_{10}$$

Then finally we get

$$(\alpha_7\varphi_6 + \alpha_{13}\varphi_7)\varphi_6\alpha_8(\alpha_8 + 1)\alpha_9\alpha_{10}\alpha_{11}\alpha_{12}\varphi_8\varphi_{10} =$$
$$\alpha_7\varphi_6\varphi_6\alpha_8(\alpha_8 + 1)\alpha_9\alpha_{10}\alpha_{11}\alpha_{12}\varphi_8\varphi_{10}$$
$$+ \alpha_{13}\varphi_7\varphi_6\alpha_8(\alpha_8 + 1)\alpha_9\alpha_{10}\alpha_{11}\alpha_{12}\varphi_8\varphi_{10} =$$
$$\alpha_7\varphi_6\alpha_8(\alpha_8 + 1)\alpha_9\alpha_{10}\alpha_{11}\alpha_{12}\varphi_8\varphi_{10}$$

This means that the story space can be simplified to

$$\alpha_1((\varphi_0\alpha_2 + \varphi_1\alpha_3(\alpha_5 + 1)\varphi_3 + \varphi_2\alpha_4(\alpha_6 + 1)\varphi_4)^*\varphi_5)$$
$$\alpha_7\varphi_6\alpha_8(\alpha_8 + 1)\alpha_9\alpha_{10}\alpha_{11}\alpha_{12}\varphi_8\alpha_{20}\varphi_{10}$$

This simply means that for a user who is looking for a home loan application the part of the story space that deals with mortgage application will be cut out.

5   Conclusion

In this paper we addressed the problem of formal reasoning about web information systems (WISs). We argued that the underlying application story must be well designed, especially for large systems. Stories can be expressed by some form of process algebra, e.g. using the language SiteLang from [6]. For the most relevant reasoning problems it is sufficient to assume that such story algebras are propositional, i.e. we ignore assignments and treat atomic operations instead.

Doing this we demonstrated that Kleene algebras with tests (KATs) are adequate to decribe the stories. We added sorts to KATs in order to enhance the model by scenes, i.e. abstract bundles of user activities at the same location in a WIS.

Then we demonstrated the use of many-sorted KATs to the problems of personalisation and satisfaction of information needs. These cover two highly relevant aspects of WISs. Thus, the use of KATs demonstrates a huge potential for improving the quality of WISs.

There are further applications for our approach such as equivalence proofs or static analysis of story space specifications, but these still have to be explored. However, as static analysis, optimisation, equivalence, etc. have already been investigated as application areas of KATs in program analysis, we are confident that our approach will be powerful enough to solve these application problems as well.

Furthermore, our research can be extended towards dynamic logic [8], in which case we would drop the restriction to ignore assignments. Of course we lose decidability properties, but we gain a more complete view of WISs, in which the structure and the dynamics of the underlying database is taken into account. This, however, implies that we have to deal not just only with storyboarding, but also with the subsequent step of defining database schemata, views and media types as outlined in [7,16].

References

1. ATZENI, P., GUPTA, A., AND SARAWAGI, S. Design and maintenance of data-intensive web-sites. In *Proceeding EDBT'98*, vol. 1377 of *LNCS*. Springer-Verlag, Berlin, 1998, pp. 436–450.
2. BARESI, L., GARZOTTO, F., AND PAOLINI, P. From web sites to web applications: New issues for conceptual modeling. In *ER Workshops 2000*, vol. 1921 of *LNCS*. Springer-Verlag, Berlin, 2000, pp. 89–100.
3. BINEMANN-ZDANOWICZ, A., KASCHEK, R., SCHEWE, K.-D., AND THALHEIM, B. Context-aware web information systems. In *Conceptual Modelling 2004 – First Asia-Pacific Conference on Conceptual Modelling* (Dunedin, New Zealand, 2004), S. Hartmann and J. Roddick, Eds., vol. 31 of *CRPIT*, Australian Computer Society, pp. 37–48.
4. BONIFATI, A., CERI, S., FRATERNALI, P., AND MAURINO, A. Building multi-device, content-centric applications using WebML and the W3I3 tool suite. In *ER Workshops 2000*, vol. 1921 of *LNCS*. Springer-Verlag, Berlin, 2000, pp. 64–75.
5. CERI, S., FRATERNALI, P., BONGIO, A., BRAMBILLA, M., COMAI, S., AND MATERA, M. *Designing Data-Intensive Web Applications*. Morgan Kaufmann, San Francisco, 2003.
6. DÜSTERHÖFT, A., AND THALHEIM, B. SiteLang: Conceptual modeling of internet sites. In *Conceptual Modeling – ER 2001*, H. S. K. et al., Ed., vol. 2224 of *LNCS*. Springer-Verlag, Berlin, 2001, pp. 179–192.
7. FEYER, T., KAO, O., SCHEWE, K.-D., AND THALHEIM, B. Design of data-intensive web-based information services. In *Proceedings of the 1st International Conference on Web Information Systems Engineering (WISE 2000)*, Q. Li, Z. M. Ozsuyoglu, R. Wagner, Y. Kambayashi, and Y. Zhang, Eds. IEEE Computer Society, 2000, pp. 462–467.
8. HAREL, D., KOZEN, D., AND TIURYN, J. *Dynamic Logic*. The MIT Press, Cambridge (MA), USA, 2000.
9. HOARE, C. A. R. An axiomatic basis for computer programming. *Communications of the ACM 12*, 10 (1969), 576–580.
10. KOZEN, D. On Kleene algebra and closed semirings. In *Mathematical Fundamentals of Computer Science* (1990), pp. 26–47.
11. KOZEN, D. A completeness theorem for Kleene algebras and the algebra of regular events. *Information & Computation 110*, 2 (1994), 366–390.
12. KOZEN, D. Kleene algebra with tests. *ACM Transactions on Programming Languages and Systems 19*, 3 (1997), 427–443.
13. KOZEN, D. On Hoare logic and Kleene algebra with tests. In *Logic in Computer Science* (1999), pp. 167–172.
14. ROSSI, G., SCHWABE, D., AND LYARDET, F. Web application models are more than conceptual models. In *Advances in Conceptual Modeling*, P. C. et al., Ed., vol. 1727 of *LNCS*. Springer-Verlag, Berlin, 1999, pp. 239–252.
15. SCHEWE, K.-D., KASCHEK, R., WALLACE, C., AND MATTHEWS, C. Modelling web-based banking systems: Story boarding and user profiling. In *Advanced Conceptual Modeling Techniques: ER 2002 Workshops* (2003), vol. 2784 of *LNCS*, Springer-Verlag, pp. 427–439.
16. SCHEWE, K.-D., AND THALHEIM, B. Modeling interaction and media objects. In *Natural Language Processing and Information Systems: 5th International Conference on Applications of Natural Language to Information Systems, NLDB 2000*, M. Bouzeghoub, Z. Kedad, and E. Métais, Eds., vol. 1959 of *LNCS*. Springer-Verlag, Berlin, 2001, pp. 313–324.

Component Framework for Strategic Supply Network Development

Antonia Albani, Bettina Bazijanec, Klaus Turowski, and Christian Winnewisser

Business Informatics and Systems Engineering
Business Faculty, University of Augsburg,
Universitätsstraße 16, 86135 Augsburg, Germany
{antonia.albani,bettina.bazijanec,klaus.turowski,
christian.winnewisser}@wiwi.uni-augsburg.de

Abstract. This paper presents a component framework for inter-organizational collaboration in value networks in the domain of strategic supply network development. The domain chosen extends the traditional frame of reference in strategic sourcing from a supplier-centric to a supply-network-scope. The basic functionality provided by the component framework and discussed in this paper is the *dynamic modeling* of strategic supply networks and the *collaboration* between requestors and suppliers in a dynamic network. The corresponding component model is introduced and the functionality provided by the modeling component discussed in detail. The problems of heterogeneity that come up in inter-organizational communication and collaboration will be addressed by introducing a collaboration component that guarantees correct interchange and representation of application data. It is shown what kind of interoperability problems will be encountered in the strategic supply network development scenario as well as how the communication and collaboration component is able to cope with these problems.

1 Introduction

With the emergence of the Internet and the continuous innovations in information and communication technologies, new possibilities and challenges for improving and automating intra- and inter-enterprise business processes arise. Technological innovations such as global, web-based infrastructures, communication standards and distributed systems enable the integration of business processes between companies thus increasing flexibility of the business system and improving inter-company collaboration in value networks, often referred as inter-organizational systems (IOS), e-collaboration and collaboration commerce [16]. Companies can therefore more and more focus on their core competencies and increasingly collaborate with, and outsource business tasks to business partners, forming value networks in order to better react to fast changing market requirements. An increasing amount of practice initiatives arose in order to not only support intra- but also inter-organizational collaboration in value networks. The concept of value networks itself with companies flexibly collaborating to design, produce, market and distribute products and services is not new and had been well established, e.g. by [18, 32], even before the above mentioned

A. Benczúr, J. Demetrovics, G. Gottlob (Eds.): ADBIS 2004, LNCS 3255, pp. 67–82, 2004.
© Springer-Verlag Berlin Heidelberg 2004

technology had become available. However, at present IT-enabled value networks can be largely found in the form of rather small, flexible alliances of professionalized participants. The support of large value networks with multiple tiers of suppliers – as they can be found in many traditional production- oriented industries – still causes considerable difficulties.

One of the most analyzed objects of reference in research centered around inter-organizational systems, virtual enterprises and value networks is the supply chain; especially with respect to the perceived business value. However, failed initiatives, primarily in the field of supply chain management, have spurred concern about the practicability of present approaches and theories and have shown the need for further refinement and adaptation. According to [17], one of the main reasons for this is the high degree of complexity that is connected with the identification of potential suppliers and the modeling of the supply chain structure, as well as the high coordination effort between entities in the supply chain. Despite the fact that both, the modeling of supply chains and the coordination between supply chain entities are basic principles in order to succeed e.g. in supply chain management, many research efforts have been based on the more operative interpretation of supply chain management [14, 15], primarily focusing on the optimization of forecast and planning accuracy, and the optimization of material flows over the whole supply chain.

In order to analyze the basic principles, such as value chain modeling and collaboration between value chain entities, in collaborative networks the authors see the necessity to set the focus primarily on strategic tasks, such as long term supplier development, before dealing with operative tasks of supply chain management, such as operative purchasing put in a network context. Strategic tasks have not been widely discussed in a network perspective yet even if current research work, such as [9], give an extended interpretation of supply chain management partly considering supplier relationships as part of supply chain management. Therefore the domain of *Strategic Supply Network Development (SSND)*, which extends the traditional frame of reference in strategic sourcing from a supplier-centric to a supply-network scope, is used in this paper to develop a generic framework for inter-enterprise collaboration providing the basic, but essential, functionalities needed in an IT-enabled value network.

In the domain of strategic supply network development two goals are persecuted. The first goal is the dynamic modeling of supply networks, supporting requestors of products or services to keep track of all suppliers or service providers contributing to a specific request in a dynamic changing environment. Therefore the concept of *self modeling demand driven value networks* is introduced in chapter 2 by means of the domain of strategic supply network development. Having explained the concept of self modeling demand driven value networks, the generic component model for the domain of SSND is introduced in chapter 3, giving a description of the basic components of the framework.

The second goal which is persecuted by using the domain of strategic supply network development in order to develop a component framework for the inter-enterprise collaboration is pointed out in chapter 4. The focus there is set on the description of the collaboration component, which aims at providing an infrastructure for collaboration and communication between requestors, suppliers and service providers. The problems of heterogeneity that come up in inter-organizational communication and collaboration will be addressed by introducing the collaboration component that guarantees correct interchange and representation of application data. It is shown what kind of interoperability problems will be encountered in the strategic supply network development scenario as well as how the communication and collaboration component is able to cope with these problems.

A first prototype implementation of the component framework for the domain of strategic supply network development is presented in chapter 5 addressing specific implementation details regarding the collaboration between network elements. Conclusion and future work are given in chapter 6.

2 Strategic Supply Network Development and the Concept of Self Modeling Demand Driven Value Networks

Purchasing has become a core function in enterprises in the 90ies. Current empiric research shows a significant correlation between the establishment of a strategic purchasing function and the financial success of an enterprise, independent from the industry surveyed [8]. One of the most important factors in this connection is the buyer-supplier-relationship. At many of the surveyed companies, a close cooperation between buyer and supplier in areas such as long-term planning, product development and coordination of production processes led to process improvements and resulting cost reductions that were shared between buyer and suppliers [8].

In practice, supplier development is widely limited to suppliers in tier-1. With respect to the above demonstrated, superior importance of supplier development we postulate the extension of the traditional frame of reference in strategic sourcing from a supplier-centric to a supply-network-scope i.e., the further development of the strategic supplier development to a *strategic supply network development (SSND)*. This refocuses the object of reference in the field of strategic sourcing by analyzing supplier networks instead of single suppliers. Embedded in this paradigm shift is the concept of the value network.

2.1 Strategic Supply Network Development

The main tasks in the domain of strategic supply network development derive from the tasks of strategic sourcing. The most evident changes regard the functions with cross-enterprise focus. The process of *supplier selection* from strategic purchasing undergoes the most evident changes in the shift to a supply network perspective. The expansion of the traditional frame of reference in strategic sourcing requires more information than merely data on existing and potential suppliers in tier-1. Instead, the supply networks connected with those suppliers have to be identified and evaluated, e.g. by comparing alternative supply networks in the production network. As a consequence, the task supplier selection is only part of the process that leads to the *modeling of strategic supply networks* in SSND. In addition to the modeling, identification and selection of suitable supply networks and composition of alternative supply networks, the *qualification of strategic supply networks* is another major goal of SSND – according to qualification of suppliers in strategic sourcing. Main prerequisite is the constant evaluation of the actual performance of selected supply networks by defined benchmarks. This is important because of the long-term character of strategic supply network relationships. For a detailed description of the domain of SSND please refer to [2, 1], where the domain has been introduced in more detail as an example domain for the identification and modeling of component based business applications and for the standardization of collaborative business applications.

2.2 Concept of Self Modeling Demand Driven Value Networks

SSND supports companies in identifying and developing their strategic networks in order to improve their productivity and to compete on the daily market. The concept of the supply network as a *self modeling demand driven network* constitutes the basis for the identification of strategic supply networks.

The concept is based on requests for information regarding a specific product (demands) and specified by a producer (OEM). The demands can either be fulfilled by the own production company or need to be sent to existing or potential suppliers in order to receive information about product's producibility. Since not only information about the supplier in tier-1 is required by the OEM in order to strategically develop the supply network, the demands are split on each node in sub-demands, which are then forwarded to the next suppliers in the value network. Every node in tier-x receives demands from clients in tier-(x-1) and communicates sub-demands, depending on the demand received, to relevant suppliers in tier-(x+1). Since every node repeats the same procedure, a requestor receives back aggregated information from the whole dynamically built network based on a specific demand sent at a specific time.

At the core of the concept of self modeling demand driven networks is the notion, that network nodes of a supply network can be identified by applying the pull principle. With the pull principle (OEM requesting information from suppliers), a network node at the beginning of a (sub-)network can identify potential nodes, i.e. suppliers, in a subsequent tier by performing a bill of materials explosion. With this information, primary requirements and dependent requirements can be identified and the respective information can be communicated – sending a demand – to the respective network nodes, i.e. potential suppliers for dependent requirements, in the subsequent tier, as these suppliers are generally known by the initiating lot.

The concept is illustrated in the following by means of an example supply network, as shown in Fig. 1. The figure on the left shows a complete demand driven network constituted of existing (highlighted nodes) and alternative supply sub-networks. Existing sub-networks are those with whom the producer already collaborates. Alternative sub-networks are networks which are built by sending a demand for a specific product to new chosen suppliers, with yet no relation to the producer. The whole network is demand driven since the producer communicates a specific strategic demand, by performing a bill of materials explosion, to existing and selected alternative suppliers in tier-1. Subsequently, the suppliers in tier-1 perform themselves a bill of materials explosion reporting the corresponding sub-demands to their own respective suppliers.

E.g., for supplier 1-2, these are the suppliers 2-2, 2-3 and 2-4 in tier-2. In the following, these suppliers report the newly defined sub-demands to their related suppliers in tier-3, which split-lot transfer the requested information including e.g. ability of delivery for the requested product, capacity per day, minimum volume to be ordered, time of delivery. The requestors aggregate the information received from all suppliers contacted for a specific request with the own information and send it back to the supplier 1-2 in tier-1. Having aggregated the information of all suppliers, the supplier 1-2 adds its own information before split-lot transferring it to the producer.

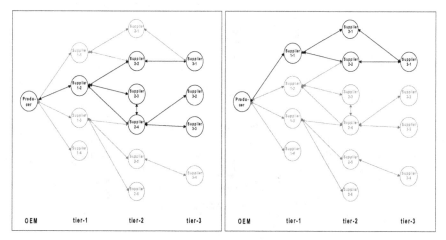

Fig. 1. Left: Supplier network, Right: Alternative supply network

With the suppliers' data locally available, the producer can visualize the selected sub-network, in which each participant constitutes a network hub. Based on that data, the producer is able to evaluate the performance of that selected sub-network by self defined benchmarks. In order to optimize sub-networks, alternative demand driven sub-networks can be visualized and modeled by applying the same concept as described above to newly defined suppliers. Fig. 1 on the right highlights an alternative virtual supply sub-network fulfilling the requirements for a product of the specific demand sent. In the event of this alternative supply sub-network being the best performing one in the whole network, the existing supply sub-network can be modified, substituting supplier 1-2 in tier-1 with the new supplier 1-1, while keeping supplier 2-2 in tier-2 and supplier 3-1 in tier-3. Having the fact that requestor-supplier relationship may change over time, new dynamically modeled supply networks – which may differ from the actual ones – are build whenever sending out new demands to the suppliers in the subsequent tiers.

3 Component Framework

To provide a basis for modeling demand driven value networks, (described in chapter 2.2), a *component framework* (see Fig. 2) for the domain of strategic supply network development has been developed offering basic functionality for the modeling of, and for the collaboration in value networks.

The component framework is based on the business component technology as defined in [25]. The underlying idea of business components combines components from different vendors to an application which is individual to each customer. The principle of modular black-box design has been chosen for the framework allowing different configurations of the SSND system – by combining different components regarding the need of the specific node – ranging from a very simple configuration of the system – to a very complex and integrated solution of the system. The framework therefore provides not only the basic functionality needed on each network node in

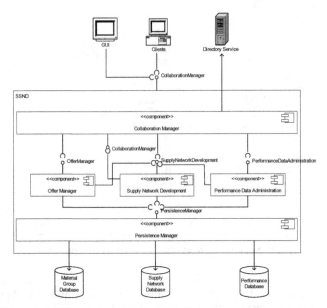

Fig. 2. Component framework for the domain of strategic supply network development

order to participate in the value network but it also provides the possibility of adding new functionality while composing additional components to the framework e.g. adding a component for the evaluation of supply networks.

The core part of the component framework is the component model *SSND* as shown in the middle of Fig. 2 in accordance with the notation of the Unified Modeling Language [21]. Five components have been identified and designed for the SSND framework. The *supply network development-, performance administration- and offer manager-components* provide the business logic for the domain of SSND. The business components have been derived based on the Business Component Modeling (BCM) process as introduced by [1] and are developed and specified according to the Memorandum of Standardized Specification of Business Components [26]. The component *supply network development* is the main business component responsible for the self modeling of demand driven value networks in the domain of strategic supply network development, as introduced in chapter 0. The component provides services for the administration of demands (specifying demands, accessing stored demands, deleting demands etc.) and for the administration of strategic supply networks (storing supply networks, updating strategic supply networks etc.) and provides the core business functionality for the component framework. In order to find potential suppliers for a specific demand, each company in the network has to provide catalogue information about products offering. The component *offer manager* therefore provides functionality for the administration of such catalogues. The catalogue information and the companies' contact information are made available to all network participants through a central organized *directory service* (see Fig. 2). The reason therefore is to provide new companies with the possibility of publishing their catalogue information in order to enable them to participate in the value network. This provides added value for the network allowing companies to find and contact new potential suppliers over the directory service while directly sending demands to existing suppliers. When sending out demands to suppliers, in order to strategically develop the value network, it is relevant not only to receive information about products' producibility but also to receive information about companies' performance. Enterprises participating in the value network have therefore to provide *self information*; that means e.g. information about the legal status of the company, year of creation, name of CEO, workforce, volume of sales, profit and loss calculations etc. The business component responsible for the administration of self information is called *performance data administration* in the component framework. The three business components presented, provide the basic business functionality needed in order to strategically develop supply networks based on demands and companies' performance data.

Additionally to the business components introduced, the component framework provides two system components – *persistence manager* and *collaboration manager* – responsible for the technical administration of the data and for the collaboration between network nodes. The information managed by the *offer manager-*, *supply network development-* and *performance data administration-*component is made persistent through the *persistence manager*. The main reason of introducing the persistence manager is based on the idea of having business components concentrating on the business logic while having system components taking care of implementation specific details. This has an impact on the distribution of the SSND system on network nodes, having the fact that different companies use different physical database systems as data storage. The framework handles that situation in having the persistent manager taking care of implementation specific details without affecting the business logic of SSND. The framework provides three semantic storages for SSND data. The *supply network database* stores all supply networks containing the aggregated information of suppliers contributing to a specific demand. For each demand, a new supply network is generated by split-lot transferring data from all suppliers and aggregating the information in the supply network development component. Such a network is then stored in the supply network database through the services provided by the persistent manager and called by the supply network development component. The information can e.g. be retrieved in order to visualize and strategically develop the supply networks. The *performance database* provides storage for the companies' self information and the *material group database* is responsible for storing the products offered by the company. The material group database additionally stores information for mapping the material group numbers of suppliers to the own internal representation of material group numbers. A mapping can either be based on product classification standards such as eCl@ss [10] or UN/SPSC [28] or – if a supplier does not make use of a specific standard – on tables cross referencing the product numbers of the two companies [13].

Example clients requesting collaboration services from SSND can either be graphical user interfaces (GUI), asking for data e.g. to visualize strategic networks, or other network nodes sending demands to suppliers. The collaboration in the SSND framework is executed by the *collaboration component*. Regarding the complexity of collaboration in inter-enterprise systems a detailed description of the collaboration component is given in chapter 4.

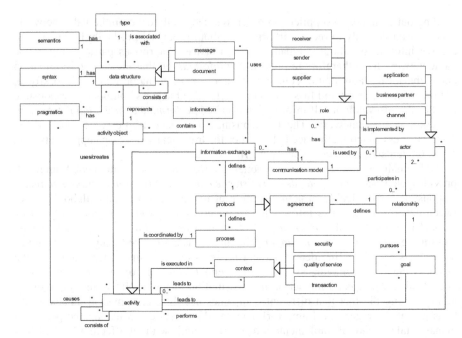

Fig. 3. Semantic model of inter-organizational collaboration

4 Collaboration Component

Successful inter-organizational collaboration is based on a suitable communication infrastructure that allows the coordination of tasks to achieve a given goal. Therefore a reusable collaboration component needs to support all basic functionality necessary in different information exchange scenarios. In order to illustrate the significance of the generic collaboration component for information exchange, a generic semantic model for inter-organizational collaboration has been developed. Fig. 3 shows a fragment of the general model to illustrate the collaboration problems in the domain of strategic supply network development.

The basic principle is the participation of *actors* in *relationships* in order to pursue a *goal* (see Fig. 3). This could be two or more *business partners* that want to exchange strategic supply network information in order to plan their demands, but also *software applications* sending data to each other in a distributed environment. In order to achieve the goal defined in such a relationship *activities* need to be performed. These activities are coordinated by a *process* that defines in what order and under which circumstances they are executed to reach the desired final state. As indicated in Fig. 3 activities can consist of other activities so that even complex operations or process chains can be represented. Typical activities are: *send, receive, transform,* and *define.* Note that even a simple activity like *send* can contain more than one subtask that can be described as activity.

Activities always use or create *activity objects* like *demand, address,* or *process description* that contain relevant *information.* Each of these activity objects can be represented by an arbitrarily complex *data structure*. The *syntax* of a data structure describes the rules how to build up correct expressions based upon a set of characters and how to arrange these expressions to get the data structure itself. Every data structure is associated with a corresponding *type* i.e. if a demand document and its corresponding *demand type* are defined, then every document with the same data structure is considered to be a demand. Ideally two separately defined types with the same name should have the same information content, but that is dependent on the actors that agreed upon this definition. The information content is also referred as the *semantics* of a data structure [22]. So the semantics provides the meaning of a data structure based on its type. In an inter-organizational scenario with many participants it is desirable to agree upon a data description standard to avoid problems with differently defined types. This can not always be achieved; in this case data structures have to be syntactically and/or semantically transformed in order to be understood by the receiver.

With activities and activity objects it is possible to model actions like *send demand*, *process answer* or *get self-information*. Activities are executed in a *context* that determines additional properties like *quality of service*, *security* or *transactional* behavior. A particular context can cause other activities that need to be performed in order to meet the criteria e.g. if an activity is executed in a secure context then e.g. data needs to be encrypted with a certain algorithm where a key must be exchanged between business partners in advance.

The activity *information exchange* (see center of Fig. 3) plays a special role in an inter-organizational setting. It represents the communication functionality that allows to coordinate activities of participating actors by passing the activity objects needed between them. For example it is necessary that a supplier receives a description of its customer's demand before it can check order information for this particular demand. A so called *protocol* defines the details of an information exchange such as message sequence and types of exchanged information. Protocols need to be mapped to the processes that coordinate the activities within participating organizations i.e. information that is contained in an incoming message must be extracted and routed to the appropriate application (actor) in order to be used in an activity at that time the process flow schedules this activity. Since every organization has only insight into its own processes and doesn't want to show any of its process details to its business partners, corresponding *public processes* are defined to model inter-organizational aspects of the overall process. A public process describes the sequence of sending and receiving information types from one organization's point of view [29, 7]. As this sequence is determined by the previously mentioned protocols, public processes provide an interface between protocols and private processes.

When exchanging information, *messages* are used to transport the actual activity object. They contain communication specific meta-information like sender and receiver address. The activity *information exchange* can be decomposed into three specific activities *send message*, *transport message*, and *receive message* that are subject to a specific underlying *communication model* which then can be implemented by a concrete *channel*. Depending on the communication model properties, these activities can have different functionalities. The *exchange flow* defines how messages are transported from sender to receiver (directly or indirectly over one or more intermediaries). *Data exchange* specifies whether data is exchanged physically or only a reference to data somewhere else is used. *Addressing* describes the method how the phyisical address of the message receiver is determined. Addressing can be static i.e. the address is known in advance, or it can be dynamic i.e. it is determined at runtime [3]. The *Response behavior* defines the degree of coupling between the actors. Messages that are exchanged synchronically between actors form a tightly coupled conversation whereas asynchronous communication allows a looser coupling between the actors.

By looking at the explained inter-organizational model based on information exchange one can now identify problems that could arise because of conflicting assumptions in a collaboration scenario and which need to be handled by a collaboration component. Regarding to [12] conflicting assumptions are the following:

Assumptions about incoming and outgoing data: As already mentioned, information represented as data structure is exchanged between actors. Problems can arise if either the syntax or the semantics of a data structure is not as expected. To change the syntax of a data structure its information content has to be transformed in a way that it is expressed according to the target syntax rules [33]. Semantical transformation must handle different terminologies [11] and different information content. Therefore, a collaboration component has to provide a transformation engine. Not only is this necessary in communication with other organizations but also internally when data is needed to be read from legacy applications. So called *adapters* have to be provided to integrate data from all known data sources. These adapters are also based on syntactical and semantical transformations.

Assumptions about patterns of interaction characterized by protocols: As private processes, especially those concerning business logic, are often already defined before inter-organizational collaboration is initiated, problems with the expected message sequence of the information exchange could arise. Protocols concerning the connectivity of applications are often standardized and do not affect higher-level protocols. A flexible collaboration component should therefore support different concrete channels that implement these standards i.e. it must be capable to send and receive data over these channels (e.g. HTTP, SMTP, SOAP). On the contrary, business protocols do highly affect private processes. So if the message sequence does not fit to the private process and necessary information is not available at time, the process can not be executed although the information is available at the sender's side [11]. Therefore a wrapper is needed to generate or delete certain messages according to the target process.

Assumptions about the topology of the system communication and about the presence of components or connectors: Even if a collaboration component implements various communication channels it has to know which one to use when sending information to a particular receiver. This information, including the actual address, must be available for each potential receiver. If some activity needs a special context, this must be recognized by all participants; for example, if encrypted information is sent then the receiver must be able to decrypt this information. Sometimes additional protocols must be included into the existing protocol infrastructure to meet a certain context agreement (e.g. acknowledgment messages for reliable communication). Again these protocols have to be supported on both sides. They can also be standardized protocols that every participant integrates into its existing protocol infrastructure, e.g. transaction protocols like parts of BTP [20] or WS-Transaction [5], or protocols that can not be easily integrated without affecting private processes. In this case problems can arise as mentioned above when discussing sequence mismatches in business protocols.

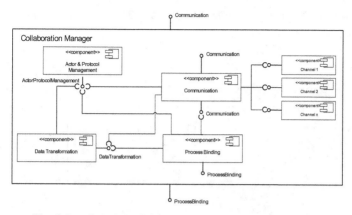

Fig. 4. Detailed view of the collaboration manager component

Regarding the functionality needed for inter-organizational collaboration in hetero-geneous environments in order to solve collaboration conflicts – as already introduced – the internal view of the collaboration manager component has been developed (see Fig. 4) and the interfaces provided by the collaboration manager specified in detail.

The *Actor & Protocol Management* component manages all information concern-ing potential communication partners and all corresponding collaboration specific data e.g. supported channels, supported protocols (communication, context, and busi-ness logic), and supported data formats. Depending on this information the collabora-tion manager component can be configured for each partner. The *Communication* component for example can choose the right send and receive functionality based on a selected channel. The same is true for the *Data Transformation* component that plugs in appropriate transformation adapters (not shown in Fig. 4). If necessary the *Process Binding* component implements the wrapper functionality to solve problems related to the message sequence as discussed above. It also integrates additional protocols caused by a specific context into the process.

5 Prototype Implementation of the Component Framework

For prove of concept, a first prototype implementation of the SSND component framework has been developed and an example supply network for the development of an electronic motor ranging from the OEM to tier-5 has been built. Therefore the SSND prototype has been installed on each node of the supply network including the OEM node. In this chapter a quick overview of the SSND prototype and some imple-mentation details focusing on the collaboration component are given.

An example view of a dynamic modeled supply network for the production of an electronic motor executed by the SSND system is shown in Fig. 5. Only a selected area of the whole supply network is shown.

The rectangles represent the different companies of the supply network visualized with important information about the node contributing to the supply network of the electronic motor. Relevant information for the requestor about the suppliers is e.g. name of the company, material group the supplier is producing, minimum volume

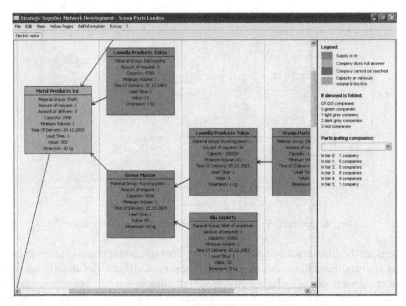

Fig. 5. Dynamic modeled supply network for the production of an electronic motor

necessary to be ordered and capacity per day. The companies are visualized in the SSND prototype in different colors, differentiating between a) suppliers able to deliver the product and amount requested b) suppliers not answering to the demand sent c) suppliers which are not online or where a communication problem exists and d) suppliers which do not have enough capacity for producing the required product, or where the order volume required by the client is too low. The tool provides different modes of visualizing the network – adding more detailed information to the nodes, showing just parts of the network, etc. – in order to support the requestors with all necessary information for developing their strategic supply networks. Giving a detailed description of the tool would go beyond the scope of this paper.

To implement the pull technology of self modeling demand driven networks in SSND, the concept of asynchronous communication (as introduced in chapter 4) has been implemented in the prototype application and has been combined with the Web Service technology responsible for the exchange of messages between components distributed on different nodes. Web services are a new promising paradigm for the development of modular applications accessible over the Web and running on a variety of platforms.

The Web service standards are SOAP [30] – supporting platform independency – WSDL [31] – specifying the interfaces and services offered – and UDDI [27] – used for the publication of the Web services offered by a specific company. All standards are based on the eXtensible Markup Language (XML) [6]. An overview of standards and related technologies for Web services is given in [24]. The communication component therefore implements the Web Service interface (called W3SSND in the SSND prototype) in order to provide access to the component through Web Services. The services offered are e.g. *process requests*, *process replies* providing different addresses for the different message types and exchanging the data not by reference but by including it in the messages (see communication model properties in Sect. 4).

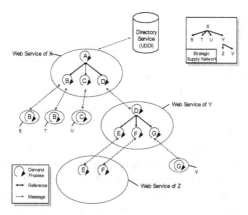

Fig. 6. SSND System Logic

The Web Service interface, the contact information and the products offered by a specific company are described in a WSDL document and made publicly available over the directory service (UDDI). Therefore new companies can be identified through the UDDI directory service while searching for potential suppliers of a specific product and addressing is dynamic being determined at runtime. Additionally the services provided by each company are globally available and accessible by any other node in the SSND network, allowing the exchange of messages between network nodes. The exchange of messages using the Web Service technology is shown in Fig. 6.

The ovals in the picture represent company nodes in the network of SSND. Each company has the SSND prototype installed, containing all components shown in Fig. 2. Every node offers therefore services provided by the collaboration component as Web Service, which are made publicly available over the UDDI directory service. A company defines sub-demands required for a specific product by a bill of material explosion, e.g. the sub-demands required from company X for the product A are B, C and D. For each demand and sub-demand a process is started on the network node waiting for a response while communicating the sub-demands by messages to the companies. Company X calls therefore the Web services *process request* of the companies S, T, U and Y. Since the companies S, T and U do not need any material from other companies, they send back the information about ability of delivery calling the Web Service *process reply* of company X. Each response is handled by the corresponding sub-demand process. Company Y instead identifies products needed from the own suppliers by a bill of material explosion, starting sub-demand processes E, F and G and communicating the sub-demands to the own suppliers.

Receiving back the information about delivery abilities, the company Y aggregates the information and returns the own supply network for that specific demand to the company X. Company X, aggregating the information from all suppliers, is then able e.g. to visualize the suppliers' network (top-right in Fig. 6) for further evaluation.

Regarding the exchange flow in the distributed system – as introduced by the communication model properties in chapter 4 – messages are transported directly from the sender to the receiver. As defined by [23], the network of independent systems that constitute the strategic supply network appears to the user of a single node inside that network as a single system and therefore represents a distributed system. It is an open peer group of loosely coupled systems. Every node is autonomous and implements functions for its own view of the network, no hierarchy exists. Regarding the different roles a node can play – e.g. being the *producer* sending a demand to known suppliers or being a *supplier* receiving demands from a client and either sending the related sub-demands to the known suppliers or sending the answer back the client – each node in its context of the application is able to store data, to send and receive demands or answers from other nodes in the network. The communication takes place between peers without guaranty that a node is always online and contributing to the network. Regarding all those aspects mentioned, the application for strategic supply network development can be considered as a peer-to-peer application having all main features – client-server functionality, direct communication between peers and autonomy of the single nodes – of today's peer-to-peer applications as defined by [4] and [19]. The only difference of the SSND system to today's understanding of peer-to-peer applications is the initialization of new nodes in such a peer-to-peer network. In a peer-to-peer network a new node can contact any other node of the network in order to become a member. In the SSND network a new node does always have to contact a specific node, namely the directory service. The advantage of such a solution is that the companies building new strategic networks can request information about new companies from the directory service and alternatively send a demand to a new member in tier-1 additionally to the known nodes.

6 Conclusion and Future Work

This paper presents a component framework for inter-organizational communication in the domain of strategic supply network development, based on the concept of self modeling demand driven networks. The core of the framework builds the component model. The business components provide the main business logic for the development of strategic supply networks, whereas the system components are handling data persistency and problems of heterogeneity that come up in inter-organizational communication and collaboration. A first prototype implementation of the framework has been introduced, focusing on implementation details regarding collaboration between network nodes.

While in the first prototype application the focus was set on the feasibility of the concept of self modeling demand driven networks and the exchange of messages within a more homogeneous environment, having all nodes installed the same system, in further extensions of the prototype collaboration concepts introduced in the component framework to solve the problems of heterogeneity need to be implemented. Additionally, as product related information used in the bill of material explosion constitutes the basis of the concept of self modeling networks, interfaces to existing PDM, ERP and PPS systems have to be defined to enhance the applicability of the system.

References

[1]   A. Albani, A. Keiblinger, K. Turowski and C. Winnewisser, *Domain Based Identification and Modelling of Business Component Applications*, in L. Kalinichenko, R. Manthey, B. Thalheim and U. Wloka, eds., *7th East-European Conference on Advances in Databases and Informations Systems (ADBIS-03), LNCS 2798*, Springer Verlag, Dresden, Deutschland, September 2003, pp. 30-45.

[2]   A. Albani, A. Keiblinger, K. Turowski and C. Winnewisser, *Domain Specific Standardisation for Collaborative Business Applications*, in R. Gonçalves-Jardim, J. Cha and A. Steiger-Garção, eds., *Proceedings of the 10th ISPE International Conference on Concurrent Engineering: Research and Applications*, A.A. Balkema, Madeira, July 2003, pp. 399 - 410.

[3]   G. Alonso, F. Casati, H. Kuno and V. Machiraju, *Web Services: Concepts, Architectures, and Applications*, Springer Verlag, 2003.

[4]   D. Barkai, *Peer-to-Peer Computing*, Technologies for Sharing and Collaboration on the Net. Intel Press (2001).

[5]   BEA, IBM and Microsoft, *Web Services Transaction (WS-Transaction)*, http://www-106.ibm.com/developerworks/webservices/library/ws-transpec/, accessed 23.03.2004.

[6]   T. Bray, J. Paoli and C. M. Sperberg-McQueen, *Extensible Markup Language (XML) 1.0*, Recommendation, World Wide Web Consortium (W3C), 02.10.1998 1998.

[7]   C. Bussler, *The Role of B2B Engines in B2B Integration Architectures*, ACM SIGMOD Record, Special Issue: Data management issues in electronic commerce, 31 (2002), pp. 67-72.

[8]   A. S. Carr and J. N. Pearson, *Strategically managed buyer - supplier relationships and performance outcomes*, Journal of Operations Management, 17 (1999), pp. 497 - 519.

[9]   A. S. Carr and L. R. Smeltzer, *The relationship of strategic purchasing to supply chain management*, European Journal of Purchasing & Supply Management, 5 (1999), pp. 43-51.

[10]   *eCl@ss*, Version 5.0. http://www.eclass.de, accessed 22.03.2004.

[11]   D. Fensel and C. Bussler, *The web service modeling framework WSMF*, White paper, Vrije Unversiteit, Amsterdam, 2002.

[12]   D. Garlan, R. Allen and J. Ockerbloom, *Architecture Mismatch: Why Reuse is so Hard*, IEEE Software, 12 (1995), pp. 17-26.

[13]   M. Hepp, *Measuring the Quality of Descriptive Languages for Products and Services.*, in F.-D. Dorloff, J. Leukel and V. Schmitz, eds., *Mulitkonferenz Wirtschaftsinformatik (MKWI), Track E-Business - Standardisierung und Integration*, Cuvillier Verlag Göttingen, Essen, 2004, pp. 157-168.

[14]   J. B. Houlihan, *International Supply Chain Management*, International Journal of Physical Distribution and Logistics Management, 15 (1985), pp. 22-38.

[15]   T. Jones and D. Riley, *Using Inventory for Competitive Advantage through Supply Chain Management*, International Journal of Physical Distribution and Logistics Management, 5 (1985), pp. 16-22.

[16]   E. Kopanaki, S. Smithson, P. Kanellis and D. Martakos, *The Impact of Interorganizational Information Systems on the Flexibility of Organizations*, Proceedings of the Sixth Americas Conference on Information Systems (AMCIS), Long Beach, CA, 2000, pp. 1434 - 1437.

[17]   D. M. Lambert and M. C. Cooper, *Issues in Supply Chain Management*, Industrial Marketing Management, 29 (2000), pp. 65-83.

[18]   T. W. Malone and R. J. Lautbacher, *The Dawn of the E-Lance Economy*, Harvard Business Review (1998), pp. 145 - 152.

[19]   M. Miller, *Discovering P2P*, Sybex, San Francisco (2001).

[20]   OASIS, *Business Transaction Protocol Specification Version 1.0*, http://www.oasis-open.org/committees/download.php/1184/2002-06-03.BTP_cttee_spec_1.0.pdf, accessed 23.03.2004.

[21]   OMG, *OMG Unified Modelling Language Spezification Version 2.0*, (2003).

[22]   A. Sheth, *Data Semantics:what, where and how?*, in R. Meersman and L. Mark, eds., *6th IFIP Working Conference on Data Semantics (DS-6)*, Chapman and Hall, 1995.

[23]   A. S. Tanenbaum, *Distributed Operating Systems*, Prentice Hall, 1995.

[24]   A. Tsalgatidou and T. Pilioura, *An Overview of Standards and Related Technology in Web Services - Special Issue on E-Services*, International Journal of Distributed and Parallel Databases (2002), pp. 135-162.

[25]   K. Turowski, *Fachkomponenten: Komponentenbasierte betriebliche Anwendungssysteme*, Shaker Verlag, Aachen, 2003.

[26]   K. Turowski, ed., *Standardized Specification of Business Components: Memorandum of the working group 5.10.3 Component Oriented Business Application System*, University of Augsburg, Augsburg, 2002.

[27]   *UDDI Version 3.0*, http://uddi.org/pubs/uddi-v3.00-published-20020719.htm, accessed 13.03.2003.

[28]   *United Nations Standard Products and Services Code (UNSPSC)*, Version 6.1101. http://www.unspsc.org, accessed 22.03.2004.

[29]   W. M. P. van der Aalst and M. Weske, *The P2P approach to Interorganizational Workflows*, in K.R.Dittrich, A.Geppert and M.C.Norrie, eds., *Conference on Advanced Information Systems Engineering (CAiSE)*, Lecture Notes in Computer Science (LNCS), Interlaken, 2001, pp. 140-156.

[30]   W3C, *SOAP Version 1.2 Part 0: Primer*, http://www.w3.org/TR/2002/CR-soap12-part0-20021219/, accessed 13.03.2003.

[31]   W3C, *Web Services Description Language (WSDL) Version 1.2*, http://www.w3.org/TR/wsdl12/, accessed 13.03.2003.

[32]   H.-J. Warnecke, *Vom Fraktal zum Produktionsnetzwerk. Unternehmenskooperationen erfolgreich gestalten*, Berlin, 1999.

[33]   E. Wüstner, T. Hotzel and P. Buxmann, *Converting Business Documents: A Clarificatoin of Problems and Solutions using XML/XSLT*, WECWIS, 2002, pp. 61-68.

An Abstract Algebra
for Knowledge Discovery in Databases

Luciano Gerber and Alvaro A.A. Fernandes

Department of Computer Science
University of Manchester
Oxford Road, Manchester M13 9PL, UK
{l.gerber,a.fernandes}@cs.man.ac.uk

Abstract. Knowledge discovery in databases (KDD) plays an important role in decision-making tasks by supporting end users both in exploring and understanding of very large datasets and in building predictive models with validity over unseen data. KDD is an ad-hoc, iterative process comprising tasks that range from data understanding and preparation to model building and deployment. Support for KDD should, therefore, be founded on a closure property, i.e., the ability to compose tasks seamlessly by taking the output of a task as the input of another. Despite some recent progress, KDD is still not as conveniently supported as end users have reason to expect due to three major problems: (1) lack of task compositionality, (2) undue dependency on user expertise, and (3) lack of generality. This paper contributes to ameliorate these problems by proposing an abstract algebra for KDD, called **K-algebra**, whose underlying data model and primitive operations accommodate a wide range of KDD tasks. Such an algebra is a necessary step towards the development of optimisation techniques and efficient evaluation that would, in turn, pave the way for the development of declarative, surface KDD languages without which end-user support will remain less than convenient, thereby damaging the prospects for mainstream acceptance of KDD technology.

1 Introduction

In spite of great interest and intense research activity, the field of knowledge discovery in databases (KDD) is still far from benefiting from unified foundations. Research focus has been patchy by and large. Efforts are all too often devoted to devising new, or extending existing, algorithms that are very specifically tailored to very specific contexts, and hence not as widely applicable as one would hope, given the large variety of application scenarios in which KDD could have a significant impact.

At present, there is no foundational framework that unifies the different representations in use, let alone a well-founded set of generic operations that both cohere, when taken together, and are flexible enough to express a significant number of complex KDD tasks in a convenient way. The lack of such foundations

A. Benczúr, J. Demetrovics, G. Gottlob (Eds.): ADBIS 2004, LNCS 3255, pp. 83–98, 2004.

is a significant impediment in the way of mainstream acceptance, and of wider deployability, of KDD technologies. This is because without such foundational framework it is very difficult to develop declarative, surface KDD languages without which end-user support may always remain less than convenient.

This is very much reflected in the difficulties data analysts face in interacting with KDD systems. KDD is an ad-hoc, iterative process comprising tasks that range from data understanding and preparation to model building and deployment. The typical flow of work in KDD projects requires end-users (i.e., data analysts and knowledge engineers) to operate a KDD suite that, particularly with respect to the data mining phase, acts as a front-end to a collection of algorithms. Unfortunately, each algorithm tends to be very specialised, in the sense that it produces optimal outcomes only under very narrow assumptions and in very specific circumstances. Moreover, different algorithms tend to depend on specific representations of their inputs and outputs, and this often requires the end user carrying out representational mappings in order for tasks to compose in a flow of work. More importantly, if all one has is a suite of algorithms, then end users bear the ultimate responsibility for overall success, since they must choose the most appropriate algorithm at each and every step of the KDD process. Bad choices may well delay or derail the process. Given that the KDD literature has given rise to a myriad different, very specific algorithms for each phase of the KDD process, and given that sometimes the differences are subtle in the surface but with significant import in terms of effectiveness and efficiency, the choices faced by end users could be bewildering. Thus, it can be seen that the state of the art in KDD still suffers from some significant shortcomings. The main issues identified above are:

1. *Lack of compositionality*, insofar as contemporary KDD suites fail to achieve seamless composition of tasks. Inputs and outputs have different representations (e.g., different file format) and the need to map across them hinders the transparency of the process. Moreover, due in part to type mismatches, there is a lack of orthogonality in the way the tasks are composed. For example, while it is possible to apply selection to (i.e., take a subset of) a dataset, that same generally does not apply to a decision tree (i.e., choose a subset of branches), despite being naturally reasonable to do so. The challenge here is to find a unified representation for KDD inputs and outputs.

2. *Dependency on user expertise*, insofar as there is a large number of candidate algorithms at almost every step, for almost every task, and each in turn has several parameters which require expertise in being set if good results are to be obtained. Often these choices affect considerably not only how satisfactory the results are but also how efficiently they are obtained. Typically, these decisions are far too complex to be undertaken by casual users. The challenge here is to find specification mechanisms that are amenable to formal manipulation by an optimisation algorithm so as to protect the end user as much as possible from inadvertent choices.

3. *Lack of generality*, insofar as it would be much more convenient if the body of algorithms proposed in the literature were better structured and if ab-

stract generalisations were available that could help the selection of concrete instances. It has been observed empirically that, despite the large number of different algorithms proposed for similar tasks, they do seem to be based on the same basic principles, differing in very particular respects that make them more applicable to certain contexts than others. The challenge here is to find abstractions that are comprehensive enough to unify the concrete, specialist algorithms that comprise the bulk of the KDD literature. This would allow the basic principles to be more vividly understood and make it possible to define, and reason about, a wide range of KDD tasks more systematically, and even mechanically.

A *unifying formal framework for KDD task composition* is a possible, concerted response to the challenges identified. As a concrete candidate for such formal framework this paper contributes the **K-algebra**, an abstract algebra for KDD whose underlying data model and primitive operations accommodate a wide range of KDD tasks. The K-algebra is a database algebra, i.e., its underlying concern is with flow throughput in situations where the volume of input at the leaves of the computation are significant enough to be the dominant factor in the efficiency of the latter. It must be stressed that the K-algebra is an *abstract algebra*, i.e., it is proposed as a candidate intermediate representation between surface languages and executable plans. It is best understood, therefore, as the proposal of an abstract machine that paves the way for systems to take decisions on behalf of the users as to how complex KDD tasks are configured and composed, similarly to what current query optimisers deliver for database systems. It is not a proposal for dealing directly with concrete effectiveness and efficiency concerns: this is what the bulk of the KDD literature is already doing so commendably.

This paper, therefore, takes the view that defining the foundations for a KDD language that can be subject to optimisation is more likely to succeed than contributing yet another too-specific tool to an already very large tool set. The motivation for our approach stems from the observation that database technology was once limited to a comparable motley collection of poorly related techniques, and the same consequences were noticed then. A historical breakthrough was the development, by Codd, of a unifying formal foundation as an abstract algebra, which was shown to be expressive enough to express complex combination of tasks, that were mappable to the concrete algorithms and techniques. The subsequent introduction of declarative languages empowered end users to query databases in an ad-hoc manner, expanding greatly the possibilities for query retrieval. Ultimately, this was all made concrete with the development of query optimisers, which can take advantage of algebraic properties to seek efficient plans to evaluate the queries over databases. This algebraic approach proved successful for other database models and languages developed subsequently, such as to object-oriented [4] and spatial [8] data, and, more recently, to XML [11] and streams [16], to name a few.

Other researchers have had similar motivations, and it seemed natural to them to consider expressing KDD tasks in a standard database language, for which a robust concretely implemented counterpart exists. However, significant technical impediments stand in the way. For example, standard database languages only have limited capability (and often none at all) to express recursion or iteration, which seem essential in KDD. For example, it is shown by Sarawagi et al. [15] that the implementation in SQL of Apriori, a classical scalable algorithm for association rule discovery, falls short in terms of performance. A similar algorithm is expressed in terms of an extended relational algebra by Ceri et al. [13]. However, it is not clear whether this approach would apply to other more challenging KDD tasks.

To illustrate the K-algebra, the paper includes a specification of a top-down decision-tree induction process in abstract-algebraic form. To the best of our knowledge, this is the first such formulation. In order to have a concrete example, the next subsections make use of the simple dataset [14] in Fig. 1. Briefly, it records weather conditions over a time period (say, days) and labels each instance with the information as to whether a particular sport was played in that day.

ID	outlook	temp	humidity	windy	play?
1	sunny	hot	high	false	no
2	sunny	hot	high	true	no
3	overcast	hot	high	false	yes
4	rainy	mild	high	false	yes
5	rainy	cool	normal	false	yes
6	rainy	cool	normal	true	no
7	overcast	cool	normal	true	yes
8	sunny	mild	high	false	no
9	sunny	cool	normal	false	yes
10	rainy	mild	normal	false	yes
11	sunny	mild	normal	true	yes
12	overcast	mild	high	true	yes
13	overcast	hot	normal	false	yes
14	rainy	mild	high	true	no

Fig. 1. The Weather Dataset

The general goal is to use such a labelled dataset to construct a decision tree that, based on the values of certain of the attributes (e.g., outlook and windy) can determine the value of the desired attribute (called the *class*) play. In other words, the decision tree hypothesises a label given an non-labelled instance. Fig. 2 depicts the de-

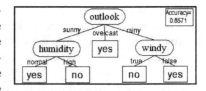

Fig. 2. Example Decision Tree

cision tree that Quinlan's ID3 [14] outputs given the dataset in Fig. 1. The remainder of this paper is structured as follows. Section 2 describes the K-algebra informally. Section 3 shows how it can express top-down decision-tree induction. Section 4 briefly discusses related work. Section 5 draws some conclusions.

2 The K-Algebra: An Abstract Algebra for KDD

2.1 The Key Underlying Concepts

The K-algebra is based on an abstract view of the KDD process as consisting of arbitrarily complex compositions of steps that *expand, compress, evaluate, accumulate, filter out* and *combine*, in a *iterative* fashion, *collections* of *summaries of data.* The italicised terms in the previous sentence denote the key underlying concepts of the K-algebra. They underpin the expression of a wide range of KDD tasks.

The K-algebra has two carriers: *K-cubes*, which are annotated multi-dimensional structures to represent individual summaries; and *K-cube-lists*, which, unsurprisingly, collect K-cubes into lists, in order to support iterative collection-at-a-time processing of K-cubes.

The typical strategy for specifying KDD tasks in the K-algebra is to obtain a most-detailed K-cube from which further candidates are derived, directly or indirectly. At each iteration, this base K-cube is often used to give rise to derived ones through the application of operations that either *expand* or *compress* a K-cube into one or more K-cubes. By 'expanding' (resp., 'compressing') is meant applying operations that, given a K-cube, increase (resp., decrease) its dimensionality or its cardinality, to yield a (usually slightly) different summarised perspective on the data. These derived summaries are *evaluated*, as a result of which they are annotated with one or more measures of interestingness [1].

The interesting ones, i.e., those who meet or exceed a given threshold, are *accumulated*, whereas the remaining ones are either refined further or *filtered out*. Alternatively, the K-cubes in the current accumulation may be *combined* (assembled back) into a single K-cube for further exploration.

2.2   The K-Algebra Carriers

The fundamental carrier of the K-algebra is a set of structures referred to as *K-cubes*. It is designed to unify the inputs and outputs of a range of KDD tasks. Informally, a K-cube is a hypercube to which is associated a vector of attributes called *annotations*. A *hypercube* is an aggregated representation of extensional data in a multi-dimensional space, in which attributes called *dimensions* play the roles of axes. The (discrete) dimensional domains divide the space into units called *cells*. Attributes called *measures* represent properties, usually aggregated values, of the data inside cells. For example, a K-cube representing a contingency table from the weather dataset is depicted in Fig. 3 in its flat representation. The attributes outlook and play are dimensions. Absolute frequency, denoted by af, is an *aggregate measure*. These are usually associated with functions on *sets of values* such as Sum, Max and Min. In contrast, rf is a *scalar measure* denoting the relative frequency obtained by a function on scalars (in this case, $rf \leftarrow af/aftotal$, where $aftotal = 14$). Each row in the (flat representation of a) K-cube corresponds to a cell.

outlook	play	af	rf
overcast	yes	4	0.286
rainy	no	2	0.143
rainy	yes	3	0.214
sunny	no	3	0.214
sunny	yes	2	0.143
aftotal: 14			

Fig. 3. Example K-Cube

---

[1] Note that, here, the concept of interestingness is inspired by, but more loosely construed than is the case in, [3].

Annotations decorate the summarised information (represented as a hyper-cube) with *interestingness* values. For example, here, it might range from grand totals and global measures, such as the total frequency aftotal in Fig. 3, to more specific measures such as the predictive accuracy of a decision tree. As it is shown later, in the K-algebra, annotations result from the computation of measures. K-cubes are collected in *K-cube-lists*, which are the second carrier of the K-algebra. There is no significant import on using lists as the concrete collection type: they are chosen because they simplify the presentation of those K-algebraic functions that operate on collections of K-cubes.

2.3   The K-Algebraic Operations

Recall that the K-algebra was said to be based on an abstract view of the KDD process as consisting of arbitrarily complex compositions of steps that *expand*, *compress*, *evaluate*, *accumulate*, *filter out* and *combine*, in a *iterative* fashion, *collections* of *summaries of data*. The previous subsection threw some light into what is meant by 'collections of summaries of data'. This subsection presents the operations that support the above steps and that provide the means for iterating over intermediate results. The full formal definition [7] is not given here for reasons of space.

Figs. 4 and 5 list the signatures for the operations and organise them in categories. In Figs. 4 and 5, the intended domains and ranges are as follows: N denotes a finite segment of the natural numbers. K is instantiated by a single K-cube, L by a K-cube-list. For example, the signatures of the operations in Fig. 10(g) reflect the conversion of a K-cube into a K-cube-list. D, M and A are, respectively, instantiated by a set of names of dimensions, measures and annotations. For example, generalise (Fig. 4(a)) requires the identification of the dimensions to be removed from a K-cube. In turn, G denotes generators that as-sign the result of an expression, usually involving scalar and aggregate elements, to an attribute. This is illustrated by the signature of the operation add-scalar-measure in Fig. 6(c), where G represents the association of a new measure with an expression as a composition of scalar functions and values. F is instanti-ated by an aggregation function, such as Max or Min, applied on a particular measure. V and E apply to higher-order functions only. The former denotes a binding variable to K-cube elements in the lists being processed, whereas the latter represents an algebraic expression (over the binding variables) to be ap-plied to a K-cube-list. Finally, R is concerned only with bridge operations: it is instantiated by a relation in the extensional layer, as explained later in this subsection.

To see the intended structure in Fig. 4, note that Fig. 4(a) lists the oper-ations on dimensions, Fig. 5(b) those on annotations, Fig. 6(c) those on mea-sures, Fig. 7(d) those on attributes, and, finally, Fig. 8(e) those on cells. As ex-pected, the basic design is that one can add, remove, convert and rename dimen-sions (e.g., specialise, generalise), annotations and measures (e.g., add-aggregate-measure, add-scalar-measure, copy-mea-as-ann). The first four categories comprise specialise $\lhd : K \times K \times 2^D \times 2^G \to K$

generalise $\rhd : K \times 2^D \times 2^F \to K$

rename-dimension $\nu^d : K \times 2^G \to K$

(a) Manipulating Dimensions

remove-annotation $\rho^a : K \times 2^A \to K$

rename-annotation $\nu^a : K \times 2^G \to K$

(b) Manipulating Annotations

add-scalar-measure $\epsilon : K \times 2^G \to K$

add-aggregate-measure $\alpha : K \times 2^D \times 2^G \to K$

remove-measure $\rho^m : K \times 2^M \to K$

rename-measure $\nu^m : K \times 2^G \to K$

(c) Manipulating Measures

copy-mea-as-dim ${}^{m\square}\kappa^d : K \times 2^G \to K$ copy-dim-as-mea ${}^{d\square}\kappa^m : K \times 2^G \to K$

copy-ann-as-mea ${}^{a\square}\kappa^m : K \times 2^G \to K$ copy-mea-as-ann ${}^{m}\kappa^a : K \times 2^G \to K$

(d) Copying Attributes

select $\sigma : K \times P \to K$

union $\cup : K \times K \to K$

difference $- : K \times K \to K$

natural-join $\bowtie : K \times K \to K$

theta-join $\bowtie : K \times K \times P \to K$

select-n $\lambda : K \times N \to K$

intersection $\cap : K \times K \to K$

cartesian-product $\times : K \times K \to K$

union-join $\bowtie : K \times K \to K$

select-kcube-on-ann $\mathbb{F} : K \times K \times P \to K$

(e) Manipulating Cells

map^1 $\mu : V \times L \times E \to L$ map^2 $\mu^2 : V \times V \times L \times L \times E \to L$

map^{2x} ${}^x\mu : V \times V \times L \times L \times E \to L$ reduce $\Delta : V \times V \times L \times E \to L$

filter $\phi : V \times L \times E \to L$ flatten $\Downarrow : L \to L$

iterate $\circlearrowright : V \times P \times N \times L \times E \to L$

(f) Higher-Order

partition-into-n $\pi^n : K \times N \to L$ partition-by-dim $\pi^d : K \times 2^D \to L$

gen-subsets $\bigtriangledown : K \times 2^G \to L$ gen-supersets $\bigtriangleup : K \times K \times 2^G \times 2^F \to L$

(g) Expanding a K-Cube into a K-Cube-List

Fig. 4. K-Algebraic Operations (1)

relation-to-kcube $\boxplus : R \times 2^D \times 2^G \to K$ kcube-to-relation $\square : K \to R$

kcube-to-kcube-list $[\,] : K \to L$ kcube-list-to-kcube $\boxdot : L \to K$

(a) Bridging Between Layers

Fig. 5. K-Algebraic Operations (2)

operations that reshape a K-cube without direct reference to its cells. These operations make a K-cube grow or shrink in dimensionality, or be evaluated by more or less measures, or be annotated in more or less ways. The operations in Fig. 5(b) provide means to assign a different role to a particular attribute in a K-cube. For example, copy-dim-as-mea adds a new measure, to a K-cube, whose values are replicated from those of an existing dimension. In contrast, the last category (in Fig. 8(e)) comprises operations that make direct reference to the cells of K-cube, and this explains the analogies with classical database-algebraic operations (e.g., select, select-n, and natural-join). This is indicative of the fact that the K-algebra can be seen to operate on (possibly aggregated) data (as in standard database algebras) but, in addition to that, it wraps that data with metadata of interest for the identification of descriptive and predictive models of the data.

The other carrier structure employed in the K-algebra is the *K-cube-list*, which collects K-cubes in (possibly nested) lists. To see the intended structure, note firstly that Fig. 9(f) lists operations that either iterate over a K-cube-list or are higher-order functions that transform a K-cube-list in some way (e.g., by mapping, by filtering, by flattening, or by folding). Fig. 10(g) lists operations that expand a single K-cube into a K-cube-list, either by partitioning it (e.g., partition-into-N, partition-by-dim) or by replacing it by its super- or subsets (e.g., gen-supersets, gen-subsets) in a controlled manner. Finally, all the operations so far could be said to be *intra-carrier operations*. However, the K-algebra is a layered algebra in the sense that closure is ensured by *inter-carrier operations* that bridge across layers.

The layers are as follows. The *extensional layer* represents the extensional data from which K-cubes are initially obtained and to which K-cubes are eventually deployed. The carrier is that of the relational model; the operations stem from an relational algebra extended with grouping and aggregation [5]. The *K-cube layer* comprises those operations that manipulate K-cubes one-at-a-time. The carrier is the K-cube. The *K-cube-list layer* provides higher-order and operations that manipulate lists of K-cubes. The carrier is the K-cube-list. Thus, the operations in Fig. 5(a) allow values to move between layers. This is necessary for deriving summaries from, and deploying models in, the extensional data layer, as well as for moving from K-cubes to K-cube-lists.

The case study in Section 3 concretely illustrates all the most important operations introduced in Figs. 4 and 5.

3   A Concrete Example: Decision-Tree Induction

This section applies the K-algebra to a concrete example of building an ID3-like classifier. Its subsections provide a quick overview of top-down decision tree building algorithms, an overview of the algorithmic strategy for constructing the classifier in K-algebraic fashion, and how the K-algebraic concepts employed correspond to the original algorithmic template for the kind of classifiers addressed.

3.1   Top-Down Decision Tree Inducers

A decision tree for the weather dataset was introduced in Fig. 2. Decision-tree models are the result of a separate-and-conquer approach and classify instances into classes. The attribute play constitutes the class one wants to predict based on the other attributes, in the given example. The branches of the tree define partitions of data and label the instances that traverse them with the class values at their leaves. For example, when applied to the weather dataset, it determines that all instances in which outlook has the value overcast, the class value (i.e., play) be yes.

A classical top-down decision tree algorithm is *ID3* [14]. It constructs a decision tree from a training dataset by recursively partitioning the data, using the attributes but the class, until it is discriminating enough with respect to the class values. Ascertaining the latter requirement relies on a measure of the purity of a partition (such as the *information gain ratio* employed in ID3-like techniques or the *Gini index* used in *CART* [1]) which essentially reflects the variability of the class distribution. The algorithm proceeds in a depth-first fashion, using a greedy heuristic strategy to decide on the best splits at each node of the tree. A high-level procedural specification of ID3 is shown in Algorithm 1.

Algorithm: ID3(T, D, b, A)

T: the tree being built
D: the current partition of data
b: the current branch of the tree
A: the set of attributes to possibly split D further

1 **if** D *is pure or* $A = \emptyset$ **then**

2 $\quad$ ⌞ Build class node for D under b
3 **else**

4 $\quad$ | Using the information gain, determine the best attribute $a \in A$ to split D
5 $\quad$ | Create a node n for a and add it to T
6 $\quad$ | Create and add to T a branch b_i for each value v in $dom(a)$
7 $\quad$ | **for** *each branch* b_i **do**

8 $\quad$ | $\quad$ ⌞ ID3(T, D_i, b_i, A) # where D_i is the subset of D determined by b_i

---

Algorithm 1. High-Level Procedural Specification of ID3

3.2   An Overview of the Algorithmic Strategy

In this subsection, the K-algebraic approach to an ID3-like classifier is presented. The algorithmic strategy used for that consists of three phases, viz., *preparation*, *iteration* and *combination and deployment*. Due to lack of space, the description here is rather high-level and is only meant to illustrate how the key concepts of the algebra are concretely applied to a classical, challenging KDD task. The outcome is the construction of (a K-cube that is operationally equivalent to) a decision-tree model. Some of the most important operations employed are discussed in somewhat more detail.

Section 2 described the general algorithmic strategy for specifying KDD tasks in the K-algebra. For the decision tree inducer, that strategy takes the following concrete form: (1) the preparation phase constructs the most detailed K-cube (K_{base}), which other computations will elaborate upon, and the initial K-cube (K_{class}) to be input into the iterative part, which provides sufficient aggregate information with respect to the dimension (play) for further evaluation of interestingness; (2) the iterative part expands K_{class} into different specialisations and partitions, evaluates interestingness (based on the Gini index, in this case), and, at each step, accumulates those with top interestingness (i.e., smallest Gini index); finally, (3) the combination and deployment phase assembles back the resulting accumulated K-cubes into one that is the desired (classification) model (K_{model}), and deploys it at the extensional layer using the appropriate bridge operation.

Phase 1: Preparation. Algorithm 2 gives the K-algebraic expressions for the preparation phase. Its purpose and intermediate steps are as follows.

Algorithm: **K-Algebraic Expressions for Preparation**

// obtain the most detailed K-cube from the extensional data

1   $K_{base} \leftarrow \boxplus_{\blacksquare outlook, humidity, windy, play\square, \square af: Count()\square}(weather R)$

2   $L_{base} \leftarrow [K_{base}]$

// obtain the K-cube with frequency distribution for the dimension play (the class)

3   $K_1 \leftarrow \alpha_{\square play\square, \square af: Sum(af)\square}(K_{base})$

4   $K_{class} \leftarrow \triangleright^{\blacksquare\blacksquare}_{\square \backslash \square play\square}(K_1)$

5   $L_{class} \leftarrow [K_{class}]$

Algorithm 2. The Preparation Phase

Firstly, the most detailed K-cube K_{base} (Fig. 6(a)) is obtained by means of the corresponding bridge operation relation-to-K-cube (denoted by $\boxplus$). This is an essential component of the algebraic strategy, as the process typically evolves in an less-to-more-specific fashion. *Specialisations* of K-cubes are obtained at each step, which requires the existence of a more detailed K-cube from which information is recovered. For instance, take a K-cube with dimensions (outlook, play) and a measure of absolute frequency (af). In order to specialise a K-cube into (outlook, humidity, play), it is not possible to de-aggregate the information from the former (i.e., af), unless it is recovered from another K-cube with the information in non-aggregated form. This explains why operations such as specialise and gen-supersets require two K-cubes as arguments: the one to specialise and the one from which information is to be recovered. This K-cube is then converted into in a singleton list L_{base} with the operation K-cube-to-K-cube-list (denoted by $[\ldots]$), for the benefit of list-processing operations in the iterative phase.

This phase also comprises the construction of the initial K-cube to be pumped into the iterative part. In lines 3 to 4, the K-cube K_{class} (Fig. 6(b)) is constructed to yield the class distribution, i.e., the absolute frequency of the dimension play. It is obtained by the combination of an add-aggregate-measure (denoted by α), which computes the aggregate values on partitions of cells determined by the distinct values of play, and a remove-dimension, which removes all the dimensions but play from the newly aggregated K-cube. The K-cube K_{class} is the start-

outlook	humidity	windy	play	af
overcast	high	false	yes	1
overcast	high	true	yes	1
overcast	normal	false	yes	1
overcast	normal	true	yes	1
rainy	high	false	yes	1
rainy	high	true	no	1
rainy	normal	false	yes	2
rainy	normal	true	no	1
sunny	high	false	no	2
sunny	high	true	no	1
sunny	normal	false	yes	1
sunny	normal	true	yes	1

(a) K_{base}

play	af
no	5
yes	9

(b) K_{class}

Fig. 6. Example Outcome Preparation

ing point for the iterative part, which will process specialisations of it with a view towards minimising the Gini index for combinations of the class with other dimensions. The initial list of K-cubes to be processed in the iterative part is assigned to L_{class}, as shown in line 5.

Phase 2: Iteration. Most of the effort in computing the classifier lies in the iterative phase of this K-algebraic approach. Algorithm 3 presents the corresponding K-algebraic expressions, whose output represented by L_{iter} feeds phase 3.

The iterate operation (denoted by $\circlearrowright$) characterises this phase. It takes as input the initial K-cube-list obtained from the preparation phase (L_{class}), and also the criteria to decide on when to continue accumulating K-cubes or leave the iteration. It is assumed that when a K-cube has the annotation gini evaluated to 0, it shall be accumulated and not specialised further. As an example, the maximum number of iterations is set to 10. When a pass of the iteration is completed, the accumulated K-cubes are assigned to L_{iter}, which is the input to the combination and deployment phase. Fig. 7 shows the intermediate results in the 3-pass iteration that leads to the desired result. (K-cube subscripts suggest which dimensions and subsets of cells led to its derivation.)

Algorithm: K-Algebraic Expressions for Iteration

// plug in the iterate operation the parameters for the termination condition
// and the initial list to be processed

1   $L_{iter} \leftarrow \circlearrowleft_{gini=0,\,10}^{L_{current}} (L_{class})($

// generate supersets, of dimensionality one degree higher, of each K-cube

2   $L_1 \leftarrow \mu_{\blacksquare\ \langle\rangle\ (af:\ Sum(af))}^{x^{k_1,k_2}}(k_1,k_2) (L_{current}, L_{base})$

// evaluate interestingness

3   $L_2 \leftarrow \mu_{interest(k)}^{k}(L_1)$

// reduce nested lists to choose best of each

4   $L_3 \leftarrow \Delta_{\text{If}_{k_1.gini<k_2.gini}(k_1,k_2)}^{k_1,k_2}(L_2)$

// partition by dimensions

5   $L_4 \leftarrow \mu_{\pi_{*\backslash\langle play\rangle}^{d}(k)}^{k}(L_1)$

// evaluate interestingness

6   $L_5 \leftarrow \mu_{interest(k)}^{k}(L_4)$

// flatten K-cube-list

7   $L_6 \leftarrow \Downarrow (L_5)$

$)$

Algorithm 3. The Iteration Phase

0th Iteration
$L_{current} = [\,K_{class}\,]$
$L_{iter} = [\,]$
1st Iteration
$L_2 = [\,[K_{out}, K_{hum}, K_{windy}]\,]$
$L_3 = [\,K_{out}\,]$
$L_5 = [\,[\,K_{outra}, K_{outov}, K_{outsu}\,]\,]$
$L_6 = [\,K_{outra}, K_{outov}, K_{outsu}\,]$
$L_{current} = [\,K_{outra}, K_{outsu}\,]$
$L_{iter} = [\,K_{outov}\,]$
2nd Iteration
$L_2 = [\,[\,K_{outraHum}, K_{outraWindy}\,], [\,K_{outsuHum}, K_{outsuWindy}\,]\,]$
$L_3 = [\,K_{ourraWindy}, K_{outsuHum}\,]$
$L_5 = [\,[\,K_{outraWindyf}, K_{outraWindyf}\,], [\,K_{outsuHumhi}, K_{outsuHumno}\,]\,]$
$L_6 = [\,K_{outraWindyf}, K_{outraWindyf}, K_{outsuHumhi}, K_{outsuHumno}\,]$
$L_{current} = [\,]$
$L_{iter} = [\,K_{outov}, K_{outraWindyf}, K_{outraWindyf}, K_{outsuHumhi}, K_{outsuHumno}\,]$

Fig. 7. Iteration Phase: Intermediate Results

K-cubes represent different ways of partitioning the data. The aim of this iterative process is to find those that best discriminate the desired class. The Gini index is a measure of how good each K-cube is in this regard, and is associated with the K-cube in the form of an annotation. All K-cubes processed in this phase have the dimension play, since we are interested in obtaining statistical information of its interaction with other dimensions.

Each iterative step starts by obtaining specialisations of the K-cubes being processed. From the initial K-cube with only the dimension play, immediate specialisations (with dimensionality one degree higher) are derived, using the gen-supersets ($\triangledown$) operation (line 2). These are evaluated, and the most promising one, i.e., the one with lowest gini, is kept, by applying a combination of reduce (Δ) and select-kcube-on-ann (If) operations. The details of the computation of the gini index for the current K-cube-list are abstracted away by a K-algebra equation *interesting*(K), which is evaluated in lines 3 and 6. Candidate specialisations are obtained for each K-cube until it has reached the desired interestingness, at which point it is saved and removed from further consideration. For example, in the first iteration, L_2 contains the specialisations [(outlook, play), (humidity, play), (windy, play)]. Each specialisation is evaluated in terms of how discriminative they are with regard to the values of play. The one with lowest gini, in this case, the one with outlook, is kept and expanded further until the termination criteria is reached. Notice that, as a K-cube is an aggregated representation of a partition of data, each of its immediate specialisations correspond to sub-partitions of the original one, corresponding to what a decision tree builder must do in practise.

Once the best candidate is retained, the next step is to explore further the partitions of data defined by each cell of a K-cube. For example, from the K-cube with outlook, distinct K-cubes for the subset of cells corresponding to outlook:rainy, outlook:overcast and outlook:sunny are obtained, using the partition-by-dimensions (π^d) in line 5. These have their interestingness evaluated in line 6. Subsequently, the functionality of the iterative operation guarantees that the pure ones are accumulated and the remaining ones are fed back for further refinement. The iteration ends when the K-cube-list $L_{current}$ becomes empty (or the maximum number of passes is reached).

Phase 3: Model Combination and Deployment. The K-cube-list resulting from phase 2 collects distinct k-cubes, which were judged to be interesting in the iterative process. They provide aggregate perspectives on (non-overlapping) partitions of the available data to help determine the class values assigned to each of the latter. The purpose of this final phase is twofold: (1) to assemble these collections of K-cubes back into a single K-cube representing the computed classification model, and (2) to deploy the model in the extensional layer by means of the appropriate bridge operation, which labels the dataset with the corresponding class values given by the cells of the K-cube model. The algebraic specification is given in Algorithm 4.

outlook	humidity	windy	play
sunny	normal	false	yes
sunny	normal	true	yes
sunny	high	false	no
sunny	high	true	no
overcast	normal	false	yes
overcast	normal	true	yes
overcast	high	false	yes
overcast	high	true	yes
rainy	normal	false	yes
rainy	normal	true	no
rainy	high	false	yes
rainy	high	true	no
gini: 0.0000			

Fig. 8. K_{m4}: The Final Model

Algorithm: **K-Algebraic Expressions for Combination and Deployment**

// combine K-cubes into a model and obtain class

1 $L_7 \leftarrow \Delta^{k_1,k_2}_{k_1 \overset{\cup}{\bowtie} k_2} (L_{iter})$

2 $K_{m1} \leftarrow \boxdot(L_7)$

3 $K_{m2} \leftarrow {}^{d\blacksquare \atop \kappa}{}^{m}_{\blacksquare play_m : play\blacksquare}(K_{m1})$

4 $K_{m3} \leftarrow \triangleright^{\blacksquare Max(rf)\blacksquare}_{play}(K_{m2})$

5 $K_{m4} \leftarrow \nu^{m}_{\blacksquare play : play_m \blacksquare}(K_{m3})$

// deploy model

6 $R_{model} \leftarrow \Box(K_{m4})$

7 $R_{test} \leftarrow \pi_{\blacksquare \setminus \{play\}}(weather R)$

8 $R_{predicted} \leftarrow R_{model} \bowtie R_{model}$

Algorithm 4. The Combination and Deployment Phase

The first step is to merge the collection in L_{iter} into a single k-cube using union-join, which takes as input two K-cubes and merges them into a single schema-compatible (.e., with the same set of dimensions, measures and annotations) one. Since the operation is binary and on a list, the higher-order reduce (Δ) operations is used, and the result is assigned to L_7. L_7 is then converted into the single K-cube representing the classification model and shown in Fig. 8. Subsequently, the steps in line 3 and 4 (which correspond to an induction leap) output the final model K_{m4} (which can be seen to be equivalent to the tree in Fig. 2). The dimensional values of play are replicated as measures in line 3 using the copy-dim-as-mea ($^{d \to m}\kappa$) operation. Then, determining which class value is representative per partition is handled by the generalise ($\triangleright$) operation in line 4, which removes the dimension play. As the K-cube shrinks in terms of its dimensionality, each partition of cells (determined by the remaining dimensions) is generalised (i.e., a representative cell is chosen) according to the maximum value of rf, as shown by the input of the operation (Max(rf)). In the deployment stage, firstly the model is converted into a relation using the kcube-to-relation ($\Box$) bridge operation. Then, in the extensional layer, the model can be applied to any unlabelled dataset (e.g., R_{test}) using the relational natural-join to yield the predictions in $R_{predicted}$ (weather R is a relation representing the weather dataset introduced earlier).

4   Related Work

There have been proposals for KDD algebras, e.g., the 3W algebra [12] and the proposal in [6]. Both are based on constraint database systems. They manipulate data and models together using a single carrier, but data mining is seen as a black box, with a single operation as a wrapper for a specific algorithm. Some of the work [13,10] on integrating knowledge discovery and database research has focused, on a narrow range of tasks, typically association rules, or else confines itself to the proposal of a surface language, which fails to throw light on what computations can be defined with it, either in abstract or concretely. Some work [9,2] covers a wider range of tasks, but proceeds in a tool set mode rather than being based on general principles, and, as such fail to provide formal framework for the integration of the two research areas. Finally, researchers [17, 15] have been attracted to the idea of using user-defined functions for implementing data mining algorithms that are strongly coupled to database query engines, but again only algorithms have been attempted and there is a distinct lack of higher-level abstractions.

5   Conclusions

This paper has presented two main contributions: (1) the K-algebra and (2) a specification of decision-tree induction in the K-algebra. The latter is, to the best of our knowledge, the first logical-algebraic specification of a KDD task that requires more expressiveness than available in classical database algebras. This shows that the K-algebra opens the way for the expression of challenging KDD tasks in purely algebraic form. In particular, the K-algebra can express the iterative aspects of the KDD process and, through its layered design, covers a wider range of tasks in the KDD process than previous work. More importantly, the K-algebra is a database algebra insofar as it is designed to operate on collections (and hence, flows). It should be noted that the K-Algebra has been designed to model discovery tasks in the symbolic tradition and, hence, the question as to whether it can be used to model tasks that are expressive in, say, connectionist of genetically-inspired approaches (e.g., neural networks, genetic algorithms) has not yet been investigated. The goal of this proposal is to address the issues identified, viz., lack of compositionality, lack of generality and dependency on user expertise. The K-algebra response to lack of compositionality is to exhibit closure through its layered design. Its response to lack of generality is to be founded on generic algorithmic elements (viz., expand, compress, evaluate, accumulate, filter out and combine). Its response to dependency on user expertise is to be formulated and formalised at a logical, abstract level upon which optimisation algorithms can, in future work, be developed. There also remains the important task of trying to capture more kinds of discovery approaches[2] and investigate empirically the practicality of the K-Algebra, especially the development of tools that may be necessary for its usability aspect.

References

1. L. Breiman, J. H. Friedman, R. Olshen, , and C. J. Stone. *Classification and Regression Trees*. CRC Press, 1984.
2. M. Corporation. Ole db for data mining specification, v1.0, July 2000.

---

[2] No claims are made regarding the expressiveness that results from the set of operations proposed other than that it is, as pointed out, sufficient to express ID3 which, in an algebraic setting, is a novel contribution.

3. U. M. Fayyad, G. Piatetsky-Shapiro, and P. Smyth. From Data Mining to Knowledge Discovery: An Overview. In *Advances in Knowledge Discovery and Data Mining*, pages 1–34. AAAI/MIT Press, 1996.
4. L. Fegaras and D. Maier. Optimizing Object Queries Using an Effective Calculus. *ACM Transactions on Database Systems*, 25(4), December 2000.
5. H. Garcia-Molina, J. D. Ullman, and J. Widom. *Database System Implementation*. Prentice-Hall, 2000.
6. I. Geist and K. Sattler. Towards Data Mining Operators in Database Systems: Algebra and Implementation. In *Proc. of 2nd Int. Workshop on Databases, Documents, and Information Fusion*, 2002.
7. L. Gerber and A. A. A. Fernandes. The K-Algebra for Knowledge Discovery in Databases. Technical report, University of Manchester, Department of Computer Science, March 2004.
8. R. H. Güting and M. Schneider. Realm-Based Spatial Data Types: The ROSE Algebra. *VLDB Journal*, 4(2):243–286, 1995.
9. J. Han, Y. Fu, W. Wang, K. Koperski, and O. Zaiane. DMQL: A Data Mining Query Language for Relational Databases. SIGMOD'96 Workshop on Research Issues on Data Mining and Knowledge Discovery, 1996.
10. T. Imielinski and A. Virmani. MSQL: A Query Language for Database Mining. *Data Mining and Knowledge Discovery*, 3(4):373–408, 1999.
11. H. V. Jagadish, L. V. S. Lakshmanan, D. Srivastava, and K. Thompson. TAX: A Tree Algebra for XML. In *Database Programming Languages, 8th International Workshop*, volume 2397 of *LNCS*, pages 149–164, 2002.
12. T. Johnson, L. V. S. Lakshmanan, and R. T. Ng. The 3W Model and Algebra for Unified Data Mining. In *Proceedings of 26th International Conference on Very Large Data Bases*, pages 21–32, 2000.
13. R. Meo, G. Psaila, and S. Ceri. An Extension to SQL for Mining Assocation Rules. *Knowledge Discovery and Association Rules*, 2(2):195–224, 1998.
14. J. R. Quinlan. Induction of Decision Trees. *Machine Learning*, 1:81–106, 1986.
15. S. Sarawagi, S. Thomas, and R. Agrawal. Integrating Mining with Relational Database Systems: Alternatives and Implications. Technical Report RJ 10107 (91923), IBM Almaden Research Center, San Jose, California, March 1998.
16. P. A. Tucker, D. Maier, T. Sheard, and L. Fegaras. Exploiting Punctuation Semantics in Continuous Data Streams. *IEEE Transactions on Knowledge and Data Engineering*, 15(3):555–568, May/June 2003.
17. H. Wang and C. Zaniolo. ATLaS: A Native Extension of SQL for Data Mining. In *Proceedings of the Third SIAM International Conference on Data Mining*, 2003.

Beyond Databases: An Asset Language for Conceptual Content Management

Hans-Werner Sehring and Joachim W. Schmidt

Technical University Hamburg-Harburg, Software Systems Department,
Harburger Schloßstraße 20, D-21073 Hamburg, Germany
{hw.sehring,j.w.schmidt}@tu-harburg.de

Abstract. Innovative information systems such as content management systems and information brokers are designed to organize a complex mixture of *media content* – texts, images, maps, videos, ... – and to present it through domain specific *conceptual models*, for example, on sports, stock exchange, or art history.
In this paper we extend the currently dominating computational container models into a coherent content-concept model intended to capture more of the meaning – thereby improving the value – of content. Integrated content-concept views on entities are modeled using the notion of *assets*, and the rationale of our asset language is based on arguments for *open language expressiveness* [19] and *dynamic system responsiveness* [8]. In addition, we discuss our experiences with a component-based implementation technology which substantially simplifies the implementation of open and dynamic asset management systems.

1   Introduction: On Content-Concept Integration

Important classes of innovative information systems such as content management systems and information brokers are designed to organize a complex mixture of *media content* – texts, images, maps, videos, ... – and to present it through domain specific *conceptual models* [6], for example, on sports, stock exchange, or art history.

Traditional implementations of such information systems reflect this complexity through their software intricacy resulting from a heterogeneous mix of conventional database technology, various augmentations by text, image or geo functionality (or just by blobs) and through additional organizational principles from domain ontologies [25,5].

In this paper we argue for a homogeneous basis for conceptual content management and present

- an integrated content-concept model – based on so-called *assets* [21] –,
- an asset language and its conceptual foundation [19], [8], as well as
- an implementation technology and architecture.

A. Benczúr, J. Demetrovics, G. Gottlob (Eds.): ADBIS 2004, LNCS 3255, pp. 99–112, 2004.

Our work is inventive essentially due to the following three contributions:

1. Content is *always* associated with its concept and represented by assets, i.e., *content-concept-pairs*. In a sense, assets generalize the notion of typed values or schema-constrained databases. Assets represent application entities, concrete or abstract ones;
2. Asset schemata are *open* in the sense that users can change asset attributes on-the-fly and any time, thus guaranteeing best correspondence with the entity-at-hand;
3. Asset management systems are *dynamic*, i.e., the system implementation changes dynamically following any on-the-fly modification of an asset schema; this requirement demands a specific system modularization and an innovative system architecture.

Our paper is structured as follows: after a short introduction of our asset language (section 2) we discuss the essentials of open and dynamic asset-based modeling and present an extensive example from the domain of art history (section 3). In section 4 we argue the benefits of asset compilation and its advantages for software system construction. The overall modularization and architecture of asset-based information systems are presented in section 5. We conclude with a short summary and an outlook into further applications of asset-based technology.

2   An Asset Language for Integrated Information Management

Assets represent application entities by content-concept-pairs (fig. 1). Following observations of [8] and others, neither content nor a conceptual model of an entity can exist in isolation. The conceptual part is needed to explain the way content refers to an entity. Content serves as an existential proof of the validity of concepts.

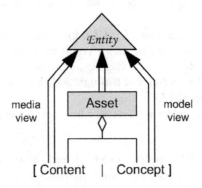

Fig. 1. Assets represent entities by [content | concept]-pairs

The content facet of assets is managed through object-oriented multimedia container technology. Assets contain handle objects referring to pieces of content.

To support *expressive* entity representations the concept facet is given by three contributions:

1. characteristic values,
2. relationships between assets, and
3. rules (types, constraints, ...).

Characteristic values describe entities by their immanent properties. Though the values may change one value is always assigned. Relationships between assets describe entities by their relation to others. Such relations may be changed or – in contrast to characteristic values – even be removed. Regular assertions describe facts about a set of similar assets. Type and value constraints on characteristics and relationships fall in this category.

Thus, the notion of assets follows closely the theoretical work of [19] (firstness, secondness, thirdness) and [8] (indivisibility of content and concept).

As already argued in the introduction, a conceptual content management system has to be based on a *responsive* dynamic model to adequately represent changing entities [21]. For expressive entity description and responsive domain modeling we propose an asset language to be employed to notate individual asset definitions and their systematics. Our asset language syntax corresponds to modern class-based languages [1].

An alternative to such a linguistic approach would be the use of a generic model to which the intended domain model is mapped. In this case users would have to face all the problems implied by an on-the-fly translation between their intended entity model and the generic model ("mentally compile and decipher" [10]).

As an *asset definition language* the language is used to define asset classes. The following code gives an example of an asset class definition:

```
class Equestrian {
  content reproduction : java.awt.Image ...
  concept
    characteristic yearOfCreation : java.util.Calendar
    characteristic medium : de.tuhh.sts.wel.Media
    relationship painter : Artist
    relationship epoch   : Epoch
    constraint epoch = painter.epoch
    ...
}
```

The body of a class definition contains two sections. Under **content** references to pieces of content are defined by content handles. Their type is given in the class definition. Valid types are defined by some object-oriented language underlying the asset language. Currently we use Java for this purpose.

The conceptual part of entity descriptions is formalized in the `concept` section. Here the contributions discussed above can be found: characteristics, relationships, and rules.

Definitions starting with `characteristic` and `relationship` define attributes which can be set for any instance of a defined class. Each of these is identified by a name. A type for actual values or bindings is given after the colon. In the case of characteristics this is a Java class again. In the example shown above the standard Java class `Calendar` and the application-specific class `Media` are used. For relationships an asset class is given which constrains the type of assets referred to. If the class name is followed by an asterisk ("*") it is a many-to-many relationship binding a set of asset instances.

Constraints pose value restrictions on the attributes of all instances of one asset class. In the above example it is defined that the epoch of the equestrian artwork has to be the same as the epoch of the artist (if one is bound). In constraint statements all attributes of the current class can be used plus the attributes of bound assets.

In the example the epoch binding for the current `Equestrian` instance is compared to the corresponding binding of the related `Artist` instance. For this to work the asset class `Artist` needs to define an epoch relationship to `Epoch` assets, just like `Equestrian`.

Possible comparators in constraint expressions test for equality ("="), lesser ("<"), greater (">"), different ("#"), or similar ("~") values or bindings. How the comparator is actually evaluated depends on the compared attributes' types. For characteristics, evaluation is done according to a Java `Comparator`. For relationships the comparisons are mapped to set relations (equality, inclusion, ...). In both cases, similarity is decided in an implementation-dependent manner (see below). Expressions can be combined using the logical operators `and`, `or`, and `not`.

Classes can be defined as subclasses of existing ones using the `refines` keyword:

```
class MedievalEquestrian refines Equestrian {
    concept constraint epoch = middleAges
}
```

This way definitions are inherited by the subclass. Here, a constraint on `epoch` is added. Inherited definitions can be overridden.

Another way to define asset classes is by giving an extensional definition. This is done by naming a set of asset instances which define a class. There are two variants of the extensional class definition. The first one gives a fixed set of instances which are the complete extent of an asset class:

```
class Equestrian definedby { e1, e2, e3 }
```

This way the asset class `Equestrian` is introduced as an enumeration type with possible instances e1, e2, and e3.

For the second variant the set of asset instances serves as an example for the intended extent of the new asset class. A definition like

```
class Equestrian definedby ~ { e1, e2, e3 }
```

defines **Equestrian** to be the class of all instances similar to e1, e2, and e3. To decide upon similarity, conceptual content management systems incorporate retrieval technology [3]. The set of asset instances is used as a training set.

For the management of asset instances statements of the asset language serve as an *asset query and manipulation language*. A **create** operation is used for the creation of asset instances. The following is an example for the instantiation of an **Equestrian** instance:

```
create Equestrian {
   medium  := de.tuhh.sts.wel.Media.STATUE
   painter := rubens
}
```

Here, **STATUE** is a constant class variable of **Media** holding a Java object for the media type "Statue" (singleton [12]). **rubens** is the name of an **Artist** asset instance.

A variant of the **create** operation allows to name a prototype instance instead of the set of initial bindings: **create** Equestrian eqProto.

For updates the **modify** operation is used. For example, the update of an **Equestrian** instance named **eq1** is done by:

```
modify eq1 {
   medium  := de.tuhh.sts.wel.Media.STATUE
   painter := rubens
}
```

A variant similar to that of **create** allows the naming of a prototype instance instead of the set of new value and instance bindings: **modify** eq1 eqProto.

The **lookfor** operation is used to retrieve asset instances. It searches for all instances of a given class. As query parameters all characteristic and relationship attributes can be constrained. An example query for **Equestrian** instances which are statues by Rubens is:

```
lookfor Equestrian {
   medium  = de.tuhh.sts.wel.Media.STATUE
   painter = rubens
}
```

Due to space limitations not all aspects of the asset language can be explained in this section. The detailed definition of the asset language can be found in [23].

3   Asset-Based Modeling: A Case for Open and Dynamic Information Systems

Asset definitions usually depend on considerations like the state of the entities to describe, the users' expertise, their current task, etc. For various reasons such influencing factors may change over time (see [8]):

title	"Bonaparte Crossing the Alps..."
artist	Jacques-Louis David : Painter
regent	Napoleon I. : Emperor
motives	mountain, alps, horse, hand
text	Bonaparte, Hannibal, Carolus
reference	Carolus Magnus Crossing the Alps, Hannibal Crossing the Alps

(a) Media Content for the Concept "Equestrian Statue"

(b) Conceptual Model of one "Equestrian Statue"

Fig. 2. Asset Facets

– The observed entities change. Thus, their descriptions have to be adjusted. This is true even for class definitions because in different states an entity is described by different sets of contents, characteristics, relationships, and constraints.
– The users' expertise influences their information needs. Usually users are not willing to (explicitly) provide data they do not consider interesting. For communication with others, though, assets need to be tailored to the receiver's needs.
– A user can view an entity while being in different contexts, e.g., depending on the task for which an asset is needed. Different asset definitions may be needed when changing context.

Thus, openness and dynamics as defined in the introduction are important properties of conceptual content management systems for a variety of reasons.

In application projects we observed that knowledge about application entities is captured by modeling the processes in which they have been created and used. Soft-goals like reasons, intentions, etc. of the creation of entities are recorded in such applications (see also [29]).

In the project *Warburg Electronic Library* (*WEL*) a prototypical open dynamic conceptual content management system has been developed [22]. In application projects our project partners create large numbers of assets modeling their domain. One primary application is art history [7]. Our project partners from art history use the WEL to pursue research in the field of Political Iconography. For content they collect reproductions of artworks (see fig. 2(a)).

The conceptual part of assets records the historical events which prove that the artifact under consideration has been used to achieve political goals. Typical information is the creation date and location of a piece of art, relationships to

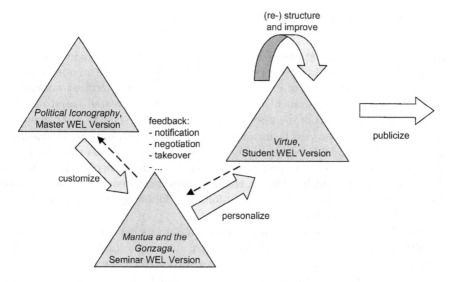

Fig. 3. Open Dynamic Asset Use in the WEL for E-Learning

the regent ordering it and the artist who created it, relationships to other works which are influential, information on the way it has been presented, etc. (see fig. 2(b)). Sets of asset instances define categories which name political phenomena. Additional constraints reveal how products of art work for political reasons.

From a computer science perspective the WEL is an important project for understanding the nature of conceptual content management systems. It serves as a field study with students and scientists. The WEL has been online for several years now [27]. Its services are used by some hundred scientists worldwide, mainly from the humanities. In cooperation with our project partners it has been used as an e-learning tool in several seminars during the past years.

As a research tool the WEL maintains a set of assets available to a research community. Researchers employ openness and dynamics to model their hypotheses. They can do so without interfering with others and without allowing them to see their results. When there are valuable findings a community can choose to integrate the assets of one of its members. For this, the WEL maintains open asset models and the corresponding asset instances on a per-user basis. Within scopes controlled through group membership asset instances can be shared among users.

In e-learning scenarios assets are prepared as course material. The body of asset instances is maintained for teaching purposes or, as is the case with the WEL, research efforts being carried out. Openness is needed by both teachers and students [ML95]. Teaching staff can select and adapt assets as teaching material for a course to be supported. In seminars and lab classes students can modify this material. Such a process is illustrated in fig. 3. This way, students get hands-on experience with the definition of concepts, the validation of models, the creation of content, etc.

4   Information System Construction by Asset Compilation

Domain experts formulate asset models using the asset language introduced in section 2. As discussed in the previous section there is a demand for open systems allowing the modification of existing assets. For asset management systems to meet the openness requirement these are automatically created based on such domain models. As part of the asset technology this is done by an *asset compiler*.

The compilation process bears a resemblance to modern software-engineering approaches like Model Driven Architecture (MDA) [18]. The asset compiler creates a platform independent model from a domain model. The platform independent model is then translated into a running software system. The translation of domain models is described in this section. The following section concentrates on actual implementations.

As a first step in the compilation process a data model is created from asset definitions given in the asset language (comparable, for example, to the interface modules of [14]). The current asset compiler uses Java as its target language. The data model consists of Java interfaces. Additional parameterizations of standard components are created as needed (see next section). Examples are schemata for databases or content management systems, XML schemata, etc.

For each asset class a Java interface is created. Definitions of subclasses are mapped to subtypes. The interfaces adhere to the JavaBeans standard [13]. Access methods ("getter" and "setter") are defined for characteristics and relationships. Class-level (thirdness) contributions are implemented in the operations of classes generated according to the interface definitions: constraints are mapped to constrained properties which throw a **VetoException** when the constraint is violated (see also [15]). Rules are expressed by bound properties which cause the invocation of further methods under the condition set by a constraint.

The UML class diagram in fig. 4 gives an overview of the generated code. The packages **lifecyclemodel** and **implementation** contain generic interfaces and classes which are part of the runtime environment of a conceptual content management system. A package like *some.project* is generated by the asset compiler.

The interfaces from package **lifecyclemodel** reflect possible states in the life of an asset instance. They define methods which allow state transitions as shown in the state chart in fig. 5.

Interfaces reflecting an asset model are created as subtypes of those generic ones. In fig. 4 the interfaces shown in package *some.project* are created for a defined asset class *A*. These introduce methods which reflect the asset classes' characteristics, relationships, and constraints as explained above.

Not shown in fig. 4 are additional interfaces which describe the management of asset instances:

- Class objects carry the asset class definitions into the data model (meta level). They offer reflection comparable to object-oriented programming languages.
- Instances are created following the factory method pattern [12].

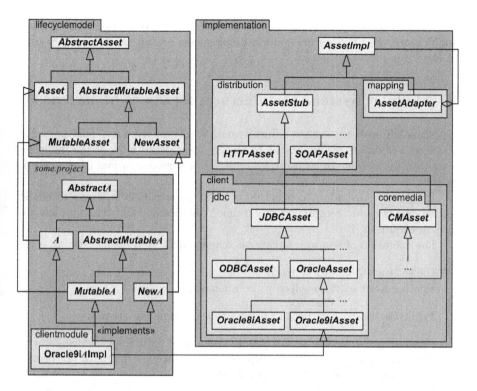

Fig. 4. Conceptual Class Diagram of Code Generated from Asset Definitions

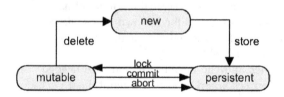

Fig. 5. State Diagram for the Asset Instance Life Cycle

- Query interfaces define possible queries to retrieve assets instances. They are equipped with methods to formulate query constraints. These constrain methods are generated for each defined characteristic and relationship and each comparison operator.
- For collections of asset instances iterators [12] are defined for each asset class.

The generated interfaces reflect the domain model. The abstract classes from the **implementation** package shown on the right of figure 4 introduce platform independent functionality. Classes which implement the interfaces and make use of the abstract classes are generated by the compiler. For an example see Oracle9i*A*Impl in package **clientmodule** in the class diagram (a subpackage of the application-specific package *some.project*). Sets of classes form modules which make up a conceptual content management system. These are described in the subsequent section.

5   Modular System Architectures for Asset Management

Open modeling allows users to adjust domain models at any time. This may affect the model of one user who wishes to change asset definitions, or the models of a user group and one of its users, who creates a personal variant of the group's model.

To dynamically adapt conceptual content management systems to changing models they are recompiled at runtime. The demand for dynamics leads to system evolution [17].

The evolution of conceptual content management systems has two aspects:

- the software needs to be modified, and
- existing asset instances need to be maintained.

Typical issues with respect to these two aspects of evolution are:

- Changes performed on behalf of individual users should not have any impact on others. Therefore, dynamic support for system evolution must not prevent continuous operation of the software system.
- On the one hand, assets as representations of domain entities cannot automatically be converted in general. On the other hand, manual instance conversion is not feasible for typical amounts of asset instances.
- If a user personalizes assets for his own needs, he still will be interested in changes applied to the original. Through awareness [11] measures he can be informed about such changes. To be able to review the changes, access to both the former and the current versions are needed. That is, revisions of assets and their schemata need to be maintained.

Crucial for both aspects of evolution – software as well as asset instances – is a modularized system architecture. On evolution steps distinguished system modules maintain sets of asset instances created under different schemata. They are produced by the asset compiler and dynamically added or replaced.

For our asset technology we identified a small set of module kinds of a conceptual content management system. The conceptual content management system architecture supports the dynamic combination of instances of the various module kinds. These modules share some similarities with components [26,2] (combinability, statelessness, ...), but in contrast to these they are generated for a concrete software system. Modules constitute the minimal compilation units of the generated software which the compiler can add or replace.

Figure 6 shows an example of the evolution of a user's domain model. Assume that the conceptual content management system shown in fig. 6(a) is in operation. It simply consists of one module m as the application layer and a

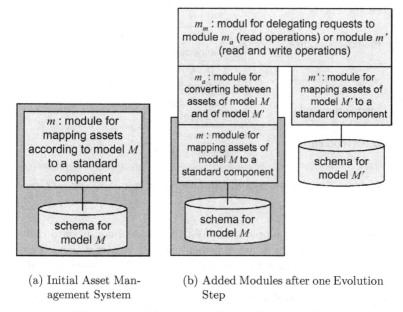

(a) Initial Asset Management System

(b) Added Modules after one Evolution Step

Fig. 6. Asset Management System Evolution Step

database as the data layer of a layered architecture. Both have been generated according to a domain model M.

If model M is redefined to become model M' the system is recompiled. This leads to the generation of additional modules which are incorporated for dynamic system evolution. The result is shown in fig. 6(b). First note that the original conceptual content management system is maintained as a subsystem of the new system version. This way existing asset instances are kept intact.

In this example a second database is set up to store asset instances following model M'. A module m' for accessing the database is created similar to m found in the original conceptual content management system. Two further modules are added to combine the two subsystems for models M and M'. These follow the mediator architecture [28], an important building block of the conceptual content management system architecture. The mapping module m_a serves as a wrapper lifting assets of M to M' (compare [20]). Mapping issues are covered by a module kind of its own rather than integrating it into the other kinds of modules so that mappings can be plugged dynamically [16]. The mediation module m_m reflects M' in the application layer of the new system version. It routes requests to either m_a or m'. Lookups are forwarded to both these modules and the results are unified. New asset instances are always created in m' according to M'. Update requests of instances of M lead to their deletion in the subsystem for M and their recreation in m'.

The two issues with evolution mentioned above are taken into consideration by this approach. Preserving the existing software as part of a new system ver-

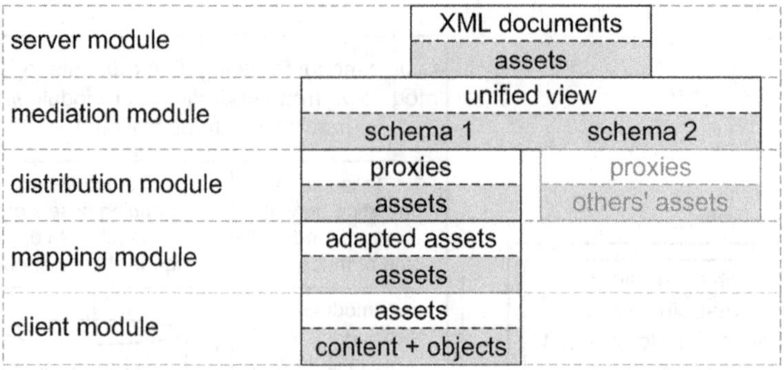

server module	XML documents	
	assets	
mediation module	unified view	
	schema 1	schema 2
distribution module	proxies	proxies
	assets	others' assets
mapping module	adapted assets	
	assets	
client module	assets	
	content + objects	

Fig. 7. Asset Management System: Module Kinds and Architectural Overview

sion leaves it in continuous operation. With the mentioned update policy asset instances are incrementally converted when needed. This way, users can perform the task of reviewing the asset instances one by one. More sophisticated policies might take the mediation module to batch mode when only a certain amount of instances is left in the outdated schema.

In a similar way configurations for other functionality are set up. E.g., to store revisions of asset instances these are maintained by distinct subsystems. A mediation module takes care of the revision control.

The above example introduces the three most important module kinds: *client modules* to access standard components managing the assets' content and data, *mapping modules* to adjust schemata, and *mediation modules* to glue the modules of a conceptual content management system together. These form the core of any conceptual content management system. In addition to these, figure 7 shows the remaining two module types. *Distribution modules* allow the incorporation of modules residing on different networked computers. Fig. 4 indicates two possible implementations in package `distribution`: the HTTP-based transmission of XML documents with a schema generated from the asset definitions (comparable to the suggestion of [24]) and one for remote method calls using SOAP. *Server modules* (not shown in fig. 4) offer the services of a conceptual content management system following a standard protocol for use by third party systems. One example is a server module for Web Services [4] with generated descriptions given in the WDL [9].

6   Concluding Remarks

Our asset model abstracts and generalizes an essential part of the core experience in database design and information system development. Initial applications demonstrate that asset-based modeling simplifies information system projects and increases the reusability of system functionality.

The degree of open schema and dynamic system changeability is substantially improved by a better understanding of the appropriate architecture and modularization of conceptual content management systems.

In addition we expect that asset-based modeling will greatly improve typical standard tasks in information systems administration. The very same methodology used for domain-specific entity modeling may also be applied to software entities and, therefore, to information systems themselves. Typical examples include naming and messaging services, user and rights management or visualization tasks. User interfaces, for example, will benefit significantly from an asset-based GUI model and UI description. A presentation logic which associates assets from the application domain and the GUI realm can then be used by a GUI engine to render such UI descriptions and exploit the dynamic openness of asset management for user interface adaptation.

References

1. Martín Abadi and Luca Cardelli. *A Theory of Objects*. Monographs in Computer Science. Springer-Verlag New York, Inc., 1996.
2. U. Aßmann. *Invasive Software Composition*. Springer-Verlag, 2003.
3. Thomas Büchner. Entwurf und Realisierung eines Java-Frameworks zur inhaltlichen Erschließung von Informationsobjekten. Master's thesis, Software Systems Department, Technical University Hamburg-Harburg, Germany, 2002.
4. David Booth, Hugo Haas, Francis McCabe, Eric Newcomer, Michael Champion, Chris Ferris, and David Orchard. Web Services Architecture, W3C Working Group Note. http://www.w3.org/TR/ws-arch/, 11 February 2004.
5. Alex Borgida and Ronald J. Brachman. Conceptual Modeling with Description Logics. In Franz Baader, Diego Calvanese, Deborah McGuinness, Daniele Nardi, and Peter Patel-Schneider, editors, *The Description Logic Handbook: Theory, Implementation and Applications*, pages 349–372. Cambridge University Press, 2003.
6. Michael L. Brodie, John Mylopoulos, and Joachim W. Schmidt, editors. *On Conceptual Modelling: Perspectives from Artificial Intelligence, Databases, and Programming Languages*. Topics in Information Systems. Springer-Verlag, 1984.
7. Matthias Bruhn. The Warburg Electronic Library in Hamburg: A Digital Index of Political Iconography. *Visual Resources*, XV:405–423, 2000.
8. Ernst Cassirer. *Die Sprache, Das mythische Denken, Phänomenologie der Erkenntnis*, volume 11-13 Philosophie der symbolischen Formen of *Gesammelte Werke*. Felix Meiner Verlag GmbH, Hamburger Ausgabe edition, 2001-2002.
9. Roberto Chinnici, Martin Gudgin, Jean-Jacques Moreau, Jeffrey Schlimmer, and Sanjiva Weerawarana. Web Services Description Language (WSDL) Version 2.0 Part 1: Core Language. www.w3.org/TR/wsdl20/, March 2004.
10. Dov Dori. The Visual Semantic Web: Unifying Human and Machine Knowledge Representations with Object-Process Methodology. In Isabel F. Cruz, Vipul Kashyap, Stefan Decker, and Rainer Eckstein, editors, *Proceedings of SWDB'03, The first International Workshop on Semantic Web and Databases, Co-located with VLDB 2003*, Humboldt-Universität, Berlin, Germany, 7.-8. September 2003.
11. P. Dourish and V. Bellotti. Awareness and Coordination in Shared Workspaces. In *Proceedings of ACM CSCW 92 Conference on Computer-Supported Work*, pages 107–114, 1992.

12. Erich Gamma, Richard Helm, Ralph Johnson, and John Vlissides. *Design Patterns: Elements od Reusable Object-Oriented Software.* Addison-Wesley, 1994.
13. Graham Hamilton. *JavaBeans (Version 1.01-A).* Sun Microsystems, Inc., 8. August 1997.
14. Manfred A. Jeusfeld. Generating Queries from Complex Type Definitions. In Franz Baader, Martin Buchheit, Manfred A. Jeusfeld, and Werner Nutt, editors, *Reasoning about Structured Objects: Knowledge Representation Meets Databases, Proceedings of 1st Workshop KRDB'94,* CEUR Workshop Proceedings, 1994.
15. H. Knublauch, M. Sedlmayr, and T. Rose. Design Patterns for the Implementation of Constraints on JavaBeans. In *Tagungsband Net.Object Days 2000, Erfurt, 9.-12. Oktober.* tranSIT GmbH, 2000.
16. Mira Mezini, Linda Seiter, and Karl Lieberherr. Component integration with pluggable composite adapters. In *Software Architectures and Component Technology.* Kluwer, 2000.
17. Giorgio De Michelis, Eric Dubois, Matthias Jarke, Florian Matthes, John Mylopoulos, Joachim W. Schmidt, Carson Woo, and Eric Yu. A Three-Faceted View of Information Systems. *Communications of the ACM,* 41(12):64–70, 1998.
18. Joaquin Miller and Jishnu Mukerji. MDA Guide Version 1.0.1. Technical Report omg/2003-06-01, OMG, 12th June 2003.
19. C.S. Peirce. *Collected Papers of Charles Sanders Peirce.* Harvard University Press, Cambridge, 1931.
20. Erhard Rahm and Philip A. Bernstein. A survey of approaches to automatic schema matching. *VLDB Journal,* 10(4):334–350, 2001.
21. Joachim W. Schmidt and Hans-Werner Sehring. Conceptual Content Modeling and Management: The Rationale of an Asset Language. In Manfred Broy and Alexandre V. Zamulin, editors, *Perspectives of System Informatics, 5th International Andrei Ershov Memorial Conference, PSI 2003,* volume 2890 of *Lecture Notes in Computer Science,* pages 469–493. Springer, July 2003.
22. J.W. Schmidt, H.-W. Sehring, M. Skusa, and A. Wienberg. Subject-Oriented Work: Lessons Learned from an Interdisciplinary Content Management Project. In Albertas Caplinskas and Johann Eder, editors, *Advances in Databases and Information Systems, 5th East European Conference, ADBIS 2001,* volume 2151 of *Lecture Notes in Computer Science,* pages 3–26. Springer, September 2001.
23. Hans-Werner Sehring. Report on an Asset Definition, Query, and Manipulation Language. Version 1.0. Technical report, Software Systems Department, Technical University Hamburg-Harburg, Germany, 2003.
24. German Shegalov, Michael Gillmann, and Gerhard Weikum. XML-enabled workflow management for e-services across heterogeneous platforms. *VLDB Journal,* 10(1):91–103, 2001.
25. John F. Sowa. *Knowledge Representation, Logical, Philosophical, and Computational Foundations.* Brooks/Cole, Thomson Learning, 2000.
26. C. Szyperski. *Component Software: Beyond Object-Oriented Programming.* Addison-Wesley, 1998.
27. Homepage of the Warburg Electronic Library. http://www.welib.de, 2004.
28. G. Wiederhold. Mediators in the Architecture of Future Information Systems. *IEEE Computer,* 25:38–49, 1992.
29. E. Yu. *Modelling Strategic Relationships for Process Reengineering.* PhD thesis, University of Toronto, 1995.

Component-Based Modeling of Huge Databases

Peggy Schmidt and Bernhard Thalheim

Computer Science and Applied Mathematics Institute, Kiel University,
Olshausenstrasse 40, 24098 Kiel, Germany
thalheim@is.informatik.uni-kiel.de, contact@peggy-schmidt.de

Abstract. Database modeling is still a job of an artisan. Due to this approach database schemata evolve by growth without any evolution plan. Finally, they cannot be examined, surveyed, consistently extended or analyzed. Querying and maintenance become very difficult. Distribution of database fragments becomes a performance bottleneck. Currently, databases evolve to huge databases. Their development must be performed with the highest care.
This paper aims in developing an approach to *systematic* schema composition based on components. The approach is based on the internal skeletal meta-structures inside the schema. We develop a theory of database components which can be composed to schemata following a architecture skeleton of the entire database.

1 Introduction

Observations

Database modeling is usually carried out by handicraft. Database developers know a number of methods and apply them with high craftman's skills. Monographs and database course books usually base explanations on small or 'toy' examples. Therefore database modeling courses are not the right school for people handling database applications in practice. Database applications tend to be large, carry hundreds of tables and have a very sophisticated and complex integrity support.

Database schemata tend to be large, unsurveyable, incomprehensible and partially inconsistent due to application, the database development life cycle and due to the number of team members involved at different time intervals. Thus, consistent management of the database schema might become a nightmare and may lead to legacy problems. The size of the schemata may be very large, e.g., the size of the SAP R/3 schema consisting of more than 21.000 tables. In contrast, [Moo01] discovered that diagrams quickly become unreadable once the number of entity and relationship types exceeds about twenty.

It is a common observation that large database schemata are error-prone, difficult to maintain and to extend and not-surveyable. Moreover, development of retrieval and operation facilities requires highest professional skills in abstraction, memorization and programming. Such schemata reach sizes of more than

A. Benczúr, J. Demetrovics, G. Gottlob (Eds.): ADBIS 2004, LNCS 3255, pp. 113–128, 2004.
© Springer-Verlag Berlin Heidelberg 2004

1000 attribute, entity and relationship types. Since they are not comprehensible any change to the schema is performed by extending the schema and thus making it even more complex.

Possible Approaches to Cope with Complexity

Large database schemata can be drastically simplified if techniques of modular modeling such as *design by units*[Tha00a] are used. Modular modeling is an abstraction technique based on principles of hiding and encapsulation. Design by units allows to consider parts of the schema in a separate fashion. The parts are connected via types which function similar to bridges. [FeT02] already observed that each large schema can be separated into a number of application dimensions such as the specialization dimension, the association dimension, the log, usage and meta-characterization dimension, and the data quality, lifespan and history dimension.

Modularization on the basis of components supports handling of large systems. The term "component" has been around for a long time. Component-based software has become a "buzzword" since about ten years beyond classical programming paradigms such as structured programming, user-defined data types, functional programming, object-orientation, logic programming, active objects and agents, distributed systems and concurrency, and middleware and coordination. Various component technologies have been developed since then: Source-level language extensions (CORBA, JavaBeans); binary-level object models (OLE, COM, COM+, DCOM, .NET); compound documents (OLE, OpenDoc, BlackBox). We may generalize components to sub-schemata.

Hierarchy abstraction enables in considering objects in a variety of levels of detail. Hierarchy abstraction is based on a specific form of the general join operator [Tha02]. It combines types which are of high adhesion and which are mainly modeled on the basis of star sub-schemata. *Specialization* is a well-known form of hierarchy abstraction. For instance, an *Address* type is specialized to the *GeographicAddress* type. Other forms are role hierarchies and category hierarchies. For instance, *Student* is a role of *Person*. *Undergraduate* is a category of *Student*. The behavior of both is the same. Specific properties have been changed. *Variations* and *versions* can be modeled on the basis of hierarchy abstraction.

Codesign [Tha00a] of database applications aims in consistent development of all facets of database applications: structuring of the database by schema types and static integrity constraints, behavior modeling by specification of functionality and dynamic integrity constraints and interactivity modeling by assigning views to activities of actors in the corresponding dialogue steps. First, a skeleton of components is developed. This skeleton can be refined during evolution of the schema. Then, each component is developed step by step. If this component is associated to another component then its development must be associated with the development of the other component as long as their common elements are concerned.

Goals of the Paper

The paper develops a methodology for *systematic development of large schemata*. Analyzing a large number of applications it has been observed in [Tha00b] that large schemata have a high internal similarity. This similarity can be used to reason on the schema in various levels of detail. At the same time, similarity can be used for improvement and simplification of the schema.

At the same time, each schema has building blocks. We call these blocks or cells in the schema *component*. These components are combined with each other. At the same time, schemata have an internal many-dimensionality. Main or kernel types are associated with information facets such as meta-characterization, log, usage, rights, and quality information. The schemata have a meta-structure. This meta-structure is captured by the *skeleton* of the schema. This skeleton consists of the main modules without capturing the details within the types. The skeleton structure allows to separate parts of the schema from others. The skeleton displays the structure at a large. At the same time, schemata have an internal *meta-structure*.

2   Skeletons and Components Within Database Schemata

Component Sub-schemata

We use the extended ER model [Tha00a] for representation of structuring and behavior. It has a generic algebra and logic, i.e., the algebra of derivable operations and the fragment of (hierarchical) predicate logic may be derived from the HERM algebra whenever the structure of the database is given.

A database type $\mathcal{S} = (S, O, \Sigma)$ is given by

- a structure S defined by a type expression defined over the set of basic types B, a set of labels L and the constructors product (tuple), set and bag, i.e. an expression defined by the recursive type equality
  $t \ = \ B \,|\, t \times ... \times t \,|\, \{t\} \,|\, [t] \,|\, l : t \quad ,$
- a set of operations defined in the ER algebra and limited to S, and
- a set of (static and dynamic) integrity constraints defined in the hierarchical predicate logic with the base predicate P_S.

Objects of the database type $\mathcal{S}^C$ are S-structured. Classes $\mathcal{S}^C$ are sets of objects for which the set of static integrity constraints is valid.

Operations can be classified into "retrieval" operations enabling in generating values from the class $\mathcal{S}^C$ and "modification" operations allowing to change the objects in the class $\mathcal{S}^C$ if static and dynamic integrity constraints are not invalidated.

A database schema $\mathcal{D} = (\mathcal{S}_1, ..., \mathcal{S}_m, \Sigma_G)$ is defined by

- a list of different database types and
- a set of global integrity constraints.

The HERM algebra can be used to define (parameterized) views $\mathcal{V} = (V, O_V)$ on a schema $\mathcal{D}$ via

- an (parameterized) algebraic expression V on $\mathcal{D}$ and
- a set of (parameterized) operations of the HERM algebra applicable to V.

The view operations may be classified too into retrieval operations O_V^R and modification operations O_V^M. Based on this classification we derive an *output view* O^V of $\mathcal{V}$ and an *input view* I^V of $\mathcal{V}$.

In a similar way (but outside the scope of this paper) we may define transactions, interfaces, interactivity, recovery, etc.

Obviously, I^V and O^V are typed based on the type system. Data warehouse design is mainly view design [Tha00a].

A **database component** is *database scheme that has an import and an export interface for connecting it to other components by standardized interface techniques.* Components are defined in a data warehouse setting. They consist of input elements, output elements and have a database structuring. Components may be considered as input-output machines that are extended by the set of all states S^C of the database with a set of corresponding input views I^V and a set of corresponding output views O^V. Input and output of components is based on channels K. The structuring is specified by S_K. The structuring of channels is described by the function $type : C \rightarrow \mathcal{V}$ for the view schemata $\mathcal{V}$. Views are used for collaboration of components with the environment via data exchange. In general, the input and output sets may be considered as abstract words from M^* or as words on the database structuring.

A **database component** $\mathcal{K} = (S_K, I_K^\mathcal{V}, O_K^\mathcal{V}, S_K^C, \Delta_K)$ is specified by

(static) **schema** S_K describing the database schema of $\mathcal{K}$,
syntactic interface providing names (structures, functions) with parameters and
    database structure for S_K^C and $I_K^\mathcal{V}, O_K^\mathcal{V}$,
behavior relating the $I^\mathcal{V}, O^\mathcal{V}$ (view) channels
$$\Delta_K : (S_K^C \times (I_K^\mathcal{V} \rightarrow M^*)) \rightarrow \mathcal{P}(S_K^C \times (O_K^\mathcal{V} \rightarrow M^*)).$$

Components can be associated to each other. The association is restricted to domain-compatible input or output schemata which are free of name conflicts.

Components $\mathcal{K}_1 = (S_1, I_1^\mathcal{V}, O_1^\mathcal{V}, S_1^C, \Delta_1)$ and $\mathcal{K}_2 = (S_2, I_2^\mathcal{V}, O_2^\mathcal{V}, S_2^C, \Delta_2)$ are free of name conflicts if the set of attribute, entity and relationship type names are disjoint.

Channels C_1 and C_2 of components $\mathcal{K}_1 = (S_1, I_1^\mathcal{V}, O_1^\mathcal{V}, S_1^C, \Delta_1)$ and $\mathcal{K}_2 = (S_2, I_2^\mathcal{V}, O_2^\mathcal{V}, S_2^C, \Delta_2)$ are called *domain-compatible* if
$dom(type(C_1)) = dom(type(C_2))$.

An output O_1^V of the component $\mathcal{K}_1$ is *domain-compatible* with an input I_2^V of the component $\mathcal{K}_2$ if $dom(type(O_1^V)) \subseteq dom(type(I_2^V))$

Component operations such as merge, fork, transmission are definable via application of superposition operations [Kud82,Mal70]: Identification of channels, permutation of channels, renaming of channels, introduction of fictitious channels, and parallel composition with feedback displayed in Figure 1.

The star schema is the main component schema used for construction. A star schema for a database type C_0 is defined by

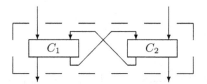

Fig. 1. The Composition of Database Components

- the (full) (HERM) schema $\mathcal{S} = (C_0, C_1, ..., C_n)$ covering all types on which C_0 has been defined,
- the subset of *strong types* $C_1, ..., C_k$ forming a set of keys $K_1, ..., K_s$ for C_0, i.e., $\cup_{i=1}^{s} K_i = \{C_1, ..., C_k\}$ and $K_i \to C_0$, $C_0 \to K_i$ for $1 \leq i \leq s$ and $card(C_0, C_i) = (1, n)$ for $(1 \leq i \leq k)$.
- the extension types $C_{k+1}, ..., C_m$ satisfying the (general) cardinality constraint $card(C_0, C_j) = (0, 1)$ for $((k + 1) \leq i \leq n)$.

The extension types may form their own $(0, 1)$ specialization tree (hierarchical inclusion dependency set). The cardinality constraints for extension types are partial functional dependencies.

There are various variants for representation of a star schemata:

- Representation based on an entity type with attributes $C_1, ..., C_k$ and $C_{k+1}, ..., C_l$ and specializations forming a specialization tree $C_{l+1}, ..., C_n$.
- Representation based on a relationship type C_0 with components $C_1, ..., C_k$, with attributes $C_{k+1}, ..., C_l$ and specializations forming a specialization tree $C_{l+1}, ..., C_n$. In this case, C_0 is a *pivot element* [BiP00] in the schema.
- Representation by be based on a hybrid form combining the two above.

The schema in Figure 2 is based on the first representation option. It shows the different facets of product characterizations.

Thus, a *star component schema* is usually characterized by a kernel entity type used for storing basic data, by a number of dimensions that are usually based on subtypes of the entity type such as **Service** and **Item**, and on subtypes which are used for additional properties such as *AdditionalCharacteristics* and *ProductSpecificCharacteristics*. These additional properties are clustered according to their occurrence for the things under consideration. Furthermore, products are classified by a set of categories. Finally, products may have their life and usage cycle, e.g., versions. Therefore, we observe that the star schema is in our case a schema with four dimensions: subtypes, additional characterization, life cycle and categorization.

Star schemata may be extended to snowflake schemata. Database theory folklore uses star structures on the basis of α-acyclic hypergraphs [Tha91,YuO92]. Snowflake structuring of objects can be caused by the internal structure of functional dependencies. If for instance, the dependency graph for functional dependencies forms a tree then we may decompose the type into a snowflake using the functional dependency $X \to Y$ for binary relationship types R on X, Y with $card(R, X) = (1, 1)$ and $card(R, Y) = (1, n)$.

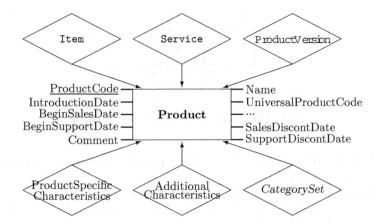

Fig. 2. Star Component Schema *Product_Intext_Data* for the *Product* Application

A snowflake schema is a

- star schema $\mathcal{S}$ on C_0 extended or changed by
  - variations $\mathcal{S}^*$ of star schema (with renaming)
  - with strong 1-n-composition by association (glue) types $A_{\mathcal{S}}^{\mathcal{S}'}$ associating the star schema with another star schema $\mathcal{S}'$ either with full composition restricted by the cardinality constraint $card(A_{\mathcal{S}}^{\mathcal{S}'}, S) = (1,1)$ or with weak, referencing composition restricted by $card(A_{\mathcal{S}}^{\mathcal{S}'}, S) = (0,1)$,
- which structure is potentially C_0-acyclic.

A schema $\mathcal{S}$ with a 'central' type C_0 is called *potentially C_0-acyclic* if all paths p, p' from the central type to any other type C_k are

- either entirely different on the database, i.e., the exclusion dependency $p[C_0, C_k] \| p'[C_0, C_k]$ is valid in the schema
- or completely identical, i.e. the pairing inclusion constraints $p[C_0, C_k] \subseteq p'[C_0, C_k]$ and $p[C_0, C_k] \supseteq p'[C_0, C_k]$ are valid.

The exclusion constraints allow to form a tree by renaming the non-identical types. In this case, the paths carry different meanings. The pairing inclusion constraints allow to cut the last association in the second path thus obtaining an equivalent schema or to introduce a mirror type C_k' for the second path. In this case, the paths carry identical meaning.

Skeleton of a Schema

Skeletons form a framework and survey the general architecture or plan of an application to which details such as the types are to be added. Plans show how potential types associated to each other in general.

The skeleton is defined by units and their associations:

Units and components: The basic element of a unit is a component. A set of components forms a unit if this set can be semantically separated from all other components without loosing application information. Units may contain entity, relationship and cluster types. The types have a certain affinity or adhesion to each other.

Units are graphically represented by rounded boxes.

Associations of units: Units may be associated to each other in a variety of ways. This variety reflects the general associations within an application. Associations group the relation of units by their meaning. Therefore different associations may exist between the same units.

Associations can also relate associations and units or associations. Therefore, we use an inductive structuring similar to the extended entity-relationship model [Tha00a].

Associations are graphically represented by double rounded boxes.

The skeleton is based on the *repulsion* of types. The measure for repulsion can be based on natural numbers with zero. A zero repulsion is used for relating weak types to their strong types. The repulsion measure $r(x, y)$ is a norm in the Mathematical sense, i.e. $r(x, y) \geq 0$, $r(x, x) = 0$, $r(x, y) \leq r(x, z) + r(z, y)$. The repulsion measure allows to build i-shells $\{ T' \mid r(T, T') \leq i \}$ around the type T.

Repulsion is a semantic measure that depends on the application area. It allows to separate types in dependence on the application. We may enhance the repulsion measure with application points of view $\mathcal{V}$, i.e., introduce a measure $r_V(T, T')$ for types T, T' and views V from $\mathcal{V}$.

These views are forming the associations of the units. Associations are used for relating units or parts of them to each other. Associations are often representing specific facets of an application such as points of view, application areas, and workflows that can be separated from each other.

Let us consider a database schema used for recording information on production processes:

the *Party* unit with components such as *Person*, *Organization*, the variety of their subtypes, address information, and data on their profiles, their relationship, etc., the *Work* unit with components *Product*, specializations of *Product* such as *Good* and *Service*, *Consumption* of elements in the production process, and the *WorkEffort* component which enables in describing the production process, the *Asset* unit consisting of only one component *Asset* with subtypes such as *Property*, *Vehicle*, *Equipment*, and *Other Asset* for all other kinds of assets, and the *Invoice* unit which combines components *Invoicing* with *InvoiceLineItem* which lists work tasks and work efforts with the cost and billing model, *Banking*, and *Tracking*.

These units have a number of associations among them:

the *WorkTask-WorkAssignment* association combines facets of work such *PartyAllocation*, *PartyWorkTaskAssignment*, *TrackOfWorkTasks*, and *ControllingOfWorkTasks*,

the *PartyAssetAssignment* association combines the units *Party* and *Asset*,
the *Billing* association is relationship among *Work* and *Invoices* and has components such as *Tracking*, *Controlling*, and *Archieving*,
the *AssetAssignment* association allows to keep track on the utilization of fixed assets in the production process and thus associates *Work* and *Asset*.

The four main units can be surveyed in a form displayed in Figure 3. We assume that billing is mainly based on the work effort. Work consumes assets and fixed assets.

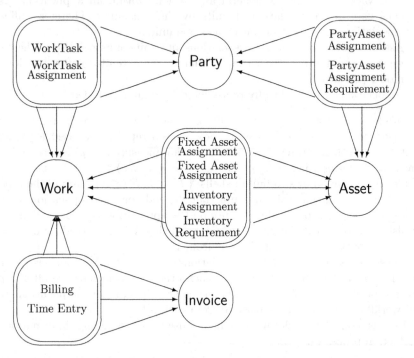

Fig. 3. Skeleton of a Schema Supporting *Production* Applications

The full schema for the *Production* application has been discussed in [Tha00b]. It generalizes schemata which have been developed in production applications and consists of more than more 150 entity and relationship types with about 650 attribute types.

Meta-characterization of Components, Units, and Associations

The skeleton information is kept by a meta-characterization information that allows to keep track on the purpose and the usage of the components, units, and associations. Meta-characterization can be specified on the basis of dockets [ScS99] that provide information:

- on the content (*abstracts* or *summaries*),
- on the delivery instruction,
- on the parameters of functions for treatment of the unit (opening with(out) zooming, breath, size, activation modus for multimedia components etc.)
- on the tight association to other units (versions, releases etc.),
- on the meta-information such as resources, restriction, copyright, roles, distribution policy etc.
- on the content providers, content reviewers and review evaluators with quality control policies,
- on applicable workflows and the current status of completion and
- on the log information that enable in tracing the object's life cycle.

Dockets can be extended to general descriptions of the utilization. The following definition frame is appropriate which classifies meta-information into mandatory, good practice, optional and useful information:

header			
content	name	developer	copyright
problem area		motivation	source
solution	intention	also known as	see too
variants	application area		
application			
applicability	consequences of application	sample applications	known applications
usability profile	experience reports	DBMS	
description			
structuring: structure, static constraints	functionality: operations, dynamic constraints, enforcement procedures	interactivity: story space, actors, media objects, representation	context: tasks, intention, history, environment, particular
implementation			
implementation	code sample	associated framework	
associated unit	collaboration	integration strategy	
`mandatory`	`good practice`	`optional`	`useful`

The frame follows the codesign approach [Tha00a] with the integrated design of structuring, functionality, interactivity and context. The frame is structured into general information provided by the header, application characterization, the content of the unit and *documentation* of the implementation.

3   Composition of Schemata Based on Components

Composition by Constructors

We distinguish three main methods for composition of components: *construction by combination* or association on the basis of constructors, *construction by folding* or combining schemata to more general schemata and *construction by categorization.* It is not surprising that these methods are based on principles of component abstraction [SmS77]. Composition is based on the skeleton of the application and uses a number of composition constructors.

Constructor-Based Composition: Star and snowflake schemata may be composed by the composition operations such as *product, nest, disjoint union, difference* and *set* operators. These operators allow to construct any schema of interest since they are complete for sets. We prefer, however, a more structural approach following [Bro00]. Therefore, all constructors known for database schemata may be applied to schema construction.

Bulk Composition: Types used in schemata in a very similar way can be clustered together on the basis of a classification. Let us exemplify this generalization approach for *Ordering processes.* The types *PlacedBy, TakenBy,* and *BilledTo* in Figure 4 are similar. They associate orders with both *PartyAddress* and *PartyContactMechanism.* They are used together and at the same objects, i.e. each order object is at the same time associated with one party address and one party contact mechanism. Thus, we can combine the three relationship types into the type *OrderAssociation.* The type *OrderAssociationClassifier* allows to derive the three relationship type. The domains *dom(ContractionDomain)* = {*PlacedBy, TakenBy, BilledTo*} and *dom(ContractionBinder)* = ∀ can be used to extract the three relationship types.

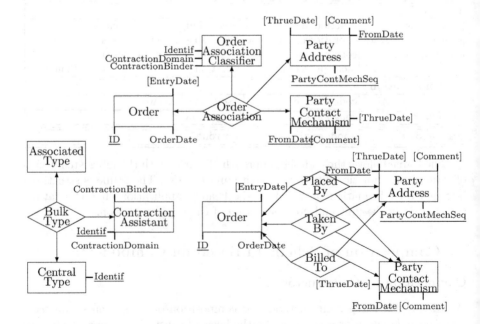

Fig. 4. The Bulk Composition Within The *Order* Application

Handling of classes which are bound by the same behavior and occurrence can be simplified by this construct. In general, the composition by folding may be described as follows:

Given a *CentralType* C and associated types which are associated by a set of relationship types $\{A_1, ..., A_n\}$ by the occurrence frame F. The occurrence frame can be $\forall$ (if the inclusion constraints $A_i[C] \subseteq A_j[C]$ are valid for all $1 \leq i, j \leq n$) or a set of inclusion constraints. Now we combine the types $\{A_1, ..., A_n\}$ into the type *BulkType* with the additional component *ContractionAssistant* and the attributes *Identif* (used for identification of objects in the type *ContractionAssisitant* if necessary), *ContractionDomain* with *dom(ContractionDomain)* = $\{A_1, ..., A_n\}$ and *dom(ContractionBinder)* = F.

Architecture Composition: Categorization-based composition have been widely used for complex structuring. The architecture of SAP R/3 often has been displayed in the form of a waffle. For this reason, we prefer to call this composition *waffle composition* or architecture composition. Architecture composition enables in associating through categorization and compartmentalization. This constructor is especially useful during modeling of distributed systems with local components and with local behavior. There are specific solutions for interface management, replication, encapsulation and inheritance. The cell construction is the main constructor in component applications and in data warehouse applications. Therefore, composition by categorization is the main composition approach used for in component-based development and in data warehouse approaches.

Lifespan Composition

Evolution of things in application is an orthogonal dimension which must represented in the schema from one side but which should not be mixed with constructors of the other side. We observe a number of lifespan compositions: **Evolution composition** records the *stages* of the life of things and or their corresponding objects and are closely related to *workflows*, **circulation composition** displays the phases in the lifespan of things, **incremental composition** allows to record the development and specifically the enhancement of objects, their aging and their own lifespan, **loop composition** supports nicely chaining and scaling to different perspectives of objects which seems to rotate in the workflow, and **network composition** allows the flexible treatment of objects during their evolution, support to pass objects in a variety of evolution paths and enable in multi-object collaboration.

Evolution Composition: Evolution composition allows to construct a well-communicating set of types with a point-to-point data exchange among the associated types. Such evolution associations often appear in workflow applications, data flow applications, in business processes, customer scenarios and during identification of variances.The *flow* constructor allows to construct a well-communicating set of types with a point-to-point data exchange among the associated types. Such flow associations often appear in workflow applications, data flow applications, in business processes, customer scenarios and during identification of variances.

Evolution is based on the specific treatment of **stages** of objects. Things are passed to teams which work on their further development. This workflow is well-specified. During evolution, things obtain a number of specific properties. The record of the evolution is based on evolution composition of object classes. Therefore, we define a specific composition in order to support the modeling, management and storage of evolution.

Circulation Composition: Things may be related to each other by life cycle stages such as repetition, evolution, self-reinforcement and self-correction. Typical examples are objects representing iterative processes, recurring phenomena or time-dependent activities.

Circulation composition allows to display objects in different phases. For instance, paper handling in a conference paper submission system is based on such phases: *PaperAbstract, SubmittedPaper, PaperInReviewing, AcceptedPaper, RejectedPaper, FinalVersionPaper, ScheduledPaperPresentation,* and *ArchievedPaperVersion.* The circulation model is supported by specific phase-based dynamic semantics [Tha00a]. Circulation forms thus an iterative process.

Incremental Composition: Incremental composition enables in production of new associations based on a core object. It is based on containment, sharing of common properties or resources and alternatives. Typical examples are found in applications in which processes generate multiple outcomes, collect a range of inputs, create multiple designs or manage inputs and outputs.

Incremental development enables in building layers of a system, environment, or application thus enabling in management of systems complexity. Incremental constructions may be based on intervals, may appear with a frequency and modulation. They are mainly oriented towards transport of data. Typical applications of the incremental constructor lead to the n-tier architecture and to versioning of objects. Furthermore, cooperation and synergy is supported. Typical incremental constructions appear in areas such as facility management. For instance, *incremental database schemata* are used at various stages of the architectural, building and maintenance phases in construction engineering.

A specialized incremental constructor is the *layer constructor* that is widely used in frameworks, e.g., the OSI framework for communicating processes. Incremental lifespan modeling is very common and met in almost all large applications. For instance, the schema[1] displayed in Figure 5 uses a specific composition frame. The type *Request* is based on the the type *Quote.* Requests may be taken

---

[1] We use the extended ER model that allows to display subtypes on the basis of unary relationship types and thus simplifies representation.

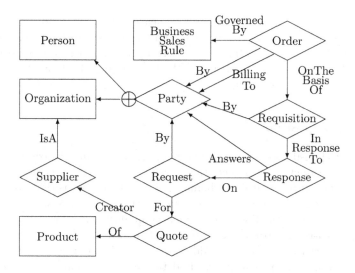

Fig. 5. Incremental Composition in the *Order* Schema

on their own. They are, however, coupled to quotes in order to be sent to suppliers. Thus, we have a specific variant of quote objects. The same observation can be made for types such as *Order*, *Requisition*, and *Response*.

Loop Composition: Loop composition is applied whenever the lifespan of objects is cyclic or looping. They are applied for representation of objects that store chaining of events, people, devices or products. The loop composition is a companion of the circulation composition since it composes non-directional, non-hierarchical associations. Different modes of connectivity may be applied. Loops may be centralized and decentralized.

Loop composition models chaining and change of perspectives of events, people, devices, and other things. Loops are usually non-directional and cyclic. Temporal assignment and sharing of resources and its record, temporal association and integration, temporal rights, roles and responsibilities can be neatly represented and scaled by loop composition as long as the association is describable.

Network Composition: Network or web composition enables in collecting a network of associated types to a multipoint web of associated types with specific control and data association strategies. The web has a specific data update mechanism, a specific data routing mechanism and a number of communities of users building their views on the web.

Networks are quickly evolving. The have usually an irregular growth, are built in an opportunistic manner, are rebuilt and renewed and must carry a large number of variations. Network composition enables in growth control and change management. Usually, they are supported by a multi-point center of connections, by controlled routing and replication, by change protocols, by controlled assignment and transfer, scoping and localization abstraction, and trader architecture. Further export/import converters and wrappers are supported. The database farm architecture [Tha01] with check-in and check-out facilities supports flexible network extension.

Context Composition

According to [Wis01] we distinguish between the *intext* and the *context* of things which are represented by object. Intext reflects the internal structuring, associations among types and sub-schemata, the storage structuring and the representation options. Context reflects general characterizations, categorization, utilization, and general descriptions such as quality. Therefore, we distinguish between **meta-characterization composition** which is usually orthogonal to the intext structuring and can be added to each of the intext types, **utilization-recording composition** which is used to trace the running of the database engine and to restore an older state or to reason on previous steps, and **quality composition** which allow to reason on the quality of the data provided and to apply summarization and aggregation functions in a form that is consistent with the quality of the data. The dimensionality [FeT02] inside schemata allows to extract other context compositions. We concentrate, however, on the main compositions. All these compositions are orthogonal to the other compositions, i.e., they can be associated to any of the compositions.

Meta-Characterization Composition: The meta-characterization is an orthogonal dimension applicable to a large number of types in the schema. Such characterizations in the schema in Figure 2 include language characteristics and utilization frames for presentation, printing and communication. Other orthogonal meta-characterizations are insertion/update/deletion time, keyword characterization, utilization pattern, format descriptions, utilization restrictions and rights such as copyright and costs, and technical restrictions. Meta-characterizations apply to a large number of types and should be factored out. For instance, in e-learning environments e-learning object, elements and scenes are commonly characterized by educational information such as interactivity type, learning resource type, interactivity level, age restrictions, semantic density, intended end user role, context, difficulty, utilization interval restrictions, and pedagogical and didactical parameters.

Utilization-Recording Composition: Log, usage and history composition is commonly used for recording the lifespan of the database. We distinguish between history composition used for storing and record the log computation history in a small time slice, usage scene composition used to associate data to their use in business processes at a certain stage, workflow step, or scenes in an application story, and structures used to record the actual usage .

Data in the database may depend directly on one or more aspects of time. We distinguish three orthogonal concepts of time: temporal data types such as instants, intervals or periods, kinds of time, and temporal statements such as current (now), sequenced (at each instant of time) and nonsequenced (ignoring time). Kinds of time are: transaction time, user-defined time, validity time, and availability time.

Quality Composition: Data quality is modeled by a variety of compositions. Data quality is essential whenever we need to distinguish versions of data based on their quality and reliability: source dimension(data source, user responsible for the data, business process, source restrictions), intrinsic data quality parameters (accuracy, objectivity, believability, reputation), accessibility data quality (accessibility, access security, contextual data quality (relevancy, value-added, timelineness, completeness, amount of information), and representational data quality (interpretability, ease of understanding, concise representation, consistent representation, ease of manipulation).

4 Conclusion

Huge databases are usually developed over years, have schemata that carry hundreds of types and which require high abilities in reading such diagrams or schemata. We observe, however, that a large number of similarities, repetitions, and - last but not least - of similar structuring in such schemata. This paper is aiming in extraction of the main meta-similarities in schemata. These similarities are based on on **components** which are either kernel components such as star and snowflake structures, or are build by application of compositions such as association, architecture, bulk or constructor composition, or lifespan composition such as evolution, circulation, incremental, loop, and network compositions, or are context compositions such as meta-characterization, utilization or deployment and quality compositions.

Therefore, we can use these meta-structuring of schemata for *modularization* of schemata. Modularization eases querying, searching, reconfiguration, maintenance, integration and extension. Further, re-engineering and reuse become feasible.

Modeling based on meta-structures enables in systematic schema development, systematic extension, systematic implementation and thus allows to keep consistency in a much simpler and more comprehensible form. We claim that such structures already can be observed in small schemata. They are however very common in large schemata due to the reuse of design ideas, due to the design skills and to the inherent similarity in applications.

Meta-structuring enable also in component-based development. Schemata can be developed step-by-step on the basis of the skeleton of the meta-structuring. The skeleton consists of units and associations of units. Such associations combine relationship types among the types of different units. Units form components within the schema.

Component-based development enables in **industrial development** of database applications instead of handicraft developments. Handicraft developments cause later infeasible integration problems and lead to unbendable, intractable and incomprehensible database schemata of overwhelming complexity which cannot be consistently maintained. We observe, however, the the computer game industry is producing games in a manufactured, component-based fashion. This paper shows that database systems can be produced in a similar form.

References

[BiP00]   J. Biskup and T. Polle, Decomposition of database classes under path functional dependencies and onto contraints. Proc. FoIKS'2000, LNCS 1762, Springer, 2000, 31-49.

[Bro97]   M. Broy, Compositional refinement of interactive systems. Journal of the ACM, 44, 6, 1997, 850-891.

[Bro00]   L. Brown, Integration models - Templates for business transformation. SAMS Publishing, New York, 2000.

[FeT02]   T. Feyer and B. Thalheim, Many-dimensional schema modeling. Proc. ADBIS'02, Bratislava, LNCS 2435, Springer, 2002, 305-318.

[Kud82]   V.B. Kudrjavcev, Functional systems. Moscov Lomonossov University Press, Moscov, 1982 (in Russian).

[Mal70]   A.I. Malzew, Algebraic systems. Nauka, Moscow, 1970 (in Russian).

[Moo01]   D.L. Moody, Dealing with complexity: A practical method for representing large entity-relationship models. PhD., Dept. of Information Systems, University of Melbourne, 2001.

[ScS99]   J.W. Schmidt and H.-W. Schring, Dockets: a model for adding value to content. Proc. ER'99, LNCS 1728, Springer, Berlin, 1999, 248-262.

[SmS77]   J.M. Smith and D.C.W. Smith, Data base abstractions: Aggregation and generalization. ACM TODS 2, 2, 1977.

[Tha91]   B. Thalheim. Dependencies in Relational Databases. Leipzig, Teubner Verlag 1991.

[Tha00a]   B. Thalheim, Entity-relationship modeling – Foundations of database technology. Springer, Berlin, 2000.

[Tha00b]   B. Thalheim, The person, organization, product, production, ordering, delivery, invoice, accounting, budgeting and human resources pattern in database design. Preprint I-07-2000, Computer Science Institute, Brandenburg University of Technology at Cottbus, 2000.

[Tha01]   B. Thalheim, Abstraction layers in database structuring: The star, snowflake and hierarchical structuring. Preprint I-13-2001, Computer Science Institute, Brandenburg University of Technology at Cottbus, 2001.

[Tha02]   B. Thalheim, Component construction of database schemes. Proc. ER'02, Tampere, LNCS 2503, Springer, 2002, 20-34.

[Wis01]   P. Wisse, Metapattern - Context and time in information models. Addison-Wesley, Boston, 2001.

[YuO92]   L.-Y. Yuan and Z. M. Ozsoyoglu, Design of desirable relational database schemes. JCSS, 45, 3, 1992, 435-470.

Cognitive Load Effects on End User Understanding of Conceptual Models: An Experimental Analysis

Daniel L. Moody[1,2]

[1] Gerstner Laboratory, Department of Cybernetics, Czech Technical University
Prague, Czech Republic
dmoody@labe.felk.cvut.cz
[2] School of Business Systems,
Monash University
Melbourne, Australia 3800
dmoody@infotech.monash.edu.au

Abstract. According to Cognitive Load Theory (CLT), presenting information in a way that cognitive load falls within the limitations of working memory can improve speed and accuracy of understanding, and facilitate deep understanding of information content. This paper describes a laboratory experiment which investigates the effects of reducing cognitive load on end user understanding of conceptual models. Participants were all naïve users, and were given a data model consisting of almost a hundred entities, which corresponds to the average-sized data model encountered in practice. One group was given the model in standard Entity Relationship (ER) form and the other was given the same model organised into cognitively manageable "chunks". The reduced cognitive load representation was found to improve comprehension and verification accuracy by more than 50%, though conflicting results were found for time taken. The practical significance of this research is that it shows that managing cognitive load can improve end user understanding of conceptual models, which will help reduce requirements errors. The theoretical significance is that it provides a theoretical insight into the effects of complexity on understanding of conceptual models, which have previously been unexplored. The research findings have important design implications for all conceptual modelling notations.

1 Introduction

1.1 Cognitive "Bandwidth" and Cognitive Overload

One of the most pervasive characteristics of life in technologically advanced societies is the growing prevalence of sensory and information overload [31]. The human organism can be viewed as an information processing system [39]. Due to limits on *working memory*, this system has a strictly limited processing capacity, which is estimated to be "the magical number seven, plus or minus two" concepts at a time [3, 34]. This has been described as the "inelastic limit of human capacity" [56], "human channel capacity" [34] or "cognitive bandwidth" [35], and represents one of the enduring laws of human cognition [3]. Working memory is used for active processing and transient storage of information, and plays an important role in comprehen-

A. Benczúr, J. Demetrovics, G. Gottlob (Eds.): ADBIS 2004, LNCS 3255, pp. 129–143, 2004.
© Springer-Verlag Berlin Heidelberg 2004

sion [2]. When the stimulus input exceeds working memory capacity, a state of *information* or *cognitive overload* ensues and comprehension degrades rapidly [14, 23].

1.2 End User Understanding of Conceptual Models

The understandability of conceptual models is of critical importance in IS development. Conceptual models must be readily comprehensible so that they can be understood by all stakeholders, particular end users [40]. If end users cannot effectively understand the conceptual model, they will be unable to verify whether it meets their requirements [30]. If the model does not accurately reflect their requirements, the system that is delivered will not satisfy users, no matter how well designed or implemented it is [36]. The large number of systems that are delivered which do not meet user requirements suggests that end users have significant difficulties understanding and verifying conceptual models [e.g. 7, 15, 47, 48, 58]. Empirical studies show that more than half the errors which occur during systems development are the result of inaccurate or incomplete requirements [29, 33]. Requirements errors are also the most common reason for failure of systems development projects [47, 48]. This suggests that improving understanding of conceptual models should be a priority area for research.

1.3 The Entity Relationship (ER) Model

The Entity Relationship (ER) Model [9] is the international standard technique for data modelling, and has been used to design database schemas for over two decades [55]. Despite the emergence of object oriented (OO) analysis techniques and in particular UML, it remains the most popular method for defining information requirements in practice [43, 46, 53]. A recent survey of practice showed that it was not only the most commonly used data modelling technique, but also the most commonly used IS analysis technique generally [12]. One of the widely quoted advantages of the ER Model is its ability to communicate with end users [e.g. 6, 10, 17, 33]. However field studies show that in practice, ER models are poorly understood by users, and in most cases are not developed with direct user involvement [21, 22]. Experimental studies also show that comprehension of data models is very poor and that a large percentage of data model components are not understood [40]. While ER modelling has proven very effective as a method for database design (as evidenced by its high level of adoption in practice), it has been far less effective for communication with users [19, 44].

1.4 Complexity Effects on Understanding of ER Models

One of the most serious practical limitations of the ER model is its inability to cope with complexity [1, 16, 45, 54, 59, 60]. Neither the standard ER Model or the Extended Entity Relationship (EER) model provide suitable abstraction mechanisms for managing complexity [60]. In the absence of such mechanisms, ER models are typically represented as single interconnected diagrams, often consisting of more than a hundred entities. Surveys of practice show that application data models consist of an average of 95 entities, while enterprise data models consist of an average of 536 entities [32]. Such models exceed human cognitive capacity by a factor of ten or more, which provides a possible explanation for why ER models are so poorly understood in practice.

1.5 Cognitive Load Theory

Cognitive Load Theory (CLT) is an internationally known and widely accepted theory, which has been empirically validated in numerous studies [5]. It is based on theories of human cognitive architecture, and provides guidelines for presenting information in a way that optimises human understanding by reducing load on working memory [27]. CLT simultaneously considers the structure of information and the cognitive architecture that people use to process the information [42]. *Cognitive load* is the amount of mental activity imposed on working memory at a point in time, and is primarily determined by the number of elements that need to be attended to [49, 50]. When cognitive load exceeds the limits of working memory, understanding is reduced. Cognitive load consists of two aspects:

- *Intrinsic cognitive load (ICL)*, which is due to the inherent difficulty of the information content. This derives from the complexity of the underlying domain and cannot be reduced.
- *Extraneous cognitive load (ECL)*, which is due to the way the information is presented. By changing how the information is presented, the level of cognitive load may be reduced, which can be used to improve understanding of subject matter.

Manipulating extraneous cognitive load so that it falls within the limitations of working memory has been found to improve both speed and accuracy of understanding [8, 37], and to facilitate deep understanding of information content [41]. However the effectiveness of this depends on the expertise of the audience. People with higher levels of expertise can handle larger amounts of information because they have more highly developed knowledge *schemas*, and require fewer elements of working memory to understand the same amount of information [49, 50]. Reducing cognitive load is likely to have little or no effect on their understanding, and may even have a negative effect: this is called the *expertise reversal effect* [24]. Novices need to attend to all elements individually, so will be significantly affected by how information is presented.

The implications of this for representing large ER models are:

- The root cause of problems in understanding large ER models is not their size *per se* (ICL), which is a function of the underlying domain and cannot be reduced, but how they are presented (ECL).
- Understanding can be improved by manipulating extraneous cognitive load so that it falls within the limitations of working memory.
- End users will be more affected by cognitive overload than analysts: this may help to explain why ER modelling has been highly effective for database design but less effective for communication with users.

1.6 Levelled Data Models

To address problems in understanding large and complex ER models, a method was developed for representing ER models in a way that reduces cognitive load to within the limitations of working memory. This is done by dividing the model into a set of cognitively manageable subsystems, called *subject areas*. Each subject area represents a subset of the ER model that is small enough to be understood by the human mind. The resulting representation is called a Levelled Data Model (LDM), and consists of three primary components (Fig. 1):

- *Context Data Model:* This provides an overview of the model and how it is divided into subject areas. This is shown in pictorial form, with each subject area represented by a graphical image.
- *Subject Area Data Models:* These show a subset of the model in detail. These are represented as standard ER models, with *foreign entities* used to show relationships to entities on other subject areas. Subject areas are limited to "seven, plus or minus two" entities, to ensure that working memory is not overloaded.
- *Entity Index:* this lists all entities alphabetically with their subject area reference, and is used to help locate specific entities within the model.

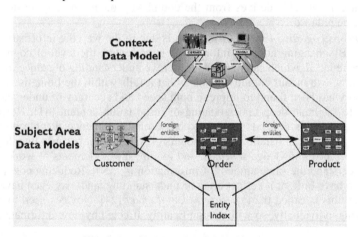

Fig. 1. Levelled Data Model Architecture

The model may be organised into any number of levels, depending on the size of the underlying data model. This results in a hierarchy of diagrams at different levels of abstraction. The "seven, plus or minus two" principle is applied at each level to ensure that *marginal cognitive load* (the cognitive load imposed by each diagram) is within the limitations of working memory.

Subject Areas as a "Chunking" Mechanism

A wide range of experimental studies have shown that humans organise items into logical groups or "chunks" in order to expand working memory capacity [e.g. 3, 11, 34, 38, 39]. The process of recursively developing information saturated chunks is the primary mechanism used by the human mind to deal with complexity in everyday life [18]. The ER model already provides one level of chunking, by allowing attributes to be grouped into entities. However this is inadequate in situations of real world complexity. A higher level chunking mechanism is needed once the number of entities exceeds human cognitive capacity (which is almost always the case in practice [32]). The LDM method provides a way of *recursively* grouping entities into higher level chunks (subject areas), which provides a general-purpose complexity management mechanism which is capable of handling any level of complexity. The size of these chunks are matched to the processing capacity of the human mind, which ensures that working memory is not overloaded.

According to cognitive load theory, the *grain size* of information should be matched to the processing ability of the intended audience [52, 57]. ER models are intended for communicating with non-experts (end users), which means that the grain size (which in this case corresponds to the number of elements per diagram) should not exceed seven, plus or minus two. Expert modellers (analysts) will be able handle much more complex diagrams because they can use their internal knowledge schemas to group elements together, but end users will need to attend to all elements individually.

Cognitive Integration: Understanding Multiple Diagrams

Diagrams facilitate problem solving by showing all relevant information in a single place [20, 28]. Dividing an ER model into subject areas reduces the number of entities which must be understood simultaneously, thus reducing cognitive load. However because information is distributed across multiple diagrams, it reduces understanding of the problem as a whole [61]. Kim et al [25] argue that for information from multiple diagrams to be integrated in the problem solver's mind, the notation must explicitly support *perceptual integration* and *conceptual integration* processes. The LDM representation supports these processes in the following ways:

- Perceptual integration: *Foreign entities* provide visual cues to show how elements on an SADM are related to elements on all other SADMs. This supports perceptual integration by aiding navigation between related diagrams.
- Conceptual integration: The *Context Data Model* provides an overview of the system in a single diagram, and thus represents what Wood and Watts [62] call a "longshot" diagram. This allows the user to integrate information from multiple diagrams into a coherent representation of the system.

1.7 Research Question Addressed

This paper describes a laboratory experiment which evaluates the effectiveness of reducing cognitive load on end user understanding of large ER models. The broad research question addressed is:

- Are data models represented using the LDM method more easily understood by end users than models represented in standard ER form?

Based on cognitive load theory, we predict that the LDM representation will improve both speed and accuracy of understanding.

2 Research Design

2.1 Experimental Design

A two group, post-test only design was used, with one active between-groups factor (Representation Method). The experimental groups consisted of a control group (using the standard ER representation) and a treatment group (using the LDM representation). Participants were trained in the conventions of one of the methods (experimental treatment), and were then given an experimental data model represented using this method. They were then given a set of questions to answer about the model (*comprehension task*) and a description of user requirements against which they were asked to verify the model (*verification task*).

2.2 Participants

There were 29 participants in the experiment, all of whom were first year Accounting students. Subjects had no prior experience in the use of data modelling techniques (which was a condition of selection for the experiment), so were considered as proxies for naïve users. All participated voluntarily in the experiment and were paid $25 on completion. Subjects were randomly assigned to experimental groups.

2.3 Materials

Experimental Data Models

The experimental data model used in this experiment was a data model taken from practice, defining the requirements for a customer management and billing system in a utility company. It consisted of 98 entities (109 including subtypes) and 480 attributes, so was very close to the average size for an application data model. As well as the diagrams, a Data Dictionary was supplied with entity and attribute definitions. Two different representations of the data model were prepared for use in the experiment, one in standard ER form and one using the LDM method. The two sets of experimental materials contained exactly the same requirements information but were presented differently. In other words, they were *informationally equivalent*, but not necessarily *computationally equivalent* [28].

Comprehension Task

A set of 25 True/False questions was used to test comprehension performance. Participants were required to answer these questions in the comprehension task.

Verification Task

A one page textual description of requirements was used to test verification performance. Participants were required to identify discrepancies between the stated requirements and the data model in the verification task. There were 15 discrepancies between the data model and the set of requirements.

2.4 Independent Variable

The independent variable is the method used to represent the experimental data model (Representation Method). This has two levels, corresponding to the different representation methods being evaluated:

- Standard ER representation (control): this represents the model as a single diagram.
- LDM representation (treatment): this is the cognitive-load reduced representation, where each diagram is of cognitively manageable size.

The independent variable was operationalised through the experimental treatment (training) and the experimental data models.

2.5 Dependent Variables

User validation of data models consists of two separate cognitive processes: comprehension and verification [26]. Users must first *comprehend* the meaning of the model, then they must *verify* the model by identifying any discrepancies between the model and their (tacit) knowledge of their requirements. Comprehension performance reflects *syntactic or surface-level understanding*: the person's competence in understanding the constructs of the modelling formalism, while verification performance reflects *semantic or deep understanding*: the person's ability to apply that understanding.

In defining measures of understanding, we therefore distinguish between two *types* of performance:

- Comprehension performance: the ability to answer questions about a data model
- Verification performance: the ability to identify discrepancies between a data model and a set of user requirements.

We also distinguish between two *dimensions* of performance:

- Efficiency: the cognitive effort required to understand a model (this requires measuring task *inputs*).
- Effectiveness: how well the data model is understood (this requires measuring task *outputs*)

In this experiment, four dependent variables were defined, which cover all aspects of understanding performance (Table 1).

- D1: Comprehension Time. This was measured by the time taken to perform the comprehension task.
- D2: Comprehension Accuracy. This was measured by the percentage of comprehension questions correctly answered.
- D3: Verification Time. This was measured by the time taken to complete the verification task.
- D4: Verification Accuracy. This was measured by the number of discrepancies correctly identified expressed as a percentage of the total number of discrepancies.

Table 1. Classification of Dependent Variables

	Efficiency	Effectiveness
Comprehension Performance	D1: Comprehension Time	D2: Comprehension Accuracy
Verification Performance	D3: Verification Time	D4: Verification Accuracy

2.6 Hypotheses

The research question defined in Section 1 is broken down into several *hypotheses*, each of which relates to a single dependent variable. This results in six hypotheses.

- H1: Participants using the LDM will perform the comprehension task faster than those using the standard ER Model (Comprehension Time)
- H2: Participants using the LDM will perform the comprehension task more accurately than those using the standard ER Model (Comprehension Accuracy)
- H3: Participants using the LDM will perform the verification task faster than those using the standard ER Model (Verification Time)
- H4: Participants using the LDM will perform the verification task more accurately than those using the standard ER Model (Verification Accuracy)

The rationale for these hypotheses is that the standard ER Model lacks adequate mechanisms for dealing with complexity. This will result in cognitive overload for participants in performing the experimental tasks, as the experimental data model exceeds working memory capacity by a factor of more than ten. This will reduce their comprehension (surface-level understanding) performance and also their verification (deep understanding) performance [4, 31]. The LDM representation, because it organises the data model into cognitively manageable chunks, reduces cognitive load to within the limitations of working memory. This will improve both speed and accuracy of performance compared to the standard ER model [50, 51].

3   Results

An independent samples t-test was used to test for differences between groups.

3.1   Comprehension Time

Table 2 summarises the results for Comprehension Time. The difference between groups was found to be statistically significant, but in the reverse direction to that predicted. Subjects using the standard ER model took significantly less time to complete the task than subjects using the LDM ($\alpha < .05$). This means that H1 was *not* supported.

Table 2. Comprehension Time Statistics

EXPERIMENTAL GROUP	MEAN (μ)	STDEV (δ)
Standard ER Model	26.67	7.99
Levelled Data Model	34.00	6.02

3.2 Comprehension Accuracy

Table 3 shows the results for Comprehension Accuracy. Participants using the LDM scored 17% better than those using the standard ER model (this represents the *unstandardised effect size*). The difference between groups was statistically significant ($\alpha <$ .01), which strongly confirmed H2.

Table 3. Comprehension Accuracy Statistics

EXPERIMENTAL GROUP	MEAN (μ)	STDEV (δ)
Standard ER Model	69.60%	9.66%
Levelled Data Model	81.43%	10.48%

Comprehension Time Versus Accuracy

In comparing the results for comprehension time and accuracy, it appears that subjects made clear trade-offs between time and accuracy. Subjects using the standard ER model performed the comprehension task significantly faster but also less accurately. The explanation for this may be that they generated an initial hypothesis, but were unable to effectively use the information in the model to refine their hypothesis due to the effects of cognitive overload [25]. This would have led to a faster decision, but also a less accurate one, as it was primarily based on their initial judgement rather than a thorough analysis of problem information. In other words, their inability to find relevant (confirming or disconfirming) information increased their speed of response but decreased accuracy by a similar margin. Subjects using the LDM representation may have spent more time testing and refining hypotheses, which took longer but led to a more accurate result.

3.3 Verification Time

Table 4 summarises the results for verification time. The mean time taken by each group was almost identical, and the difference between groups was not significant (α < .05). This means that H3 was *not* supported.

Table 4. Verification Time Statistics

EXPERIMENTAL GROUP	MEAN (μ)	STDEV (δ)
Standard ER Model	31.87	7.58
Levelled Data Model	31.71	7.47

3.4   Verification Accuracy

Table 5 shows the results for verification accuracy. Participants using the LDM scored 59% better than those using the standard ER model. The difference between groups was statistically significant ($\alpha < .01$), which means that H4 was strongly supported.

Table 5. Verification Accuracy Statistics

EXPERIMENTAL GROUP	MEAN (μ)	STDEV (δ)
Standard ER Model	37.87%	21.37%
Levelled Data Model	60.06%	21.78%

A point worth noting is the low score for the control group on this task: participants using the standard ER model scored less than 40% on this task. In practice, ER models are often distributed to end users for the purpose of identifying discrepancies between the model and their (tacit) requirements. The inability of users to perform the verification task effectively may explain the high level of requirements errors reported in practice [29, 33].

Verification Time Versus Accuracy

In the comprehension task, speed and accuracy were inversely related, while on this task, both groups took almost exactly the same time. This suggests that the apparent tradeoffs between time and accuracy on the comprehension task were due to other reasons. Most subjects were able to finish the experiment well within the allotted time, so there was little need for subjects to make time-accuracy trade-offs. An alternative explanation is that in the face of overwhelming complexity, subjects in the control group resorted to guessing some of their answers in the comprehension task. Because the comprehension questions were all in True/False format, participants had a 50% chance of getting the answer right by guessing. This may be a particular problem with using students as participants, as they are likely to understand this "law of probabilities" very well! In the verification task, guessing was taken out of the equation, which would explain why both groups took a similar amount of time to perform the task.

If this interpretation is correct, the comprehension results overstate the performance of both groups, because participants would have scored 50% based on chance alone. When the scores are adjusted for chance (Table 6), the results obtained are almost identical to those for Verification Accuracy which provides support for this interpretation of the data . Using this measure, participants using the LDM representation scored 63% better than those using the standard ER model, which is similar to the difference found on the comprehension task.

Table 6. Comprehension Accuracy Adjusted for Chance

EXPERIMENTAL GROUP	MEAN (μ)
Standard ER Model	39.20%
Levelled Data Model	62.86%

This suggests a systematic flaw in previous experimental studies which have evaluated comprehension of data models, almost all of which have used True/False questions. Data models naturally lend themselves to questions in a True/False format e.g. Can a project have many employees? Can an employee manage many projects? However True/False questions introduce a significant amount of measurement error, as subjects can score 50% simply by guessing. A better approach in future may be to use multiple choice questions, with an "Unable to Tell" option.

4 Conclusion

4.1 Summary of Findings

Of the four hypotheses originally proposed, two were supported (H2, H4), one was not supported (H3), with a reverse finding in one case (H1). The conclusions are that:
- H1 (contra): Subjects using the LDM representation took longer to comprehend the model.
- H2: Subjects using the LDM representation were able to more accurately comprehend the model.
- H4: Subjects using the LDM representation were able to more accurately verify the model.

Speed of Understanding

Neither of the hypotheses relating to speed of understanding (H1, H4) was supported, and the reverse result was found for H1. The conclusion from this is that reducing cognitive load has no effect on speed of understanding of data models, as the reverse result obtained for H1 was attributed to guessing. This is inconsistent with the predictions of cognitive load theory, but may be explained by the graphical nature of the subject matter. According to Kim et al [25], distributing information across multiple diagrams results in additional cognitive overheads to search for relevant information and integrate it together. Thus any increase in speed of understanding as a result of the reduction in cognitive load may have been offset by the time taken to navigate between different diagrams.

Accuracy of Understanding

The significant improvement in both comprehension and verification accuracy using the LDM representation provides strong evidence that reducing cognitive load improves both surface (syntactic) understanding and deep (semantic) understanding of data models. By dividing a large ER model into chunks of cognitively manageable size, the LDM representation reduces extraneous cognitive load to within the limitations of working memory, thereby improving understanding. This is consistent with the predictions of cognitive load theory. Since the experimental material for the two groups was *informationally equivalent*, the way the models were presented must have been responsible for the difference in performance between the experimental groups. This suggests that decisions regarding the presentation of conceptual models are far from trivial and should be approached with as much care as decisions on their content [20, 25, 40].

4.2 Practical Significance

This research has important implications for conceptual modelling practice. The experimental results show that reducing cognitive load improves end user comprehension and verification of ER models by more than 50%. Improving end user understanding and verification will help to increase the accuracy of conceptual models in practice, and thereby reduce incidence of requirements errors and increase the likelihood that systems will meet user requirements. As the ER model is the most commonly used requirements analysis technique [12], this research has the potential to significantly improve requirements analysis effectiveness.

4.3 Theoretical Significance

This is the first experimental analysis of the effects of cognitive overload on understanding of conceptual models. The largest model used in any previous experimental study of data model understanding is 15 entities, which means the effects of complexity on end user understanding have been previously unexplored. The results provide strong evidence for the existence of cognitive overload effects on end user understanding of ER models, which provides a possible explanation for why they are so poorly understood in practice. CLT is used to provide a theoretical explanation for why end users have difficulties understanding large ER models and also why analysts do not have similar difficulties. The experiment also provides evidence that reducing extraneous cognitive load can improve end user understanding of conceptual models.

4.4 Wider Significance

Conceptual models are used for understanding a system and communicating this understanding to others. For this reason, it is essential that conceptual modelling notations take into account the characteristics of human information processing as well as the characteristics of the problem situation [7, 20, 25]. One of the most important constraints on human information processing is the capacity of working memory: in an IS context, the sheer volume of requirements information can quickly overwhelm working memory capacity [7, 13]. This is an issue which has been previously unexplored in conceptual modelling research. The findings of this experiment thus have general implications for developing more effective conceptual modelling techniques. In order to improve understanding, conceptual modelling notations should be designed to reduce cognitive load to within the limitations of working memory. This is particularly important when diagrams are used to communicate with non-technical people (as is almost always the case in conceptual modelling), as they are likely to be more affected by cognitive overload [49, 51].

References

[1]   AKOKA, J. and I. COMYN-WATTIAU (1996): Entity Relationship And Object Oriented Model Automatic Clustering, *Data And Knowledge Engineering*, **20** (1): p. 87-117.

[2]   BADDELEY, A. and G. HITCH (1974): Working Memory, In *The Psychology of Learning and Motivation: Volume 8*, G.H. Bower (Ed.), Academic Press: London.

[3]   BADDELEY, A.D. (1994): The Magical Number Seven: Still Magic After All These Years?, *Psychological Review*, **101** (2): p. 353-356.

[4]   BADDELEY, A.D. (1999): *Essentials of Human Memory*, Cognitive psychology,, Hove, England: Psychology Press, xi, 356.

[5]   BANNERT, M. (2002): Managing Cognitive Load: Recent Trends in Cognitive Load Theory, *Learning and Instruction*, **12** (1): p. 139-146.

[6]   BATINI, C., S. CERI, and S.B. NAVATHE (1992): *Conceptual Database Design: An Entity Relationship Approach*, Redwood City, California: Benjamin Cummings.

[7]   BROWNE, G.J. and V. RAMESH (2002): Improving Information Requirements Determination: A Cognitive Perspective, *Information & Management*, **39**: p. 625-645.

[8]   CHANDLER, P. and J. SWELLER (1996): Cognitive Load While Learning to Use a Computer Program, *Applied Cognitive Psychology*, **10**.

[9]   CHEN, P.P. (1976): The Entity Relationship Model: Towards An Integrated View Of Data, *ACM Transactions On Database Systems*, **1** (1), March: p. 9-36.

[10]   CHEN, P.P. (2002): Entity-Relationship Modeling: Historical Events, Future Trends, and Lessons Learned, In *Software Pioneers: Contributions to Software Engineering*, M. Broy and E. Denert (Eds.), Springer-Verlag: Berlin, p. 100-114.

[11]   COFER, C.N. (1965): On Some Factors in the Organisational Characteristics of Free Recall, *American Psychologist*, April: p. 261-272.

[12]   DAVIES, I., P. GREEN, and M. ROSEMANN (2003): Modelling in Australian Practice - Preliminary Insights, *Information Age*, February: p. 34-42.

[13]   DAVIS, G.B. (1982): Strategies for Information Requirements Determination, *IBM Systems Journal*, **21** (1).

[14]   DRIVER, M. and T. MOCK (1975): Human Information Processing Decision Style Theory and Accounting Information Systems, *Accounting Review*, **50**.

[15]   EWUSI-MENSAH, K. (1997): Critical Issues in Abandoned Information Systems Projects, *Communications of the ACM*, **40**: p. 74-80.

[16]   FELDMAN, P. and D. MILLER (1986): Entity Model Clustering: Structuring A Data Model By Abstraction, *The Computer Journal*, **29** (4): p. 348-360.

[17]   FINKLESTEIN, C. (1989): *An Introduction to Information Engineering: From Strategic Planning to Information Systems*, Singapore: Addison-Wesley.

[18]   FLOOD, R.L. and E.R. CARSON (1993): *Dealing With Complexity: An Introduction To The Theory And Application Of Systems Science*: Plenum Press.

[19]   GOLDSTEIN, R.C. and V.C. STOREY (1990): Some Findings On The Intuitiveness Of Entity Relationship Constructs, In F.H. Lochovsky (Ed.) *Entity Relationship Approach To Database Design And Querying*, Amsterdam: Elsevier Science,

[20]   HAHN, J. and J. KIM (1999): Why Are Some Diagrams Easier to Work With?: Effects of Diagrammatic Representation on the Cognitive Integration Process of Systems Analysis and Design, *ACM Transactions on Computer-Human Interaction*, **6** (3), September: p. 181-213.

[21]   HITCHMAN, S. (1995): Practitioner Perceptions On The Use Of Some Semantic Concepts In The Entity Relationship Model, *European Journal of Information Systems*.

[22]   HITCHMAN, S. (2004): The Entity Relationship Model And Practical Data Modelling, *Journal of Conceptual Modelling*, **31**, March.

[23]   JAKOBY, J., D. SPELLER, and C. KOHN (1978): Brand Choice As A Function Of Information Load, *Journal Of Applied Psychology*, **63**.

[24] KALYUGA, S., P. AYRES, S.K. CHANG, and J. SWELLER (2003): The Expertise Reversal Effect, *Educational Psychologist*, **38** (1): p. 23-31.

[25] KIM, J., J. HAHN, and H. HAHN (2000): How Do We Understand a System with (So) Many Diagrams? Cognitive Integration Processes in Diagrammatic Reasoning, *Information Systems Research*, **11** (3), September: p. 284-303.

[26] KIM, Y.-G. and S.T. MARCH (1995): Comparing Data Modelling Formalisms, *Communications of the ACM*, **38** (6).

[27] KIRSCHNER, P.A. (2002): Cognitive Load Theory: Implications of Cognitive Load Theory on the Design of Learning, *Learning and Instruction*, **12** (1): p. 1-10.

[28] LARKIN, J.H. and H.A. SIMON (1987): Why a Diagram is (Sometimes) Worth Ten Thousand Words, *Cognitive Science*, **11** (1).

[29] LAUESEN, S. and O. VINTER (2000): Preventing Requirement Defects, In *Proceedings of the Sixth International Workshop on Requirements Engineering: Foundation for Software Quality (REFSQ'2000)*, Stockholm, Sweden, June 5-6 2000.

[30] LINDLAND, O.I., G. SINDRE, and A. SØLVBERG (1994): Understanding Quality In Conceptual Modelling, *IEEE Software*, **11** (2), March: p. 42-49.

[31] LIPOWSKI, Z.J. (1975): Sensory And Information Inputs Overload: Behavioural Effects, *Comprehensive Psychiatry*, **16** (3), May/June: p. 105-124.

[32] MAIER, R. (1996): Benefits And Quality Of Data Modelling: Results Of An Empirical Analysis, In B. Thalheim (Ed.) *Proceedings Of The Fifteenth International Conference On The Entity Relationship Approach*, Cottbus, Germany: Elsevier, October 7-9.

[33] MARTIN, J. (1989): *Information Engineering*, Englewood Cliffs, N.J.: Prentice Hall, 3 v.

[34] MILLER, G.A. (1956): The Magical Number Seven, Plus Or Minus Two: Some Limits On Our Capacity For Processing Information, *The Psychological Review*, **63**, March: p. 81-97.

[35] MOODY, D.L. (2001): *Dealing with Complexity: A Practical Method for Representing Large Entity Relationship Models (PhD Thesis)*, Melbourne, Australia: Department Of Information Systems, University of Melbourne.

[36] MOODY, D.L. and G.G. SHANKS (2003): Improving the Quality of Data Models: Empirical Validation of a Quality Management Framework, *Information Systems*, **28** (6), August: p. 619-650.

[37] MOUSAVI, S., R. LOW, and J. SWELLER (1995): Reducing Cognitive Load by Mixing Auditory and Visual Presentation Modes, *Journal of Educational Psychology*, **77**: p. 272-284.

[38] MURDOCK, B.B. (1993): TODAM3: A Model Of Storage And Retrieval Of Item, Associative And Serial Order Information, *Psychological Review*, **100** (2): p. pp. 183-203.

[39] NEWELL, A.A. and H.A. SIMON (1972): *Human Problem Solving*: Prentice-Hall.

[40] NORDBOTTEN, J.C. and M.E. CROSBY (1999): The Effect of Graphic Style on Data Model Interpretation, *Information Systems Journal*, **9**.

[41] PAAS, F. (1992): Training Strategies for Attaining Transfer of Problem Solving Skill in Statistics: A Cognitive Load Approach, *Journal of Educational Psychology*, **84**: p. 429-434.

[42] PAAS, F., A. RENKL, and J. SWELLER (2003): Cognitive Load Theory and Instructional Design: Recent Developments, *Educational Psychologist*, **38** (1): p. 1-4.

[43] PIATTINI, M., M. GENERO, and C. CALERO (2002): Data Model Metrics, In *Handbook of Software and Knowledge Engineering (Volume 2)*, S.K. Chang (Ed.), World Scientific: New Jersey.

[44] SHANKS, G.G. (1997): The Challenges Of Strategic Data Planning In Practice: An Interpretive Case Study, *Journal of Strategic Information Systems*, **6**.

[45] SIMSION, G.C. (1989): A Structured Approach To Data Modelling, *The Australian Computer Journal*, **21** (3), August: p. 108-117.

[46] SIMSION, G.C. and G.C. WITT (2001): *Data Modeling Essentials: Analysis, Design, and Innovation (2nd Ed)*, The Coriolis Group.

[47] STANDISH GROUP (1995): *The CHAOS Report into Project Failure*, The Standish Group International Inc. Available on-line at http://www.standishgroup.com/visitor/chaos.htm.

[48] STANDISH GROUP (1996): *Unfinished Voyages*, The Standish Group International Inc. available on-line at http://www.standishgroup.com/visitor/voyages.htm.

[49] SWELLER, J. (1988): Cognitive Load During Problem Solving: Effects on Learning, *Cognitive Science*, **12**: p. 257-285.

[50] SWELLER, J. (1994): Cognitive Load Theory, Learning Difficulty and Instructional Design, *Learning and Cognition*, **4**.

[51] SWELLER, J. and P. CHANDLER (1994): Why Some Material is Difficult to Learn, *Cognition and Instruction*, **12** (3).

[52] SWELLER, J., J.J.G. VAN MERRIËNBOER, and F. PAAS (1998): Cognitive Architecture and Instructional Design, *Educational Psychology Review*, **10** (3): p. 251-296.

[53] TEOREY, T.J. (1999): *Database Modelling And Design (3rd Edition)*, San Francisco: Morgan Kaufmann Publishers.

[54] TEORY, T.J., G. WEI, D.L. BOLTON, and J.A. KOENIG (1989): ER Model Clustering As An Aid For User Communication And Documentation In Database Design, *Communications Of The ACM*, August.

[55] THALHEIM, B. (2000): *Entity Relationship Modeling: Foundations of Database Technology*, Berlin: Springer, xii, 627.

[56] UHR, L., C. VOSSIER, and J. WEMAN (1962): Pattern Recognition over Distortions by Human Subjects and a Computer Model of Human Form Perception, *Journal of Experimental Psychology: Learning*, **63**.

[57] VAN MERRIËNBOER, J.J.G. (1997): *Training Complex Skills: A Four Component Instructional Design Model for Technical Training*, Englewood Cliffs, New Jersey, USA: Educational Technology Publications.

[58] VESSEY, I. and S. CONGER (1994): Requirements Specification: Learning Object, Process and Data Methodologies, *Communications of the ACM*, **37** (102-113).

[59] WAND, Y. and R.A. WEBER (1993): On the Ontological Expressiveness of Information Systems Analysis and Design Grammars, *Journal of Information Systems*, **3** (4), October: p. 217-237.

[60] WEBER, R.A. (1997): *Ontological Foundations Of Information Systems*, Melbourne, Australia: Coopers And Lybrand Accounting Research Methodology Monograph No. 4, Coopers And Lybrand.

[61] WOODS, D. (1995): Towards a Theoretical Base for Representation Design in the Computer Medium: Ecological Perception and Aiding Human Cognition, In *Global Perspectives on the Ecology of Human-Machine Systems*, J. Flach, et al. (Eds.), Lawrence Erlbaum Associates: New Jersey.

[62] WOODS, D.D. and J.C. WATTS (1997): How Not to Have to Navigate Through Too Many Displays, In *Handbook of Human Computer Interaction*, M.G. Helander, T.K. Landauer, and P.V. Prabhu (Eds.), Elsevier Science: Amsterdam, Netherlands, p. 617-650.

Template Based, Designer Driven Design Pattern Instantiation Support[*]

Vladimír Marko

Institute of Informatics and Software Engineering
Faculty of Informatics and Information Technologies,
Slovak University of Technology, Ilkovičova 3, SK-84216 Bratislava, Slovakia
Vladimir.Marko@fiit.stuba.sk

Abstract. This paper proposes a process of applying design patterns to design model of a software system. The process facilitates multi-step design pattern instantiation involving interaction with a designer. It results in enrichment of software design model with explicit and implicit information about interplaying entities forming a meaningful design pattern instance. The pattern template models significant aspects of design pattern and provides set of constraints to make possible to allow guiding the designer through the process of instantiation. Emphasis has been put on supporting the interactive, iterative and incremental instantiation process. The designer is prompted with a list of tasks based on pattern template and momentary state of each pattern instance. Designer's actions consequently alter the state of particular pattern instance and comple the closed loop of the process. As a demonstration we have developed a prototype CASE tool.

1 Introduction and Motivation

Recent advances in software engineering made the usage of design patterns a sound engineering practice. Using design pattern is a preferred way of solving recurring problems among development teams. It allows to avoid "reinventing the wheel" and to ease communication of partial solutions that are specific to the problem being solved.

Pattern catalogs are collections of generally usable patterns [1,2] or patterns specific for certain application domain or development activity [3,4]. Significant effort is being put into discovering, defining particular design pattern and describing its various aspects to capture the essence of recurring solution in order to make possible to apply existing knowledge repeatedly. By applying a pattern to a new recurrence of the problem, or by instantiating it [5], one gets an instance of the pattern adapted to be the solution of the problem in particular context.

There are many concerns being addressed by scientific community regarding usage of design patterns. They range from identification of design patterns in

---

[*] The work reported here was partially supported by Slovak Scientific Agency, Grant No. VG 1/0162/03.

A. Benczúr, J. Demetrovics, G. Gottlob (Eds.): ADBIS 2004, LNCS 3255, pp. 144–158, 2004.

legacy software models (e.g. for improving documentation), through advising developers to choose the right pattern in the right context, to helping to apply the pattern correctly and to obtain consistent pattern instance. This is a broad area of problems demanding different approaches; therefore we decided to address the latter task, i.e. to focus on supporting pattern instantiation process by assisting the developer.

Applying the idea behind the design pattern in a real-world case is not a trivial task. A design pattern is generally a complex structure consisting of several entities with different responsibilities, which should be embedded into software model. This is done by mapping those responsibilities to actual elements of software model. Additionally, existing pattern instances should become a part of software model being developed in order to become the benefit of documentation itself.

To relieve the developer from complexity of creating and maintaining pattern instances, it is important to provide tool support to enable efficient exploitation of knowledge gathered and published in form of design pattern.

In practice, design problems are addressed in the design phase of software development lifecycle, but standard modeling techniques like Unified Modeling Language [6] do not provide efficient way to capture and store information about solutions based on design patterns. Mostly, design patterns are applied in design phase in a way that turn them into specific solutions, but there is missing explicit information about design pattern instance. Alternatively, solving well known design problems is being postponed into implementation phase, thus implementing software and applying design pattern take place concurrently, often by means of assisted refactoring [7]. Unfortunately, such approach adds little value except reusing proven implementation solutions. The benefit of improved communication and documentation does not apply, because design pattern instance gets lost in vast implementation model (in this case, it is actual code in arbitrary programming language).

Obviously, the sooner the design pattern is applied, the greater is the benefit from additional informations. This is due to the fact that such an approach allows better design reuse, because the same design may be shared by several implementations or subsequent development process iterations. Facts mentioned above lead to the conclusion that it is beneficial to facilitate design pattern instantiation in design phase, and to retain explicit information about existing instances in design model. Therefore in our research we have focused on supporting design phase of software development.

The atomic approach which is suitable for working with primitives like classes, operations, attributes and relations among them, may not be suitable for creating more complex structures that represent solution induced from design pattern description called design pattern instance. These structures consist of primitives, but should also carry additional information about the way how these primitives play together to form a solution. Moreover, patterns instances are not isolated in the design model, they are usually overlapped and some primitives may participate in several design pattern instances.

We adopted the three basic properties of design pattern instantiation support method as stated in [8] and applied them:

- **Interactive.** The interactivity involves multiple interactions with designer during formation of pattern instance. Moreover, the process should also be able to suggest possible steps of instantiation. For example, we found very useful a possibility to generate primitives taking part in selected pattern instance. Such primitives may be consequently extended to carry out tasks specific to developed system. As the design pattern described in discovery phase includes constraints on individual primitives (e.g. "the operation/method should be abstract"), we can use this information to set properties of generated primitives that may be deduced from design pattern description.
- **Incremental.** The pattern may not be instantiated at once. Desired instance may be too complex to make considering all facets of the problem at once impossible. Moreover, the requirement of incremental process is implied by need to evolve the pattern instance as designer proceeds with the design work and/or accepts new requirements.
- **Iterative.** Most activities of software engineering are iterative, thus it is natural to go back to improve design, to fix mistakes or to solve several problems simultaneously.

The rest of this paper is structured as follows. In Section 2, we briefly introduce several basic concepts that need to be explained before going on. Section 3 describes proposed design pattern instance representation. Section 4 focuses on the main goal of this paper, the mechanisms of instantiation. In Section 5 we describe a CASE tool prototype we have created to evaluate our approach. We conclude with related work in Section 6 and some conclusions and future work in Section 7.

2   Basic Concepts

It is often said that design patterns are discovered rather than invented [3]. Existing solutions of similar problems are abstracted and described. Our approach takes such description as a basis enabling to apply design pattern to solve new recurrence of the problem of which the pattern is an abstracted solution. Due to fact that the pattern is instantiated in design model, we refer to the person who instantiates it as a designer.

In this paper we consider work with UML model. More specifically class model is the target in which the design patterns are instantiated. The motivation stems from availability of design pattern description based on UML/OMT diagrams and by ubiquity of class diagrams as a foundation of object-oriented design. Design patterns in catalogs are often described by defining their static structure in the form of class diagrams.

The following subsection introduces design pattern representation which is crucial for proposed instantiation process.

2.1   Design Pattern Representation

Suitable formal description of design pattern which captures the most important aspects and properties of the pattern is crucial for developing instantiation support method. The presented approach proposes *pattern template* to be such a description. The pattern must be represented as pattern template in order to be instantiated using the suggested approach.

Role modeling approach [9] has been used to realize mapping of pattern elements to target model elements. Each responsibility in design pattern corresponds to a role. Each role is typed to enforce the type of design model primitive (class, operation or attribute) which can be *cast* to that particular role. Casting is equivalent to making mapping between role and particular design model primitive.

The pattern template inherits existing knowledge stored as a description in a pattern catalogs and enriches it with additional information. Information is added to enable definition of a set of possible outcomes that can be achieved by instantiating the pattern. It also defines the way in which the resulting pattern instance integrates into the model of the system being designed.

Pattern template consists of three basic components: pattern structure, role graph and compatibility matrix. Each component carries distinctive knowledge about design pattern as follows:

- **Pattern Structure.** It is a description of structural and partly behavioral properties of pattern instance from the pattern catalog. There is significant effort to factor out as much metamodel dependencies as possible from design pattern representation, therefore almost all the metamodel specific properties are concentrated in pattern structure. To form a structural model, it is required to identify roles, to remove duplicate primitives representing the same role and to rename them to represent the name of role instead of a concrete actor. The design pattern structure then defines the properties of actual design primitives cast in roles and the type of relations between them (e.g. relation of generalization, association in the case of UML model).
- **Role Graph.** The role graph defines dependencies between roles, and constraints the quantity of instances of any role in regard to any other role. This property is called multiplicity as defined in [10]. It is the lower and upper bound to the number of contracts each role may possess. Cited approach has been extended to allow representation of relative multiplicity. Dependencies in role graph are directed edges; each endpoint is characterized by multiplicity constraint, similar to UML relation multiplicity constraint. An example role graph for prototype pattern is shown in Fig. 1.
  If there are dependencies in both directions between any two roles, then there is only one edge drawn between them without arrows, thus denoting it is a bidirectional dependency.
- **Compatibility Matrix.** The knowledge of which roles may be combined (in other words they are compatible) is included neither in pattern template structure nor in the role graph. The compatibility matrix defines which pairs of roles are compatible. The notion of compatibility is similar to notion of

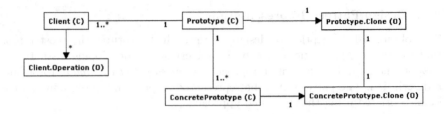

Fig. 1. Prototype pattern role graph

role constraint matrix as described in [9]. If the two roles are compatible, then the same model primitive may be cast into both roles of the same pattern instance.

3   Pattern Instance Representation

Setup and maintenance of information about existence of design pattern instance in the software design model is very important. In order to fulfil the requirement of interactivity, the pattern instance should represent not only grouping of primitives forming it, but should also offer steps which the designer may wish to take to develop the design further.

The pattern instance is represented by an instance graph. It is defined as an undirected graph whose nodes are role instances and edges are dependency instances. It defines momentary state of each pattern's instance and evolves with each step the designer takes. Every instance graph in the software's model represents single distinct design pattern instance. The example of instance graph is shown in Fig. 2. The graphic representation describes a sample instance of Decorator pattern.

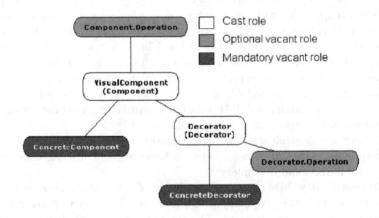

Fig. 2. Instance graph of example Decorator instance

There are three basic states of a node:

- Optional vacant role (e.g. Component.Operation, Decorator.Operation)
- Mandatory vacant role (e.g. ConcreteComponent, ConcreteDecorator)
- Cast role (e.g. VisualComponent, Decorator)

Figure 3 shows a statechart depicting transitions between node states. Vacant role forms an offer to cast the role. Cast roles are created by designer by accepting an offer and making new contract. However, iterative and incremental nature of proposed instantiation process demands the ability to cancel existing contract, effectively removing cast role and updating the instance graph accordingly. Vacant roles are generated according to rules derived from Pattern template. These rules are described in detail in next section.

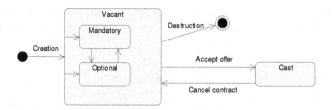

Fig. 3. Role instance lifecycle

There are two kinds of offers: optional and mandatory [8]. Mandatory offers must be turned into cast roles in order for pattern instance to meet multiplicity requirements as defined by role graph.

The edges of the instance graph are dependency instances and their existence is crucial for evaluation of actual relative number of contracts.

The pattern instance itself is also characterized by its state, which is updated after each change in the structure of representing graph. We have adopted following two notions to define the state of the pattern instance as introduced in [11]:

- **Completeness.** Complete pattern instance does not contain mandatory vacant roles. The bounding condition for completeness is as follows: For each cast role c, for each role graph dependency d ending in role c:

$$m_{min}(d) \leq |I_d(d)| \leq m_{max}(d) \qquad (1)$$

where $|I_d(d)|$ is number of instances; m_{min} is lower and m_{max} is upper bound of multiplicity of role graph dependency d.
- **Correctness.** Correctness bounds the number of created instances of each role. The condition simply disallows to create more contracts than it is dictated by the role graph. For each cast role c, for each role graph dependency d ending in role c:

$$|I_d(d)| \leq m_{max}(d) \qquad (2)$$

We have abandoned the notion of inconsistency as described in [11], thanks to strong control applied to the process of instantiation, which does not allow the designer to create instances not satisfying the condition of correctness. Also, each change to class model results in change of the pattern instance graph, if it is applicable (e.g. deleting a class participating in pattern instance results in instance graph update).

4   Pattern Instantiation Process

The heart of the proposed method is the instantiation process. It is the process whose input is a pattern template. The process results into pattern instance integrated into class model of software system being developed and into an instance graph which maintains relationships between role instances. The process consists of multiple iterative steps and is driven by interaction with designer. Conceptual block scheme in Fig. 4 shows the inputs and results of instantiation process.

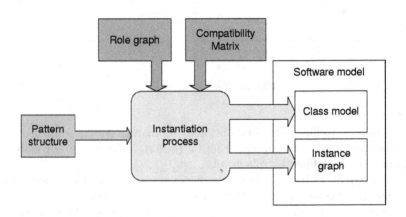

Fig. 4. Instantiation block diagram

Pattern structure, which is based on description of the design pattern, is a basis for how the actual pattern instance will look in the target class model. It is complemented by role graph and compatibility matrix that provide the rules and mandatory constraints for controlling the formation of an instance. Instantiation results in a design pattern instance in its implicit (classes with responsibilities, properties and relations based on pattern structure) and explicit form (instance graph).

4.1   The Designer's View

Iteration of pattern instantiation process (Fig. 5) is bounded by the action of designer. Designers are allowed to make new contracts as well as to cancel existing contracts.

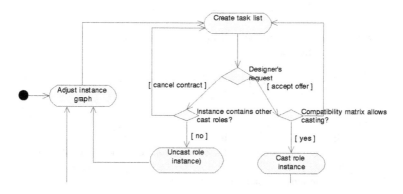

Fig. 5. Iterative instantiation process

The designer is prompted with the list of cast and vacant roles – a task list. It is in fact different graphical representation of an instance graph. Roles are displayed as a two level nested list. At the first level, class role instances are listed. At the second level, there are listed attribute and operation role instances grouped by encapsulating class. Concrete examples of task lists are shown in Fig. 7.

The rationale behind transforming graph structure into a task list lies in improved quick navigation the list provides.

Each edge of the role graph may be annotated with a short description of the responsibility of depending roles [10]. E.g. dependency of ConcretePrototype from Prototype may be read: "implements interface of cloning" and this will be expanded into the hint: "Vacant role ConcretePrototype implements interface of cloning Graphic playing role of Prototype" in the list of offers. The hint is placed between dependee and the name of the role the dependee depends to with names of concrete primitives substituted. The goal is to enlighten the purpose of vacant roles within the pattern instance to provide additional guidance for the designer.

4.2   Instance Graph Adjustment

All iterations of the process include adjustment of instance graph. This adjustment adds possible offers to the graph, which do not break rules of relative multiplicity. Therefore the condition of correctness (2) is checked each time the pattern instance is about to be updated. Note that the conditions of correctness and completeness are related to cast roles only. There may be any vacant roles, but casting any one of them may not break the rule of correctness.

The simplified skeleton algorithm of adjustment is shown in Fig. 6.

The initial adjustment includes offering vacant instances for all roles. These role instances form the origin to allow the designer to start casting roles from.

A weak side of the above mentioned approach is the way it copes with ambiguity of role relationships. When there is large number of possibilities how to add an instance, the graph adjustment results in creating a vacant role for each

```
repeat
   for all role graph dependency d do
      s ← start point role of d
      e ← end point role of d
      for all sᵢ ← cast role s do
         if |I_d| ending in sᵢ ≥ m_max then
            continue
         end if
         for all eᵢ ← instance of e do
            if adding dependency instance of (sᵢ, eᵢ) does not generate duplicate role
            instance eᵢ then
               add dependent instance (sᵢ, eᵢ)
            end if
         end for
         if creating of eᵢ ← vacant role of e and adding dependency instance of
         (sᵢ, eᵢ) does not generate duplicate role instance eᵢ then
            eᵢ ← new vacant instance of e
            add dependent instance (sᵢ, eᵢ)
         end if
      end for
   end for
until no dependency instances added
```

Fig. 6. Adjusting of instance graph

combination of depending roles. Example of such a situation is when there are roles A, B, C. B depends on A and C. If the dependency type is "one-to-one" the result is creation of a vacant instance of B role for each combination of A and C instances. This is desired behavior. On the other side, if the A to B and C to B relationships are "many", then there is only one B vacant role of B created. This happens, because the algorithm is unsure what subset of A and C instances should B instance depend on. The possible resolution of this caveat is being researched (e.g. by considering transitive evaluation of multiplicities that takes also dependencies of A and C with each other into account).

4.3   Accepting and Canceling Contracts

Both accepting and canceling contracts is a designer initiated activity resulting in changing the internal state of an instance. Necessary checking of constraints is part of them. Existing or newly created primitive may be cast into role. The process of casting comprises of:

1. **Type check.** Only primitives of the role type are allowed to be cast.
2. **Compatibility matrix check.** It refuses to cast role so that compatibility matrix constraint would be violated.
3. **Changing the role instance state.** The state of the node is set to cast. This will trigger adjusting the instance graph for next iteration.

4. **Setting properties on primitive.** As pattern structure of pattern template uses the same metamodel as target model, the properties of primitive being cast to role are copied from the template. This step includes recursive checking of transitional generalization/realization relationship in pattern structure. If there is such relationship between the two primitives in pattern template, identical relationship is enforced between instances cast into respective roles.

The contracts may be cancelled only if role instance does not contain any encapsulated role instances. Of course with every role cast there are all properties specific to that role added to the class design model (e.g. class stereotype, UML relationships with other primitives cast into depending roles).

4.4   Example

An example of two successive steps of Prototype pattern instance formation is in Fig. 7, the example is taken from [1]. It is a fragment of musical notation editor design model. In the first step shown (marked as Step n), there is an excerpt from target class model, which includes only entities related to this particular pattern instance. It is a situation after certain number of steps of instantiation process.

There are two cast roles. Class GraphicTool is cast in role Client and class Graphic is cast in role Prototype. The instance graph reflects actual state of an instance. There are optional vacant roles for another Client, as well as for operation, which may be cast to role Client.Operation. Moreover, there are two mandatory vacant roles: ConcretePrototype and Prototype.Clone. Designer must cast these two roles in order to make pattern instance complete (grayscale coding is identical as in Fig. 2) .

The next step (n+1) shows the situation after the designer decides to cast newly created class Staff into the role of ConcretePrototype. As part of the contract creation process, generalization relation between Graphic and Staff classes are enforced (if there is already such relation, even transitive, it is taken into account).

As it can be seen, another vacant role ConcretePrototype jumps out, because according to multiplicity constraint there may be any number of classes cast into the role of ConcretePrototype (Fig. 1). This time, mentioned vacant role is optional because there is already existing ConcretePrototype cast role depending from Graphic cast to role Prototype, so local condition of correctness is satisfied. However, clone operations of both Graphic and Staff classes are not cast to respective roles, yet. Therefore global condition of completeness is not yet satisfied. After casting roles Prototype.Clone and ConcretePrototype.Clone, the pattern instance will be complete, because it will contain cast and optional vacant roles only.

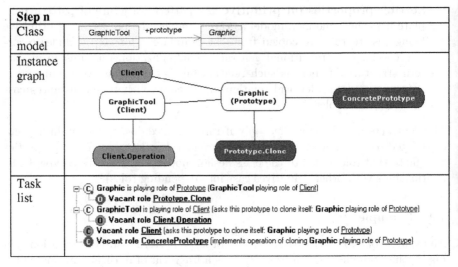

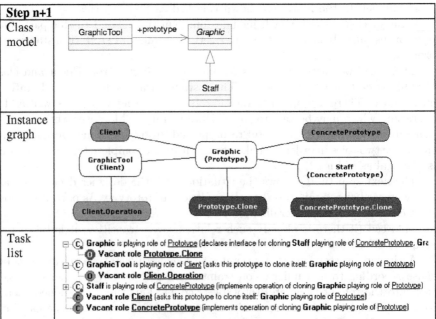

Fig. 7. Example of instance evolution

5   Prototype CASE Tool Implementation

To evaluate proposed approach we have designed and implemented a CASE tool [14] as an environment enabling work with pattern instance in conjunction with traditional object-oriented design. With our declared effort not to duplicate existing tool support and to reuse and enrich it instead, we have decided to make the tool as an add-in to a renowned CASE tool. Rational Rose became our selection as a host environment.

To make such a tool possible, defined external representation of pattern template as well as pattern instance has been defined. The pattern template consists of pattern structure defined as a Rational Rose class model, role graph and compatibility matrix are supplied as a XML file. We have represented all 23 patterns described in [1] as pattern templates to be acceptable for implemented CASE tool. The resulting pattern instances are not only integrated into class model but there is also XML representation of instance graph for each pattern instance included in Rose model. This pattern instance representation is directly embedded into Rational Rose file, to reduce the possibility of inconsistency between Rose model and pattern instance model. By storing both parts of model in single file, easier distribution of models has been achieved.

The main window of the tool remains always visible during design work as a slightly sophisticated "toolbar" (Fig. 8). Therefore the designer can seamlessly switch between working with common design primitives and working with patterns. The role may be cast by selecting existing primitive meeting the constraints imposed by pattern template or there may be generated new primitive which become cast into the selected role, thus it is combining the top-down and bottom-up approaches [12], but in an incremental way.

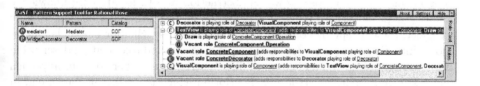

Fig. 8. CASE tool user interface

The tool also allows pinpointing any pattern instance as a newly created class diagram including all primitives participating in it and pattern induced relations among them.

6   Related Work

There is quite high number of commercial and non-commercial CASE environments, more or less supporting applying design patterns.

Rational XDE [15] is a full-fledged CASE tool focused on design. The designer is guided through the process of pattern instantiation through the set of wizards presenting sequence of predefined steps. The downside is the need of predefinition of one or few possible sequences of instantiation steps for each pattern and further modifications of the existing pattern instance are more complicated. Borland Together [16] is more focused on doing UML design and Java code generation simultaneously. The pattern instantiation is again controlled by a wizard.

Similar way of role system modeling using a graph is described in [17]. In this case the ambiguity of relations between role instances is resolved by "slicing" the pattern definition graph into unambiguous subgraphs interconnected with common nodes representing roles.

One of the most perspective tools is the FRED (Framework Editor) [18]. Its principle is similar to that of Borland Together except it is less focused on code generation and more concentrated on the design patterns and architectural view of software frameworks, however it contains quite elaborate code generation. Our research is significantly based on the results that this working group achieved. In their reports [13,8,10], they conceived statement of needing iterative, incremental and interactive way of supporting software design. The specialization pattern is modeled using a pattern graph and a set of constraints. Pattern graph itself defines relations between roles as well as properties and constraints of actual model elements cast into the roles (in this case Java language structural constructs). This pattern graph is then used to induce casting graph, which describes relations among actual role instances and is used to generate the framework specialization instructions for developer using the product.

We found the above mentioned idea of describing relations between roles using a graph allowing inducing a task list to guide developer to be a sound one. To compare, our aim was to support design pattern instantiation in software design, thus lifting it a level closer towards abstraction and to isolate core knowledge about design pattern to make it possible to be instantiated. Consequently we extended the concept by consolidating information specific for particular metamodel into a pattern structure and independent role and role relation description into separate role graph and compatibility matrix views. Therefore our approach enables to reuse pattern structure description which is readily available, e.g. in form of class models. Additionally, role graph and compatibility matrix allows relaxing the structural constraints on pattern instances. All these components form different views of the same design pattern considering different aspects of instantiation process.

7   Conclusions

The main purpose of this paper is to present the foundation of design pattern support method which has been designed to fill the gaps in design pattern support in current mainstream CASE tools. Most importantly, we decided to bring design pattern support to the same level of flexibility characteristic to working with basic design primitives as classes, operations and attributes using major CASE tools. Of course, the specific nature of working with design patterns has been taken into account.

To meet the research goals, development focused on enabling interactive pattern instantiation process which generates the meaningful offers for the designer. The purpose is flexible creation of consistent and correct pattern instances. The instantiation process is neither atomic, nor does it rely on predefined wizard-like steps. It is designed to make possible to start with any part of the design pattern and incrementally evolve the instance as needed to allow the designer to be focused on designed system-specific matters and not on recurring pattern itself. Another realized feature is the iterative way of working with patterns as the process allows modifications of already instantiated parts of a pattern while keeping it consistent.

The process relies on formalized description of design pattern properties in form of pattern template. This description adds a set of properties needed to make instantiation possible, but leaves the representation of pattern structure separate to ensure not to be dependent on particular design metamodel or technique. To appropriately represent pattern instance we have also designed formalized representation of pattern instance, which became part of design model of developed software system.

Implementing the CASE tool prototype based on intermediate results of the research gave us valuable feedback for planning further improvements to the method and to evaluate its current performance. We have used the tool to document the design model of the mid-sized software system – of the tool itself. By using this method, we have interactively instantiated 11 different patterns in design model of the tool. Although we have used the tool especially in the post-design phase (when almost all design work has been already done), and not concurrently with the design as it is intended, we have appreciated the seamless integration of work with patterns and work with classes and their properties.

A few shortcomings of designed method have been identified. They include efficient representation of certain combinations role relationships. Another potential improvement would be checking of role compatibility across all pattern instances instead of checking in scope of every single instance. The task is to determine a set of properties, which would describe how patterns may be composed to form larger unit while still checking the compatibility of responsibilities assigned to shared primitives. The future research will focus on tackling these issues.

Extending pattern template with additional views and instantiating such views is another challenging research direction. Such views could describe behavioral properties of the pattern in form of sequence diagrams and customized sequence diagrams. This behavioral model would become created and evolved during pattern instantiation just like class diagrams in current state.

References

1. Gamma, E., Helm, R., Johnson, R., Vlissides, J.: Design Patterns: Elements of Reusable Object-Oriented Software. Addison Wesley Longman (1995)
2. Rohnert, H., Buschmann, F., Regine, M., Sommerland, P.: Patterns of Software Architecture: A System of Patterns. Addison Wesley, First ed. (1996)
3. Fowler, M.: Analysis Patterns: Reusable Object Models. Addison Wesley, First. ed. (1997)
4. EventHelix.com: Real-Time Pattern Catalog, http://www.eventhelix.com/RealtimeMantra/PatternCatalog/ (12. 3. 2004)
5. Smolárová, M., Návrat, P.: Reuse with Design Patterns: Towards Pattern-Based Design. In: Feng, Y., Notkin D., Gaudel, M.C. (eds.): Proc. Software: Theory and Practice. PHEI - Publishing House of Electronics Industry, China (2000) 232–235
6. Object Management Group: OMG Unified Modeling Language Specification, Version 1.5, March 2003.
7. Eden, A.H., Gil, J., Yehudai, A.: Precise specification and automatic application of design patterns. In: Automated Software Engineering (1997) 143–152
8. Hakala, M.: Task-Based Tool Support for Framework Specialization. In: Proceedings of OOPSLA'00 Workshop on Methods and Tools for Framework Development and Specialization, Tampere University of Technology, Software Systems Laboratory, Report 21 (2000)
9. Riehle, D., Gross, T: Role Model Based Framework Design and Integration. In: Proc. of Conference on Object-Oriented Programming Systems, Languages and Applications (OOPSLA'98), Canada (1998) 117–133
10. Viljamaa, R., Viljamaa, J.: Creating Framework Specialization Instructions for Tool Environments. In: Osterbye, K. (ed.): Proc. of the Nordic Workshop on Software Development Tools and Techniques (NWPER'2002) (2002)
11. Smolárová, M., Návrat, P.: Representing Design Patterns as Design Components. In: Eder, J., Rozman, I., Welzer, T. (eds.): Proc. of Short Papers Advances in Databases and Information Systems (ADBIS'99), Maribor, Slovenia (1999) 140–148
12. Florijn, G., Meijers, M., Winsen, P.: Tool Support for Object-Oriented Patterns. In: Askit, M., Matsuoka, S. (1997, eds.): ECOOP'97. Lecture Notes in Computer Science, Vol. 1241. Springer-Verlag, Germany (1997)
13. Hautamäki, J.: Task-Driven Framework Specialization - Goal-Oriented Approach. Licentiate thesis, University of Tampere (2002)
14. Marko, V.: Using Patterns in Software Design. Master Thesis (in Slovak), Slovak University of Technology Bratislava (2003)
15. Rational XDE, http://www.ibm.com/developerworks/rational/products/xde (23. 3. 2004)
16. Borland Together, http://www.borland.com/together (4. 2. 2004)
17. Maplesden, D., Hosking, J., Grundy, J.: A Visual Language for Design Pattern Modelling and Instantiation. In: Proc. of IEEE 2001 Symposia on Human Centric Computing Languages and Environments (HCC'01) (2001) 338–340
18. Fred: Framework Editor, http://practise.cs.tut.fi (4. 2. 2004)

A High-Level Language for Specifying XML Data Transformations

Tadeusz Pankowski

Institute of Control and Information Engineering,
Poznan University of Technology, Poland,
Tadeusz.Pankowski@put.poznan.pl

Abstract. We propose a descriptive high-level language XDTrans devoted to specify transformations over XML data. The language is based
on unranked tree automata approach. In contrast to W3C's XQuery or
XSLT which require programming skills, our approach uses high-level
abstractions reflecting intuitive understanding of tree oriented nature of
XML data. XDTrans specifies transformations by means of rules which
involve XPath expressions, node variables and non-terminal symbols denoting fragments of a constructed result. We propose syntax and semantics for the language as well as algorithms translating a class of
transformations into XSLT.

1 Introduction

Transformation of XML data becomes increasingly important along with development of web-oriented applications (e.g. Web Services, e-commerce, information
retrieval, dissemination and integration on the Web), where data structures of
one application must be transformed into a form accepted by another one. A
transformation of XML data can be carried out by means of W3C's languages
XSLT [1] or XQuery [2]. However, every time when an XML document should
be transformed into some other form, a new XSLT (or XQuery) program must
be written, which requires programming skills. Thus, the operational nature of
XSLT and XQuery makes them less desirable candidates for high-level *transformation specification* [3]. To avoid programming, other transformation languages
have been proposed [3,4,5].

In this paper we propose a new language called XDTrans that is devoted to
specify transformations for XML data. Some preliminary ideas of the approach
underlying XDTrans were presented in [6] and [7]. We discuss both syntax and
semantics of the language as well as some representative examples illustrating
using of it. We assume that the user perceives XML documents as data trees
according to DOM model [8], and is familiar with syntax and semantics of XPath
expressions [9]. Main advantages and novelties of the approach are as follows:

- XDTrans expressions are high-level transformation rules reflecting intuitive
  understanding how an output data tree is constructed from input data trees,
  and involve XPath expressions, node variables and some non-terminal symbols (*concepts*) denoting subtrees in a constructed data tree;

A. Benczúr, J. Demetrovics, G. Gottlob (Eds.): ADBIS 2004, LNCS 3255, pp. 159–172, 2004.
© Springer-Verlag Berlin Heidelberg 2004

- expressive power of XDTrans corresponds to structural recursion [10] and a fragment of top-down XSLT (without functions), however, in XDTrans we can join arbitrary number of different documents (not supported by XSLT [11]);
- a transformation of a single XML document can be translated into XSLT program – we propose algorithms for such translations;
- in contrast to XSLT, which can be used for transforming documents having only a standard form, XDTrans semantic functions could be applied to transform non-standard representations of XML documents (e.g. in relational databases [6],[12],[13]).

The structure of the paper is as follows. In Section 2 we propose XDTrans as a language for high-level transformation specification. We formulate its syntax and semantics, and discuss some examples illustrating its use. In Section 3, algorithms translating a class of XDTrans programs into XSLT are proposed. Section 4 concludes the paper.

2   High-Level Transformation Specification – XDTrans

2.1   Syntax of XDTrans

According to W3C standard, any XML document can be represented as a data tree [8], where a node conforms to one of the seven node types: *root, element, attribute, text, namespace, processing instruction*, and *comment*. In this paper, we restrict our attention to four first of them. Every node has a unique *node identifier* (nid). A data tree can be formalized as follows [7]:

Definition 1. *A data tree is an expression defined by the syntax:*

$$
\begin{aligned}
&data\ tree ::= nid(tree),\\
&tree \qquad ::= e\text{-}tree \mid a\text{-}tree \mid t\text{-}tree,\\
&e\text{-}tree \qquad ::= <e,nid>(tree,...,tree), \qquad (element\ tree),\\
&a\text{-}tree \qquad ::= <a,nid>(s), \qquad\qquad\quad (attribute\ tree),\\
&t\text{-}tree \qquad ::= nid(s), \qquad\qquad\qquad\quad (text\ tree),
\end{aligned}
$$

where nid, e, a, and s are from, respectively, a set $\mathcal{N}$ of node identifiers, a set Σ_E of element labels, a set Σ_A of attribute labels, and a set $\mathcal{S}$ of string values. By $\mathcal{D}_{\Sigma,\mathcal{S}}(\mathcal{N})$, where $\Sigma = \Sigma_E \cup \Sigma_A$, will be denoted a set of all data trees over Σ and $\mathcal{S}$ with node identifiers from $\mathcal{N}$. □

Further on we assume that $\mathcal{C}$ is a set of *non-terminal symbols* called *concepts*, and $\mathcal{P}$ is a set of *XPath expressions* in which some *variables* can appear.

The goal of *transformation* is to convert a set of input data trees into an expected single output data tree. A transformation can be specified by a set of *transformation rules* (or *rules* for short). Every rule determines a type of expected *final* or *intermediate* result data tree in a form of a *terminal* or *non-terminal tree expression*.

Definition 2. *A tree expression over* Σ, $\mathcal{C}$, $\mathcal{S}$ *and* $\mathcal{P}$ *conforms to the following syntax:*

$$\tau ::= s \mid E \mid a(s) \mid a(E) \mid C(E) \mid e(\tau, ..., \tau),$$

where: $s \in \mathcal{S}, E \in \mathcal{P}, a \in \Sigma_A, C \in \mathcal{C}, e \in \Sigma_E$. *The set of all tree expressions will be denoted by* $\mathcal{T}_{\Sigma,\mathcal{S}}(\mathcal{C},\mathcal{P})$. □

Definition 3. *A transformation specification language is a system*

$$XDTrans = (\Sigma, \mathcal{C}, \mathcal{S}, \mathsf{START}, \mathcal{P}, \mathcal{R}),$$

where $\mathsf{START} \in \mathcal{C}$ *is the initial concept, and* $\mathcal{R}$ *is a finite set of rules of the following two forms:*

$$(C, E) \to \tau,$$
$$(C, (\$v_1 : E_1, ..., \$v_p : E_p)) \to \tau,$$

where $C \in \mathcal{C}$, *any* E *(possibly with subscripts) is from* $\mathcal{P}$, *$v (possibly with subscripts) is a node variable,* $\tau \in \mathcal{T}_{\Sigma,\mathcal{S}}(\mathcal{C},\mathcal{P})$, *and every node variable (if any) occurring in the body occurs also in the head of the rule.* □

The head of a rule includes a concept C which will be rewritten by the body of the rule. A rule with concept C in the head *defines* this concept. We assume that any concept in a given set of rules must be defined, and that every concept has exactly one definition. So, our system is deterministic. Recursive definitions for concepts are allowed (e.g. SUB_PART in Example 3(1)). There must be exactly one rule, the *initialization rule*, defining the initial concept START. In order to refer to the root of a document we use "/" (if the document is understood) or a *root node* identifying the document (e.g. function *document("URI")* returning the root node).

In Fig. 1 there is an example of XML document *suppliers*, its DTD and data tree. The document *parts* in Fig. 2 is a transformed form of (a selection of) the document from Fig. 1 (see Example 1).

The following example illustrates how XDTrans can be used to transform *suppliers* into *parts*:

Example 1. Transform suppliers into parts, where each part has as attributes name of the part and name of its supplier, include only two first parts of each supplier.

(1) transformation specification without variables:

```
(START, /suppliers)                        → parts(PART(.))
(PART, supplier/part[position() ≤ 2]) → part(PNAME(.), SNAME(.))
(PNAME,.)                                  → @pname(text())
(SNAME,.)                                  → ../@sname
```

(2) transformation specification with variables:

```
(START, /suppliers)                        → parts(PART(.))
(PART, ($v:supplier,
        $p:$v/part[position()≤2],
        $s:$v/@sname))                      → part(PNAME($p), $s)
(PNAME,.)                                  → @pname(text())
```

□

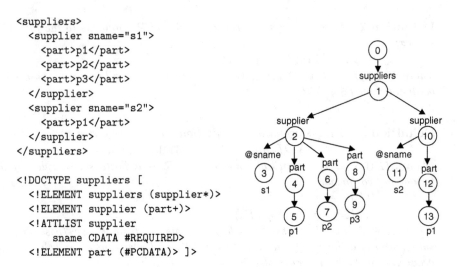

```
<suppliers>
  <supplier sname="s1">
    <part>p1</part>
    <part>p2</part>
    <part>p3</part>
  </supplier>
  <supplier sname="s2">
    <part>p1</part>
  </supplier>
</suppliers>

<!DOCTYPE suppliers [
  <!ELEMENT suppliers (supplier*)>
  <!ELEMENT supplier (part+)>
  <!ATTLIST supplier
      sname CDATA #REQUIRED>
  <!ELEMENT part (#PCDATA)> ]>
```

Fig. 1. XML document *suppliers*, its DTD and date tree

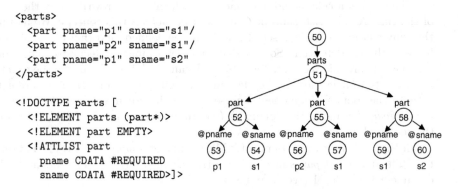

```
<parts>
  <part pname="p1" sname="s1"/
  <part pname="p2" sname="s1"/
  <part pname="p1" sname="s2"
</parts>

<!DOCTYPE parts [
  <!ELEMENT parts (part*)>
  <!ELEMENT part EMPTY>
  <!ATTLIST part
    pname CDATA #REQUIRED
    sname CDATA #REQUIRED>]>
```

Fig. 2. XML document *parts*, its DTD and date tree

2.2 Semantics for XDTrans

Every XDTrans rule is evaluated in an *evaluation context* (or *context* for short) like XPath expressions are [9], [14]. We will write $(C, E)\langle S, n\rangle$ to denote that the head of a rule is evaluated in a *context* $\langle S, n\rangle$, where S is an ordered set of distinct nodes (a *context set*), and n is a *context node*, $n \in S$ ($\langle\rangle$ denotes the *empty context*). A context is used to evaluate XPath expression(s) included in the head of the rule. Evaluation of the head produces a new context set (the *output context set*). Every *output context* determined by the output context set is then used to process the body of the rule, where recursively the same or other rules can be invoked.

A rule is formulated against an input data tree(s) and the result of the rule is an output data tree (possibly non-terminal). An XPath expression (or a sequence of XPath expressions labeled with variables) occurring in the head of the rule, determines a number of (sub)trees instantiated from the tree expression being the body of the rule. All trees developed from the tree expression have a common structure but each of them has unique nodes (node identifiers). If each leaf of such a tree does not contain any concept then the tree is a *terminal tree* otherwise it is a *non-terminal tree*.

Now we define how a rule transforms input date tree(s) into an output data tree. By $N_E\langle S, n\rangle$ we denote an ordered set of nodes obtained by evaluating E in a context $\langle S, n\rangle$. For example, for the data tree from Fig. 1, we have: $N_{supplier/part}\langle(1), 1\rangle = (4, 6, 8, 12)$.

We will use a Skolem function $new()$ that for every invocation returns a unique node identifier. Now, we will define a semantics for heads of XDTrans rules and next a semantics for bodies of the rules.

Evaluation of $(C, E) \to \tau$ in the context $\langle\rangle$ and $\langle S, n\rangle$

1. First, the head of the rule must be evaluated in a given context:
   - the result of the evaluation is an ordered set $S_1 = N_E\langle S, n\rangle = (n_1, ..., n_m)$, $m \geq 1$, referred to as an *output context set*,
   - for any output context $\langle S_1, n_i\rangle, 1 \leq i \leq m$, the body τ of the rule must be processed;
   - it follows from the restrictions on XML documents that for an initialization rule its head qualification E must return a singleton, i.e. $S_1 = N_E\langle\rangle = (n_1)$, i.e. $m = 1$.
2. In the next step, τ should be evaluated in m contexts, i.e. the expression $\tau(\langle S_1, n_1\rangle, ..., \langle S_1, n_m\rangle), m \geq 1$ must be processed:

   H1. For an initialization rule we start from the expression $(\mathtt{START}, E)\langle\rangle$ and rewrite it by the expression $new()(\tau\langle(n_1), n_1\rangle)$, where (n_1) is the result of evaluation E in the empty context, Fig. 3.

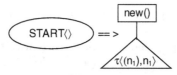

Fig. 3. Rewriting specified by a transformation rule $(\mathtt{START}, E) \to \tau$ in the empty context.

   H2. For a non initialization rule $(C, E) \to \tau$ and a context $\langle S, n\rangle$, where $N_E\langle S, n\rangle = S_1 = (n_1, ..., n_m)$, the expression $x((C, E)\langle S, n\rangle)$ is rewritten by $x(\tau\langle S_1, n_1\rangle, ..., \tau\langle S_1, n_m\rangle)$, Fig. 4.

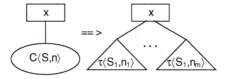

Fig. 4. Rewriting specified by a rule $(C, E) \to \tau$ in a context $\langle S, n\rangle$.

Evaluation of $(C, (\$v_1 : E_1, ..., \$v_p : E_p)) \to \tau$ in the context $\langle\rangle$ and $\langle S, n\rangle$

1. The result of processing an expression $(\$v_1 : E_1, ..., \$v_p : E_p)$ in a context $\langle S, n\rangle$ (or in $\langle\rangle$) is an ordered set $\Omega = (\omega_1, ..., \omega_m), m \geq 1$, of distinct *valuations* of variables. Every valuation $\omega \in \Omega$ assigns a node of the input data tree to $\$v_i$ such that $\omega(\$v_i) \in N_{E_i}\langle S, n\rangle$ (or $\omega(\$v_i) \in N_{E_i}\langle\rangle$), for every i, $1 \leq i \leq p$. For an initialization rule, Ω must have at most one element.

H3. An initialization rule $(\mathtt{START}, (\$v_1 : E_1, ..., \$v_p : E_p))\langle\rangle$ is rewritten by $new()(\tau\langle(\omega_1), \omega_1\rangle)$, where ω_1 is the single valuation satisfying the expression $(\$v_1 : E_1, ..., \$v_p : E_p)$ in the empty context, Fig. 5.

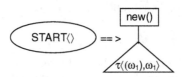

Fig. 5. Rewriting specified by a rule $(\mathtt{START}, (\$v_1 : E_1, ..., \$v_p : E_p)) \to \tau$ in the empty context.

H4. For a non initialization rule $(C, (\$v_1 : E_1, ..., \$v_p : E_p)) \to \tau$ and a context $\langle S, n\rangle$, where $\Omega = (\omega_1, ..., \omega_m), m \geq 1$, $x(C, (\$v_1 : E_1, ..., \$v_p : E_p))\langle S, n\rangle)$ is converted into $x(\tau\langle\Omega, \omega_1\rangle, ..., \tau\langle\Omega, \omega_m\rangle)$, Fig.6.

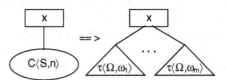

Fig. 6. Rewriting specified by a rule $(C, (\$v_1 : E_1, ..., \$v_p : E_p)) \to \tau$ in a context $\langle S, n\rangle$.

2. Let $E[\$v]\langle\Omega, \omega'\rangle$ denote that an expression E with the only variable $\$v$ is to be evaluated in a context $\langle\Omega, \omega'\rangle$ (see e.g. Fig. 5 and Fig. 6.). In this case the context is given by means of valuations, so it should be *resolved* first. The resolution is achieved by replacing every valuation with its value for the variable $\$v$. Thus the resolved version of the expression is: $E[\$v]\langle S, n\rangle$, where $S = \{\omega(\$v) \mid \omega \in \Omega\}$, and $n = \omega'(\$v)$.

Evaluation of the body of a rule

The meaning of transformations specified by expressions of the form $\tau\langle S, n\rangle$ is illustrated in Fig. 7. If the result does not depend on a whole context we use the notation $\langle., .\rangle$.

For the all possible tree expressions forming the body of a rule (according to Definition 2), we have:

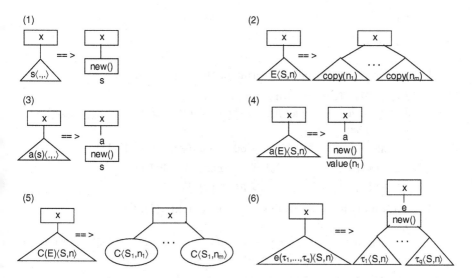

Fig. 7. Graphical interpretation of rewritings specified by bodies of rules

B1. The body of the form s creates a text node with the string value s. Rewriting imposed by the expression is independent of a context, Fig. 7(1):

$$x(s\langle S,n\rangle) \Rightarrow x(new()(s)).$$

B2. For an expression of the form E in a context $\langle S,n\rangle$, where $\mathbb{N}_E\langle S,n\rangle = (n_1,...,n_m)$, subtrees from the input tree(s) identified by $n_i, 1 \leq i \leq m$, are copied into the output tree. The expression $copy(n_i)$ recursively copies a source subtree denoted by n_i and creates a new node identifier for any copy of a source node, Fig. 7(2):

$$x(E\langle S,n\rangle) \Rightarrow x(copy(n_1),...,copy(n_m)).$$

B3. An expression of the form $a(s)$ creates an attribute node labeled a with the string value s. Rewriting defined by the expression is independent of a context, Fig. 7(3):

$$x(a(s)\langle S,n\rangle) \Rightarrow x(< a, new() > (s)).$$

B4. For an expression of the form $a(E)$ in a context $\langle S,n\rangle$, where $\mathbb{N}_E\langle S,n\rangle = (n_1)$, an attribute node labeled a with the string value equal to $value(n_1)$ is created, Fig. 7(4):

$$x(a(E)\langle S,n\rangle) \Rightarrow x(< a, new() > (value(n_1))).$$

B5. If $S_1 = \mathbb{N}_E\langle S,n\rangle = (n_1,...,n_m)$, then an expression $x(C(E)\langle S,n\rangle)$ is replaced by the expression $x(C\langle S_1,n_1\rangle,...,C\langle S_1,n_m\rangle)$, where $C\langle S_1,n_i\rangle$ denotes an invocation of the rule identified by C in a context $\langle S_1,n_i\rangle, 1 \leq i \leq m$, Fig. 7(5):

$$x(C(E)\langle S,n\rangle) \Rightarrow x(C\langle S_1,n_1\rangle,...,C\langle S_1,n_m\rangle).$$

B6. For an expression $e(\tau_1,...,\tau_q)$ in a context $\langle S,n\rangle$ a new element node labeled e is created with q subtrees, where i-th subtree will be developed by evaluating expressions τ_i in the context $\langle S,n\rangle, 1 \leq i \leq q$, Fig. 7(6):

$$x(e(\tau_1,...,\tau_q)\langle S,n\rangle) \Rightarrow x(< e, new() > (\tau_1\langle S,n\rangle,...,\tau_q\langle S,n\rangle)).$$

Transformations from Example 1 are carried out as follows:

Transformation (1)

1. Evaluation of the initialization rule in the empty context:
   - *Rule:* $(\text{START}, /\text{suppliers}) \to \text{parts}(\text{PART}(.))$
   - *Value of the head qualifier in the evaluation context:* $\mathbb{N}_{/\text{suppliers}}\langle\rangle = (1)$
   - *Rewritings:*

     $\text{START}\langle\rangle \quad\quad\quad \overset{H1}{\Rightarrow} 50(\text{parts}(\text{PART}(.)\langle(1),1\rangle)$

     $\text{parts}(\text{PART}(.)\langle(1),1\rangle) \overset{B6}{\Rightarrow} <\text{parts},51>(\text{PART}(.)\langle(1),1\rangle)$

     $\text{PART}(.)\langle(1),1\rangle \quad\quad \overset{B5}{\Rightarrow} \text{PART}\langle(1),1\rangle$

2. Evaluation of the rule defining PART in context $\langle(1),1\rangle$:
   - *Rule:*
     $(\text{PART}, \text{supplier}/\text{part}[\text{position}() \leq 2]) \to \text{part}(\text{PNAME}(.), \text{SNAME}(.))$
   - *Value of the head qualifier in the evaluation context:*
     $\mathbb{N}_{\text{supplier}/\text{part}[\text{position}()\leq 2]}\langle(1),1\rangle = (4,6,12)$
   - *Rewritings:*

     $\text{PART}\langle(1),1\rangle \overset{H2}{\Rightarrow} (\text{part}(\text{PNAME}(.),\text{SNAME}(.))\langle(4,6,12),4\rangle,$
     $\quad\quad\quad\quad\quad\quad \text{part}(\text{PNAME}(.),\text{SNAME}(.))\langle(4,6,12),6\rangle,$
     $\quad\quad\quad\quad\quad\quad \text{part}(\text{PNAME}(.),\text{SNAME}(.))\langle(4,6,12),12\rangle)$

     $\text{part}(\text{PNAME}(.),\text{SNAME}(.))\langle(4,6,12),6\rangle \overset{B6}{\Rightarrow}$

     $\overset{B6}{\Rightarrow} <\text{part},52>(\text{PNAME}(.)\langle(4,6,12),4\rangle,\text{SNAME}(.)\langle(4,6,12),4\rangle)$

     $\ldots$

     $\text{PNAME}(.)\langle(4,6,12),4\rangle \overset{B5}{\Rightarrow} \text{PNAME}\langle(4),4\rangle, \text{ since } \mathbb{N}_{.}\langle(4,6,12),4\rangle = (4)$

     $\text{SNAME}(.)\langle(4,6,12),4\rangle \overset{B5}{\Rightarrow} \text{SNAME}\langle(4),4\rangle$

     $\ldots$

3. Evaluation of the rule defining PNAME in context $\langle(4),4\rangle$:
   - *Rule:* $(\text{PNAME}, .) \to @\text{pname}(\text{text}())$
   - *Value of the head qualifier in the evaluation context:* $\mathbb{N}_{.}\langle(4),4\rangle = (4)$
   - *Rewritings:*

     $\text{PNAME}\langle(4),4\rangle \quad\quad\quad \overset{H2}{\Rightarrow} @\text{pname}(\text{text}())\langle(4),4\rangle$

     $@\text{pname}(\text{text}())\langle(4),4\rangle \overset{B4}{\Rightarrow} <@\text{pname},53>(\text{value}(5)),$
     $\quad\quad\quad\quad\quad\quad\quad \text{since } \mathbb{N}_{\text{text}()}\langle(4),4\rangle = 5$

4. Evaluation of the rule defining SNAME in context $\langle(4),4\rangle$:
   - *Rule:* $(\text{SNAME}, .) \to ../@\text{sname}$
   - *Value of the head qualifier in the evaluation context:* $\mathbb{N}_{.}\langle(4),4\rangle = (4)$
   - *Rewritings:*

     $\text{SNAME}\langle(4),4\rangle \quad\quad \overset{H2}{\Rightarrow} ../@\text{sname}\langle(4),4\rangle$

     $../@\text{sname}\langle(4),4\rangle \overset{B2}{\Rightarrow} \text{copy}(3), \text{ since } \mathbb{N}_{../@sname}\langle(4),4\rangle = (3)$

5. Analogously for the remaining cases.

Transformation (2)

1. Evaluation of the initialization rule in the empty context - as for transformation (1).
2. Evaluation of the rule defining `PART` in context $\langle(1),1\rangle$:
   - *Rule:*
     ```
     (PART, ($v:supplier,
             $p:$v/part[position()≤2],
             $s:$v/@sname))              → part(PNAME($p),$s)
     ```
   - *Value of the head qualifier in the evaluation context:*
     a sequence $\Omega = (\omega_1, \omega_2, \omega_3)$ of three valuations defined as follows:
     $$\omega_1 : (\omega_1(\$v) = 2, \quad \omega_1(\$p) = 4, \quad \omega_1(\$s) = 3),$$
     $$\omega_2 : (\omega_2(\$v) = 2, \quad \omega_2(\$p) = 6, \quad \omega_2(\$s) = 3),$$
     $$\omega_3 : (\omega_3(\$v) = 10, \omega_3(\$p) = 12, \omega_3(\$s) = 11).$$
   - *Rewritings:*
     $$\text{PART}\langle(1),1\rangle \overset{H4}{\Rightarrow} (\text{part}(\text{PNAME}(\$p),\$s))\langle\Omega,\omega_1\rangle,$$
     $$\text{part}(\text{PNAME}(\$p),\$s))\langle\Omega,\omega_2\rangle,$$
     $$\text{part}(\text{PNAME}(\$p),\$s))\langle\Omega,\omega_3\rangle)$$
     $$\text{part}(\text{PNAME}(\$p),\$s))\langle\Omega,\omega_1\rangle \overset{B6}{\Rightarrow}$$
     $$\overset{B6}{\Rightarrow} \texttt{<part,52>}(\text{PNAME}(\$p)\langle\Omega,\omega_1\rangle,\$s\langle\Omega,\omega_1\rangle)$$
     . . .
     $$\text{PNAME}(\$p)\langle\Omega,\omega_1\rangle \overset{B5}{\Rightarrow} \text{PNAME}\langle(4),4\rangle, \text{ since } \text{N}_{\$p}\langle\Omega,\omega_1\rangle = (\omega_1(\$p)) = (4)$$
     . . .
     $$\$s\langle\Omega,\omega_1\rangle \overset{B2}{\Rightarrow} \text{copy}(3), \text{ since } \text{N}_{\$s}\langle\Omega,\omega_1\rangle = (\omega_1(\$s)) = (3)$$
     . . .
3. Evaluation of the rule `PNAME` in the context $\langle(4),4\rangle$: in the same way as for the transformation (1).
4. Similarly for the remaining cases.

2.3   Examples

The transformation discussed in Example 1 can be formulated without using variables (specification 1) or with variables (specification 2). Now we will show examples of transformations, where it is necessary to use variables. In general, variables are necessary when the transformation requires a join condition comparing two or more XML values belonging to the same or to two different documents.

Example 2. (Join) Join *books* and *papers* documents into a *bib* document.

Input "papers.xml":	Output: `<bib>`
`<papers>...</papers>`	`<papers>...</papers>`
Input "books.xml":	`<books>...</books>`
`<books>...</books>`	`</bib>`

Transformation specification:
```
(START, ($p:document("papers.xml")/papers,
         $b:document("books.xml")/books)  → bib($p,$b)
```
□

Example 3. (Recursion) Convert a flat list of part elements, *partlist*, into a tree representation, *parttree*, based on *partof* attributes [15], and do the inverse transformation.

Input DTD:

```
<!DOCTYPE partlist [
  <!ELEMENT partlist (part*)>
  <!ELEMENT part EMPTY>
  <!ATTLIST part
      partid CDATA #REQUIRED
      partof CDATA #IMPLIED
      name   CDATA #REQUIRED>]>
```

Output DTD:

```
<!DOCTYPE parttree [
  <!ELEMENT parttree (part*)>
  <!ELEMENT part (part*)>
  <!ATTLIST part
      partid CDATA #REQUIRED
      name   CDATA #REQUIRED>]>
```

(1) Transformation specification:

$$(\text{START},/\texttt{partlist}) \rightarrow \texttt{parttree(MAIN\_PART(.))}$$
$$(\text{MAIN\_PART},\texttt{part[not(@partof)]}) \rightarrow \texttt{part(@partid,@name,SUB\_PART(.))}$$
$$(\text{SUB\_PART},(\$v_1:\texttt{@partid},$$
$$\$v_2:\texttt{../part[@partof=}\$v_1\texttt{]})) \rightarrow \texttt{part(}\$v_2\texttt{/@partid,}\$v_2\texttt{/@name,}$$
$$\texttt{SUB\_PART(}\$v_2\texttt{))}$$

(2) Inverse transformation specification:

$$(\text{START},/\texttt{parttree}) \rightarrow \texttt{partlist(MAIN\_PART(.),SUB\_PART(.))}$$
$$(\text{MAIN\_PART},\texttt{part}) \rightarrow \texttt{part(@id,@name)}$$
$$(\text{SUB\_PART},\texttt{part//part}) \rightarrow \texttt{part(@id,@name,@partof(../@id))}$$

□

The enrich the expression power of transformation, we will use a *filtering of a set of contexts*. We explain it by the following example.

Example 4. (Context filtering) Let us assume that we want to set a filter on a contexts using the position of a context node. For example, the transformation (1) defined in Example 1 would have the form:

$$(\text{START, /suppliers}) \rightarrow \texttt{parts(PART(.))}$$
$$(\text{PART, supplier/part[position()} \leq 2]) \rightarrow \texttt{part(PNAME(.[\$currpos != 2]))}$$
$$(\text{PNAME,.)} \rightarrow \texttt{@pname(text())}$$

Note that in **PART** rule we want to ignore the second context which is passed to the right-hand side of the rule. As we have seen, in our example we have three contexts determined by the context set $(4,6,12)$ – so, the evaluation in the context $\langle(4,6,12),6\rangle$ must be ignored. □

We assume that an XPath expression can use the following context variables:

- $curr$, denoting the current context node – the same as the dot (.);
- $currpos$, denoting the position of the context node in a context set;
- $size$, denoting a size (number of elements) of a context set.

3   Translation from XDTrans to XSLT

The following two algorithms transform a specification made in XDTrans into an XSLT program which carries out transformation on document instances. In general, there are many possible XSLT programs that can perform a given transformation. This method can be applied only to transformations over one document because joining of many documents is not supported by XSLT.

Algorithm 1 defines translation for the head of a rule and uses Algorithm 2 to translate the bode of a rule. As the result, an XSLT program (*stylesheet*) is obtained.

Algorithm 1 *(generating XSLT templates).*
Input: a specification rule $r \in \mathcal{R}$
Output: XSLT template $\Lambda(r)$
$\Lambda(r) = $ **case** r **of**
   $(\text{START},E) \to \tau$:

        \<xsl:template name="START" match="/">
        \<xsl:for-each select="E">
         $\rho(\tau)$
        \</xsl:for-each>
        \</xsl:template>

   $(C, E) \to \tau$:

        \<xsl:template name="C"
        \<xsl:param name="curr"> 1 \</xsl:param>
        \<xsl:param name="currpos"> 2 \</xsl:param>
        \<xsl:param name="size"> 3 \</xsl:param>
        \<xsl:for-each select="$curr/$E$">
         $\rho(\tau)$
        \</xsl:for-each>
        \</xsl:template>

   $(C, (\$v_1 : E_1, ..., \$v_n : E_n)) \to \tau$:

        \<xsl:template name="C"
        \<xsl:param name="curr"> 1 \</xsl:param>
        \<xsl:param name="currpos"> 2 \</xsl:param>
        \<xsl:param name="size"> 3 \</xsl:param>
        \<xsl:for-each select="$curr/$E_1$">
         \<xsl:variable name="v_1" select="." />
         ...
         \<xsl:for-each select="$curr/$E_n$">
          \<xsl:variable name="v_n" select="." />
          $\rho(\tau)$
         \<xsl:for-each>
         ...
        \<xsl:for-each>
        \</xsl:template>
endcase

Algorithm 2 *(generating XSLT elements).*
Input: a non-terminal tree expression $\tau \in \mathcal{T}_{\Sigma,S}(\mathcal{C},\mathcal{P})$
Output: XSLT element $\rho(\tau)$
$\rho(\tau) = $ **case** τ **of**

        s : <xsl:text>
             s
        </xsl:text>
     E : <xsl:for-each select="E"/>
        <xsl:copy-of select="."/>
        </xsl:for-each>
  $a(s)$: <xsl:attribute name="a">
          s
        </xsl:attribute>
  $a(E)$: <xsl:attribute name="a">
        <xsl:value-of select="E"/>
        </xsl:attribute>
  $C(E)$: <xsl:for-each select="E"/>
        <xsl:call-template name="C">
         <xsl:with-param name="curr" select="."/>
         <xsl:with-param name="currpos" select="position()"/>
         <xsl:with-param name="size" select="last()"/>
        </xsl:call-template>
        </xsl:for-each>
$e(\tau_1, ..., \tau_n)$: <xsl:element name="e">
        $\rho(\tau_1)$ ... $\rho(\tau_n)$
        </xsl:element>
endcase

Example 5. Application of Algorithm 1 (and Algorithm 2) to the transformation specification from Example 3(1), produces the XSLT script listed in Fig. 8.

4   Conclusions

In the paper we proposed a method and a high-level language, XDTrans, devoted to high-level specification for XML data transformation. The language is both descriptive and expressive, and is based on ideas rooted in tree automata [16]. From the user point of view, the specification can be perceived as a refinement process in which properties of constructed output document are systematically specified and refined. The method supports the user's intuition for defining trees according to the top-down way of thinking. A program in XDTrans consists of a set of rules (possibly recursive). Each rule defines a *concept* (i.e. a non-terminal symbol) included in the head of the rule, which is either an initial concept or occurs in leaves of the current state of a constructed tree. The rule specifies how the concept should be replaced. Finally, a terminal tree (without occurrences of any concept) should be obtained.

```
<xsl:template name="START" match="/">
<xsl:for-each select="/partlist">
<xsl:element name="parttree">
<xsl:for-each select=".">
  <xsl:call-template name="MAIN_PART">
  <xsl:with-param name="curr" select="."/>
  </xsl:call-template>
</xsl:for-each>
</xsl:element>
</xsl:for-each>
</xsl:template>

<xsl:template name="MAIN_PART">
<xsl:param name="curr">1</xsl:param>
<xsl:for-each select="$curr/part[not(@partof)]">
<xsl:element name="part">
  <xsl:for-each select="@partid">
  <xsl:copy-of select="."/>
  </xsl:for-each>
  <xsl:for-each select="@name">
  <xsl:copy-of select="."/>
  </xsl:for-each>
  <xsl:for-each select=".">
  <xsl:call-template name="SUB_PART">
  <xsl:with-param name="curr" select="."/>
  </xsl:call-template>
  </xsl:for-each>
```

```
</xsl:element>
</xsl:for-each>
</xsl:template>

<xsl:template name="SUB_PART">
<xsl:param name="curr">1</xsl:param>
<xsl:for-each select="$curr/@partid">
<xsl:variable name="v1" select="."/>
<xsl:for-each
     select="$curr/../part[@partof=$v1]">
  <xsl:variable name="v2" select="."/>
  <xsl:element name="part">
  <xsl:for-each select="$v2/@partid">
  <xsl:copy-of select="."/>
  </xsl:for-each>
  <xsl:for-each select="$v2/@name">
  <xsl:copy-of select="."/>
  </xsl:for-each>
  <xsl:for-each select="$v2">
  <xsl:call-template name="SUB_PART">
  <xsl:with-param name="curr" select="."/>
  </xsl:call-template>
  </xsl:for-each>
  </xsl:element>
</xsl:for-each>
</xsl:for-each>
</xsl:template>
```

Fig. 8. XSLT program generated for transformation specification in Example 3(1)

The semantics defined for XDTrans rules provides a way for implementation in any repository storing XML data. An algorithm doing this task must be able to process XPath expressions in such repositories. In particular, in [6] and [13] we discussed this problem when the repository is a relational database system. In this paper we show that a broad class of XDTrans specifications, except from those which join different documents, can be translated into XSLT programs which carry out the expected transformation over the standard representation of XML data. Since our specification is independent of the way in which XML data are represented, it could be also used to integrate heterogeneous data specifying appropriate transformations over them.

References

1. XSL Transformations (XSLT) 2.0. W3C Working Draft. www.w3.org/TR/xslt20 (2002)
2. XQuery 1.0: An XML Query Language. W3C Working Draft. www.w3.org/TR/ xquery (2002)
3. Tang, X., Tompa, F.W.: Specifying transformations for structured documents. In Mecca, G., Simeon, J., eds.: Proc. of the 4th International Workshop on the Web and Databases, WebDB 2001. (2001) 67–72
4. Kuikka, E., Leinonen, P., Penttonen, M.: Towards automating of document structure transformations. In: Proc. of ACM Symposium on Document Engineering 2002 DocEng'02, ACM Press (2002) 103–110
5. Krishnamurthi, S., Gray, K., Graunke, P.: Transformation-by-example for XML. 2nd Int. Workshop of Practical Aspects of Declarative Languages PADL'00, Lecture Notes in Computer Science **1753** (2000) 249–262

6. Pankowski, T.: Transformation of XML data using an unranked tree transducer, In: E-Commerce and Web Technologies, 4th International Conference, EC-Web 2003. Lecture Notes in Computer Science **2738** (2003) 259–269
7. Pankowski, T.: Specifying transformations for XML data. In: Proceedings of the Pre-Conference Workshop of VLDB 2003, Emerging Database Research in East Europe. (2003) 86–90
8. XQuery 1.0 and XPath 2.0 Data Model. W3C Working Draft. www.w3.org/TR/query-datamodel (2002)
9. XML Path Language (XPath) 2.0, W3C Working Draft: (2002) www.w3.org/TR/xpath20.
10. Buneman, P., Fernandez, M., Suciu, D.: UnQL: A query language and algebra for semistructured data based on structural recursion. VLDB Journal **9** (2000) 76–110
11. Bonifati, A., Ceri, S.: Comparative analysis of five XML query languages. SIGMOD Record **29** (2000) 68–79
12. Pankowski, T.: XML-SQL: An XML query language based on SQL and path tables, In: XML-Based Data Management and Multimedia Engineering - EDBT 2002 Workshops. Lecture Notes in Computer Science **2490** (2002) 184–209
13. Pankowski, T.: Processing XPath expressions in relational databases, In: Theory and Practice of Computer Science, SOFSEM 2004. Lecture Notes in Computer Science **2932** (2004) 265–276
14. Gottlob, G., Koch, C., Pichler, R.: Efficient algorithms for processing XPath queries. In: Proc. of the 28th International Conference on Very Large Data Bases, VLDB 2002, Hong Kong, China. (2002) 95–106
15. XML Query Use Cases W3C Working Draft. www.w3.org/TR/xquery-use-cases/ (2003)
16. Martens, W., Neven, F.: Typecheking top-down uniform unranked tree transducers. In: Database Theory - ICDT 2003, 9th International Conference. Lecture Notes in Computer Science **2572** (2003) 64–78

Implementing a Query Language for Context-Dependent Semistructured Data

Yannis Stavrakas, Kostis Pristouris, Antonis Efandis, and Timos Sellis

National Technical University of Athens, 15773 Athens, Greece
{ys,timos}@dblab.ntua.gr
{kprist,aefan}@freemail.gr

Abstract. In today's global environment, the structure and presentation of information may depend on the underlying *context* of the user. To address this issue, in previous work we have proposed *multidimensional semistructured data* (*MSSD*), where an information entity can have alternative variants, or *facets*, each holding under some *world*, and *MOEM*, a data model suitable for representing MSSD. In this paper we briefly present *MQL*, a query language for MSSD that supports *context-driven queries*, and we attempt to motivate the direct use of context in data models and query languages by comparing MOEM and MQL with equivalent, context-unaware forms of representing and querying information. Specifically, we implemented an evaluation process for MQL during which MQL queries are translated to equivalent Lorel queries, and MOEM databases are transformed to corresponding OEM databases. The comparison between the two query languages and data models demonstrates the benefits of treating context as first-class citizen. We illustrate this query translation process using a *cross-world* MQL query, which has no direct counterpart in context-unaware query languages and data models.

1 Introduction

The Web posed a number of new problems to the management of data, and the need for metadata at a semantic level was soon realized [9]. One such problem is that, while in traditional databases and information systems the number of users is more or less known and their background is to a great extent homogeneous, Web users do not share the same background and do not apply the same conventions when interpreting data. Such users can have different perspectives of the same entities, a situation that should be taken into account by Web data models and query languages. A related issue is that information providers often need to manage different variations of essentially the same information, which are targeted to different consumer groups.

Those problems call for a way to represent and query information entities that manifest different facets, whose contents can vary in structure and value. As a simple example imagine a product (car, laptop computer, etc.) whose specification changes according to the country it is being exported. Or a Web page that is to be displayed on devices with different capabilities, like mobile phones, PDAs, and personal computers. Another example is a report that must be represented at various degrees of detail and in various languages.

A. Benczúr, J. Demetrovics, G. Gottlob (Eds.): ADBIS 2004, LNCS 3255, pp. 173–188, 2004.

In previous work we proposed *multidimensional semistructured data* (*MSSD*) [2,14,16], which are semistructured data [3] that present different *facets* under different *contexts*. We argued [4] that Web data should be able to adapt to different *contexts*, and that this capability should be managed in a uniform way at the level of database and information systems. Context-aware data models and query languages can be applied on a variety of cases and domains; in [6,7,15] we showed how they can be used to represent and query histories of semistructured databases that evolve over time.

Context has been used in diverse areas of computer science as a tool for reasoning with viewpoints and background beliefs, and as an abstraction mechanism for dealing with complexity, heterogeneity, and partial knowledge. A formal framework for reasoning upon a subset of a global knowledge base can be found in [17], while examples of how context can be used for partitioning an information base into manageable fragments of related objects can be found in [8,13]. Our perception of context has also been used in *OMSwe*, a web-publishing platform described in [1,12]. OMSwe is based on an Object DBMS, which has been extended to support a flexible, domain-independent model for information delivery where context plays a pivotal role.

In this paper, we give a short overview of *Multidimensional Query Language* (*MQL*) [4,7] that treats context as first-class citizen and can express *context-driven queries*, in which context is important for selecting the right data. MQL is based on key concepts of Lorel [5], and its data model is *Multidimensional OEM* (*MOEM*) [2], an extension of OEM [3] suitable for MSSD. We present an evaluation process for MQL queries that we have implemented in a prototype system. As part of this evaluation process, MQL queries are translated to "equivalent" Lorel queries, and MOEM databases are transformed to corresponding OEM databases. Our purpose is to intuitively compare the two query languages and data models: although OEM and Lorel are not aware of the notion of context, they are in principle capable of handling context-dependent information encoded in a graph. Through this comparison, we demonstrate the benefits of directly supporting context as first-class citizen: MQL and MOEM are much more elegant and expressive when context is involved, while they become as simple as Lorel and OEM when context is not an issue. The query translation process is illustrated using a *cross-world* MQL query. Cross-world queries relate facets of information that hold under different worlds, and have no counterpart in context-unaware query languages and data models.

The paper is structured as follows. Section 2 reviews preliminary material on MSSD. Section 3 introduces MQL. Section 4 presents in detail the MQL evaluation process: the transformation of MOEM to OEM is specified first, and then the translation of MQL to Lorel is explained. Finally, Section 5 summarizes the conclusions.

2 Multidimensional Semistructured Data

The main difference between conventional and multidimensional semistructured data is the introduction of *context specifiers*. Context specifiers are syntactic constructs that are used to qualify pieces of semistructured data and specify sets of *worlds* under which those pieces hold. In this way, it is possible to have variants of the same information entity, each holding under a different set of worlds. An information entity that encompasses a number of variants is called *multidimensional entity*, and its variants are called *facets* of the entity. Each facet is associated with a context that defines the conditions under which the facet becomes a *holding facet* of the multidimensional entity.

2.1 Dimensions and Worlds

The notion of *world* is fundamental in MSSD. A world is specified using parameters called *dimensions*, and represents an environment under which data obtain a substance. The notion of world is defined [2] with respect to a set of dimensions **D** and requires that every dimension in **D** be assigned a single value.

In MSSD, sets of worlds are represented by *context specifiers* (or simply *contexts*), which are constraints on dimension values. The use of dimensions for representing worlds is shown through the following context specifiers:

(a)   [time=07:45]
(b)   [language=greek, detail in {low,medium}]
(c)   [season in {fall,spring}, daytime=noon
           a. | season=summer]

Context specifier (a) represents the worlds for which the dimension time has the value 07:45, while (b) represents the worlds for which language is greek and detail is either low or medium. Context specifier (c) is more complex, and represents the worlds where season is either fall or spring and daytime is noon, together with the worlds where season is summer. For a set of (*dimension, value*) pairs to represent a world with respect to a set of dimensions **D**, it must contain exactly one pair for each dimension in **D**. Therefore, if **D** = {language, detail} with domains $V_{language}$ = {english, greek} and V_{detail} = {low, medium, high}, then {(language, greek), (detail, low)} is one of the six possible worlds with respect to **D**. This world is represented by context specifier (b), together with the world {(language, greek), (detail, medium)}. It is not necessary for a context specifier to contain values for every dimension in **D**. Omitting a dimension implies that its value may range over the whole domain.

The context specifier [ ] is a *universal context* and represents the set of all possible worlds with respect to any set of dimensions **D**, while the context specifier [-] is an *empty context* and represents the empty set of worlds with respect to any set of dimensions **D**. In [2,4] we have defined operations on context specifiers, such as *context intersection* and *context union* that correspond to the conventional set operations of intersection and union on the related sets of worlds. We have also defined how a context specifier can be transformed to the set of worlds it represents with respect to a set of dimensions **D**. Moreover, *context equality* and *context subset* allow to compare contexts based on their respective set of worlds.

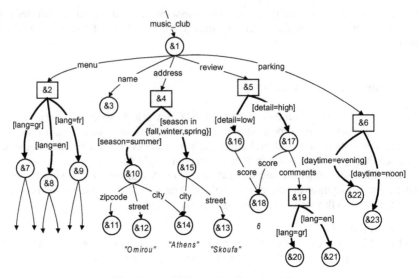

Fig. 1. A multidimensional music-club

2.2 Multidimensional OEM

Multidimensional Data Graph [4] is an extension of *Object Exchange Model* (OEM) [3,5], suitable for representing multidimensional semistructured data. Multidimensional Data Graph extends OEM with two new basic elements:

- *Multidimensional nodes* represent multidimensional entities, and are used to group together nodes that constitute facets of the entities. Graphically, multidimensional nodes have a rectangular shape to distinguish them from conventional circular nodes.
- *Context edges* are directed labeled edges that connect multidimensional nodes to their facets. The label of a context edge pointing to a facet, is a context specifier defining the set of worlds under which that facet holds. Context edges are drawn as thick lines, to distinguish them from conventional (thin-lined) OEM edges.

In Multidimensional Data Graph the conventional circular nodes of OEM are called *context nodes* and represent facets associated with some context. Conventional OEM edges (thin-lined) are called *entity edges* and define relationships between objects. All nodes are considered objects, and have unique *object identifiers* (*oids*). Context objects are divided into *complex objects* and *atomic objects*. Atomic objects have a value from one of the basic types, e.g. integer, real, strings, etc. A context edge cannot start from a context node, and an entity edge cannot start from a multidimensional node. Those two are the only constraints on the morphology of Multidimensional Data Graph.

As an example, consider the simple Multidimensional Data Graph in Figure 1, which represents context-dependent information about a music club. For simplicity, the graph is not fully developed and some of the atomic objects do not have values attached. The music_club with oid &1 operates on a different address during the summer than the rest of the year (in Athens it is usual for clubs to move south close to the sea in the summer period, and north towards the city center during the rest of the year). Except from having a different value, context objects can have a different structure, as is the case of &10 and &15 which are facets of the multidimensional object address with oid &4. The menu of the club is available in three languages, namely English, French and Greek. In addition, the club has a couple of alternative parking places, depending on the time of day as expressed by the dimension daytime. The music-club review has two facets: node &16 is the low detail facet containing only the review score with value 6, while the high detail facet &17 contains in addition review comments in two languages. In what follows we formally define Multidimensional Data Graph.

   Let CS be the set of all context specifiers, L be the set of all labels, and A be the set of all atomic values. A **Multidimensional Data Graph** G is a finite directed edge-labeled multigraph $G = (V_{mld}, V_{cxt}, E_{cxt}, E_{ett}, r, v)$, where:

1. The set of nodes V consists of **multidimensional nodes** and **context nodes**, $V = V_{mld} \cup V_{cxt}$. Context nodes are divided into **complex nodes** and **atomic nodes**, $V_{cxt} = V_c \cup V_a$.
2. The set of edges E consists of **context edges** and **entity edges**, $E = E_{cxt} \cup E_{ett}$, such that $E_{cxt} \subseteq (V_{mld} \times CS \times V)$ and $E_{ett} \subseteq (V_c \times L \times V)$.
3. $r \in V$ is the **root**, with the property that there exists a path from r to every other node in V.
4. v is a function that assigns values to nodes, such that: $v(x) = M$ if $x \in V_{mld}$, $v(x) = C$ if $x \in V_c$, and $v(x)=v'(x)$ if $x \in V_a$, where M and C are reserved values, and v' is a value function v': $V_a \to A$ which assigns values to atomic nodes.

   Two fundamental concepts related to Multidimensional Data Graphs are *explicit context* and *inherited context* [2,4]. The explicit context of a context edge is the context specifier assigned to that edge, while the explicit context of an entity edge is considered to be the universal context specifier [ ]. The explicit context can be considered as the "true" context only within the boundaries of a single multidimensional entity. When entities are connected together in a graph, the explicit context of an edge is not the "true" context, in the sense that it does not alone determine the worlds under which the destination node holds. The reason for this is that, when an entity e_2 is part of (pointed by through an edge) another entity e_1, then e_2 can have substance only under the worlds that e_1 has substance. This can be conceived as if the context under which e_1 holds is inherited to e_2. The context propagated in that way is combined with (constraint by) the explicit context of each edge to give the *inherited context* for that edge. The inherited context of a node is the union of the inherited contexts of incoming edges (the inherited context of the root is [ ]). As an example, node &18 in Figure 1 has inherited context [detail in {low, high}]. Worlds where detail is low are inherited through node &16, while worlds where detail is high are inherited through node &17.

   In Multidimensional Data Graph leaves are not restricted to atomic nodes, and can be complex or multidimensional nodes as well. This raises the question under which worlds does a path lead to a leaf that is an atomic node. Those worlds are given by *context coverage*, which is symmetric to inherited context, but propagates to the opposite direction: from the leaves up to the root of the graph. The context coverage of a node or an edge represents the worlds under which the node or edge has access to leaves that are atomic nodes. The context coverage of leaves that are atomic nodes is [], while the context coverage of leaves that are complex nodes or multidimensional nodes is [-]. The context coverage of node &19 in Figure 1 is [lang in {gr, en}] (all leaves in Figure 1 are considered atomic nodes).

For every node or edge, the context intersection of its inherited context and its context coverage gives the *inherited coverage* of that node or edge. The inherited coverage represents the worlds under which a node or edge may actually hold, as determined by constraints accumulated from both above and below. A related concept is *path inherited coverage*, which is given by the context intersection of the inherited coverages of all edges in a path, and represents the worlds under which a complete path holds.

A *context-deterministic* Multidimensional Data Graph is a Multidimensional Data Graph in which context nodes are accessible from a multidimensional node under mutually exclusive inherited coverages (hold under disjoint sets of worlds). Intuitively, context-determinism means that, under any specific world, at most one context node is accessible from a multidimensional node. A *Multidimensional OEM*, or *MOEM* for short, is a context-deterministic Multidimensional Data Graph whose every node and edge has a non-empty inherited coverage. In an MOEM all nodes and edges hold under at least one world, and all leaves are atomic nodes. The Multidimensional Data Graph in Figure 1 is an MOEM.

Given a world *w*, it is possible to *reduce* an MOEM *to a conventional OEM* graph holding under *w*, by eliminating nodes and edges whose inherited coverage does not contain *w*. A process that performs such a *reduction to OEM* is presented in [2]. In addition, given a set of worlds, it is possible to *partially reduce* an MOEM into a new MOEM, that encompasses exactly the OEM facets for the given set of worlds.

3 Multidimensional Query Language

Multidimensional Query Language (MQL) [4], is a query language designed especially for MOEM databases, and is essentially an extension of Lorel [5]. An important feature of MQL is *context path expressions*, which are path expressions qualified with context specifiers and *context variables*. Context path expressions take advantage of the fact that every Multidimensional Data Graph can be transformed to a *canonical form* [4,7], where every context node is child of solely multidimensional node(s), and vice-versa. The canonical form of the MOEM in Figure 1 contains an additional multidimensional node which is pointed by the entity edge labeled name, and whose only facet under every possible world (explicit context []) is the context node &3. It also contains similar multidimensional nodes for the context nodes &11, &12, &13, &14, &18, and &1 (the root of a graph in canonical form is always a multidimensional node). If a graph is in canonical form, every possible path is formed by a repeated succession of one context edge and one entity edge. Context path expressions are built around the canonical form, and therefore consist of a number of *entity parts* and *facet parts* succeeding one another. Entity parts follow a dot (.) and are matched against entity edges, while facet parts follow a double colon (::) and are matched against context edges:

```
[detail=high]music_club::[-].review::[-]   X
```

In this context path expression, `music_club` and `review` are entity parts, while the two empty context specifiers `[-]` are facets parts. A facet part matches a corresponding context edge, if it is subset of the explicit context of the edge, in other words, if every world it defines is covered by the explicit context of the edge. Consequently, the empty context `[-]` as a facet part matches any context edge. The context specifier `[detail=high]` is an *inherited coverage qualifier* and is matched against the *path inherited coverage* of a path. For a path to match an inherited coverage qualifier, it must hold under every world specified by the qualifier. An inherited coverage qualifier may precede any entity part or facet part in a context path expression. Facet parts can often be omitted, implying the empty context `[-]`. Therefore, the above context path expression can also be written as:

```
[detail=high]music_club.review   X
```

Evaluated on the graph of Figure 1, this context path expression causes the *context object variable* X to bind to node &17. Had we used a *multidimensional object variable*, denoted <X>, we would have caused it to bind to the multidimensional node &5.

Consider the following MQL query:

```
select name: P, winter_street: Y
from music_club X,
 X.[season=winter]address.street Y,
 X.[season=summer]address.street Z,
 X.name P
where Z="Omirou"
```

This is a *cross-world* query, which returns the name and the street address in winter of a music club whose summer address is known. Evaluated on the database of Figure 1, variable P binds to node &3 and Y binds to &13. The result of an MQL query is always a Multidimensional Data Graph in the form of an *mssd-expression* [2].

4 Evaluating MQL Queries with LORE

We have implemented MQL on top of LORE [10], analogously to Lorel, which has been implemented on top of an object database [5]. We have chosen LORE as a basis for implementing MQL, because our purpose was to see: (a) how an MQL query compares with an "equivalent" Lorel query, and (b) how an MOEM can be expressed through a conventional OEM.

The overall architecture is shown in Figure 2. The process we want to implement is depicted as a dashed line, which starts from an MQL query, passes through an MOEM database, and concludes with a Multidimensional Data Graph that is the result of the query.

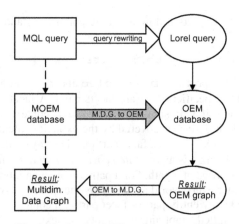

Fig. 2. Evaluating MQL queries using LORE

The process that actually takes place is depicted as a normal line, and shows a Lorel query evaluated on an OEM database that returns an OEM graph as a result. This line together with the ellipse-shaped boxes is part of LORE, which is controlled by our system through the programming interface that it provides.

The main issue is to define a transformation T from Multidimensional Data Graphs M to OEMs O = T(M), with the following properties:

- The reverse transformation T^{-1} exists, and if O is given then $M = T^{-1}(O)$ can be recovered.
- It is possible to translate an MQL query q_M to an "equivalent" Lorel query q_L.

By equivalent we mean that if q_M evaluated on M returns M′ and q_L evaluated on O returns O′, then T(M′) = O′. Then, the answer to q_M can be computed by evaluating q_L on T(M), and by applying the reverse transformation $T^{-1}(O′)$ to the results of q_L.

Those transformations and the MQL query translation are depicted in Figure 2 as thick horizontal arrows. The system, among other things, implements those arrows and performs the following key steps:

1. Converts an MOEM database to an OEM database, which becomes the database of LORE.
2. Translates an MQL query to a Lorel query, which is passed over to LORE for evaluation on the OEM database.
3. Gets the results from LORE, and converts them from OEM back to Multidimensional Data Graph.

Step 1 initializes the database and corresponds to the gray horizontal arrow in the middle of Figure 2, while steps 2 and 3 are carried out every time an MQL query is submitted. The Multidimensional Data Graph of step 3 is the result of the MQL query of step 2 evaluated on the MOEM database of step 1.

In the following sections, we specify the three key steps listed above. The actual application that implements them is part of a more comprehensive platform [11] for MSSD, and is presented in Section 4.4.

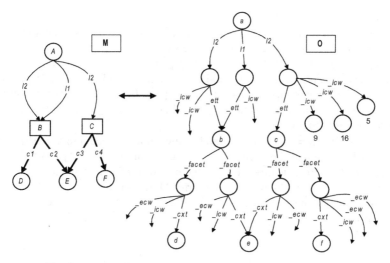

Fig. 3. Representing Multidimensional Data Graph using OEM

4.1   Transforming MOEM Databases to OEM

In order to transform MOEM to OEM, we must use special OEM structures to represent MOEM elements that do not have a counterpart in OEM, namely context edges and multidimensional nodes: context edges can be represented by OEM edges that have some special label, while multidimensional nodes correspond to OEM nodes from which these special edges depart. Moreover, we must encode context in OEM in a way Lorel can understand and handle. Contexts that must be encoded include explicit contexts and inherited coverages of edges.

Figure 3 gives an intuition of the transformation. It presents a simple Multidimensional Data Graph M together with its OEM counterpart O. Nodes with a capital letter in M correspond to nodes with the respective lowercase letter in O. Observe that for each edge in M an additional node exists in O, splitting the edge in two OEM edges. The role of this node is to group the encoded context(s) for the corresponding Multidimensional Data Graph edge. A number of reserved labels with special meaning are used. All reserved labels start with an underscore, and they are: _ett, _facet, _cxt, _icw, and _ecw. An entity edge is represented by an edge with the same label and a following edge labeled _ett. A context edge is represented by an edge labeled _facet and a following edge labeled _cxt. Explicit contexts and inherited coverages of edges are converted to the worlds they represent, and all possible worlds are mapped to integers. Edges that are labeled _icw point to the enumerated worlds (integer-valued nodes) that belong to inherited coverages, while edges labeled _ecw point to the enumerated worlds that belong to explicit contexts.

The actual transformation process of a Multidimensional Data Graph M = (V_{mld}, V_{cxt}, E_{cxt}, E_{ett}, r, v) to an OEM O is given below.

O ← MDGToOEM (M) is:

1. For every world, add a new atomic node w to V_{cxt} that corresponds to that world, having as value the integer mapped to the world.
2. Move all (multidimensional) nodes from V_{mld} to V_{cxt} (complex nodes).
3. For every edge h = (q, l, p) ∈ E_{ett} add a new complex node u to V_{cxt}. Then, replace h with the new edges (q, l, u) and (u, _ett, p) in E_{ett}. Next, for every world represented by the inherited coverage of h, add an edge (u, _icw, w) to E_{ett}, where w corresponds to that world.
4. For every edge h = (q, c, p) ∈ E_{cxt} add a new complex node u to V_{cxt}. Then, remove h from E_{cxt}, and add the edges (q, _facet, u) and (u, _cxt, p) to E_{ett}. Next, for every world represented by the inherited coverage of h, add an edge (u, _icw, w) to E_{ett}, where w corresponds to that world. Moreover, for every world represented by the explicit context of h, add an edge (u, _ecw, w) to E_{ett}, where w corresponds to that world.
5. Return O = (V_{cxt}, E_{ett}, r, v).

4.2 Translating MQL Queries to Lorel

MQL queries can be translated to "equivalent" Lorel queries, which are evaluated on the OEM given by the transformation defined in the previous section. For this translation to work, the MOEM database *must be in canonical form* when the transformation to OEM takes place. This allows context path expressions, which are built around the canonical form, to be translated to "equivalent" Lorel path expressions.

In this section we specify such a translation that supports the major features of MQL. We have not addressed some features of MQL that seemed difficult or impossible to translate, like regular expressions in context path expressions (*general context path expressions* [4]).

Converting Context Path Expressions to Path Expressions. To facilitate the comprehension of translated Lorel queries, we use E-HUB as identifier for nodes from which a _ett edge departs, MLD for nodes from which a _facet edge departs, and C-HUB for nodes from which a _cxt edge departs. In addition, we use w1, w2, ... to denote the integers that have been mapped to worlds.

We start with a very simple MQL from clause:

```
from X.[c]label Y
```

We assume [c] is a context specifier representing the worlds that correspond to w_4, w_7, and w_9. As shown in [4], [c] is implied throughout the path it qualifies, and the clause can be written as:

```
from X.[c]label::[c][-] Y
```

This from clause can also be written in MQL using a multidimensional object variable <V> as:

```
from X.[c]label <V>,
     <V>::[c][-] Y
```

The equivalent Lorel expression is:

```
from X.label E-HUB, E-HUB._ett MLD,
     MLD._facet C-HUB, C-HUB._cxt Y
where       E-HUB._icw{W4} = w₄
       and E-HUB._icw{W7} = w₇
       and E-HUB._icw{W9} = w₉
       and C-HUB._icw{W4} = w₄
       and C-HUB._icw{W7} = w₇
       and C-HUB._icw{W9} = w₉
```

The `where` clause states that the inherited coverages of the two MOEM edges must contain all the worlds specified by `[c]`. Observe the use of the variables $W4$, $W7$, and $W9$, which declare that it is *not* the same node that must be equal to w_4, to w_7, and to w_9 (otherwise the condition would always be false).

We now use the MQL query example of Section 3, and apply the same process to its `from` clause. For brevity, we use `[c1]` to denote the context specifier `[season=winter]`, and `[c2]` to denote `[season=summer]`. The MQL query can now be written as:

```
select name: P, winter_street: Y
from [-]music_club <V1>, <V1>::[-][-] X,
  X.[c1]address <V2>, <V2>::[c1][-] V3,
  V3.[c1]street <V4>, <V4>::[c1][-] Y,
  X.[c2]address <V5>, <V5>::[c2][-] V6,
  V6.[c2]street <V7>, <V7>::[c2][-] Z,
  X.[-]name <V8>, <V8>::[-][-] P
where Z="Omirou"
```

The equivalent Lorel query is:

```
select name: P, winter_street: Y
from
    music_club E-HUB1, E-HUB1._ett V1,
    V1._facet C-HUB1, C-HUB1._cxt X,
    X.address E-HUB2, E-HUB2._ett V2,
    V2._facet C-HUB2, C-HUB2._cxt V3,
    V3.street E-HUB3, E-HUB3._ett V4,
    V4._facet C-HUB3, C-HUB3._cxt Y,
    X.address E-HUB4, E-HUB4._ett V5,
    V5._facet C-HUB4, C-HUB4._cxt V6,
    V6.street E-HUB5, E-HUB5._ett V7,
    V7._facet C-HUB5, C-HUB5._cxt Z,
    X.name E-HUB6, E-HUB6._ett V8,
    V8._facet C-HUB6, C-HUB6._cxt P
where
    Z="Omirou"
    and predicate(E-HUB2) and predicate(C-HUB2)
    and predicate(E-HUB3) and predicate(C-HUB3)
    and predicate(E-HUB4) and predicate(C-HUB4)
    and predicate(E-HUB5) and predicate(C-HUB5)
```

The expressions *predicate*(VAR) ensure that the corresponding edges have a proper inherited coverage. Therefore, each expression *predicate*(VAR) must be replaced by

```
        VAR._icw{W1} = w₁
and     VAR._icw{W2} = w₂
and     VAR._icw{W3} = w₃
and     ...
```

where w_1, w_2, w_3, ... are the integers that correspond to worlds of the respective inherited coverage qualifier: for E–HUB2, C–HUB2, E–HUB3, and C–HUB3 the inherited coverage qualifier is [season=winter], while for E–HUB4, C–HUB4, E–HUB5, and C–HUB5 the inherited coverage qualifier is [season=summer]. The edges that correspond to variables E–HUB1, C–HUB1, E–HUB6, and C–HUB6 can have any inherited coverage because their implied inherited coverage qualifier is the empty context [-], thus they are not included in where.

Using the above framework, it is straightforward to translate MQL queries that contain multidimensional object variables. Actually, the analytical form of our MQL query example contains the multidimensional object variables <V1>, <V2>, <V4>, <V5>, <V7>, and <V8>, which correspond to the variables V1, V2, V4, V5, V7, and V8 of the equivalent Lorel query. In addition, it is easy to accommodate explicit context qualifiers. A facet part :: [c_I][c_E] will result in a predicate of the form:

```
        VAR._icw{W1} = w₁
and     VAR._icw{W2} = w₂
and     VAR._icw{W3} = w₃
and     ...
and     VAR._ecw{W2} = w₂
and     VAR._ecw{W6} = w₆
and     ...
```

where w_1, w_2, w_3, ... correspond to the worlds of the inherited coverage qualifier [c_I], and w_2, w_6, ... correspond to the worlds of the explicit context qualifier [c_E].

Context Variables and "within" Clause. MQL uses an additional within clause to express conditions on contexts. Consider the MQL query:

```
select comments: Y
from music_club.[X]review.comments Y
within [X] * [detail=high] <= [lang=gr]
```

The *context variable* [X] binds to the path inherited coverage of the path

```
review::[-].comments::[-]
```

and the condition in within requires that the context intersection (denoted *) between this path inherited coverage and [detail=high] be context subset (denoted <=) of [lang=gr]. Consequently, this condition ensures that the query returns comments facets in Greek in high detail (node &20 in Figure 1). Note that there are more intuitive ways to express the same query in MQL, but with less demonstrative value.

The first step is to express context specifiers as Lorel queries. Suppose that [detail=high] represents the worlds that correspond to the integers w_1, w_2, and w_3. The following Lorel query evaluates to the respective nodes:

```
select W
from music_club.#._icw W
where W=w₁ or W=w₂ or W=w₃
```

Lets use $L_{[detail=high]}$ to refer to this query, and $L_{[lang=gr]}$ to refer to an analogous Lorel query that expresses [lang=gr]. In addition, we use the symbol L_{CXT_VAR} to refer to a Lorel query expressing the path inherited coverage bound to the context variable [X]. This Lorel query is:

```
E-HUB2._icw intersect C-HUB2._icw
intersect
E-HUB3._icw intersect C-HUB3._icw
```

The query evaluates to the "worlds" under which all edges of the path hold. Now that we have expressed all contexts as queries evaluating to sets of nodes that represent worlds, we can express context subset as a relation between the queries. Assuming that *query1* expresses a context [c1] and *query2* a context [c2], the condition [c1] <= [c2] ([c1] context subset of [c2]) is implemented by the predicate:

```
for all LEFT in (query1):
    exists RIGHT in (query2): LEFT = RIGHT
```

where LEFT and RIGHT are Lorel variables that range over the "worlds" to the left and to the right side of the symbol <=, respectively.

The MQL query can now be translated to the following Lorel query:

```
select comments: Y
from
    music_club E-HUB1, E-HUB1._ett V1,
    V1._facet C-HUB1, C-HUB1._cxt V2,
    V2.review E-HUB2, E-HUB2._ett V3,
    V3._facet C-HUB2, C-HUB2._cxt V4,
    V4.comments E-HUB3, E-HUB3._ett V5,
    V5._facet C-HUB3, C-HUB3._cxt Y
where
    for all LEFT in
    (L_CXT_VAR intersect L_[detail=high]):
        exists RIGHT in (L_[lang=gr]):
            LEFT = RIGHT
```

By combining in similar ways Lorel queries that express sets of worlds, it is straightforward to implement any context condition in the within clause.

4.3 Transforming OEM Results to M.D.G.

LORE returns the result of a Lorel query as an OEM graph. As stated, this OEM graph can be transformed to a Multidimensional Data Graph, which is the result of the original MQL query.

The process that transforms an OEM $O = (V, E, r, v)$ to a Multidimensional Data Graph M is given below.

M ← OEMToMDG (O) is:

1. Represent O as a Multidimensional Data Graph $M = (V_{mld}, V_{cxt}, E_{cxt}, E_{ett}, r, v)$, where $V_{ett} = V$, $E_{ett} = E$, and V_{mld}, E_{cxt} are empty sets.
2. For every edge $h = (q, l, u) \in E_{ett}$ where l is not a reserved label, remove u from V_{cxt}. Then remove h and $(u, \_ett, p)$ from E_{ett}, and add the edge (q, l, p) to E_{ett}. Remove all edges $(u, \_icw, w)$ from E_{ett}.
3. For every edge $h = (q, \_facet, u) \in E_{ett}$, move q from V_{cxt} to V_{mld} (if not already moved), and remove u from V_{cxt}. For all nodes w, where $(u, \_ecw, w) \in E_{ett}$, apply context union to the corresponding worlds to get a context specifier c. Then remove h and $(u, \_cxt, p)$ from E_{ett}, and add the edge (q, c, p) to E_{cxt}. Remove all edges $(u, \_ecw, w)$ and $(u, \_icw, w)$ from E_{ett}.
4. Remove from V_{cxt} all nodes that correspond to worlds (unreachable from the root at this time).
5. Return $M = (V_{mld}, V_{cxt}, E_{cxt}, E_{ett}, r, v)$.

Notice that, in order to reconstruct context specifiers, step 3 needs the *same* mapping of worlds to integers that was initially used while transforming the MOEM database to OEM.

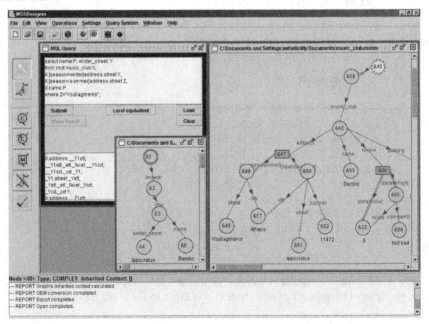

Fig. 4. Evaluating an MQL query and displaying the results in *MSSDesigner*

4.4 Prototype Implementation

Our prototype system is implemented in Java and interfaces with LORE, which is used as a back-end. The system is initialized with an MOEM database, receives MQL queries, and returns Multidimensional Data Graphs as results. The system actually constitutes the Query Subsystem of *MSSDesigner* [11], a more general platform for managing multidimensional semistructured data, and is shown in Figure 4. It relies on this platform to perform basic functions, like carrying out context operations and calculating the inherited coverage of MOEMs.

5 Conclusions

In this paper we demonstrated some of the benefits of treating context as first-class citizens in Web data models and query languages. We briefly introduced MQL, a context-aware query language for semistructured data, and discussed in detail an evaluation process for MQL queries. We defined a transformation from MOEM graphs to corresponding OEM graphs and vice-versa, and specified how MQL queries can be translated to equivalent Lorel queries. We presented a prototype system that implements the above, and uses LORE to evaluate MQL queries. This evaluation process gave an opportunity for an intuitive comparison between the two query languages and data models: MQL and MOEM are much more elegant and expressive when context is involved, while they become as simple as Lorel and OEM when context is not an issue. Moreover, MQL and MOEM directly support cross-world queries, which have no counterpart in context-unaware query languages.

References

1. M. C. Norrie, and A. Palinginis. From State to Structure: an XML Web Publishing Framework. In the *15th International Conference on Advanced Information Systems Engineering (CAiSE'03)*, Austria, June 2003.
2. Yannis Stavrakas, and Manolis Gergatsoulis. Multidimensional Semistructured Data: Representing Context-Dependent Information on the Web. In the *14th International Conference on Advanced Information Systems Engineering (CAiSE'02)*, Toronto, Canada, May 2002.
3. Dan Suciu. An Overview of Semistructured Data. *SIGACT News*, 29(4): 28-38, 1998.
4. Yannis Stavrakas. *Multidimensional Semistructured Data: Representing and Querying Context-Dependent Multifaceted Information on the Web*. PhD Thesis, Department of Electrical and Computer Engineering, National Technical University of Athens, Greece, June 2003.
5. S. Abiteboul, D. Quass, J. McHugh, J. Widom, and J. L. Wiener. The Lorel Query Language for Semistructured Data. *International Journal on Digital Libraries*, 1(1): 68-88, April 1997.
6. Y. Stavrakas, M. Gergatsoulis, C. Doulkeridis, and V. Zafeiris. Accommodating Changes in Semistructured Databases Using Multidimensional OEM. In the *6th Conference on Advances in Databases and Information Systems (ADBIS'02)*, Slovakia, September 2002.

7. Yannis Stavrakas, Manolis Gergatsoulis, Christos Doulkeridis, and Vassilis Zafeiris. Representing and Querying Histories of Semistructured Databases Using Multidimensional OEM. To appear in *Information Systems* journal.
8. John Mylopoulos, and Renate Motschnig-Pitrik. Partitioning Information Bases with Contexts. In the *3rd International Conference on Cooperative Information Systems (CoopIS'95)*, pages 44-55, Vienna, Austria, May 1995.
9. The World Wide Web Consortium (W3C). Resource Description Framework (RDF) Schema Specification, 1999. http://www.w3.org/ TR/PR-rdf-schema
10. J. McHugh, S. Abiteboul, R. Goldman, D. Quass, and J. Widom. LORE: A Database Management System for Semistructured Data. *SIGMOD Record*, 26(3): 54-66, September 1997.
11. Vassilis Zafeiris, Christos Doulkeridis, Yannis Stavrakas, and Manolis Gergatsoulis. An Infrastructure for Manipulating Multidimensional Semistructured Data. In the *1st Hellenic Data Management Symposium (HDMS'02)*, Athens, Greece, July 2002.
12. Moira C. Norrie, and Alexios Palinginis. Empowering Databases for Context-Dependent Information Delivery. *CAiSE'03 Workshop on Ubiquitous Mobile Information and Collaboration Systems (UMICS'03)*, Austria, June 2003.
13. Manos Theodorakis, Anastasia Analyti, Panos Constantopoulos, and Nikos Spyratos. Context in Information Bases. In the *3rd International Conference on Cooperative Information Systems (CoopIS'98)*, New York City, 1998.
14. Manolis Gergatsoulis, Yannis Stavrakas, and Dimitris Karteris. Incorporating Dimensions to XML and DTD. In the *12th Conference on Database and Expert Systems Applications (DEXA'01)*, Munich, Germany, September 2001.
15. Manolis Gergatsoulis, and Yannis Stavrakas. Representing Changes in XML Documents Using Dimensions. In *XML Database Symposium (XSym 2003)* in Conjunction with VLDB 2003, Berlin, Germany, September 2003.
16. M. Gergatsoulis, Y. Stavrakas, D. Karteris, A. Mouzaki, and D. Sterpis. A Web-based System for Handling Multidimensional Information through MXML. In *the 5th Conference on Advances in Databases and Information Systems (ADBIS 2001)*, Lithuania, 2001.
17. Chiara Ghidini, and Fausto Giunchiglia. Local Model Semantics, or contextual reasoning = locality + compatibility. *Artificial Intelligence* 127, pages 221 - 259, 2001.

Static Analysis of Structural Recursion in Semistructured Databases and Its Consequences

András Benczúr and Balázs Kósa

Department of Information Systems
Eötvös Loránd University Faculty of Science
Pázmány Péter sétány 1/C, Budapest, Hungary, H-1117
abenczur@ludens.elte.hu, balhal@cs.elte.hu

Abstract. Structural recursion is a graph traversing and restructuring operation in UnQL [7], [8], a query language for semistructured data. In this paper we consider satisfiability questions mainly in the presence of schema graphs [2], [9], which are used for describing the structure of semistructured data. We introduce a new kind of simulation between schema graphs, with which the relationships can be represented in more subtle ways. By means of operational graphs we also develop a new way for defining the semantics of structural recursions. Our results give us algorithms for checking whether a given query will satisfy the restrictions imposed by schema graphs and techniques with which these can be involved in queries. Query optimizing methods are also developed.

1 Introduction

In our days it is almost a banality to talk about the importance of semistructured [1] and XML [6] data. They are modelled with very similar structures, namely rooted, labeled, directed graphs, hence several questions of these researh fields can be discussed simultaneously [2]. However, there are also differences. Several query languages were developed for both structures: for instance Lorel [4], UnQL [7], [8] for semistructured data and XSL [11], XML-QL [12], XQuery [5] for XML, just to mention some. Each of them contains operations by means of which data graphs can be traversed and restructured. In our paper we pay attention to such an operation, the structural recursion. It was introduced in UnQL [7], [8]. It is related to top-down tree transducers [16], but it is more powerful than these because it can express joins and cartesian products [7]. Here we consider only structural recursions without conditions. Bunemann et al. have proven that they are closed under composition and offered powerful optimizations [7]. Dan Suciu showed their very advantageous characteristics in distributed systems [17]. In addition they form the core language of XSL [11], the first commercial XML query language. There is no doubt that structural recursions have their interests of their own and may become a useful tool on other fields of computer science.

The data model of UnQL uses edge labels. An example can be found in Figure 1. There is a simple syntax for textual representation of trees. Structured values (internal nodes) can be denoted as $\{l_1 : t_1, \ldots, l_n : t_n\}$, here l_i stands for

A. Benczúr, J. Demetrovics, G. Gottlob (Eds.): ADBIS 2004, LNCS 3255, pp. 189–203, 2004.

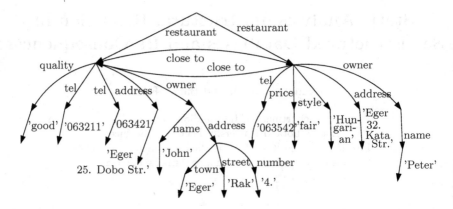

Fig. 1. An example of a data graph.

labels and t_i for other structured or atomic values. $\{\}$ denotes the empty graph, a graph consisting a node only. Note that $\{l_1: t_1, \ldots, l_n: t_n\}$ is a set of label/value (label/tree) pairs in contrast to other models, where to each node a unique object identifier is assigned. Thus the UnQL model, like the relational model, is "value based" [7]. Since sets of label/tree pairs are considered, trees can be constructed by means of three basic constructors: the union, $\cup$, the singleton set, $\{l: t\}$ and the empty graph, $\{\}$ [7].

We present UnQL through an example. We shall not enter into details, the interested reader should consult [7], [8].

```
Q:= select {result: {D: {owner: {name: C}} ∪
     {(select{address: E}
             where {D: {owner: {name: C}, address: E}} in db)}}}
     where {D: {owner: {name: C}}} in db.
```

The query accomplishes a group by operation, i.e., under an *owner* edge it inserts the owner's name and the set of the addresses of their restaurants. UnQL has a simple `select...where...` structure with pattern matching. Patterns are given in terms of regular path expressions. Nested queries and other possibilities can be used.

Semistructured data is often described as "schema-less" or "self-describing", since information, which is part of the schema in traditional databases, is intermingled with data [2]. However, even partial knowledge of the structure can help in improving storage, optimizing query evaluation etc. [2], hence various methods were developed for this purpose. One of them, which suits well the data model of UnQL, uses schema graphs and dual schema graphs [9]. The optimization of regular path expressions in the presence of schema graphs were discussed in [14]. Regular path expressions can be encoded as structural recursions [7]. One of our method is a generalization of a result of [14].

In the course of static analysis certain properties of queries given with their syntax is examined without running them. One possible question is that, for a given query q whether there exists an instance I s.t. $q(I)$ is not empty. In case of relational algebra the preceding problem is undecidable in general [3]. Hence it is also undecidable in the case of UnQL, because for tree data graphs encoding relational databases and queries mapping such tree data graphs to tree data graphs also encoding relational databases, the two languages have the same expressive power [7].

For answering this satisfiability question in case of structural recursions we shall present a new way for defining the semantics for them. Using this it will turn out that our problem can be answered easily in linear time.

Owing to its relation with query optimization mentioned in the first paragraph, we shall also examine the satisfiability question in that case, when the inputs and outputs of a query q are restricted by means of schema graphs and dual schema graphs respectively. We introduce a new kind of simulation between schema graphs to be able to represent more subtle relationships. Our algorithms answering these problems also give us methods for checking whether the result of a given query will satisfy the above restrictions and query rewriting techniques with which these can be involved in the query. We shall also present two optimization possibilities. One of them is an easy generalization of the result of [14] as it was already mentioned. The other one is different from it, but in the background we always use the same idea given by our semantics. If we set aside the time needed to check the satisfaction of a unary formula, then all algorithms work in polinomial time.

The usefulness and strength of our semantics become more transparent, if structural recursions with conditions introduced in the underlying algebra of UnQL, UnCal, are examined. Here there may be unnecessary conditions. These should be eliminated. A natural extension of our semantics will turn out to be a very good tool for describing the complex relationships between conditions. We plan to review our results in another paper.

In section 2 the basic concepts are described formally. In section 3 the track semantics is introduced. The algorithms answering static analitical questions, checking restrictions and the optimizing methods are in section 4. In section 5 we present the query rewriting technique through an example.

2   Basic Concepts

As it was mentioned semistructured data can be modelled with rooted, edge-labeled, directed graphs. Formally, let $\mathcal{U}$ be the universe of all constants ($\mathcal{U} = Int \cup String \cup Bool \cup \ldots$) and it also contains a special constant, ε. For those who are familiar with automata theory, the role of ε can be described as it is similar to that of silent transitions. Then a data graph DB is a triple, $DB = (V, E, v_0)$, where V is the set of nodes, $E \subset V \times \mathcal{U} \times V$ is the set of edges and v_0 is the distinguished root. We shall use the notations $V.DB$, $E.DB$ for the sets of nodes and edges of a data graph DB respectively. Usually atomic values are represented by the leaves, however, in case of UnQL for the sake of convenience

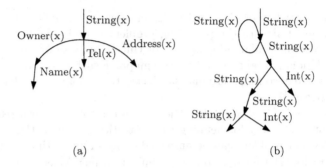

(a)   (b)

Fig. 2. The data graph in Figure 1. conforms dually to the schema graph in (a) and conforms to the one in (b). The schema graph in (b) subsumes the one in (a).

it is assumed that the last edges of branches represent them. See Figure 1. for an example. A *path* in a graph is a sequence of subsequent edges of that graph.

Two data graph is considered equivalent if they are bisimilar. Formally, two data graphs DB, DB' are bisimilar if there exists a binary relation $\simeq$ between $V.DB$ and $V.DB'$, s.t. (i) $v_0 \simeq v_0'$, where v_0, v_0' are the roots (ii) whenever $u \simeq u', u \in V.DB, u' \in V.DB', (u, \varepsilon^*.a, v) \in E.DB$ then $\exists v' \in V.DB'$ s.t. $(u', \varepsilon^*.a, v') \in E.DB'$ $v \simeq v'$ and if $(u', \varepsilon^*.b, v') \in E.DB'$ then $\exists v \in V.DB$ s.t. $(u, \varepsilon^*.b, v) \in E.DB, v \simeq v'$ [7]. Here $(u, \varepsilon^*.a, v) \in E.DB$ is a sloppy shorthand for that there is a path from u to v starting with arbitrary number of ε edges and ending with an a edge. If there exists a bisimulation between DB and DB', then there always exists a maximal bisimulation which can be found in time $O(m \log(m + n))$, here $n = |V.DB| + |V.DB'|, m = |E.DB| + |E.DB'|$ [7], [15]. In the sequel we shall always consider this maximal bisimulation. It can be seen that it is enough to take into account that subgraph, which is reachable from the root, for it is bisimilar to the whole graph. It is also clear that the concept of equivalence introduced by bisimulation well fits the set semantics of trees [7].

Now consider a set of base predicates $P_1, P_2, \ldots$ and an interpretation over $\mathcal{U}$. A unary formula is a formula with at most one free variable. A schema graph is a rooted, labeled, directed graph, whose edges are labeled unary formulas [9]. Typical predicates include $Int(x), String(x)$ etc. and user-defined unary predicates, $P(x)$. The generated theory $\mathcal{T}$ is decidable [9]. A schema graph is a rooted, labeled graph, whose edges are labeled with unary formulas [9].

A data graph, DB, conforms to a schema graph S, $DB \preccurlyeq^+ S$, if (i) $v_0 \preccurlyeq^+ v_0'$, where v_0, v_0' are the roots (ii) whenever $u \preccurlyeq^+ u', u \in V.DB, u' \in V.S, (u, \varepsilon^*.a, v) \in E.DB$ then $\exists v' \in V.S$ s.t. $(u', \varepsilon^*.p, v') \in E.S, v \preccurlyeq^+ v'$ and $\mathcal{U} \models p(a)$ [9]. In this case one cannot enforce the presence of a label with some property on a level of a data graph, only the allowable labels on that level can be specified. An example is shown in Figure 2.b.

In case of its dual counterpart the possibilities are reversed. One can specify the required edges on a level, but cannot avoid the appearance of arbitrary labels there. There is a hint to this notion in [2], however, as far as we know the correct definition is given in this paper first time. A data graph DB conforms to a schema graph S dually, $S \preccurlyeq^- DB$, if (i) $v_0 \preccurlyeq^- v'_0$, where v_0, v'_0 are the roots (ii) whenever $u \preccurlyeq^- u'$, $u \in V.S$, $u' \in V.DB$, $(u, \varepsilon^*.p, v) \in E.S$ then $\exists v' \in V.DB$ and $\exists a \in \mathcal{U}$ s.t. $(u', \varepsilon^*.a, v') \in E.DB$, $v \preccurlyeq^- v'$ and $\mathcal{U} \models p(a)$. See an example in Figure 2.a. Note that data graphs can be considered as special schema graphs, because constants in $\mathcal{U}$ can be substituted with unary predicates becoming true iff the constant in question appears in its argument. For a given constant a, denote the appropriate predicate $a(x)$ or p_a. Hence in the rest of the paper we shall sometimes blur the distinction between constants and predicates, and we shall consider data graphs as special cases of schema graphs.

In the sequel we shall need three basic notions concerning schema graphs.

(a) Let S_1, S_2 be schema graphs. S_2 subsumes S_1, $S_1 \preccurlyeq^+ S_2$, if (i) $v_{0_1} \preccurlyeq^+ v_{0_2}$, where v_{0_1}, v_{0_2} are the roots (ii) whenever $u_1 \preccurlyeq^+ u_2$, $u_1 \in V.S_1$, $u_2 \in V.S_2$, $(u_1, \varepsilon^*.p_1, v_1) \in E.S_1$ then $\forall a \in \mathcal{U}$, $\mathcal{U} \models p_1(a)$, there exists $v_2 \in V.S_2$ and $(u_2, \varepsilon^*.p_2, v_2) \in E.S_2$ s.t. $\mathcal{U} \models p_2(a)$, $v_1 \preccurlyeq^+ v_2$ [9]. An example can be seen in Figure 2. The term *subsume* is well-justified, because if $[S] = \{DB \mid DB \preccurlyeq^+ S\}$, then one can prove that $S_1 \preccurlyeq^+ S_2$ iff $[S_1] \subseteq [S_2]$ [9]. S_1, S_2 is considered equivalent, if both $S_1 \preccurlyeq^+ S_2$ and $S_2 \preccurlyeq^+ S_1$ holds. It can be checked in time $m^{O(1)}t$ whether $S_1 \preccurlyeq^+ S_2$, where t is the time needed to check the validity of a sentence in the theory $\mathcal{T}$ [9].

(b) Sometimes the previous property is too strong for describe the relationships between schema graphs. Hence we introduce the dual counterpart of this relation, which is introduced in this paper first time as far as we know. S_2 subsumes S_1 dually, $S_1 \preccurlyeq^- S_2$ if (i) $v_{0_1} \preccurlyeq^- v_{0_2}$, where v_{0_1}, v_{0_2} are the roots (ii) whenever $u_1 \preccurlyeq^- u_2$, $u_1 \in V.S_1$, $u_2 \in V.S_2$, $(u_1, \varepsilon^*.p_1, v_1) \in E.S_1$ then $\exists a \in \mathcal{U}$, $\mathcal{U} \models p_1(a)$ and $\exists v_2 \in V.S_2$, $(u_2, \varepsilon^*.p_2, v_2) \in E.S_2$ s.t. $v_1 \preccurlyeq^- v_2$ and $\mathcal{U} \models p_2(a)$. Note that $S_1 \preccurlyeq^- S_2$ informally means that S_2 has a subgraph with the "same" structure as S_1.

(c) The intersection of schema graphs will play a decisive role in our algorithms and proofs. Denote S the intersection of S_1 and S_2, $S := S_1 \sqcap S_2$. Then (i) $V.S = \{(u_1, u_2) \mid u_i \in V.S_i, (i = 1, 2)\}$ (ii) $E.S = \{((u_1, u_2), p, (v_1, v_2)) \mid (u_1, u_2), (v_1, v_2) \in V.S, p = p_1 \wedge p_2$, where $(u_i, p_i, v_i) \in E.S_i (i = 1, 2)$ and $\exists a \in \mathcal{U}, \mathcal{U} \models p_1(a) \wedge p_2(a)\}$ [9]. See an example in Figure 3. The followings can be shown: (i) $S \preccurlyeq^+ S_i (i = 1, 2)$ (ii) if $S' \preccurlyeq^+ S_i (i = 1, 2)$ also holds, then $S' \preccurlyeq^+ S$ (iii) $[S] = [S_1] \cap [S_2]$ [9].

ε edges can be eliminated similarly as in the case of automata. Namely, for a given ε edge, add edges to its starting node s.t. all nodes, reachable through a p edge from the endpoint, should also be reachable from it through a p edge. An example can be found in Figure 3.e. Note that a schema graph is always equivalent with its counterpart without ε edges [7].

In the sequel we shall need to consider the union of arbitrary schema graphs S_1, S_2. Let u be a new node different from the nodes of S_1 and S_2 respectively. Add ε edges from u to the roots. This new graph is defined to be the union of S_1 and S_2. Note that in case of tree data graphs the two semantics of union is equivalent [7]. An example can be found in Figure 3.f.

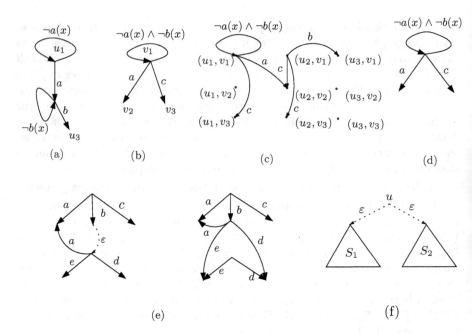

Fig. 3. (a), (b) schema graphs, (c) the intersection of the schema graphs of (a) and (b), (d) the maximal subgraph of the schema graph in (c) reachable from the root, (e) an example for the elimination of ε edges, (f) the union of schema graphs

Eventually we explain by means of an example how structural recursions work on trees. The semantics on arbitrary data graphs will be described later. Consider the following two structural recursions:

$$f_1(t_1 \cup t_2) \quad = f_1(t_1) \cup f_1(t_2)$$
$$f_1(\{owner: t\}) = \{owner: f_2(t)\}$$
$$f_1(\{l: t\}) \quad = f_1(t)$$
$$f_1(\{\}) \quad\quad = \{\}.$$

$$f_2(t_1 \cup t_2) = f_2(t_1) \cup f_2(t_2)$$
$$f_2(\{l: t\}) = \{l: f_2(t)\}$$
$$f_2(\{\}) \quad = \{\}$$

These stuctural recursions copy the subgraphs under an *owner* edge of the data graph in Figure 1. The semantics of structural recursion is the following: as it reaches a node which has several outgoing edges, it calls itself recursively on each branch, and it takes the union of the results, $f_1(t_1 \cup t_2) = f_1(t_1) \cup f_1(t_2)$ (there are several ways to split the graph as $t_1 \cup t_2$, however, all choices leads to the same result). It does the construction eagerly as it processes an edge with a label followed by a subgraph, $f_2\{l: t\} = \{l: f_2(t)\}$ (here l match every labels). In the example it can be observed that recursive calls to other structural recursions are allowed. Some syntactic restrictions were introduced in order to guarantee termination [7]. These are the followings: (i) the right side of $f(t_1 \cup t_2)$ should always be $f(t_1) \cup f(t_2)$ (ii) each result of recursive calls on the right side of $f(\{l: t\})$ can be used only by constructors, calls like $f_1(f_2(t))$, $f(\{a: \{b: t\}\})$ are not allowed (iii) the result of $f(\{\})$ should always be $\{\}$, recall that $\{\}$ denotes

Algorithm: Construction of the Operational Graph
Input   : $f = (f_1, \ldots, f_n)$
Output   : U_f
Method   : $used := \{\}$; $default := \perp$; /* $\perp$ denotes the unsatisfiable predicate */
           /* assume f_1 has the control first */
           create a new node, label it with f_1;
           $used := used \cup \{f_1\}$; $builder(next\_row(f_1), f_1)$;

$builder(label_1, label_2, control, current)$:
  if $label_1 \neq null$ then
    if $control$ has not been processed in course of the algorithm then
      create a new node labeled $control$;
    if $label_1 = l$ then $label_1 := default$;
      else $default := default \wedge \neg label_1(x)$;
    draw an edge from $current$ to $control$, label it with $label_1$ and $label_2$;
    if $control$ not in $used$ then $used := used \cup \{control\}$;
                             $builder(next\_row(control), control)$;
    if $current \neq control$ then $builder(next\_row(current), current)$;
  else return$(())$;

Fig. 4. The algorithm constructing the operational graph of a structural recursion.

the empty graph. Since the $f(t_1 \cup t_2)$, $f(\{\})$ rows are always the same, we shall write down only the remaining parts of structural recursions in the sequel. Note that the order of rows is important, because for example an *owner* edge of the input in f_1 matches both $\{owner: t\}$ and $\{l: t\}$. In such cases the first matching row counts.

3   The Track Semantics of Structural Recursions

In this section we shall develop a new way for defining the semantics for structural recursions on arbitrary inputs. First we shall construct an auxiliary graph, the *operational graph* U_f for a structural recursion $f = (f_1, \ldots, f_n)$. Here f consists of n recursive structural recursions. By means of its operational graph one will be able to track the run of a structural recursion. In addition it tells which subgraphs of the input may have an impact on the result. It also "describes" the structure of the output, and it will establish the connection between schema graphs and structural recursions. The algorithm constructing the operational graph can be found in Figure 4.

The nodes of U_f are labeled f_i-s $(1 \leq i \leq n)$ and its edges labeled binary lists of constants or predicates. If f_i constructs a b edge as a result of an a edge and calls f_j for the subgraph under the a edge, then there is an $(f_i, [a, b], f_j)$ edge in U_f. The $next\_row(f_i)$ $(1 \leq i \leq n)$ function takes the subsequent row of the last processed row of f_i. If neither of its rows has been processed yet, then it takes the first row. It returns three values: the label in the singleton set on the left hand side of the equation and the label and the name of the structural recursion in the singleton set on the right hand side respectively. If there is no other row to proceed, then it returns three nulls. If the label on the right side misses, i.e, nothing will be constructed, then the second value becomes ε. These values are given to the variables $label_1$, $label_2$, $control$ in the argument of the function $builder$. The fourth parameter tells which structural recursion has the control now. Virtually the function $builder$ constructs the operational graph calling itself recursively. Note that the construction can be done in $O(n)$ time in the size of the input (here the size of the input is the number of rows in f). As an example, consider the following structural recursions:

$$f_1 : (\{a: t\}) = \{a: f_2(t)\}$$
$$(\{b: t\}) = \{b: f_3(t)\}$$
$$(\{l: t\}) = f_1(t)$$

$$f_3 : (\{c: t\}) = \{a: f_4(t)\}$$
$$(\{d: t\}) = \{\}$$
$$(\{l: t\}) = f_3(t)$$

$$f_2 : (\{a: t\}) = f_1(t)$$
$$(\{l: t\}) = \{l: f_2(t)\}$$

$$f_4 : (\{d: t\}) = \{e: f_4(t)\}$$
$$(\{l: t\}) = f_4(t)$$

U_f, $f = (f_1, \ldots, f_4)$, can be found in Figure 5.a.

Now we are to define the semantics by means of operational graphs. The processing of an input consists of three steps. Suppose that we are to process the subgraph t, which is assumed to be a tree at first. (i) Split t into branches, process each of them and then take the union of the results. (ii) Assume that we are to process the (u, a_1, v) edge of t according to f_i. Because of the construction of the $default$ label, there is a unique edge from f_i, $(f_i, [p, b_1], f_j)$, s.t. $\mathcal{U} \models p(a_1)$. The result of (u, a_1, v) will be an edge (u', b_1, v') and f_j will carry on the processing. Remember that an ε edge means that nothing will be constructed. Assume that next we are to process (v, a_2, w) and its result is (v'', b_2, w'). Then add an ε edge from v' to v'' in the result. Note that u' should also be linked to the endpoint of the result of the edge processed right before (u, a_1, v). (iii) If t has cycles, then for a given cycle assume that (u', b_1, v') was constructed as a result of its first processed edge, and (w', b_2, z') as a result of its last processed one. Then add an ε edge from z' to u'. In this paper we consider looping edges as cycles. Eventually ε edges can be eliminated. An example can be found in Figure 5.b, which uses the operational graph of the previous example.

We shall call this method as the *track semantics* of structural recursions. Its equivalence with the other semantics defined in [7] is quite natural.

4   Static Analysis and Optimizing Methods

4.1   Preparing Concepts and Observations

For answering static analitical questions, first we shall need some concepts. Consider only the first elements of edge labels in U_f, this graph will be D_f. Similarly, the second elements will give G_f. Note that D_f is deterministic, i.e., $\nexists a \in \mathcal{U}$ s.t. $\mathcal{U} \models p_1(a) \wedge p_2(a)$, where p_1, p_2 are labels of two neighbouring edges in D_f. Next note that if S_1 subsumes (dually) S_2, $S_1 \preccurlyeq S_2$, then each node and each

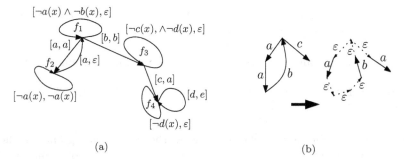

(a)   (b)

Fig. 5. (a) an operational graph (b) an example of the track semantics

edge of S_1 have at least one pair in S_2 given by the $\preccurlyeq$ relation. The subgraph constituted by these nodes and edges are called the *correspondence* of S_1 in S_2, in notation $S_2^{S_1}$. Formally $V.S_2^{S_1} := \{u_2 \mid u_2 \in V.S_2, \exists u_1 \in V.S_1, u_1 \preccurlyeq u_2\}$ and $E.S_2^{S_1} := \{(u_2, p_2, v_2) \mid (u_2, p_2, v_2) \in E.S_2, \exists(u_1, p_1, v_1) \in E.S_1, u_1 \preccurlyeq u_2, v_1 \preccurlyeq v_2, \exists a \in \mathcal{U}, \mathcal{U} \models p_1(a) \wedge p_2(a)\}$. The ε-*extension* of a subgraph $\hat{S}$ of a schema graph S, in notation $\hat{S}^{\varepsilon}$, is the following: (i) $V.\hat{S}^{\varepsilon} := \{v \mid v \in V.\hat{S}$ or $\exists(u, \varepsilon^*, v) \in E.S$ s.t. $u \in V.\hat{S}\}$ (ii) $E.\hat{S}^{\varepsilon} := \{(u, c, v) \mid (u, c, v) \in E.\hat{S}$ or $c = \varepsilon$ and $u, v \in V.\hat{S}^{\varepsilon}\}$.

Next we make some observations, which will turn out to be useful in the sequel. First note that for an arbitrary edge of U_f, there exists an instance I, s.t. this edge is traversed in the processing of I. Namely, take a path in D_f ending in the corresponding edge. Leave the node labels, and change the formulas to constants satisfying them. Let I be this path. It is obvious that I has the required property. Similarly, we get a lemma as follows:

Lemma 1 *For an arbitrary rooted subgraph of U_f with the same root as U_f, there exists an instance I, s.t. this subgraph is traversed in the processing of I.*

Note that the question that for a given structural recursion f whether there exists an instance I s.t. $f(I)$ is not empty, can be answered easily by means of Lemma 1. Namely, the following statement holds: there is an instance I for a given structural recursion f s.t. $f(I)$ is not empty iff G_f contains at least one edge having a label different from ε. Moreover we have another lemma:

Lemma 2 *For a given instance I and structural recursion $f = (f_1, \ldots, f_n)$, $(u_I, p_I, v_I) \in I$ will be processed by the structural recursion f_i, and f_j will get the control afterwards iff $((u_I, u_{D_f}), p_I \wedge p_{D_f}, (v_I, v_{D_f})) \in E.I \sqcap D_f$. Here f_i, f_j are the node labels of u_{D_f} and v_{D_f} respectively.*

Proof. Assume that the first edge of I, which is to be processed, is (u_I, a, v_I). If $((u_I, u_{D_f}), p_a \wedge p_{D_f}, (v_I, v_{D_f})) \in E.I \sqcap D_f$, then $\mathcal{U} \models p_{D_f}(a)$. Hence (u_I, a, v_I) will be processed according to $(u_{D_f}, p_{D_f}, v_{D_f})$. Conversely, if (u_I, a, v_I) is processed according to $(u_{D_f}, p_{D_f}, v_{D_f})$, then $((u_I, u_{D_f}), p_a \wedge p_{D_f}, (v_I, v_{D_f}))$ is in $E.I \sqcap D_f$. Note that this edge in U_f is unambiguous, since D_f is deterministic. The proof can be continued in a similar manner. Note that each node of I has at most one pair in $V.I \sqcap D_f$ and hence in D_f.

At the end of this subsection we prove four easy technical lemmas.

Lemma 3 *Let S_1, S_2 be schema graphs and I an instance s.t. $S_1 \preccurlyeq^- I \preccurlyeq^+ S_2$, then $S_1 \preccurlyeq^- S_2$.*

Proof. We construct a $\preccurlyeq^-$ relation between the two schema graphs in the following manner. First $v_{1_0} \preccurlyeq^- v_{2_0}$, here v_{1_0}, v_{2_0} are the roots. Suppose that $u_1 \preccurlyeq^- u_2$, $u_1 \in S_1$, $u_2 \in S_2$ and $\exists u_I \in I$, $u_1 \preccurlyeq^- u_I$, $u_I \preccurlyeq^+ u_2$, the three roots meet this requirement. Consider $(u_1, p_1, v_1) \in E.S_1$. Then $\exists (u_I, a, v_I) \in E.I$ s.t. $v_1 \preccurlyeq^- v_I$ and $\mathcal{U} \vDash p_1(a)$. Moreover $\exists (u_2, p_2, v_2) \in E.S_2$ s.t. $v_I \preccurlyeq^+ v_2$ and $\mathcal{U} \vDash p_2(a)$. Thus the $\preccurlyeq^-$ relation can be extended with $v_1 \preccurlyeq^- v_2$. The proof can be continued inductively.

Lemma 4 *Let S_1, S_2, S_3 be schema graphs. If $S_1 \preccurlyeq^+ S_2$ and $S_2 \preccurlyeq^+ S_3$, then $S_1 \preccurlyeq^+ S_3$.*

Proof. Recall that $S_1 \preccurlyeq^+ S_2$ iff $[S_1] \subseteq [S_2]$ [9]. Owing to the transitivity of the $\subseteq$ relation, the $\preccurlyeq^+$ relation is also transitive.

Lemma 5 *Let S_1, S_2 be schema graphs. Suppose that $S_1 \preccurlyeq^+ S_2$. Then S_1 is equivalent to $S_1 \sqcap S_2$.*

Proof. From the (i) property of intersection $S_1 \sqcap S_2 \preccurlyeq^+ S_1$ holds. Furthermore $S_1 \preccurlyeq^+ S_1$ trivially, $S_1 \preccurlyeq^+ S_2$ was supposed, hence from the (ii) property of intersection $S_1 \preccurlyeq^+ S_1 \sqcap S_2$.

Lemma 6 *Let S_1, S_2, S_3 be schema graphs. Then $(S_1 \sqcap S_2) \sqcap S_3$ is equivalent with $S_1 \sqcap (S_2 \sqcap S_3)$.*

Proof. Applying the definition of intersection we get the followings: $V.(S_1 \sqcap S_2) \sqcap S_3 = \{((u_1, u_2), u_3) \mid (u_1, u_2) \in V.S_1 \sqcap S_2, u_3 \in V.S_3\}$, $E.(S_1 \sqcap S_2) \sqcap S_3 = \{(((u_1, u_2), u_3), ((p_1 \wedge p_2) \wedge p_3), ((v_1, v_2), v_3)) \mid ((u_1, u_2), u_3), ((v_1, v_2), v_3) \in V.(S_1 \sqcap S_2) \sqcap S_3, ((u_1, u_2), p_1 \wedge p_2, (v_1, v_2)) \in E.S_1 \sqcap S_2, (u_3, p_3, v_3) \in E.S_3$ and $\exists a \in \mathcal{U}, \mathcal{U} \vDash (p_1(a) \wedge p_2(a)) \wedge p_3(a)\}$.

$V.S_1 \sqcap (S_2 \sqcap S_3) = \{(u_1, (u_2, u_3)) \mid (u_2, u_3) \in V.S_2 \sqcap S_3, u_1 \in V.S_1\}$, $E.S_1 \sqcap (S_2 \sqcap S_3) = \{((u_1, (u_2, u_3)), (p_1 \wedge (p_2 \wedge p_3)), (v_1, (v_2, v_3)) \mid (u_1, (u_2, u_3)), (v_1, (v_2, v_3)) \in V.S_1 \sqcap (S_2 \sqcap S_3), ((u_2, u_3), p_2 \wedge p_3, (v_2, v_3)) \in E.S_2 \sqcap S_3, (u_1, p_1, v_1) \in E.S_1$ and $\exists a \in \mathcal{U}, \mathcal{U} \vDash p_1(a) \wedge (p_2(a) \wedge p_3(a))\}$. It can be seen that $V.(S_1 \sqcap S_2) \sqcap S_3 = V.S_1 \sqcap (S_2 \sqcap S_3)$ and $E.(S_1 \sqcap S_2) \sqcap S_3 = E.S_1 \sqcap (S_2 \sqcap S_3)$.

4.2   Practical Problems and Their Solutions

The preceding lemmas have some corollaries, which may play an important role in real world situations. Firstly suppose that one would like to insert some data from a database into another one in a well-known *insert into-select-from-where* fashion, but here an UnQL query is used instead of an SQL query. Assume that this query can be translated into a structural recursion f. It is a certain assumption that the target database has some restrictions, which we can translate to our "jargon", as there exists two schema graphs S_1, S_2 s.t. $S_1 \preccurlyeq^- f(I) \preccurlyeq^+ S_2$ should hold for every instance I. Note that in case of XML documents there may be several properties prescribed by DTDs that can be expressed using schema graphs in such a manner. Hence one may also apply the following discussions to that case.

Secondly suppose that the inputs are typed, i.e., all of them should conform to a given schema graph S. This can be the situation, when we are to process results of another query, for example. It can also be a natural question that for a given structural recursion f, whether there exists a typed input s.t. the result is not empty. These are both satisfiability questions and as we solve them, we shall also develop some methods for checking these restrictions as well as for optimizing query evaluation.

For the first problem remember that in the proof of Lemma 2. we have observed that each node of the input has at most one pair in D_f as we process it. Note that these are given by $D_f^{I \sqcap D_f}$. Since both D_f, G_f are derived from U_f, it is obvious that each node and edge of D_f have a corresponding node and edge in G_f. For a given subgraph of D_f, D'_f, call the corresponding subgraph as the G_f-*correspondence* of D'_f. Note that the D_f-*correspondence* of a subgraph of G_f could be defined similarly as well as the U_f-*correspondence*. Moreover we can say that each node of the input has a corresponding node in G_f. In the course of processing do the following: whenever an ε edge is drawn as a consequence of a cycle in I, draw an edge between the appropriate nodes in G_f. Denote this new graph G_f^I. Clearly, from the track semantics $f(I) \preccurlyeq^+ G_f^I$ holds. The $\preccurlyeq^+$ relation are constituted by means of the aforementioned pairs of nodes of I and G_f respectively. Thereafter for a given node u in G_f, add ε edges from the nodes reachable from u to u. If it has not been done, then add also a looping ε edge to u. Denote this graph $\hat{G}_{f,\varepsilon}$. Eliminate the ε edges and denote the result graph $\hat{G}_f$. Obviously for every instance I, $G_f^I \preccurlyeq^+ \hat{G}_f$. Consequently by Lemma 4. $f(I) \preccurlyeq^+ \hat{G}_f$ holds. Now, we get a nearly straightforward proposition.

Proposition 1 *For a given structural recursion f and schema graph S there exists an instance I s.t. $f(I) \preccurlyeq^- S$ holds iff $S \preccurlyeq^- \hat{G}_f$.*

Proof. If there is an instance I s.t. $S \preccurlyeq^- f(I)$, then by Lemma 3., $S \preccurlyeq^- \hat{G}_f$.

If $S \preccurlyeq^- \hat{G}_f$, then consider $\hat{G}_f^S$. It can be seen that $S \preccurlyeq^- S \sqcap \hat{G}_f$. Namely let (u, p, v) be an edge of S. Here u denotes the root. We know that there is an edge (u', p', v') in $\hat{G}_f$ s.t. $v \preccurlyeq^- v'$ and $\exists a, \mathcal{U} \vDash p(a) \wedge p'(a)$. Here u' denotes the root. Then $((u, u'), p \wedge p', (v, v'))$ will be an edge of $S \sqcap \hat{G}_f$. Moreover $u \preccurlyeq^- (u, u')$ and $v \preccurlyeq^- (v, v')$ hold. The $\preccurlyeq^-$ relation between S and $S \sqcap \hat{G}_f$ can be constructed further along the same lines. We also know that $S \sqcap \hat{G}_f \preccurlyeq^+ S$ holds. Hence S and $S \sqcap \hat{G}_f$ have the same structure, so $\hat{G}_f^S$ and $\hat{G}_f^{S \sqcap \hat{G}_f}$ are equivalent to each other.

Consider the D_f-correspondence of $\hat{G}_f^{S \sqcap \hat{G}_f}$. By Lemma 1., there is an instance I s.t. this graph is traversed as we process I. From the definition of the track semantics $S \preccurlyeq^- f(I)$ holds clearly. Note that $S \sqcap \hat{G}_{f,\varepsilon}$ would not have a sense, because the intersection was not defined for schema graphs having ε edges.

The proof also gives us a method for checking that whether the output of a given input will satisfy the restriction in question or not. So we would like to prescibe that $f(I)$ should conform dually to a schema graph S, i.e., on each level the required edges are given. It has become clear, that only $\hat{G}_f^{S \sqcap \hat{G}_f}$ is important from this point of view, i.e., its edges should be used in the construction. Hence clearly $S^{S \sqcap \hat{G}_f}$ should be equivalent with S, otherwise the restriction could not be satisfied. Note that by means of $\hat{G}_{f,\varepsilon}$ one can rewrite the ε edges in $\hat{G}_f^{S \sqcap \hat{G}_f}$, hence we get a subgraph, $\hat{G}_{f,\varepsilon}^{S \sqcap \hat{G}_f}$, of $\hat{G}_{f,\varepsilon}$. Denote its D_f-correspondence $D_{f,-}^S$. Obviously $D_{f,-}^S$ should be traversed for the satisfaction of the restriction. Hence $D_{f,-}^S$ should be a subgraph of $D_f^{I \sqcap D_f}$. This is a necessary and sufficient condition, if $S^{S \sqcap \hat{G}_f}$ is equivalent with S. We have just proven the necessity. However, the sufficiency is also straightforward from the preceding train of thoughts.

On the other hand, if one would like to prescribe that $f(I)$ should conform to a schema graph S, $f(I) \preccurlyeq^+ S$, then by similar train of thoughts $\hat{G}_f^{S \sqcap \hat{G}_f}$ should be considered again. Remember that here on each level the allowable edges are given. Consequently edges of $\hat{G}_f$ not in $\hat{G}_f^{S \sqcap \hat{G}_f}$ should not be used for constructions. Certainly ε edges do not have an impact on the result. Hence the ε-extension of $\hat{G}_{f,\varepsilon}^{S \sqcap \hat{G}_f}$ should be considered. Denote its D_f-correspondence $D_{f,+}^S$. As it can be seen only the edges of $D_{f,+}^S$ can be used in the processing, i.e., $I^{I \sqcap D_{f,+}^S}$ should be equivalent to I. This a necessary and sufficient condition again. Moreover instead of $I \sqcap D_f$, $I \sqcap D_{f,+}^S$ should be taken into account in the construction of the result. Thus it is enough to use the U_f-correspondence of $D_{f,+}^S$ instead of U_f. This could mean considerable improvement in query evaluation. In the next paragraph a similar result will be presented, whose effect was tested empirically in [14].

The beauty of the previous considerations is that, if we return to our second practical problem, when typed inputs are considered, the solution can be given along the same lines. Accordingly I conforms to a schema graph S, $I \preccurlyeq^+ S$, and by Lemma 2. only $D_f^{I \sqcap D_f}$ is used for the construction of the result. By Lemma 4. $I \sqcap D_f \preccurlyeq^+ S$ also holds. Now as we apply Lemma 5. and Lemma 6. we get that $I \sqcap D_f$ is equivalent with $I \sqcap D_f \sqcap S$. Hence in the process of an instance only the appropriate subgraph of $S \sqcap D_f$ should be considered instead of D_f. This result is a slight generalization of another one given in [14], because regular path expressions can be translated into structural recursions. As it was mentioned this fact may eventuate considerable improvements again, when a query is to be executed [14].

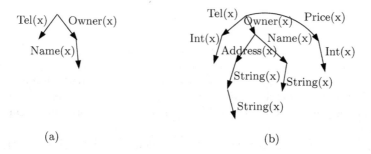

(a)   (b)

Fig. 6. Examples of a dual schema (a) and a schema graph (b) for query rewriting.

5   Query Rewriting

Consider the first practical problem of Section 4.2 again, when the structure of the output was restricted by means of schema gaphs, i.e., keeping the notations $S_1 \preccurlyeq^- f(I) \preccurlyeq^+ S_2$ should hold. Suppose that the user was careless and he or she has written a query, whose results cannot satisfy the restrictions, because of the structure of the query. There are two possibilities. Either the database system displays an error message, or the query is rewritten in such a way that the restrictions are involved in the query as in case of the *chase* algorithm in relational tableux [3]. This latter option can be achieved by means of the results of the previous section.

Recall that the equivalence of $S_1^{S_1 \cap \hat{G}_f}$ and S_1 was a necessary and sufficient condition for the satisfiability of the given restriction. Furthermore only the edges of $D_{f,+}^S$ should be considered in the processing. These two subgraphs and the schema graphs shows, how the syntax of the original structural recursion should be changed. We present the method through an example. From this it is not difficult to develop a general algorithm. Consider the data graph in Figure 1. S_1, S_2 are given in Figure 6.a and b. For the sake of simplicity suppose that the following query was asked.

$$f(\{l\colon t\} = \{l\colon f(t)\}$$

The rewritten query will be the following.

$$f \colon (\{owner\colon t\}) = \{owner\colon g_2(t)\} \cup \{owner\colon g_1(t)\} \qquad g_1 \colon (\{l\colon t\}) = \{l\colon h(t)\}$$
$$(\{tel\colon t\}) \quad = \{tel\colon g_1(t)\} \qquad\qquad\qquad\qquad g_2 \colon (\{l\colon t\}) = \{l\colon g_1(t)\}$$
$$(\{price\colon t\}) = \{price\colon g_1(t)\} \qquad\qquad\qquad h \colon (\{l\colon t\}) = \{\}$$
$$(\{l\colon t\}) \quad = \{\}$$

It can be seen that for the rewritten query there exist instances for sure s.t. their result satisfy the restrictions. Note that we cannot check whether an edge after a *tel* edge has an *integer* label. In this case we may assume that this is guaranteed by the source. As another opportunity structural recursions can be extended easily to be able to check such prescriptions. Namely, conditions like $\{Int(l)\colon t\}$ should be allowed on the left hand side for example.

Conclusions

We have developed a new way for defining semantics for structural recursions by means of which the relationships between structural recursions and schema graphs can be apprehended. We have also given some methods for answering satisfiability questions, checking restrictions and optimizing queries. As it is usual after solving the satisfiability problems, questions of containment can also be solved.

We have not discussed those cases, when the right sides of the equations of structural recursions consist of a more complex structure, for instance $\{a: f_1(t)\} \cup \{b: f_2(t)\}$ or $\{a: \{b: f_1(t)\}\}$, than a singleton set. However, note that the track semantics can be extended without difficulties to handle such cases and the result can also be constructed in polinomial time.

Yet we have not examined deeply the relationships between schema graphs and DTDs and how our methods should be changed in the presence of DTDs. Perhaps this will be done in the future. Structural recursion with conditions have also not been considered here, but we plan to analyse them in another paper.

References

1. S. Abiteboul. Querying semi-structured data. In *Proceedings 6th International Conference on Database Theory,* 1997, pp. 1-18.
2. S. Abiteboul, P. Buneman, D. Suciu. *Data on the Web: From Relations to Semistructured Data and XML.* Morgan Kaufmann Publishers, 2000.
3. S. Abiteboul, R. Hull, V. Vianu. *Foundations of Databases.* Addison-Wesley, 1995.
4. S. Abiteboul, D. Quass, J. McHugh, J. Widom, J. Wiener. The Lorel query language for semistructured data. *International journal on digital libraries,* 1(1):68-88, April 1997.
5. Scott Boag, D. Chamberlain, M. Fernandez, D. Florescu, J. Robie, Jérome Simeon. XQuery 1.0: An XML query language. W3C Working Draft 2003.
   http://www.w3.org./TR/xquery/.
6. T. Bray, J. Paoli, C. M. Sperberg-McQueen. Extensible Markup Language (XML) 1.0. W3C Recommendation REC-xml-19980210. Available as
   http://www.w3.org/REC-xml.
7. P. Buneman, M. Fernandez, D. Suciu. UnQL: a query language and algebra for semistructured data based on structured recursion. *The VLDB Journal (2000) 9:* 76-110.
8. P. Buneman, S. Davidson, G. Hillebrand, D. Suciu. A query language and optimization techniques for unstructured data. In *Proceedings of ACM-SIGMOD International Conference on Management of Data,* pages 505-516, 1996.
9. P. Buneman, S. Davidson, M. Fernandez, D. Suciu. Adding Structure to Unstructured Data. University of Pennsylvania, Computer and Information Science Department, 1996.
10. James Clark. Xml path language (xpath), 1999.
    http://www.w3.org./TR/xpath.
11. James Clark. XSL transformations (xslt) specification, 1999.
    http://www.w3.org./TR/WD-xslt.

12. A. Deutsch, M. Fernandez, D. Florescu, A. Levy, D. Suciu. A query language for XML. In *Proceedings of the Eights International World Wide Web Conference (WWW8)*, Toronto, 1999.
13. Wenfei Fan and Leonid Libkin. On XML integrity constraints in the presence of DTDs. In *PODS'01*, pages 114-125.
14. M. Fernandez and D. Suciu. Optimizing regular path expressions using graph schemas. In *Proceedings of the International Conference on Data Engineering*, pages 14-23, 1998.
15. R. Paige, R. Tarjan. Three partition refinement algorithms. *SIAM Journal of Computing*, 16:973-988, 1987.
16. G. Rozenberg, A Salomaa. *Handbook of Formal Languages*. Springer Verlag, 1997.
17. Dan Suciu. Distributed Query Evaluation on Semistructured Data. *ACM Transactions on Database Systems*, Vol. 27, No. 1, March 2002, Pages 1-62.

Catalogues from a New Perspective: A Data Structure for Physical Organisation

Gábor M. Surányi[1], Zsolt T. Kardkovács[2], and Sándor Gajdos[3]

[1] FZI Research Center for Information Technologies,
Database Systems Research Group
Haid-und-Neu-Strasse 10–14, D-76131 Karlsruhe, Germany
Gabor.Suranyi@fzi.de
[2] Budapest University of Technology and Economics,
Department of Telecommunications and Media Informatics,
Database Education Laboratory
H-1117, Budapest, Magyar tudósok körútja 2., Hungary
kardkovacs@db.bme.hu
[3] Hewlett–Packard Hungary
H-1117, Budapest, Neumann János u. 1., Hungary
sandor.gajdos@hp.com

Abstract. If vast quantities of data elements are considered, catalogues provide an intuitive way of organisation. While in common use the term catalogue refers to a tree-shaped specialisation hierarchy, we allow any transitively reduced acyclic digraph of a transitive relation such as the specialisation relationship to be a representation of a catalogue. This conforms to real-life scenarios, where each element can be classified differently depending on the actual point of view. As shown by the application of catalogues for database integration purposes, the inherent definition of similarity among categories is extremely useful. In this paper, we investigate whether catalogues as a physical organisation method also have some benefit. We accomplish this task by precisely defining the data structure and thoroughly analysing the time and space complexity properties of its management routines. The results are also compared to those of relevant alternative organisation methods.

Keywords: Physical organisation, catalogue, similarity query

1 Introduction

Efficiency in cost and time is a major issue in the development of computer systems. Efficiency is also the key of business success at customers of such systems. As a consequence, solution providers are forced to deliver software for constantly evolving requirements. This phenomenon hinders software *re-use* literally, but makes vendors produce systems which *utilise* already existing solutions as subcomponents.

The previous statement also applies to information systems which manage massive amount of data. Their common property is that although the underlying Database Management Systems (DBMS's) support either navigation or

A. Benczúr, J. Demetrovics, G. Gottlob (Eds.): ADBIS 2004, LNCS 3255, pp. 204–214, 2004.

value-based search to query and update data elements, the business logic needs more sophisticated retrieval and management functions. Therefore, these must be implemented outside the DBMS, contrary to the original concept of data management. To illustrate this, consider the following simple scenario, which is rather typical in any data retrieval or analysing environment.

Example 1 (Travel agency). Diverse information about holiday resorts is stored at a travel agency. For customers, probably the most important details are daily price, accessibility and facilities. On demand the best matching places should be returned for a given preference list. If the potential number of facilities and accessibilities is large, there is a great chance of not finding any resort which exactly matches the specification. Then approximate (quasi-similar) hits are to be delivered. While in the case of price, the definition of similarity is straightforward, at accessibility and facilities there is no obvious interpretation of similarity. The most likely definition for this purpose is the inherent set inclusion. However, the usage of such a proximity function is not supported by any DBMS directly.

Database management systems have been designed to provide efficient retrieval and update of data elements based on the values of fields and *inter*-field relationships. But for most applications, relationships within single fields (*intra*-field) are of great importance nowadays. For instance, considering the travel agency again, set inclusion of facilities or accessibility is such a relation, they are necessary for the evaluation of similarity queries and other queries which specify minimum and/or maximum conditions to be satisfied.

Although there is no hurdle creating new data models which are capable of representing intra-field relationships, without proper counterparts in the physical layer such extensions cannot be exploited. Unfortunately, no physical organisation technique provides them currently. The commonly used methods either focus on inter-field relationships and create clusters[1], simplify the calculation of joined data elements[2], or they enforce predefined intra-field relationships (indexes[3]), or they fully neglect them (hashes[3]). This means that current physical organisation methods are fairly sub-optimal for the purposes of modern applications with sophisticated models. It should be noted, however, that supporting intra-field relationship-aware data models by the physical layer does not necessarily contradict the principle of (physical) data independence[4] since physical organisation particulars can be changed without altering the data model.

In this paper, we investigate if the use of so-called catalogues as a physical organisation method is reasonable to provide access to intra-field relationships that are defined by pre orders. These catalogues were originally designed to integrate heterogeneous databases and described in details in [5]. To begin with, we briefly introduce catalogues in the next section. Since catalogues are mainly used to accelerate lookup-by-value operations, other physical organisation methods with similar functionality are also pointed out there. Section 3 deals with space requirements of each method. Time estimation of duration of important operations is done in Section 4. Section 5 lists several options to improve the performance of catalogues and concludes the paper.

2 Catalogues and Quasi-alternative Methods

Physical organisation methods can be classified into two groups based on their concrete goal. Some methods deal with the structuring of data elements so that dereferencing inter-entity links are on average inexpensive considering block accesses. The rest of methods build auxiliary structures in order to speed up other operations (again, measured in medium accesses), e.g. the lookup by value, insertion, deletion, modification of data elements.

As catalogues aim at representing intra-field relationships, they belong to the second group. It means that the efficiency of catalogues must be compared to other methods managing auxiliary structures. Interestingly, according to [3] none of the basic structures has fundamentally changed since it was enumerated in [4]. Among them only hashes and sparse indexes are considered in this paper. Dense and several other, less known indexes are omitted because they are less frequently employed and the space and time complexity of their management routines are similar to the ones of sparse indexes. Bitmap indexes are pretty young on the scene and they were originally used in Decision Support Systems to accelerate data search based on low-cardinality fields [6,3]. Since we impose no limit on the size of a field's domain, bitmap indexes are unsuitable for our purposes and not included in our comparison either.

There also exist more sophisticated structures for special purposes. For example, techniques for computing join, the key operation of the relational data model have their own literature (see e.g. [2,7]). But these methods are usually add-ons in the sense that they are not normally used in basic lookup operations. Consequently, we do not deal with them in this paper but we manifest that their interaction with catalogues must clearly be addressed in the future.

Based on [5], we define catalogues for physical organisation purposes as follows.

Definition 1 (Catalogue). *Let $\precsim$ be a given pre order on the universe of an attribute and $\preceq$ a partial order on the equivalence classes specified by $\precsim$. A catalogue is basically the digraph representation of $\preceq$ where each node is an equivalence class and reflexive and transitive links are omitted. Finally, each node of the catalogue, similarly to the leaves of sparse indexes, points to a set of data elements which contain any value assigned to the node in their corresponding attribute.*

Example 2 (prev. contd.). For the travel agency scenario, several simple data elements and their corresponding catalogues determined by different orders are shown in Fig. 1. In the case of price the usual arithmetical order, while at accessibility and facilities set inclusion are employed as orders. Inter-node edges of the catalogues are depicted by $\longrightarrow$ arrows. Entities are identified by the abbreviations of their name, and are connected to the nodes by $\longmapsto$ arrows.

Name	Price	Accessibility	Facilities
Student Hostel I.	30	{bus}	{}
Student Hostel II.	30	{train}	{sauna}
Transatlantic Motel	60	{bus}	{golf, sea}
Seaside Hotel	800	{plane, train}	{golf, tennis, sauna, sea}
Golden Beach	1000	{plane, ship}	{casino, golf, tennis, sauna, sea}

a) Sample data elements

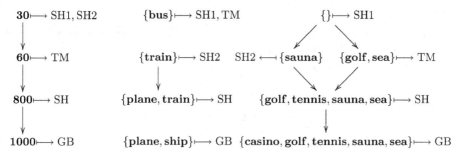

b) Catalogue for price c) Catalogue for accessability   d) Catalogue for facilities

Fig. 1. Sample data and catalogues for a travel agency

3   Space Allocation

In the rest of the paper let k stand for the number of fields for which auxiliary structures can be built. Let $n_1, \ldots, n_k$ denote the cardinality of the $1^{st}, \ldots, k^{th}$ field respectively. The number of all data elements equals to N $(n_1, \ldots, n_k \leq N)$. Furthermore, we adopt two commonly used symbols to specify computational complexity. As usual, $\mathcal{O}(X)$ means that the complexity is at most $c_1 X$, while $\Theta(X)$ means that the complexity lies between $c_2 X$ and $c_3 X$, where c_1, c_2, c_3 are constants.

If hashing is used as a speed-up method, the whole structure occupies $\Theta(N)$ space irrespectively of the cardinality of fields.

If indexes are employed, the size (the number of nodes) of each index tree is proportional to n_i. This is a consequence of the fact that an index tree is always balanced and the number of pointers starting from a node is limited. Obviously, leaves have variable length as they store reference to each data element which contain the value in question. But the total length of leaves is $\Theta(N)$.

Although catalogues also have n_i nodes, there is a substantial difference: they may contain $\mathcal{O}(n_i^2 + N)$ pointers in total as proven next.

Example 3 ('Dense' catalogue). Consider the sets of $\lfloor \frac{n_i}{2} \rfloor$ and $\lceil \frac{n_i}{2} \rceil$ nodes where each node in the former is connected to each node in the latter and the rest of pointers determine which data elements contain each value.

The quadratic limit signifies that a catalogue *can* occupy much more space than an index. Example 1 demonstrates, however, that the subset relation plays a distinguished and important role in simple catalogues, i.e. in catalogues built on a single attribute. The reason for that is that the subset relation is a natural pre order on the power set of the values if no other pre order is identifiable on the domain. Hence, probably the most common catalogues are based on the subset relation, and the following calculation gives a favourable upper limit on their space allocation.

Example 4 (Catalogue of all subsets). The catalogue of all possible subsets of the set containing l elements has

$$L = 2^l$$

nodes and

$$\sum_{i=0}^{l}(l-i)\binom{l}{i} = \frac{l}{2}2^l = \frac{L\log_2 L}{2}$$

inter-node edges, i.e. its space requirement is linearithmic.

4   Time Complexity

We need an additional parameter for time analyses. Directly or indirectly all operations on physical structures are given a value for the ith field, for which the structure in question is built. The number of data elements storing the same value as specified by the argument is denoted by N_i ($N_i \leq N$). M_i stands for the size of the result set if it does not equal to N_i.

4.1   Lookup

As well known, the hash-based search method locates the desired data elements in a single step (assuming a 'good' hash function), then only the dereferencing of pointers is needed which takes $\Theta(N_i)$ time.

Indexes are more robust then hashes in the sense that they do not depend on non-data parameters such as the selection of a function, but they theoretically can not operate as fast as hashes: a lookup always consumes $\Theta(\log n_i + N_i)$ time.

Before analysing catalogues, we should exactly define the lookup method. For this the definition of a new concept, a relation and the introduction of a notation are necessary.

Definition 2 (Entry point). *A node which has no predecessor is considered an entry point.*

Parts b, c and d of Fig. 1 illustrate catalogues with 1, 3 and 1 entry point respectively.

Definition 3 (Value equivalence). *u is equivalent to w denoted by $u \equiv w$ if and only if $u \precsim w$ and $w \precsim u$.*

It should be noted that although in the examples of Fig. 1 value equivalence is the same as value identity, they are distinct notions in general.

Originally, both $\precsim$ and $\equiv$ are relations over values. From now on, we apply them to nodes as well. It is interpreted as any value of the node was given as the argument. This definition is unambiguous because of the properties of the relations and the way catalogues are constructed.

The lookup procedure is specified as follows. Its correctness is proven in [8].

Algorithm 1 (Search in a Catalogue).

simpleSearch(v_i)—find all data elements containing v_i in the ith field

1. Let *node* be an unprocessed entry point, if any, otherwise go to step 5.
2. *result* := **simpleSearchNode**(*node*, v_i)
3. If *result* $\neq$ 'not found', return the data elements belonging to *result*.
4. Go to step 1.
5. Return 'not found'.

simpleSearchNode(*node*, v_i)

1. If $v_i \equiv_i$ *node*, return *node*.
2. Let *nextNode* be any of the direct successors of *node*, for which

$$nextNode \precsim_i v_i$$

holds. If there is no such *nextNode*, return 'not found'.
3. Call and return **simpleSearchNode**(*nextNode*, v_i).

This implementation of lookup runs in $\mathcal{O}(e_i + d_i + N_i)$ time, where e_i is the number of entry points and d_i is the length of the longest path in the catalogue. (Note that $e_i + d_i \leq n_i$ always holds.) It means that with respect to this operation, it is worth building a catalogue if $e_i + d_i \ll n_i$ only.

Example 5 (prev. contd.). The longest path in the catalogue of all subsets is l, and there is a sole entry point, the empty set. Therefore, $d_i = \log_2 L$ and the time complexity of search is the same as at an index.

4.2   Insert, Delete

Inserting a data element does not involve any non-constant time task besides lookup in the case of hashes. At indexes, all levels of the tree may have to be re-organised. Thus, insertion takes $\mathcal{O}(\log n_i + N_i)$ time.

In catalogues re-organisation because of a new element is also necessary. The new node may reside in the middle of all other nodes, requiring the modification of all edges to maintain the reduced property of the graph. As an extreme case, insertion of such a new node into the catalogue outlined in Example 3 runs in $\Theta(L^2)$, i.e. in quadratic time. The following implementation is not more time-consuming since it basically searches for directly preceding nodes and then modifies edges as needed.

Algorithm 2 (Insertion into a Catalogue).

insert(v_i, *item*)—insert data element *item* which has v_i as value of the ith field

1. *prevNodes* := $\emptyset$
2. Let *node* be an unprocessed entry point, if any, otherwise go to step 7.
3. *result* := **predecessors**(*node*, v_i, *item*)
4. If *result* = 'inserted', exit procedure.
5. *prevNodes* := *prevNodes* $\cup$ *result*
6. Go to step 2.
7. Create a new node *newNode* for v_i, and assign the single element *item* to it.
8. Let *prevNode* be an unprocessed element of *prevNodes*, if any, otherwise exit procedure.
9. Let *nextNode* be an unprocessed successor of *prevNode*, if any, otherwise go to step 13.
10. If *newNode* $\precsim_i$ *nextNode* does not hold, go to step 9.
11. Remove the edge between *prevNode* and *nextNode*.
12. Create an edge from *newNode* to *nextNode*.
13. Create edge from *prevNode* to *newNode*.
14. Go to step 8.

predecessors(*node*, v_i, *item*)

1. If *node* $\precsim_i v_i$ does not hold, return $\emptyset$.
2. If *node* $\equiv_i v_i$ is not true, jump to step 5.
3. If *item* is not already assigned to *node*, add *item* to *node*.
4. Return 'inserted'.
5. *prevNodes* := $\emptyset$
6. Let *nextNode* be an unprocessed successor of *node*, if any, otherwise return *prevNodes*.
7. *result* := **predecessors**(*nextNode*, v_i, *item*)
8. If *result* = 'inserted', return *result*.
9. *prevNodes* := *prevNodes* $\cup$ *result*.
10. Go to step 6.

The deletion of a data element from a catalogue is conservative in the sense that if the element to be deleted was just inserted, the resulting catalogue is always the same as it was before the insertion. As a consequence, deletion has al least the same time complexity as insertion if catalogues are utilised.

Algorithm 3 (Deletion from a Catalogue).

delete(v_i, *item*)—delete data element *item* which has v_i as value of the ith field

1. Let *node* be an unprocessed entry point, if any, otherwise go to step 5.
2. *result* := **simpleSearchNode**(*node*, v_i)
3. If *result* $\neq$ 'not found', go to step 6.
4. Go to step 1.
5. Return 'not found'.

6. If *item* is not assigned to *result*, return 'not found'.
7. If the only data element assigned to *result* is *item*, go to step 10.
8. Remove *item* from the list of data elements assigned to *result*.
9. Return 'success'.
10. Let *prevNodes* be the predecessor, *nextNodes* the successor nodes of *result*.
11. Remove all edges starting from or ending at *result*.
12. For each *node* $\in$ *prevNodes*, compute the set of nodes reachable from *node* by a directed path and assign it to *succ[node]*.
13. Let $\langle prevNode, nextNode \rangle$ be an unprocessed pair from *prevNodes* $\times$ *nextNodes*, if any, otherwise return 'success'.
14. Create edge from *prevNode* to *nextNode* if *nextNode* $\notin$ *succ[prevNode]*.
15. Go to step 13.

The previous implementation indeed runs in $\mathcal{O}(n_i^2)$ time. Only Step 12 needs further attention, but it is easy to see that it can be executed for all nodes of the catalogue in one step by applying a graph-traversal algorithm. The running time of such algorithms is proportional to the number of vertices and edges [9], hence it is at most quadratic in the number of nodes.

Hash structures are also conservative. Trees are not, but it is true that no more than $\mathcal{O}(\log n_i)$ re-structuring modifications are needed after the naive deletion.

4.3   Additional Lookup Operations

Apart from the update of data elements, which requires a deletion/insertion pair in general, all conventional operations have been discussed. Since all these operations must be supported by all physical organisation structures, the usefulness of a structure is rather determined by the other facilities it provides for applications. In accordance with the Introduction, the most important operations and their complexity are discussed next.

Data elements which meet a minimum requirement are easily retrievable from any index but not from hashes. Analogously, a maximum requirement can also be specified. These methods are called lower and upper bound queries respectively and can be implemented for catalogues as follows.

Algorithm 4 (Lower Bound Search in a Catalogue).
lowerSearch(v_i)—find all data elements containing at least v_i in the ith field

 – For each entry point as *node*, call **lowerSearchNode**(*node*, v_i).

lowerSearchNode(*node*, v_i)

1. If $v_i \precsim_i node$, call **lowerSearchAll**(*node*) and return.
2. Call **lowerSearchNode**(*nextNode*, v_i) with all successors of *node* as *nextNode* for which
$$nextNode \precsim_i v_i.$$

lowerSearchAll(*node*)

1. Emit the elements of *node* as result.
2. Call **lowerSearchAll**(*nextNode*) with all successors of *node* as *nextNode*.

Algorithm 5 (Upper Bound Search in the Catalogue).
upperSearch(v_i)—find all data elements containing at most v_i in the ith field

– For each entry point as *node*, call **upperSearchNode**(*node*, v_i).

upperSearchNode(*node*, v_i)

1. If *node* $\precsim_i v_i$ does not hold, return.
2. Emit the elements of *node* as result.
3. Call **upperSearchNode**(*nextNode*, v_i) with all successors of *node* as *nextNode*.

Because interval queries inherently require the scan of a part of data elements, namely the ones to be returned, the cost of scanning usually dominates the cost of the operation both at indexes and catalogues. But the upper bound search in a catalogue has the advantage of delivering partial results while processing, not all hits once at the end. Furthermore, it should be noted that catalogues are more flexible since they allow the use of pre orders, not only total orders as indexes do.

Value-based neighbouring relationship cannot be interpreted in hash structures, and it is in general of no interest in indexes. Catalogues, by means of pre orders, enable the modelling of more complex, more realistic situations, where the relationship of being a neighbour is ambiguous. In accordance with common requirements as demonstrated in Example 1, we propose posing similarity and not neighbouring queries to catalogues. It makes difference only if the given value is contained in the catalogue, then similarity responds with data elements containing the specified value. (In the other case data elements assigned to nodes which would be neighbours if the value were represented are returned.)

Algorithm 6 (Similarity Search in a Catalogue).
similarSearch(v_i)—find all data elements containing similar value to v_i in the ith field

– For each entry point as *node*, call **similarSearchNode**(*node*, NULL, v_i).

similarSearchNode(*node*, *prevNode*, v_i)

1. If *node* $\precsim_i v_i$ does not hold, jump to step 10.
2. Select all *nextNode* successors of *node* into *nextLess* for which

$$nextNode \precsim_i v_i.$$

3. If *nextLess* = ∅, jump to step 6.
4. For each *nextNode* ∈ *nextLess* call *similarSearchNode*(*nextNode*, *node*, v_i).
5. Return

6. If
$$v_i \precsim_i node \wedge prevNode \neq \text{NULL}$$
holds, emit the elements of $prevNode$ as result.

7. If
$$v_i \precsim_i node$$
is not true, emit the elements of $node$ as result.

8. Emit all elements of $nextNode$ successors of $node$ as result for which
$$v_i \precsim_i nextNode.$$

9. Return

10. If $v_i \precsim_i node$, emit the elements of $node$ as result.

Like the classical search method, this implementation runs in $\mathcal{O}(e_i + d_i + M_i)$ time, where N_i is replaced by the quantity M_i. Parts of the result are delivered here before completing the operation, too.

5 Conclusion

The main goal of the paper has been to verify that the use of catalogues in the physical layer of a database is feasible and beneficial. Clearly, catalogues based on pre orders provide better support for modern database applications by enabling the database manager to answer lower-bound, upper-bound and similarity queries even if it is ambiguous.

We have analysed the memory footprint of the catalogue structure and the time complexity of conventional operations (data element lookup, insertion and deletion) in terms of block accesses. The results of complexity comparison with the commonly used physical organisation techniques show that either parallel operation of catalogues and classical methods is required, or obvious improvements that are applicable to the algorithms (such as parallelisation, traversing common subtrees only once, or processing subcatalogues earlier which have delivered more hits so far) should be employed.

In our future endeavour we will verify that comparison time has no significant effect on performance and consider the aforementioned modifications. Based on the currently existing prototype implementation a test environment will be set up so that we can analyse how many percent of real-life problems provide appropriate ordering relations which are applicable for catalogue construction.

References

1. Kemper, A., Moerkotte, G.: Physical object management. In Kim, W., ed.: Modern Database Systems: The Object Model, Interoperability, and Beyond. ACM Press and Addison-Wesley Publishing Co. (1995) 175–202
2. Mishra, P., Eich, M.H.: Join processing in relational databases. ACM Computing Surveys **24** (1992) 63–113

3. Ramakrishnan, R., Gehrke, J.: Database Management Systems. 2nd edn. McGraw-Hill Higher Education (2000)
4. Ullman, J.D.: Principles of Database and Knowledge-Base Systems. Volume I. Computer Science Press Inc. (1988)
5. Kardkovács, Zs.T., Surányi, G.M., Gajdos, S.: Application of catalogues to integrate heterogeneous data banks. In Meersman, R., Tari, Z., eds.: OTM Workshops. Volume 2889 of Lecture Notes in Computer Science., Springer (2003) 1045–1056
6. Chan, C.Y., Ioannidis, Y.E.: Bitmap index design and evaluation. In Haas, L.M., Tiwary, A., eds.: SIGMOD 1998, ACM Press (1998) 355–366
7. Harris, E.P., Ramamohanarao, K.: Join algorithm costs revisited. The VLDB Journal 5 (1996) 64–84
8. Kardkovács, Zs.T., Surányi, G.M., Gajdos, dr., S.: On the integration of large data banks by a powerful cataloguing method. Periodica Polytechnica, Series Electrical Engineering (2004) To appear.
9. Cormen, T.H., Leiserson, C.E., Rivest, R.L., Stein, C.: Introduction to Algorithms. 2nd edn. MIT Press (2001)

Database Caching – Towards a Cost Model for Populating Cache Groups

Theo Härder and Andreas Bühmann

Department of Computer Science, University of Kaiserslautern,
P. O. Box 3049, D-67653 Kaiserslautern, Germany
{haerder, buehmann}@informatik.uni-kl.de

Abstract. Web caching keeps single Web objects ready somewhere in caches in the user-to-server path, whereas database caching uses full-fledged database management systems as caches to adaptively maintain sets of records from a remote database and to evaluate queries on them. Using so-called cache groups, we introduce the new concept of constraint-based database caching. These cache groups are constructed from parameterized cache constraints, and their use is based on the key concepts of value and domain completeness. We show how cache constraints affect the correctness of query evaluations in the cache and which optimizations they allow. Cache groups supporting practical applications must exhibit controllable load behavior for which we identify necessary conditions. For such safe cache groups, the cost trade-off for record loading and predicate evaluation saving has to be observed during their design. Therefore, we analyze their load overhead and propose a population estimation algorithm to be used for a cache group advisor.

1 Introduction

Transactional Web applications (TWAs) in various domains (often called e*-applications) dramatically grow in number and complexity. At the same time, each application faces increasing demands regarding data volumes and workloads to be processed efficiently. In such situations, caching is a proven concept to improve response time and scalability of the applications as well as to minimize communication delays in wide-area networks. For this reason, a broad spectrum of techniques has emerged in recent years to keep static Web objects (like HTML pages, XML fragments, or images) in caches in the user-to-server path (client-side caches, proxies of various types, CDNs).

As the TWAs must deliver more and more dynamic and frequently updated content, this so-called *Web caching* [9,11] should be complemented by techniques that are aware of the consistency and completeness requirements of cached data (whose source is dynamically changed in backend databases) and that, at the same time, adaptively respond to changing workloads. Attempts targeting these objectives are called *database caching*, for which several different solutions have been proposed in recent years [2,3,4]. Currently many database vendors are developing prototype systems or are just extending their current products [8,10].

A. Benczúr, J. Demetrovics, G. Gottlob (Eds.): ADBIS 2004, LNCS 3255, pp. 215–229, 2004.

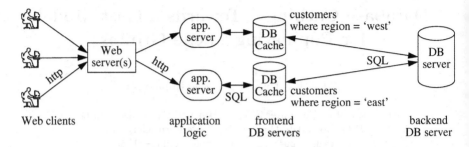

Fig. 1. Database caching for Web applications

What is the technical challenge of all these approaches? When user requests require responses to be assembled from static and dynamic contents somewhere in a Web cache, the dynamic portion is generated by a remote application server, which in turn asks the backend DB server for up-to-date information, thus causing substantial latency. An obvious reaction to this performance problem is the migration of application servers to data centers closer to the users: Figure 1 illustrates that clients select one of the replicated Web servers "close" to them in order to minimize its response time. This optimization is amplified if the associated application servers can instantly provide the expected data – frequently indicated by geographical contexts. But the displacement of application servers to the edge of the Web alone is not sufficient; conversely it would dramatically degrade the efficiency of DB support because of the frequent round trips to the then remote backend DB server. As a consequence, primarily used data should be kept close to the application servers in so-called DB caches. A flexible solution should not only support database caching at mid-tier nodes of central enterprise infrastructures [10], but also at edge servers of content delivery networks or remote data centers.

Another important aspect of a practical solution is to achieve full *cache transparency* for the applications, i. e., modifications of the application programming interface are not tolerated. Such a property gives the cache manager the choice at run time to process a query locally or to send it to the backend DB server, e. g., to comply with strict consistency requirements. Cache transparency typically requires that each DB object is represented only once in a cache and that it exhibits the same properties (name, type, etc.) as in the backend.

The use of SQL implies another challenge because of its declarative and set-oriented nature. This means that, to be useful, the cache manager has to guarantee that queries can be processed in the DB cache, i. e., the sets of records (of various types) satisfying the corresponding predicates – denoted as *predicate extensions* – must be completely in the cache. This *completeness condition*, the so-called *predicate completeness*, ensures that the query evaluation semantics is equivalent to the one provided by the backend.

A federated query facility [2,8] allows cooperative predicate evaluation by multiple DB servers. This property is very important for cache use, because local evaluation of some (partial) predicate can be complemented by the work of the backend DB server on other (partial) predicates whose extensions are not in the cache. Hence, in the following we refer to predicates meaning their portions to be evaluated in the cache.

2   Constraint-Based Database Caching

We take a look at the concepts developed and realized in the DBCache project [2] and explore the underlying ideas. This work has lead us to a class of techniques which we term *constraint-based database caching* [7]. In particular, we analyze techniques which support the evaluation of specific PSJ queries (projection-selection-join queries) in the cache.

For the specification of cache contents, we refer to a particular approach called *cache groups*. In short, a cache group is a collection of related cache tables. Cache constraints defined on and between them determine the records of the corresponding backend tables that have to be kept in the cache. The technique does not rely on the specification of static predicates: The constraints are parameterized, which makes this specification adaptive; it is completed when the parameters are instantiated by values of so-called cache keys. An "instantiated constraint" then corresponds to a predicate and, when the constraint is satisfied – i. e., all related records have been loaded – the predicate extension delivers correct answers to eligible queries.

The key idea of constraint-based caching is to start with very simple base predicates (here equality predicates) and to extend them by other types of predicates (equi-join predicates in our case) in a constructive way, such that cache maintenance can always guarantee the presence of the corresponding predicate extensions in the cache. Hence, there are no or only simple decidability problems whether a complete predicate evaluation can be performed. Only a simple probe query is required in the cache at run time to determine the availability of eligible predicate extensions. Furthermore, because all columns of the corresponding backend tables are kept in the cache, all project operations possible in the backend can also be performed in the cache thereby enabling PSJ queries. Since full DB functionality is available, the results of these queries can further be refined by operations like group-by, having, or order-by.

2.1   How Do Cache Groups Work?

As introduced above, a cache group is a collection of related cache tables. For simplicity, the names of tables and columns are identical in the cache and in the backend DB. Considering a cache table S, we denote by S_B its corresponding backend table, by $S.c$ a column c of S. Note, a cache usually contains only subsets of records pertaining to a small fraction of backend tables. Its primary task is to support query processing for TWAs which typically contain up to 3 or 4 joins [2]. Hence, we expect the number of cache tables – featuring a high degree of reference locality – to be in the order of 10 or less, even if the backend DB consists of hundreds of tables.

If we want to be able to evaluate a given predicate in the cache, we must keep a collection of records in the cache tables such that the completeness condition for the predicate is satisfied. For simple equality predicates like $S.c = v$ this completeness condition takes the shape of *value completeness*.

Definition 1 (Value completeness, VC). *A value v is said to be value complete in a column $S.c$ if and only if all records of $\sigma_{c=v}S_B$ are in S.*

If we know that a value v is value complete in a column $S.c$, we can correctly evaluate $S.c = v$, because all rows from the corresponding backend table S_B that carry that value are in the cache. But how do we know that v is value complete? This is easy if we maintain *domain completeness* of specific table columns.

Definition 2 (Domain completeness, DC). *A column $S.c$ is said to be domain complete (DC) if and only if all values v in $S.c$ are value complete.*

Given a domain-complete column $S.c$, if a probe query confirms that value v is in $S.c$ (a single record suffices), we can be sure that v is value complete and thus evaluate $S.c = v$ in the cache. Note that unique (U) columns of a cache table (defined by SQL constraints "unique" or "primary key" in the backend DB schema) are DC per se (*implicit* domain completeness). Non-unique (NU) columns in contrast need extra enforcement of DC.

So far, we can evaluate only equality predicates, i. e., simplest selection queries, in the cache. To enhance such queries with equi-join predicates, we introduce *referential cache constraints* (RCCs), which guarantee the correctness of equi-joins between cache tables. Such RCCs are specified between two cache table columns: a source column $S.a$ and a target column $T.b$. The tables S and T need not be different, not even the columns themselves.

Definition 3 (Referential cache constraint, RCC). *RCC $S.a \rightarrow T.b$ between columns $S.a$ and $T.b$ is satisfied if and only if all values v in $S.a$ are value complete in $T.b$.*

RCC $S.a \rightarrow T.b$ ensures that, whenever we find a record s in S, all join partners of s with respect to $S.a = T.b$ are in T. Note, the RCC alone does not allow us to correctly perform this join in the cache: Many rows of S_B that have join partners in T_B may be missing from S. But using an equality predicate on a DC column $S.c$ as an "anchor", we can restrict this join to records that exist in the cache: RCC $S.a \rightarrow T.b$ expands the predicate extension of $S.c = x$ to the predicate extension of $(S.c = x$ and $S.a = T.b)$. In this way, DC columns serve as *entry points* for queries.

Domain completeness of a column $S.c$ is equivalent to an RCC $S.c \rightarrow S.c$, a so-called *self-RCC* on its defining column $S.c$. By specifying such a self-RCC, the DBA can enforce domain completeness of $S.c$ and thus create an entry point for query evaluation explicitly.

How do the records that constitute a predicate extension get into the cache? And how are these predicate extensions actually chosen? For these tasks, we introduce the second kind of cache constraint, the so-called *cache key*.

Definition 4 (Cache key). *A cache key column S.k is always kept domain complete. Only values in $\pi_k S_B$ initiate cache loading when they are referenced by user queries.*

You can imagine that the specification of a cache key includes a self-RCC; similar to it, a cache key can always be used as an entry point. (In both cases the columns get *explicitly* domain complete.) But in addition, a cache key serves as a *filling point* for a distinguished *root table R* (the only table in a cache group that contains cache keys) and – via the (paths of) RCCs specified between R and related cache tables – for the *member tables* of the cache group. Whenever a query references a particular cache key value that is not in the cache, the backend DB must evaluate this query. But as a consequence of this cache miss attributed to a cache key, the cache manager satisfies the value completeness for the missing cache key value by fetching all required records from the backend and loading them into the cache table R (thus keeping the cache key column domain complete). To satisfy the RCCs, the member tables of the cache group are loaded in a similar way (details are provided in [2]). Hence, a reference to a cache key value x serves as something like an indicator that, in the immediate future, locality of reference is expected on the predicate extension determined by x. Cache keys therefore carry information about the future workload and sensitively influence caching performance. Hence, DBAs must select them carefully[1].

2.2 Types of RCCs and Their Use in Cache Groups

Depending on the types of the source and target columns, we classify RCCs as $(1\!:\!1)$, $(1\!:\!n)$, $(n\!:\!1)$, and $(n\!:\!m)$ and denote them as follows:

- U → U or U → NU: member constraint (MC)
- NU → U: owner constraint (OC)
- NU → NU: cross constraint (XC).

Using RCCs we implicitly introduce something like a value-based table model intended to support queries. Despite similarities, MCs and OCs are not identical to the PK/FK (primary key/foreign key) relationships in the backend DB: Those can be used for join processing symmetrically, RCCs only in the specified direction. XCs have no counterparts at all. Because a high fraction of all SQL join queries refers exclusively to PK/FK relationships – they represent real-world relationships captured by the DB design –, almost all RCCs are expected to be of type MC or OC; accordingly XCs and multiple RCCs ending on a NU column seem to be rare.

---

[1] Low-selectivity cache key columns may cause cache filling actions involving huge sets of records never used later. It may therefore be necessary to control the use of cache key values with stop-word or recommendation lists.

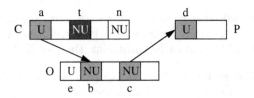

Fig. 2. Cache group OP for order processing

Assume a cache group OP with tables C, O, and P and cache key $C.t$, formed by $C.a \to O.b$ and $O.c \to P.d$, where $C.a$ and $P.d$ are U columns and $C.t$, $O.b$ and $O.c$ are NU columns (Fig. 2). In a common real-world situation, C, O, and P could correspond to backend DB tables Customer, Order and Product. Hence, both RCCs would typically characterize PK/FK relationships that will be used for join processing in the cache. Additional RCCs, for example, $C.t \to O.b$ or $O.c \to C.n$, are conceivable; such RCCs, however, have no counterparts in the backend DB schema and, when used for a cross join of C and O, their contributions to the query semantics remain in the user's responsibility.

As we know, if a probing operation on some domain-complete column $T.c$ identifies value x, we can use $T.c$ as an entry point for evaluating $T.c = x$. Now, any enhancement of this predicate with equi-join predicates is allowed if these predicates correspond to RCCs reachable from cache table T.

Assume, we find 'gold' in $C.t$ (of cache group OP), then the predicate ($C.t =$ 'gold' and $C.a = O.b$ and $O.c = P.d$) can be processed in the cache correctly. Because the predicate extension (with all columns of all cache tables) is completely accessible, any column may be specified for output. Of course, a correct predicate can be refined by "and-ing" additional selection terms (referring to cache table columns) to it; e. g. ($C.t =$ 'gold' and $O.e > 42$ and $C.n$ like 'Smi%' and ...).

3 Cache Group Design and Analysis

At this point, we know how to configure a cache group by specifying the participating tables, the RCCs connecting them, and the cache keys, which initiate the population of the cache group. We can use domain-complete columns as entry points to obtain correct query results for eligible query predicates. Is this all we need to know to design and to effectively make use of cache groups?

On the one hand, a cache group should enable as flexible use for predicate evaluation as possible: We should not leave any entry point or RCC unexploited. This requires that we know about all of them, not just about those we specified explicitly. On the other hand, we want to design safe cache groups which exhibit controllable load behavior.

Definition 5 (Reachability graph). *A reachability graph γ is a directed graph implicitly defined for a cache group G. It has G's tables and RCCs as nodes and edges. γ is composed by starting from G's root table and following all RCCs transitively thereby connecting all reachable tables (as nodes of γ).*

Definition 6 (Paths and cycles). *A path in a reachability graph starts at a source table and ends at a sink table. It connects a collection of cache tables via a sequence of RCCs. No RCC may appear twice in a path. A cycle is a path that starts and ends at the same table.*

Definition 7 (Homogeneous and heterogeneous cycles). *A cycle is homogeneous, if only a single column per table is involved, heterogeneous otherwise.*

Heterogeneous RCC cycles can lead to excessive population of cache groups primarily caused by recursive filling actions. Such "dangerous" load behavior must clearly be identified and prevented.

3.1 Entry Points for Query Evaluation

So far, we have argued that a cache table column can be tested and used by an equality predicate correctly only if it is domain complete. But how do we know that? Of course, cache table columns that carry either a self-RCC or a cache key (i. e., at least all filling points) are explicitly domain complete; columns of type U are implicitly domain complete. Cache-supported query evaluation gains much more flexibility and power, if we can correctly decide that other cache columns are domain complete as well.

Let us refer again to OP. Because $C.a \to O.b$ is the only RCC that induces filling of O, we know that $O.b$ is domain complete (denoted as *induced domain completeness*). Hence, we can correctly evaluate the query predicate ($O.b = y$ and $O.c = P.d$) if we encounter value y in $O.b$ – in addition to ($C.a = x$ and $C.a = O.b$ and $O.c = P.d$) if value x is in $C.a$.

Note, additional RCCs ending in $O.b$ would not destroy the DC of $O.b$, though any additional RCC ending in a column different from $O.b$ would do[2]: Assume an additional RCC ending in $O.e$ induces a new value v, which implies the insertion of $\sigma_{e=v}O_B$ into O – just a single record o. Now a new value w of $o.b$, so far not present in $O.b$, may appear, but all other records of $\sigma_{b=w}O_B$ fail to do so. For this reason, a cache table filled by RCCs (or cache keys) on more than one column cannot have an induced DC column. This means that induced DC is *context dependent*; in contrast to explicit or implicit DC (i. e., DC of cache key, self-RCC, or U columns), it can be lost when a cache group configuration is modified. This leads us to the following definition:

Definition 8 (Induced domain completeness). *A cache table column is induced domain complete, if it is the only column of a cache table filled[2] via one or more RCCs or via a cache key definition.*

Let us summarize our findings concerning the population of cache tables and the domain completeness of their columns: A cache table T can be filled via

---

[2] We must distinguish between RCCs that only reach a column and RCCs that fill it: RCCs that never cause any record to be loaded (e. g., a self-RCC on a U column) do not disturb induced DC. How to effectively classify an arbitrary RCC is unsettled.

cache key columns or RCCs ending in one or more of its columns. A column of T can be domain complete due to specifications in the backend (implicitly: U columns), due to specifications in the cache (explicitly: cache keys, self-RCCs), or as a result of the interaction of specified items (induced).

Analogous to extra DC columns, one can discover *optimization RCCs* in a cache group, i.e., RCCs that have not been specified, but hold in the given context. For example, in OP the (optimization) RCC $O.b \rightarrow C.a$ allows an additional join direction.

3.2 Safeness of Cache Groups

It is unreasonable to accept all conceivable cache group configurations, because cache misses on cache key columns may provoke unforeseeable load operations. Although the cache can be populated asynchronously to the transaction observing the cache miss, avoiding a burden on its response time, uncontrolled loading is undesirable: Substantial extra work, which can hardly be estimated, may be required by the frontend and backend DB servers, which will influence the transaction throughput in heavy workload situations.

Specific cache group configurations may even exhibit a recursive loading behavior that jeopardizes their caching performance. Once cache filling is initiated, the enforcement of cache constraints may require multiple phases of record loading. Such behavior typically occurs, when two NU-DC columns a and b of a cache table X must be maintained. A set of values appears in a, for which X is loaded with the corresponding records of X_B to keep column a domain complete. These records populate b with a set of (new) values that have to be made value complete, which possibly introduces new values into a again. As a result, a and b may receive new values in a recursive way.

Cache groups are called *safe* if no recursive load behavior is possible. Upon a cache key miss, we want the initiated cache loading to stop after a *single pass* of filling operations through the tables of the cache group.

Obviously, recursive loading requires that there is a cyclic structure among the specified RCCs (remember, every cache key also contains an RCC). Simple examples show that there are not only unsafe RCC cycles, but also safe ones (consider a homogeneous cycle) [2,7]. We analyzed cycles in detail and derived safeness conditions for cache group configurations. These conditions are more sophisticated than a simple exclusion of pairs of NU-DC columns (as sketched above), because the mutual introduction of new values can span several tables and can also be neutralized by compensating effects. Nevertheless the safeness conditions can be stated as a single rule that requires the designer of a cache group to inspect all contained cycles for certain patterns of U and NU columns.

4   Loading Behavior of Cache Groups

So far, we have discussed the correctness and safeness conditions of cache groups. To analyze the loading behavior, we will derive a simple quantitative cost model.

It is aimed at estimating the approximate cost (depending on column selectivities and RCCs specified) for the population of a cache group caused by a single cache key value.

4.1 Model Assumptions

For quantitative modeling, we generally assume uniform value distribution in columns and stochastic independence between columns (i.e., the standard assumptions of query processing). Each column of a cache table T inherits the cardinality of the corresponding column of backend table T_B. Hence, $T.j$ has cardinality $c_{T.j}$ (i.e., it has up to $c_{T.j}$ distinct values). We define the selectivity of column $T.j$ to be $s_{T.j} = 1/c_{T.j}$. Thus, the smaller the value $s_{T.j}$, i.e., the larger the value $c_{T.j}$, the higher is the column selectivity. For example, if T contains N_T records, an equality predicate on $T.j$ qualifies $N_T \cdot s_{T.j} = N_T/c_{T.j}$ records ($1 \leq c_{T.j} \leq N_T$) implying that NULL values are excluded.

When n_T records are filled into a table T, e.g., to satisfy a cache constraint on a given column $T.i$, how many distinct values d are entered into a stochastically independent column $T.j$? The result for the boundary values is obvious: If $T.j$ is unique, $d = n_T$, and if the cardinality of $T.j$ is 1, $d = 1$. In general, an accurate determination of d demands for a stochastic model which evaluates the expected number of distinct values of $T.j$ [12]. In abstract terms: Given natural numbers N, c, n ($1 \leq c \leq N, n \leq N$), what is the expected number d of colors when n balls are drawn without replacement from a bucket with N balls. These balls occur in c different colors and are uniformly distributed, i.e., there are N/c balls per color. The following model, which we have derived for the sketched situation, is used throughout the paper and referenced by $f(N, c, n)$:

$$d = f(N, c, n) = c \cdot \left(1 - \binom{N - N/c}{n} \Big/ \binom{N}{n} \right) .$$

In frequent situations, more than one record set is independently filled into table T. Instead of computing the sum of the various set sizes, we could improve our population estimation by modeling such situations of a combination of events. Then the expected size n_T of T's population induced by m independent cache constraints could be calculated with the following considerations. If $A_1, \ldots, A_m$ are m events, what is the probability of the event that at least one among the m A_j occurs. In symbols, this event is $A_{1\ldots m} = A_1 \cup A_2 \cup \cdots \cup A_m$. It is not sufficient to know the probabilities of the individual events A_j, but we must have complete information concerning all possible overlaps. Fortunately, due to the stochastic-independence assumption, we can easily compute for each pair (i, j), each triple (i, j, l), etc., the probability of events $A_i \cap A_j$ or $A_i \cap A_j \cap A_l$, etc. Furthermore, we can compose our formula iteratively, thereby computing the probabilities of the following events [5]: $(A_1 \cup A_2), (A_{12} \cup A_3), (A_{123} \cup A_4), \ldots$.

This abstract model for the combination of events can easily be applied to our problem of determining the number of distinct records when independent record sets are filled into a table. By multiplying the (filling) probabilities with table cardinality N_T, we immediately yield $n_{T1...m}$ as the number of distinct records for m overlapping record sets. If n_{T1} and n_{T2} records are to be filled independently into table T, n_{T12} is the number of records actually loaded, etc.:

$$n_{T12} = n_{T1} + n_{T2} - n_{T1} \cdot n_{T2}/N_T \ ,$$

$$n_{T123} = n_{T12} + n_{T3} - n_{T12} \cdot n_{T3}/N_T \ ,$$

$$n_{T1234} = n_{T123} + n_{T4} - n_{T123} \cdot n_{T4}/N_T \ , \ldots$$

The rationale of our somewhat simplified estimation model, the calculation of average record populations in cache tables, is considered to be a great help for cache group design, e. g., when applied by a cache group advisor. A model refinement is only possible at the expense of substantially increased model complexity. The actual value distributions in columns and the size of record sets induced by RCCs (equivalently, (intermediate) join results) could be approached more accurately by introducing histograms, describing the frequency of individual values or of values belonging to value ranges, and join selectivities.[3] This would require additional and more accurate statistical data for cache tables and cache groups which is, due to its dynamic nature, hard to derive and to maintain.

4.2   Effective Cache Keys and Applicable RCCs

To keep the population model simple, but at the same time as accurate as possible, we need the "right" concepts. As argued in the following, two essential concepts for the population estimation of a cache group G are *applicable RCC* and *effective cache key*.

Any filling action in a cache group is path-dependent and depends on the type of RCC traversed. For example, an optimization RCC does not change G's filling and need therefore not be considered for G's population estimation. (In Fig. 3, $Q.e \rightarrow O.a$ and $V.g \rightarrow O.a$ would be such optimization RCCs.) Otherwise, we would have to deal with MC $\rightarrow$ OC cycles (the reverse owner constraint for an already traversed member constraint) adding unnecessary complexity. In Fig. 3, all four RCCs shown are applicable for the population estimation.

Conversely, if a reverse *member* constraint is specified explicitly, this RCC is considered a design error. The resulting homogeneous cycle would only lead to excessive load situations without benefiting the transaction's queries.

When more than one cache key is specified for a root table, we can always reduce such a set of cache keys to a single effective cache key (ck_{eff}) as far as cost estimations for the filling process are concerned.[4] ck_{eff} is the only non-unique

---

[3] However, this would only improve certain situations. Since values in a column, distributed according to a histogram, are used in RCCs which enforce the filling of these values in columns of other tables, the model complexity seems to be very hard to control.

[4] Consider two cache keys, $T.u$ unique and $T.n$ non-unique. If a value of u causes a cache miss, the single qualified record is loaded into the cache. The new value of $T.n$ has to be made value complete which determines the set of records to be loaded (except in the case of a NULL value in $T.n$, which we exclude from our estimations).

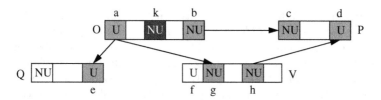

Fig. 3. Cache group G

cache key, if any; otherwise, it is any unique cache key. When $O.a$ and $O.k$ are defined as cache keys in Fig. 3, then $O.k$ is the effective one.

The column ck_{eff} determines the number n_S of records to be loaded into the root table S upon any cache miss, which is caused by probing an equality predicate on a cache key column of S. Furthermore, it guarantees that domain completeness for all cache key columns of S is satisfied after loading these n_S records. In fact, for the computation of n_S, only the cardinality of the ck_{eff} column matters (together with N_S, the cardinality of S_{B}). Therefore, we always deal with ck_{eff} in the following.

A computation step considers a source table S – for the initial step, the root table –, an applicable RCC R, and a target table T. Given N_S and N_T, the expected filling size n_T of T enforced by R can be derived from n_S and from the cardinalities of the columns connected by R. In a subsequent step, table T may become the new source table S', and an outgoing RCC together with its target table T' is selected as the component under consideration.

4.3   Population Estimation – A Simple Example

To derive a general scheme of cache group filling, the basic step and its quantitative description can be studied using the situation illustrated in Fig. 3. It covers the essential column and RCC types: $O.k$ labels a NU (effective) cache key, whereas $O.a$ and $O.b$ denote U and NU (non-domain-complete) columns.

In the following, a new value v of cache key $O.k$ is assumed to be filled into cache table O, enforcing the load of $n_{O.k}$ records of type O to guarantee DC of $O.k$. Because $O.a$ is unique, the number of new $O.a$ values is $n_{O.k}$. But what is the number $n_{O.b}$ of $O.b$ values that appear in the cache as a consequence of v? Furthermore, how many records of types Q, V, and P have to be loaded to satisfy the RCCs $O.a \rightarrow Q.e$, $O.a \rightarrow V.g$, and $O.b \rightarrow P.c$?

Of course, when a column is unique, its cardinality is equal to the number of records in the corresponding backend table, e.g., $c_{O.a} = N_O$. Using the uniform-value-distribution assumption, we can immediately compute $n_O = n_{O.k} = N_O/c_{O.k}$, which is the number of records of type O to be loaded. The computation of $n_{O.b}$ is much more difficult and requires additional thoughts which led to our model $f(N, c, n)$. Hence, by substituting $n_{O.b}$ for d and N_O, $c_{O.b}$, and n_O in $f(N, c, n)$, we can compute $n_{O.b} = f(N_O, c_{O.b}, n_O)$.[5]

---

[5] The formula for $f(N_O, c_{O.b}, n_O)$ is only one possible option. If available, any other (possibly more efficiently computable) approximation could act as a substitute.

A fundamental difficulty prohibits the more accurate approximation of the case where both $O.k$ and $O.b$ are non-unique. All the $n_{O.b}$ values computed by our formula become effective for the first $O.k$ value only. In a subsequent filling initiated by a new $O.k$ value v', some $O.b$ values qualified by v' may already reside in the root table, and, therefore, only $n_{\text{eff}} \leq n_{O.b}$ values may trigger further fillings via RCCs. A more accurate approximation would require to consider the filling history of the cache group which seems to be impractical and is definitely beyond the rationale of our estimation model. Moreover, this case does not seem so important to justify additional model complexity. Therefore, we always put up an inequality relation in formulas where $n_{O.b}$ is involved: $n_{\text{eff}} \leq n_{O.b} = f(N_O, c_{O.b}, n_O)$.

In case of a unique source column $O.a$ of an RCC (i.e., a membership constraint), always all $n_{O.a} = n_O$ values are new and lead to the loading of the corresponding values in the target column of the participating table (let's say Q or V). Hence, always n_Q (n_V) records of type Q (V) are to be filled into the cache table Q (V): $n_Q = n_O \cdot N_Q/c_{Q.e}$ ($n_V = n_O \cdot N_V/c_{V.g}$). In case of a non-unique source column $O.b$ of an RCC (i.e., an OC or XC), all $n_{O.b} \leq n_O$ values are assuredly new only when O is empty. In general, some of these values may already have been brought into the cache table by a previously referenced $O.k$ value. Therefore, the resulting cache load for the target table P can only be estimated by $n_{P1} \leq n_{O.b} \cdot N_P/c_{P.c} = f(N_O, c_{O.b}, n_O) \cdot N_P/c_{P.c}$.

As indicated in Fig. 3, P is reached by an additional RCC loading path $O.a \rightarrow V.g, V.h \rightarrow P.d$, the contribution of which has to be approximated. According to our assumptions, n_V records cause $d = f(N_V, c_{V.h}, n_V)$ different values to be loaded into $V.h$, which, in turn, need d different owner records in P. Because there are already records in P loaded via $O.b \rightarrow P.c$, we may encounter some of these owner records there. Hence, we can expect $n_P = n_{P1} + n_{P2} - n_{P1} \cdot n_{P2}/N_P$ records to be loaded into P where $n_{P2} = f(N_V, c_{V.h}, n_V) \cdot N_P/c_{P.d} = f(N_V, c_{V.h}, n_V)$.

4.4   General Scheme for a Single Evaluation Step

After having discussed, by referring to the example in Fig. 3, the various parameters influencing the filling of a cache group caused by a single cache key value, we can generalize our notation and summarize our findings. In the following, we use S and T for source and target table, or for a table in general. Compiled in Tab. 1, we have derived a general schema for determining the cache table filling of a single evaluation step i. There we assess the effects of a single RCC R of a given type U/NU $\rightarrow$ U/NU.[6] Initiated by n_S records filled into S, the listed value n_T is the expected size of the record set that is to be filled into T to satisfy RCC R. For the initial step ($i = 1$), n_S is derived from the effective cache key of the root table. Note again, a target table becomes the source table of the subsequent evaluation step $i + 1$: $T_i \mapsto S_{i+1}$ and $n_{T_i} \mapsto n_{S_{i+1}}$.

---

[6] We assume a lossless join along an RCC. If, for example, an RCC connects a unique column of S with a unique column of T, then $N_S = N_T$, i.e., NULL values do not occur in these columns.

Table 1. General scheme for the table population induced by an RCC

| target table filling n_T | | target column $T.j$ | |
		U	NU
	U	$n_S \cdot 1$	$n_S \cdot N_T/c_{T.j}$
source column $S.i$	NU, DC	$n_S \cdot c_{S.i}/N_S \cdot 1$	$n_S \cdot c_{S.i}/N_S \cdot N_T/c_{T.j}$
	NU, non-DC	$f(N_S, c_{S.i}, n_S) \cdot 1$	$f(N_S, c_{S.i}, n_S) \cdot N_T/c_{T.j}$

Whether a non-unique column $S.i$ becomes domain complete, is context dependent (see Sect. 3.1). If it is domain complete, all its values cause new record sets of size $N_S/c_{S.i}$ to be loaded into S.

5 Evaluation of Single Cache Groups

So far, we have considered the effect of a single RCC on cache group filling. Note, since n_S and n_T are context dependent, it is not sufficient to sum the individual RCC filling results. Starting from an empty cache group G, our next goal is the estimation of G's population induced by a single ck_{eff} value. This estimation is an upper bound (in the average-case sense) for subsequent fillings due to a further ck_{eff} value, because, in case of a NU, non-DC source column $S.i$ of an RCC, some of the values estimated by $f(N, c, n)$ may already reside in column S. Hence, only some of these values may lead to a filling activity in the target table. The effective set of values is usually smaller than estimated by our formula – a rare situation that, however, has to be taken into account due to limited model accuracy.

We propose a population-estimation algorithm PE that refers to G's reachability graph γ built from its applicable RCCs only; we assume that γ is cycle free. PE starts at the given filling point and computes – once and for all – the number of records n_S to be filled into the root table. Each member table T has $m \geq 1$ incoming RCCs originating from source tables $S_1, \ldots, S_m$. In order to avoid multiple evaluation of T's outgoing RCCs (for each incoming RCC separately), we need the expected size $n_{T\text{act}}$ of T's population based on all incoming RCCs, before we compute the populations of tables directly reachable from T.[7] Furthermore, in order to compute T's table population at once, we must know $n_{S_i\text{act}}$ of all source tables S_i. Since this rule applies to all S_i in their role as a target table as well, we have to compute the individual table populations in cache group G in such an order that, for the estimation of each T, the estimated populations of all S_i are already known. In other words, we have to perform a topological sort TS of G's reachability graph[8] to determine the order in which

---

[7] Although G is assumed to be cycle-free, this is the reason why a single traversal (e. g. left-most depth-first) of G's reachability graph is not sufficient for the population estimation.

[8] Since a topological sort detects cycles, it is a consistency check whether the PE algorithm is applicable to G's reachability graph.

---

1. Using its reachability graph, list the topological sort order of G's tables in TSO.
2. Visit the first (root) table S in TSO and compute the expected population n_S using the cardinality of ck_{eff}.
3. While there are tables in TSO not visited, visit the next table T and obtain the expected table population n_T:
   a) For each incoming RCC $R_i = S_i.a \to T.b_i$, compute the population n_{Ti} using the already computed $n_{S_i\text{act}}$ of its source table S_i, the type of R_i, and the cardinality of its target column $c_{T.b_i}$.
   b) $n_{T\text{act}}$ is obtained by applying the combination-of-events model using all determined n_{Ti}.

Fig. 4. Algorithm PE, estimating the population of a cache group G caused by a reference to a single ck_{eff} value.

the table populations can be computed. Since only the root table of G lacks incoming arcs, it is the starting point of TS.

Knowing $n_{S_i\text{act}}$ for all source tables $S.i$ connected to T via incoming RCCs, we can apply the appropriate formula of Tab. 1 and compute the population sizes n_{Ti} $(i = 1, \ldots, m)$ expected from each of the m RCCs. Since the corresponding record sets are considered stochastically independent, we can eliminate the expected duplicates from our population estimation by computing $n_{T\text{act}} = n_{T1\ldots m}$ as sketched in Sect. 4.1. Figure 4 summarizes the steps of PE.

6   Conclusion and Future Work

We have introduced constraint-based database caching using as an example a specific kind of cache groups tailored to PSJ queries, which frequently occur in TWAs. Cache groups provide predicate completeness for predicates built constructively from simple base predicates, which are specified as parameterized constraints on cache tables. This use of parameters gives cache groups a simple kind of adaptability.

The analysis of the basic type of cache groups has shown that one must be aware of the consequences of a set of specified cache constraints: On the one hand, performance problems due to uncontrolled cache loading must be prevented; on the other hand, one must know which kinds of predicates can be evaluated correctly in the cache and must have efficient probe operations to check the availability of predicate extensions. Furthermore, for each variation of constraint-based caching, quantitative analyses must help to understand which cache configurations are worth the effort. Therefore, we have developed the basic principles to quantitatively estimate the loading costs of a given cache group configuration.

Our framework can be used for the design of a cache group advisor supporting the DBA in the specification of a cache group, when the characteristics of the workload are known. Then, the expected costs for cache maintenance and the savings gained by predicate evaluation in the cache can be determined thereby identifying the trade-off point of cache operation. For example, starting with the cache tables and join paths exhibiting the highest degrees of reference locality, the cache group design can be expanded by additional RCCs and tables until the optimum point of operation is reached. Such a tool may also be useful during cache operation by observing the workload patterns and by proposing or automatically invoking changes in the cache group specification. This kind of self-administration or self-tuning opens a new and complex area of research often referred to as autonomic computing.

There are many other issues that wait to be resolved: For example, we have not said anything about the invalidation of predicates, about the removal of overlapping predicate extensions from the cache, or about different strategies how updates can be applied to cache and backend DB. We also want to explore, how the idea of constraint-based caching can be extended to other types of predicates (e.g., range or aggregation predicates).

Acknowledgments. We want to thank M. Altinel, Ch. Bornhövd, and C. Mohan for many fruitful discussions during the first author's sabbatical at ARC of IBM in San Jose. This cooperation led to deep insights into the problems of constraint-based database caching.

References

1. Akamai Technologies Inc.: Akamai EdgeSuite. http://www.akamai.com/
2. Mehmet Altinel, Christof Bornhövd, Sailesh Krishnamurthy, C. Mohan, Hamid Pirahesh, Berthold Reinwald: Cache Tables: Paving the Way for an Adaptive Database Cache. VLDB Conference 2003: 718–729
3. Khalil Amiri, Sanghyun Park, Renu Tewari, Sriram Padmanabhan: DBProxy: A Dynamic Data Cache for Web Applications. ICDE Conference 2003: 821–831
4. Jesse Anton, Lawrence Jacobs, Xiang Liu, Jordan Parker, Zheng Zeng, Tie Zhong: Web Caching for Database Applications with Oracle Web Cache. SIGMOD Conference 2002: 594–599
5. William Feller. *An Introduction to Probability Theory and Its Application.* 3rd edition, John Wiley & Sons, 1968
6. Jonathan Goldstein, Per-Åke Larson: Optimizing Queries Using Materialized Views: A Practical, Scalable Solution. SIGMOD Conference 2001: 331–342
7. Theo Härder, Andreas Bühmann:Datenbank-Caching – Eine systematische Analyse möglicher Verfahren, Informatik – Forschung und Entwicklung, Springer (2004)
8. Per-Åke Larson, Jonathan Goldstein, Jingren Zhou: MTCache: Mid-Tier Database Caching in SQL Server. ICDE Conference 2004
9. Stefan Podlipinig, Laszlo Böszörmenyi: A Survey of Web Cache Replacement Strategies. ACM Computing Surveys 35:4, 374–398 (2003)
10. The TimesTen Team: Mid-tier Caching: The TimesTen Approach. SIGMOD Conference 2002: 588–593
11. Gerhard Weikum: Web Caching. In: *Web & Datenbanken – Konzepte, Architekturen, Anwendungen.* Erhard Rahm/Gottfried Vossen (Hrsg.), dpunkt.verlag, 191–216 (2002)
12. S. Bing Yao: An Attribute Based Model for Database Access Cost Analysis. ACM Trans. Database Syst. 2(1): 45–67 (1977)

Towards Quadtree-Based
Moving Objects Databases[*]

Katerina Raptopoulou[1], Michael Vassilakopoulos[2], and Yannis Manolopoulos[1]

[1] Department of Informatics, Aristotle University,
GR-54006 Thessaloniki, Greece.
{katerina,manolopo}@delab.csd.auth.gr
[2] Department of Informatics, Technological Educational Institute of Thessaloniki,
GR-54101 Thessaloniki, Greece.
vasilako@it.teithe.gr

Abstract. Nowadays, one of the main research issues of great interest is the efficient tracking of mobile objects that enables the effective answering of spatiotemporal queries. This line of research is relevant to a number of modern applications spanning many contexts. In this paper, we consider the organization of a moving object database by quadtree based structures (structures obeying the Embedding Space Hierarchy). In this context, we adapt an indexing method, called XBR trees, to support range queries about the history of trajectories of moving objects. The XBR tree is a quadtree like external memory, balanced and compact structure that follows regular decomposition. Apart from the presentation of the new method, we experimentally show that it outperforms the only previous Embedding Space Hierarchy approach (based on PRM quadtrees) for indexing moving objects.

Keywords: Quadtrees, Moving Objects, Spatiotemporal Queries, Spatiotemporal Databases

1 Introduction

In the past few years, the focus of the research in Geographic Information Systems (GISs) has drastically evolved from traditional data management issues (such as modeling, indexing, querying) to new and exciting challenges raised by the emergence of new technologies. Two of the major recent achievements of these technologies, namely the World Wide Web and the development of accurate positioning systems, have a strong impact on GISs. In particular, positioning systems constitute a very challenging area. The Global Positioning System (GPS) and the new European Galileo satellite project (its launching has been decided very recently, at the end of March 2002), are able to determine the position of a moving object with a very high precision (e.g. a few centimeters).

---

[*] Research funded by the ARCHIMEDES project 2.2.14 "Management of Moving Objects and the WWW" of the Technological Educational Institute of Thessaloniki (EPEAEK II) and the bilateral Greek-Serbian scientific protocol.

A. Benczúr, J. Demetrovics, G. Gottlob (Eds.): ADBIS 2004, LNCS 3255, pp. 230–245, 2004.

On the other hand, there undoubtedly exists a necessity for numerous applications related to moving objects. Technologies involving mobile computing have appeared to show a great evolution, particularly in the last few years. Devices such as mobile phones and Internet terminals have become ubiquitous.

There are also applications, which include vehicle navigation, tracking and monitoring, where the positions of air, sea or land-based equipment, such as airplanes, fishing boats and cars (e.g. taxis or ambulances) are of interest. An example of such applications is the tracking of fighter planes in air-force combat situations. Being able to correctly locate the planes (that move very fast) at a present time and in the near future can be used to avoid enemy targets and also guide the of fighter planes towards proper targets. Other real life examples that involve objects with positions changing over time, are traffic control, fleet management, fire or hurricane front monitor and weather forecast.

The topic of querying and indexing moving objects has been addressed by several researchers. As far as the theoretical background is concerned, Sistla et al. in [11] proposed a data model, called Moving Objects Spatio-Temporal (MOST) model, for representing moving objects and a query language, called Future Temporal Logic. Wolfson et al. [18] addressed the uncertainty issues, which determine the frequency with which the database has to update the locations of the moving objects, in order to provide an error bound.

Several papers have appeared that base the indexing of moving objects on structures that belong in the family of R-trees [4]. For example, in [10] Saltenis et al. proposed an R*-tree based access method (the TPR-tree) to index the current and future locations of moving objects aiming at handling range queries. Pfoser et al. [9] proposed the STR-tree as an R-tree based indexing scheme suitable for storing the history of moving objects and for trajectory-based queries. Furthermore, the Historical R-tree was proposed by Nascimento et al. [8] as an indexing method for spatiotemporal data and range queries. Finally, in [19], Zhu et al. proposed octagon trees (OT-tree, O-tree) as extensions to the R*-tree to index moving objects and handle range queries.

All these methods are based on the concept of Object Space Hierarchy (the partitioning of regions depends on the data) that is followed by structures of the R-tree family. In this paper, we focus on methods based on the concept of Embedding Space Hierarchy (the partitioning of regions follows a regular fashion) that is followed by structures of the quadtree family. To the authors knowledge, the only paper that addresses the problem of indexing moving points by such a method is presented in [12]. In the present paper, a new such technique is presented and compared to the method of [12].

These structures allow processing of range time and space queries (e.g. which objects will appear in a specific area within a given time interval), or to predict the future position of an object, or to follow the history of the movement of an object.

An alternative perspective to tackle the issue of moving objects is the use of transformations to index their trajectories. In [6] Kollios et al. used the dual transformation with a view to improve the performance during range queries.

Similarly, Chon et al [3], proposed the SV-model as an alternative method of transformation. The use of moving objects can also be applied in multimedia environments. For example, Tzouramanis et al. in [14,15,16] presented several spatiotemporal access methods (i.e. the OLQ-trees Overlapping Linear Quadtrees and the MVLQ-tress Multiversion Linear Quadtrees) for storing and retrieving evolving raster images.

In [5], Hadjieleftheriou et al., suggested the Partially Persistent (PPR-tree) as a method for indexing and querying the history of moving objects with changing extend (e.g. shrinking). Furthermore, the object movement was described by polynomial and not by linear functions and the queries examined were range ones. Finally, other researchers proposed the use of techniques rooted in computational geometry (for example, in [1] external Range Trees are presented and use for indexing moving points).

The indexing scheme that we propose here, the External Balanced Regular trees (XBR trees), is based on quadtrees, and more specifically on hierarchical and regular subdivision of space. The key ideas behind its design were originally presented in [17] for managing spatial objects, in general. In this paper, we use XBR-trees in the context of spatiotemporal databases. More specifically, we use XBR-trees to index the trajectories of moving objetcs and to answer spatiotemporal queries about these objects. In addition to the material appearing in [17], in this paper, we present a modified algorithm for splitting internal nodes of XBR-trees to deal with extreme conditions and we also describe the steps of the deletion process in XBR-trees.

We experimentally compare the resulting method (that could be used as the physical layer of a Moving Objects Database) with the only analogous (quadtree based) method that is based on the PMR quadtree and was presented in [12] by Tayeb et al. An important difference between two techniques is that the indexing part of the PMR resides in main memory use, whereas the indexing part of XBR trees is a multiway disk-based tree. However, the experiments conducted in the present paper cannot be compared directly with the ones presented in [12], since they are performed under completely different conditions and assumptions (in [12] only the present status of moving objects is maintained, while in this paper the trajectory of each object through time is kept).

The XBR trees constitute a family of new secondary memory structures, which are suitable for storing and indexing multi-dimensional points and line segments. In 2 dimensions, the resulting structure is an External Balanced Quadtree, in 3 dimensions an External Balances Octtree, and in higher dimensions an External Balanced Hyper Quadtree. The main characteristic of all these structures is that they subdivide space (in an hierarchical and regular fashion) into disjoint regions. These spatial access methods are fully dynamic, while insertions are not complicated to program as they affect a single tree path only. Moreover, XBR trees are variable resolution structures. That is, the number of space subdivisions is not predefined, making these structures suitable for very large amounts of data. Due to the balanced nature of these structures and the disjointness of the resulting regions, searches and other queries in these trees are processed very efficiently. The interested reader will find a short qualitative comparison of XBR-trees with other well known structures, such as R-trees, R+trees, hB-trees and GBD trees, in [17]

The rest of the paper is organized as follows. Section 2 describes the assumptions made with respect to the movement of the objects, Section 3 gives a detailed description of the new structure and a short description of PMR quadtrees. Section 4 exposes the experimental results as far as query performance of the two trees is concerned. Finally, Section 5 presents briefly the conclusions and further research directions.

2   Monitoring of Moving Objects

We assume that time is discrete and that the location and velocity of each object is updated only at predefined time points that divide time in a number of time intervals. For each time interval of the past (up to the current time point), a line segment that expresses the movement of the object during this interval is maintained. For the interval starting at the current time point, a line segment that express the initial location and velocity of the object is maintained. All these line segments make up a polyline that expresses the trajectory of the object from the starting time point to the point that follows the current time point. Especially, the last line segment expresses not the actual trajectory, but the expected trajectory from the current time point to the next one.

When time advances to the next time point, each object notifies the system of its actual location and velocity. With this data, the last line segment of the polyline is updated (meaning that, in general, the last line segment must be deleted and reinserted to reflect the actual data) and a new segment that expresses the expected trajectory from the new current time point to the next one is inserted. The resulting line segments are stored in the (XBR, or PMR) tree leaves and information guiding the search to the leaves is stored in internal nodes.

This scheme aims at efficiently supporting range queries regarding the history of the objects movement. For example, to answer the query 'Find all the objects that were positioned inside a particular area during a specific time interval', we traverse the tree from the root, visiting only the nodes which may contain object trajectories satisfying the query. This is done by comparing the area coordinates specified by the query to the coordinates specifying each node.

Although, it is possible to handle X and Y coordinates of each object (along with time) at the same structure (with tree versions that can handle 3-dimensional data), following the approach of [12] we handle X and Y coordinates independently. This means that we keep one 2-dimensional tree for X coordinate along with time and another 2-dimensional tree for Y coordinate along with time. We answer a query using each of the trees and then combine the subanswers. Accordingly, at each time point we update both trees.

3   XBR and PMR

3.1   The XBR Tree

The XBR tree consists of two kinds of nodes: the leaves that occupy disk pages containing the actual data, namely the line segments, and the internal nodes, also occupying disk pages, which provide a multiway indexing method.

Despite the fact that XBR tree is an indexing method capable of being defined for various dimensions, for the sake of brevity, in the sequel we assume two dimensions. For 2 dimensions the hierarchical decomposition of space is the same as the quadtrees. More specifically, the space is subdivided in 4 equal subquadrants, any of which may be further subdivided recursively in 4 subquadrants.

Internal Nodes. Each internal node in the XBR tree consists of a non-predefined number of pairs of the form <address, pointer>. The number of these pairs is non-predefined because the addresses being used are of variable size. An address expresses a child node region and is paired with the pointer to this child node. Apparently, both the size of an address and the total space occupied by all pairs within a node must not exceed the node size.

More specifically, the address encoding method that we used works as follows. For a binary integer x initially we form code γ that consists of two parts. The first has $\lfloor \log_2 x \rfloor$ 0s and one 1, while the second is the number $x - 2^{\lfloor \log_2 x \rfloor}$ in binary form, expressed with $\lfloor \log_2 x \rfloor$ bits. The code that we finally use is δ that encodes the number $\lfloor \log_2 x \rfloor + 1$ with the first part of code γ (with the two parts of γ concatenaded) and with the second part the same to that of code γ (in binary form the number $x - 2^{\lfloor \log_2 x \rfloor}$). More details appear in [17].

The addresses being used constitute a representation of a specific subquadrant being produced by quadtree-like hierarchical subdivision of the current space. Each address is formed by a number of directional digits each one representing a particular subquadrant. That is, NW, NE, SW and SE subquadrants of a quadrant are distinguished by the directional digits 0, 1, 2 and 3, respectively. For example, the address 1 represents the NE quadrant of the current space, while the address 10 the NW subquadrant of the NE quadrant of the current space.

One of the main novelties of this particular indexing scheme is the fact that in reality the region of a child is the subquadrant determined by the address in its pair minus the subquadrants corresponding to the previous pairs of the internal node to which it belongs.

For example, Figure 1 depicts an internal node that points to two leaves. While the left child region is the SW quadrant of the original space, the right child region is the whole space minus the region of the first quadrant. Each * symbol denotes the end of a variable size address. In particular, the address of the left child is 2*, where the directional digit 2 corresponds to the SW quadrant of the original space. Moreover, the right child address is * (i.e. no directional digits exist in this address) and the region for this child is the whole space minus the first child region. Each address refers to a minimal quadrant covering the

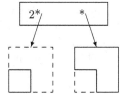

Fig. 1. An XBR tree with one internal node and two leaves.

internal node. In this specific example, the minimal subquadrant is the whole space, since the internal node under consideration is the root.

When a search or an insertion of a line segment is performed, descending the tree from the root specifies the appropriate leaves and their regions. At the root, the region that has to be checked is the whole space. When visiting an internal node, we check in turn every contained pair. The first pair with a subquadrant that contains the particular coordinates is chosen and its pointer to the next level is followed. By examining this way the pairs in each node, the path being followed determines the region under consideration by intersecting it with the subquadrant of the chosen pair and subtracting the subquadrants of the pairs appearing to the left of this pair.

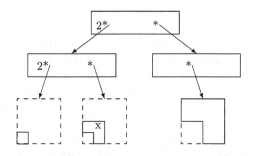

Fig. 2. An XBR tree with two levels of internal nodes.

After an insertion in the left child, this child is split and the result is shown in Figure 2. The child split has caused the split of the internal node too, and this has led to the new root creation. If someone wants to detect a data element marked with 'x' , he has to follow the following procedure. At first, he has to visit the root and the pairs that it contains. As we can see, the address 2* that belongs to the first pair, is the one whose respective subquadrant contains the coordinates of 'x'. Therefore, he has to follow the pointer of the first pair. In this node, the address of the first pair, 2*, determines the SW subquadrant of the SW quadrant of the whole space, which does not contain the coordinates of 'x' and the address of the second pair, *, determines the rest of the SW quadrant of the whole space, which contains the coordinates of 'x'. We follow the pointer of this pair and reach the leaf containing 'x'.

The multi-way nature of the XBR tree is not explicitly depicted by the two examples presented previously. This is done in purpose, only for the sake of brevity.

Leaf Nodes. Each external node (leaf) in the XBR tree may contain a number of line segments, which is limited by a predefined capacity C. When an insertion causes the number of line segments of a particular leaf to exceed C, then the leaf is spit following a hierarchical decomposition analogous to the quadtree decomposition, until the resulting regions contain line segments that are less than $x \times C$ and more than $(1 - x) \times C$, where $0.5 < x < 1$.

The constant x is chosen in order to affect the number of necessary subdivisions and the size of addresses that are created after the split. A choice of a value close to 0.5 has proven to cause more subdivisions and larger sizes of addresses. This is due to the fact that hardly ever does a partition split the leaf in subregions that contain almost equal numbers of elements.

With such a value assigned to x, we can achieve a better guarantee as far as the space occupancy of leaves is concerned. On the contrary, the PMR quadtree partitions each leaf once and only once. Such a method requires overflow pages. This is not the case for the XBR leaf however, which is guaranteed to contain at most C line segments plus the number of directional digits needed to reach this leaf. Furthermore, in PMR quadtrees there is no minimum occupancy of leaf nodes.

If we consider that x is assigned the value 0.75, then after continuous insertions of line segments in the NW corner of the right leaf region of Figure 2, the region of this leaf splits in four. If from the subregions formed none contains less than $3C/4$ and more than $C/4$ line segments, then the subregion containing the larger number of data elements is split in four. This procedure is repetitively applied until there exists a region with less than $3C/4$ and more than $C/4$ line segments. Then the original leaf will split in two leaves: the subregion created above will represent the region of the left of the two resulting leaves. The rest of the original region is the new right leaf region. Following this policy, both leaves created will be at least 1/4 full. This situation is depicted in Figure 3.

Splitting of Internal Nodes. An internal node overflow causes a split in two in a way that achieves a good balance between the space use in the two nodes. In order to perform the split, first of all we construct a quadtree that has as nodes the quadrants existing in the XBR internal node to be spit. This is shown in Figure 4a. This node contains addresses that subdivide the node region. Each address corresponds to a quadtree node represented by a square. By following the path to this node, all intermediate quadtree nodes are marked as circles. There also exists the possibility, that a square may be the ancestor of others squares (for example, the square of address 0* is a parent for the squares of addresses 00*, 01* and 02*). The address * specifies the quadtree root.

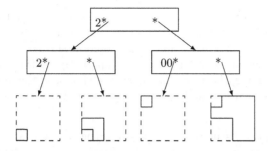

Fig. 3. The XBR tree after splitting the rightmost leaf of the tree in Figure 2.

To each node, we assign the number of squares that will be freed, when we eliminate the subtree rooted at this node. A bottom-up procedure rapidly calculates this number. In Figure 4c each external square is assigned the value 1: the squares of 100*, 101*, 00*, 01* and 02* are all assigned the value 1. Each internal square is assigned the sum of values of its children plus 1. For example, the square of 0* is assigned the value 4=1+1+1+1. Finally, a circle is assigned the sum of values of its children only. For example, the second root child is assigned 2, since it has only one child (another circle) with value 2. Next we traverse the tree in order to find a node, apart from the root, which is a square and is assigned the largest number of squares in the tree.

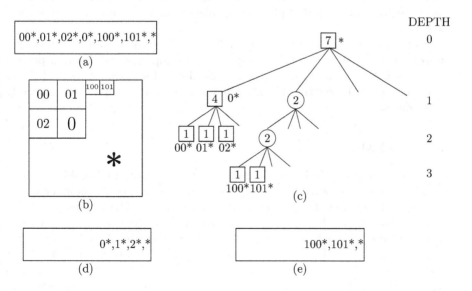

Fig. 4. Splitting of an internal XBR tree node.

For example, in the tree of Figure 4c, the node assigned with the largest number of squares, is the leftmost root child with address '0' and number of squares equal to 4. The sought subtree is rooted at this node. The resulting two nodes are depicted in Figure 4d and 4e. Apparently, in the father node of the original internal node, the entry 0*, which corresponds to the minimal quadblock of the left of the resulting nodes, should be inserted.

Deletion. Deletion is used while updating the location and velocity of each object at each time point. That is, the last line segment of the trajectory of each moving object is updated at the end of each time interval (in general, it must be deleted and reinserted to reflect the actual data) and a new line segment, expressing the expected trajectory from the new current to the next time point, is inserted.

Since a line segment may cross the regions of several XBR-tree leaf nodes, it has to be removed from all these leaf nodes. Following a procedure similar to the insertion of a line segment, at each internal node (starting from the root) we sequentialy examine the <address, pointer> pairs and recursively visit child nodes with regions that are crossed by the line segment. This way, we determine all the leaves that are crossed by the line segment (the line segment must be deleted from each of these leaves).

If a leaf node from which we remove the line segment underflows (if it contains less than $(1 - x) \times C$ line segments), then a merge occurs. First, the <address, pointer> pair corresponding to this leaf that resides in its parent internal node is deleted. Then, the rest line segments of the leaf node are added to the rightmost child of the parent internal node (the righmost brother of the leaf node). If this child overflows, then it is split (as described in the "Leaf Nodes" part of the current subsection) and the split may propage to higher levels (hosting internal nodes).

Since internal nodes do not have a minimum occupancy theshold, the merge process is not applied to internal nodes. A more sophisticated deletion process that considers alternative merging of an underflowed leaf node with other brother leaves, except for its rightmost brother and merging of internal nodes is currently under development.

3.2   The PMR Tree

The PMR tree [12] is an indexing scheme based on quadtrees, capable of indexing line segments. The internal part of the tree consists of an ordinary region quadtree (degree four tree) residing in main memory. The leaf nodes of this quadtree point to the bucket pages that hold the actual line segments and reside on disk (Table 1). Each line segment is stored in every bucket whose quadrant (region) it crosses. A line segment can cross a region of a bucket either fully or partially. The PMR tree was proposed as an access method where the index is kept in main memory, whereas the indexed data, namely the line segments, are stored in secondary storage.

Table 1. RAM and Disc usage for XBR-trees and PMR-trees.

	XBR-trees	PMR-trees
RAM	Pointer to Root	Internal Nodes
Disk	Internal Nodes and External Nodes	External Nodes

Insertion in the PMR tree. A line segment is inserted in a PMR tree by being registered in the buckets that correspond to the quadrants that it crosses. During that procedure the capacity of each bucket that is intersected by the line segment is checked in order to verify whether that insertion causes it to exceed the predefined bucket capacity. If the bucket capacity is exceeded, then the bucket is split once and only once into four equal quadrants (if the bucket has already been split, then a chain of overflow buckets is maintained). Therefore, the bucket capacity is a split threshold. When a bucket is split, four new buckets are created, each one corresponding to a single subquadrant of the quadrant of the original bucket. After this procedure is performed, the old parent bucket is no longer in use. On the contrary, the quadtree pointer (in main memory) that used to point to that bucket now points to a new quadtree node with four pointers that point to the four newly created buckets.

Deletion in the PMR tree. A line segment is deleted from a PMR quadtree by being removed from all the buckets that correspond to quadrants that it crosses. During this procedure, the capacity of the bucket and its siblings are checked in order to discover if the deletion causes the total number of lines segments in them to be less than a split threshold. If the split threshold is greater than the capacity of the bucket and its siblings, then they merge and the merge procedure is then repeated to the parent quadtree node.

4 Experimentation

For the tree implementations and the experiments execution we used a Pentium 1600-MhZ with 1024K memory. The page size used was 4k, which resulted in a leaf node containing 204 lines. After experimentation, we came to the conclusion that the use of a buffer of 100K with least-recently-used page replacement, has shown better performance in comparison to other choices. Therefore, except these 100 disk pages, the entire index comprising both the internal and the external nodes, reside on disk.

For the experiments execution, we considered 1000 time units, being separated into 100 equal time intervals, each one of 10 time units. We conducted several experiments with a varying number of moving objects N, and a different size for the range query, which is successively set to 0.1, 0.01, 0.001 of the total space into consideration. At time unit 0, we randomly generate a velocity and an initial location for each object. We assume that during each time interval the object velocity and location are constant. At the interval end though, these numbers are updated for each object. This procedure is repetitively applied until the end of the time horizon being considered is reached.

The queries performed are range queries and during an experimental execution they are repeated after 10 constant time intervals. During the experiments execution we count the I/O cost for the queries, the cost for the pages that are not found in the buffer and are read from the disk, the execution time cost, the average number of repetitions of each line and the number of nodes that reside on disk for the XBR tree and the number of nodes that reside either in disk or in memory for the PMR tree.

Since both the XBR tree and the PMR tree, belong to the quadtree families, each line segment inserted in them is not kept in a single but in more than one leaves. Therefore counting and comparing the number of the appearances of a line segment in the two trees is considered to be noteworthy.

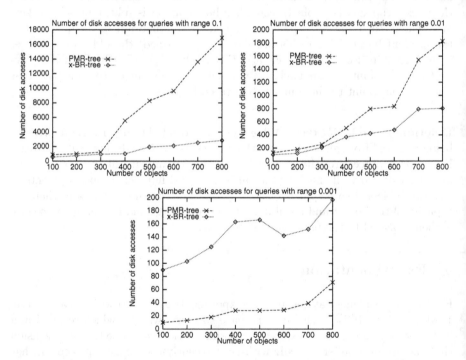

Fig. 5. Disk Accesses for queries with range 0.1 (top left), 0.01 (top right) and 0.001 (bottom).

The first three experiments presented in Figure 5 study the number of disk accesses. Namely, we counted the number of disk accesses that were required for both trees during the execution of the range queries. In each experiment the parameters are the number of objects and the size of the range query. The objects vary from 100 to 800, whereas the query size takes values 0.1, 0.01 and 0.001.

Figure 5 top left illustrates the number of disk accesses for range queries performed for a query size equal to 0.1 of the whole space under consideration. In this figure, the XBR tree requires significantly fewer disk accesses than the PMR tree. Figure 5 top right depicts the number of disk accesses for queries size equal to 0.01. As in the previous experiment, the number of disk accesses made by the XBR tree are again significantly fewer than those made by the PMR tree. Figure 5 bottom presents the number of disk accesses for the 0.001 query sizes. In this case, the PMR tree requires fewer disk accesses during the execution of the range queries. However, its difference from the XBR tree is very small (notice the scale on the y-axis). This reverse behavior is easily explained. For a very small query size, a small number of leaves is accessed. In the XBR tree (unlike the PMR tree), the internal nodes that are used to reach the leaves, also reside on disk and contribute to the number of disk accesses. This is the penalty the XBR tree has to pay, in order to be capable to handle very large amounts of data (unlike the semi-RAM based PMR quadtree). As it will be shown later in this section, in the experiments that study execution time cost, even under this situation, the XBR tree outperforms the PMR quadtree.

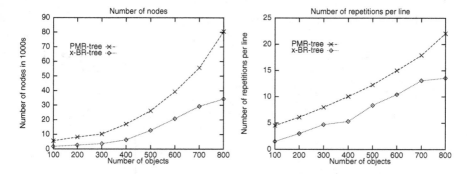

Fig. 6. Number of Nodes (left) and Medium Number of Repetitions Per Line (right).

The next two experiments presented in Figure 6, study the number of nodes required for both trees and the average number of appearances for the lines inserted. In each experiment, the parameters are the number of objects under consideration, which varies from 100 to 800.

Figure 6 left shows (in thousands) the number of nodes required by the two trees. During the experiment evolution, the PMR tree grew and was made up of nodes that resided either on disk, or in main memory. By definition, all the XBR tree nodes reside in the disk. The nodes in the former case were by far more than the ones in the latter case. This means that the XBR tree (due to its multiway nature) has a smaller height than the PMR tree, which will help the tree to answer the queries more effectively.

Since both the PMR tree and the XBR tree are quadtrees (and subdivide space in a predefined manner), it follows that the lines inserted in them are not kept in a single leaf. Each line segment may intersect and be inserted in several leaves, a fact that can delay the query processing. The average number of appearances per line inserted is presented in Figure 6 right. The parameter in this experiment is the number of objects, which again varies from 100 to 800. In this experiment, the XBR tree again stored each line segment in fewer leaves than the PMR tree.

To sum up the results from the experiments in Figure 6, we come out that the XBR tree is a more compact tree, with smaller height, occupying fewer nodes than the PMR tree. Furthermore, the lines inserted in the XBR tree are not repeated as many times as in the PMR case. The second result, namely that the inserted lines are repeated more times in the PMR tree is a logical conclusion drawn from the fact that the PMR has more nodes. This means that the lines inserted in the tree have to be repeated in more nodes.

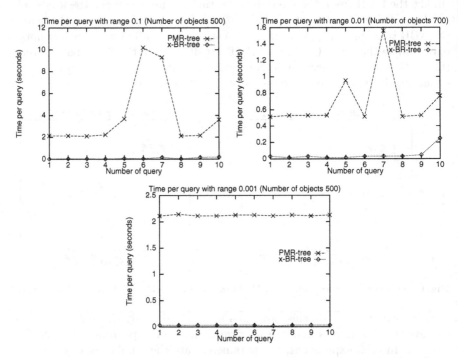

Fig. 7. Elapsed time for queries with range 0.1 (top left), range 0.01 (top right) and range 0.001 (bottom).

The next three experiments study the time elapsed during each query execution (execution time cost). For each tree, we performed 10 queries, each one during a constant time interval. The parameters in these experiments are the number of the query from 1 to 10, the query range that takes values 0.1, 0.01 and 0.001 and the number of objects, which takes values 500, 700 and 500. Since in each experiment there are 10 queries performed, in each figure there are 10 numbers corresponding to the elapsed time.

In Figure 7 top left the experiment was conducted with 500 moving objects and query size equal to 0.1. In this figure, the execution time for the XBR tree

is significantly less than the time for the PMR tree. Another observation, as far
as the experiment is concerned, is that the time spent for the PMR tree shows
an instant great increase during the queries from 5 to 8. This instability in the
PMR tree shows that there is no guarantee for the time needed, which can be
either small or bigger. In Figure 7 top right 700 moving objects are considered in
combination with 0.01 queries. As in the previous experiment, the time needed
by the XBR tree in this figure is significantly less. Furthermore, the time spent
by the PMR tree still appears to show a great instant increase during the queries
from 4 to 8. Finally, in Figure 7 bottom there are 500 moving objects and 0.001
range queries. In this case, again, the XBR tree consumes significantly less time
than the PMR tree for all the range queries conducted. Note that this happens
contrary to the higher number of disk accesses needed by the XBR tree (Figure
5 bottom). In other words, although for 0.001 range queries the PRM quadtree
slightly outperfoms the XBR tree in disk accesses, overall (in execution time)
the XBR tree significantly outperforms the PMR quadtree.

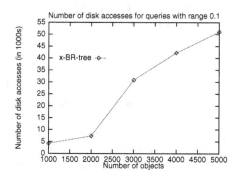

Fig. 8. Node Accesses.

As a final experiment, in Figure 8 we counted the number of disk accesses
that were required for the XBR tree. The parameter in this experiment is the
number of moving objects, which varies from 1000 to 5000, whereas the query
range into consideration is 0.1 of the whole space. The reader may ask why we
have not presented results for the PMR quadtree also. The answer is that, for
these cardinalities of moving objects, the execution needed to gather such results
for the PMR quadtree was excessive.

5   Conclusions and Future Work

Considering the great application demands for monitoring of mobile objects, to
be able to efficiently locate and answer queries related to the position of these
objects in time is very important. More specifically, modern applications, such as
Mobile Computing and Geographic Information Systems, make the development
of research within this field inevitable.

In this paper, we proposed a method, XBR trees, that follows the Embedding Space Hierarchy and can efficiently keep track of the moving objects history and answer spatiotemporal range queries. According to the experimentation presented, this scheme is indeed efficient. In all experiments conducted, the XBR tree outperforms the PMR quadtree (the only Embedding Space Hierarchy method up to now that has been proposed for monitoring moving objects). Even in the case of very small query ranges, where the PRM quadtree slightly outperformed the XBR tree in disk accesses, overall (in execution time) the XBR tree significantly outperformed the PMR quadtree.

The queries answered during experimentation were statiotemporal range queries that tracked the history of the motion of the moving objects. One possible future extension to this investigation is the implementation and experimentation with other types of spatiotemporal queries. Such types may include

- nearest neighbor queries (e.g. 'indicate the nearest neighbor of an object at each position of its trajectory', a query of great importance), or
- spatiotemporal joins, namely queries that deal with moving objects combined with moving regions (e.g. 'Find all airplanes that intersect clouds while they move').

Future research may also include

- experimenting with 3-dimensional versions of the quad-based trees (to combine time and the two coordinates X and Y in a single indexing structure),
- employing alternative buffering methods to improve tree performance, or
- comparing the XBR tree indexing method with other spatiotemporal trees (especially ones following the Object Space Hierarchy, like R-tree based structures), so that we can come up with more general conclusions about the winner structure for moving objects management.

References

1. P.K. Agarwal, L. Arge, J. Erickson: "Indexing Moving Points", *Proceedings 19th ACM Symposium on Principles of Database Systems (PODS'2000)*, pp.175-186, Madison, WI, 2000.
2. N. Beckmann, H. Kiegel, R. Scheider, B. Seeger: "The R*-tree: an Efficient and Robust Access Method for Points and Rectangles", *Proceedings ACM SIGMOD International Conference on Management of Data*, pp.322-331, Atlantic City, NJ, 1990.
3. H.D. Chon, D. Agarwal, A.E. Abbadi: "Storage and Retrieval of Moving Objects", *Proceedings 2nd International Conference on Mobile Data Management*, pp.173-184, Hong-Kong, China, 2001.
4. A. Guttman: "R-trees: a Dynamic Index Structure for Spatial Searching", *Proceedings ACM SIGMOD International Conference on Management of Data*, pp.47-57, Boston, MA, 1984.
5. M. Hadjieleftheriou, G. Kollios, V.J. Tsotras, D. Gunopoulos: "Efficient Indexing of Spatiotemporal Objects", *Proceedings 8th International Conference on Extending Database Technology (EDTB'2002)*, pp.251-268, Prague, Czech Republic, 2002.

6. G.Kollios, D. Gunopoulos, V.J. Tsotras: "On Indexing Mobile Objects", *Proceedings 18th ACM Symposium on Principles of Database Systems (PODS'99)*, pp.261-272, Philadelphia, PA, 1999.

7. G. Kollios, D. Gunopoulos, V.J. Tsotras, A.Delis, M. Hadjieleftheriou: "Indexing Animated Objects Using Spatiotemporal Access Methods", *IEEE Transactions on Knowledge and Data Engineering*, Vol.13, No.5, pp.758-777, 2001.

8. M.A. Nascimento, J.R.O. Silva: "Towards Historical R-trees", *Proceedings ACM Symposium on Applied Computing (SAC'98)*, pp.235-240, Atlanta, GA, 1998.

9. D. Pfoser, C. Jensen, Y. Theodoridis: "Novel Approaches to the Indexing of Moving Object Trajectories", *Proceedings 26th International Conference on Very Large Databases (VLDB'2000)*, pp.189-200, Cairo, Egypt, 2000.

10. S. Saltenis, C.S. Jensen, S.T. Leutenegger, M.A. Lopez: "Indexing the Positions of Continuously Moving Objects", *Proceedings ACM SIGMOD International Conference on Management of Data*, pp.331-342, Dallas, TX, 2000.

11. A.P. Sistla, O. Wolfson, S. Chamberlain, S. Dao: "Modeling and Querying Moving Objects", *Proceedings 13rd IEEE International Conference on Data Engineering (ICDE'97)*, pp.422-432, Birmingham, UK, 1997.

12. J. Tayeb, O. Ulusoy, O. Wolfson: "A Quadtree based Dynamic Attribute Indexing Method", *The Computer Journal*, Vol.41, No.3, pp.185-200, 1998.

13. Y .Theodoridis, M. Vazirgiannis, T. Sellis: "Spatio-Temporal Indexing for a Large Multimedia Applications" *Proceedings 3rd IEEE International Conference on Multimedia Computing and Systems*, pp.441-448, Hiroshima, Japan, 1996.

14. T. Tzouramanis, M. Vassilakopoulos, Y. Manolopoulos: "Overlapping Linear Quadtrees: a Spatiotemporal Indexing Method", *Proceedings 6th ACM Symposium on Advances in Geographic Information Systems (ACM-GIS'98)*, pp.1-7, Bethesda, MD, 1998.

15. T. Tzouramanis, M. Vassilakopoulos, Y. Manolopoulos: "Multiversion Linear Quadtrees for Spatiotemporal Data", *Proceedings 4th East-European Conference on Advances in Databases and Information Systems (ADBIS-DASFAA'2000)*, pp.279-292, Prague, Czech Republic, 2000.

16. T. Tzouramanis, M. Vassilakopoulos and Y. Manolopoulos: "Overlapping Linear Quadtrees and Spatio-temporal Query Processing", *The Computer Journal*, Vo.43, No.4, pp.325-343, 2003.

17. M. Vassilakopoulos and Y. Manolopoulos: "External Balanced Regular (x-BR) Trees: new Structures for Very Large Spatial Databases", *Proceeding of the 7th Panhellenic Conference on Informatics*, pp.III.61-III.68, Ioannina, Greece, 1999,

18. O. Wolfson, B. Xu, S. Chamberalin, L. Jiang: "Moving Objects Databases: Issues and Solutions", *Proceedings 10th International Conference on Scientific and Statistical Database Management (SSDBM'98)*, pp.111-122, Capri, Italy, 1998.

19. H. Zhu, J. Su, O.H. Ibarra: "Trajectory Queries and Octagons in Moving Object Databases", *Proceedings 11th ACM International Conference on Information and Knowledge Management (CIKM'2002)*, pp.413-421, McLean, VA, 2002.

A Content-Based Music Retrieval System Using Multidimensional Index of Time-Sequenced Representative Melodies from Music Database

Kyong-I Ku, Jae-Yong Won, Jaehyun Park, and Yoo-Sung Kim

School of Information and Communication Engineering,
Inha University, Incheon 402-751, Korea
yskim@inha.ac.kr

Abstract. In content-based music retrieval systems, since both the correctness and the performance of retrievals are important, a few content-based music retrieval systems have the melody index which contains the representative melodies of music to be likely used as users' queries. In this paper, we describe the development of a content-based music retrieval system in which the multidimensional index of time-sequenced representative melodies extracted appropriately based on musical composition forms is used to support quick and appropriate retrievals to users' melody queries. From the experimental results, we can see that the developed system can retrieve more relevant results than previous systems with smaller storage overhead than whole melody index.

1 Introduction

Most of currently working music retrieval systems are based on only metadata of music, such as title, name of composer, name of singer, and words of song([1], [2]). In these traditional music retrieval systems, users should recall and specify metadata of music they want as users' queries. However, this type of querying is unnatural due to the general fact that people prefer to remember a part of music itself rather than its metadata. Therefore, content-based music retrieval system in which users can query by some melodies they remember is essentially required.

As content-based music retrieval systems, a few systems have been developed([3], [4], [5], [6]). In these systems, users specify query melodies by humming, by playing, or by drawing a part of music remembered as the representative melodies. Here, by the representative melodies of music we mean that they are semantic delegation of music's melodies such as the first melody, the climax melody, and the repeated theme melodies of the music, and people can remember these melodies for the music so that users are likely to use these melodies as query melodies([7]). Then, the system retrieves the music information according to the similarity between user's query melody and the melodies of music database.

However, since most of the previous content-based music retrieval systems do not have the effective indexing mechanism, users may face with long response time due to the time-consuming syntactic processing for retrievals in which an approximate matching between query melody and all melodies of underlying music database

A. Benczúr, J. Demetrovics, G. Gottlob (Eds.): ADBIS 2004, LNCS 3255, pp. 246–258, 2004.

should be performed. Other some of the previous systems([6], [8]) have the first melody index in which only the beginning part of each music is included as the indexed melody. In general, however, since people are likely to remember music by its representative melodies not by only its first beginning part, these systems with the first melody index cannot support user queries of all possible representative melodies including climax melody and repeated theme melodies of music.

To remedy the above problem, some researches([9], [10], [11], [12]) have concentrated on extracting repeated theme melodies from a music file. In [9] and [10], since authors consider only the exactly repeated patterns not approximately repeated patterns as theme melody in a music file, the theme melody index that contains only the exactly repeated theme melodies extracted by the mechanism of [9] or [10] is not enough to support users' queries of the representative melodies. However, an our previous work([12]) proposed a theme melody extraction mechanism in which an extended graphical clustering algorithm is used for grouping the approximately repeated melodies into one cluster with considering musical composition forms and a melody is extracted from each cluster as an approximately repeated theme melody. In addition to the approximately repeated theme melodies of music, the first melody and the climax melody of the music are augmented into the final representative melody set. Thus, the representative melody index can well support users' queries in which these kinds of melodies are used.

In another our previous work([13]), we developed a content-based music retrieval system in which the 2-dimensional representative melody index is used. In this system, since the dimension of the metric space for the representative melody index is just 2, several melodies that have totally different music patterns may be placed within a close distance. Hence, even though the signature of melody that stands for the melody's variation patterns is used to distinguish these melodies, we have slightly inappropriate results sometimes in the previous system. These inappropriate retrievals mainly come from the excessive reduction of semantic features of melody into a point of 2-dimensional metric space with two-axes, average length variation and average pitch variation of melody.

In this paper, we discuss the development of a content-based music retrieval system in which the multidimensional index of time-sequenced representative melodies is used to enhance the correctness and the performance of retrievals from users' incomplete melody queries. Basically, since melody comes out from continuous arrangement of notes as time goes, a melody can be transformed into a time sequence data. In this work, a representative melody of motif length is transformed into an 8-dimensional time-sequenced data, and it is mapped into a point of 8-dimensional metric space of M-tree([14]) for the representative melody index. We also discuss the procedure for content-based retrieval using the multidimensional time-sequenced representative melody index and compare the performance of the proposed system to that of the previous one.

The rest of this paper is organized as follows. Section 2 discusses the overall architecture of the developed content-based music retrieval system. In section 3, we discuss the systematic construction of the multidimensional time-sequenced representative melody index. In section 4, we discuss the procedures and the appropriateness of the content-based music retrievals using the multidimensional time-sequenced representative melody index. We also discuss the performance of the system. Finally, this paper is concluded with future works in section 5.

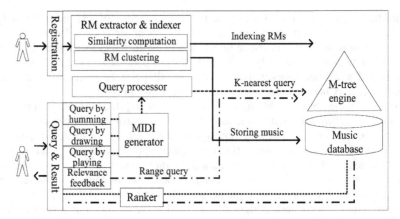

Fig. 1. Architecture of the Proposed Content-based Music Retrieval System

2 Architecture of Content-Based Music Retrieval System

The overall architecture of the content-based music retrieval system using the multi-dimensional time-sequenced representative melody index is shown in Fig. 1. It consists of Registration interface, RM extractor & indexer, M-tree engine, Music database, Query & Result interface, MIDI generator, Query processor, and Ranker.

From the new music file submitted via Registration interface, RM extractor & indexer extracts the representative melodies. This work is accomplished by the unit of motif since it is the minimum meaningful unit in music semantics([15]). This module has two primary sub-modules; Similarity computation and RM clustering. Similarity computation module computes the similarity values of all pairs of motifs of music. And, RM clustering module classifies motifs of the music file into one or more groups in each of which only the similar motifs to each other are included. The more detail of extracting representative melodies from a music file is discussed in section 3.1.

The appropriately extracted representative melodies from a music file are stored in the multidimensional time-sequenced representative melody index implemented by M-tree([14]), a well-known multidimensional indexing scheme. To place the extracted representative melodies into the multidimensional metric space of M-tree, a representative melody of motif length is transformed into an 8-dimensional time-sequenced data, and it is mapped into a point of 8-dimensional metric space of M-tree. The more detail on converting a melody of one motif into 8-dimensional time-sequenced data is discussed in section 3.2.

Query & Result Interface consists of three querying modules and one for the relevance feedback. Up to now, since the drawing interface is well tested and is good for viewing the user's query melody, we will use this interface hereafter.

In this work, we assume that music file is in MIDI(musical instrument digital interface) format since it is a well-known standard for computer music. MIDI generator transforms a query melody of humming, drawing, or playing into MIDI format as the intermediate format. Then, Query processor makes the retrieval features of query melody. It retrieves the relevant melodies from the multidimensional time-sequenced representative melody index of M-tree by using k-nearest neighbor search algorithm.

Ranker decides ranks of the retrieval results according to the distances between the query melody and the retrieval results. Since a query melody is of different length from representative melodies in the representative melody index, we use a time-warping distance function([16], [17]) to compute the distance between them. To enhance the appropriateness of retrieval results, users can go through the user relevance feedback phase via the relevance feedback module of Query & Result interface. The more details concerned on retrieval and user relevance feedback are discussed in section 4.

3   Systematic Construction of the Representative Melody Index

3.1   Extraction of Representative Melodies

The summarized procedure for the extraction of the representative melodies(RMs) from a music file is shown in Fig. 2.

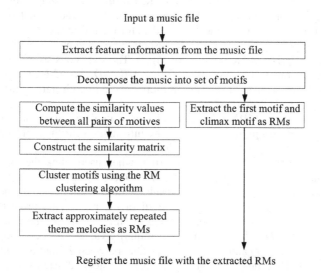

Fig. 2. Procedure for Extracting Representative Melodies from Music File

When a music file is submitted, the features such as time signature, pitch and length of notes are extracted from the submitted music file. By using the feature information, we decompose a music file into the set of motifs, since a motif is the semantic unit of music composition. Then we compute the similarity values between all pairs of the motifs by using the similarity computation algorithm([18]). Then, the similarity matrix can be constructed. The motifs of a music file are clustered based on the similarity values by using the proposed RM clustering algorithm that considers the musical composition forms. The detail of the clustering algorithm is in [12].

From each clusters, we extract an approximately repeated theme melody as a representative melody based on the position or role of the motif within the music. If a cluster includes the first motif or the climax motif, we extract that motif as the repre-

Fig. 3. The Music Score of a Korean Children Song 'Spring of Hometown'

sentative melody from the corresponding cluster. Otherwise, we extract a RM from each cluster to allow the extracted melody to be the center position of the cluster in metric space of M-tree. After extraction of RM from each cluster, if the first motif or the climax motif of a music file does not exist in the extracted melody set, we add them to the final set of representative melodies for the music file.

As an example of extracting the representative melodies, we will use a Korean children song, 'Spring of Hometown' of Fig. 3. The song consists of 8 motifs and has a pattern as its musical composition form, A-B-C-D-E-B'-C-D. From the musical composition form, we can expect that 8 motifs should be clustered into three similar groups, $\{B, B'\}$, $\{C, C\}$, and $\{D, D\}$.

When we input the MIDI of 'Spring of Hometown' in Fig. 3 for registration, we can see the screen of Fig. 4. We can see the information for the representative melodies extracted from the music file at the lower window.

To see the more details of RM clustering, when users click the 'Representative' button of the rightmost frame we can see the screen of Fig. 5. In this screen, we can see the similarity matrix, the clustering results with threshold value by the RM extraction algorithm of [12], and the climax motif of the music file. From the similarity matrix, we can easily recognize that 'Spring of Hometown' has the musical composi tion form of A-B-C-D-E-B'-C-D since the similarity values between 3rd and 7th motifs, 4th and 8th motifs are 100 and the similarity value between 2nd and 6th is almost near to 100, exactly 99. That means we have final three clusters $\{2, 6\}$, $\{3, 7\}$, $\{4, 8\}$. From these clusters, as shown in Fig. 5, we extract the motifs 6, 3, 8 as the representative melodies, respectively. And 1st motif is augmented into the final set as the first melody. Note that 3rd motif is also the climax melody of the music file.

3.2 Multidimensional Index of Representative Melodies

To place an extracted melody into the multidimensional metric space of representative melody index of M-tree, since we regard the melody of music as time-series data that consists of sequences of values or events as time goes, we transform a representative melody into 8-dimensional time-sequenced data. That is, melody of a representative motif is translated into a time-sequenced data of $<t_1, t_2, t_3, t_4, t_5, t_6, t_7, t_8>$. From the analysis of our experimental music database of 300 songs, we can see that the de-

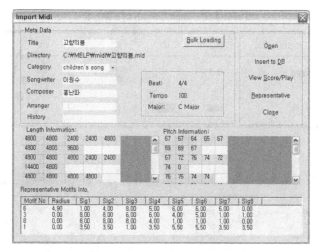

Fig. 4. Registration Window for 'Spring of Hometown'

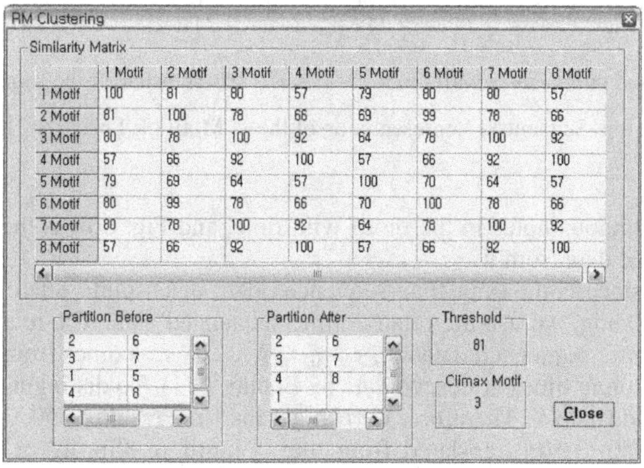

Fig. 5. RM Clustering Result for 'Spring of Hometown'

nominator of time-meter is either 4 or 8. Therefore, we translate representative melody into a time-sequenced data of 8 sequences.

To translate a representative motif into a time-sequenced data of 8 sequences, we revised the length of a musical note with time. In a motif, the length of a musical note is revised according to Table 1, and the pitch value of note is revised according to the pitch value of MIDI format, respectively. For example, a quarter note($\quarternote$) of 'C5' is represented as the note whose length is 8 and pitch is 60.

So, we intermediately translate a representative melody of n/m time-meters into $16n$ sequences and re-organize them into 8 sequences by using the average value of each $2n$ sequences from the original $16n$ sequences. Fig. 6 shows an example of translation of the 1st motif of a Korean Children Song 'Spring of Hometown' in Fig. 3 into an 8-dimensional time-sequenced data. Fig. 6(a) denotes the graph of the revised pitch

Table 1. Revised Length of a Musical Note

Revised length value	32	16	8			1
Note	𝅝	𝅗𝅥	𝅘𝅥	𝅘𝅥𝅮	𝅘𝅥𝅯	𝅘𝅥𝅰
Rest	𝄻	𝄼	𝄽	𝄾	𝄿	𝅀

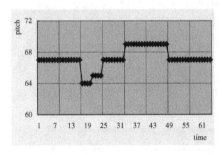
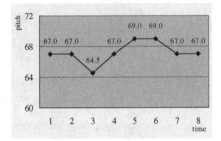

(a) Revised pitch values with time   (b) Translated time-sequenced data

Fig. 6. Time-Sequenced Representation of the 1st Motif of 'Spring of Hometown'

values of continuous notes in the motif with time, and Fig. 6(b) is the 8-dimensional time-sequenced data from it.

However, since comparing time-sequenced data of absolute pitch values depends on the key of song, we use the relative time-sequenced data. The relative pitch of 8-dimensional time-sequenced data $<s_1, s_2, s_3, s_4, s_5, s_6, s_7, s_8>$ comes from the normalization of the absolute time-sequenced data by Equation (1). To distinguish between note and rest, we add 1 to s_i. Therefore, we can get the final result {3.50, 3.50, 1.00, 3.50, 5.50, 5.50, 3.50, 3.50} translated from the 1st motif of 'Spring of Hometown' as shown in the lower window of Fig. 4.

$$s_i = t_i - \text{MIN}\{t_1, .., t_8\} + 1 \qquad (1)$$

The time-sequenced data transformed from a representative melody is mapped into a point of the metric space for the representative melody index implemented by M-tree. Since we translate a melody into an 8-dimensional time-sequenced data, the dimension of M-tree becomes 8 and a representative melody is mapped into a point of 8-dimensional metric index space with radius. Here, radius stands for the largest distance computed by Euclidean distance function between the selected representative melody and other melody in the cluster.

4   Content-Based Music Retrieval from Melody Query

4.1   Procedure of Content-Based Music Retrieval

The summarized procedure for the content-based music retrievals using the multidimensional time-sequenced representative melody index(for short in figure, MDTSRM index) is in Fig. 7. When a user's melody query with the expected number of results n is submitted to the query interface, the system extracts the feature information from the query and translate the query melody into an 8-dimensional time-sequenced data by the same way for indexing. With these features of the query, we do k-nearest neighbor searching from M-tree of the multidimensional time-sequenced representative melody index. In this work, we use $2n$ as k value in k-nearest neighbor searching in order to enrich the candidates for more appropriate retrieval results.

To filter out inappropriate melodies from $2n$ candidates and to rank the retrieval results, we compute the similarities between the query and $2n$ candidates by time-warping distance function. As well known, time-warping is able to compute the distance between two melodies of different lengths. Hence, we can retrieve the appropriate melodies from the representative melody index even though users submit query melodies that are not of one motif length. According to the similarity values, we choose top n melodies from $2n$ candidates and decide the ranks of the final retrieval results.

Users view the final retrieval results based on their ranks and check the relevance for each music file in the retrieval results via viewing its music score with a visual interface and/or listening the music with an auditory interface. If users do not satisfy the retrieval results, users do over again the relevance feedback from the previous query or the previous results until they get music files they want. In the relevance feedback phase, we do range searching within in the multidimensional time-sequenced representative melody index. The retrieval range of the relevance feedback is adjusted according to the degree of user's satisfaction to the previous retrieval results.

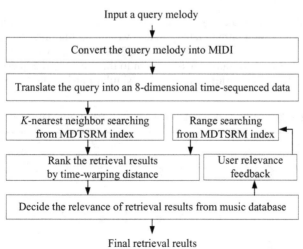

Fig. 7. Procedure of Content-based Music Retrievals Using the Representative Melody Index

4.2   Content-Based Music Retrieval Using the Representative Melody Index

For content-based music retrievals in the developed system, we use the query inter-face as shown in Fig. 8. In this interface, user can draw the music scores of query with the selection of expected number of results at 'Result Num'. 'Play' and 'Stop' buttons are to start and to stop listening the query melody, respectively. After drawing a query melody, by click 'Query' button users can get the retrieval results as shown at the lower window of Fig. 8. The retrieval results in the lower window of Fig. 8 come from the multidimensional time-sequenced representative melody index. However, when we select a row in the results, we can see the full music score that is stored in the underlying music database. After viewing and listening the retrieval results, users can advance the relevance feedback phase for a selected result at the lower window of Fig. 8 by clicking 'Feedback' button.

Fig. 8. Query and Result from 8-dimensional Time-Sequenced RM Index

To validate the appropriateness of the retrieval results from the multidimensional time-sequenced representative melody index, we list up the retrieval results from the query melody of Fig. 8 at Table 2. From Table 2, we can easily recognize that the first result melody has exactly same music pattern to the prefix of the query melody given in Fig. 8, and also other retrieval results have similar music patterns to the query mel-ody.

Table 2. Summerization of Retrieval Results for Query Melody of Fig. 8

Rank	Music Scores
1	
2	
3	

Instead of using 8-dimensional metric space of M-tree, our previous system used 2-dimensional one. That is, to place melodies into the metric space of M-tree, we compute the average length variation and the average pitch variation of each melody and the radius of each cluster. If we assume that a representative melody of n/m time-meters has k continuous notes, $[(l_1, p_1), (l_2, p_2), ..., (l_k, p_k)]$, where l_i and p_i are the length and pitch of i-th musical note in the melody, respectively. The average length variation $\bar{l}$ and the average pitch variation $\bar{p}$ are computed by Equation (2) and (3), respectively. In Equation (2), the first term denotes the average length difference of k musical notes in the representative melody to the dominator m of the times of the music and the second term denotes the average value of $k-1$ length differences between continuous k musical notes. Similarly, in Equation (3), the first term denotes the average value of pitch differences between the first musical notes and the following $k-1$ ones and the second term is for the average value of $k-1$ pitch differences between k continuous musical notes. And the distance $d(v, u)$ between two representative melodies $u(\bar{l}_u, \bar{p}_u)$ and $v(\bar{l}_v, \bar{p}_v)$ is computed by the Euclidean distance in 2-dimensional space. The radius of a cluster stands for the maximum distance between the extracted representative melody of a cluster and other melodies in the cluster in 2-dimenstional metric space of M-tree.

$$\bar{l} = ((\sum_{i=1}^{k} |m - l_i|) / k + (\sum_{i=1}^{k-1} |l_{i+1} - l_i|) / (k-1)) / 2 \qquad (2)$$

$$\bar{p} = (\sum_{i=1}^{k-1} (\frac{|p_1 - p_{i+1}| + |p_{i+1} - p_i|}{2})) / (k-1) \qquad (3)$$

If we use the previous system in which a 2-dimensinal metric space is used instead of 8-dimensional metric space for the representative melody index with same music database, the retrieval result for the same query melody of Fig. 8 is shown in Fig. 9. Since the average length variation and the average pitch variation of query melody are 2.74 and 1.28, respectively, the melodies which have similar values to them are retrieved and are ranked based on the distance between the query and these melodies as shown in Fig. 9.

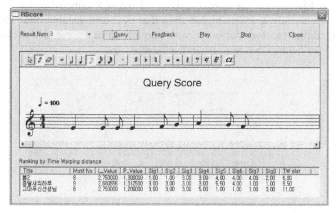

Fig. 9. Query and Result from 2-dimensional Time-Sequenced RM Index

Table 3. Summerization of Retrieval Results for Query Melody of Fig. 9

Rank	Music Score
1	
2	
3	

To compare both the music scores in Table 2 retrieved from the 8-dimensional time-sequenced representative melody index and those from the 2-dimensional one, we also list up the retrieval results in Table 3. From the comparison of retrieval results of Table 2 and Table 3, we can recognize easily that the retrieval results of Table 2 are more relevant to the query melody than those of Table 3.

4.3 Performance Evaluation

We do experiments with a music database of 300 Korean children songs. From the experimental database, we get 753 representative melodies, whereas the total number of motifs in the database is 2,151. The ratio of number of representative melodies to that of whole melodies is 0.35. It means that by using the representative melody index instead of whole melody index may save the storage overhead for index up to 65%.

In addition, to compare the correctness of the retrieval results, we do experiments with another experimental music database of 100 Korean children songs. In the experimental music database, 10 songs come from the artificial remake of the original 'Spring of Hometown', while 90 songs are selected from the first experimental music database of 300 Korean children songs. We index these representative melodies extracted from the experimental music database separately into 2-dimensional metric space of M-tree and 8-dimensional metric space of M-tree. To compare the precisions of retrieval results for two cases, we use the 1st, 3rd, 6th, 8th melodies as query melodies. As shown in Fig. 10, the average precision of using 8-dimensional time-sequenced representative melody index is higher than that of 2-dimensional one. Therefore, we can recognize that the 8-dimensional time-sequenced representative melody index is more useful for content-based music retrieval systems.

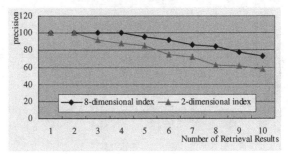

Fig. 10. Comparison of Precisions

5 Conclusions

In this paper, we discuss the development of a content-based music retrieval system in which 8-dimensional time-sequenced representative melody index is used to improve the appropriateness and the performance of retrieval from users' melody queries. Since music composition is regarded as an arrangement of continuous notes within the time-meter, music melody can be transformed into 8-dimensional time-sequenced data. Hence, we first introduce the overall architecture of the content-based music retrieval system developed in this work. We also discuss the construction of the 8-dimensional representative melody index from the extracted melodies and the content-based retrieval procedure with relevance feedback from users' melody queries. According to the experimental results, the system can save the index space up to 65% than the case of using the whole melody index while the precision of retrieval results from the proposed system is higher than that for the previous system in which 2-dimensional index is used for the representative melody index.

As the future work, we will develop a music classification scheme and recommendation system for users based on the similarity between the user's preference and the semantics of music. Then we will use this system in developing an e-commerce system for digitized music files.

Acknowledgements. This work was supported by the Korea Science and Engineering Foundation(KOSEF) through the Northeast Asian e-Logistics Research Center at University of Incheon.

References

1. Lu, G.: Indexing and Retrieval of Audio: A Survey. Journal of Multimedia Tools and Applications. 5 (2001) 269-290.
2. Kim, S., Kim, Y. S.: An Indexing and Retrieval Mechanism Using Representative Melodies for Music Databases. Proceedings of 2000 International Conference on Information Society in the 21st Century. (2000) 393-400.
3. Ghias, A., Logan, J., Charmberlin, D., Smith, B. C.: Query By Humming Musical Information Retrieval in an Audio Database. Proceedings of ACM Multimedia, (1995).
4. McNab, R., Smith, L., Witten, I.: Towards the Digital Music Library: Tune Retrieval from Acoustic Input. Proceedings of Digital Libraries, (1996).
5. Chou, T., Chen, A., Liu, C.: Music Databases: Indexing Techniques and Implementation. Proceedings of IEEE International Workshop on Multimedia Database Management Systems. (1996).
6. Hurson, D.: Themefinder. http://www.themefinder.com.
7. Meyer, L.: Explaining Music. Saegwang Publishing Co. (1990).
8. Jee, J., Oh, H.: Design and Implementation of Music Information Retrieval System Using Melodies. Journal of Korea Information Processing Society, Vol. 5(1). (1998).
9. Chen, A., Hsu J., Liu, C. C.: Efficient Repeating Pattern Finding in Music Databases. Proceedings of ACM Conference on Information and Knowledge Management. (1998).
10. Liu, C. C., Hsu, J. L., Chen, L. P.: Efficient Theme and Non-trivial Repeating Pattern Discovering in Music Databases. Proceedings of the 15th International Conference on Data Engineering. (1999).

11. Kang, Y., Ku, K., Kim, Y. S.: Extracting Theme Melodies by Using a Graphical Clustering Algorithm for Content-based Music Information Retrieval. Lecture Notes in Computer Science, Vol. 2151. Springer-Verlag. (2001).
12. Ku, K., Kim, Y. S.: Extraction of Representative Melodies Considering Musical Composition Forms for Content-based Music Retrievals. Proceedings of the IASTED International Conference on Databases and Applications. (2004).
13. Won, J., Lee, J., Ku, K., Park, J., Kim, Y. S.: A Content-Based Music Retrieval System Using Representative Melody Index from Music Databases. Proceedings of the International Symposium on Computer Music Modeling and Retrieval. (2004).
14. Ciaccia, P., Patella, M., Zezula, P.: M-tree: An Efficient Access Method for Similarity Search in Metric Spaces. Proceedings of 23rd International Conference on VLDB. (1997).
15. Lee, B., Paek, G.: Everyone can compose songs. Jackeunwoori Publishing Co. Korea. (2000).
16. Yi, B., Jagadish, H., Faloutsos, C.: Efficient Retrieval of Similar Time Sequences under Time Warping. Proceedings of IEEE International Conference on Data Engineering. (1998).
17. Kim, S., Park, S., Chu, W.: An Index-based Approach for Similarity Search Supporting Time Warping in Large Sequence Databases. Proceedings of IEEE International Conference on Data Engineering. (2001).
18. Lim, S., Ku, K., Kim, Y. S.: Similarity Computation between Music Motifs Using Cosine Measure. Proceedings of Korea Information Processing Society, Vol. 10(1). (2003).

Solving Stochastic Optimization in Distributed Databases Using Genetic Algorithms

Viorica Varga, D. Dumitrescu, and Crina Groşan

Department of Computer Science, Faculty of Mathematics and Computer Science,
Babeş-Bolyai University, Cluj-Napoca, Romania,
{ivarga,ddumitr,cgrosan}@cs.ubbcluj.ro

Abstract. Stochastic query optimization problem for multiple join is addressed. Two sites model of Drenick and Smith [2] is extended to four relations stored at four different sites. The model of three joins stored at two sites leads to a nonlinear programming problem, which has an analytical solution. The model with four sites leads to a special kind of nonlinear optimization problem (P). This problem can not be solved analytically. It is proved that problem (P) has at least one solution and two new methods are presented for solving the problem. An ad hoc constructive model and a new evolutionary technique is used for solving problem (P). Results obtained by the two considered optimization approaches are compared.

Keywords and Phrases: Adaptive representation, distributed database, evolutionary optimization, genetic algorithms, query optimization.

1 Introduction

The query optimization problem for a single query in a distributed database system was treated in great detail in the literature. Many algorithms were elaborated for minimizing the costs necessary to perform a single, isolated query in a distributed database system. Some methods can be found in [9], [1], [12]. Most approaches look for a deterministic strategy assigning the component joins of a relational query to the processors of a network that can execute the join efficiently and determine an efficient strategy for the data transferring.

A distributed system can receives different types of queries and processes them at the same time. Query processing strategies may be distributed over the processors of a network as probability distributions. In this case the determination of the optimal query processing strategy is a stochastic optimization problem. There is a different approach to query optimization if the system is viewed as one which receives different types of queries at different times and processes more than one query at the same time.

The multiple-query problem is not deterministic; the multiple-query-input stream constitutes a stochastic process. The strategy for executing the multiple-query is distributed over the sites of the network as a probability distribution.

A. Benczúr, J. Demetrovics, G. Gottlob (Eds.): ADBIS 2004, LNCS 3255, pp. 259–274, 2004.

The "decision variables" of the stochastic query optimization problem are the probabilities that component operators of the query are executed at particular sites of the network.

The main objective of the state-transition model is to give globally optimal query-processing strategies. [2] treat the single-join model, the general model for the join of two relations and a multiple-join with three relations, which are stored at two different sites. The general model for the join of two relations leads to linear programming problem. The multiple join model of three relations stored at two different sites leads to a nonlinear optimization problem, which can be solved analytically. The stochastic model for the join of three relations, which are stored at three different sites is presented in [13] and [14]. This model leads to a nonlinear programming problem, which is a specific one. Stochastic query optimization model using semijoins is presented in [8].

The aim of this paper is to extend the stochastic model to the join of four relations. In Section 2 the case when the relations are stored at four sites is considered. The stochastic query optimization problem in case of four relations leads to a constrained nonlinear optimization problem. In Section 3 a constructive method for solving the nonlinear programming problem is given. We consider an evolutionary technique based on a dynamic representation [3] [4]). This technique called *Adaptive Representation Evolutionary Algorithm* (AREA) is described in Section 4. The results obtained by applying these different approaches are presented in Section 5. Two sets of values for constants are used in these experiments. Solutions are nearly the same. The CPU time required for solving the optimization problem by using evolutionary algorithm is less than the CPU time required by the constructive method. Due to the very short execution time of the evolutionary algorithm the method can be applied in real-time systems.

2   Stochastic Query Optimization Problem of Four Relations Join

Consider four relations stored in different sites of the distributed database. The join of these four relations will be defined in the context of stochastic model of [2]. Consider relations A, B, C, D stored at the sites 1,2,3 and 4 respectively.

Denote by Q_4 the single-query type consisting of the join of four relations:

$$Q_4 = A \bowtie B \bowtie C \bowtie D.$$

Initial state of relations referenced by the query Q_4 in the four-site network is the column vector defined as:

$$s_0 = \begin{pmatrix} A \\ B \\ C \\ D \end{pmatrix}$$

where the i-th component of the vector s_0 is the set of relations stored at site i, $i \in \{1, 2, 3, 4\}$ at time $t = 0$.

Initial state s_0 is given with time-invariant probability $p_0 = p(s_0)$ i.e. p_0 is the probability that relation A is available at site 1, relation B at site 2, relation C at site 3, and relation D at site 4. The four relations are not locked for updating or are unavailable for query processing for any other reason. We assume that the input to the system consists of a single stream of type Q_4.

For the purpose of stochastic query optimization we enumerate all logically valid joins in the order in which they may be executed. Let us suppose that Q_4 has three valid execution sequences:

$$Q_4 S_1 = (((A \bowtie B) \bowtie C) \bowtie D),$$

$$Q_4 S_2 = ((A \bowtie B) \bowtie (C \bowtie D)),$$

$$Q_4 S_3 = (A \bowtie (B \bowtie (C \bowtie D))).$$

Sequence $Q_4 S_1$ can be applied if $A \cap B \neq \emptyset$. So the join $B' = A \bowtie B$ is executed before the join $C' = B' \bowtie C$. The last executed join will be $D' = C' \bowtie D$. The sequence $Q_4 S_2$ is adequate for parallel execution.

The system that undergoes transition in order to execute the join of four relations is described in this section as in [2]. The strategy for executing the multiple join is distributed over the sites of the network. Conditional probabilities are associated with the edges of the state-transition graph. Executing a multiple join is equivalent to solve an optimization problem. This problem is referred as *stochastic query optimization model*. Theorem 1 states, that the stochastic query optimization model for the multiple join query defines a nonlinear optimization problem.

With respect to the stochastic query optimization model we can state the following Theorem, see [5].

Theorem 1. *The stochastic query optimization model for the multiple join query of type Q_4 defines a nonlinear optimization problem.*

Stochastic query optimization problem for the query $Q_4 S_1$ is given by:

$$(P_1) \begin{cases} \text{minimize } \Delta_1 \\[4pt] \quad \text{subject to:} \\ \tau_i \leq \Delta_1, i = 1, 2, 3, 4 \\[4pt] p_{0,11} + p_{0,21} = 1, \\ p_{11,12} + p_{11,22} = 1, \\ p_{21,32} + p_{21,42} = 1, \\ p_{12,13} + p_{12,23} = 1, \\ p_{22,33} + p_{22,43} = 1, \\ p_{32,53} + p_{32,63} = 1, \\ p_{42,73} + p_{42,83} = 1, \\[4pt] p_{0,11}, p_{0,21}, p_{11,12}, p_{11,22}, p_{21,32}, p_{21,42}, p_{12,13} \in [0,1], \\[4pt] p_{12,23}, p_{22,33}, p_{22,43}, p_{32,53}, p_{32,63}, p_{42,73}, p_{42,83} \in [0,1]. \end{cases}$$

where the mean processing times $\tau_i, i = 1, 2, 3, 4$ are expressed as:

$$\tau_1 = T_{11}(B')p_{0,11} + T_{12}(C')p_{0,11}p_{11,12} + T_{13}(D')p_{0,11}p_{11,12}p_{12,13},$$
$$\tau_2 = T_{21}(B')p_{0,21} + T_{32}(C')p_{0,21}p_{21,32} + T_{53}(D')p_{0,21}p_{21,32}p_{32,53}$$
$$\tau_3 = T_{22}(C')p_{0,11}p_{11,22} + T_{42}(C')p_{0,21}p_{21,42} + T_{33}(D')p_{0,11}p_{11,22}p_{22,33}$$
$$+ T_{73}(D')p_{0,21}p_{21,42}p_{42,73}, \tag{2.1}$$
$$\tau_4 = T_{23}(D')p_{0,11}p_{11,12}p_{12,23} + T_{43}(D')p_{0,11}p_{11,22}p_{22,43}$$
$$+ T_{63}(D')p_{0,21}p_{21,32}p_{32,63} + T_{83}(D')p_{0,21}p_{21,42}p_{42,83}.$$

The obtained problem (P_1) is a constrained nonlinear optimization problem. In the next section we propose a constructive approach for solving the optimization problem (P_1).

The number of relations and sites in one distributed database can be different. Resulting nonlinear optimization problem has different number of variables and constraints. Therefore we have to generalize problem (P_1) for an arbitrary number of relations and sites.

Let us consider p continous functions

$$f_1, ..., f_p : [0, 1]^n \to R_+,$$

where p is the number of sites in the distributed database and $f_i, (i = 1, \ldots, p)$ represents the mean processing time at site i.

Our optimization problem (P_1) may be generalized to the following optimization problem (P_p).

$$(P_p) \begin{cases} \text{minimize } \Delta_1 \\ \quad \text{subject to:} \\ f_1(x_1, x_2, \ldots, x_n) \leq \Delta_1, \\ \vdots \\ f_p(x_1, x_2, \ldots, x_n) \leq \Delta_1, \\ x_1, x_2, \ldots, x_n \in [0, 1]. \end{cases}$$

A new framework is necessary for establishing conditions under which problem (P_p) has a solution.

Let (X, d) be a compact metric space and

$$f_1, ..., f_p : X \to R_+$$

be continuous strictly positive functions.

Consider the next generic optimization problem:

$$(P) \begin{cases} \text{minimize } y, y \in R \\ \quad \text{subject to:} \\ \quad x \in X, (X \text{ is a compact metric space}), \\ y > 0, \\ f_1(x) \leq y, \\ \vdots \\ f_p(x) \leq y. \end{cases}$$

With respect to problem (P) we can state the following Theorem, see [5].

Theorem 2. *Problem (P) has at least one solution.*

3 A Constructive Method for Solving General Stochastic Query Problem

Now we are ready to give a constructive method for solving problem (P). This method generates a sequence converging to a solution of the problem (P). Theorem 3 ensures that the constructed sequence really converges towards a solution of the optimization problem (P).

Let $f : X \to R$ be the function defined by

$$f(x) = \max\{f_1(x), ..., f_p(x)\}.$$

and y_0 the global minimum value of the function f, i.e.

$$y_0 = \min_{x \in X} f(x).$$

Let $A_1 \subset A_2 \subset A_3 \subset \ ... \ \subset A_n \subset \ ...$ be a sequence of finite subsets of X such that $\overset{\infty}{\underset{n=1}{\cup}} A_n$ is dense (see [11]) in X, i.e. $\overline{\cup A_n} = X$ equivalent to the fact, that for $\forall x \in X, \exists x_n \in \underset{n \in N}{\cup} A_n$ such that $x_n \to x$.

We consider

$$A_1 = \{u_1, u_2, ..., u_{q_1}\}, \qquad u_i \in X, i = 1, ... q_1,$$
$$A_2 = \{v_1, v_2, ..., v_{q_2}\}, \qquad v_j \in X, j = 1, ... q_2,$$
$$\vdots$$
$$A_n = \{w_1, w_2, ..., w_{q_n}\}, \qquad w_k \in X, k = 1, ... q_n,$$

where $q_i \in N^*, i = 1, ..., n$ and $q_n \to \infty$.

Let us consider the sequence $(y_n)_{n \geq 1}$ defined as folows:

$$y_1 = \min\{\max\{f_1(u_1), f_2(u_1), ..., f_p(u_1)\}, ..., \max\{f_1(u_{q_1}), f_2(u_{q_1}), ..., f_p(u_{q_1})\},$$
$$y_2 = \min\{\max\{f_1(v_1), f_2(v_1), ..., f_p(v_1)\}, ..., \max\{f_1(v_{q_2}), f_2(v_{q_2}), ..., f_p(v_{q_2})\},$$

$$\vdots$$

$$y_n = \min\{\max\{f_1(w_1), f_2(w_1), ..., f_p(w_1)\}, ..., \max\{f_1(w_{q_n}), f_2(w_{q_n}), ..., f_p(w_{q_n})\}.$$

It is easy to see that sequence $(y_n)_{n \geq 1}$ is monotone decreasing and bounded. Therefore the sequence is convergent.

With respect to the convergent sequence $(y_n)_{n \geq 1}$ we can state the following Theorem, see [6].

Theorem 3. *The sequence $(y_n)_{n \geq 1}$ converges to a solution of the problem (P).*

In the case of solving problem (P_p) using Theorem 3 we have

$$X = [0, 1]^n.$$

In order to obtain an approximate solution of problem (P_p) in the Constructive Algorithm we take a uniform grid G of the hypercube $[0,1]^k$.
We may choose the sets $(A_i)_{i \in N^*}$ in the folowing way:

$$A_1 = \left\{ \left(\frac{i_0}{n}, \frac{i_1}{n}, \cdots, \frac{i_n}{n} \right) | i_0, i_1, \ldots, i_n \in \{0, 1, \ldots, n\} \right\},$$

$$A_2 = \left\{ \left(\frac{j_0}{2n}, \frac{j_1}{2n}, \cdots, \frac{j_{2n}}{2n} \right) | j_0, j_1, \ldots, j_{2n} \in \{0, 1, \ldots, 2n\} \right\},$$

$$\vdots$$

$$A_k = \left\{ \left(\frac{l_0}{2^{k-1}n}, \frac{l_1}{2^{k-1}n}, \cdots, \frac{l_{2^{k-1}n}}{2^{k-1}n} \right) | l_0, l_1, \ldots, l_{2^{k-1}n} \in \{0, 1, \ldots, 2^{k-1}n\} \right\},$$

where

$$i_0 < i_1 < \ldots < i_n,$$
$$j_0 < j_1 < \ldots < j_{2n},$$
$$l_0 < l_1 < \ldots < l_{2^{k-1}n}.$$

Our grid is that induced by $A_1, A_2, \ldots, A_k$. The sets $(A_i)_{i \in N^*}$ constructed in the above way verify the conditions of Theorem 2. For our purposes we may consider $n = 10$.

For each point of the grid G we compute the values $f_s, s = 1, \ldots, p$. Choosing the maximum $f_s, s = 1, \ldots, p$, we ensure that each inequality in the problem (P_p) holds. Problem solution will be the minimum of all selected maximums.

The previous considerations enable us to formulate an algorithm for solving problem (P_p). This technique will be called *Constructive Algorithm* (CA) and may be outlined as bellow.

Constructive Algorithm

Input:
    n $//$ the number of divisions;
    Functions $f_1, f_2 ..., f_p$ $//$ express the problem constraints.
begin
Initializations:
    $h = \frac{1}{n}$ $//$ the length of one division;
    $valx_j = 0, j = 1, ..., k$ $//$ initial values for x_j;
    for $s = 1$ **to** p **do** $//$ initial values for functions f_s
      $valf_s = f_s(valx_1, valx_2, \ldots, valx_k)$
    end for
    $valmax = \max\{valf_s, s = 1, ..., p\}$
    $valmin = valmax$
    for $j = 1$ **to** k **do** $//$ in $xmin_j$ we store the x_j values for which we
      $xmin_j = valx_j$ $//$ have the minimum of f_s
    end for
Constructing the grid:
    for $i_1 = 1$ **to** n **do**
      $valx_1 = i_1 * h$
      for $i_2 = 1$ **to** n **do**
        $valx_2 = i_2 * h$
           $\vdots$

        for $i_k = 1$ **to** n **do**
          $valx_k = i_{k*}h$
          for $s = 1$ **to** p **do** $//$ calculate the values for functions f_s for
            $valf_s = f_s(valx_1, valx_2, \ldots, valx_k)$ $//$ the current values of x_j
          end for
          $valmax = \max\{valf_s, s = 1, ..., p\}$
          if $(valmax < valmin)$ **then**
            $valmin = valmax$
            for $j = 1$ **to** k **do** $//$ store in $xmin_j$ the new x_j values
              $xmin_j = valx_j$ $//$ for which we have the
            end for $//$ minimum of f_s
          end if
          end for $// i_k$
           $\vdots$

      end for $// i_2$
    end for $// i_1$
end

Remark. $valmin$ denote the minimum value of Δ_1 from problem (P_p) and $xmin_j$, $j = 1, ..., k$ denote the values for x_j, $j = 1, ..., k$ for which the minimum is reached.

The Constructive Algorithm should be repeated for a new value of n, so that the divisions have to include the old divisions, in this way we obtain a new subset A_i of the set X.

Solution obtained by the Constructive Algorithm can be refined using a *Refinement Algorithm* (RA) (see [6]).

Algorithms CA and RA can be used to solve the general stochastic optimization problem (P). The problem of four relations join is formulated as the problem (P_1), which is a particularization of general problem (P).

Numerical experiments for solving problem (P_1) using the Constructive Algorithm and Refinement Algorithm are presented in Section 5.

4   Solving Problem (P_p) Using an Evolutionary Algorithm

In this section an evolutionary technique used for solving stochastic optimization problem (P_p) is proposed.

Let us denote

$$g_i = x_i + x_{i+1}, i = 1, \ldots, p.$$

Using these notations general problem (P) (see Section 2) can be reformulated as the following constrained optimization problem:

$$(P') \begin{cases} \text{minimize } y \\ \quad \text{subject to:} \\ y > 0, \\ f_i(x) \leq y, \ i = 1, \ldots, p, \\ g_i(x) - 1 = 0, \ i = 1, \ldots n, \\ x = (x_1, \ldots, x_n). \end{cases}$$

The evolutionary method for solving problem (P') implies the next steps:

Step 1. Maximize the p functions $f_1, \ldots, f_p$.
Let us denote by

$$f^*(x) = \max_{i=1,\ldots,p} f_i(x), \ x \in X.$$

Step 2. Minimize function f^* by using an evolutionary algorithm.
In this case the fitness of the solution x may be defined as:

$$eval(x) = f^*(x)$$

Let us denote by x^* the obtained minimum.

Step 3. The solution y of the problem can be obtained by setting

$$y = x^* + \varepsilon,$$

where $\varepsilon > 0$, is a small number.

Remark. The constraints g_i were treated by considering each x_i, i not odd, as being $(1 - x_i)$. The advantage of applying an evolutionary technique for solving problem (P') is that the involved function f^* is not necessary effectively computed. Only the values of function f^* for the candidate solution are needed. An evolutionary algorithm called *Adaptive Representation Evolutionary Algorithm* (AREA) is proposed for solving problem (P'). AREA technique will be described in what follows.

4.1 AREA Technique

The main idea of AREA technique is to use a dynamical encoding allowing each solution be encoded over a different alphabet. This approach is similar to that proposed in [7]. Solution representation is adaptive and may be changed during the search process as the effect of mutation operator.

Each AREA individual consists of a pair (x, B) where x is a string encoding object variable and B specifies the alphabet used for encoding x. B is an integer number such that $B \geq 2$ and x is a string of symbols over the alphabet $\{0, 1, \ldots, B - 1\}$. If $B = 2$, the standard binary encoding is obtained.

Each solution has its own encoding alphabet. The alphabet over which x is encoded may be changed during the search process.

An example of AREA chromosome is the following:
$$C = (301453, 6).$$

Remark. The genes of x may be separated by comma if required (for instance when $B \geq 10$).

4.2 Search Operator

Within AREA mutation is the unique search operator. Mutation can modify object variables as well as the last chromosome position (fixing the representation alphabet).

When the changing gene belongs to the object variable sub-string (x – part of the chromosome), the mutated gene is a symbol randomly chosen from the same alphabet.

Example
Let us consider the chromosomes can be represented over the alphabets $B_2, \ldots, B_{30}$, where
$$B_i = \{0, 1, \ldots, i - 1\}.$$
Consider the chromosome C represented over the alphabet B_8:
$$C = (631751, 8).$$

268   V. Varga, D. Dumitrescu, and C. Groşan

Consider a mutation occurs on the position 3 in the x part of the chromosome and the mutated value of the gene is 4. Then the mutated chromosome is:
$$C_1 = (634751, 8).$$
If the position specifying the alphabet is changed, then the object variables will be represented using symbols over the new alphabet, corresponding to the mutated value of B.

Consider again the chromosome C represented over the alphabet B_8:
$$C = (631751, 8).$$
Consider a mutation occurs on the last position and the mutated value is 5. Then the mutated chromosome is:
$$C_2 = (23204032, 5).$$
C and C_2 encode the same value over two different alphabets (B_8 and B_{10}).

Remark. A mutation generating an offspring worst than its parent is called a *harmful mutation*. A constant called MAX_HARMFUL_MUTATIONS is used to determinate when the chromosome part represented the alphabet will be changed (mutated).

4.3 AREA Procedure

During the initialization stage each AREA individual (chromosome, solution) is encoded over a randomly chosen alphabet. Each solution is then selected for mutation. If the offspring obtained by mutation is better than its parent than the parent is removed from the population and the offspring enters the new population. Otherwise, a new mutation of the parent is considered. If the number of successive harmful mutations exceeds a prescribed threshold (denoted by MAX_HARMFUL_MUTATIONS) then the individual representation (alphabet part) is changed and with this new representation it enters the new population.

The reason behind this mechanism is to dynamically change the individual representation whenever it is needed. If a particular representation has no potential for further exploring the search space then the representation is changed. In this way we hope that the search space will be explored more efficiently.

The AREA technique may be depicted as follows.

AREA technique

begin
    Set $t = 0$;
    Random initializes chromosome population $P(t)$;
    Set to zero the number of harmful mutations for each individual in $P(t)$;

    while ($t <$ number of generations) **do**
        $P(t+1) = \emptyset$;
        for $k = 1$ **to** PopSize **do**
            Mutate the kth chromosome from $P(t)$. An offspring is obtained.
            Set to zero the number of harmful mutations for offspring;

    if the offspring is better than the parent **then**
      the offspring is added to $P(t + 1)$;
    else
      Increase the number of harmful mutations for current individual;
      if the number of harmful mutations for the current individual $=$
        MAX_HARMFUL_MUTATIONS **then**
        Change the individual representation;
        Set to zero the number of harmful mutations for the current
          individual;
        Add individual to $P(t+1)$;
      else
        Add current individual (the parent) to $P(t+1)$;
      end if
    end if
   end for;
   Set $t = t + 1$;
  end while;
end

5 Numerical Experiments

We consider two numerical experiments for solving problem (P_1) using Constructive Algorithm and evolutionary technique above described. Results obtained by applying AREA technique are compared with the results obtained by applying Constructive Algorithm (and after that, Refinement Algorithm).

The obtained results in the case of a communication network with a speed of $6 \cdot 10^4$ bps are presented. The model allows different transfer speed for the distinct connections. But in our experiment the transfer speed is assumed to be constant for each connection. In the Table 1 and Table 4 appear two cases and in every case the number of bits for every relation and the necessary time to transfer the relations through the network.

We have to approximate the size of B', where $B' = A \bowtie B$ and the size of C', where $C' = B' \bowtie C$.

Table 1. Relation sizes and transfer times for Experiment 1.

	Number of bits	Transfer time
Relation A	8,000,000	133.33s
Relation B	4,000,000	66.66s
Relation C	10,000,000	166.66s
Relation D	5,000,000	83.33s
Relation B'	10,400,000	173.33s
Relation C'	25,600,000	426.66s

Table 2. Parameters used by AREA technique.

AREA Parameters	
Population size	100
Number of generations	100
Mutation probability	0,01
Number of variable	14
Number of alphabets	30
MAX_HARMFUL_MUTATIONS	5

The database management system can take these sizes from the database statistics. In our computation we ignore the local processing time, because it is unessential compared to the transmission time.

5.1   Experiment 1

Consider problem (P_1), where the mean processing times at the four sites are:

$$\tau_1 = 66.66p_{0,11} + 166.66p_{0,11}p_{11,12} + 83.33p_{0,11}p_{11,12}p_{12,13},$$
$$\tau_2 = 133.33p_{0,21} + 166.66p_{0,21}p_{21,32} + 83.33p_{0,21}p_{21,32}p_{32,53},$$
$$\tau_3 = 173.33p_{0,11}p_{11,22} + 173.33p_{0,21}p_{21,42} + 83.33p_{0,11}p_{11,22}p_{22,33} \qquad (5.2)$$
$$\qquad + 83.33p_{0,21}p_{21,42}p_{42,73},$$
$$\tau_4 = 426.66p_{0,11}p_{11,12}p_{12,23} + 426.66p_{0,11}p_{11,22}p_{22,43}$$
$$\qquad + 426.66p_{0,21}p_{21,32}p_{32,63} + 426.66p_{0,21}p_{21,42}p_{42,83}.$$

Parameters used within AREA technique are given in Table 2:

The results obtained by applying AREA technique and Constructive Algorithm (and Refinement Algorithm after that) are outlined in Table 3.

Remark. Final result obtained by AREA technique and CA is very similar. Only CPU time is different: CPU time obtained by AREA technique is 0.05s, and the CPU time obtained by CA is 11 minutes.

5.2   Experiment 2

Consider the experimental conditions given in Table 4. The mean processing times in this case at the four sites are:

$$\tau_1 = 16.66p_{0,11} + 33.33p_{0,11}p_{11,12} + 16.66p_{0,11}p_{11,12}p_{12,13},$$
$$\tau_2 = 133.33p_{0,21} + 33.33p_{0,21}p_{21,32} + 16.66p_{0,21}p_{21,32}p_{32,53},$$
$$\tau_3 = 173.33p_{0,11}p_{11,22} + 173.33p_{0,21}p_{21,42} + 16.66p_{0,11}p_{11,22}p_{22,33} \qquad (5.3)$$
$$\qquad + 16.66p_{0,21}p_{21,42}p_{42,73},$$
$$\tau_4 = 213.33p_{0,11}p_{11,12}p_{12,23} + 213.33p_{0,11}p_{11,22}p_{22,43}$$
$$\qquad + 213.33p_{0,21}p_{21,32}p_{32,63} + 213.33p_{0,21}p_{21,42}p_{42,83}.$$

Table 3. Solutions obtained by AREA technique and CA for the first set of constants considered.

Transfer probabilities	Solutions obtained by AREA	Solutions obtained by the CA + RA
$p_{0,11}$	0.701	0.7
$p_{0,21}$	0.298	0.3
$p_{11,12}$	0.404	0.4
$p_{11,22}$	0.595	0.6
$p_{21,32}$	0.901	0.9
$p_{21,42}$	0.098	0.1
$p_{12,13}$	0.513	0.55
$p_{12,23}$	0.486	0.45
$p_{22,33}$	0.755	0.75
$p_{22,43}$	0.244	0.25
$p_{32,53}$	0.970	0.95
$p_{32,63}$	0.029	0.05
$p_{42,73}$	0.978	0.85
$p_{42,83}$	0.0213	0.15
Δ_1	106.251	106.372

Table 4. Relation sizes and transfer times for Experiment 2.

	Number of bits	Time to transfer
Relation A	8,000,000	133.33s
Relation B	1,000,000	16.66s
Relation C	2,000,000	33.33s
Relation D	1,000,000	16.66s
Relation B'	10,400,000	173.33s
Relation C'	12,800,000	213.33s

Table 5. Parameters used by AREA algorithm.

AREA Parameters	
Population size	100
Number of iterations	10000
Mutation probability	0,01
Number of variables	14
Number of alphabets	30
MAX_HARMFUL_MUTATIONS	5

Parameters used by AREA in this case are given in Table 5.

The results obtained by applying AREA algorithm and CA + RA are given in Table 6.

Remark. According to Table 6 the final solutions obtained by these two algorithms are very close. CPU time obtained by AREA technique is 0.05 s, less than

Table 6. Solutions obtained by AREA technique and CA for the second set of constants considered.

Transfer probabilities	Solutions obtained by AREA	Solutions obtained by the CA + RA
$p_{0,11}$	0.778	0.75
$p_{0,21}$	0.221	0.25
$p_{11,12}$	0.75	0.75
$p_{11,22}$	0.249	0.25
$p_{21,32}$	0.962	0.875
$p_{21,42}$	0.037	0.125
$p_{12,13}$	0.75	1
$p_{12,23}$	0.25	0
$p_{22,33}$	0.996	0.875
$p_{22,43}$	0.003	0.125
$p_{32,53}$	0.891	0.25
$p_{32,63}$	0.108	0.75
$p_{42,73}$	0.771	0.875
$p_{42,83}$	0.228	0.125
Δ_1	39.7492	40.3232

the CPU time obtained by CA, which is 15 minutes. Evolutionary algorithms seem to be useful technique for practical optimization proposes.

6 Stochastic Model Versus Heuristic Strategy

We compare our stochastic optimization model and a very popular transfer heuristic. According to the *transfer heuristic* (see [9]) the smallest relation from the operands of a join is transfered to the other operand relation. A query against a database is executed several times (not only once). Stochastic model takes it into account and tries to share the execution of the same query between the sites of the network.

We say that a strategy is *"pure"* if the execution path of the respective query in the state-transition graph is the same in every case the query is executed. If the query is executed several times, one of the joins of the query is executed in each case by the same site, and this is valid for each join of the query.

In the following we compare the results of the proposed stochastic model and the results given by a *"pure"* strategy.

In step 1 of Experiment 1 the transmission of relation B is chosen several times, because its size is smaller than the size of relation A. Therefore the system undergoes transition from state s_0 in state s_{11} in 7 cases from 10.

Transition from state s_{11} states s_{12} and s_{22} are chosen in a balanced mode. This because the size of relation B' ($B' = A \bowtie B$) is approximately equal to the size of relation C.

This balance is not so evident from state s_{21}. This can be explained by the heuristic character of the methods proposed in this paper.

In the third step of query strategy, which is the join of relation D with the resulted relation C' ($C' = B' \bowtie C$.), nearly in every case relation D is chosen for transfer. This because the size of D is much smaller than the size of relation C'.

Consider the "*pure*" strategy (deduced from transfer heuristic): s_0, s_{11}, s_{12}, s_{13}. Every join is executed in site 1, and the necessary time is: 66.66s + 166.66s + 83.33s = 316.65s, which is much greater than the mean processing time given by the stochastic query optimization model (i.e. 106.251s).

In Experiment 2 the situation is similar. As the size of relation B is smaller than in case of Experiment 1 the transfer of B is chosen more often than in case of Experiment 1.

In step 3 in most cases the transfer of relation D is chosen. The size of D is much smaller than the size of the result relation C'. In this case a "*pure*" strategy with the same transfer heuristic may be s_0, s_{11}, s_{12}, s_{13}. The necessary time for this "pure" strategy in site 1 is: 16.66s + 33.33s + 16.66s = 66.65s, which is greater than the mean processing time given by the stochastic optimization model (i.e. 39.7492s).

7   Conclusions

Stochastic query optimization problem of four relations stored in four different sites leads to a constrained nonlinear optimization problem. For solving this problem two different approaches are considered: a constructive (exhaustive) one and an evolutionary one. The results obtained by applying these two methods are very similar. The difference consist in CPU time: by considering evolutionary method for solving the problem the execution time is less than the running time obtained by applying the constructive method. Evolutionary approach seems thus to be more suitable for solving real world applications in real time.

Acknowledgments. We are grateful to professors A. Benczúr and Cs. Varga for their valuable suggestions.

References

1. Date, C.J.: An Introduction to Database Systems, Addison-Wesley Publishing Company, Reading, Massachusetts (2000)
2. Drenick, P.E., Smith, E.J.: Stochastic query optimization in distributed databases, ACM Transactions on Database Systems, Vol. 18, No. 2 (1993) 262-288
3. Dumitrescu, D., Grosan, C., Oltean, M.: A new evolutionary adaptive representation paradigm, Studia Universitas "Babes-Bolyai", Seria Informatica, Volume XLVI, No. 1 (2001) 15-30
4. Grosan, C., Dumitrescu, D.: A new evolutionary paradigm for single and multiobjective optimization, Seminar on Computer Science, "Babes-Bolyai" University of Cluj-Napoca (2002)

5. Dumitrescu, D., Grosan, C., Varga, V.: Stochastic Optimization of Querying Distributed Databases I. Theory of four Relations Join, Studia Univ. "Babes-Bolyai" Cluj-Napoca, Informatica, vol. XLVIII, No. 1 (2003) 79-88.
6. Dumitrescu, D., Grosan, C., Varga, V.: Stochastic Optimization of Querying Distributed Databases II. Solving Stochastic Optimization, Studia Univ. "Babes-Bolyai" Cluj-Napoca, Informatica, vol. XLVIII, No. 2 (2003) 17-24
7. Kingdon, J., Dekker, L.: The shape of space, Technical Report, RN-23-95, Intelligent System Laboratories, Department of Computer Science, University College, London (1995)
8. Markus, T., Morosanu, C., Varga V.: Stochastic query optimization in distributed databases using semijoins, Annales Universitatis Scientiarum Budapestinensis de Rolando Eötvös Nominatae Sectio Computatorica 20 (2001) 107-131
9. Özsu, M. T., Valduriez, P.: Principles of Distributed Database Systems, Prentice-Hall (1991)
10. Ramakrishnan, R.: Database Management Systems, WCB McGraw-Hill (1998)
11. Rudin, W.: Principles of Mathematical Analysis, McGraw-Hill, New York (1976)
12. Ullman, J.D.: Principles of Database and Knowledge-Base Systems, Vol. I-II, Computer Science Press (1988)
13. Varga, V.: Stochastic optimization for the join of three relations in distributed databases I. The theory and one application, Studia Universitas "Babes-Bolyai", Seria Informatica, Volume XLIII, No. 2, (1998) 37-46
14. Varga, V.: Stochastic optimization for the join of three relations in distributed databases II. Generalization and more applications, Studia Universitas "Babes-Bolyai", Seria Informatica, Volume XLIV, No. 1, (1999) 55-62

ML-1-2PC: An Adaptive Multi-level Atomic Commit Protocol

Yousef J. Al-Houmaily[1] and Panos K. Chrysanthis[2]

[1] Dept. of Computer and Information Programs
Institute of Public Administration
Riyadh 11141, Saudi Arabia
houmaily@ipa.edu.sa
[2] Department of Computer Science
University of Pittsburgh
Pittsburgh, PA 15260, USA
panos@cs.pitt.edu

Abstract. The one-two phase commit (1-2PC) protocol is a combination of a one-phase atomic commit protocol, namely, implicit yes-vote, and a two-phase atomic commit protocol, namely, presumed commit. The 1-2PC protocol integrates these two protocols in a dynamic fashion, depending on the behavior of transactions and system requirements, in spite of their incompatibilities. This paper extends the applicability of 1-2PC to the multi-level transaction execution model, which is adopted by database standards. Besides allowing incompatible atomic commit protocols to co-exist in the same environment, 1-2PC has the advantage of enhanced performance over the currently known atomic commit protocols making it more suitable for Internet database applications.

1 Introduction

The *two-phase commit* (2PC) protocol [9,12] is one of the most widely used and optimized *atomic commit protocols* (ACPs). It ensures atomicity and independent recovery but at a substantial cost during normal transaction execution which adversely affects the performance of the system. This is due to the costs associated with its *message complexity* (i.e., the number of messages used for coordinating the actions of the different sites) and *log complexity* (i.e., the amount of information that needs to be stored in the stable storage of the participating sites for failure recovery). For this reason, there has been a re-newed interest in developing more efficient ACPs and optimizations. This is especially important given the current advances in electronic services and electronic commerce environments that are characterized by high volume of transactions where commit processing overhead is more pronounced. Most notable results that aim at reducing the cost of commit processing are *one-phase commit* (1PC) protocols such as *implicit yes-vote* (IYV) [4,6] and *coordinator log* (CL) [19].

Although 1PC protocols are, in general, more efficient than 2PC protocols, 1PC protocols place assumptions on transactions or the database management

A. Benczúr, J. Demetrovics, G. Gottlob (Eds.): ADBIS 2004, LNCS 3255, pp. 275–290, 2004.

systems (DBMSs). Whereas some of these assumptions are realistic (i.e., reflect how DBMSs are usually implemented), others can be considered restrictive in some applications [1,6]. For example, 1PC protocols restrict the implementation of applications that wish to utilize *deferred consistency constraints validation*, an option that is specified in the SQL standards.

The *one-two phase commit* (1-2PC) protocol attempts to achieve the best of the two worlds. Namely, the performance of 1PC and the wide applicability of 2PC. It is essentially a combination of 1PC (in particular, *IYV*) and 2PC (in particular, *Presumed Commit – PrC* [16]). It starts as 1PC and dynamically switches to 2PC when necessary. Thus, 1-2PC achieves the performance advantages of 1PC protocols whenever possible and, at the same time, the wide applicability of 2PC protocols. In other words, 1-2PC supports deferred constraints without penalizing those transactions that do not require them. Furthermore, 1-2PC achieves this advantage on a participant (cohort) basis within the same transaction in spite of the incompatibilities between the 1PC and 2PC protocols.

This paper extends the applicability of 1-2PC to the multi-level transaction execution (MLTE) model, the one adopted by database standards and implemented in commercial systems. The MLTE model is specially important in the context of Internet transactions since they are hierarchical in nature, making 1-2PC more suitable for Internet database applications.

In Section 2, we review PrC, IYV and 1-2PC. *Multi-level 1-2PC* is introduced in Section 3. The performance of 1-2PC is analytically evaluated in Section 4.

2   Background

A distributed/Internet transaction accesses data by submitting operations to its *coordinator*. The coordinator of a transaction is assumed to be the *transaction manager* at the site where the transaction is initiated. Depending on the data distribution, the coordinator decomposes the transaction into a set of *subtransactions*, each of which executes at a single participating database site (*cohort*).

In the *multi-level transaction execution* (MLTE) model, it is possible for a cohort, to decompose its assigned subtransactions further. Thus, a transaction execution can be represented by a multi-level execution tree with its coordinator at the root, and with a number of intermediate and leaf cohorts. When the transaction finishes its execution and submits its final commit request, the coordinator initiates an atomic commit protocol.

2.1   Presumed Commit Two-Phase Commit Protocol

Presumed Commit (PrC) [16] is one of the best known variants of the two-phase commit protocol which consist of a *voting phase* and a *decision phase*. During the voting phase, the coordinator requests all cohorts to *prepare to commit* whereas, during the decision phase, the coordinator either commits the transaction if *all* cohorts are prepared-to-commit (voted "yes"), or aborts the transaction if any cohort has decided to abort (voted "no").

In general, when a cohort receives the final decision and complies with the decision, it sends an acknowledgment (ACK). ACKs enable a coordinator to discards all information pertaining to a transaction from its *protocol table* (that is kept in main memory), and forgets the transaction. Once the coordinator receives ACKs from all the cohorts, it knows that all cohorts have received the decision and none of them will inquire about the status of the transaction in the future. In PrC, cohorts ACK only abort decisions and not commit ones. A coordinator removes a transaction from its protocol table either when it makes a commit decision or when it receives ACKs from all cohorts in the case of abort decision. This means that in case of a status inquiry, a coordinator can interpret lack of information on a transaction to indicate a commit decision.

In PrC, misinterpretation of missing information as a commit after a coordinator's failure is avoided by requiring coordinators to record in a force written initiation log record all the cohorts for each transaction before sending prepare to commit messages to the cohorts. To commit a transaction, the coordinator force writes a commit record to logically eliminate the **initiation** record of the transaction and then sends out the commit decision. When a cohort receives the decision, it writes a non-forced commit record and commits the transaction without having to ACK the decision. After a coordinator or a cohort failure, if the cohort inquires about a committed transaction, the coordinator, not remembering the transaction, will direct the cohort to commit it (by presumption).

To abort a transaction, the coordinator does not write an abort decision in its log. Instead, it sends out the abort decision and waits for ACKs. When a cohort receives the decision, it force writes an abort record and sends an ACK.

In the MLTE model, the behavior of the root coordinator and each leaf cohort remains the same as in two-level transactions. The only difference is the behavior of *cascaded coordinators* (i.e., non-root and non-leaf cohorts) which behave as leaf cohorts with respect to their direct ancestors and root coordinators with respect to their direct descendants. In *multi-level PrC*, each cascaded coordinator has to force write an initiation record before propagating the prepare to commit message to its descendant cohorts. On abort decision, it notifies its descendants, force writes an abort record and, then, acknowledge its ancestor. It forgets the transaction when it receives ACKs from all its descendants. On commit decision, a cascaded coordinator propagates the decision to its descendants, writes a non-forced commit record and, then, forgets the transaction.

2.2   Implicit Yes-Vote One-Phase Commit Protocol

Unlike PrC, the *implicit yes-vote* (IYV) [4,6] protocol consist of only a single phase which is the decision phase. The (explicit) voting phase is eliminated by overlapping it with the ACKs of the database operations. IYV assumes that each site deploys (1) a *strict two-phase locking* and (2) *physical page–level replicated–write–ahead logging* with the undo phase *preceding* the redo phase for recovery.

In IYV, when the coordinator of a transaction receives an ACK from a cohort regarding the completion of an operation, the ACK is *implicitly* interpreted to mean that the transaction is in a prepared-to-commit state at the cohort. When the cohort receives a new operation for execution, the transaction becomes active again at the cohort and can be aborted, for example, if it causes a deadlock or violation to any of the site's database consistency constraints. If the transaction is aborted, the cohort responds with a *negative ACK* message (NACK). Only when all the operations of the transaction are executed and acknowledged by their perspective cohorts, the coordinator commits the transaction. Otherwise, it aborts the transaction. In either case, the coordinator propagates its decision to all the cohorts and waits for their ACKs.

IYV handles cohort failures by partially replicating its log rather than force writing the log before each ACK. Each cohort includes the *redo* log records that are generated during the execution of an operation in the operation's ACK. Each cohort also includes the *read* locks acquired during the execution of an operation in the ACK in order to support the option of *forward recovery* [6]. After a crash, a cohort reconstructs the state of its database, which includes its log and lock table as it was just prior to the failure with the help of the coordinators. To limit the number of coordinators that need to be contacted after a site failure, each cohort maintains a *recovery-coordinators' list* (RCL) which is kept in the stable log. At the same time, by maintaining a local log and using WAL, each cohort is able to undo the effects of aborted transactions locally using only its own log.

In *multi-level IYV*, the behavior of a root coordinator and leaf cohorts remains the same as in IYV, whereas cascaded coordinators are responsible about the coordination of ACKs of individual operations.

As in the case of the (two-level) IYV, only a root coordinator maintains a replicated redo log for each of the cohorts. When a cascaded coordinator receives ACKs from all its descendants that participated in the execution of an operation, it sends an ACK to its direct ancestor containing the redo log records generated across all cohorts and the read locks held at them during the execution of the operation. Thus, after the successful execution of each operation, root coordinator knows all the cohorts (i.e., both leaf and cascaded coordinators) in a transaction. Similarly, each cohort knows the identity of the root coordinator which is reflected in its RCL. The identity of the root coordinator is attached to each operation send by the root and cascaded coordinators.

While the execution phase of a transaction is multi-level, the decision phase is not. Since the root coordinator knows all the cohorts at the time the transaction finishes its execution it sends its decision directly to each cohort without going through cascaded coordinators. Similarly, each cohort sends its ACK of the decision directly to the root coordinator. This is similar to the flattening of the commit tree optimization [17].

2.3 The 1-2PC Protocol

1-2PC is a composite protocol that inter-operates IYV and PrC in a practical manner in spite of their incompatibilities. In 1-2PC, a transaction starts as 1PC at each cohort and continuous this way until the cohort executes a deferred consistency constraint. When a cohort executes such a constraint, it means that the constraint needs to be synchronized at commit time. For this reason, the cohort switches to 2PC and sends an *unsolicited deferred consistency constraint* (UDCC) message to the coordinator. The UDCC is a flag that is set as part of a *switch* message, which also serves as an ACK for the operation's successful execution. When the coordinator receives the switch message, it switches the protocol used with the cohort to 2PC.

When a transaction sends its final commit primitive, the coordinator knows which cohorts are 1PC and which cohorts are 2PC. If all cohorts are 1PC (i.e., no cohort has executed deferred constraints), the coordinator behaves as an IYV coordinator. On the other hand, if all cohorts are 2PC, the coordinator behaves as a PrC coordinator with the exception that the initiation log record (of PrC) is now called a *switch* log record.

When the cohorts are mixed 1PC and 2PC in a transaction's execution, the coordinator resolves the incompatibilities between the two protocols as follows: (1) It " talks" IYV with 1PC cohorts, and PrC with 2PC cohorts and (2) initiates the voting phase with 2PC cohorts before making the final decision and propagating the final decision to all cohorts. This is because a "no" vote from a 2PC cohort is a *veto* that aborts a transaction. Further, in order to be able to reply to the inquiry messages of the cohorts after failures, 1-2PC synchronizes the timing at which it forgets the outcome of terminated transactions. A coordinator forgets the outcome of a committed transaction when all 1PC cohorts ACK the commit decision, and the outcome of an aborted transaction when all 2PC cohorts ACK the abort decision. In this way, when a cohort inquires about the outcome of a forgotten transaction, the coordinator replies with a decision that matches the presumption of the protocol used by the cohort which is always consistent with the actual outcome of the transaction.

1-2PC has been optimized for *read-only* transactions and for context-free transactions with a *forward* recovery option [3] but never extended for multi-level transactions which is done in the next section.

3   The Multi-level 1-2PC Protocol

Extending the 1-2PC for multi-level transactions, there are three cases to consider: (1) all cohorts are 1PC, (2) all cohorts are 2PC and (3) cohorts are mixed 1PC and 2PC. We discuss each of these cases in the following three sections.

3.1   All Cohorts Are 1PC

In the multi-level 1-2PC, the behavior of the root coordinator and each leaf cohort in the transaction execution tree remains the same as in two-level 1-2PC. The only difference is the behavior of cascaded coordinators which is similar to that of the cascaded coordinators in the multi-level IYV. Since an operation's ACK represents the successful execution of the operation at the cascaded coordinator and all its descendants that have participated in the operation's execution, the cascaded coordinator has to wait until it receives ACKs from the required descendants before sending the (collective) ACK and redo log records to its direct coordinator in the transaction execution tree. Thus, when a transaction finishes its execution, all its redo records are replicated at the root coordinator's site. As in the two-level 1-2PC, only root coordinators are responsible for maintaining the replicated redo log records and a root coordinator knows all the cohorts (i.e., both leaf and cascaded coordinators).

The identity of the root coordinator is attached to each operation send by the root and cascaded coordinators. When a cohort receives an operation from a root coordinator for the first time, it records the coordinator's identity in its RCL and force writes its RCL into stable storage. A cohort removes the identity of a root coordinator from its RCL, when it commits or aborts the last transaction submitted by the root coordinator.

As in IYV, if a cohort fails to process an operation, it aborts the transaction and sends a NACK to its direct ancestor. If the cohort is a cascaded coordinator, it also sends an abort message to each implicitly prepared cohort Then, the cohort forgets the transaction. When the root or a cascaded coordinator receives NACK from a direct descendant, it aborts the transaction and sends abort messages to all direct descendants and forgets the transaction. The root coordinator behaves similarly when it receives an abort request from a transaction.

On the other hand, if the root coordinator receives a commit request from the transaction after the successful execution of all its operations, the coordinator commits the transaction. On a commit decision, the coordinator force writes a commit log record and then sends commit messages to each of its direct descendants. If a descendant is a leaf cohort, it commits the transaction, writes a non-forced log record and, when the log record is flushed into the stable log, it acknowledges the commit decision.

If the cohort is a cascaded coordinator, the cohort commits the transaction, forwards a commit message to each of its direct descendants and writes a non-forced commit log record. When the cascaded coordinator receives ACKs from all its direct descendants and the commit log record that it wrote had been flushed into the stable log, the cohort acknowledges the commit decision to its direct ancestor. Thus, the ACK serves as a collective ACK for the entire cascaded coordinator's branch.

3.2   All Cohorts Are 2PC

At the end of the transaction execution phase, the coordinator declares the transaction as 2PC if all cohorts have switched to 2PC. When all cohorts are 2PC, 1-2PC can be extended to the MLTE model in a manner similar to the multi-level PrC which we briefly discussed in Section 2.1 and detailed in [5]. However, multi-level 1-2PC is designed in such a way that 1-2PC does not realize the commit presumption of PrC on every two adjacent levels of the transaction execution tree. In this respect, it is similar to the *rooted PrC* which reduces the cost associated with the initiation records of PrC [5].

Specifically, cascaded coordinators do not force write switch records which are equivalent to the *initiation* records of PrC and, consequently, do not presume commitment in the case that they do not remember transactions. For this reason, in multi-level 1-2PC, the root coordinator needs to know *all* the cohorts at all levels in a transaction's execution tree. Similarly, each cohort needs to know *all* its ancestors in the transaction's execution tree. The former allows the root coordinator to determine when it can *safely* forget a transaction while the latter allows a prepared to commit cohort at any level in a transaction's execution tree to find out the final *correct* outcome of the transaction, even if intermediate cascaded coordinators have no recollection about the transaction due to a failure.

In order for the root coordinator to know the identities of all cohorts, each cohort includes its identity in the ACKs of the *first* operation that it executes. When a cascaded coordinator receives such an ACK from a cohort, it also includes its identity in the ACK. In this way, the identities of all cohorts and the chain of their ancestors are propagated to the root coordinator. When the transaction submits its commit request, assuming that that all cohorts have requested to switch to 2PC during the execution of the transaction, the coordinator force writes a *switch* record, as in two-level 1-2PC. The switch log record includes the identities of all cohorts in the transaction execution tree. Then, it sends out prepare to commit messages to its direct descendants.

When the coordinator sends the prepare to commit message, it includes its identity in the message. When a cascaded coordinator receives the prepare to commit message, it appends its own identity to the message before forwarding it to its direct descendants. When a leaf cohort receives a prepare to commit message, it copies the identities of its ancestors in the prepared log record before sending its "Yes" vote. When a cascaded coordinator receives "Yes" votes from all its direct descendants, the cascaded coordinator also records the identities of its ancestors as well as its descendants in its prepared log record before sending its collective "Yes" vote to its direct ancestor.

If any direct descendant has voted "No", the cascaded coordinator force writes an abort log record, sends a "No" vote to its direct ancestor and an abort message to each direct descendant that has voted "Yes" and waits for their ACKs. Once all the abort ACKs arrive, the cascaded coordinator writes a non-forced end record and forgets the transaction.

As in multi-level PrC, when the root coordinator receives "Yes" votes from all its direct descendants, it force writes a commit record, sends its decision to its direct descendants and forgets the transaction. When a cascaded coordinator receives a commit message, it commits the transaction, propagates the message to its direct descendants, writes a non-forced commit record and forgets the transaction. When a leaf cohort receives the message, it commits the transaction and writes a non-forced commit record.

If the root coordinator receives a "No" vote, it sends an abort decision to all direct descendants that have voted "Yes" and waits for their ACKs, knowing that all the descendants of a direct descendant that has voted "No" have already aborted the transaction. When the coordinator receives all the ACKs, it writes a non-forced end record and forgets the transaction. When a cascaded coordinator receives the abort message, it behaves as in multi-level PrC. That is, it propagates the message to its direct descendants and writes a forced abort record.

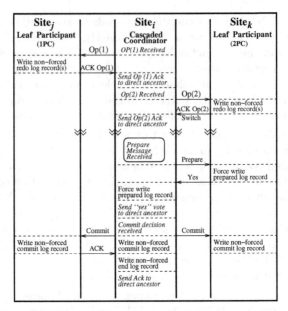

Fig. 1. Mixed cohorts in a 2PC cascaded coordinator's branch (commit case).

Then, it acknowledges its direct ancestor. Once the cascaded coordinator has received ACKs from all its direct descendants, it writes a non-forced end record and forgets the transaction. When a leaf cohort receives the abort message, it first force writes an abort record and, then, acknowledges its direct ancestor.

3.3   Cohorts Are Mixed 1PC and 2PC

Based on the information received from the different cohorts during the execution of a transaction, at commit time the coordinator of the transaction knows the protocol of each of the cohorts. It also knows the execution tree of the transaction. That is, it knows all the ancestors of each cohort and whether a cohort is a cascaded coordinator or a leaf cohort. Based on this knowledge, the coordinator considers a direct descendant to be 1PC if the descendant and *all* the cohorts in its branch are 1PC, and 2PC if the direct descendant or *any* of the cohorts in its branch is 2PC. For a 1PC branch, the coordinator uses the 1PC part of multi-level 1-2PC with the branch, as we discussed above (Section 3.1). For a 2PC branch, the coordinator uses 2PC regardless of whether the direct descendant is 1PC or 2PC. That is, the coordinator uses the 2PC part of multi-level 1-2PC discussed in the previous section (Section 3.2). Thus, with the exception in the way a coordinator's decide on which protocol to use with each of its direct descendants, the coordinator's protocol proceeds as in the two-level 1-2PC.

For leaf cohorts, each cohort behaves exactly in the same way as in two-level 1-2PC regardless of whether the leaf cohort descends from a 1PC or 2PC branch. That is, a cohort behaves as 1PC cohort if it has not requested to switch protocol or as 2PC if has made such a request during the execution of the transaction.

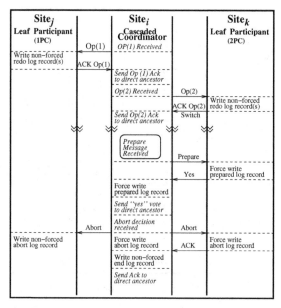

Fig. 2. Mixed cohorts in a 2PC cascaded coordinator's branch (abort case).

On the other hand, the behavior of cascaded coordinators is different and depends on the types of its descendant cohorts in the branch. A cascaded coordinator uses multi-level 1PC when all the cohorts in its branch, including itself, are 1PC. Similarly, a cascaded coordinator uses multi-level 2PC when all the cohorts in the branch, including itself, are 2PC. Thus, in the above two situations, a cascaded coordinator uses multi-level 1-2PC as we discussed it in the previous two sections, respectively.

When the protocol used by a cascaded coordinator is different than the protocol used by at least one of its descendants (not necessarily a direct descendant), there are two scenarios to consider. Since, for each scenario, cascaded coordinators behave the same way at any level of the transaction execution tree, below we discuss the case of the last cascaded coordinator in a branch.

2PC cascaded coordinator with 1PC cohort(s). When a 2PC cascaded coordinator receives a prepare message from its ancestor after the transaction has finished its execution, the cascaded coordinator forwards the message to each 2PC cohort and waits for their votes. If any cohort has decided to abort, the cascaded coordinator force writes an abort log record, then, sends a "no" vote to its direct ancestor and an abort message to each prepared cohort (including 1PC cohorts). Then, it waits for the ACKs from the prepared 2PC cohorts. Once it receives the required ACKs, it writes a non-forced end log record and forgets the transaction. On the other hand, if all the 2PC cohort have voted "yes" and the cascaded coordinator's own vote is a "yes" vote too, the cascaded coordinator force writes a prepared log record and then sends

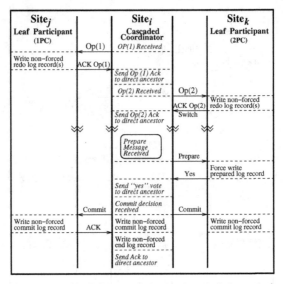

Fig. 3. Mixed cohorts in a 1PC cascaded coordinator's branch (commit case).

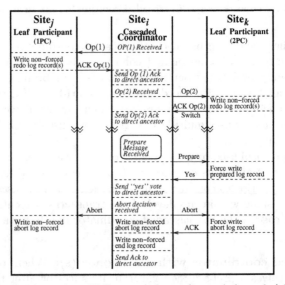

Fig. 4. Mixed cohorts in a 1PC cascaded coordinator's branch (abort case).

a (collective) "yes" vote of the branch to the its direct ancestor, as shown in Figure 1. Then, it waits for the final decision.

If the final decision is a commit (Figure 1), the cascaded coordinator forwards the decision to each of its direct descendants (both 1PC and 2PC), and writes a commit log record. The commit log record of the cascaded coordinator is written in a non-forced manner, following PrC protocol. Unlike PrC, however, a cascaded coordinator expects each 1PC cohort to acknowledge the commit message but not 2PC cohorts since they follow PrC. When a cascaded coordinator receives ACKs from 1PC cohorts, it writes a non-forced end log record. When the end record is written into the stable log due to a subsequent forced write of a log record or log buffer overflow, the cascaded coordinator sends a collective ACK to its direct ancestor and forgets the transaction.

On the other hand, if the final decision is an abort (Figure 2), the cascaded coordinator sends an abort message to each of its descendants and writes a forced abort log record (following PrC protocol). When 2PC cohorts acknowledge the abort decision, the cascaded coordinator writes a non-forced end log record. Once the end record is written onto stable storage due to a subsequent flush of the log buffer, the cascaded coordinator sends an ACK to its direct ancestor and forgets the transaction.

Notice that, unlike two-level 1-2PC, a 2PC cohort that is cascaded coordinator has to acknowledge both commit and abort decisions. A commit ACK reflects the ACKs of all 1PC cohorts while an abort ACK reflects the ACKs of all 2PC cohorts (including the cascaded coordinator's ACK).

1PC cascaded coordinator with 2PC cohort(s). As mentioned above, a 1PC cascaded coordinator with 2PC cohorts is dealt with as 2PC with respect to messages. Specifically, when a 1PC cascaded coordinator receives a prepare message from its ancestor, it forwards the message to each 2PC cohort and waits for their votes. If any cohort has decided to abort, the cascaded coordinator force writes an abort log record, then, sends a "no" vote to its direct ancestor and an abort message to each prepared cohort (including 1PC cohorts). Then, it waits for the abort ACKs from the prepared 2PC cohorts. Once the cascaded coordinator receives the required ACKs, it writes a non-forced end log record and forgets the transaction. On the other hand, if all the 2PC cohort have voted "yes", the cascaded coordinator sends a (collective) "yes" vote of the branch to the its direct ancestor, as shown in Figure 3, and waits for the final decision.

If the final decision is a commit (Figure 3), the cascaded coordinator forwards the decision to each of its direct descendants (both 1PC and 2PC), and writes a commit log record. The commit log record of the cascaded coordinator is written in a non-forced manner, following IYV protocol. Unlike IYV, however, a cascaded coordinator expects each 1PC cohort to acknowledge the commit message but not 2PC cohorts since they follow PrC. When a cascaded coordinator receives ACKs from 1PC cohorts, it writes a non-forced end log record. When the end record is written into the stable log due to a subsequent forced write of a log record or log buffer overflow, the cascaded coordinator sends a collective ACK to its direct ancestor and forgets the transaction.

On the other hand, if the final decision is an abort (Figure 4), the cascaded coordinator sends an abort message to each of its descendants and writes a non-forced abort log record (following IYV protocol). When 2PC cohorts acknowledge the abort decision, the cascaded coordinator writes a non-forced end log record. Once the end record is written onto stable storage due to a subsequent flush to the log buffer, the cascaded coordinator sends an ACK to its direct ancestor and forgets the transaction.

As in the case of a 2PC cascaded coordinator with mixed cohorts, a 1PC cohort that is cascaded coordinator has to acknowledge both commit as well as abort decisions. A commit ACK reflects the ACKs of all 1PC cohorts (including the cascaded coordinator's ACK) while an abort ACK reflects the ACKs of all 2PC cohorts.

3.4   Recovering from Failures

As in all other atomic commit protocols, site and communication failures are detected by *timeouts*. If the root coordinator times out while awaiting the vote of one of its direct descendants, it makes an abort final decision, sends abort messages to all its direct descendants and wait for their ACKs to complete the protocol. Similarly, if a cascaded coordinator times out while awaiting the vote of one of its direct descendants, it makes an abort decision. It also force writes an abort log record, sends a "no" vote to its direct ancestor and abort messages to all its direct descendants and waits for their abort ACKs.

After a site failure, during its recovery process, a 2PC leaf cohort inquires its direct ancestor about the outcome of each prepared to commit transaction. In its inquiry message, the cohort includes the identities of its ancestors recorded in the prepared log record. In this way, if the direct ancestor of the prepared cohort does not remember the transaction, it uses the list of ancestors included in the inquiry message to inquire its own direct ancestor about the transaction's outcome rather than replying with a commit message by presumption. (Recall that a 2PC cascaded coordinator does not write initiation records for transactions, therefore, it cannot presume commitment in the absence of information about a transaction.) Eventually, either one of the cascaded coordinators in the path of ancestors will remember the transaction and provide a reply, or the inquiry message will finally reach the root coordinator. The root coordinator will respond with the appropriate decision if it remembers the outcome of the transaction or will respond with a commit decision by presumption. Once the cohort receives the reply message, it enforces the decision and sends an ACK only if the decision is abort.

On the other hand, if the leaf cohort is a 1PC cohort, the cohort uses its list of RCL to resolve the status of those transactions that were active prior to the failure, as in IYV. Specifically, the cohort inquires each of the coordinators recorded in its RCL with a recovering message. Once the repair messages arrive from the listed coordinators, the cohort repairs its log by applying the missing redo records and finish its recovery procedure. If the failure is a communication failure and the cohort is left blocked in an implicit prepared state, the cohort keeps inquiring its direct ancestor until it receives a final decision. Once the final decision arrives, the cohort continues its protocol as during normal processing.

In the event that the root coordinator fails, during its recovery process, the root coordinator identifies and records in its protocol table each transaction with a switch log record without a corresponding commit or end record. These transactions have not finished their commit processing by the time of the failure and need to be aborted. For each of these transactions, the coordinator sends an abort message to its direct descendants, as recorded in the switch record, along with their lists of descendants in the transaction execution tree. The recipient of the abort message can be either a cascaded coordinator or a leaf cohort. In the case of a cascaded coordinator, if it is in a prepared-to-commit state, the cascaded coordinator behaves as in the case of normal processing discussed above. Otherwise, it responds with a *blind* ACK, indicating that it has already aborted the transaction. Similarly, if the abort message is received by a leaf cohort, the cohort behaves as in the case of normal processing if it is in a prepared-to-commit state or replies with a blind ACK.

Similarly, for each transaction with each that has a commit log record but without corresponding switch and end record, the coordinator knows that all cohorts in this transaction execution are 1PC and the transaction has not finished the protocol before the failure. For each of these transactions, the coordinator adds the transaction in its protocol table and sends a commit message to each of its direct ancestors. Then, the coordinator waits for the ACKs of the direct descendants. Once the required ACKs arrive, the coordinator writes an end log record and forgets the transaction.

In the case of a 2PC cascaded coordinator failure, during the recovery process, the cascaded coordinator adds to its protocol table each *undecided* transaction (i.e., a transaction that has a prepared record without a corresponding final decision record) and each decided (i.e., committed or aborted) transaction that has not been fully acknowledged by its direct descendants prior to the failure. For each undecided transaction, the cascaded coordinator inquires its direct ancestor about the outcome of the transaction. As in the case of a leaf cohort failure, the inquiry message contains the identities of all ancestors as recorded in the prepared record. Once the cascaded coordinator receives the final decision, it completes the protocol as in the normal processing case discussed above. For each decided but not fully acknowledged transaction, the cascaded coordinator re-sends decision messages to its direct descendants (according to the protocol specification) and waits for all their ACKs before completing the protocol as during normal processing, e.g., by writing a non-forced end log record.

4 Analytical Evaluation

In this section, we evaluate the performance of 1-2PC and compare it with the performance of PrC and IYV. In our evaluation, we also include the *presumed abort* (PrA) protocol [16] which is the other best known 2PC variant. As opposed to PrC, PrA coordinators assume that lack of information on a transaction indicates an aborted transaction. This eliminates the need for an abort log record at the coordinator and the need of an ACK and force write abort decision log records at the cohorts.

Our evaluation method is based on evaluating the *log, message* and *time* (message delay) complexities. In the evaluation, we consider the number of coordination messages and forced log writes that are due to the protocols only

Table 1. The cost of the protocols to *commit* a transaction.

	PrC	PrA	IYV	1-2PC (1PC)	1-2PC (2PC)	1-2PC (MIX)
Log force delays	$2d-1$	d	1	1	$d+1$	$3 \sim (d+1)$
Total forced log writes	$2c+l+2$	$2c+2l+1$	1	1	$c+l+2$	$n-p+2$
Message delays (Commit)	$2(d-1)$	$2(d-1)$	0	0	$2(d-1)$	$2 \sim (2d-1)$
Message delays (Locks)	$3(d-1)$	$3(d-1)$	$d-1$	$d-1$	$3(d-1)$	$(2+d) \sim 3(d-1)$
Total messages	$3n$	$4n$	$2n$	$2n$	$3n$	$4c_{Mix}+2p_{1PC}+3p_{2PC}$
Total messages with piggybacking	$3n$	$3n$	n	n	$3n$	$3c_{Mix}+2p_{1PC}+3p_{2PC}$

Table 2. The cost of the protocols to *abort* a transaction.

	PrC	PrA	IYV	1-2PC (1PC)	1-2PC (2PC)	1-2PC (MIX)
Log force delays	$2d-2$	$d-1$	0	0	d	$2 \sim d$
Total forced log writes	$3c+2l+1$	$c+l$	0	0	$2c+2l+1$	$2(n-p)+1$
Message delays (Abort)	$2(d-1)$	$2(d-1)$	0	0	$2(d-1)$	$2 \sim (2d-1)$
Message delays (Locks)	$3(d-1)$	$3(d-1)$	$d-1$	$d-1$	$3(d-1)$	$(2+d) \sim 3(d-1)$
Total messages	$4n$	$3n$	n	n	$4n$	$4c_{Mix}+p_{1PC}+4p_{2PC}$
Total messages with piggybacking	$3n$	$3n$	n	n	$3n$	$3c_{Mix}+p_{1PC}+3p_{2PC}$

(e.g., we do not consider the number of messages that are due to the operations and their acknowledgments). The costs of the protocols in both commit and abort cases are evaluated during normal processing.

Tables 1 and 2 compare the costs of the different protocols for the commit case and abort case on a per transaction basis, respectively. The column titled "1-2PC (1PC)" denotes the 1-2PC protocol when *all* cohorts are 1PC, whereas the column titled "1-2PC (2PC)" denotes the 1-2PC protocol when *all* cohorts are 2PC. The column titled "1-2PC (MIX)" denotes the 1-2PC protocol in the presence of a mixture of both 1PC and 2PC cohorts. In the table, n denotes the total number of sites participating in a transaction's execution (excluding the coordinator's site), p denotes the number of 1PC cohorts (in the case of 1-2PC protocol), c denotes a cascaded coordinator, l denotes a leaf cohort and d denotes the depth of the transaction execution tree assuming that the root coordinator resides at level "1".

The row labeled "Log force delays" contains the sequence of forced log writes that are required by the different protocols up to the point that the commit/abort decision is made. The row labeled "Message delays (Decision)" contains the number of sequential messages up to the commit/abort point, and the row labeled "Message delays (Locks)" contains the number of sequential messages that are involved in order to release all the locks held by a committing/aborting transaction at the cohorts' sites. In the row labeled "Total messages with piggybacking", we apply *piggybacking* of the ACKs, which is a special case of the lazy commit optimization to eliminate the final round of messages.

It is clear from Tables 1 and 2 that 1-2PC performs as IYV when all cohorts are 1PC cohorts, outperforming the 2PC variants in all performance measures including the number of log force delays to reach a decision as well as the total number of log force writes. For the commit case, the two protocols require only one forced log write whereas for the abort case neither 1-2PC nor IYV force write any log records. When all cohorts are 2PC, 1-2PC performs by about d less in the number of sequential forced log writes and c less in the total forced log writes for both the commit as well as the abort case. This makes the performance enhancement of 1-2PC much more significant in the presence of deep execution trees. This performance enhancement is reflected on the 1-2PC when there is a cohorts' mix where the costs associated with log force delays, message delays to reach a decision and message delays to commit depends on the number of sequential 2PC cohorts as well as their positions in the execution tree.

Piggybacking can be used to eliminate the final round of messages for the commit case in PrA, IYV and 1-2PC (1PC). That is not the case for PrC, and 1-2PC (2PC) because a commit decision is never acknowledged in these protocols. Similarly, this optimization can be used in the abort case with PrC and 1-2PC (2PC) but not with PrA, IYV or 1-2PC (1PC) since a cohort in the latter set of protocols never acknowledges an abort decision. 1-2PC (MIX) benefits from this optimization in both commit and abort cases. This is because, in a commit case, a 1PC leaf cohort and each cascaded coordinator with mixed cohorts acknowledge the commit decision, whereas in an abort case, a 2PC leaf cohort and each cascaded coordinator with mixed cohorts acknowledge the abort decision, which can be both piggybacked.

Finally, the performance of multi-level 1-2PC can be further enhanced by applying three optimizations: read-only, forward recovery and flatting of the commit tree. These were not discussed in this paper due to space limitations.

5 Conclusions

Recently, there has been a re-newed interest in developing new atomic commit protocols for different database environments. These environments include gigabit-networked, mobile and real-time database systems. The aim of these efforts is to develop new and optimized atomic commit protocols that meet the special characteristics and limitations of each of these environments.

The 1-2PC protocol was proposed to achieve the performance of one-phase commit protocols when they are applicable, and the (general) applicability of two-phase commit protocols, otherwise. The 1-2PC protocol clearly alleviates the applicability shortcomings of 1PC protocols in the presence of (1) deferred consistency constraints, or (2) limited network bandwidth. At the same time, it keeps the overall protocol overhead below that of 2PC and its well known variants, namely presumed commit and presumed abort. For this reason, we extended 1-2PC to the multi-level transaction execution model, the one specified by the database standards and adopted in commercial database systems. We also evaluated its performance and compared it to other well known commit protocols. Our extension to 1-2PC and the results of our evaluation demonstrates the practicality and efficiency of 1-2PC, making it a specially important choice for Internet transactions that are hierarchical in nature.

References

1. Abdallah, M., R. Guerraoui and P. Pucheral. One-Phase Commit: Does it make sense? *Proc. of the Int'l Conf. on Parallel and Distributed Systems*, 1998.
2. Abdallah, M., R. Guerraoui and P. Pucheral. Dictatorial Transaction Processing: Atomic Commitment without Veto Right. *Distributed and Parallel Databases*, 11(3):239-268, 2002.
3. Al-Houmaily, Y. J. and P. K. Chrysanthis. 1-2PC: The One-Two Phase Atomic Commit Protocol. *Proc. of the ACM Annual Symp. on Applied Computing*, pp 684-691, 2004.
4. Al-Houmaily, Y. J. and P. K. Chrysanthis. Two Phase Commit in Gigabit-Networked Distributed Databases. *Proc. of the Int'l Conf. on Parallel and Distributed Computing Systems*, pp. 554-560, 1995.
5. Al-Houmaily, Y., P. Chrysanthis and S. Levitan. An Argument in Favor of the Presumed Commit Protocol. *Proc. of the Int'l Conf. on Data Engineering*, pp. 255-265, 1997.
6. Al-Houmaily, Y. J. and P. K. Chrysanthis. An Atomic Commit Protocol for Gigabit-Networked Distributed Database Systems. *Journal of Systems Architecture*, 46(9):809-833, 2000.
7. Attalui and Salem. The Presumed-Either Two-Phase Commit Protocol, *IEEE TKDE*, 14(5):1190-1196, 2002.
8. Chrysanthis, P. K., G. Samaras and Y. Al-Houmaily. Recovery and Performance of Atomic Commit Processing in Distributed Database Systems. *Recovery Mechanisms in Database Systems*, V. Kumar and M. Hsu, Eds., Prentice Hall, 1998.
9. Gray, J. Notes on Data Base Operating Systems. In Bayer R., R.M. Graham, and G. Seegmuller (Eds.), *Operating Systems: An Advanced Course*, LNCS-60:393-481, 1978.
10. J. Gray and A. Reuter. *Transaction Processing: Concepts and Techniques*. Morgan Kaufmann, 1993.
11. Gupta, R., J. Haritsa and K. Ramamritham. Revisiting Commit Processing in Distributed Database Systems. *Proc. of ACM SIGMOD*, pp. 486-497, 1997.
12. Lampson, B. Atomic Transactions. *Distributed Systems: Architecture and Implementation - An Advanced Course*, B. Lampson (Ed.), LNCS-105:246-265, 1981.
13. Lampson, B. and D. Lomet. A New Presumed Commit Optimization for Two Phase Commit. *Proc. of VLDB*, pp. 630-640, 1993.
14. Liu, M., D. Agrawal and A. El Abbadi. The Performance of Two Phase Commit Protocols in the Presence of Site Failures. *Distributed and Parallel Databases*, 6(2):157-182, 1998.
15. Mohan, C. and B. Lindsay. Efficient Commit Protocols for the Tree of Processes Model of Distributed Transactions. *Proc. of the ACM Symp. on Principles of Distributed Computing*, 1983.
16. Mohan, C., B. Lindsay and R. Obermarck. Transaction Management in the R^* Distributed Data Base Management System. *ACM TODS*, 11(4):378-396, 1986.
17. Samaras, G., K. Britton, A. Citron and C. Mohan. Two-Phase Commit Optimizations in a Commercial Distributed Environment. *Distributed and Parallel Databases*, 3(4):325-360, 1995.
18. Samaras, G., G. Kyrou, P. K. Chrysanthis. Two-Phase Commit Processing with Restructured Commit Tree. *Proc. of the Panhellenic Conf. on Informatics*, LNCS-2563:82-99, 2003.
19. Stamos, J. and F. Cristian. Coordinator Log Transaction Execution Protocol. *Distributed and Parallel Databases*, 1(4):383-408, 1993.
20. Tal, A. and R. Alonso. Integration of Commit Protocols in Heterogeneous Databases. *Distributed and Parallel Databases*, 2(2):209-234, 1994.

Making More Out of an Inconsistent Database

Jef Wijsen

Université de Mons-Hainaut, Mons, Belgium,
jef.wijsen@umh.ac.be,
http://staff.umh.ac.be/Wijsen.Jef/

Abstract. Repairing a database means making the database consistent
by applying changes that are as small as possible. Nearly all approaches
to repairing have assumed deletions and insertions of entire tuples as
basic repair primitives. A negative effect of deletions is that when a
tuple is deleted because it contains an error, the correct values contained
in that tuple are also lost. It can be semantically more meaningful to
update erroneous values in place, called update-based repairing.
We prove that a previously proposed approach to update-based repairing
leads to intractability. Nevertheless, we also show that the complexity
decreases under the rather plausible assumption that database errors
are mutually independent.
An inconsistent database can generally be repaired in many ways. The
consistent answer to a query on a database is usually defined as the
intersection of the answers to the query on all repaired versions of the
database. We propose an alternative semantics, defining the consistent
answer as being maximal homomorphic to the answers on all repairs. This
new semantics always produces more informative answers and ensures
closure of conjunctive queries under composition.

1 Introduction

Database textbooks generally explain that integrity constraints are used for capturing the set of all "legal" databases and hence should be satisfied at all times.
Nevertheless, many operational databases contain data that is known or sus-
pected to be inconsistent. Inconsistency may be caused, among other reasons, by
data integration and underspecified constraints. For example, the rule "No employee has more than one contact address" gives rise to an error if two databases
to be integrated store different addresses for the same employee. The FIRSTNAME
CHAR(20) declaration in SQL does not protect us from inputting illegal first
names like "Louis14". When later on we specify that first names cannot contain
numbers, the database may already turn out to be inconsistent.

Since database inconsistency is a widespread phenomenon, it is important
to understand how to react to it. The seminal work of Arenas et al. [1] has
roused much research in the construct of *repair* for dealing with inconsistency.
In broad outline, a repair of an inconsistent database I is a database J that is
consistent and "as close as possible" to I. Closeness can be captured in many
different ways, giving rise to various definitions of repair. Under any definition,

A. Benczúr, J. Demetrovics, G. Gottlob (Eds.): ADBIS 2004, LNCS 3255, pp. 291–305, 2004.
© Springer-Verlag Berlin Heidelberg 2004

a given database I can generally be repaired in more than one way. When there are multiple repairs, the question arising is which repair to use for answering queries. The generally accepted query semantics is to execute the query on each repair and return the intersection of all query answers, the so-called *consistent query answer*. Intuitively, all repairs are equally possible and only tuples that appear in all answers are certainly true.

Nearly all approaches so far have assumed that databases are repaired by deleting and inserting entire tuples. A problem with deletion/insertion-based repairing is that a single tuple may contain both correct and erroneous components. When we delete a tuple because it contains an error, we also lose the correct components as an undesirable side effect. For example, it might be undesirable to delete the entire tuple:

⟨Firstname : Louis14, Name : De Funès, Nickname : Fufu, Born : 1914, Died : 1983⟩

from a movie star database at the time the first name is found to be illegal. To overcome this problem, we proposed in [2] a notion of repairing that allows to update the erroneous components in place, while keeping the consistent ones. In the current example, the effect of such "update-based repairing" would be to ignore Louis14 while keeping all other components. Although update-based repairing is attractive from a semantics point of view, it remained unclear up to now whether it is tractable in general. We prove in this paper that the approach to update-based repairing introduced in [2] leads to intractability. Nevertheless, we also introduce an elegant variant with decreased complexity.

Technically, our repair construct differs from other approaches in that it relies on homomorphisms instead of subset relationships between databases and repairs. Homomorphisms also naturally lead to a revised notion of consistent query answer. We define a consistent query answer as being maximal homomorphic to the query answers on all repairs. This definition not only gives us more informative answers, but also ensures closure of conjunctive queries under composition. Closure is interesting because it allows for consistent views. Intersection-based consistent answers, on the other hand, do not give us closure.

The paper is organized as follows. In Sect. 2, we give an overview of several repair constructs and show how they differ on a simple example. In Sect. 3, we show that under update-based repairing in its purest form, recognizing repairs is already intractable for very simple constraints. We gain tractability by adding a condition that captures a plausible hypothesis about the nature of errors. The so-called "independence-of-errors" thesis says that if the same constant has more than one erroneous occurrence in the same relation, then there is no reason to believe that all these errors should be corrected in the same way. Eventually, this leads to a new repair construct, called *uprepair*. Section 4 introduces a homomorphism-based definition of consistent answer and shows that under this new semantics, we obtain closure of conjunctive queries under composition. Finally, Sect. 5 concludes the paper.

2   Overview of Repair Constructs

A manufacturer of beauty products stores data about his production capacity. The single row in the relation I expresses that soap with mint flavor can be manufactured by the LA production plant at a fast rate. We introduce column headings for readability.

I	Prod	Flavor	City	Rate
	soap	mint	LA	fast

For simplicity, we assume a unirelational database in the examples and the technical treatment; nevertheless, all results extend to databases with multiple relations.

All products that can be produced in LA can be produced in NY at a fast rate (τ_1), and mint products cannot be produced at a fast rate outside NY (ϵ_1). Furthermore, the production rate is fully determined by the product, the flavor, and the city (ϵ_2).

$$\tau_1 : \forall w, x, z \big(P(w, x, \text{LA}, z) \Longrightarrow P(w, x, \text{NY}, \text{fast}) \big)$$

$$\epsilon_1 : \forall w, y \big(P(w, \text{mint}, y, \text{fast}) \Longrightarrow y = \text{NY} \big)$$

$$\epsilon_2 : \forall w, x, y, z, z' \big(P(w, x, y, z) \wedge P(w, x, y, z') \Longrightarrow z = z' \big)$$

The symbols ϵ and τ refer to equality-generating and tuple-generating full dependencies [3], respectively. Note, however, that many results apply to larger classes of constraints. The predicate symbol P is to be interpreted by the relation I.

Clearly, the relation I falsifies both τ_1 and ϵ_1. The relation I can be repaired by simply deleting its single tuple. However, we can be more subtle and assume that one of the values "mint," "LA," or "fast" is erroneous. These diverging ways of repairing are formalized next.

The notion of repair is defined relative to a fixed set Σ of integrity constraints. In general, a *repair* of a (possibly inconsistent) relation I is a consistent relation J that is "as close as possible" to I. Different ways of capturing closeness have resulted in different definitions of repair. Most authors have relied on set inclusion to define closeness. In [4], a repair of I is a maximal (w.r.t. $\subseteq$) consistent subset of I. This boils down to considering tuple deletions as a repair primitive. Other approaches also take care of extensions of the original relation. In [1], the symmetric difference between a relation and its repairs is required to be minimal (w.r.t. $\subseteq$). This boils down to considering insertions and deletions as repair primitives, and to treat both symmetrically. An asymmetric treatment of insertions and deletions is proposed by Calì et al. [5]: under what they call the "loosely-sound" semantics, they minimize (w.r.t. $\subseteq$) the set of tuples deleted during repairing, irrespective of the tuples to be inserted. Importantly, in the running example, under each of these semantics, the only repair of I relative to $\{\tau_1, \epsilon_1, \epsilon_2\}$ would be the empty relation.

In [2], we expressed the closeness criterion between a database and its repairs in terms of homomorphisms instead of subset relationships. In this approach,

F_1	Prod	Flavor	City	Rate
	soap	x	LA	fast

U_1	Prod	Flavor	City	Rate
	soap	x	LA	fast
	soap	x	NY	fast

F_2	Prod	Flavor	City	Rate
	soap	mint	y	fast

U_2	Prod	Flavor	City	Rate
	soap	mint	NY	fast

F_3	Prod	Flavor	City	Rate
	soap	mint	LA	z

U_3	Prod	Flavor	City	Rate
	soap	mint	LA	z
	soap	mint	NY	fast

Fig. 1. The tableaux F_1, F_2, and F_3 are fixes of I and $\{\tau_1, \epsilon_1, \epsilon_2\}$. The tableaux U_1, U_2, and U_3 are minimal (w.r.t. $\succeq$) extensions of these fixes that satisfy each constraint of $\{\tau_1, \epsilon_1, \epsilon_2\}$.

repairs can contain (existentially quantified) variables, i.e. repairs are tableaux. Definition 1 recalls the definition of tableau and introduces the homomorphism relationship underlying our work.

Definition 1. *We assume a fixed arity n. A tuple is a sequence $\langle p_1, \ldots, p_n \rangle$ where each p_i is either a variable or a constant. A tableau is a finite set of tuples. A tuple or tableau without variables is called* ground; *a ground tableau is also called a* relation. *If T is a tableau, then* ground(T) *is the set of ground tuples in T.*

A homomorphism from tableau S to tableau T is a substitution θ for the variables in S that preserves tuples, i.e. $\langle p_1, \ldots, p_n \rangle \in S$ implies $\langle \theta(p_1), \ldots, \theta(p_n) \rangle \in T$, where it is understood that θ is the identity on constants. If such a homomorphism exists, then S is said to be homomorphic *to T, denoted $T \succeq S$.*

S and T are equivalent, *denoted $S \sim T$, iff $S \succeq T$ and $T \succeq S$.*

In Fig. 1, each of F_1, F_2, F_3 is homomorphic to I. Furthermore, F_1, F_2, F_3 are homomorphic to U_1, U_2, U_3, respectively. It can be easily verified that the relation $\succeq$ is reflexive and transitive, and that $\sim$ is an equivalence relation. In the database community, homomorphisms are well-known tools used in the context of query containment [3]. We now introduce a stronger homomorphism, which not only preserves tuples but also cardinality.

Definition 2. *Tableau S is said to be* one-one homomorphic *to tableau T, denoted $T \sqsupseteq S$, iff there exists a homomorphism θ from S to T that identifies no two tuples of S, i.e. if s_1, s_2 are distinct tuples of S, then $\theta(s_1) \neq \theta(s_2)$.*

To see the difference between $\succeq$ and $\sqsupseteq$, consider the following tableau E:

E	Prod	Flavor	City	Rate
	soap	x	y	fast
	soap	mint	y	z

The substitution $\theta = \{x/\text{mint}, y/\text{LA}, z/\text{fast}\}$ is a homomorphism from E to I, hence $I \succeq E$. However, $I \not\sqsupseteq E$ because any homomorphism from E to I must map the two tuples of E onto the single tuple of I.

At the center of each theory on repairing is the notion of consistency:

Definition 3. *A constraint is a formula σ equipped with a semantics that allows us to determine whether a tableau T satisfies σ, denoted $T \models \sigma$. For a set Σ of constraints, we write $T \models \Sigma$ iff $T \models \sigma$ for each $\sigma \in \Sigma$.*

A tableau T is said to be consistent *(w.r.t. Σ) iff $T \models \Sigma$; otherwise T is* inconsistent. *A tableau T is said to be* subconsistent *(w.r.t. Σ) iff it is homomorphic to a consistent tableau, i.e. $U \succeq T$ for some consistent tableau U.*

Significantly, we require that satisfaction of constraints be defined for tableaux. Often, semantics for $\models$ defined on relations naturally carries over to tableaux. This is the case for full dependencies:

Definition 4. *Let τ be a full tuple-generating dependency, and ϵ a full equality-generating dependency, i.e.*

$$\tau : \forall^* \big(P(\boldsymbol{x_1}) \wedge \ldots \wedge P(\boldsymbol{x_m}) \Longrightarrow P(\boldsymbol{x_{m+1}}) \big) \ ,$$

$$\epsilon : \forall^* \big(P(\boldsymbol{x_1}) \wedge \ldots \wedge P(\boldsymbol{x_m}) \Longrightarrow p = q \big) \ ,$$

where every variable occurring at the right-hand of $\Longrightarrow$ also occurs at the left-hand of $\Longrightarrow$. Let T be a tableau. Then, $T \models \tau$ iff for every substitution θ, if $\theta(\boldsymbol{x_i}) \in T$ for each i, $1 \leq i \leq m$, then $T \sim T \cup \theta(\boldsymbol{x_{m+1}})$. Next, $T \models \epsilon$ iff for every substitution θ, if $\theta(\boldsymbol{x_i}) \in T$ for each i, $1 \leq i \leq m$, then $\theta(p)$, $\theta(q)$ are not two distinct constants and T is $\sim$-equivalent to the tableau obtained from T by identifying $\theta(p)$ and $\theta(q)$.

The tableaux U_1, U_2, and U_3 in Fig. 1 are consistent according to Def. 4. On the other hand, both F_1 and F_3 falsify τ_1, and F_2 falsifies ϵ_1. Nonetheless, F_1, F_2, and F_2 are subconsistent because they are homomorphic to the consistent tableaux U_1, U_2, and U_3, respectively.

Using homomorphisms instead of subset relationships naturally leads to the following generalization of deletion-based repairing.

Definition 5. *Let Σ be a set of constraints. A* downrepair *of I and Σ is a maximal (w.r.t. $\succeq$) consistent tableau D satisfying $I \sqsupseteq D$.*

In the running example, two downrepairs D_1 and D_2 are as follows:

D_1	Prod	Flavor	City	Rate
	soap	x	y	fast

D_2	Prod	Flavor	City	Rate
	soap	mint	y	z

It can be verified that D_1 and D_2 are consistent, but that this would no longer be the case if one of x, y, or z were replaced by "mint," "LA," or "fast," respectively. Moreover, every other downrepair is equal to D_1 or D_2 up to a renaming of variables. Intuitively, both downrepairs assume an error in column City: the

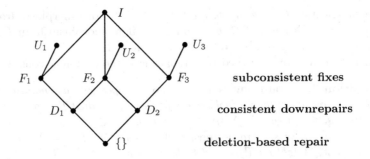

Fig. 2. Tableaux of the running example ordered by $\succeq$. Each of U_1, U_2, U_3 is consistent.

faulty value "LA" is replaced by y. In addition, D_1 assumes an error in column Flavor (x instead of "mint"), and D_2 in column Rate (z instead of "fast"). Both downrepairs believe that soap is somehow produced.

Note that the tableau $E = D_1 \cup D_2$ shown earlier is also consistent. However, E is not a downrepair because $I \not\supseteq E$. The requirement that a downrepair be one-one homomorphic ($\supseteq$) to the original relation guarantees a one-one relationship between original and repaired tuples. Moreover, since the cardinality of each downrepair is bounded by the cardinality of the original relation, there can be only finitely many nonequivalent downrepairs of a given relation I.

A further refinement consists in taking care of extensions of the original relation, which gives us the notion of *fix*:

Definition 6. *Let Σ be a set of constraints. A* fix *of I and Σ is a maximal (w.r.t. $\succeq$) subconsistent tableau F satisfying $I \supseteq F$.*

The difference with downrepairs is that downrepairs need to be consistent, while fixes need only be subconsistent. Intuitively, each fix retains a maximal amount of data from the original database under the restriction that the retained data be reconcilable with the integrity constraints.

In the running example, F_1, F_2, and F_3 are three fixes, and all other fixes are equal to one of these three up to a renaming of variables. Intuitively, F_1, F_2, and F_3 assume errors in columns Flavor, City, and Rate, respectively.

Figure 2 shows the different tableaux of the running example ordered by $\succeq$ (one edge corresponding to $U_3 \succeq U_2$ has been deliberately omitted because it is nonessential). Intuitively, the higher a tableau in this lattice, the more information it contains. Obviously, each downrepair must necessarily be homomorphic to some fix. Also, since $I \supseteq D$ implies $I \succeq D$, every repair obtained by simply deleting tuples is homomorphic to some downrepair—on the other hand, as pointed out by Chomicki and Marcinkowski (unpublished), a downrepair may have no deletion-based repair homomorphic to it. We will focus on fixing hereinafter. Unfortunately, fixing in its purest form leads to intractability (see Sect. 3). We will therefore need to impose further restrictions on fixes in order to gain tractability.

$$\epsilon_5 : \forall x, y, z \big(P(x,y) \wedge P(x,z) \Longrightarrow y = z\big)$$

I	Name	Sal
	Ed	195
	Ed	205
	An	195

F_4	Name	Sal
	Ed	195
	x	205
	An	195

F_5	Name	Sal
	x	195
	Ed	205
	An	195

F_6	Name	Sal
	Ed	y
	Ed	205
	An	y

$$\sim$$

F_5'	Name	Sal
	Ed	205
	An	195

Fig. 3. Example shedding light on the difference between fixes and i_fixes.

3   I_fixes and Uprepairs

Let Σ be a set of constraints. Fix checking is the following problem: on input of a relation I and tableau F, decide whether F is a fix of I and Σ. The corresponding problem for deletion/insertion-based repairing has been studied in detail in [4, 6]. All complexity results in this paper refer to *data complexity*, i.e. the set of constraints and the arity are fixed, and the complexity is in terms of the cardinality of the input tableaux. Unfortunately, fix checking is intractable, even for very simple constraints.

Theorem 1. *Let*

$$\epsilon_3 : \forall x, y \big(P(x,y) \Longrightarrow x = a\big)$$
$$\epsilon_4 : \forall x, y \big(P(x,y) \Longrightarrow y = a\big)$$

*Given a relation I and a tableau F (both of arity 2), it is **NP**-hard to decide whether F is a fix of I and $\{\epsilon_3, \epsilon_4\}$.*

Proof. Crux. Reduction from GRAPH-3-COLORABILITY [7].   □

Consistent query answering (see Sect. 4) can be expected to be at least as hard as fix checking. Hence, the **NP**-hardness result of Theorem 1 means that the fix construct, though semantically clean, is unlikely to be practical for querying purposes. It can be shown that downrepair checking is also **NP**-hard.

Fortunately, fix checking becomes tractable if we require that no variable occurs more than once in a fix. Interestingly, this requirement is often quite natural and even desirable, as illustrated by the following example. The relation I of Fig. 3 stores employee salaries, and the constraint ϵ_5 expresses that no employee has more than one salary. Clearly, I is inconsistent; three fixes are

F_4, F_5, and F_6. Note that these fixes are not comparable by $\succeq$, and that F_5 is equivalent to the smaller relation F_5'.

The fix F_6 contains two occurrences of the same variable y. In this way, F_6 preserves the information that two tuples of I record the same salary for Ed and An. In addition, the second tuple of F_6 states that Ed earns 205. The conclusion should be that An earns 205 as well. In fact, the following relation U_6 is the smallest (w.r.t. $\succeq$) consistent tableau satisfying $U_6 \succeq F_6$. Practically, U_6 can be obtained by a chase [8] of F_6 by $\{\epsilon_5\}$.

U_6	Name	Sal
	Ed	205
	An	205

However, repairing I into U_6 may be counterintuitive: looking at I, it seems weird to believe that An's salary is not 195. Intuitively, the fact that Ed and An earn the same salary in I is just a coincident which should not be taken too far.

From now on, we will require that no variable occurs more than once in a fix. The practical motivation is the "independence-of-errors" thesis: if multiple occurrences of the same value are erroneous, then this should be considered a coincident not to be taken into account during repairing. With this thesis, only F_4 and F_5 would be legal ways of fixing.

I_tableaux and i_fixes differ from tableaux and fixes in that they cannot contain multiple occurrences of the same variable. The prefix "i" may be read as "independence."

Definition 7. *An* i_tableau *is a tableau* T *in which no variable occurs more than once.*

Let I *be a relation and* Σ *a set of constraints. An* i_fix *of* I *and* Σ *is a maximal (w.r.t.* $\succeq$*) subconsistent* i_tableau F *such that* $I \sqsupseteq F$.

We know that fix checking is intractable (Theorem 1). Theorem 2 concerns the tractability of i_fix checking: given a fixed set Σ of constraints, on input of a relation I and an i_tableau F, decide whether F is an i_fix of I and Σ. The result applies to all constraints for which tableau subconsistency can be checked in polynomial time.

Definition 8. *A set* Σ *of constraints is said to be in* **SUBCON^P** *iff for every tableau* F, *it can be decided in polynomial time in* $|F|$ *whether* F *is subconsistent.*

Proposition 1. *Every finite set of full dependencies is in* **SUBCON^P**.

Theorem 2. *Let* Σ *be a set of constraints in* **SUBCON^P**. *For every relation* I *and* i_tableau F, *deciding whether* F *is an* i_fix *of* I *and* Σ *is in* **PTIME**.

The next natural step is to pass from subconsistent i_fixes to consistent tableaux, called *uprepairs*. The prefix "up" is used to emphasize the difference with down-repairs (see Def. 5) and with other repair notions in the literature.

Definition 9. *Let I be a relation and Σ a set of constraints. An* uprepair *of I and Σ is a minimal (w.r.t. $\succeq$) consistent tableau U such that $U \succeq F$ for some i_fix F of I and Σ.*

If Σ is a set of full dependencies and F an i_fix, then the uprepair corresponding to F is unique up to $\sim$ and can be computed in polynomial time in $|F|$ by an algorithm known as *the chase* [8].

The fixes F_1, F_2, and F_3 of Fig. 1 are also i_fixes since no variable occurs more than once in each of them; the corresponding uprepairs are U_1, U_2, and U_3, respectively.

4   Consistent Query Answers and Consistent Views

Our notion of uprepair is homomorphism-based rather than subset-based. The advantage is that homomorphisms allow us to "hide," through the use of variables, erroneous values in a tuple while preserving the consistent ones. We now provide a homomorphism-based notion of consistent query answer, and discuss its advantages over the commonly used intersection-based definition.

4.1   Infimum

Given a set $\mathbf{S}$ of tableaux, one can construct a unique (up to $\sim$) maximal (w.r.t. $\succeq$) tableau T that is homomorphic to each tableau of $\mathbf{S}$ [2,9].

Definition 10. *Let $\mathbf{S}$ be a finite set of tableaux. An* infimum *of $\mathbf{S}$ is a tableau T satisfying:*

1. *$S \succeq T$ for each $S \in \mathbf{S}$, and*
2. *for each tableau T', if $S \succeq T'$ for each $S \in \mathbf{S}$, then $T \succeq T'$.*

Any set $\mathbf{S}$ of tableaux has an infimum, which is necessarily unique up to $\sim$, i.e. the set of infimums of $\mathbf{S}$ is an equivalence class of $\sim$. We assume there is an arbitrary selection rule that picks a representative of this $\sim$-equivalence class and denote it "inf $\mathbf{S}$". The results hereafter do not depend on the actual representative chosen.

In what follows, let $\mathbf{U} = \{U_1, U_2, U_3\}$, the set of uprepairs of our running example (see Fig. 1). The infimum of $\mathbf{U}$ is the following tableau:

inf U	Prod	Flavor	City	Rate
	soap	x	NY	fast

Intuitively, the information common to each uprepair is that soap is produced in NY at a fast rate.

4.2   New Notion of Consistent Answer

In what follows, we focus on conjunctive queries expressed as rules [3], staying within a unirelational database perspective.

Definition 11. *A* conjunctive query *is a rule*

$$Q : \langle \boldsymbol{x_0} \rangle \leftarrow P(\boldsymbol{x_1}), \ldots, P(\boldsymbol{x_m})$$

where every variable occurring in $\boldsymbol{x_0}$ also occurs at the right-hand of $\leftarrow$. The answer to Q on input of a tableau T, denoted $Q(T)$, is the smallest tableau containing the (not necessarily ground) tuple t if there exists a substitution θ such that $\theta(\boldsymbol{x_0}) = t$ and $\theta(\boldsymbol{x_i}) \in T$ for each i, $1 \leq i \leq m$. The arity of the predicate symbol P is called the input arity *of Q; the arity of $\boldsymbol{x_0}$ is the* output arity.

The query answer $Q(T)$ can contain variables that occur in T; it generally suffices to know T, and hence $Q(T)$, up to a variable renaming.

A database repair need not be unique, so we can assume a set $\mathbf{S}$ of repairs. Accordingly, consistent query answering extends query semantics from a single tableau T to a set $\mathbf{S}$ of tableaux. In the following definitions, one may think of the set $\mathbf{S}$ as the set of all repairs (uprepairs in our framework). The general practice for answering a query Q is to return the intersection of the query answers on each repair, denoted $Q^{\cap}$. We also propose an alternative semantics, denoted Q^{inf}, which returns the infimum of the query answers on each repair.

Definition 12. *Let $\mathbf{S}$ be a finite set of tableaux and Q a conjunctive query. We define* intersection-based *and* infimum-based *query semantics, as follows:*

$$Q^{\cap}(\mathbf{S}) := \bigcap \{\mathbf{ground}(Q(T)) \mid T \in \mathbf{S}\}$$
$$Q^{\text{inf}}(\mathbf{S}) := \inf \{Q(T) \mid T \in \mathbf{S}\}$$

Note that $Q^{\cap}$ semantics first applies $\mathbf{ground}(\cdot)$ (see Def. 1) to remove tuples with variables. Alternatively, we could assume w.l.o.g. that no two distinct tableaux of $\mathbf{S}$ have a variable in common, which makes the use of $\mathbf{ground}(\cdot)$ superfluous. To determine $Q^{\cap}(\mathbf{S})$ or $Q^{\text{inf}}(\mathbf{S})$, it suffices to know the tableaux of $\mathbf{S}$ up to $\sim$-equivalence:

Proposition 2. *Let $\mathbf{S}_1$ and $\mathbf{S}_2$ be two finite sets of tableaux such that for each tableau in either set, there exists an equivalent tableau in the other set. For each conjunctive query Q, $Q^{\cap}(\mathbf{S}_1) = Q^{\cap}(\mathbf{S}_2)$ and $Q^{\text{inf}}(\mathbf{S}_1) \sim Q^{\text{inf}}(\mathbf{S}_2)$.*

Consequently, to determine consistent query answers in our framework, it suffices that $\mathbf{S}$ is a finite set containing, for each uprepair U, a tableau equivalent to U. The following proposition expresses that Q^{inf} always provides more informative answers than $Q^{\cap}$:

Proposition 3. *Let $\mathbf{S}$ be a finite set of tableaux. For each conjunctive query Q, $Q^{\text{inf}}(\mathbf{S}) \supseteq Q^{\cap}(\mathbf{S})$.*

Assume a query V asking which products can be manufactured in which flavors in NY:

$$V : \langle w, x \rangle \leftarrow P(w, x, \mathrm{NY}, z)$$

For the set $\mathbf{U} = \{U_1, U_2, U_3\}$ of uprepairs, we obtain:

$$V^\cap(\mathbf{U}) = \{\} \qquad \text{and} \qquad V^{\inf}(\mathbf{U}) = \{\langle \mathrm{soap}, x \rangle\} \ .$$

That is, the consistent answer under infimum-based semantics is that soap is produced in some (unknown) flavor. This is more informative than the empty answer obtained under intersection-based semantics.

4.3 Consistent Views

We saw that one advantage of $Q^{\inf}$ over $Q^\cap$ is that it always yields more informative answers (Prop. 3). We now show a second advantage: $Q^{\inf}$ semantics supports consistent views, while $Q^\cap$ does not.

An appealing property of the relational model, known as *closure*, is that the result of a query on a database is a new relation that can be queried further. This allows, among others, for the construct of *view*. A view on a database I is specified by a view name and a view definition; the view definition is some query V on I. If this view is queried further by a query Q, then the answer returned should be $Q(V(I))$. The "intermediate" result $V(I)$ need not be materialized because the same answer can be obtained by executing $Q \circ V(I)$, where $Q \circ V$ is a single new query that is the composition of Q and V. Computing the composition is also known as "view substitution." The closure of conjunctive queries under composition [3, Theorem 4.3.3] motivates the following definition:

Definition 13. *Let Q and V be conjunctive queries such that the output arity of V is equal to the input arity of Q. We write $Q \circ V$ for the conjunctive query satisfying for each tableau T, $Q \circ V(T) = Q(V(T))$.*

Importantly, under $Q^{\inf}$ semantics, conjunctive queries remain closed under composition:

Theorem 3. *Let $\mathbf{S}$ be a finite set of tableaux. Let Q, V be conjunctive queries such that the output arity of V is equal to the input arity of Q.*
Then, $(Q \circ V)^{\inf}(\mathbf{S}) \sim Q(V^{\inf}(\mathbf{S}))$.

Proof. Crux. It takes some effort to show that inf and conjunctive queries commute, i.e. $Q^{\inf}(\mathbf{S}) \sim Q(\inf \mathbf{S})$ for any conjunctive query Q. Then, $(Q \circ V)^{\inf}(\mathbf{S}) \sim Q \circ V(\inf \mathbf{S}) = Q(V(\inf \mathbf{S})) \sim Q(V^{\inf}(\mathbf{S}))$.

For example, let Q be the following query on the output of V defined in Sect. 4.2:

$$Q : \langle w \rangle \leftarrow V(w, x)$$

Obviously, the composition of V followed by Q asks for products manufactured at NY:

$$Q \circ V : \langle w \rangle \leftarrow P(w, x, \mathrm{NY}, z)$$

We have $(Q \circ V)^{\mathrm{inf}}(\mathbf{U}) = Q(V^{\mathrm{inf}}(\mathbf{U})) = \{\langle \mathrm{soap} \rangle\}$.

To conclude, the consistent answer to $Q \circ V$ under infimum-based semantics can be obtained by executing Q on the consistent answer to V. It is easy to see that this nice property does not hold for intersection-based semantics. Indeed,

$$(Q \circ V)^{\cap}(\mathbf{U}) = \{\langle \mathrm{soap} \rangle\} \ ,$$

but since $V^{\cap}(\mathbf{U})$ is empty (see Sect. 4.2), the answer $\{\langle \mathrm{soap} \rangle\}$ cannot be obtained by issuing Q (or any other query) on $V^{\cap}(\mathbf{U})$. Consequently, intersection-based semantics does not support consistent views.

5   Discussion and Related Work

5.1   Related Work

Although theoretical approaches to reasoning with inconsistent information date back to the 80s, the distinction between "consistent" and "inconsistent" answers to queries on databases that violate integrity constraints, seems to be due to Bry [10], who founded the idea on provability in minimal logic. Consistent query answering gained momentum with the advent of a model-theoretic construct of repair [1]. Different logic programming paradigms [11,12,13] have been used to characterize database repairs and consistent query answers. Other formalisms used to this extent include analytic tableaux [14] (unrelated to our tableaux) and annotated predicate calculus [15]. Given a consistent deductive database and an update that may render the database inconsistent, Mayol and Teniente [16] define minimal insertions, deletions, and modifications for restoring the database to a consistent state. They mention that these integrity maintenance techniques can be adapted to repair an inconsistent database.

All approaches cited so far (including ours) assume a single database context. The data integration setting of [17,18] considers a global database which is retrieved by queries over local source databases. Inconsistency can arise relative to integrity constraints expressed over the global schema. Lembo et al. [17] study the computation of consistent answers to queries over the global schema when the constraints are key and inclusion dependencies. Complexity results of consistent query answering under key and inclusion dependencies appear in [5].

Consistent query answering also appears in the context of data integration in [19,20]. From [19], it follows that under certain acyclicity conditions, sets of not-necessarily-full tuple-generating dependencies are in **SUBCON^P** and hence are covered by our results. This observation is important because not-necessarily-full tuple-generating dependencies are needed to capture foreign key constraints in general.

We have noticed (e.g. in Prop. 2) that it is often a waste of time to examine more than one representative of an $\sim$-equivalence class. For space efficiency reasons, we may be interested in finding the representative of the smallest size; finding minimal (w.r.t. size) representatives within an $\sim$-equivalence class subject to certain conditions is at the center of [20].

Recent comprehensive overviews of database repairing and consistent query answering appear in [6,21].

5.2   Concluding Remarks

Let I be a database that is replaced by a consistent database J (possibly $I = J$ if I is consistent). All repair notions that have appeared in the literature [1,5,11, 13,14,15,17,22] measure the distance between a database and its repairs in terms of the tuples inserted $(J \setminus I)$ and deleted $(I \setminus J)$ during repairing. Insertions and deletions can be treated symmetrically [1,12,13] or asymmetrically [5]. In [4], only tuple deletions are possible as repair primitive.

In [2], we first proposed to use homomorphisms instead of subset relationships for comparing a database and its repairs. This allows rectifying a value within a tuple while preserving other correct values within the tuple. This is significant as many operational databases contain "long" tuples, and errors seldom affect the entire tuple. In general, our approach cannot be simulated by deletion/insertion-based repairing.

We have shown (Theorem 1) that for the construct of update-based repairing proposed in [2], it is already **NP**-hard (data complexity) to decide whether a given tableau F is a fix of a relation I and a set Σ of equality-generating full dependencies. Fortunately, we were able to show (Theorem 2) that the problem is in **PTIME** if no variable occurs more than once in F, i.e. if F is an i-fix. This restriction to i-fixes accomplishes the quite natural "independence-of-errors" assumption.

By requiring that i-fixes be maximal (w.r.t. $\succeq$), we retain as much information as possible from the original database; only data that cannot possibly be reconciled with the integrity constraints is removed. This is similar in nature to the "loosely-sound" semantics proposed in [5] for deletion/insertion-based repairing. A consistent minimal extension of an i-fix is an uprepair. Uprepairs, in general, preserve more consistent information than other repair constructs in the literature.

Nearly all research on consistent query answering has focused on (the complexity of) computing consistent answers. So far, little attention has been paid to revisiting existing database theory under this new query semantics. In this respect, we showed that to maintain the closure of conjunctive queries under composition (and hence the principle of view substitution), consistent query answers should be infimum-based rather than intersection-based (see Theorem 3). Moreover, we showed (Prop. 3) that the newly proposed semantics always yields more informative answers.

References

1. Arenas, M., Bertossi, L., Chomicki, J.: Consistent query answers in inconsistent databases. In: Proc. 18th ACM SIGACT-SIGMOD-SIGART Symposium on Principles of Database Systems, ACM Press (1999) 68–79
2. Wijsen, J.: Condensed representation of database repairs for consistent query answering. In: Proc. 9th Int. Conf. on Database Theory, ICDT 2003. LNCS 2572, Springer (2002) 378–393
3. Abiteboul, S., Hull, R., Vianu, V.: Foundations of Databases. Addison-Wesley (1995)
4. Chomicki, J., Marcinkowski, J.: Minimal-change integrity maintenance using tuple deletions. Information and Computation (To appear)
5. Calì, A., Lembo, D., Rosati, R.: On the decidability and complexity of query answering over inconsistent and incomplete databases. In: Proc. 22nd ACM Symposium on Principles of Database Systems, ACM Press (2003) 260–271
6. Chomicki, J., Marcinkowski, J.: On the computational complexity of minimal-change integrity maintenance in relational databaes. In Bertossi, L., Hunter, A., Schaub, T., eds.: Inconsistency Tolerance. Springer-Verag (To appear)
7. Garey, M.R., Johnson, D.S.: Computers and Intractability. A Guide to the Theory of NP-completeness. W.H. Freeman and Company (1979)
8. Beeri, C., Vardi, M.Y.: A proof procedure for data dependencies. Journal of the ACM **31** (1984) 718–741
9. Nienhuys-Cheng, S.H., de Wolf, R.: Least generalizations and greatest specializations of sets of clauses. Journal of Artificial Intelligence Research **4** (1996) 341–363
10. Bry, F.: Query answering in information systems with integrity constraints. In: First IFIP WG 11.5 Working Conference on Integrity and Internal Control in Information Systems: Increasing the Confidence in Information Systems, Zurich, Switzerland, December 4-5, 1997, Chapman Hall (1997) 113–130
11. Arenas, M., Bertossi, L., Chomicki, J.: Answer sets for consistent query answering in inconsistent databases. Theory and Practice of Logic Programming **3** (2003) 393–424
12. Greco, G., Greco, S., Zumpano, E.: A logic programming approach to the integration, repairing and querying of inconsistent databases. In: Proc. 17th Int. Conf. on Logic Programming (ICLP 2001). Volume 2237 of LNCS., Springer (2001) 348–364
13. Greco, G., Greco, S., Zumpano, E.: A logical framework for querying and repairing inconsistent databases. IEEE Trans. on Knowledge and Data Engineering **25** (2003) 1389–1408
14. Bertossi, L., Schwind, C.: Database repairs and analytic tableaux. Annals of Mathematics and Artificial Intelligence **40** (2004) 5–35
15. Arenas, M., Bertossi, L., Kifer, M.: Applications of Annotated Predicate Calculus to Querying Inconsistent Databases. In: Proc. 1st Int. Conf. on Computational Logic (CL 2000). Volume 1861 of LNAI., Springer (2000) 926–941
16. Mayol, E., Teniente, E.: Consistency preserving updates in deductive databases. Data & Knowledge Engineering **47** (2003) 61–103
17. Lembo, D., Lenzerini, M., Rosati, R.: Source inconsistency and incompleteness in data integration. In: Proc. 9th Int. Workshop on Knowledge Representation meets Databases (KRDB 2002). Number 54 in CEUR Workshop Proceedings (2002)
18. Calì, A., Calvanese, D., Giacomo, G.D., Lenzerini, M.: Data integration under integrity constraints. Information Systems **29** (2004) 147–163

19. Fagin, R., Kolaitis, P.G., Miller, R.J., Popa, L.: Data exchange: Semantics and query answering. In: Proc. 9th Int. Conf. on Database Theory, ICDT 2003. LNCS 2572, Springer (2002) 207–224
20. Fagin, R., Kolaitis, P.G., Popa, L.: Data exchange: Getting to the core. In: Proc. 22nd ACM Symposium on Principles of Database Systems, ACM Press (2003) 90–101
21. Bertossi, L., Chomicki, J.: Query answering in inconsistent databases. In Chomicki, J., van der Meyden, R., Saake, G., eds.: Logics for Emerging Applications of Databases. Springer (2003) 43–83
22. Arenas, M., Bertossi, L., Chomicki, J., He, X., Raghavan, V., Spinrad, J.: Scalar aggregation in inconsistent databases. Theoretical Computer Science **296** (2003) 405–434

Process Query Language:
A Way to Make Workflow Processes More Flexible*

Mariusz Momotko[1] and Kazimierz Subieta[2,3]

[1] Rodan Systems,
ul. Pulawska 465, 02-844 Warszawa, Poland
Mariusz.Momotko@rodan.pl
http://www.rodan.pl
[2] Institute of Computer Science PAS,
ul. J.K. Ordona 21, 01-237 Warszawa, Poland
[3] Polish-Japanese Institute of Information Technology,
ul. Koszykowa 86, 02-008 Warszawa, Poland
subieta@pjwstk.edu.pl

Abstract. Many requirements for a business process depend on the workflow execution data that includes common data for all the population of processes, state of resources, state of processes, etc. The natural way to specify and implement such requirements is to put them into the process definition. In order to do it, we need: (1) a generalised workflow metamodel that includes data on the workflow environment, process definitions, and process execution; (2) a powerful and flexible query language addressing the metamodel; (3) integration of a query language with a business process definition language. In this paper the mentioned workflow metamodel together with the business process query language BPQL is presented. BPQL is integrated with the XML Process Definition Language (XPDL) increasing significantly its expressiveness and flexibility. We also present practical results for application of the proposed language in the OfficeObjects® WorkFlow system.

1 Introduction

During the last decade workflow management systems (WfM systems) made a successful career. The WfM systems have been used for implementing various types of business processes. Despite many advantages resulted from application of such systems, there were also observed significant limitations. One of the major restrictions was assumption that business processes do not change too often during their execution. While such assumption may be satisfied for majority of production processes, for less rigid processes, such as administration ones, this is not true. Because of the nature of the latter processes, they need to adapt frequent changes in workflow environment (i.e. resources, data and applications) as well as workflow itself (e.g. the current workload of participants) [21], [1], [23].

---

* This work was supported by the European Commission project ICONS, IST-2001-32429.

A. Benczúr, J. Demetrovics, G. Gottlob (Eds.): ADBIS 2004, LNCS 3255, pp. 306–321, 2004.
© Springer-Verlag Berlin Heidelberg 2004

An approach to increase processes adaptability is to make their definition more flexible. In this context flexible means that it is possible to express complex dynamic requirements that depend on process execution history as well as current organisational and application data (referred further to as relevant data). An alternative is manual control of processes and their resources at run time and this may be the only way for complex and unpredictable cases. However for many quite complex requirements, such as workflow participant assignments and transition conditions, this approach seems to be the closest to the real business process behaviour.

In order to express the mentioned requirements, we need to define an appropriate process metamodel, then to develop a language to query this model, and finally to integrate this language with a process definition language. The process metamodel has to be generic and include both process definition as well as process execution entities. So far, there is at least one widely known process definition metamodel proposed in [24] standard by Workflow Management Coalition (WfMC). While this metamodel is well defined, there is no standard process execution metamodel provided neither by WfMC standards nor by other process management body (e.g. BPMI). In addition, process execution models provided by WfM systems seem to be tool oriented and mainly focusing on entities implemented within a given system. Recently, there is some effort in defining such generalised process execution model (e.g. [11]). However, it does not include some process features proposed within the last workflow research such as advanced time management [9] or flexible workflow participant assignment [14].

In order to make process definition more flexible, in the next step we need to develop a language to query the mentioned metamodel. This language should be able to express all possible queries on the metamodel, and should be readable and clear for process designers which are not necessarily software programmers.

In Section 2 we propose a generalised process metamodel as an extension of the WfMC's metamodel; the extension concerns entities related to process execution. In Section 3 on the basis of this metamodel we define a Business Process Query Language (BPQL). First we specify process definition elements where this language may be used and then define its syntax and semantics followed by some aspects of its pragmatics. In Section 4 we present integration of BPQL with XML Process Definition Language (XPDL). In Section 5 we present practical results of application the mentioned language in a commercial workflow management system that is OfficeObjects® WorkFlow. In Section 6 we discuss related work. Section 7 concludes.

2 Process Metamodel

In order to specify a workflow query language in the first stage an appropriate workflow process metamodel should be defined. It should represent two parts of 'workflow process puzzle': process definition and process execution. The former part is mainly used by workflow engines to execute workflow processes while the latter helps monitoring and analysing workflow process execution.

Since WfM systems are only a part of IT applications, there is a need to specify requirements for the workflow environment. From the workflow point of view such systems have three dimensions: processed data, provided services and registered resources that may execute the services operating on the data. A part of these data is

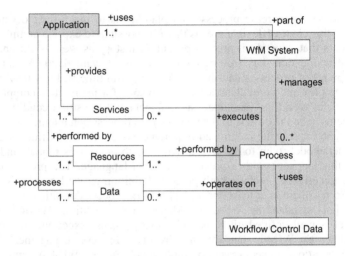

Fig. 1. Workflow system as a part of IT application

used by WfM systems to control execution of workflow processes (i.e. flow conditions, and workflow participant assignment). WfM systems have rights only to read these data, not to modify them. In WfMC terms these data are referred to as *workflow relevant data*. Services provided by information systems may be used to express process activities. During execution of activities WfM systems call these services with appropriate parameters In the WfMC terminology these data are called *applications*. There are also resources that include users or automatic agents that may perform some activities within workflow processes.

Resources may be also selected using roles, groups or organizational units. A resource that may participate in process execution is called a *workflow participant*. In addition to the mentioned elements WfM systems use *workflow control data*. These data are managed only by WfM systems and store workflow specific information such as number of active process instances, international setting, etc.

The workflow process metamodel defines workflow entities, their relationships and basic attributes. It consists of two parts, namely a workflow process definition metamodel and a workflow process instance metamodel. The former part defines the top-level entities contained within process definition, their relationships and basic attributes. It is used to design and implement a computer representation of business processes. The latter part defines the top-level entities contained within process instantiation, their relationships and basic attributes. This metamodel is used to represent process execution that is done according to the process definition model. The workflow process metamodel also shows how individual process definition entities are instantiated during process execution.

The main entity of the definition metamodel is *process definition*. It provides basic information about the computer representation of a business process. For every process a set of *data container attributes* is defined. This attributes are used during process execution in the evaluation of conditional expressions, such as transition conditions or pre and post conditions. The set of container attributes (i.e. number, types, and names) depends on individual process definitions.

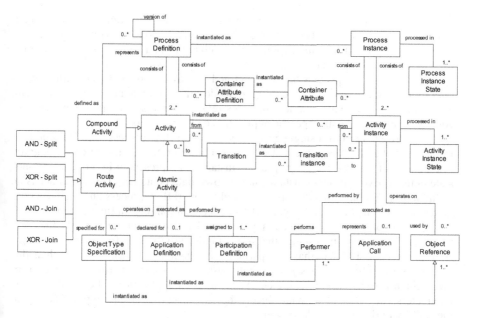

Fig. 2. Process metamodel

Process definition consists of activities. An *activity* defines a piece of work that forms one logical step within a process. There are three types of activities: atomic, route and compound ones. An *atomic activity* is a smallest logical step within the process that may not be further divided. For every atomic activity it is possible to define *who* will perform it, *how* it will be executed and *what* data will be processed. An atomic activity may be performed by one or more workflow participants. Basically, a workflow participant is a user (or their group), a role or an organizational unit. In addition, the system can be treated as a special workflow participant. Specification of workflow participants that may perform a given activity is called *workflow participant assignment*. The way how activity will be performed is specified by *application* which is executed on behalf of it.

Such specification also includes a set of parameters that will be passed to the application. Since the mentioned application operates on data, also object types that will be processed (i.e. created, modified, read or deleted) by this activity has to be defined. Object types may be considered as workflow relevant data that is a part of application data related to and processed by workflow processes.

The second type of activity is a compound activity. This type of activity represents a sub process and usually is defined to simplify process definition and make use of common activities that exist in many business processes. The last type of activity is a route activity. It is used to express control flow elements, namely split and join operations. For both split and join operations two basic control flow operators are defined: AND and XOR. On the basis of these operators it is possible to express more complex flow operations. A route activity is performed by the system. Since this type of activity is a skeletal one, it performs no work processing, neither object types nor application is associated with it.

The order of activities within the process is defined by transitions. A transition defines the relation between two activities. Transition from one activity to another one may be conditional (involving expressions which are evaluated to permit or inhibit the transition) or unconditional.

When a workflow process has been defined, it may be executed many times. Execution of a workflow process according to its definition is called a process enactment. The context of such an enactment includes real performers (workflow participants), concrete relevant data, and specific application call parameters.

The representation of a single enactment of a workflow process is called a process instance. Its behavior is expressed by states and described as a state chart diagram. The history of states for a given process instance is represented by process instance state entities. Every process instance has its own data container. This container is an instantiation of a data container type defined for workflow process and includes container attributes that are used to control process execution (e.g. in flow conditions).

Execution of a process instance may be considered as execution of a set of activity instances. Every activity instance that is an atomic activity is performed by one workflow participant. If more that one participant is assigned to the activity, then this activity is instantiated as a set of activity instances with one performer for each of them. Such activity instance may be executed as an application called with specific parameters and operates on data objects that are instances of data types assigned to the activity during process definition.

If an activity instance is a route activity it is performed automatically by the system and there is neither application nor data objects assigned to it. In the case when activity instance is a *sub-process*, it is represented by another process instance executed according to the definition of the mentioned sub-process.

Similarly to the process instance, behaviour of an activity instance is represented by state diagram and stored as activity instance state entities.

Flow between activity instances is represented by *transition instances*. When an activity instance is finished, the system checks which transitions that are going from this activity may be instantiated. If a transition has no condition or transition condition is satisfied, it is automatically instantiated by the system. A transition instance may be considered as a relation 'predecessor-successor' between two activities.

3   Business Process Query Language

The process metamodel described in the previous section specifies basic workflow entities and relationships between them. In order to extract information from this metamodel, it is necessary to define a query language addressing business processes.

This language like other standard query languages should have clear syntax and unambiguous semantics. It should be able to express complex queries. It also needs to be coherent and complete to ask all possible queries to the process model. It should be an object-oriented language rather than a relational one since the process metamodel is much easier to represent through objects and associations.

This language should also provide core workflow specific functionality, namely:

- functions to simplify operations on process definition/instance graphs, especially to retrieve information about the first activity, current activity, its predecessors as well as possible successors,

- functions to extract some information about the context of calling a given query, e.g. in the case of using function to retrieve the activity that is currently processed it is required to know which process that query is asking for.

It seems that these two kinds of requirements for business process query languages may be satisfied by selecting the most suitable standard query language and extend it by a set of process specific features/functions.

Because of popularity of XML the family of XML query languages (e.g. XQuery) comes as the first candidate for the mentioned standard language [22]. They have quite clear syntax and reasonable set of operators. However, these languages address a hierarchical data structure with no cycles and many-to-many relationships. This kind of relationship is used quite often in the process model, for instance, the predecessor-successor association between activities or activity instances is a many-to-many one. The next candidate is the family of SQL query languages. These languages are very popular and widely used. They are able to operate on relational data and query various types of relationships between entities. Despite many advantages of these languages their syntax is quite complicated (see successive specifications of SQL-89, SQL-92 [12] and SQL-99 [13]). Some constructs of SQL introduce limitations and semantic reefs (e.g. group by operator or null values) and sometimes are criticised for their ambiguous semantics. While SQL-99 covers not only relational, but also object-relational structures, implementation of it presents too big challenge (ca. 1500 pages of specification), clearly out of the potential of a small software enterprise.

The last alternative is the family of object-oriented query languages. They seem to be the most appropriate to express various types of queries to the business process metamodel. As far as well known specifications of object-oriented or object-relational specifications are concerned, it seems that there is no good solution for the requirements specified at the beginning of this section. There are many opinions that the most known ODMG OQL [15] does not provide clear and coherent specification [2, 19]. Moreover, lack of convincing formal semantics causes that query optimisation in OQL is still an open question. Fortunately, there is one more candidate that has recently joined the group, that is the Stack-Based Query Language (SBQL) [17, 18, 20] Unlike other presented candidates this language has simple, formal and coherent semantics. SBQL has very powerful query optimisation methods, in particular, methods based on query rewriting, methods based on indices and methods based on removing dead queries. Currently it has several implementations, in particular, for the European project [9], for XML repositories based on the DOM model, and for the object-oriented DBMS Objectivity/DB. SBQL syntax (at it is shown in the next sections) is very simple and seems to be easier to understood and use.

3.1   Syntax, Semantics, and Pragmatics of BPQL

The BPQL syntax is defined as a context-free grammar specified in the EBNF notation. Semantics of BPQL follows the semantics of SBQL and it is based on the operational method (abstract implementation machine). Pragmatics of BPQL concerns how it can be used properly and what is the reason to use it. Pragmatics includes some visualisation of the process metamodel and rules of developing BPQL queries according to the metamodel and according to the assumed business ontology. In this section,

BPQL pragmatics will be illustrated by examples showing definitions of a business processes and corresponding queries.

The fundamental concepts of BPQL are taken from the stack-based approach (SBA) to query languages. In SBA a query language is considered a special kind of a programming language. Thus, the semantics of queries is based on mechanisms well known from programming languages like the environment (call) stack. SBA extends this concept for the case of query operators, such as selection, projection/navigation, join, quantifiers and others. Using SBA one is able to determine precisely the operational semantics of query languages, including relationships with object-oriented concepts, embedding queries into imperative constructs, and embedding queries into programming abstractions: procedures, functional procedures, views, methods, modules, etc.

SBA is defined for a general object store model. Because various object models introduce a lot of incompatible notions, SBA assumes some family of object store models which are enumerated M0, M1, M2 and M3. The simplest is M0, which covers relational, nested-relational and XML-oriented databases. M0 assumes hierarchical objects with no limitations concerning nesting of objects and collections. M0 covers also binary links (relationships) between objects. Higher-level store models introduce classes and static inheritance (M1), object roles and dynamic inheritance (M2), and encapsulation (M3). For these models the formal query language SBQL (Stack-Based Query Language) is defined. SBQL is based on abstract syntax and full orthogonality of operators, hence it follows the mathematical flavour of the relational algebra and calculi. SBQL, together with imperative extensions and abstractions, has the computational power of programming languages. Concrete syntax, special functionality, special features of a store model and a concrete metamodel allow one to make from SBQL a concrete query language, in particular BPQL.

SBA respects the naming-scoping-binding principle, which means that each name occurring in a query is bound to the appropriate run-time entity (an object, an attribute, a method a parameter, etc.) according to the scope of its name. The principle is supported by means of the environment stack. The classical stack concept implemented in almost all programming languages is extended to cover database collections and all typical query operators occurring e.g. in SQL and OQL. The stack also supports recursion and parameters: all functions, procedures, methods and views defined by SBA can be recursive by definition. Rigorous formal semantics implied by SBA creates a very high potential for query optimization. Full description of SBA and SBQL is presented in [20].

Following SBQL, a BPQL query can return a simple or complex value that is constructed from object identifiers, atomic values and names. The definition of a query result is recursive and involves basic structure and collection constructs (struct, bag, sequence). In particular, a query can return an atomic value (e.g. for query 2+2), a bag of references to attributes (e.g. for query *Performer.Name*), a collection of named references to objects (e.g. for query *Performer as p*). BPQL is based on the modularity rule which means that semantics of a complex query is recursively composed from semantics of its components, up to atomic queries which are literals, object names and function calls.

BPQL includes all basic non-algebraic operators (SBA term), such as quantifiers, selection, dependent join, projection, navigation (path expressions). There is also many algebraic operators, among them a conditional query *if q_1 then q_2 else q_3*, aliasing (operator *as*), typical arithmetic/string operators and comparisons, boolean operators, and others. A simplified syntax of BPQL is presented in Appendix.

A BPQL query can also include a function call. A function may have arguments, which are BPQL queries too. A function returns a result, which is compatible with query results (e.g. can be a collection of OIDs) hence function calls can be freely nested in BPQL queries. BPQL introduces a set of core functions, both standard ones and workflow specific ones. The standard functions includes mathematical functions (e.g. COS, SIN, SQRT), string functions (e.g. CONCAT, SUBSTRING), date and time functions (e.g. CURRDATE, YEAR, MONTH), and aggregate functions (e.g. AVG, COUNT, MAX).

So far, there are four workflow-specific functions. They were implemented in BPQL in advance to simplify queries.

- *FirstActInst(ProcessInstance): ActivityInstance* – returns an object that represents the start activity for a process instance which is passed as the argument of the function.
- *PrevActInst(ActivityInstance): ActivityInstance []* – returns a list of objects that represent direct predecessors of the activity passed as the argument of the function.
- *ActInst(ProcessInstance, ActId): ActivityInstance []* – returns a list of activity instances that are instantiation of the activity within a process instance. Both process instance object and identifier of the activity are passed as the function arguments.
- *NextActInst(ActivityInstance): ActivityInstance []* – returns a list of objects that represent direct successors of the activity passed as the argument of the function.

In addition to the above functions, two context-related functions are provided:

- *ThisProcessInst: ProcessInstance* – returns the object that represents the process instance on behalf of which a given query is executed.
- *ThisActivityInst: ActivityInstance* - returns the object that represents the activity instance on behalf of which a given query is executed.

All the class and attribute names as well as function names and their parameters are stored in the internal BPQL dictionary. A couple of examples of using BPQL are presented below.

Example 1 – Optional Activity
The 'advanced verification' activity should be performed only if the deadline for a given process instance is greater then 2 days and exists an expert which the current workload is less than 8 working hours.

```
(ThisProcessInst.deadline – Currdate) > 2 and
    exists (Performer as P where
            sum( (P.performs.ActivityInst where status = 'open').duration) < 8)
```

Example 2 – Participant Assignment
An activity should be executed by the performer of the first activity or, if this performer has more than five delayed tasks to perform, by the performer of the previous activity.

```
if
   count(FirstActInst(ThisProcessInst).performedBy.
   Performer.performs.ActivityInst where
      (delayed = 'yes' and status = 'open') <= 5
then FirstActInst(ThisProcessInst).performedBy.Performer
else  PrevActInst(ThisActInst).performedBy.Performer
```

3.2 BPQL and Process Definition

BPQL may be used to generalise process definition. It is able to express some requirements on the process definition that depends on process execution data (e.g. the performer of this activity is a seller with the minimal work-load). As will be shown in the next section, BPQL queries may simplify process definition reducing the number of defined activities which have to be 'artificially' introduced to cope with the mentioned requirements.

BPQL may be used in the process definition in all the elements that operate on relevant or workflow control data such as transition condition, workflow participant assignment, pre and post-activity conditions, and event handling (condition part).

Moreover, BPQL exposes the mentioned requirements directly in the process definition giving more knowledge of its elements to the process designers. Before, these element had to be hidden to the process designers and written as programming procedures. Such situation makes process modification harder since very often it is necessary to modify the code of procedures instead of modifying the process definition itself. BPQL gives the chance to the process designers to change process definition without (or with less) interfering in the programming stuff.

3.3 How It Works – An Example

Let us assume that there is a simplified version of a process for ordering laptops. Every registered customer may order any number of laptops. An order made by a customer is then accepted by a company seller which is responsible for verifying financial status of the customer and ability to meet the order at the requested time. For a bigger order or if there is not too much time for its acceptance, the order is served by a senior-seller. Otherwise, it is served by a plain seller. In addition, the order should be served by a seller that has minimal work-load. At this stage of process implementation 'minimal' means a person which has minimal number of tasks assigned. If the order was accepted, it is sent to the production department for completing. It is an assumption that all the orders are processed by the company.

Even in this simplified example some of the requirements for the process have to be defined on the basis of process execution data. For instance, the 'minimal work-load' requirement may be only expressed using a query on the current task assignment. Yet, to select a kind of a seller for accepting the order may be defined by a condition on process relevant data (workflow environment). The requirement may be easily expressed using BPQL. What is more, their definition in BPQL simplifies the definition of the process making it more generalised. Instead of defining two activities for accepting the order: one for 'Senior-seller' and another for 'Seller', it is possible to define only one for both mentioned workflow participants. Such approach seems to be more adequate the real business process that is modelled and computerized. The role 'seller' may be defined in BPQL as follows[1]:

1.	(**if** Order.Value > 30000 **or** Order.DeliverDate - CurrDate ≤ 2
2.	**then**
3.	User **where** position = 'Senior-Seller' **and**
4.	*count*(is.Performer.performs.ActivityInst **where** status='open')
5.	=
6.	*min*((User **where** position = 'Senior-Seller').
7.	*count*(is.Performer.performs.ActivityInst **where** status='open'))
8.	**else**
9.	User **where** position = 'Seller' **and**
10.	*count*(is.Performer.performs.ActivityInst **where** status='open')
11.	=
12.	*min*((User **where** position = 'Seller').
13.	*count*(is.Performer.performs. ActivityInst **where** status='open'))

Line 1 defines the condition to select either a senior-seller (lines 3-7) or a seller (lines 9-13). A senior-seller that will perform a given activity is a person employed at the position 'Senior-seller' (line 3) and which has the minimal work-load (line 4) among all senior sellers (lines 6-7). Similarly for the users with the 'Seller' position. The condition *status='open'* specifies only those tasks that are currently being performed. The function *count* determines the number of activity instances that are currently performed by a given user. Similarly, the function *min* determines a minimal number of tasks assigned to 'Senior-seller' (lines 6-7) and a 'Seller' (lines 12-13). Association *is* connects User objects to Performer objects, and association *performs* connects Performer objects to ActivityInst objects (note corresponding path expressions). Because in general the query may return several users (all with minimal workload), the additional function is necessary that takes randomly one of them. The query can be optimised by using an index on the User position attribute and by factoring out independent sub-queries (in this case both sub-queries starting from *min*).

4 Integration of BPQL and XPDL

It seems that the best way of using BPQL in process definition is to integrate it with a well known and widely used process definition language. Nowadays, there are several standard process definition languages such as XML Process Definition Language (XPDL) [25], Business Process Modelling Language [6] or more web-oriented languages such as Business Process Execution Language for Web Services (BPEL4WS) [5] and Web Service Description Language [26].

So far it seems that XPDL and BPEL(4WS) are the most mature and complete process definition languages. Both these languages may be easily extended of BPQL. This integration will much extend the functionality of the existing language. As an example we present in the next sub-sections how it may be done in XPDL.

---

[1] The object *User* represents an application user. The corresponding class is a part of application resource data.

4.1 Transition Condition

In XPDL [25] a transition condition is expressed by the XML tag *Transitions/Transition/Condition* with type *CONDITION*. However there is no specification how this condition should look like. Usually it is represented as a text. In this situation, the XPDL definition may be extended by more precise definition which requires a condition to be written in BPQL. If a BPQL query returns one or more objects as the result, then the condition is satisfied. Otherwise, if the result is empty, it is not. An example written in XPDL may look like:

```
<Transition Id="b1" From="ChckBalance" To="ProcRequest">
<Condition Type="CONDITION">
Order where
    (id = ThisProcessInstance.hasDataContainer.orderId and
    (value > 30000 or quantity > 100))
</Condition> <Transition/>
```

4.2 Workflow Participant Assignment

According to the WfMC's definition [24], a Workflow Participant Assignment (WPA) defines the set of participants that will perform a given workflow activity. A participant can be one of the following types: a resource (specific resource agent), resource set, organisational unit, role (a function of a human within an organisation), human (a user) or system (an automatic agent).

To be coherent with the above definition it is suggested to use BPQL to define a participant. BPQL definition could be included as an extended attribute of the participant specification, if the participant is represented as a role. In this case, the WPA definition would remain the same while the participant definition would be expressed as a function that returns a set of participants. A BPQL query would return a set of workflow participants that would satisfy it. In addition, also WPA decision and the modifier introduced in [14] could be used to specify a workflow participant. An example written in XPDL may look like:

```
<Participant Id="p1" Name="Seller">
<ParticipantType Type="ROLE">
<Description>Seller</Description>
<ExtendedAttributes>
<ExtendedAttribute Name="Definition">
    User where (position = 'Seller')
    </ExtendedAttribute> </ExtendedAttributes>
</Participant>
```

4.3 Pre and Post-activity Condition

So far, pre and post conditions for workflow activities are not defined directly in XPDL. However, it is possible to use the tag *ExtendedAttribute* to express these conditions which, once again, would be defined in BPQL. If a BPQL query returns one or more objects as the result, then the condition is satisfied. Otherwise, if the result is empty, it is not. An example written in XPDL may look like:

```
<Activity Id="56" Name="Compose Acceptance Message">
 <Implementation>
  <Tool Id="composeMessage" Type="APPLICATION">
   <ActualParameters>
    <ActualParameter>status</ActualParameter>
    <ActualParameter>orderNumber</ActualParameter>
   </ActualParameters>
  </Tool>
 </Implementation>
 <ExtendedAttributes>
  <ExtendedAttribute Name="Pre-Condition">
   Order where (id = ThisProcessInstance.hasDataContainer.orderId and status = 'closed')
  </ExtendedAttribute>
 </ExtendedAttributes>
</Activity>
```

5 Practical Results

The first version of BPQL has been implemented for workflow participant and integrated in *OfficeObjects*® *WorkFlow* (*OO WorkFlow*) from Rodan System. This system has been deployed at major Polish public institutions (e.g. Ministry of Labour and Social Policy, Ministry of Infrastructure) as well as at private companies (e.g. Sanplast Ltd.).

XPDL, used in *OO WorkFlow* to represent process definition, has been recently extended of BPQL according to the suggestions about workflow participant assignment presented in the previous section.

First practical verification of BPQL was done for the system for electronic document exchange between Poland and European Council (referred further to as EWDP). In this system *OO WorkFlow* was used to implement the process for preparation of the Polish standpoint concerning a given case that was discussed at the European Council, COREPERS or its working groups. The process consists of more than 40 activities and includes about 10 process roles. It is going to be used by all nineteen Polish Ministries and central offices with about 12000 users registered. Daily, there are about 200 documents processed. On the average, preparation of the Polish standpoint lasts about two or three days.

Owing to BPQL, it was possible to generalise this process and make it suitable for all the offices. Complex rules to assign appropriate workflow participants have been quite easily expressed in BPQL, especially for (1) main coordinator which assigns Polish subjects to individual EU documents, (2) leading and supporting coordinators which assign experts to the processed document, (3) leading expert and supporting experts. These workflow participants are selected on the basis of possessed roles, their competence, current work-load and availability. Competence data are extracted from the system ontology.

In addition, also the process owners got the better chance to modify the process definition without modifying the code of the system. So far, there were twelve medium-scale changes of the process that were done only by modification of the process definition (early production phase).

6   Related Work

So far, there are a few other approaches to define a business process query language and use it in process definition. Firstly, in [7] the authors presented a language to model web applications – WebML. This language provides functionality to define business processes and make them more flexible. To define a condition or a workflow participant it is possible to use an attribute whose value may be calculated by a complex program. Despite its huge flexibility (every algorithm may be written as a procedure), this approach, however, seems to be less appropriate for non-programming process owner and to hide the algorithms to calculate these attributes inside the program code. In addition, at the best our knowledge this language is not compliant with any of the existing well known standard process definition languages.

In [14] the authors proposed WPAL – a functional language to define workflow participant assignment. This language is able to use workflow control data (e.g. the performer of a given activity, reference to the objects represents the start activity). Despite its flexibility, it has similar problems as WebML has. BPQL defined in this article may be treated as a continuation and significant extension of WPAL.

Finally, there is some work on a business process query language carried out by BPMI. It is promised that this language will offer facilities for process execution and process deployment (process repository). However, after two years of this work, still there is no official, even a draft version available [3].

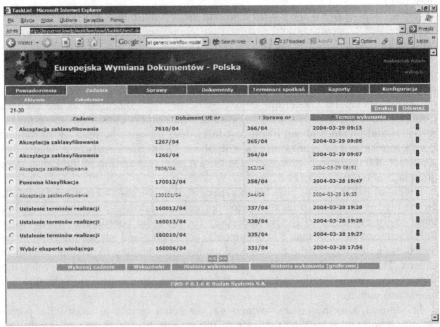

Fig. 3. Work list for an EWDP user (in Polish)

On the other hand there are many workflow management systems that provide some selected elements of business process query languages. For example in Staffware [16], there is a set of workflow functions (i.e. SW functions) that can be used to define a conditions and a workflow participant. In Lotus Workflow [8], it is possible to call a lotus script function in order to define the above elements. *OfficeObjects WorkFlow* in her previous version implemented WPAL [14]. Unfortunately, all these examples of query languages do not provide clear and coherent semantics. In addition, the problem with moving algorithms form process definition into application still remains.

7 Conclusion

In this paper we have defined a workflow process metamodel and a business process query language BPQL to operate on this metamodel. In order to assure clear syntax and complete semantics of the language, SBQL has been used as the core specification. On the top of it BPQL was defined. The article also shows how BPQL may be used to make process definition more flexible and easy to modify. BPQL, following SBQL, can work on all data models that can be used for a workflow process metamodel, starting from the relational one, through XML-oriented, up to most advanced object oriented models.

Despite these advantages the presented approach leaves several open issues. In some cases where relevant data come from several data sources it is impossible to make a BPQL query. Also BPQL is not helpful when the current control of process resources depends on factors that are not present in the metamodel, or factors that are too random. In such cases the workflow processes must be controlled manually.

The first version of BPQL has been developed in *OfficeObjects® WorkFlow* and implemented in the system for electronic document exchange between Poland and European Council to define process for answering European documents. Owing to BPQL it was possible to reduce flow complexity of the process and make it easier for further modifications.

References

1. Van der Aalst, W.M.P.: Generic Workflow models: How to Handle Dynamic Change and capture management Information?, CoopIS'99, Edinburgh, Scotland
2. Alagic, S.: The ODMG Object Model: Does it Make Sense?, OOPSLA'97, Atlanta, USA
3. Business Process Management Initiative: Business Process Query Language Web Page, http://www.bpmi.org/bpql.esp
4. Bussler, C.: Keynote – Semantics Workflow Management, presentation at BPM'2004, Potsdam, Germany
5. IBM developer works: Business Process Execution Language for Web Services, ver. 1.0, Jul 2002
6. Business Process Management Initiative: Business Process Modelling Language, Nov 2002
7. Ceri, S., Manolescu I.: Constructing and integrating Data-Centric Web Applications; Methods, Tools and Techniques, VLDB'2003, Berlin, Germany

8. Lotus Development Corporation, Lotus Workflow Process Designer's Guide, ver. 3.0, 2001
9. Eder, J., Paganos, E.: Managing Time in Workflow Systems, in Workflow Handbook 2001, Layna Fischer (Ed.), Future Strategies Inc., USA
10. Intelligent Content Management System, IST-2001-32429, 5th EC Framework Programme, www.icons.rodan.pl
11. List B., Schiefer J., Bruckner R.: Process Data Store: A Real-Time Data Store for Monitoring Business Processes, DEXA'2003, Prague, Czech Republic
12. Melton, J., Simon, A.: Understanding the New SQL: A Complete Guide. Morgan Kaufmann, 1993
13 Melton, J., Simon, A., R., Gray, J.: SQL:1999 - Understanding Relational Language Components. Morgan Kaufmann Publishers, 2001
14 Momotko, M., Subieta. K.: Dynamic change of Workflow Participant Assignment, ADBIS'2002, Bratislava, Slovakia
15. Object Data Management Group: The Object Database Standard ODMG, Release 3.0. R.G.G.Cattel, D.K.Barry, Ed., Morgan Kaufmann, 2000
16. Staffware, Procedure Definer's Guide; Staffware Plc, Issue 2, March 1999
17. Subieta K., Beeri, C., Matthes, F., Schmidt, J.,W., A Stack-Based Approach to Query Languages. East-West Database Workshop, 1994, Springer Workshops in Computing, 1995
18. Subieta, K., Kambayashi, Y., and Leszczyłowski, J.: Procedures in Object-Oriented Query Languages. VLDB'1995, Zurich, Switzerland
19. Subieta, K.: Object-Oriented Standards: Can ODMG OQL be Extended to a Programming Language? (In) Cooperative Databases and Applications, World Scientific, 459-468, 1997
20. Subieta, K.: Theory and Construction of Object-Oriented Query Languages. Editors of the Polish-Japanese Institute of Information Technology, 2004, 520 pages (in press)
21. Sadiq, S., Handling Dynamic Schema Changes in Workflow Processes, 11th Australian database Conference, Canberra, Australia, 2000
22. W3C: XQuery 1.0: An XML Query Language. W3C Working Draft 12, Nov 2003, http://www.w3.org/TR/xquery
23. Weske, M., Vossen, G., Flexibility and Cooperation in Workflow Management Systems, Handbook on Architectures of Information Systems., pp 359–379. Berlin: Springer 1998
24. Workflow Management Coalition: The Workflow Reference Model, WfMC-TC-1003 issue 1.1, Jan 1995
25. Workflow Management Coalition: Workflow process definition language – XML process definition language, WfMC-TC-1025, ver. 1.0, Oct 2002
26. W3C Consortium: Web Service Description Language, ver. 1.1, W3C, March 2001

Appendix: The (Simplified) Syntax of BPQL

<query>	::=	<literal>
	|	<name>
	|	exists <query> (<query>)
	|	all <query> (<query>)
	|	<query> . <query>
	|	<query> where <condition>
	|	<query> join <query>
	|	<query> as <aliasName>
	|	<query> group as <aliasName>
	|	<function>
	|	(queryList)
	|	if <query> then <query> else <query>
	|	<algExpression>
queryList	::=	<query> {, <query>}
<condition>	::=	<logExpression>
<logExpression>	::=	<logSum>
<logSum>	::=	<logProduct> { or <logProduct>}
<logProduct>	::=	<logSExpression> { and <logSExpression> }
<logSExpression>	::=	not <logSum> | (<logSum>) | <logCondition>
<logCondition>	::=	<leftSide> <opComp> <rightSide>
<opComp>	::=	< | <= | = | => | > | <>
<leftSide>	::=	<algExpression>
<rightSide>	::=	<algExpression>
<algExpression>	::=	<algSum>
<algSum>	::=	<algProduct> { [+ | -] <algProduct>}
<algProduct>	::=	<algExpression> { [* | / | %] <algExpression>}
<algExpression>	::=	(<algExpression>)
	|	<symbol> | <literal> | (<query>)
<function>	::=	<fName> | <fName> (<queryList>)
<symbol>	::=	<objName> {. <objName>}
<literal>	::=	<text> | <integer> | <float> | <boolean>
<boolean>	::=	true | false

Triggering Replanning in an Integrated Workflow Planning and Enactment System

Hilmar Schuschel and Mathias Weske

Hasso-Plattner-Institute at the University of Potsdam,
Prof.-Dr.-Helmert-Strasse 2-3, 14482 Potsdam, Germany,
{Schuschel,Weske}@hpi.uni-potsdam.de

Abstract. Workflow management systems support and automate the enactment of business processes. For this purpose, workflow management systems use process definitions that have been manually planned and modeled at build time. Recent research approaches try to enhance this concept by automating the creation of process definitions, using planning algorithms. This avoids the need for predefined process definitions and thus increases flexibility and allows to save costs. An important aspect of flexibility is the ability to react to unanticipated events that might occur during runtime. This Reaction can imply replanning and dynamically adapting the process. This paper shows how replanning can be triggered automatically in an integrated workflow planning and enactment system. Triggers for monitoring process executions are presented and events are defined which lead to the evaluation of corresponding conditions for deciding when replanning is necessary. Finally, advantages, limitations and areas of application of this approach are discussed.

1 Introduction

In todays dynamic markets, organizations have to take advantage of information technology to improve their business and stay competitive. A crucial point for the competitiveness of organizations is the performance of their processes [7,22]. Workflow management systems [6,9,10] are applied to support and automate process enactment. For this purpose, process definitions are use that have been manually planned and modeled at build time. Recent research approaches propagate the feature to plan processes definitions automatically to improve quality and flexibility [1,11,12,18,25]. An important aspect of flexibility is the ability to react to unanticipated events that might occur during runtime, by replanning and dynamically adapting the process. This paper shows how replanning can be triggered automatically in an integrated workflow planning and enactment system. Triggers for monitoring process executions are presented. Therefore, events are defined which lead to the evaluation of corresponding conditions for deciding when replanning is necessary.

   A *process* is a defined set of partially ordered steps intended to reach a goal [4]. It is the means to change a given situation in order to fulfill a company's goal. The information about this situation including all relevant documents is

A. Benczúr, J. Demetrovics, G. Gottlob (Eds.): ADBIS 2004, LNCS 3255, pp. 322–335, 2004.

called a *case*. Examples of cases are an incoming purchase order that has to be handled or a sick patient who has to be cured. From an organizational point of view, the life cycle of a process includes the phases planning and enactment. *Planning* is the generation of a description called a *process definition* of what has to be done in which order to reach a particular goal. The subsequent phase is *enactment*, which is the organizational task to schedule the work in accordance to the process definition. Workflow management systems take a process definition as input and use it to support and automate process enactment. Traditionally, planning and supplying the process definition to the workflow management system has to be done manually. Recently, advances in the automation of business process planning has been made. Automated planning allows to generate individual process definitions for every case. Thus, quality and flexibility can be improved. An important aspect of flexibility is the ability to react to unanticipated events that might occur during runtime, by generating a new process definition and dynamically adapting the process. Basically, there are three main steps in replanning:

1. Trigger replanning when necessary
2. Generate a new process definition
3. Adapt process enactment to the changed process definition

To fully automate replanning, all three steps have to be taken into account. While research in workflow management concentrates on step 3 to enhance flexibility, the integration of automated process planning allows to fully support replanning.

This paper is based on the integrated planning and enactment system presented in [18] and adds a concept for automated initiation of replanning. Triggers are specified to monitor process executions and start replanning if necessary. In principle, replanning is necessary, if the process definition assigned to a case is no longer adequate for further enactment. This paper defines two degrees of adequateness and identifies events that may threaten this adequateness. To each event a condition is assigned, specifying the exact circumstances under which the event makes replanning necessary.

Related work is presented in Section 2. Section 3 introduces the relevant foundations on AI planning algorithms and workflow management. Section 4 describes the overall workflow planning and enactment system and adds a concept for automatically triggering replanning. Finally, in Section 5 areas of application, and unsolved problems are discussed.

2   Related Work

There are two major areas of related work: research on dynamic adaption of workflows and approaches to automatically generate workflow process definitions.

Dynamic adaption of workflows deals with adjusting running process instances to changes in the process definition [3,15,17,8]. Nevertheless, all this work is concentrated on step 3 of replanning – the adaption of process enactment – as described in Section 1. Triggering replanning and generating a new process definition is expected to be done manually.

Recent research approaches present options to automate the generation of processes definitions: For instance, in [1] ontologies of domain services and domain integration knowledge are used that serve as a model for workflow integration rules. DY_{flow} [25] avoids the use of predefined process definitions and allows the dynamic composition of Web services to business processes by applying backward-chain, forward-chain and data flow inference. Another approach dealing with automated composition of web-services is described in [14]. Semantics for a subset of DAML-S [21] are defined in terms of a first-order logical language, to enable automated planning. In [11] the composition of single tasks or subgraphs of workflows is embedded in a case-based framework for workflow model management. In [12] the application of contingent planners to existing workflow management systems is discussed. To generate process definitions some of these approaches use Artificial Intelligence (AI) planning algorithms, while others use proprietary developed algorithms. Although AI planning algorithms have been in research for more than 30 years [5], advances in recent years make their application on real business domains promising [13,23]. The issue of replanning is discussed by some of these approaches, but step 1 of replanning – triggering replanning – is not explicitly taken into account.

3 Preliminaries

There has already been done a lot of research on planning and workflow enactment in the areas of AI planning algorithms and workflow management systems respectively. This section presents the concepts from both research areas that are important for an integration of workflow planning and enactment. In the remainder of this paper, common concepts of both areas are described using one continuous terminology, instead of applying the area specific terminology at each case. The example introduced in this section will be used throughout the paper to illustrate the integration to an overall system.

3.1 Planning Algorithms

In this section, foundations on AI planning are presented which are relevant for triggering replanning in an integrated workflow planning and enactment system. Furthermore, an example is introduced that is used throughout the paper.

Planning algorithms [5,24] take a description of the current state of a case, a goal, and a set of activity definitions as input. The *goal* constitutes the desired state of the case and where required a metric to optimize. The means to transform the case from its actual state to the desired state are the activities. An *activity* is a piece of work that forms one logical step within a process. An *activity definition* defines the conditions under which an activity can be executed, called *preconditions* and its impacts on the state of the case, called *effects*:

Definition. An *activity definition d* consists of

- a set $prec_d$ of preconditions
- a set eff_d of effects

A *domain* is a set of activities definitions. To sum up, the input of a planner is a *planning problem* defined as follows:

Definition. A *planning problem P* consists of

- a domain dom_P
- an initial state $init_P$
- a goal $goal_P$

The initial state and the goal are logical descriptions of the state of the case. *Planning* is the task of finding a partially ordered set of activities that, when executed, transforms the case from its current state to the goal. The description of this set of activities and their ordering – the *process definition* – is the output of the planning algorithm. To illustrate the basic procedure of a planning algorithm and the relationship between its input and output, the planning of a simple process is presented. The example domain D consists of five activity definitions d_1 to d_5 that are described using the Planning Domain Definition Language [16] (PDDL). The corresponding definition given in extracts:

```
(define (domain D)
...
  (:action d1
     :precondition (and (v) (t))
     :effect (and (y) (increase (costs) 50)))

  (:action d2
     :precondition (x)
     :effect (and (z) (u) (increase (costs) 20)))

  (:action d3
     :precondition (x)
     :effect (and (v) (t) (not (z)) (increase (costs) 30)))

  (:action d4
     :precondition (z)
     :effect (and (w) (increase (costs) 10)))

  (:action d5
     :precondition (x)
     :effect (and (w) (increase (costs) 40)))

  (:action d6
     :precondition (x)
     :effect (and (t) (increase (costs) 10)))
)
```

Process Definition p_1:

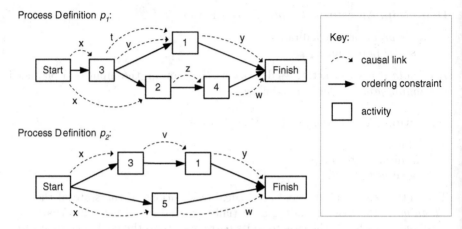

Fig. 1. Process Definitions p_1 and p_2

Activity definition d_1 has the precondition v and the effect y. For instance, v is the fact that a customer name is determined and y is the fact that the address of the customer is determined. Thus, activity definition d_1 determines the address of a customer based on his name. Besides these functional properties, non-functional properties are specified: The costs for the execution of d_1 are 50. To define a concrete planning problem, not only the domain has to be specified, but also the initial state and the goal. The corresponding PDDL definition given in extracts:

```
(define (problem P)
  (:domain D)
  ...
  (:init (x) (= (costs) 0)
  (:goal (and (w) (y)))
  (:metric minimize (costs))
)
```

The planning problem P is specified as follows: The initial state is $x \land (costs = 0)$ and the goal is $w \land y$ with the costs to minimize. To complete the input for a planning algorithm, two extra activity definitions are introduced: an activity definition *Start* without preconditions and whose effect is the initial state of the case and an activity definition *Finish* with the goal as a precondition and no effects. The task of a planning algorithm is to find a process definition that solves P. Process definition p_1 depicted in Fig. 1 is a solution for P. The activities are partially ordered in a way that the effects of preceding activities satisfy the preconditions of subsequent activities. For example, d_2 has the effect z that is needed by d_4 as a precondition. Such a link between the effect of one activity that satisfies the precondition of another activity is expressed by a *causal link*, depicted as a dashed arrow. Every causal link implies an *ordering constraint*. For example, the ordering constraint from d_3 to d_1 is derived from the causal link between these activities. Additionally, ordering constraints are also inserted to protect causal links. For example, the ordering constraint from d_3 to d_2 is inserted to protect the causal link from d_2 to d_4. If there would be no ordering constraint from d_3 to d_2, d_3 could be executed between d_2 and d_4. This would be problematic, because d_3 negates the effect z of d_2 that is needed by d_4 as a precondition.

Process definition p_1 is a solution of P. The minimized, overall costs are 110. There exists another process definition p_2 depicted in Fig. 1 that also produces the facts w and y, if started in an initial state in which fact x holds. Since the overall costs of p_2 are not minimal, it is no solution of P.

3.2   Workflow Management

The purpose of workflow management systems [6,9,10,19] is to support and automate the enactment of business processes. During workflow enactment pieces of work have to be passed to the right participant at the right time with the support of the right tool. A central property of a workflow management system is that this functionality is not hard coded for a specific process, but implemented in a way that the system can take any process definition as input. For a workflow management system, the relationship between effects and preconditions as the causal origin of the ordering of the activities is not relevant. Therefore, a process definition as input for a workflow management system contains only ordering constrains and no information on preconditions, effects nor causal links. Next to the process definition, the workflow management system needs information on the potential participants of the process and the available tools.

Before the execution of a process, all activities are in the state *init*. The execution of a process starts with the activities in the process definition that have no predecessors. For example in process definition p_1 depicted in Fig. 1 activity 3 is scheduled first. When an activity is executed the workflow management systems automatically starts the appropriate tool with the data that has to be processed in this activity. By starting an activity its state changes to *running*. After execution completes, the state of an activity changes to *done* and its subsequent activities are started. This iterates until all activities are in the state done and the process is completed.

4   Replanning in an Integrated Planning and Enactment System

This section is divided into three subsections: In Section 4.1, the overall framework for an integrated workflow planning and enactment system is presented. Section 4.2 carries on by adding a concept for replanning. Finally, Section 4.3 describes triggers for replanning in detail.

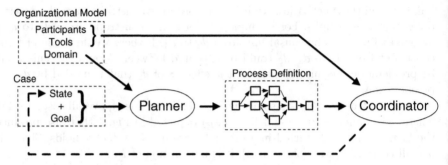

Fig. 2. Integrated Planner and Coordinator

4.1 Framework

The two central sub-systems of the framework are the planner and the coordinator. The planner generates a process definition for each case. The coordinator then uses the process definition to schedule the activities. In the following, the basic functional and behavioral aspects of the interaction of these components are described. Fig. 2 gives an overview of the interrelation of input and output between planner and coordinator. The basis for the overall system is the formal description of the domain, the participants and the tools. They describe the means of the company to process individual cases. A case is defined as follows:

Definition. A *case* c consists of

- a state $state_c$
- a goal $goal_c$

To plan a process definition to handle a case c, a corresponding problem definition P has to be specified. This is done by mapping $state_c$ to $init_P$ and $goal_c$ to $goal_P$. The domain of the problem definition is the domain of the organizational model. The planner takes the problem definition as input and generates a process definition as output. A process definition is defined as follows:

Definition. A *process definition* p consists of

- a set $inst_p$ of activity instances
- a set $conn_p \subseteq inst_p \times inst_p$ of control connectors

Definition. An *activity instance* i based on activity definition d consists of

- an execution state $exec_i \in \{\text{init, running, done}\}$
- a set act_i of actual effects
- a set $rel_i \subseteq eff_d$ of relevant effects

An activity instance is the representation of an activity definition in a process definition. In addition to the information in its corresponding activity definition, an activity instance contains information on its execution state and its effects. This information is important for triggering replanning as it is explained in Section 4.3. The limitation to three different execution states of activity instances is a strong simplification for the purpose of this paper. The set act_i contains the effects the activity actually had during execution. The set rel_i contains the effects of eff_d that are relevant for the process. An effect $e \in eff_d$ is relevant iff, ceteris paribus, the planner would generate another process definition, if $e \notin eff_d$. The relevance of an effect in eff_d depends on the problem definition. Consider the example introduced in Section 3.1. The activity definition d_2 has the effects $z \wedge u \wedge$ increase costs by 20. The effect u is not relevant for p_1, because the same process definition would be generated, no matter if d_2 has the effect u or not. Thus, the relevant effects rel_2 are $z \wedge$ increase costs by 20.

After the process definition is planned, it is assigned to the case. The process definition combined with information on participants and tools, is the input of the coordinator. This allows the coordinator to schedule the execution of the activities in accordance to the process definition until the goal is reached. The dashed arrow from the coordinator to the state of the case depicted in Fig. 2 illustrates the effects of the activities on the case, which are scheduled by the coordinator.

To illustrate the behavior of the overall system the example from Section 3.1 is carried on. Let us assume a case c should be handled that is specified as follows: $state_c$ is x and $goal_c$ is $w \wedge y$ with the costs to optimize. First, a corresponding problem definition P has to be specified. Therefore, $state_c$ is mapped to $init_P$ and $goal_c$ is mapped to $goal_P$. A solution for P is the process definition p_1 depicted in Fig. 1. The rectangles stand for the activity instances i_1 to i_4 that represent the activity definitions d_1 to d_4 in p_1. All activity instances are in the state init. p_1 is given to the coordinator. Execution begins by starting i_3. While running, i_3 has the anticipated effects $v \wedge t \wedge \neg z$. After i_3 completes, the subsequent activity instances i_1 and i_2 are started. The execution continues until all activity instances are in the state done and the goal is reached.

4.2   Replanning

An integrated planning and enactment system allows to automatically replan process definitions if necessary and adapt the process enactment. Therefore, the interaction between planner and coordinator becomes more interlaced . Consider the example above. Let us assume that i_3 completes without having all anticipated effects. For example it has the effects v and $\neg z$ but not the effect t. In this case replanning becomes necessary, because a precondition of the subsequent activity instance i_1 is not satisfied. The coordinator that monitors the execution of the process, notes the missing effect and triggers replanning. Replanning is done by planning a new process definition based on the current state of the case. In the example, the current state of the case $state_c$ is $x \wedge v \wedge \neg z$. A new planning problem P' is defined and the planner generates a process definition p_3 shown in Fig. 3 i_3 is not part of p_3, because the effect v is not needed any more, and the missing effect t can also be produced by i_6 at a lower cost. p_3 is assigned to the

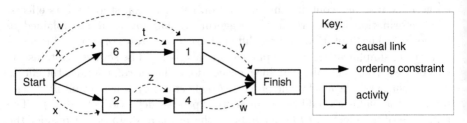

Fig. 3. Process Definition p_3

case and given to the coordinator, which then adapts the process enactment to the new process definition. In the example above replanning became necessary, because an activity instance completed and an anticipated effect was missing. Next to anticipated effects that are missing, other events can occur that make replanning necessary. In the following, a general approach to trigger replanning automatically is presented.

As a basic principle, replanning is necessary, if the process definition that is assigned to a case becomes inadequate. While initially the planner generates an optimal process definition, the example above shows that certain circumstances can make it inadequate for further enactment. To state the adequateness of a process definition more precisely, the properties *working* and *optimal* are defined:

Definition. A process definition p is *working* for case c, iff applied on c, it transforms $state_c$ to $goal_c$.

Definition. A process definition p is *optimal* for case c, iff it is working for c and no other process definition working for c is better in relation to the optimization metric.

For example, initially the process definition p_1 is optimal for a case c. Process definition p_2 is also working for c, but it is not optimal. It has to be considered that the properties working and optimal also refer to process definitions that have already been started: The state of the case may already have changed and that the execution state of the activity instances may already be running or done. In this case the the properties working and optimal refer to the unfinished part of the process definition and the current state of the case. For example, let us assume that the process definition p_1 is already partially executed. i_3 has completed and has all anticipated effects. p_1 is still optimal, because it transforms the current state $state_c$: $x \land v \land t \land \neg z$ to the goal state $goal_c$: $y \land w$. If i_3 completes without having the anticipated effect t, p_1 is not working for the case c any more. As will be shown, process definitions can also loose the property optimal without loosing the property working.

The purpose of replanning is that a case is always assigned to an optimal process definition. It is assumed, that a planner initially generates an optimal process definition for a case. The process definition is then assigned to a case for execution. During execution, the process definition may loose the property optimal. In this case, replanning has to be triggered to generate a new, optimal process definition. If a new process definition is found, proess enactment is adapted. If the planner is unable to find a new process definition, the goal can not be reached any more and human intervention becomes necessary.

4.3   Triggers for Replanning

In this subsection a detailed description of triggers for replanning is given. The presented set of triggers does not claim to be complete, but it covers typical causes for replanning. The triggers are specified in form of Event Condition Action (ECA) rules [2]. Events are identified that threaten the property optimal of the associated process definition. To avoid unnecessary replanning, conditions are defined for every event to specify the exact circumstances under which the event may threaten the property optimal. The triggers in detail:

Trigger 1:
Event: activity instance i has effect e
Condition: $e \notin eff_d$ with activity instance i based on activity definition d
Action: Replan

In the domain, effects are defined for each activity that are anticipated from its execution. For example, the effect y is anticipated form the execution of i_1. The planner uses this information to plan an optimal process definitions for a case. During execution, an activity may have effects that are not anticipated. In this case, the input of the planner was incorrect. Thus, it can no longer be guaranteed that the process definition is optimal. For example, if i_3 has an unanticipated effect v, p_1 is still working for c, but it is not optimal any more. p_1 is working, because if the remaining activities are scheduled in accordance to p_1, the goal will be reached. Nevertheless, p_1 is not optimal, because p_3 is also working for c and has lower costs. In contrast to this example, activities can also have effects threatening the property working. The trigger to handle unanticipated effects is defined as follows: The event for Trigger 1 is an activity instance i having an effect e. The condition of Trigger 1 checks, if the effect was anticipated. The domain defines the anticipated effect for each activity. Therefore, it is checked, whether the effect e was defined in the activity definition d of the activity instance i. If this is the case, the input of the planner was correct and it is guaranteed that the process definition is still optimal. Otherwise, the process definition may have lost this property and replanning is necessary.

Trigger 2:
Event: activity instance i completes
Condition: $rel_i - act_i \neq \emptyset$
Action: Replan

Next to unanticipated effects, an activity can have less effects than anticipated. This complies with the example given at the beginning of Section 4.2, where i_3 is missing the effect t. This can make the process definition loose the property working. In the example above, p_1 looses the property working, because a precondition of the subsequent activity instance i_1 is not satisfied. As an activity can have effects as long as it is running, the proper time to check if it had all anticipated effects is when it completes. Therefore, the event for Trigger 2 is an activity i that completes. If $eff_d - act_i \neq \emptyset$ there is at least one effect $e \in eff_d$ defined in the activity definition that did not occur during the execution of the activity instance. Thus, the input of the planner was not correct and it can not be guaranteed that the process definition is still optimal. Nevertheless, not all effects in the activity definition are always relevant for planning a concrete process definition as explained in Section 4.1. Given the set rel_i of relevant effects for each activity instance, unnecessary replanning can be avoided by defining $rel_i - act_i \neq \emptyset$ as the condition for Trigger 2. In the example above, the relevant effects rel_2 for i_2 are $z \land$ increase costs by 20. If i_2 completes and the effect u is missing, there is no need to replan. In contrast, if the effect z is missing, replanning is necessary. This example shows that additional information on relevant effects for each activity instance allows to avoid unnecessary replanning. For this reason the planner adds this information to each activity instance when generating the process definition. Please note that a check $act_i - eff_d \neq \emptyset$ is not necessary, because unanticipated effects have already been taken into account by Trigger 1.

Trigger 3:
Event: $goal_c$ of case c changes
Condition: *true*
Action: Replan

The event for Trigger 3 is a change in the goal of a case. As a result the associated process definition may loose the property optimal. For example, consider the execution of p_1. Let us assume that i_3 is in the state running. Due to an external event, e.g. a customer request, the goal state $goal_c$ is changed from $w \land y$ to y. As a result, p_1 is not optimal any more, because i_2 and i_4 have become needless. Furthermore, if $goal_c$ is changed to m, p_1 even looses the property working. From this it follows that a change in the goal of a case must trigger replanning to assure to have an optimal process definition.

Trigger 4:
Event: external effect on state $state_c$ of case c
Condition: *true*
Action: Replan

Trigger 4 handles external effects on the state of the case. External effects are ad hoc effects that can not be assigned to the execution of an activity instance.

For example, p_1 is executed and i_3 is running. The coordinator has assigned i_3 to a participant for execution. Now external events may occur that have an effect w on the case, for example: a customer calls, pieces of information are lost or a new law is implemented in the company. Due to the effect w, i_2 and i_4 become needless. Thus, p_1 is not optimal any more. Generally speaking, an external effect is always an unanticipated effect and thus replanning becomes necessary.

Trigger 5:
Event: activity definition d changes
Condition: $\exists$ an activity instance i based on d with $exec_i \in \{$init, running$\}$
Action: Replan

The triggers 5 and 6 deal with changes in the domain. The event for Trigger 5 is a change in an activity definition d. The preconditions or effects of d may change or d becomes unavailable. This event make replanning necessary, if the process definition assigned to the case contains at least one activity instance based on d that is not already done. Changes in activity definitions of finished activity instances are not threatening the properties working and optimal, because the domain only specifies the anticipated behavior of activities instances. Thus, activity instances that are already finished are not affected by domain changes.

Trigger 6:
Event: additional activity definition becomes available
Condition: *true*
Action: Replan

If additional activities become available, the current process definition may not be optimal any more. For example, p_1 is executed and i_3 is running. Consider a new activity definition d_7 that is equal to d_5 with the exception that is costs only 10. Thus, another process definition p_4 that replaces i_2 and i_4 is better in matters of costs. As new activities can make the current process definition loose the property optimal, replanning should to be triggered. Please note that in contrast to Trigger 5 an additional activity definition only threatens the property optimal and not the property working. Thus, if it is sufficient to have a working process definition, Trigger 6 can be renounced to save replanning effort.

5   Discussion

In this paper we specified triggers that enable automated initiation of replanning. For this purpose, events were identified that threaten the adequateness of process definitions. Conditions were assigned to every event, to specify the exact circumstances under which the event makes replanning necessary. In particular, a set of relevant effects rel_i for an activity instance i was defined and it was shown, how it can help to avoid unnecessary replanning. It is important to mention that relevant effects are not part of the standard output of an AI planner. It is possible to check if an effect is relevant, by planning again without this effect and comparing the resulting process definition with the original – that is the way relevance was defined. This approach may not be feasible, because for every effect of every activity instance a process definition has to be planned to check relevance. Instead relevant effects can be determined directly during planning. Basically, the information on causal links and causal link protection generated during planning, has to be analyzed. A detailed description is beyond the scope of this paper. The presented approach is a step towards fully automating replanning. Especially, applications in which replanning is time crucial or has to be done without human interaction, can benefit form the ability to automatically trigger replanning. The presented triggers are part of the replanning concept of an integrated planning and enactment system called Plængine. Currently a first prototype is realized that is able to take a domain and problem definition in PDDL as input, to generate a process definition in the Business Process Execution Language for Web Services [20]. The process definition is then given to the coordinator for process enactment. Automated triggering of replanning is included in the second prototype that is currently in the design phase.

Acknowledgments. The authors would like to thank Jens Hündling for his valuable suggestions on this paper.

References

1. S. A. Chun, V. Atluri, and N. R. Adam. Domain knowledge-based automatic workflow generation. In *Proceedings of the 13th International Conference on Database and Expert Systems Applications*, pages 81–92. Springer-Verlag, 2002.
2. U. Dayal, B. T. Blaustein, A. P. Buchmann, U. S. Chakravarthy, M. Hsu, R. Ledin, D. R. McCarthy, A. Rosenthal, S. K. Sarin, M. J. Carey, M. Livny, and R. Jauhari. The HiPAC Project: Combining Active Databases and Timing Constraints. *SIGMOD Record*, 17(1):51–70, 1988.
3. C. Ellis, K. Keddara, and G. Rozenberg. Dynamic change within workflow systems. In *Proceedings of conference on Organizational computing systems*, pages 10–21. ACM Press, 1995.
4. P. H. Feiler and W. S. Humphrey. Software process development and enactment: Concepts and definitions. In *Proceedings of the Second International Conference on Software Process*, pages 28–40. IEEE CS Press, 1993.
5. R. E. Fikes and N. Nilsson. Strips: A new approach to the application of theorem proving to problem solving. *Artificial Intelligence*, 2:189–208, 1971.
6. D. Georgakopoulos, M. F. Hornick, and A. P. Sheth. An overview of workflow management: From process modeling to workflow automation infrastructure. *Distributed and Parallel Databases*, 3(2):119–153, 1995.
7. M. Hammer and J. Champy. *Reengineering the corporation*. Harper Collins Publishing, New York, 1993.
8. S. Horn and S. Jablonski. An approach to dynamic instance adaption in workflow management applications. In *Conference on Computer Supported Cooperative Work (CSCW)*, 1998.

9. S. Jablonski and C. Bussler. *Workflow Management: Modeling Concepts, Architecture, and Implementation.* International Thomson Computer Press, 1996.
10. F. Leymann and D. Roller. *Production workflow: concepts and techniques.* Prentice Hall, 2000.
11. T. Madhusudan and J. L. Zhao. A case-based framework for workflow model management. In *Proceedings of the Business Process Management Conference,* volume 2678 of *LNCS,* pages 354–369. Springer, 2003.
12. MD R-Moreno, D. Borrajo, and D. Meziat. Proces modelling and AI planning techniques: A new apporach. In *Proceedings of the 2nd International Workshop on Information Integration and Web-based Applications Services,* 2000.
13. K. Myers and P. Berry. The boundary of workflow and ai. In *Proceedings of the AAAI-99, Workshop on Agent-Based Systems in the Business context,* 1999.
14. S. Narayanan and S. McIlraith. Simulation, verification and automated composition of web services. In *11th International World Wide Web Conference,* 2002.
15. G. J. Nutt. The evolution towards flexible workflow systems. *Distributed Systems Engineering,* 3:276–294, Dec 1996.
16. Planning Competition Committee. PDDL – The planning domain definition language. AIPS-98, 1998.
17. M. Reichert and P. Dadam. ADEPT flex -supporting dynamic changes of workflows without losing control. *Journal of Intelligent Information Systems,* 10(2):93–129, 1998.
18. H. Schuschel and M. Weske. Integrated workflow planning and coordination. In *14th International Conference on Database and Expert Systems Applications,* volume 2736 of *LNCS,* pages 771–781. Springer, 2003.
19. A. P. Sheth, D. Georgakopoulos, S. Joosten, M. Rusinkiewicz, W. Scacchi, J. C. Wileden, and A. L. Wolf. Report from the NSF workshop on workflow and process automation in information systems. *SIGMOD Record,* 25(4):55–67, 1996.
20. S. Thatte, T. Andrews, F. Curbera, H. Dholakia, Y. Goland, J. Klein, F. Leymann, K. Liu, D. Roller, D. Smith, I. Trickovic, and S. Weerawarana. Business Process Execution Language for Web Services, version 1.1. Published on the WWW by BEA Corp., IBM Corp., Microsoft Corp., SAP AG and Siebel Systems, March 2003.
21. The DAML Services Coalition. DAML-S: Web service description for the semantic web. In *The First International Semantic Web Conference (ISWC),* 2002.
22. D. Wastell, P. White, and P. Kawalek. A methodology for business process redesign: experiences and issues. *Journal of Strategic Information Systems,* 3(1):23–40, 1994.
23. D. S. Weld. Recent advances in AI planning. *AI Magazine,* 20(2):93–123, 1999.
24. Q. Yang. *Intelligent Planning: A Decomposition and Abstraction Based Approach.* Springer, 1997.
25. L. Zeng, B. Benatallah, H. Lei, A. H. H. Ngu, D. Flaxer, and H. Chang. Flexible composition of enterprise web services. *Electronic Markets - Web Services,* 13(2), 2003.

Grouped Processing of Relational Algebra Expressions over Data Streams

Janusz R. Getta[1] and Ehsan Vossough[2]

[1] School of Information Technology and Computer Science
University of Wollongong
Wollongong, NSW 2522, Australia
jrg@uow.edu.au
[2] Department of Computing and Information Technology
University of Western Sydney Campbelltown
Campbelltown, NSW, Australia
e.vossough@uws.edu.au

Abstract. Implementation of the data stream processing applications requires a method for formal specification of the computations at a dataflow level. The logical models of stream processing hide the lower level implementation details. To solve this problem, we propose a new model of data stream processing based on the concepts of relational data stream, extensible system of elementary operations on relational streams, and data stream processing network integrating the dataflows and elementary operations. Next, we present the transformations of grouped data stream processing applications into data stream processing networks. The transformations proposed in the paper integrate the networks and optimize the implementations through elimination of the redundant elementary operations and dataflows. Finally, the paper introduces a timestamp based synchronization of data flows in our model and discusses its correctness.

1 Introduction

Data streams naturally occur in many modern applications of information technologies [1]. Processing of data streams includes storing, manipulating, and filtering the theoretically unlimited sequences of data items propagated by the sensor devices [2], financial institutions, traffic monitoring systems, etc. At the logical level, a traditional SQL based specification of a data stream application makes it very similar to a traditional database application [3,4]. Unfortunately, due to the performance reasons, the implementation techniques developed for the conventional database systems cannot be directly applied to the processing of rapidly changing sequences of data items [5]. Specification of the computations performed on the elements of data streams requires a different system of elementary operations and different organization of data flows among the operations.

This work introduces a concept of relational data stream and defines a new system of dataflow level operations on the relational streams. The new system

A. Benczúr, J. Demetrovics, G. Gottlob (Eds.): ADBIS 2004, LNCS 3255, pp. 336–347, 2004.

allows for transformation of the grouped data stream applications, i.e. different applications that operate on common data streams, into the data stream processing networks and optimization of the networks. The data flow operations reflect the principles of reactivity, adaptability, and extensibility of data stream processing. Reactivity means the processing of a new data element as soon as it is appended to a stream. Adaptability means automatic reaction of the system to the dynamically changing situations. For example, shifting more computational power into the processing of data streams that suddenly increased the frequencies, or changing the processing priorities in order to eliminate the bottlenecks. Extensibility means the ability of the system to create the complex operations from the elementary ones through pipelining, symmetric composition, or encapsulation of the elementary operations. To enforce the principles listed above we extend the traditional models of data streams with the concepts of composite data items (tuples) combined with **insert** or **delete** operations. A template for the elementary operations rather than a fixed set of operations assures the extensibility of the system. The elementary operations concurrently processing the data items against the varying contents of relational tables provide a high level of reactivity of the system. Adaptability of the system can be achieved through the identification of equivalent transformations of the common designs into a number of data stream processing networks.

The paper is organised as follows. Section 2 contains a brief review of the origins and recent contributions in the area of data stream processing systems. Section 3 presents a formal model of relational data streams and extensible system of operations on the streams. Section 4 introduces the concepts of paths, data stream processing networks and proposes the transformations of the relational algebra based data stream applications into the data stream processing networks. Optimization of the grouped applications is discussed in the same section. Section 5 considers synchronization of elementary operations and data flows between the operations. Finally, section 6 concludes the paper.

2   Previous Works

The origins of data stream processing techniques can be traced back to adaptive query processing [6,7,8,9,10] continuous query processing, [11,12,4,13], online algorithms [14,15,16], and large number of works on data flow processing, see the reviews [17,18]. A comprehensive review of many works that contributed to the various aspects of data stream processing can be found in [1].

A typical data stream processing model applies the pipes and/or queues to connect the operations on the elements of data streams in a way that outputs of one operation become the inputs of another operation [19]. The STREAM project [20] expresses the query execution plans as the expressions over the unary and binary operations directly derived from the relational algebra. The operations are linked with the queues and have access to the synopsis data structures that implement the most up-to-date views on data streams. Execution of the operations is controlled by a central scheduler that dynamically determines amount of time available to each one of them. The CACQ [19] and TelegraphCQ [5] systems treat the data streams as the infinite relational tables. The system uses the "Eddy" [21] operator to dynamically process the items appended to data streams. The Aurora and Medusa projects [22] target implementation of high performance stream processing engine. Optimization of stream processing described in [23] is based on a model of computations where the relational algebra like operations on data streams are linked with the queues. Approximate computation of relational join over the data streams and the complexity of set expression processing are presented in [24] and [25].

3   Data Stream Processing Model

3.1   Basics

A *raw data stream* is an unlimited sequence of elementary values, usually numbers. A *prepared data stream* is an unlimited sequence of composite data elements like records, tuples, objects, etc. A *prepared data stream* is obtained by "zipping" of a number of *raw data streams*. A *relational data stream* is a *prepared data stream* such that all its elements are pairs $<\alpha,t>$ where $\alpha\in\{$insert, delete$\}$ and t is a tuple of elementary data items. When a pair $<$insert,$t>$ is collected from a stream, a tuple t obtains the most up to date timestamp and it is recorded in a fixed size window over the stream. If the window is full then the tuple t' with the oldest timestamp is removed from the window and pair $<$delete,$t'>$ is inserted into an output stream of the recording operation. An empty slot in the window is filled with t and pair $<$insert,$t>$ is inserted into an output stream of the recording operation. If a pair $<$delete,$t>$ is collected from a stream by the recording operation then a tuple t it is removed from the window and the pair is inserted into an output stream. The recording operation is always the first operation executed after a new element is collected from a stream.

The semantics of the data stream applications are expressed at the logical level in the terms of *windows* and operations on prepared data streams. Let $w_{s_1},\ldots,w_{s_n}$ be the windows on data streams $s_1,\ldots,s_n$. Consider application a expressed as a relational algebra expression $e_a(w_{s_1},\ldots,w_{s_n})$. Let $t_1,\ldots,t_k$ denote the time spots when the new data elements are collected from the input streams. Then, the evaluation of expression e_a at $t_1,\ldots t_k$ provides a sequence of values $e_a(t_1),\ldots e_a(t_k)$. These values are the results of the continuous processing of application a at $t_1,\ldots,t_k$. Obviously, the recomputation of entire expression $e_a(w_{s_1},\ldots,w_{s_n})$ at $t_1,\ldots,t_k$ is not feasible. We need the operations that describe the minimal sequence of actions required to recompute an application after an arrival of a new data item.

3.2   Elementary Operations

A system of elementary operation on data streams includes the housekeeping operations like *recorder* described in the previous section and *injector* used to

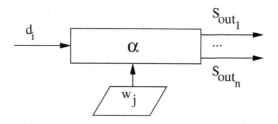

Fig. 1. An operation template

merge the data streams. The other group includes the operations similar to the relational algebra operations and derived from an operation template. An *injector* operation $(\delta \Rightarrow s)$ takes on input an element δ from a data stream and inserts it into a processing sequence on another data stream s. A *recorder* operation $(\delta \rightarrow w_s)$ acts either on a window on input stream w_s or on a set of tuples that play a role of an intermediate data container. When the recorder processes $<$insert,$t>$ on a set r then t becomes a member of r and $<$insert,$t>$ is appended to the output stream of the recorder. Processing of $<$delete,$t>$ removes t from r and sends $<$delete,$t>$ to the output stream. The operations derivable from the template take on input a single element $\delta = <\alpha, t>$, $\alpha \in \{$insert, delete$\}$ from a stream s_i, optionally the contents of window w_j on a data stream s_j, and send the results to n output streams $s_{out_1}, \ldots s_{out_n}$, see Figure 1. The template is a set of pairs $\{(\Phi_1, \Theta_1), \ldots, (\Phi_n, \Theta_n)\}$ where for $i = 1, \ldots n$, Φ_i is a *filtering expression* and Θ_i is a *transformation expression*. A *filtering expression* is a formula that evaluates to either **true** or **false** over a tuple t and the static contents of window w_j on stream s_j. A transformation expression is a sequence $[\theta_1, \ldots, \theta_k]$ of elementary transformation operations like projection, aggregation, arithmetic transformations, etc on a tuple t and optionally the contents of w_j. The semantics of an operation derived from the template is equivalent to the semantics of the following pseudocode.

if $\Phi_1(t, w_j)$ then $\Theta_1(t, w_j) \rightarrow s_{out_1}$;
if $\Phi_2(t, w_j)$ then $\Theta_2(t, w_j) \rightarrow s_{out_2}$;
$\cdots \quad \cdots \quad \cdots$
if $\Phi_n(t, w_j)$ then $\Theta_n(t, w_j) \rightarrow s_{out_n}$;

The elementary operations are derived from the template by the instantiations of expressions Φ_i and Θ_i, selection of an input stream s_i, window w_j, and the output streams. For example, an operation α_{spj} that implements concatenation of selection (σ_ϕ), projection (π_x), natural join $(\bowtie)$ of a tuple t and window w_j, and projection of the results (π_x) is derived from the template by the substitutions $\Phi_1 \leftarrow \sigma_\phi(t)$ and $\Theta_1 \leftarrow \pi_x(t \bowtie w_j)$ and discarding the rest of the template. The semantics of α_{spj} is defined by a pseudocode:

if $\sigma_\phi(t)$ then $\pi_x(t \bowtie w_j) \rightarrow s_{out}$;

In another example the derivation of operation α_{avg} that selects from a window w_j all data items that have the same values of attribute a as a tuple t and computes average of all values of attribute b from the selected items provides:

> `if true then` $avg_b(\gamma(t \bowtie_a w_j)) \rightarrow s_{out}$;

A transformation operation γ creates an aggregated data item from the results of $t \bowtie_a w_j$ and function avg_b finds an average value of attribute b in the aggregated data items.

An operation $-_{left}$ that takes on input an element $<\alpha,t>$ and computes $\{t\} -_X w_j$ is derived as follows.

> `if` $\forall r \in w_j \ t[X] \neq r[X]$ `then`
>   `if` $\alpha =$ `insert then` $<$`insert,`$t> \rightarrow s_{out}$ `else` $<$`delete,`$t> \rightarrow s_{out}$ `endif`
> `endif`

The terms $<$`insert,`$t> \rightarrow s_{out}$, $<$`delete,`$t> \rightarrow s_{out}$ denote the insertions of the elements $<$`insert,`$t>$, $<$`delete,`$t>$ into an output stream of the operation. A similar operation $-_{right}$ takes an element $<\alpha,t>$ and computes $w_j -_X \{t\}$ in the following way.

> `if` $\exists r \in w_j \ r[X] = t[X]$ `then`
>   `if` $\alpha =$ `insert then` $<$`delete,`$t> \rightarrow s_{out}$ `else` $<$`insert,`$t> \rightarrow s_{out}$ `endif`
> `endif`

The implementations of $-_{left}$ and $-_{right}$ are different because a set difference operation is not commutative. The commutative operations need only one variant of the respective operation. For example, an operation α_{spj} has the same implementation for both $(t \bowtie w_j)$ and $(w_j \bowtie t)$. It is easy to show that all relational algebra like operation on a stream element and window can be derived from the template. Moreover, the template allows for the derivations of the composite "piped" operations, i.e. the operations where the data items flow from one stage of processing to another without being recorded in the persistent storage. The piped operations significantly improve performance of data stream processing. The next section shows how to implement the relational algebra operations on the data streams as the networks of the elementary operations derivable from the template.

3.3   Paths and Networks

A *data stream processing path* or just a *path*, is an expression $p{:}t_1 \mid \ldots \mid t_n$ where p is a path name and for $i{=}1,..,n$, t_i denotes either an elementary operation or *injection point*. The adjacent elementary operations in a path are "piped" such that outputs generated by t_i are consumed by its successor t_{i+1}. If an operation t_i contributes to more than one output stream then identification of an output used by a path is attached to t_i. An *injection point* is a location among two

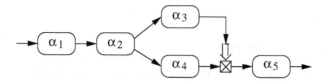

Fig. 2. The sample data stream processing paths

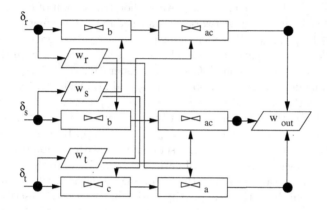

Fig. 3. A network implementation of $(r(ab) \bowtie_b s(bc)) \bowtie_{ac} t(ac)$

adjacent operations in the same path where an injection operation inserts new elements from another stream. The injection points are needed to merge two or more paths. A set of paths describes a system of operations performed on the relational streams. For example, a system of operations given in Figure 2 is described by the paths:

$$p_1 : \alpha_1 \mid \alpha_2(out_2) \mid \alpha_4 \mid x \mid \alpha_5,$$
$$p_2 : \alpha_2(out_1) \mid \alpha_3 \mid \Rightarrow x.$$

All operations in a path are binary operations. An operation is a pair αw or $w\alpha$ where α is an operation code and w is a data container read by an operation, e.g. $(w_i \bowtie_x)$ or $(-_{left}w_j)$. An operation code may be prefixed with a tag to uniquely identify the operation in another path. A symbol '|' means that elements produced on output by one operation become the input elements of its successor. An example given in Figure 3 and collection of paths given below implements a logical level expressions $r(ab) \bowtie_b s(bc)) \bowtie_{ac} t(ac)$ where r, s, ad t are the relational streams. A window w_{out} contains the results of the expression.

$$p_r :\rightarrow w_r \mid \bowtie_s w_s \mid \bowtie_{ac} w_t \mid \rightarrow w_{out},$$
$$p_s :\rightarrow w_s \mid w_r \bowtie_b \mid \bowtie_{ac} w_t \mid \rightarrow w_{out},$$
$$p_t :\rightarrow w_t \mid \bowtie_b w_s \mid \bowtie_{ac} w_r \mid \rightarrow w_{out}$$

4   Applications

4.1   Single Expressions

An implementation data stream application needs a transformation of a logical level specification of the application into its implementation in a form of a data stream processing network. Let $e(r_1, \ldots, r_n)$ be a relational algebra expression over the relational streams $r_1, \ldots, r_n$. An ad-hoc translation of e into an equivalent data stream processing network is performed in the following way. Consider a stream $r_i \in \{r_1, \ldots, r_n\}$. Consider an operation $\alpha_i(r_i, e')$ where e' is a subexpression of e. Construct a path $p_i{:}\alpha_i w_{e'}$ where $w_{e'}$ is set container with the intermediate results of subexpression e'. Consider an operation $\alpha_{i+1}(\alpha_i(r_i, e'), r_j)$ whose arguments include the result of operation α_i and argument r_j. Extend the path constructed in the previous step to $p_i{:}\alpha_i w_{e'} \mid \alpha_{i+1} r_j$. Consider the next operation and extend the path once more. Repeat the process until no more operation is left in e. Then, append an operation $\to w_{result}$ to a path p_i. Repeat, this process for all input streams $r_1, \ldots, r_n$. If $w_{e'}$ is a set container with the intermediate results then insert an operation $\to w_{e'}$ to all paths that contribute to the contents of $w_{e'}$. Add a recorder operation $\to w_i$ at the beginning all paths p_i whose inputs are directly taken from the data streams. Application of the method described above to a logical level expression $r((ab) \bowtie_b s(bc)) \bowtie_{ac} t(ac)$ provides the following paths:

$$p_r{:} \to w_r \mid \bowtie_b w_s \mid \to w_{rs} \mid \bowtie_{ac} w_t \mid \to w_{result},$$
$$p_s{:} \to w_s \mid w_r \bowtie_b \mid \to w_{rs} \mid \bowtie_{ac} w_t \mid \to w_{result},$$
$$p_t{:} \to w_t \mid \bowtie w_{rs} \mid \to w_{result}.$$

A straightforward transformation of a relational algebra expression into a set of paths always assumes that intermediate results are recorded in the persistent storage. Access and maintenance of the persistent storage decreases the performance and increases the complexity of synchronisation of dataflows. The problem can be avoided if it is possible to transform a syntax tree of the expression into a left- (right-) deep syntax tree for each one of its arguments r_i is located at the left- (right-) deep leaf level. Let $\alpha(r_i, \beta(r_j, e'(r_1, \ldots, r_{j-1})))$ be a subexpression of the expression. If the operations α and β commute then we transform the expression into $\beta(r_j, \alpha(r_i, e'(r_1, \ldots, r_{j-1})))$. The transformation brings an argument r_i closer to the left- (right-) deep leaf level. As a simple example consider an expression $r((ab) \bowtie_b s(bc)) \bowtie_{ac} t(ac)$ over the relational streams r, s, and r. The expression is equivalent to $(t(ac) \bowtie_c s(bc)) \bowtie_{ab} r(ab)$ where an argument $t(ac)$ is located at the left-deep leaf level. In such a case, construction of a path p_t from the new expression provides $p'_t{:} \to w_t \mid \bowtie_c s(bc) \mid \bowtie_{ab} r(ab)$, which does not accesses the intermediate results, see Figure 3. The dots represents the recorder operations, the trapezoids represent the data containers and edges from containers to elementary operations represent read actions performed by the operations when processing the stream elements. The edges between the elementary operations represent the flows of relational data streams. The elementary operations are implemented as simultaneously running processes that collect the stream elements from the input queue, read data containers and append the results to an output queue.

4.2   Grouped Expressions

Implementation of the grouped applications requires an optimal transformation of several logical level expressions into one data stream processing network. It is essential that operations and sub-paths common to several paths are implemented as the same processes. The main objective of the optimal transformations of grouped expressions is to minimize the total number of elementary operations involved in the implementation. As a simple example consider two data stream applications represented at a logical level as the relational algebra expressions $e_1 : r(ab) \bowtie_a s(ac)$ and $e_2 : t(cd) \bowtie_c s(ac)$ where r and s are the relational data streams. Translation of the expressions e_1 and e_2 provide the following collection of data stream processing paths:

$$p_{r_1}: \to w_r \mid \bowtie_a w_s \mid \to w_{out_1} \qquad p_{t_2}: \to w_t \mid \bowtie_d w_s \mid \to w_{out_2}$$
$$p_{s_1}: \to w_s \mid \bowtie_a w_r \mid \to w_{out_1} \qquad p_{s_2}: \to w_s \mid \bowtie_d w_t \mid \to w_{out_2}$$

To reduce a number of processes the join operations $\bowtie_a w_s$ and $\bowtie_d w_s$ can be implemented as a single join operation $\bowtie_{a|d}$ that merges the functionality of both operations. The new operation recognizes the identifiers of elements from streams r and t and outputs the results to out_r or to out_t respectively. Moreover recording of input elements of a stream s can be expressed as a single operation and operation $\prec$ that replicates a stream s on the outputs out_{s_1} and out_{s_2} for processing against r and t. The data processing paths after the optimizations use only 3 join operations (see below).

$$p_{r_1}: \to w_r \mid x \mid \bowtie_{a|d} w_s(out_r) \mid \to w_{out_1}$$
$$p'_{t_2}: \to w_t \mid \Rightarrow x$$
$$p''_{t_2}: \bowtie_{a|d} w_s(out_s) \mid \to w_{out_2}$$
$$p'_{s_1}: \to w_s \mid \prec (out_{s_1}) \mid \bowtie_d w_t \mid \to w_{out_2}$$
$$p''_{s_2}: split(out_{s_2}) \mid \bowtie_a w_r \mid \to w_{out_1}$$

Identification of the common operations and sub-paths reduces the total number of operations in the implementation. Consider two data stream processing paths $p_\alpha: \alpha_1 w_1 \mid \ldots \mid \alpha_m w_m$ and $p_\beta: \beta_1 v_1 \mid \ldots \mid \beta_n v_n$. We say that a sequence of operations τ_α in p_α matches a sequence of operations τ_β in p_β if a sequence of data containers used in τ_α is the same as a sequence of data containers used in p_β. The operations τ_α and p_β can be merged if they match each other and if the paths they belong to have been already merged over the sequences τ'_α and τ'_β such that τ'_α precedes τ_α and τ'_β follows τ_α or the opposite. For example, the paths $p_{\alpha_1}: \alpha_1 w_1 \mid \alpha_2 w_2$ and $p_{\alpha_2}: \alpha_2 w_2 \mid \alpha_1 w_1$ cannot be merged on both operations α_1 and α_2. If such a case happens we try to commute the sequence of operations in the paths whenever it is possible.

Integration of the operations αw and βw provides an operation $\alpha|\beta w$ that recognizes the stream identifiers in the data elements and computes either αw or βw. Of course the implementation of $\alpha|\beta w$ shares the common code of the operations. A typical example would be the hash based implementation of $\bowtie_x |\cap w$ where hashing of w over the attributes in x allows for the common implementation of the operations $\bowtie_x$ and $\cap$.

5   Synchronization of Data Flows

Serial processing of the data stream elements is a simple however not very effective way of performing the computations on data streams. High frequencies of the input streams and isolation of elementary operations in a data stream processing network suggest more simultaneous execution of the operations. An idea of parallel or concurrent computations immediately raises the questions about scheduling of the elementary operations and correctness of the scheduling. Assume that a data stream processing network implements a function f that processes a number of relational streams. Then, the network correctly implements a function f if for any sequence of input elements $\delta_1,\ldots,\delta_n$ the the network produces a sequence of values $f(\delta_1, S_1),\ldots,f(\delta_n, S_n)$ where $S_1,\ldots,S_n$ are the states of all data containers in the network after the arrivals of elements $\delta_1,\ldots,\delta_n$. In many cases such strict definition of correctness is not really needed. The high frequencies of the streams cause so frequent modifications of the outputs that observation of all modification in the real time is simply impossible. Therefore we introduce a concept of partial correctness. We say that the computations performed by a data stream processing network are partially correct if for any sequence of input elements $\delta_1,\ldots,\delta_n$ some of the results are equal to $f(\delta_1, S_1),\ldots,f(\delta_n, S_n)$. Partial correctness requires that only from time to time the results produced by a network reflect the present state of input data streams.

A sequence of computations along a path may be considered as a database transaction that operates on data containers. Then, at a logical level synchronization of the computations along paths is identical to synchronization of database transactions. To be correct, the executions along all paths must preserver the order serializability for all of its input elements It means that synchronization should preserve the orders of conflicting operations i.e read and write operations over the data containers. Consider a data stream processing network that has n input relational streams $s_1,\ldots,s_n$ and such that it has no containers with intermediate results of the computations. Then, in such a network the conflicts happens over the accesses to the windows on relational streams $w_{s_1},\ldots,w_{s_n}$ and to the final results in w_{out}. The input elements are recorded in the windows on relational streams and in the same moment the other operations attempt to the contents of the windows. An operation that processes an element δ_{s_i} and reads a window w_{s_j} must read from w_{s_j} only the element that arrived before δ_{s_i}. It is easy to enforce this condition by examining the timestamp of δ_{s_i} and the timestamps of data items read from w_{s_j} and processing only the data items such that their timestamps are lower than the timestamp of δ_{s_i}. The conflicts over access to the final result are sorted out with the timestamps as well. The results are recorded in an intermediate container and reordered accordingly to the values of timestamps in the final container.

It is possible use timestamping to synchronize the computations in a class of stream processing networks that write and read from the intermediate data containers and such that the operations on data containers satisfy an invariant property. Let a data stream processing network computes a function f. We say that the network is *invariant* of for any permutation of a finite sequence of elements $\delta_1,\ldots,\delta_n$ the final result produces by the network is always the same. A network processing the relational streams is an *invariant network* because processing of relational algebra operations does not depend on the order of elements, e.g. join of two relational table does not depend on the order of rows in the tables. To correctly synchronize the operations in an invariant data stream processing network we have to dynamically modify the timestamps of the elements flowing thorough the network. Each time an element is recorded in an intermediate data container it obtains a new current timestamp which is the largest timestamp in the network. It is possible to show that such method preserves the partial correctness of the computations performed by the network. A sketch of a proof is as follows. Consider an invariant network such that the operations $\rightarrow w$ and αw belong to two separate path in the newtwork. A recorder operation $\rightarrow w$ writes to an intermediate data container w and αw reads from the same container. Assume that elements δ_m and δ_n are submitted for processing and recorded in the window in input streams such that timestamp of δ_m is lower than timestamp of δ_n. Let $res(\delta_m)$ denote the results of processing of δ_m recorded in w and let $res(\delta_n)$ denote the results of processing of δ_n that trigger execution of operation α. To correctly process the elements $res(\delta_m)$ should be recorded in w before $res(\delta_n)$ triggers the execution of operation α. In such a case w is processed in a correct order because α will read all data items from w earlier inserted by the recorder. However, if recording in w of $res(\delta_m)$ is late and operation α starts its execution too early then $res(\delta_n)$ will never be processed by α against $res(\delta_m)$. It is because timestamp of $res(\delta_m)$ is lower than timestamp of $res(\delta_n)$. A modification of timestamp associated with $res(\delta_m)$ dynamically changes the order of elements δ_m and δ_n processed by the remaining part of the network. A problem is that part of the network processes the elements in order δ_m before δ_n and other part of the network process the elements in the opposite order. If a network is invariant i.e. an order of input elements has no impact on the final result then when processing of both δ_m and δ_n is completed the results should be correct. This method supports only the partial correctness because the results after processing of δ_n alone are definitely incorrect. The methods that achieve complete and partial correctness in non-invariant data stream processing networks are beyond the scope of this paper.

6   Summary and Open Problems

The modern applications of information technologies consider processing of fast evolving and theoretically unlimited sequences of data items commonly called as data streams. This work targets the grouped processing of relational algebra expressions over the relational streams. A relational stream is a sequence of tuples obtained from zipping of the raw data streams. We propose an extensible system of elementary operations on relational streams and we describe the transformations of data stream applications into the data stream processing networks. Next, we show how to merge the data stream processing paths in order to minimize the total number of elementary operations in the implementation.

The work also dicusses the synchronization of parallel computations in the data stream processing networks. We introduces the notions of correctness and partial correctness of parallel computations and shows that timestamping is sufficient to preserve the correctness of computations in the networks which do not use intermediate data containers. A way how the logical level expressions on data streams are transformed into the data stream processing networks seems to be the most important contribution of this research. A concept of operational elements in a data stream like `insert` and `delete` leads towards processing of the structured data streams.

A number of problems remains to be solved. A central problem is the implementation of a data stream processing system based on a set of elementary operations derivable from a common pattern defined in the paper and performance aspects of the system. The other group of problems includes synchronization of data stream processing in a general class of data stream processing networks and identification of the classes of data stream applications that can be translated into the data stream processing networks that do not need access to the windows on intermediate data streams.

References

1. Babcock, B., Babu, S., Datar, M., Motwani, R., Widom, J.: Models and issues in data stream systems. In Popa, L., ed.: Proceedings of the Twenty-first ACM SIGACT-SIGMOD-SIGART Symposium on Principles of Database Systems, ACM Press (2002) 1–16
2. Madden, S., Franklin, M.J.: Fjording the stream: An architecture for queries over streaming sensor data. In: 18th International Conference on Data Engineering February 26-March 1, 2002, San Jose, California, IEEE (2002)
3. Arasu, A., Babcock, B., Babu, S., McAlister, J., Widom, J.: Characterizing memory requirements for queries over continuous data streams. In Popa, L., ed.: Proceedings of the Twenty-first ACM SIGACT-SIGMOD-SIGART Symposium on Principles of Database Systems, ACM Press (2002) 221–232
4. Babu, S., Widom, J.: Continuous queries over data streams. SIGMOD Record **30** (2001) 109–120
5. Krishnamurthy, S., Chandrasekaran, S., Cooper, O., Deshpande, A., Franklin, M.J., Hellerstein, J.M., Hong, W., Madden, S.R., Reiss, F., Shah, M.A.: Telegraphcq: An architectural status report. Bulletin of the Technical Committee on Data Engineering **26** (2003) 11–18
6. Hellerstein, J.M., Franklin, M.J., Chandrasekaran, S., Deshpande, A., Hildrum, K., Madden, S., Raman, V., Shah, M.A.: Adaptive query processing: Technology in evolution. Bulletin of the Technical Committee on Data Engineering **23** (2000) 7–18
7. Cole, R.L.: A decision theoretic cost model for dynamic plans. Bulletin of the Technical Committee on Data Engineering **23** (2000) 34–41
8. Bouganim, L., Fabret, F., Mohan, C.: A dynamic query processing architecture for data integration systems. Bulletin of the Technical Committee on Data Engineering **23** (2000) 42–48
9. Ives, Z.G., Levy, A.Y., Weld, D.S., Florescu, D., Friedman, M.: Adaptive query processing for internet applications. Bulletin of the Technical Committee on Data Engineering **23** (2000) 19–26

10. Urhan, T., Franklin, M.J.: Xjoin: A reactively-scheduled pipelined join operator. In: IEEE Data Engineering Bulletin 23(2), IEEE (2000) 27–33
11. Terry, D., Goldberg, D., Nichols, D., Oki, B.: Continuous queries over append-only databases. In: Proceedings of the 1992 ACM SIGMOD International Conference on Management of Data. (1992) 321–330
12. Liu, L., Pu, C., Tang, W.: Continual queries for internet scale event-driven information delivery. IEEE Transactions on Knowledge and Data Engineering **11** (1999) 610–628
13. Hellerstein, A.R.: Eddies: Continuously adaptive query processing. In: Proc. ACM-SIGMOD International Conference on Management of Data. (1998) 106–117
14. Fiat, A., Woeginger, G.J.: On Line Algorithms, The State of the Art. Springer Verlag (1998)
15. Hellerstein, J.M., Haas, P.J., Wang, H.J.: Online aggregation. In: Proceedings of the 1997 ACM SIGMOD International Conference on Management of Data. SIGMOD Record (1997) 171–182
16. Hellerstein, J.M., Haas, P.J., Wang, H.J.: Online aggregation. In: SIGMOD 1997, Proceedings ACM SIGMOD International Conference on Management of Data, ACM Press (1997) 171–182
17. Lee, E.A., Parks, T.M.: Dataflow process networks. Technical report, Department of Electrical Engineering and Computer Science, University of California (1995)
18. Stephens, R.: A survey of stream processing. Technical Report CSRG95-05, Department of Electronic and Electrical Engineering, University of Surrey (1996)
19. Madden, S., Shah, M., Hellerstein, J.M., Raman, V.: Continuously adaptive continuous queries over streams. In: Proceedings of the 2002 ACM SIGMOD International Conference on Management of Data, Madison, Wisconsin, June 4-6, 2002, ACM Press (2002) 49–60
20. Group, T.S.: Stream: The stanford stream data manager. Bulletin of the Technical Committee on Data Engineering **26** (2003) 19–26
21. Avnur, R., Hellerstein, J.M.: Eddies: Continuously adaptive query processing. In: Proceedings of the 2000 ACM SIGMOD International Conference on Management of Data, ACM (2000) 261–272
22. Stonebraker, M., Cherniack, M., Cetintemel, U., Balazinska, M., Balakrishnan, H.: The aurora and medusa projects. Bulletin of the Technical Committee on Data Engineering **26** (2003) 3–10
23. Viglas, S.D., Naughton, J.F.: Rate-based query optimization for streaming information sources. In: Proceedings of the 2002 ACM SIGMOD International Conference on Management of Data, ACM Press (2002) 37–48
24. Das, A., Gehrke, J., Riedewald, M.: Approximate join processing over data streams. In: Proceedings of the 2003 ACM SIGMOD International Conference on Management of Data, San Diego, June9-12, 2003. (2003)
25. Ganguly, S., Garofalakis, M., Rastogi, R.: Processing set expressions over continuous update streams. In: Proceedings of the 2003 ACM SIGMOD International Conference on Management of Data, San Diego, June9-12, 2003. (2003)
26. Getta, J., Vossough, E.: Optimization of data stream processing. Submitted for publication in SIGMOD Record (2004)

Processing Sliding Window Join Aggregate in Continuous Queries over Data Streams

Weiping Wang[1], Jianzhong Li[1,2], DongDong Zhang[1], and Longjiang Guo[1,2]

[1] School of Computer Science and Technology, Harbin Institute of Technology, China
[2] School of Computer Science and Technology, Heilongjiang University, China
{wpwang,lijzh,zddhit,guolongjiang}@hit.edu.cn

Abstract. Processing continuous queries over unbounded streams require unbounded memory. A common solution to this issue is to restrict the range of continuous queries into a sliding window that contains the most recent data of data streams. Sliding window join aggregates are often-used queries in data stream applications. The processing method to date is to construct steaming binary operator tree and pipeline execute. This method consumes a great deal of memory in storing the sliding window join results, therefore it isn't suitable for stream query processing. To handle this issue, we present a set of novel sliding window join aggregate operators and corresponding realized algorithms, which achieve memory-saving and efficient performance. Because the performances of proposed algorithms vary with the states of data streams, a scheduling strategy is also investigated to maximize the processing efficiency. The algorithms in this paper not only can process the complex sliding window join aggregate, but also can process the multi-way sliding window join aggregate.

1 Introduction

Recently a new class of data-intensive applications has become widely recognized: applications in which the data is modeled best not as persistent relations but rather as transient data streams. Examples of such applications include financial applications, network monitoring, security, telecommunications data management, web applications, manufacturing, and sensor networks. The database research community has begun focusing its attention on query processing over unbounded continuous input stream. Due to their continuous and dynamic nature, querying data streams involves running a query continually over a period of time.

Unbounded streams can't be wholly stored in bounded memory. A common solution to this issue is to restrict the range of continuous queries into a sliding window that contains the last K items or the items that have arrived in the last T time units. The former is called a count-based, or a sequence-based sliding window, while the latter is called a time based or a timestamp-based sliding window [12]. Constraining all queries by sliding window predicates allows continuous queries over unbounded streams to be executed in a finite memory and in an incremental manner by producing new results as new items arrive in.

Evaluating sliding window join over streams is practical and useful in many applications. Meanwhile, in many cases it is necessary to process aggregate over the results

A. Benczúr, J. Demetrovics, G. Gottlob (Eds.): ADBIS 2004, LNCS 3255, pp. 348–363, 2004.

of sliding window join. For example, in a building monitoring system, the sensors monitoring temperature generate stream A, which contains three attributes: **Location, Time** and **Temperature**. Meanwhile, the sensors monitoring smokes generate stream B, which also contains three attributes: **Location, Time** and **Strength**. In order to find out which room might be on fire, the manager of the building may put forward a query as the following:

Q1:

SELECT location, **COUNT**(*) **FROM** A[10 MINUTE], B[10 MINUTE]

WHERE   A.location = B.location

AND A.temperature>=40

AND B.strength >0.6

GROUP BY location

HAVING COUNT (*)>5;

When Q1 is processed in continuous queries, a new count value must be output as each new item of stream arrives in. A solution for processing sliding window join aggregate is illustrated by figure 1(1), upon each arrival of a new item from stream A, four tasks must be performed:

1. Insert the new item into the sliding window of stream A.
2. Invalidate all the expired items in A's sliding window and B's sliding window.
3. Process join of A's sliding window and B's sliding window, and insert the results into a queue.
4. Compute the aggregate function by scanning the queue one pass.

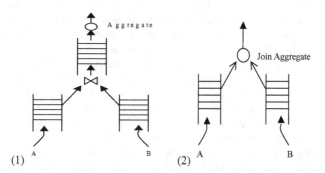

Fig. 1. (1) SW Join Aggregate Query Plan, (2) SW Join Aggregate Operator

This method consumes a great deal of memory in storing the results of sliding window join. Assume that there are 1000 items in sliding window A and sliding window B respectively, and the join selectivity is 0.1, then 100,000 join results need to be stored. Since memory is the most expensive resource in data stream query processing system, therefore it isn't a good solution. In contrast, we propose a set of novel sliding window join aggregate operators, which compute the aggregate function while processing the sliding window join. These operators needn't store the join results, thereby they can save memory effectively. For each operator, we propose several realized algorithms, which can achieve memory-saving and efficient performance. Since the performance of algorithms vary with the states of data streams, a scheduling strategy is also presented, which dynamically assign the most effective algorithm for the operator according to the states of streams. The methods presented in this paper can process not only the complex sliding window join aggregate, but also the multi-way sliding window join aggregate.

The remainder of this paper is organized as following. In section 2, we review related work. Section 3 describes the algorithms for the two-way sliding window join aggregate operator and gives the experimental study of proposed algorithms. Section 4 presents techniques for maximizing sliding window join aggregate efficiency, while section 5 extends the proposed algorithms to process multi-way sliding window join aggregate. In section 6, we give our conclusions and identify future work.

2   Related Work

There has been a great deal of recent interest in developing novel data management techniques and adapting traditional database technology to the data stream model, such as, Cougar [2], Aurora [3], Telegraph [4,5] and STREAM [1]. The first two focus on processing sensor data. STREAM addresses all aspects of stream data management, including memory management, operator scheduling, and approximate query answering via summary information. A continuous query language (CQL) has also been proposed within the STREAM project [7].

Defining sliding windows is one solution proposed in the literature for bounding the memory requirements of continuous queries and unblocking streaming operators [12]. Since it is unpractical to processing the join over unbounded streams in bounded memory, a good deal of research has been conducted on processing sliding window join over data streams. The first non-blocking binary join algorithm, symmetric hash join was presented in [11], which was optimized for in memory performance, leading into thrashing on larger inputs. Sliding window joins over two streams were studied by Kang et al. [14], who introduced incrementally computable binary joins as well as a per-unit-time cost model. Lukasz et al have discussed sliding window multi-join processing over data streams, and also proposed some join ordering heuristic rules that provides a good join order without iterating over the entire search space [15].

Processing aggregate over data streams is another related research area. Manku et al presented algorithms for computing frequency counts exceeding a user-specified threshold over data streams [8]. Correlated aggregates were studied by J. Gehrke in [9]. A. Dobra et al calculated small "sketch" summaries of the streams, and used them to provide approximate answers to aggregate queries with provable guarantees on the approximation error. Datar et al proposed an algorithm maintaining samples and simple statistics over sliding windows [12].

To the best of our knowledge, there have been to date no research works discussing the processing of sliding window join aggregate over data streams.

3   Processing Two-Way Sliding Window Join Aggregate

There are five two-way sliding window join aggregate operators according to the aggregate functions, namely SWJ-COUNT, SWJ-SUM, SWJ-AVG, SWJ-MAX and SWJ-MIN. Among them, SWJ-COUNT, SWJ-SUM and SWJ-AVG work in same way; meanwhile, SWJ-MAX and SWJ-MIN work in same way. In this paper, we only propose the realized algorithms for the operator SWJ-COUNT, which are also suitable for SWJ-SUM and SWJ-AVG. For the limitation of the space, the realized algorithms for operator SWJ-MAX and SWJ-MIN are not presented in this paper. Table 1 lists the meaning of symbols used in this paper.

Table 1. Symbols

Symbol	Meaning
SWA, SWB	Sliding window corresponding to stream A, B
a, β	Number of items in SWA, SWB respectively
T_a	Time size of time-based window SWA
λ_a	Arrival rate of stream A
M	Number of hash buckets in hash table of sliding window
C	Cost of accessing one item in sliding window
σ	Selectivity of join operator
$sizeA, sizeB$	Item size of stream A,B respectively
aob	Concatenation of item a and item b
$\times$	Join

Before illustrating algorithms in detail, we introduce several definitions.

Definition 1. A data stream is an infinite time sequence with the incremental order, $S=\{s_1, s_2, ..., s_t, ...\}$, s_t is an item appearing at time t.

Definition 2. Let T be a time interval size, and $t>T$ is the variable time, $SW_i[t-T : t]$ is defined as a time-based sliding window of data stream i, whose time size is T.

Definition 3. SW_{TK} is a snapshot of the sliding window SW at the time T_K, $SW_{TK} = SW[T_K-T : T_K]$.

3.1 SWJ-COUNT Evaluating Algorithms

The function of SWJ-COUNT operator is computing the number of sliding window join results. Three algorithms will be introduced: SC, IC and TC.

3.1.1 SC Algorithm

SC is a simple algorithm to process SWJ-COUNT. When a new item of stream A (or B) arrives in, firstly it is inserted into sliding window SWA (or SWB), and then all expired items in sliding window SWA and SWB are removed (whose timestamps are now outside the current time window). Finally, process the join of SWA and SWB, meanwhile, the aggregate value is computed along with processing join.

The most time cost of SC is processing join. Since hash join algorithm always has optimal efficiency in several join algorithms, it is chosen to process join in SC and sliding windows are constructed in hash table.

Before analyzing the cost of SC algorithm, we briefly introduce our cost model. Each arrival of an item from streams triggers the sliding window join aggregate algorithm to execute once. In this paper, the time cost we consider is the time that the algorithm executes once.

In the first step, SC algorithm inserts a new item into sliding window, and the cost of this step is C. The second step of SC scans both SWA and SWB in one pass, with a cost of $(\alpha+\beta)C$. Assuming that SWA and SWB have M buckets respectively, and each bucket of SWA ,SWB has α/M and β/M items, respectively on average. Then the cost for processing $SWA \times SWB$ is $M*(\dfrac{\alpha}{M}*\dfrac{\beta}{M})*C = \dfrac{\alpha*\beta}{M}*C$. Here we ignore the cost of computing aggregate function, because it is done along with the processing join. The total time cost for SC algorithm is

$$C+(\alpha+\beta)*C+\frac{\alpha*\beta}{M}*C \approx (\alpha+\beta+\frac{\alpha*\beta}{M})*C$$

It is easily to know that the space cost of SC is O ($\alpha*sizeA+\beta*sizeB$).

3.1.2 IC Algorithm

Since the whole items in SWA must be joined with whole items in SWB at each execution of SC algorithm, the time cost of SC is obviously very high. Because only a few items would be expired at each time sliding windows invalidation, there are much more duplicated computations between the two executions of SC algorithm. In this section, we will present a new algorithm IC, which performs more efficient than SC algorithm.

The main idea of IC algorithms is described in figure 2, IC calculates the SWJ-COUNT in an incremental manner, that is, the $(k+1)_{th}$ result of SWJ-COUNT is computed based on the k_{th} aggregate value.

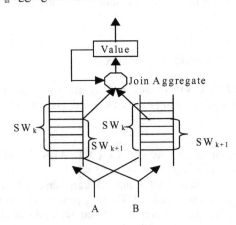

Fig. 2. IC Algorithm

Before discuss the detail of the algorithm, we introduce a theorem.

Theorem 1. Give four relations A, B, C and D, the following equation is true:
$|(C{\times}D)| = |(A{\times}B)| + |(C{\backslash}A)\ {\times}D| + |(D{\backslash}B)\ {\times}C| - |(C{\backslash}A)\ {\times}(D{\backslash}B)| - |(A{\backslash}C)\ {\times}(B{\cap}D)| - |(B{\backslash}D)\ {\times}(A{\cap}C)\ | - |(A{\backslash}C){\times}(B{\backslash}D)|$.

The proof for Theorem 1 can be found in Appendix A. Assuming that the current snapshot of SWA, SWB is SWA_{TK}, SWB_{TK}, and now the $|SWA_{TK}{\times}SWB_{TK}|$ is known, when a new item f of stream A arrives in at time T_J, the following is the description of IC algorithm.

IC Algorithm
Input: SWA, SWB, T_J, f, CountValue, T
Output: CountValue
1. Insert f into SWA
2. Invalidate every expired tuple g in SWA and SWB which satisfy T_J - $g.timestamp>T$.Push the expired tuples of SWA and SWB into collection SetA and SetB respectively;
3. $val1 = COUNT(\{f\}{\times}SWB)$;
4. $val2 = COUNT(SetA{\times}SWB)$;
5. $val3 = COUNT(SetB{\times}(SWA{\backslash}\{f\}))$;
6. $val4 = COUNT(SetA\ {\times}SetB)$;
7. $CountValue = CountValue + val1 - val2 - val3 - val4$;
8. clear collection SetA, SetB;
9. Return CountValue;

Here COUNT(A) means a function that computes the number of items in set A. After the insertion of new item f and the invalidation of SWA and SWB, the current sliding window snapshot of SWA, SWB is SWA_{TJ}, SWB_{TJ} respectively. We want to compute the $|SWA_{TJ}{\times}SWB_{TJ}|$. According to theorem 1, we can get the following equation:

$|(SWA_{TJ}{\times}SWB_{TJ})|$ = $|(SWA_{TK}{\times}SWB_{TK})|$ + $|(SWA_{TJ}{\backslash}SWA_{TK}){\times}SWB_{TJ}|$ + $|(SWB_{TJ}{\backslash}SWB_{TK}){\times}SWA_{TJ}|$ - $|(SWA_{TJ}{\backslash}SWA_{TK}){\times}(SWB_{TJ}{\backslash}SWB_{TK})|$ - $|(SWA_{TK}{\backslash}SWA_{TJ})\ {\times}(SWB_{TK}{\cap}SWB_{TJ})|$ - $|(SWB_{TK}{\backslash}SWB_{TJ}){\times}(SWA_{TK}{\cap}SWA_{TJ})\ |$ - $|(SWA_{TK}{\backslash}SWA_{TJ}){\times}(SWB_{TK}{\backslash}SWB_{TJ})|$

According to the description of IC algorithm, we know that $SWA_{TJ}{\backslash}SWA_{TK} = \{f\}$. Since there is no item of data stream B coming in, it is true that $SWB_{TJ} \subseteq SWB_{TK}$, namely $SWB_{TJ}{\backslash}SWB_{TK}=\phi$. It is easy to know that $SWA_{TK}{\backslash}SWA_{TJ} = SetA$, $SWB_{TK}{\backslash}SWB_{TJ} = SetB$, $SWA_{TK}{\cap}SWA_{TJ} = SWA_{TJ}{\backslash}\{f\}$ and $SWB_{TK}{\cap}SWB_{TJ} = SWB_{TJ}$. Then:

$|(SWA_{TJ}{\times}SWB_{TJ})|$ = $|SWA_{TK}{\times}SWB_{TK}|$ + $|\{f\}{\times}SWB_{TJ}|$ - $|SetA{\times}SWB_{TJ}|$ - $|SetB{\times}(SWA_{TJ}{\backslash}\{f\})|$ - $|SetA{\times}SetB|$.

Several join operations need to be processed in IC algorithm, here we also choose hash join algorithm to process them (excluding the join of SetA and SetB). In IC, the cost of the first step is C and the second step cost is $(a+\beta)C$. SWB consists of M buckets, and each bucket has β/M items, consequently, the cost of the third step is $(\beta/M)^*$ C. The time cost of the fourth and the fifth step are $|SetA|^*\beta/M^*\ C$ and $|SetB|^*a/M^*\ C$ respectively. We choose the nested loop join algorithm for processing the join of SetA and SetB, so the sixth step cost is $|SetA|^*|SetB|^*C$. The total time cost of IC is:

$C+(a+\beta)C+(\beta/M)C+ |SetA|*\beta/M*C+|SetB|*a/M*C+|SetA|*|SetB|*C$
$\approx (a+\beta)C+(\beta/M)* C+ |SetA|*\beta/M*C + |SetB|*a/M* C + |SetA|*|SetB|*C$

Although IC algorithm needs process several join operations, it has lower execution time cost since only a few items participate each join operation. The space cost of IC algorithm is $O(a*sizeA + \beta*sizeB)$.

3.1.3 TC Algorithm

IC algorithm performs effectively, however, there are still several join operations need to be processed, which consume much more time. In contrast, only one join should be processed in TC algorithm to calculate the aggregate by means of storing some summaries for each item in the sliding window.

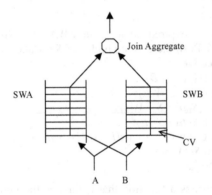

Fig. 3. TC algorithm

The concept of TC algorithm comes from the observation that, given two relations A and B, $|A \times B| = \sum_{\forall g \in A} |\{g\} \times B|$. As is shown in figure 3, each item in *SWA* and *SWB* is assigned an attribute *CV*. Assuming that *SWA* joins *SWB* based on attribute a, for each item f in the *SWA*, $f.CV = |\{ g \mid g \in SWB, g.timestamp > f.timestamp , g.a=f.a\}|$. It means that the value of $f.CV$ is the number of items in *SWB* which arrive later than f and match with item f.

It should be emphasized that the value of $f.CV$ is not the total number of items in *SWB* that matches with f. If the value of attribute *CV* is defined as that, when an item g matching with f in *SWB* is expired, the value of $f.CV$ must be decreased by one. That is, we have to process $\{g\} \times SWA$ to find out all the items in *SWA* that match with item g and decrease their *CV* attribute value by one. The join operation can't be avoided during the invalidation of sliding window if attribute *CV* is defined like that.

Adopting our definition for the attribute *CV*, the invalidation of sliding windows wouldn't modify the attribute *CV*'s value. Let's prove it.

Theorem 2. Given two sliding window *SWA*, *SWB* with *T* time size, $\forall k \in SWA, k$ has an attribute *CV*, and $k.CV = |\{ g \mid g \in SWB, g.timestamp > k.timestamp , g.a=k.a\}|$. At the time T_K, an item g in *SWB* is expired, then $\forall k \in SWA_{TK}$, the invalidation of g doesn't modify the value of $k.CV$.

Proof. Suppose that the invalidation of g modifies k's CV value. it means that equation $g.a{=}k.a$ and $g.timestamp >k.timestamp$ exists. Since the item g is expired, T_K - $g.timestamp>T$ is ture, then T_K - $k.timestamp>T$, that is $k \notin SWA_{TK,}$ which conflicts with $k{\in}SWA_{TK}$. So the supposition is wrong, and the theorem is proved.   □

According to theorem 2, it needn't process the join when invalidate sliding window.

Theorem 3. Given two sliding window SWA and SWB, $\forall f \in SWA$, $f.CV = |\{\ g\ |\ g \in SWB$, $g.timestamp >f.timestamp$, $g.a{=}f.a\}|$; $\forall g{\in}SWB$, $g.CV = |\{\ f\ |\ f \in SWA$, $f.timestamp >g.timestamp$, $f.a{=}g.a\}|$, the following equation exists:

$$|SWA{\times}SWB| \quad = \quad \sum_{\forall k\in SWA,SWB} k.CV$$

Proof. $\forall r{\in}SWA \times SWB$, then $r = f \circ g$, where $f{\in}SWA$, $g{\in}SWB$. According to the definition of attribute CV, if $f.timestamp>g.timestamp$, then $g.CV$ add 1,else $f.CV$ add 1. So $\forall r{\in}SWA \times SWB$, its contribution to $\sum_{\forall k\in SWA,SWB} k.CV$ is one . That is:

$$|SWA{\times}SWB| \quad = \quad \sum_{\forall k\in SWA,SWB} k.CV \qquad □$$

TC algorithm is designed according to theorem 3. Assuming that a new item f of stream A arrives in at time T_J, the TC algorithm is shown as following.

TC Algorithm
Input: SWA, SWB, T_J, f, T
Output: $CountValue$
1. $f.CV = 0$; $CountValue = 0$;
2.   Insert f into SWA;
1.   Invalidate every expired tuple g in SWA and SWB which satisfy T_J - $g.timestamp>T$.
2.   Find bucket B in SWB that match with f's hash value
3.   **FOR** $\forall$ tuple $g{\in}B$ **DO**
4.   **IF** $g.a = f.a$
5. $g.CV{+}{+}$;
6.   **FOR** $\forall k{\in}SWA$ **DO**
7. $CountValue = CountValue + k.CV$;
8.   **FOR** $\forall g{\in}SWB$ **DO**
9. $CountValue = CountValue + g.CV$;
10. **Return** $CountValue$;

Let's analyze the time cost of TC algorithm. We ignore the first step cost. The cost of the second step is C, and the cost of the third step is $(a{+}\beta)C$. In TC algorithm, the structure of sliding window is also a hash table, and the time cost of steps 5~7 is $(\beta/M)* C$. Steps 8~12 scan both sliding windows, with a cost of $(a{+}\beta)C$ So the whole cost of TC is:

$$C+2(a{+}\beta)C + \beta/M* C \approx 2(a{+}\beta)C+\beta/M* C$$

In TC algorithm, each item in sliding windows has an attribute CV, whose type is integer. Then the space cost of TC algorithm is:

$$O\ (\sigma*sizeA+\beta*sizeB+(\alpha+\beta)*SizeOf(Int)).$$

3.2 Performance Study

3.2.1 Experimental Setup

To examine the performance of the proposed algorithms, we implement them in C. The experiments are performed in Intel PIV 2.4Ghz with 256MB memory, running windows 2000. We generate two continuous data streams A and B randomly, stream A consisting of four attributes: **Location, Time, Temperature** and **Timestamp**, and B also with four attributes: **Location, Time, Strength** and **Timestamp**. The size of A's item and B's item are both 18 Bytes. The following query is tested in our experiments:

> **SELECT** location, **COUNT**(*)
> **FROM** A[T SECONDS], B[T SECONDS]
> **WHERE** A.location = B.location;

To compare the performance of the algorithms, we also implement PC algorithm, which computes the sliding window join aggregate with the operator tree. PC algorithm has been induced in section 1.

We test the performance of proposed algorithms in two scenarios:
- (i)   Variable time window and Constant arrival rate (VTCA)
- (ii)   Constant time window and Variable arrival rate (CTVA).

We consider CTCA in Section 3.2.2, and consider CTVA in Section 3.2.3

3.2.2 Variable Time Window and Constant Arrival Rate

In this experiment, the parameters for SWA and SWB are the same, the arrival rate of the stream is 100 items/sec, the selectivity of the join operator is 0.01, and the number of buckets in the hash table is 100. Figure 4 shows the performance of the four algorithms in the case that the window size is varying, and Figure 5 shows the amount of memory consumed by each algorithm.

As is shown in figure 4, when the stream rate is constant, IC algorithm outperforms the other algorithms, and PC algorithm has the worst performance. Let's analyze the cost of PC algorithm, suppose that a new item f of stream A come in, the cost of insertion and invalidation of PC algorithm is $(\alpha+\beta)*C$. The cost of evaluating $\{f\}\times SWB$ is $(\beta/M)*C$, and $\beta*\sigma$ join results would be produced. Insert the join results into the queue, the cost is $\beta*\sigma*C_w$, here parameter C_w is much larger than C[1]. The final step of PC algorithm scans the queue to calculate the count, whose cost is $(\alpha*\beta*\sigma)*C$. The total cost of PC algorithm is $(\alpha+\beta)*C+(\beta/M)*C+\beta*\sigma*C_w+(\alpha*\beta*\sigma)*C$. The join selectivity σ has great impact on the performance of PC algorithm according to the cost formula. In our experiment, $\sigma = 1/M$, then the cost of PC is $(\alpha+\beta)*C+(\beta/M)*C+\beta/M*C_w+(\alpha*\beta/M)*C$, which is much higher that the cost of the other algorithms.

---

[1] The cost of inserting the new item into sliding window also should be C_w. Since only one item needs to be inserted into sliding window, we approximately consider its cost as C.

Interestingly, IC executes faster than TC. The reason is that, in the case of constant stream arrival rate, only one item in sliding window would be expired when a new item arrives in, that is, $|SetA| = 1$ and $|SetB| = 1$. The time cost of IC is $(\alpha+\beta)C + (\alpha/M+\beta/M)* C + (\beta/M)* C + C$, which is less than the cost of TC, $2*(\alpha+\beta)C+\beta/M* C$. As figure 4 illustrates, the curves for PC and SC increase sharply with the growth of sliding window size, while the curve for TC goes up slowly. The sliding window size has little impact on the performance of IC algorithm.

Figure 5 shows the curves of memory used by the four algorithms. As expected, the amount of memory used by PC is greatly larger than by the other algorithms, since it stores the join results in memory. The amount of memory used by TC is a little larger than IC and SC because it requires every item in sliding window has an extra attribute CV. SC and IC have the lowest space cost.

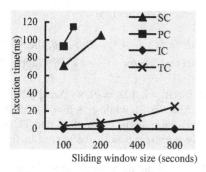

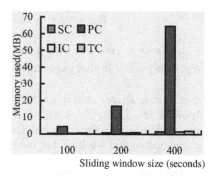

Fig. 4. Varying sliding window size
$(\lambda_a = \lambda_b = 100, M = 100, \sigma = 0.01)$

Fig. 5. Varying sliding window size
$(\lambda_a = \lambda_b = 100, M = 100, \sigma = 0.01)$

3.2.3 Constant Time Window and Variable Arrival Rate

In this scenario the data stream arrival rate is varying and the sliding window time size is constant. The parameters for SWA and SWB are also the same. We randomly generate two data streams whose arrival rates obey the Zipf distribution. At the i_{th} second the arrival rates of data streams are $\lambda_i = \dfrac{1}{i^2} \times 5000$ items/sec, where $1 \ i \ 10$.

The sliding window time size is equal to 5 seconds, the selectivity of join operator is 0.05, and the number of buckets in hash table is 20.

Figure 6 illustrates the performance of four algorithms. We begin the experiment after the sliding window is full, that is, begin at the 6_{th} second. IC and TC still outperform the other two algorithms. In the 6_{th} second, TC executes faster than IC, and in rest time, IC performs optimal. We compare the cost of IC with the cost of TC:

$IC : (\alpha+\beta)C+(\beta/M)* C+|SetA|*\beta/M* C + |SetB|*\alpha/M* C + |SetA|*|SetB|*C$
$TC: 2*(\alpha+\beta)C+\beta/M* C$

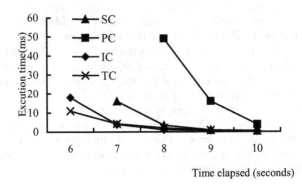

Fig. 6. Varying stream rate $(T_a=T_b=5s, M=20, \sigma=0.05)$

It is easy to conclude that, if $|SetA|*\beta/M +|SetB|*\alpha/M+|SetA|*|SetB| >\alpha+\beta$, then TC outperforms IC. In this experiment, at the 6th second, $\alpha=\beta=\sum_{i=1}^{5} \lambda_i =7318$. Suppose that an item arrives in at this time, then $|SetA| = |SetB| = \lambda_i/(2\lambda_6)=70$, so $|SetA|*\beta/M + |SetB|*\alpha/M + |SetA|*|SetB| = 2*7318*70/20+70*70 = 56126$,while $\alpha + \beta = 14636$. It means that TC execute more efficient than IC. We compute the costs of IC and TC at each second, and we find that the results exactly correspond with the curves in figure 6.

The above two experimental results show that when the data stream arrival rate is constant, IC has optimal performance; and when the data stream arrival rate varies with time rapidly, TC is the best choice to process the join aggregate. In the following section we will present a scheduling strategy that can assign the most optimal algorithm for the operator according to the states of data streams.

4   Maximize the Processing Efficiency

4.1   Scheduling Strategy

Continuous queries are the long running queries, and some parameters, such as join selectivity and stream arrival rates, will change in the running of continuous queries. It is crucial for the query optimizer to choose the most effective algorithm according to the states of steams.

In section 3, we have introduced three time-cost formulas for each proposed algorithm. There are three factors that affect the cost of SC,IC and TC: the number of items in sliding window α and β, the number of buckets in hash table M, $|SetA|$ and $|SetB|$. We can get these parameters before executing the algorithms. When an item arrives in from streams, the query optimizer computes the time cost for each algorithm and chooses the algorithm that has the lowest time cost to execute.

IC algorithm processes sliding window join aggregate based on the last aggregate value, while TC algorithm requires every item in sliding window has attribute CV and corresponding value, therefore IC and TC can't switch to each other directly. We make some modifications for the two algorithms when involving the scheduling strategy. In IC algorithm, each item also has the *CV* attribute, and its value is computed during processing {*f*}×*SWB*. In TC algorithm, the last time aggregate value is stored.

4.2 Experimental Results

We develop the algorithm HC that involving the scheduling strategy and compare the performance of HC with IC and TC. In this experiment the parameters for *SWA* and *SWB* are also the same. Two data streams are generated randomly, with the arrival rate at the i_{th} second being:

$$\lambda_i = \begin{cases} i \times 500 & i \bmod 2 = 1 \\ i^{-1} \times 500 & i \bmod 2 = 0 \end{cases}, 1 \quad i \quad 10$$

In this experiment the time size of the sliding windows are equal to 5 seconds, the selectivity of the join operator is 0.05, and the number of buckets in hash table was 20. As is shown in figure 7, the HC algorithm achieves optimal performance at any time as expected.

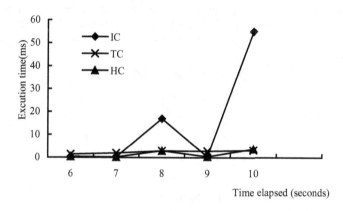

Fig. 7. Performance of scheduling strategy ($T_a=T_b=5$s , $M =20$, $\sigma=0.05$)

5 Processing Complex Sliding Window Join Aggregate

In this section, we will discuss how to extend our proposed algorithms to process complex sliding window join aggregate, such as query that contains Group By clause or multi-way sliding window join aggregate.

5.1 Processing Group By Clause

It is easy to extend the proposed algorithms to process the query that contains Group By clause. We illustrate it with an example of algorithm IC. The improved IC algorithm is termed as GIC algorithm.

GIC uses a list structure, *Glist* to store the last aggregate values for each group value. When an item from steam comes in, GIC updates the sliding window and gets the expired items set *SetA* and *SetB*, and then processes joins: $\{f\} \times SWB$, *SetA*×*SWB*, *SetB*×(*SWA*\\$\{f\}$) and *SetA*×*SetB*. GIC updates each group aggregate value stored in *Glist* according to the join results. Finally, the *Glist* is output. If the query also has the Having clause, a predicate is used to filter the *Glist* value.

5.2 Processing Multi-way Sliding Window Join Aggregate

Multi-way sliding window join processing issue has been discussed by Lukasz in [15]. They combined some binary join operators and reorganized the query plan dynamically. Viglas et al proposed the alternative of extending existed symmetric binary operators to handle more than two inputs, and completed an implementation of multiway join operator, *Mjoin* [16]. It is straight to apply *Mjoin* operator to handle multiway sliding window join. As is shown in figure 8, when a new item arrives in, it is inserted into the corresponding sliding window, and then invalidates all the sliding window's expired items. The new item probes the others sliding windows and outputs the join results.

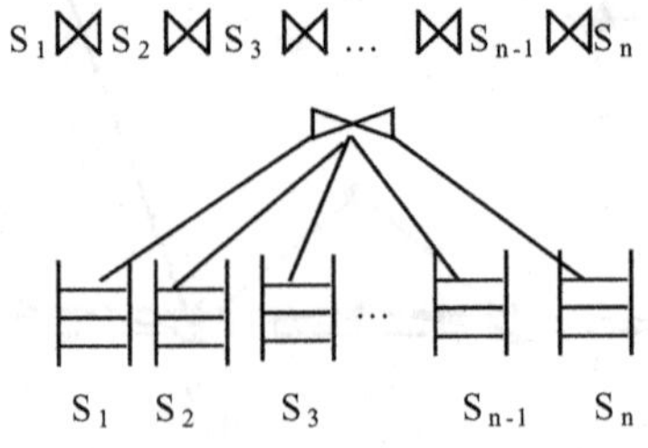

$$s_1 \bowtie s_2 \bowtie s_3 \bowtie \dots \bowtie s_{n-1} \bowtie s_n$$

Fig. 8. Mjoin operator

We process the multi-way sliding window join aggregate based on *Mjoin* operator. As an example, TC algorithm is extended to process the multi-way sliding window join aggregate. The new algorithm is named as MTC algorithm. When a new item f arrives in from stream s_1, a set of join results are produced after the execution of *Mjoin*. Each join result r can be represented as $f o g_2 o \dots o g_n$, where $g_i \in SW_i$. Because the invalidation of any g_i can cause join result r expire, the time to live for r is decide by the item g_k that arrive in system the earliest among the items g_2, g_3, ... , g_n. Since the contribution of r to the COUNT value is one, let $g_k.CV$ add one. According to theorem 3:

$$\left| SW_1 \times SW_2 \times \cdots \times SW_n \right| = \sum_{i=1}^{n} \sum_{g \in S_i} g.cv$$

MTC algorithm calculates the multi-way sliding window join aggregate according to this formula.

5.3 Experiment Results

We implement four algorithms GSC, GPC, GIC and GTC to handle the sliding window join aggregate query that contains Group By clause, which extends from SC, PC, IC and TC algorithm respectively. The performances of the four algorithms are tested in this experiment. As is shown in figure 9, in constant streaming rate, GIC has the optimal performance.

The performance of processing multi-way sliding window join aggregate is also tested. We implement three algorithms MSC, MPC and MTC, which base on SC, PC and TC correspondingly. Among the three algorithms, MTC executes the most efficient. As figure 10 illustrates, with the sliding window number grows up, the performance of MSC and MPC decrease sharply, while MTC algorithm is still efficient.

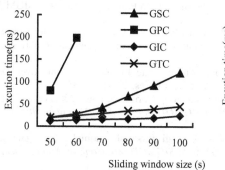

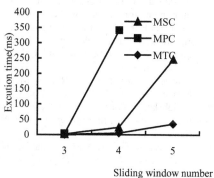

Fig. 9. Processing Group By clause ($\lambda_a = \lambda_h = 100$, $M = 100$, $\sigma = 0.01$)

Fig. 10. Processing Multi-SW join aggregate ($\lambda_a = \lambda_h = 100$, $T_a = T_h = 10s$, $M = 100$, $\sigma = 0.01$)

6 Conclusions and Future Work

Sliding window is an often-used method to restrict the range of continuous queries over unbounded data streams. Many effective methods for processing sliding windows queries have been investigated, however, to our knowledge no algorithm for processing sliding windows join aggregate has been proposed to date in the literature. We present three novel sliding window join aggregate algorithms: SC, IC and TC. Theoretical analysis and experiment results show the proposed algorithms are efficient. Since the algorithms performance vary with stream arrival rate, a scheduling algorithm is also presented to maximize the processing efficiency.

In this paper we only consider aggregate function COUNT. It is easy to extend the proposed algorithms to handle aggregate function SUM and AVG. But these methods are not suitable for processing aggregate function MAX and MIN. In future work, we plan to investigate the algorithms for processing MAX and MIN over the sliding window join results.

References

1. Brian Babcock. Shivnath Babu. Mayur Datar. Rajeev Motwani. Jennifer Widom, Models and Issues in Data Stream Systems. In Proc. ACM SIGACT\SIGMOD Symp.on Principles of Database Systems, 2002: 1-16.
2. Y. Yao, J. Gehrke. Query Processing in Sensor Networks. In Proc. 1st Biennial Conf. On Innovative Data Syst. Res (CIDR), 2003: 233-244
3. D. Carney, U. Cetintemel, M. Cherniack, C. Convey, S. Lee, G. Seidman, M. Stonebraker,N. Tatbul, S. Zdonik. Monitoring streams-A New Class of Data Management Applications. In Proc. 28th Int. Conf. on Very Large Data Bases, 2002: 215-226
4. S. Madden, M. Shah, J. M. Hellerstein, and V. Raman. Continuously Adaptive Continuous Queries over Streams. In *SIGMOD*, 2002.:49-60
5. S. Chandrasekaran, M. J. Franklin. Streaming Queries over Streaming Data. In Proc. 28th Int. Conf. on Very Large Data Bases, 2002: 203-214
6. A. Arasu, B. Babcock, S. Babu, J. McAlister, J. Widom. Characterizing Memory Requirements for Queries over Continuous Data Streams. In Proc. ACM SIGACT-SIGMOD Symp.on Principles of Database Systems, 2002 : 221-232.
7. A. Arasu, S. Babu, J. Widom. An Abstract Semantics and Concrete Language for Continuous Queries over Streams and Relations. Stanford University Technical Report 2002-57,November 2002.
8. Gurmeet Singh Manku _Rajeev Motwani. Approximate Frequency Counts over Data Streams. In Proc. 28th Int. Conf. on Very Large Data Bases, 2002: 346-357
9. J. Gehrke, F. Korn, and D. Srivastava. On Computing Correlated Aggregates over Continual Data Streams. In *Proc. of the 2001 ACM SIGMOD Intl. Conf. on Management of Data*, September 2001.
10. A. Dobra, J. Gehrke,M. Garofalakis, and R. Rastogi. Processing complex aggregate queries over data streams. In *Proc. of the 2002 ACM SIGMOD Intl. Conf. on Management of Data*, 2002.
11. A. N. Wilschut, P. M. G. Apers: Dataflow Query Execution in a Parallel Main-Memory Environment. PDIS 1991: 68-77
12. M. Datar, A. Gionis, P. Indyk, R. Motwani. Maintaining Stream Statistics over Sliding Windows. In Proc. 13th SIAM-ACM Symposium on Discrete Algorithms, 2002: 635-644.
13. P. J. Haas, J. M. Hellerstein: Ripple Joins for Online Aggregation. SIGMOD Conference 1999: 287-298
14. Jaewoo Kang. Jeffery F.Naughton. Stratis D. Viglas. Evaluating Window Joins over Unbounded Streams. ICDE Conference 2003.
15. Lukasz Golab. M.Tamer Ozsu. Processing Sliding Window Multi-Joins in Continuous Queries over Data Streams. Waterloo University Technical Report CS-2003-01. February 2003.
16. Stratis D. Viglas Jeffrey F. Naughton Josef Burger. Maximizing the Output Rate of Multi-Way Join Queries over Streaming Information Sources. In Proc. of the 2003 Intl. Conf. on Very Large Data Bases

Appendix A

Theorem 1. Given four relations: A, B, C and D, the following equation is true.

$|(C \times D)| = |(A \times B)| + |(C \backslash A) \times D| + |(D \backslash B) \times C| - |(C \backslash A) \times (D \backslash B)| - |(A \backslash C) \times (B \cap D)| - |(B \backslash D) \times (A \cap C)| - |(A \backslash C) \times (B \backslash D)|$

Proof. According to the rule $(A \backslash B) \times C = (A \times C) \backslash (B \times C)$, then

$|(C \backslash A) \times (D \backslash B)| = |(C \backslash A) \times D \backslash (C \backslash A) \times B| = |(C \backslash A) \times D| - |(C \backslash A) \times D \cap (C \backslash A) \times B| = |(C \backslash A) \times D| - |(C \backslash A) \times (D \cap B)|$, similarly, $|(A \backslash C) \times (B \backslash D)| = |(A \backslash C) \times B| - |(A \backslash C) \times (B \cap D)|$

So the right side of the equation in theorem 1, $|(A \times B)| + |(C \backslash A) \times D| + |(D \backslash B) \times C| - |(C \backslash A) \times (D \backslash B)| - |(A \backslash C) \times (B \cap D)| - |(B \backslash D) \times (A \cap C)| - |(A \backslash C) \times (B \backslash D)| = |(A \times B)| + |(C \backslash A) \times D| + |(D \backslash B) \times C| - |(C \backslash A) \times D| + |(C \backslash A) \times (D \cap B)| - |(A \backslash C) \times (B \cap D)| - |(B \backslash D) \times (A \cap C)| - |(A \backslash C) \times B| + |(A \backslash C) \times (B \cap D)| = |(A \times B)| + |(D \backslash B) \times C| + |(C \backslash A) \times (D \cap B)| - |(B \backslash D) \times (A \cap C)| - |(A \backslash C) \times B|$.

According to the follow equation:

$|(C \backslash A) \times (D \cap B)| = |C \times (D \cap B) \backslash A \times (D \cap B)| = |C \times (D \cap B)| - |C \times (D \cap B) \cap A \times (D \cap B)| = |C \times (D \cap B)| - |(C \cap A) \times (D \cap B)|$.

Similarly $|(B \backslash D) \times (A \cap C)| = |B \times (A \cap C)| - |(B \cap D) \times (A \cap C)|$. Then $|(A \times B)| + |(D \backslash B) \times C| + |(C \backslash A) \times (D \cap B)| - |(B \backslash D) \times (A \cap C)| - |(A \backslash C) \times B| = |(A \times B)| + |(D \backslash B) \times C| + |C \times (D \cap B)| - |(C \cap A) \times (D \cap B)| - |B \times (A \cap C)| + |(B \cap D) \times (A \cap C)| - |(A \backslash C) \times B| = |(A \times B)| + |(D \backslash B) \times C| + |C \times (D \cap B)| - |B \times (A \cap C)| - |(A \backslash C) \times B| = |(A \times B)| + |D \times C \backslash B \times C| + |C \times (D \cap B)| - |B \times (A \cap C)| - |A \times B \backslash C \times B| = |(A \times B)| + |D \times C| - |(D \times C) \cap (B \times C)| + |C \times (D \cap B)| - |B \times (A \cap C)| - |A \times B| + |(A \times B) \cap (C \times B)| = |(A \times B)| + |D \times C| - |(D \cap B) \times C| + |C \times (D \cap B)| - |B \times (A \cap C)| - |A \times B| + |(A \cap C) \times B| = |D \times C| = |C \times D|$.   □

How to Integrate Heterogeneous Spatial Databases in a Consistent Way?

David Sheeren[1,3], Sébastien Mustière[1], and Jean-Daniel Zucker[2,3]

[1] COGIT Laboratory, Institut Géographique National,
94165 Saint-Mandé Cedex, France
{David.Sheeren,Sebastien.Mustiere}@ign.fr
http://recherche.ign.fr/activ/cogit/index.html
[2] LIM&BIO, University of Paris 13
[3] LIP6 Laboratory, AI Section, University of Paris 6
{Jean-Daniel.Zucker}@lip6.fr

Abstract. There currently exist many geographical databases that represent a same part of the world, each with its own levels of detail and points of view. The use and management of these databases sometimes requires their integration into a single database. One important issue in this integration process is the ability to analyse and understand the differences among the multiple representations. These differences can of course be explained by the various specifications but can also be due to updates or errors during data capture. In this paper, after describing the overall process of integrating spatial databases, we propose a process to interpret the differences between two representations of the same geographic phenomenon. Each step of the process is based on the use of an expert system. Rules guiding the process are either introduced by hand from the analysis of specifications, or automatically learnt from examples. The process is illustrated through the analysis of the representations of traffic circles in two actual databases.

1 Introduction

In recent years, a new challenge has emerged from the growing availability of heterogeneous databases: their interoperability. The combination of multiple sources can be lead to several solutions: "multidatabase" systems [1], "federated" systems [2] or "distributed database" [3].

Database integration has already received much attention in the literature. Some contribution concerns the problem of *schema integration*, for which a survey of the different approaches can be found in [4,5]. The schema matching reveals various differences and conflicts between elements (semantic conflicts, structural conflicts,...) and several propositions exist to solve them [6,7]. Other works have focused on the problem of *data integration*. Procedural or declarative approaches can be adopted to achieve it [4,8]. Other contributions propose to help the integration with artificial intelligence techniques [9], in particular, with knowledge representation and reasoning techniques [10].

A. Benczúr, J. Demetrovics, G. Gottlob (Eds.): ADBIS 2004, LNCS 3255, pp. 364–378, 2004.

In the field of geographical databases (GDB), the integration becomes an issue of growing interest. The combination of multiple sources aims to increase the potentiality of applications development. It can also help the producers to maintain their databases in a more consistent way: updates can be propagated automatically and quality controls can be facilitated [11]. According to the strategy, the integration can lead to the creation of a composite product or a multi-representation system. Specific tools for merging geometrical data have been proposed [12] as data models and structures to support multiple representations [13,14,15].

Today, an important issue has still to be solved: the detection and management of inconsistencies between the geographical representations. Objects of the databases may be collected according to different specifications and can thus present various modelizations. These differences are generally normal and reflect the multiple levels of details of the databases and their application domains. However, incompatibilities can exist between representations deriving from updates or errors during the data collect. These inconsistencies are more problematic because the user of the system can be confronted with contradictory results when using one representation or an other. Incompatibilities can relate to the shape and position of the objects as well as attributes and spatial relations. Few works tackle this problem and in general, the propositions deal with the consistency of topological relations and they presuppose an order between representations [16,17].

In this paper, a new approach is proposed to assess the consistency between the geometrical representations of geographical data. The approach is based on the following points:

- The use of background knowledge and in particular, the specifications of each database, to justify the difference between multiple representations.
- The use of a rule-based system to manipulate this knowledge and check the consistency in an automatic way.
- The use of machine learning techniques to acquire the knowledge when the specifications are not available, ambiguous or incomplete.

The paper is structured as follows. First, we present the integration process for spatial databases and discuss about its particularities (section 2). Then, we detail the elements of our approach and present the architecture of the system implemented (section 3). We illustrate the feasibility of the process with a particular application (section 4). Then, we conclude the paper and give some research perspectives (section 5).

2   Spatial Database Integration Process

2.1   Specificity's

The unification of vector spatial databases requires adaptations of classical integration methodologies [18,19]. These adaptations mainly result from the existence of a geometry associated to the data. The geometry makes the correspondence identification more complex and introduce specific conflicts between the data.

For instance, particular matching tools are necessary to define the correspondences between the data of the different sources because in general, it is not possible to declare a common identifier as for the classical databases. Only the position of the objects can be exploited. Generally, the matching algorithms are thus based on the computation of distances between geometric locations. Some of them also used additional criteria as the shape of the objects and the topological relations they have [20,21,22].

Specifics conflicts also appear between the data [23]. It concerns both spatial representations and attributes. The conditions of representation of the objects can be different from one database to another and it can lead to *specifications conflicts*(figure 1). For instance, an object can be represented in one database but be absent in the other (*selection conflict*) or this object can correspond to a group of primitives in the second database (*decomposition conflict* leading to a *fragmentation conflict* at the data level). These conflicts must be identified during the declaration of correspondences, and integration techniques must be extended to solve them [18].

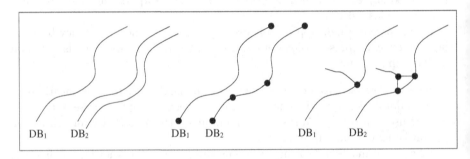

Fig. 1. Different representations of a same geographical phenomenon leading to several conflicts between data.

Another important particularity of the spatial databases, which makes the integration process more complex, is the existence of lots of implicit information. There is a gap between what we perceive when we visualise the geometrical instances and what is actually stored in the databases. For example, it is easy to identify at the screen the main road that leads to a particular town, or the most sinuous river among a set of objects of this category, but this information ("main", "leads", "sinuous") are not explicitly stored in the databases. However, the integration frequently requires the extraction of this kind of information in order to homogenise the different sources and to check the consistency of the representations (see section 4). Specifics tools of spatial analysis are generally required to achieve this extraction.

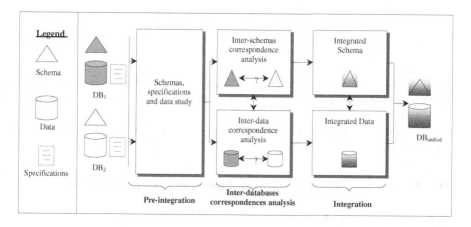

Fig. 2. Main steps of the spatial databases integration process

2.2 Main Steps of the Integration Process

The main steps of the spatial integration process are illustrated in figure 2. They can be connected with the three phases defined for classical databases: the *pre-integration*, the *correspondences investigation* and the *integration* (see [24] for a detailed description). The first task consists in the study of each database, to have a good understanding of the content, and to prepare the integration. A detailed analysis of the specifications is undertaken and several modifications at the schema and data levels are realized. The schemas are rearranged in different ways to make them more homogeneous semantically and syntactically. The spatial data are enriched by extracting the implicit information.

For this first step, an important issue concerns the specifications analysis phase. These documents are usually expressed in natural language and thus in a poorly formalised language. For geographical databases, they are particularly huge and detailed. Their manipulation is a hard task, and their automatic manipulation is almost impossible. We have recently proposed a model to better formalise these specifications and used them in a more pratical way [25], but this research is still in progress [26].

The second task aims at identifying and declaring correspondences between the elements of the schemas and the geometrical instances of the databases. Similar elements and conflicts at the schema level can be defined with a particular language. For instance, [8] proposes some clauses to specify respectively what are the related schema elements (the *Interdatabase Correspondence Assertions - ICA*), how the schemas elements are related using the relationships holds, how corresponding instances are identified (*With Corresponding Identifiers - WCI*), and how representations are related (*With Corresponding Attributes - WCA*). At the data level, the elements are put in correspondence with matching algorithms. A particular clause refers to it: the *Spatial Data Matching (SDM)* [18].

For this step, a current issue concerns the assessment of consistency between the spatial representations. It is necessary to detect errors before to integrate the data. This is our research problem and we present our approach in the next section.

The last tasks concern the actual integration. According to the specifications of the unified database, the new schema is defined. It supposes to have rules to translate and restructure the initial schemas. Data instances are also integrated. As the case may be, representations are merged or kept and transferred in the new system.

3   Consistency Assessment Between Spatial Data

3.1   Our Overall Approach

Our approach to assess the consistency between representations is illustrated in figure 3. The process is decomposed in several steps. We briefly describe it below but each phase will be detailed throughout the application developed in section 4.

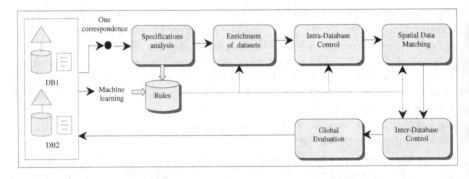

Fig. 3. The reasoning path to assess the consistency between multiple representations

The process starts with *one correspondence* between classes of the schemas of the two databases. We presume that matching at the schema level has already been carried out. It remains to compute and study the correspondences between instances at the data level. *One correspondence* can be expressed in terms of ICA [8]. For example, we know that the *building* class in DB$_1$ tallies with the *residential building* and *commercial building* classes in DB$_2$, which can be expressed in the form:

DB1.*Building* ≡ DB$_2$.(*ResidentialBuilding, CommercialBuilding*).

The task of *specifications analysis* is the next step. The specifications are analysed in order to determine several rule bases that will be used to guide each of the ensuing steps. These rules primarily describe what exactly the databases contain, what differences are likely to appear, and in which conditions. In that sense, these rules constitute the whole necessary knowledge for the assessment process. Basically, this step is performed through the analysis of documents. However, these documents are sometimes not available or their description are incomplete and ambiguous. In these cases, knowledge elicitation techniques can be used in order to learn these specifications or to complete them [27].

The next step concerns the *enrichment* of each dataset. As we have already mentioned, the aim is to extract implicit information in order to express the datasets in a more homogeneous way. The enrichment leads to the creation of new objects and relations.

A preliminary step of control is then planned: the *intra-database control*. During this step, part of the specifications is checked so as to detect some internal errors and determine how the data instances globally respect specifications.

Once the data of both databases have been independently controlled, we match them. The relationships are computed through geometric and topologic data matching. Each pair is then validated and characterised by a degree of confidence.

The *inter-database control* follows this step. It consists in the comparison of the representations of the homologous objects. This comparison leads to the evaluation of the conformity of the differences. At the end, differences existing between each matching pair are expressed in terms of *equivalence* (differences justified by the specifications), *inconsistency* (matching or capture error) or *update*.

After the interpretation of all the differences, a global evaluation is supplied: the number of equivalencies, the number of errors and their seriousness, and the number of differences due to updates.

3.2   Which Knowledge Is Required to Check the Consistency?

Our approach is founded on the use of the specifications of each GDB to guide the assessment of the consistency. These metadata enable to justify if the differences in representation are normal or not, since they define the content of the databases and the modelization of the objects. In general, the specifications are described in natural language, in paper documents. Thus, this information seems easily exploitable for the task of checking the representations. Nevertheless, it is possible that the specifications only exist through the data. They are not always explicitly described in documents. And when they exist, the description of the representation often lack of exhaustivity because it is difficult to imagine all the possible cases liable to appear in the field. In addition, the capture constraints are often insufficiently formalised and can lead to ambiguous interpretation (for instance: *when a crossroads is "vast", a polygon is created*). Other background knowledge is also required for the process. For example, information relating to the quality of the datasets is necessary in order to fix the parameters of the matching algorithms, or else, common geographical knowledge is useful when the specifications are not sufficient to explain the differences, principally in the case of updates. In fact, the main challenge to assess the consistency is the acquisition of this knowledge. Experts in the field could define the knowledge they use when the specifications are not available but in general, these experts are rarely able to supply an explicit description of it. This key problem is well-known as the "*knowledge acquisition bottleneck*".

3.3   How to Acquire the Knowledge?

To face this issue, we have decided to use supervised machine learning techniques [28,29]. This induction process is one of the solutions developed in the Artificial Intelligence field. Its aim is to automatically derive some rules from a set of labelled examples given by an expert and to apply these learning rules to classify other examples with unknown classification. In our context, these techniques can be used at several steps. First, during the specifications analysis phase, when capture criteria are too complex or imprecise to draw knowledge by hand in the form of rules. In this case, inductive tools can be performed to grasp the necessary knowledge and organise it. Second, during the enrichment phase. The learning algorithms can be used to extract implicit information. Then, during the matching step. Parameters of geometrical matching procedures can be learned (for instance, the distance threshold to select candidates). Finally, these techniques can help to describe each matching pairs in terms of *equivalence* or *inconsistency* during the inter-database control [30].

3.4   How to Manipulate the Knowledge in an Automatic Way?

We have opted for the use of an expert-system. Such systems have already proved to be efficient in numerous fields where complex knowledge needs to be introduced. They dissociate the knowledge embedded in rules and tools in order to handle them [31]. This specificity gives them a large flexibility because it is possible to introduce a large number of rules, and because the rules can be analysed, added, modified or removed in a very simple way. In addition, the *inference engine* itself determines the activation of rules while handling in a procedural way could turn out to be quite hard if not impossible. In other respects, we have split into several steps the reasonning path of the task (figure 3). In that way, we have adopted an approach of second generation expert-systems [31], considering the control over the inferences as a kind of knowledge in itself and introducing it explicitly in the system.

3.5   Architecture of the System

Two main modules compose the general architecture of our system (figure 4): the experimental *Oxygene Geographical Information System* and the *Jess* expert-system. *Oxygene* is a platform developed at the COGIT laboratory [32]. Spatial data is stored in the relational *Oracle* DBMS, and the manipulation of data is performed with the *Java* code in the object oriented paradigm. The mapping between the relational tables and the *Java* classes is done by the *OJB* library. A *Java* API exists to make the link between this platform and the second module,

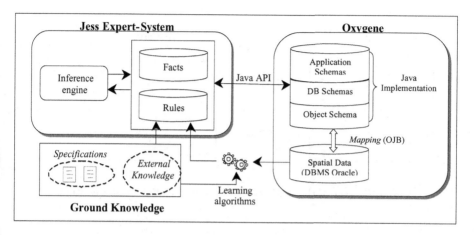

Fig. 4. Overall architecture of the system

the *Jess* rule-based system. The latter is an open source environment which can be tightly coupled to a code written in *Java* language [33]. The rules used by *Jess* originate directly from the specifications, or have been gathered with the learning tools.

4 Experimentation

4.1 The Case Study

We have decided to implement the process described above for dealing with the case of traffic circles of two databases from the French National Mapping Agency: BDCarto and Georoute. These databases have been defined according to different specifications, in order to fulfil different application domains and analysis levels. The first one present a decametric resolution and aims at satisfying application needs at regional and departmental levels. The other one, Georoute, is a database with a metric resolution dedicated to traffic applications (figure 5). Among these data, we will identify and select the traffic circles to study the inter-representations consistency.

4.2 Pre-integration

Two steps of our process can be connected to the pre-integration phase: the *specifications analysis* and the *enrichment* of spatial data.

Specification Analysis. For both databases, the specifications mention that the traffic circles may have one of the two representations: a point (simple representation) or a group of connected point and lines (complex representation). The selection of the representation is dictated by the diameter of the object in

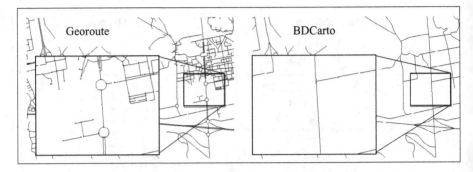

Fig. 5. Extract of the road theme of the two spatial databases studied

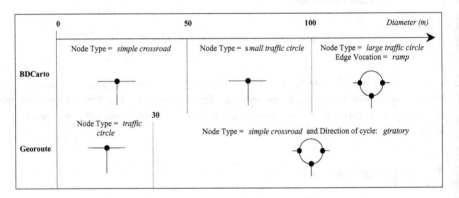

Fig. 6. Some specifications concerning the representation of the traffic circles of BD-Carto and Georoute

the real world and the presence of a central reservation. These selection criteria are different from one database to another (figure 6).

The traffic circles classes are thus not explicitly in the two databases. In the case of the point representation, a particular value of the 'node kind' attribute can be used to select them. In the case of complex representation, it is necessary to resort to specific geometric tools to extract the detailed representation. This is done in the next step of the process.

Enrichment. The enrichment of the databases concerns both data and schemas. Introducing the traffic circles in the data supposes the definition of new classes and relations at the schema level, as their instanciation (figure 7). The creation of these objects is a first step towards the identification of *federative concepts* [26], corresponding to geographical entities defined independently of the representation. The correspondence between these concepts and the objects of each database would enable to help the creation of the unified schema. It comes close to the notion of *ontology* [34].

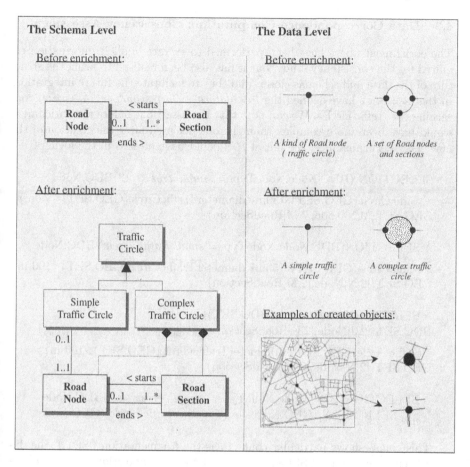

Fig. 7. The enrichment step induces modifications at the schema and data levels

The extraction of the traffic circles have required several steps for each database. First, we dealt with the *simple traffic circles*. The class was created and instanciated, as well as the relation with the *road nodes*. This task did not present any difficulty since the simple traffic circles are road nodes for which the attribute *nature* takes the value '*traffic circle*' (this is the case for Georoute). Then, we extracted the *complex traffic circle*. In a first time, we computed a topological graph (a planar graph with faces). Each face was characterised with a circularity index, the number of nodes associated and the direction of the cycle. We defined specific rules concerning those criteria and introduced them in our decision support system. Each face was analysed and finally, only faces corresponding to a traffic circle were retained. Each complex traffic circle was thus created with a polygonal geometry.

4.3   Data Correspondence Computation: Consistency Assessment

The enrichment phase have been performed to extract implicit information required for the consistency study, but it has also been realised to bring the structure of the data and schemas closer, and thus to facilitate the future integration.
In that sense, we have defined the *Interdatabase Correspondence Assertion* concerning the traffic circles. We can note that the assertions before the enrichment
would have been more complex than the one declared after the creation of the
new classes. For instance, the initial *ICA* could be expressed in the form of:

SELECTION (BDC.Node.NodeType=*'simple crossroad'*)BDC.Node
$\supseteq$trafficCircle(GEO.SET)$\wedge$(30m<diameterTrafficCircle(GEO.SET)< 50m)
GEO.SET([2,N]Node,[2,M]RoadSection)

$\wedge$ SELECTION(BDC.Node.NodeType=*'small traffic circle'*)BDC.Node
$\equiv$trafficCircle(GEO.SET)$\wedge$(50m<diameterTrafficCircle(GEO.SET)<100 m)
GEO.SET([2,N]Node,[2,M]RoadSection)

$\wedge$ SELECTION(trafficCircle(BDC.SET))
BDC.SET([2,J]Node,[2,K]RoadSection$_{\text{WHERE(BDC.RoadSection.Vocation='ramp')}}$)
$\equiv$trafficCircle(GEO.SET)$\wedge$(diameterTrafficCircle(GEO.SET)>100 m)
GEO.SET([2,N]Node,[2,M]RoadSection)

$\wedge$ SELECTION(BDC.Node.NodeType=*'simple crossroad'*)BDC.Node
$\supseteq_{\text{else}}$ SELECTION (GEO.Node.NodeType=*'traffic circle'*)GEO.Node

This clause shows particular conflicts as the fragmentation ('SET'), the different selection criteria ('SELECTION') and the decomposition conflicts (a relationship hold with a decomposition criterion). The *ICA* after the enrichment
can take the following form, much simpler:

BDC.SimpleTrafficCircle $\supseteq$ GEO.SimpleTrafficCircle OR
SELECTION(diameterTrafficCircle<100(GEO.ComplexTrafficCircle))
GEO.ComplexTrafficCircle

BDC.COMPLEXTRAFFICCIRCLE $\equiv$
SELECTION(diameterTrafficCircle>100(GEO.ComplexTrafficCircle))
GEO.ComplexTrafficCircle

Intra-Database Control. A this level, the representations of the objects are
checked to detect some internal errors. For instance, we controlled that each
simple traffic circle was not in a *cul-de-sac*. The specifications of Georoute indicate that such a node can not take the *'traffic circle'* value for the *'nature'*
attribute. Concerning the complex objects, we systematically checked the diameter, the number of nodes and the direction of the cycle. The control was

automated thanks to several rules activated by the expert-system. These rules were developed and introduced by hand. For example:

(defrule control_diameter_georoute
(if diameter < 30)
⇒
(set diameterConformity "not conform"))

In some cases, several possible interpretations were assigned for a same representation since there was some uncertainty regarding the conformity of the representation. For example, it is not possible to control the existence of a central reservation even though the presence of this object govern the selection of the traffic circles. Some of these uncertainties were removed after *the inter-database control.*

Spatial Data Matching. We developed specific tools to match our data. The algorithms use Euclidean distance and intersection criteria: objects are matched if they are close or if they intersect each other. Only 8% of matching errors have been detected interactively for a total of 124 matching pairs.

In order to increase the reliability of the matching phase and detect these errors automatically, we decided to use the results of an other matching procedure. The algorithms used and developed by [21] rely on other criteria: especially the Hausdorff's distance and the topological relationships. With these results, we only retained the identical pairs in the two procedures, that is to say, 82% of matching pairs. We considered them as certain. In general, the matching errors made with the two methods were not the same and we envisage to improve the algorithms exploiting the hole of the criteria (see figure 8).

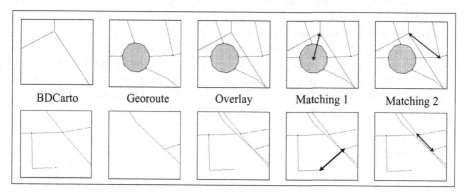

Fig. 8. Some results of the matching step computed with the two processes

Inter-database Control. Some internal errors were already detected during the first step of control but the representations of the two databases had not been compared. This is the aim of this phase.

The introduction of rules by hand in the expert-system was first considered, but because of numerous possible cases and the complexity of some rules, we decided to use supervised machine learning. An example of a rule computed by the C5.0. algorithm [35] is presented below. It enables the detection of an inconsistency:

> *If the type of the traffic circle in Georoute = 'dot'*
> *And the node type of the traffic circle in BDCarto = 'small traffic circle'*
> *Then the representations are inconsistent.*

This step, as well as the last steps, are work in progress. The comparison will lead to the classification of each matching pair in terms of *equivalence* and *inconsistency*. The rules gathered from the machine learning shall be analysed to evaluate their consistency according to the specifications. Finally, a global evaluation will be provided.

5   Conclusion

This paper has given an overview of the spatial databases integration process with its specificity's, and has pointed to several key issues, among these, the assessment of consistency between multiple representations.

We have proposed a new approach to deal with that problem, considering the specifications of the GDB as the principal knowledge to check the conformity of each representation. Because of the complexity of this knowledge and sometimes, its inadequacy, we have decided to adopt an approach combining the intervention of experts in the field and machine learning techniques to acquire these specifications. The automatic activation of the learning rules is then provided thanks to an expert-system.

The process have been tested in a real context, with two spatial databases of the French National Mapping Agency. The application developped demonstrates the feasibility of the approach . The last steps of the process are being implemented. Further research has to focus on the interpretation of differences in a context where no explicit capture constraints exist.

References

1. Hurson, A., Bright, M.: Multidatabase systems: An advanced concept in handling distributed data. Advances in Computers **32** (1992) 149–200
2. Sheth, A., Larson, J.: Federated database systems for managing distributed heterogeneous, and autonomous databases. ACM Computing Surveys **22** (1990) 183–236
3. Özsu, M., Valduriez, P.: Principles of Distributed Database Systems. Prentice-Hall (1999)

4. Batini, C., Lenzerini, M., Navathe, S.B.: A comparative analysis of methodologies for database schema integration. ACM Computing Surveys **18** (1986) 323–364
5. Rahm, E., Bernstein, P.: A survey of approaches to automatic schema matching. Very Large Database Journal **10** (2001) 334–350
6. Dupont, Y.: Resolving fragmentation conflicts in schema integration. In: Proceedings of the International Conference on Conceptual Modeling/Entity Relationship Approach, Springer-Verlag, LNCS n° 881 (1994)
7. Kim, W., Choi, I., Gala, S., Scheevel, M.: On resolving schematic heterogeneity in multidatabase systems. Distributed and Parallel Databases Journal **1** (1993) 251–279
8. Spaccapietra, S., Parent, C., Dupont, Y.: Model independant assertions for integration of heterogeneous schemas. Very Large Database Journal **1** (1992) 81–126
9. Levy, A.: Combining artificial intelligence and database for data integration. In: Special Issue, Artificial Intelligence Today, Recent Trends and Developments, Springer-Verlag, LNAI (1999)
10. Calvanese, D., Giacomo, G.D., Lenzerini, M., Nardi, D., Rosati, R.: Knowledge representation approach to information integration. In: Proceedings of AAAI Workshop on Artificial Intelligence and Information Integration, AAAI Press/The MIT Press (1998) 58–65
11. Lemarie, C., Badard, T.: Cartographic database updating. In: Proceedings of the 20th International Cartographic Conference (ICC). Volume 2. (2001) 1376–1385
12. Devogele, T.: A new merging process for data integration based on the discrete fréchet distance. In: Proceedings of the 10th International Symposium on Spatial Data Handling (SDH). (2002) 167–181
13. Vangenot, C., Parent, C., Spaccapietra, S.: Modeling and manipulating multiple representations of spatial data. In: Proceedings of the 10th International Symposium on Spatial Data Handling (SDH). (2002) 81–93
14. Kidner, D., Jones, C.: A deductive object-oriented gis for handling multiple representations. In: Proceedings of the 6th International Symposium on Spatial Data Handling (SDH). Volume 2. (1994) 882–900
15. Timpf, S., Frank, A.: A multi-scale dag for cartographic objects. In: Proceedings of Auto-Carto 12. (1995) 157–163
16. Egenhofer, M., Clementini, E., Felice, P.D.: Evaluating inconsistencies among multiple representations. In: Proceedings of the 6th International Symposium on Spatial Data Handling (SDH). Volume 2. (1994) 901–920
17. El-Geresy, B., Abdelmoty, A.: A qualitative approach to integration in spatial databases. In: Proceedings of the 9th International Conference on Database and Expert Systems Applications (DEXA), Springer-Verlag, LNCS n° 1460 (1998)
18. Devogele, T., Parent, C., Spaccapietra, S.: On spatial database integration. International Journal of Geographical Information Science **12** (1998) 335–352
19. Strauch, J., de Souza, J.M., Mattoso, M.: A methodology for gis databases integration. In: Technical Report, Federal University of Rio de Janeiro. (1998)
20. BelHadjAli, A.: Qualité géométrique des entités surfaciques. Application à lappariement et définition dune typologie des écarts géométriques. Phd thesis, Université de Marne-la-Vallée (2001)
21. Devogele, T.: Processus d'intégration et d'appariement de bases de données géographiques; application à une base de données routières multi-échelles. Phd thesis in computer science, Université de Versailles (1997)
22. Walter, V., Fritsch, D.: Matching spatial data sets: a statistical approach. International Journal of Geographical Information Science **13** (1999) 445–473

23. Parent, C., Spaccapietra, S., Devogele, T.: Conflicts in spatial database integration. In: Proceedings of the 9th International Conference on Parallel and Distributed Computing Systems. (1996) 772–778
24. Parent, C., Spaccapietra, S.: Database integration: the key to data interoperability. In: Advances in Object-Oriented Data Modeling. The MIT Press (2001)
25. Mustiere, S., Gesbert, N., Sheeren, D.: A formal model for the specifications of geographic databases. In: Proceedings of the Workshop on Semantic Processing of Spatial Databases (GeoPro). (2003) 152–159
26. Gesbert, N., Libourel, T., Mustière, S.: Apport des spécifications pour les modèles de bases de données géographiques. Revue Internationale de Géomatique (under review) (2004)
27. Mitchell, T.M.: Machine Learning. McGraw-Hill International Editions (1997)
28. Sester, M.: Knowledge acquisition for the automatic interpretation of spatial data. International Journal of Geographical Information Science **14** (2000) 1–24
29. Malerba, D., Esposito, F., Lanza, A., Lisi, F., Appice, A.: Machine learning for information extraction from topographic maps. In: Geographic Data Mining and Knowledge Discovery. Taylor and Francis (2001) 291–314
30. Sheeren, D.: Spatial databases integration: Interpretation of multiple representations by using machine learning techniques. In: Proceedings of the 21st International Cartographic Conference (ICC). (2003) 235–245
31. David, J.M., Krivine, J.P., Simmons, R.: Second Generation Expert Systems. Springer Verlag (1993)
32. Badard, T., Braun, A.: Oxygene: an open framework for the deployment of geographic web services. In: Proceedings of the 21st International Cartographic Conference (ICC). (2003) 994–1003
33. Jess: A rule engine for the java platform. In: http://herzberg.ca.sandia.gov/jess/. (2003)
34. Visser, U., Stuckenschmidt, H., Schuster, G., Vogele, T.: Ontologies for geographic information processing. Computers and Geosciences **28** (2002) 103–117
35. Quilan, J.R.: C4.5 : Programs for machine learning. Morgan Kaufmann (1993)

Vague Spatial Data Types,
Set Operations, and Predicates

Alejandro Pauly and Markus Schneider*

University of Florida
Department of Computer & Information Science & Engineering
Gainesville, FL 32611, USA
{apauly,mschneid}@cise.ufl.edu

Abstract. Many geographical applications deal with spatial objects that cannot be adequately described by determinate, crisp concepts because of their intrinsically indeterminate and vague nature. Current geographical information systems and spatial database systems are unable to cope with this kind of data. To support such data and applications, we introduce *vague spatial data types* for *vague points*, *vague lines*, and *vague regions*. These data types cover and extend previous approaches and are part of a data model called *VASA* (*Vague Spatial Algebra*). Their formal framework is based on already existing, general exact models of crisp spatial data types, which simplifies the definition of the vague spatial model. In addition, we obtain executable specifications for the operations which can be immediately used as implementations. This paper gives a formal definition of the three vague spatial data types as well as some basic operations and predicates. A few example queries illustrate the embedding and expressiveness of these new data types in query languages.

1 Introduction

The current mapping of spatial phenomena of the real world to exclusively crisp, i.e., precisely determined, spatial objects is an insufficient abstraction process for many geometric applications since often the feature of *spatial vagueness* or *spatial indeterminacy* is inherent to many geometric and geographic data [2]. Applications based on this kind of geometric data are so far not covered by current GIS and spatial database systems.

So far, often contrary to reality, spatial data modeling implicitly assumes that the positions of points, the locations and routes of lines, and the extent and hence the boundary of regions are precisely determined and universally recognized. The properties of the space at points, along lines, and within regions are given by attributes whose values are assumed to be constant over the whole objects. Examples are man-made spatial objects (e.g., monuments, highways, buildings) and predominantly immaterial spatial objects (e.g., countries, districts, land parcels with their political, administrative, and cadastral boundaries). We denote this kind of entities as *crisp* or *determinate spatial objects*.

On the other hand, there are many geometric applications in which positions of points are not exactly known, the locations and routes of lines are unclear, and regions do not

---

* This work was partially supported by the National Science Foundation under grant number NSF-CAREER-IIS-0347574.

A. Benczúr, J. Demetrovics, G. Gottlob (Eds.): ADBIS 2004, LNCS 3255, pp. 379–392, 2004.

have sharp boundaries, or their boundaries cannot be precisely determined. Examples are social or natural phenomena (e.g., terrorists' refuges and escape routes, population density, unemployment rate, soil quality, vegetation, oceans, oil fields, biotopes, deserts). We denote this kind of entities as *vague* or *indeterminate spatial objects*.

This paper presents an object model for defining *vague spatial data types* for *vague points*, *vague lines*, and *vague regions*. These types are part of a data model called *VASA* (*Vague Spatial Algebra*). The model rests on "traditional" (i.e., exact) modeling techniques and extends, rather than replaces, the current theory of spatial database systems and GIS. Further, moving from an exact to a vague domain does not necessarily invalidate conventional (computational) geometry; it is merely an extension. Hence, exact object models can be considered as special cases of our vague object model. All vague spatial data types and several vague spatial operations are defined generically, i.e., without type-specific definitions. Since our vague spatial data types and operations are based on their crisp counterparts and can be expressed by them, we obtain *executable specifications* that can be directly used as an implementation. In this paper, we do not aim at developing a type system with a "complete" set of operations and predicates. The goal is more to demonstrate the power, simplicity, and expressiveness of our model.

Section 2 discusses related work. Section 3 informally introduces the concept of vague spatial objects and motivates it by giving some application examples. Section 4 gives a generic definition of vague spatial data types and vague spatial set operations. Section 5 deals with type-specific operations. Section 6 introduces some vague topological predicates. Section 7 illustrates the embedding of vague spatial data types into query languages. Finally, Section 8 draws some conclusions and addresses future work.

2   Related Work

Spatial vagueness has to be seen in contrast to spatial uncertainty resulting from either a lack of knowledge about the position and shape of an object (*positional* uncertainty) or the inability of measuring such an object precisely (*measurement* uncertainty). Much literature, which we will not consider here, has been published on dealing with positional and measurement uncertainty; it mainly proposes probabilistic models. Spatial vagueness is an intrinsic feature of a spatial object where we cannot be sure whether certain components belong to the spatial object or not. Our vague spatial data types cover both aspects of spatial uncertainty and spatial vagueness.

Three main alternatives have been proposed as general design methods. *Models based on fuzzy sets* (e.g., [1,11]) are all based on fuzzy set theory, allow a much more fine-grained modeling of vague spatial objects, but are computationally much more expensive with respect to data structures and algorithms. *Models based on rough sets* (e.g., [13]) work with lower and upper approximations of spatial objects, which is similar to our approach. But the formal background is rather different. *Models based on exact spatial objects* (e.g., [3,4,10,6] extend data models, type systems, and concepts for crisp spatial objects to vague spatial objects. The model described in this paper belongs to this latter category.

A benefit of the exact object model approach is that existing definitions, techniques, data structures, algorithms, etc., need not be redeveloped but only modified and extended, or simply used. So far, four object models have been proposed for vague regions. The first three models use some kind of zone concept, either without holes [3,4] or with holes [10]. The central idea is to consider determined zones surrounding the indeterminate boundaries of a region and expressing its minimal and maximal extension. The zones serve as a description and separation of the space that certainly belongs to the region and the space that is certainly outside. While [3] and [4] are mainly interested in classifications of topological relationships between vague regions for which a simple model is assumed, [10] proposes a model of complex vague regions with vague holes and focuses on their formal definition. Unfortunately, the three approaches are limited to "concentric" object models and have problems with geometric closure properties. The model described in [6] also pursues the exact model approach but is much more general and much simpler than the other approaches. It is a precursor of this paper and introduces the concept of vague regions.

3 What Are Vague Spatial Objects?

The central idea of *vague spatial objects* is to base their definition on already well known, geometric modeling techniques. Our concept necessitates a general object model incorporating determinate spatial data types *point*, *line*, and *region* that are closed under (appropriately defined) geometric union, intersection, difference, and complement operations. Such *crisp* type systems have, e.g., been proposed in [9,7], and we will take them and their corresponding formal definition for granted in this paper. Informally, these models consider a *point* object as a finite set of individual points, a *line* object as a finite set of disjoint *blocks* where each block represents a finite set of curves, and a *region* object as a finite set of disjoint, connected areal components (called *faces*) possibly with disjoint holes (see Figure 1).

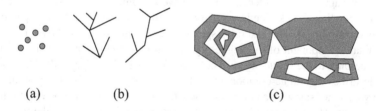

(a)   (b)   (c)

Fig. 1. Examples of a (complex crisp) point object (a), a (complex crisp) line object (b), and a (complex crisp) region object (c). Each collection of components forms a single crisp object.

As an illustrating example, we consider a homeland security scenario to introduce our concept for dealing with spatial vagueness and to demonstrate its usability. Secret services (should) have knowledge of the whereabouts of terrorists. For each terrorist, some of their refuges are precisely known, some are not and only conjectures. We can model these locations as a *vague point* object where the precisely known locations are called the *kernel point* object and the assumed locations are denoted as the *conjecture point* object. Secret services are also interested in the routes a terrorist takes to move

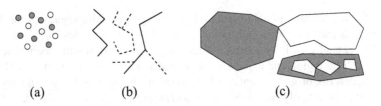

(a)   (b)   (c)

Fig. 2. Examples of a (complex) vague point object (a), a (complex) vague line object (b), and a (complex) vague region object (c). Each collection of components forms a single vague object.

from one refuge to another. These routes can be modeled as *vague line* objects. Some routes, called *kernel line* objects, have been identified. Other routes can only be assumed to be taken by a terrorist; they are denoted as *conjecture line* objects. Knowledge about areas of terroristic activities is also important for secret services. From some areas it is well known that a terrorist operates in them; we call them *kernel region* objects. From other areas we can only assume that they are the target of terroristic activity; we denote them as *conjecture region* objects. Figure 2 gives some examples. Grey shaded areas, straight lines, and grey points indicate kernel parts; areas with white interiors, dashed lines, and white points refer to conjecture parts.

Based on this scenario and taking into account spatial vagueness, we are able to pose interesting queries. We can ask for the locations where any two terrorists have taken the same refuge. We can determine those terrorists that operated in the same area. We can compute the locations where routes taken by different terrorists crossed each other. Many further queries are possible. Vague concepts offer a greater flexibility for modeling properties of spatial phenomena in the real world than determinate concepts do. Still, vague concepts comprise the modeling power of determinate concepts as a special case.

In this sense, many scenarios can be found that could make meaningful use of the concept of vague spatial objects. They all have in common that a vague spatial object (e.g., a vague line) is described by a pair of two disjoint or adjacent crisp spatial objects (e.g., two crisp lines). The first crisp spatial object, called the *kernel part*, describes the determinate component of the vague object, that is, the component that definitely and always belongs to the vague object. The second crisp spatial object, called the *conjecture part*, describes the vague component of the vague object, that is, the component from which we cannot say with any certainty whether it or subparts of it belong to the vague object or not. *Maybe* the conjecture part or subparts of it belong to the vague object, *maybe* this is not the case. Or we could say that this is *unknown*.

4   A Generic Definition of Vague Spatial Data Types and Vague Spatial Set Operations

Based on the motivation in the previous section, we now give a formal definition of vague spatial data types (Section 4.1) and vague spatial set operations (Section 4.2). An interesting observation is that these definitions can be given in a generic manner, i.e., type-specific considerations are unnecessary. At the end, Section 4.3 introduces a few other generic operations as well as predicates.

4.1 Vague Spatial Data Types

For the definition of vague points, vague lines, and vague regions we make use of the data types *point* for crisp points, *line* for crisp lines, and *region* for crisp regions. All crisp spatial data types $\alpha \in \{point, line, region\}$ are assumed to have a complex inner structure as it has been defined, e.g., on the basis of point sets and point set topology in [7], or in concrete implementations in [8]. In particular, this means that a *point* object includes a finite number of single points, a *line* object is assembled from a finite number of curves, and a *region* object consists of a finite number of disjoint faces possibly containing a finite number of disjoint holes. Further, these types must be closed under the geometric set operations *union* ($\oplus : \alpha \times \alpha \to \alpha$), *intersection* ($\otimes : \alpha \times \alpha \to \alpha$), *difference* ($\ominus : \alpha \times \alpha \to \alpha$), and *complement* ($\sim \alpha \to \alpha$). Each type α together with the operations $\oplus$ and $\otimes$ forms a boolean algebra. The identity of $\otimes$ is denoted by **1**, which corresponds to IR^2. The identity of $\oplus$ is presented by **0**, which corresponds to the empty spatial object (empty point set).

Syntactically, the extension of a crisp spatial data type to a corresponding vague type is given by a type constructor v as follows:

$$v(\alpha) = \alpha \times \alpha \qquad \forall \alpha \in \{point, line, region\}$$

That is, each vague spatial data type is represented as a pair of corresponding crisp spatial data types. For example, for $\alpha = point$ we obtain $v(point) = point \times point$, which we also name *vpoint*. Accordingly, the data types *vline* and *vregion* are defined. For a vague spatial object $w = (k, c) \in v(\alpha)$, we call $k \in \alpha$ the *kernel part* of w, and $c \in \alpha$ denotes the *conjecture part* of w.

Semantically, the kernel part represents the determinate, crisp part of w, i.e., the area which definitely and always belongs to w. The conjecture part describes the vague part of w, i.e., the area for which we cannot say with any certainty whether it or parts of it belong to w or not. *Maybe* it or parts of it belong to w, *maybe* this is not the case. We could also say that this is *unknown* or *unclear* and thus a conjecture. To enable this intended semantics, we require:

$$\forall \alpha \in \{point, line, region\} \ \forall w = (k, c) \in v(\alpha) : disjoint(k, c) \vee meet(k, c)$$

The functions *disjoint* and *meet*, which operate on complex crisp spatial objects, denote generalized versions [12] of the well known topological predicates on simple spatial objects [5].

Let *points* : $v(\alpha) \to \mathrm{IR}^2$ be an auxiliary function that yields the (unknown) point set of a vague spatial object. For an object $w = (k, c) \in v(\alpha)$ we can then conclude that

$$k \subseteq points(w) \subseteq k \oplus c$$

Hence, k can be regarded as a lower (minimal, guaranteed) approximation of w and $k \oplus c$ can be considered as an upper (maximally possible, speculative) approximation of w, which brings us near to rough set theory. Even if we do not know the exact point set of w, we assume and require that $points(w)$ is not arbitrary but compatible to α, i.e.,

$$points(w) \in \alpha \quad \text{and} \quad points(w) \ominus k \in \alpha$$

Using the characteristic function χ deciding about the existence or non-existence of an element in a set, we obtain $\chi(p) = 1$ for all $p \in k$, $\chi(p) = 0$ for all $p \in \mathbb{R}^2 - (k \cup c)$, $\chi(p) = 1 \vee \chi(p) = 0$ for all $p \in c - k$, and $\chi(p) = 1$ for all $p \in points(w) \in \alpha$. Note the deliberate use of set-theoretic operations. Especially common boundary points of k and c ($k \cap c \neq \varnothing$) are mapped to 1.

4.2 Vague Spatial Set Operations

The three vague geometric set operations **union**, **intersection**, and **difference** have all the same signature $v(\alpha) \times v(\alpha) \to v(\alpha)$. In addition, we define the operation **complement** with the signature $v(\alpha) \to v(\alpha)$. It is our goal and makes sense to define them in a type-independent and thus generic manner. In order to define them for two vague spatial objects u and w, it is helpful to consider meaningful relationships between the kernel part, the conjecture part, and the outside part of u and w. For each operation we give a table where a column/row labeled by k, c, or o denotes the kernel part, conjecture part, or outside part of u/w. Each entry of the table denotes a possible combination, i.e., intersection, of kernel parts, conjecture parts, and outside parts of both objects, and the label in each entry specifies whether the corresponding intersection belongs to the kernel part, conjecture part, or outside part of the operation's result object.

Table 1. Components resulting from intersecting kernel parts, conjecture parts, and outside parts of two vague spatial objects with each other for the four vague geometric set operations.

union	k	c	o		intersection	k	c	o		difference	k	c	o		complement	k	c	o
k	k	k	k		k	k	c	o		k	o	c	k			o	c	k
c	k	c	c		c	c	c	o		c	o	c	c					
o	k	c	o		o	o	o	o		o	o	o	o					

The *union* (Table 1) of a kernel part with any other part is a kernel part since the union of two vague spatial objects asks for membership in either object and since membership is already assured by the given kernel part. Likewise, the union of two conjecture parts or the union of a conjecture part with the outside should be a conjecture part, and only the parts which belong to the outside of both objects contribute to the outside of the union.

The outside of the *intersection* (Table 1) is given by either region's outside because intersection requires membership in both regions. The kernel part of the intersection only contains components which definitely belong to the kernel parts of both objects, and intersections of conjecture parts with each other or with kernel parts make up the conjecture part of the intersection.

Obviously, the *complement* (Table 1) of the kernel part should be the outside, and vice versa. With respect to the conjecture part, anything inside the vague part of an object might or might not belong to the object. Hence, we cannot definitely say that the complement of the vague part is the outside. Neither can we say that the complement belongs to the kernel part. Thus, the only reasonable conclusion is to define the complement of the conjecture part to be the conjecture part itself.

The definition of *difference* (Table 1) between u and w can be derived from the definition of complement since it is equal to the intersection of u with the complement of v. That is, removing a kernel part means intersection with the outside which always leads to outside, and removing anything from the outside leaves the outside part unaffected. Similarly, removing a conjecture part means intersection with the conjecture part and thus results in a conjecture part for kernel parts and conjecture parts, and removing the outside of w (i.e., nothing) does not affect any part of u.

Motivated by the just informally described, intended semantics for the four operations, we now define them formally. An interesting aspect is that these definitions can be based solely on already known crisp geometric set operations on well-understood exact spatial objects. Hence, we are able to give *executable specifications* for the vague geometric set operations. This means, if we have the implementation of a crisp spatial algebra available, we can directly *execute* the vague geometric set operations without being forced to design and implement new algorithms for them.

Let $u, w \in v(\alpha)$, and let u^k and w^k denote their kernel parts, u^c and w^c their conjecture parts, and u^o and w^o their outside parts. The outside of u, e.g., is defined as $u^o := \sim(u^k \oplus u^c)$. We define:

$$
\begin{aligned}
u \text{ union } w &:= (u^k \oplus w^k, (u^c \oplus w^c) \ominus (w^k \oplus w^k)) \\
u \text{ intersection } w &:= (u^k \otimes w^k, (u^c \otimes w^c) \oplus (u^k \otimes w^c) \oplus (u^c \otimes w^k)) \\
u \text{ difference } w &:= (u^k \otimes (\sim w^k), (u^c \otimes w^c) \oplus (u^k \otimes w^c) \oplus (u^c \otimes (\sim w^k))) \\
\text{complement } u &:= (\sim u^k, u^c)
\end{aligned}
$$

We introduce juxtaposition as an abbreviating notation for the intersection of two crisp spatial objects and assign intersection higher associativity than union and difference. Hence, the above definition for u **difference** w could also be specified more concisely as $(u^k(\sim w^k), u^c w^c \oplus u^k w^c \oplus u^c(\sim w^k))$.

In a next step, we have to prove that the definitions realize the behavior specified in Table 1. For $z = u$ **union** w we have to show the three identities (1) $z^k = u^k w^k \oplus u^k w^c \oplus u^k w^o \oplus u^c w^k \oplus u^o w^k$, (2) $z^c = u^c w^c \oplus u^c w^o \oplus u^o w^c$, and (3) $z^o = u^o w^o$. The proof for (1) leverages that $\oplus$ is idempotent. We can therefore duplicate the first term $u^k w^k$. Then using the fact that $\otimes$ distributes over $\oplus$ we can factorize both u^k and w^k and obtain: $z^k = (u^k(w^k \oplus w^c \oplus w^o)) \oplus (w^k(u^k \oplus u^c \oplus u^o)))$. Since $w^k \oplus w^c \oplus w^o = \mathbf{1} = \mathbb{R}^2$ and $u^k \oplus u^c \oplus u^o = \mathbf{1}$, where $\mathbf{1}$ is the identity of $\otimes$, we get $z^k = (u^k \otimes \mathbf{1}) \oplus (w^k \otimes \mathbf{1}) = u^k \oplus w^k$, which is the definition of the kernel part of **union**.

For proving equation (2) we know that for $r, s \in \alpha$ holds: $r \oplus s = rs \oplus r(\sim s) \oplus (\sim r)s$. We can use this identity to rewrite the conjecture part definition as $u^c w^c \oplus u^c(\sim w^c) \oplus (\sim u^c)w^c \ominus (u^k w^k \oplus u^k(\sim w^k) \oplus (\sim u^k)w^k)$. Now we evaluate all complements by using that $\sim w^c = w^k \oplus w^o$ and $\sim w^k = w^c \oplus w^o$. This leads to $u^c w^c \oplus u^c(w^k \oplus w^o) \oplus (u^k \oplus u^o)w^c \ominus (u^k w^k \oplus u^k(w^c \oplus w^o) \oplus (u^c \oplus u^o)w^k)$. Applying distributivity of $\otimes$ we obtain: $u^c w^c \oplus u^c w^k \oplus u^c w^o \oplus u^k w^c \oplus u^o w^c \ominus (u^k w^k \oplus u^k w^c \oplus u^k w^o \oplus u^c w^k \oplus u^o w^k)$. In this term, only $u^c w^k$ and $u^k v^c$ appear in both parts of the difference; all other intersections to be subtracted have no effect at all since all intersections are pairwise disjoint. We obtain: $u^c w^c \oplus u^c w^o \oplus u^o w^c$ which corresponds exactly to the condition required for z^c.

For proving equation (3) we note that in a boolean lattice for $r, s \in \alpha$ holds: $\mathbf{1} \otimes s = s$, $\mathbf{1} \oplus s = \mathbf{1}$, and $\mathbf{1} = r \oplus (\sim r)$. Therefore, we know that $s = (r \oplus (\sim r))s = rs \oplus (\sim r)s$, and it follows that $r \oplus s = r \oplus rs \oplus (\sim r)s$. We also know that $r \oplus rs = r(\mathbf{1} \oplus s) = r$ so that $r \oplus s = r \oplus (\sim r)s$. Since $(\sim r)s$ is another way of denoting the difference $s \ominus r$, we get: $r \oplus (s \ominus r) = r \oplus s$. Now we have by definition that $z^o = \sim(z^k \oplus z^c) = \sim(u^k \oplus w^k \oplus ((u^c \oplus w^c) \ominus (u^k \oplus w^k))) = \sim(u^k \oplus w^k \oplus u^c \oplus w^c)$. By commutativity and de Morgan's law this reduces to $(\sim(u^k \oplus u^c)) \otimes (\sim(w^k \oplus w^c))$ which is by the definition of complement equal to $u^o \otimes w^o$, the condition required for z^o.

Due to their lengthiness, we omit the proofs of the other three operations here whose correct behavior can be shown in a similar way.

4.3   Other Generic Operations and Predicates

Sometimes it is helpful to be able to explicitly deal with the kernel part or the conjecture part of a vague spatial object, or to swap its kernel part and conjecture part. For that purpose, we define the following generic operations for $u = (u^k, u^c) \in v(\alpha)$:

$$
\begin{aligned}
\mathbf{kernel}(u) &:= (u^k, \mathbf{0}) \\
\mathbf{conjecture}(u) &:= (\mathbf{0}, u^c) \\
\mathbf{invert}(u) &:= (u^c, u^k)
\end{aligned}
$$

All three operations have the signature $v(\alpha) \to v(\alpha)$[1]. The **kernel** operation especially facilitates computations exclusively with the exact part of a vague spatial object u, because the vague spatial operations, applied to vague spatial objects with an empty conjecture part, behave exactly like the corresponding crisp spatial operations. This can be easily seen from the definitions and is intended. Consequently, crisp spatial objects are a special case of their corresponding vague counterparts. The **conjecture** operation allows one to focus on the unclear, indeterminate part of u. The **invert** operation changes the role of kernel part and conjecture part of u.

It is also possible to identify generic predicates. The most obvious ones are $=, \neq$: $v(\alpha) \to bool$. For $u, w \in v(\alpha)$, they are defined as follows:

$$
\begin{aligned}
u = w &:= (u^k = w^k \wedge u^c = w^c) \\
u \neq w &:= (u^k \neq w^k \vee u^c \neq w^c)
\end{aligned}
$$

5   Type-Specific Spatial Operations

In this section we describe a few operations requiring particular types as operands. The operation **boundary** with the signature $vregion \to vline$ allows us to extract the boundary of a vague region as a vague line. Its definition requires the crisp operation $boundary : region \to line$ which determines the boundary of a crisp region as a crisp line. Vice versa, the operation **interior** with the signature $vline \to vregion$ determines faces in a vague line object and transforms them into a vague region. Its definition requires the crisp operation $interior : line \to region$ which calculates the faces of a crisp line and collects

---

[1] To really connect vague and crisp spatial data types and to map the kernel part or the conjecture part of a vague spatial object to the corresponding crisp spatial object, one could define projection functions $\pi_k, \pi_c : v(\alpha) \to \alpha$ with $\pi_k(u) = u^k$ and $\pi_c(u) = u^c$.

them into a crisp region. For $r \in vregion$ in particular **interior**(**boundary**(r)) $= r$ holds, i.e., the operations **interior** and **boundary** are inverse. The operation **vertices** with the signatures $vline \rightarrow vpoint$ and $vregion \rightarrow vpoint$ collects the end points of the segments of a vague line and the end points of the segments of the boundary of a vague region respectively. Its definition is based on the crisp operation $vertices$ with the signatures $line \rightarrow point$ and $region \rightarrow point$. Let further $l \in vline$. We define:

$$
\begin{aligned}
\textbf{boundary}(r) &:= (boundary(r^k), boundary(r^c)) \\
\textbf{interior}(l) &:= (interior(l^k), interior(l^c)) \\
\textbf{vertices}(l) &:= (vertices(l^k), vertices(l^c)) \\
\textbf{vertices}(r) &:= (vertices(r^k), vertices(r^c))
\end{aligned}
$$

We have so far described the **intersection** operation only for two vague spatial objects of the same type. We extend this definition now to all mixed type combinations with the signatures $vpoint \times vline \rightarrow vpoint$, $vpoint \times vregion \rightarrow vpoint$, $vline \times vregion \rightarrow vline$, $vregion \times vpoint \rightarrow vpoint$, $vregion \times vline \rightarrow vline$, and $vline \times vpoint \rightarrow vpoint$. For this purpose, we generalize the crisp intersection operation $\otimes$ to all corresponding crisp variants of the just mentioned signatures. These crisp variants are well defined. The already known definition for **intersection** can then also be applied in case of the mixed type combinations.

The operation **common_border** incorporates a special kind of intersection. It computes the shared boundary of two extended vague spatial objects as a vague line. Its signatures are $vline \times vline \rightarrow vline$, $vline \times vregion \rightarrow vline$, $vregion \times vline \rightarrow vline$, and $vregion \times vregion \rightarrow vline$. The definitions can be reduced to the well defined crisp spatial operation $common\_border : line \times line \rightarrow line$ which computes the common line parts of two crisp lines. We define for $l, m \in vline$ and $r, s \in vregion$:

$$
\begin{aligned}
\textbf{common\_border}(l, m) &:= (common\_border(l^k, m^k), common\_border(l^c, m^c)) \\
\textbf{common\_border}(l, r) &:= \textbf{common\_border}(l, \textbf{boundary}(r)) \\
\textbf{common\_border}(r, l) &:= \textbf{common\_border}(l, r) \\
\textbf{common\_border}(r, s) &:= \textbf{common\_border}(\textbf{boundary}(r), \textbf{boundary}(s))
\end{aligned}
$$

Finally, we discuss the vague operator **convex_hull** : $vpoint \rightarrow vregion$. A subset S of the plane is called *convex* if and only if for any pair of points $p, q \in S$ the line segment between p and q is completely contained in S. The well known crisp operation $convex\_hull : point \rightarrow region$ computes the smallest convex region that contains all points of a given point object. We define the convex hull of a vague point $p \in vpoint$ as

$$
\textbf{convex\_hull}(p) := (convex\_hull(p^k), convex\_hull(p^k \oplus p^c) \ominus convex\_hull(p^k))
$$

The smallest, guaranteed convex hull of p is given by the convex hull of its kernel part. If all points of the conjecture part of p lie inside or on the boundary of the convex hull of its kernel part, the conjecture part of the resulting vague region is **0**, i.e., the empty region object. Otherwise, the convex hull involving all points both from the kernel part and the conjecture part will be larger than the convex hull of the kernel part.

6   Vague Topological Predicates

Topological predicates provide information about the relative position of spatial objects towards each other. The result type of *vague topological predicates*[2] is a value of a new vague data type named $vbool = \{true, false, maybe\}$. That is, we use a three-valued logic as the range of these predicates. The definition of the *vague logical operators* **and, or,** and **not** (Table 2) parallels the definition of the vague spatial operations in Section 4.2 (t, f, and m are used as abbreviations for *true, false, maybe*).

Table 2. Vague logical operators (three-valued logic).

and	t	m	f
t	t	m	f
m	m	m	f
f	f	f	f

or	t	m	f
t	t	t	t
m	t	m	m
f	t	m	f

not	t	m	f
	f	m	t

We first consider a generic definition of the vague **inside** predicate which has the signatures $vpoint \times \alpha \rightarrow vbool$ with $\alpha \in \{vpoint, vline, vregion\}$, $vline \times \beta \rightarrow vbool$ with $\beta \in \{vline, vregion\}$, and $vregion \times vregion \rightarrow vbool$. Let u be the first operand and w be the second operand according to the signatures. Then their definition is as follows:

$$u \textbf{ inside } w := \begin{cases} true & \text{if } u^k \oplus u^c \subseteq w^k \\ false & \text{if } u^k \not\subseteq w^k \oplus w^c \\ maybe & \text{otherwise} \end{cases}$$

Hence, we can safely say that u **inside** w holds if everything of u (i.e., kernel part and conjecture part) is inside the kernel part of w. If this is not the case, we cannot simply conclude that u **inside** w is *false* since this requires definite knowledge about a part of u being outside any part of v. In other words, if we can exclude *true* as the predicate result and if $u^k \subseteq w^k \oplus w^c$, we are not sure about insideness, and we define u **inside** w as *maybe*.

Next we present a generic definition of the vague **intersects** predicate which has the signature $\alpha \times \alpha \rightarrow vbool$ with $\alpha \in \{vpoint, vline, vregion\}$. We define for $u, w \in \alpha$:

$$u \textbf{ intersects } w := \begin{cases} true & \text{if } u^k w^k \neq \mathbf{0} \\ false & \text{if } u^k w^k \oplus u^c w^c \oplus u^k w^c \oplus u^c w^k = \mathbf{0} \\ maybe & \text{otherwise} \end{cases}$$

The definition means that the predicate holds if the kernel parts of u and w intersect. This is true independent from the value of $u^c w^c$. Likewise, if $u^k \oplus u^c$ and $w^k \oplus w^c$ are disjoint, we can definitely say that u and w do not intersect at all. However, if $u^k w^k = \mathbf{0}$ and $u^c w^c \neq \mathbf{0}$, we cannot be sure about the intersection of u and w and let the predicate return the value *maybe*.

---

[2] In this paper, we deliberately omit the discussion of a "complete" collection of vague topological predicates for which we are currently designing a comprehensive concept that will be presented in a future paper.

The predicate **on_border_of** : $vpoint \times \alpha \to vbool$ with $\alpha \in \{vline, vregion\}$ checks whether a vague point is located on a vague line and a vague region respectively. Let $p \in vpoint$, $l \in vline$, and $r \in vregion$. We use the operation **boundary** defined in Section 5 to compute the boundary of a vague region as a vague line and define:

$$
\begin{aligned}
\textbf{on\_border\_of}(p, l) &:= \quad \textbf{inside}(p, l) \\
\textbf{on\_border\_of}(p, r) &:= \quad \textbf{inside}(p, \textbf{boundary}(r))
\end{aligned}
$$

The predicate **border_in_common** has the signatures $vline \times vline \to vbool$, $vline \times vregion \to vbool$, $vregion \times vline \to vbool$, and $vregion \times vregion \to vbool$. It determines whether two extended vague spatial objects share a common border. Let $l, m \in vline$ and $r, s \in vregion$. Then

$$
\textbf{border\_in\_common}(l, m) := \begin{cases}
true & \text{if } l^k m^k \neq \mathbf{0} \wedge l^k m^k \in vline \\
false & \text{if } l^k m^k \oplus l^c m^c \oplus l^k m^c \oplus l^c m^k = \mathbf{0} \vee \\
& \quad l^k m^k \oplus l^c m^c \oplus l^k m^c \oplus l^c m^k \notin vline \\
maybe & \text{otherwise}
\end{cases}
$$

$$
\begin{aligned}
\textbf{border\_in\_common}(l, r) &:= \quad \textbf{border\_in\_common}(l, \textbf{boundary}(r)) \\
\textbf{border\_in\_common}(r, l) &:= \quad \textbf{border\_in\_common}(l, r) \\
\textbf{border\_in\_common}(r, s) &:= \quad \textbf{border\_in\_common}(\textbf{boundary}(r), \textbf{boundary}(s))
\end{aligned}
$$

7 Embedding Vague Spatial Data Types into Query Languages

A few examples shall demonstrate the integration of vague spatial concepts into the relational data model and the query language VSQL (vague SQL). We do not give a full description of VSQL. Vague spatial data types are embedded as *abstract data types* into a relational schema and may be used as attribute types like standard types. That is, their internal structure is hidden from the user and can only be accessed by operations. For instance, we may specify the relation weather(climate: *string*, region: *vregion*), where the column named *region* contains vague region values for various climatic conditions given by the column *climate*, and the relation soil(quality: *string*, region: *vregion*) describing the soil quality for certain regions.

If we want to find out all regions where lack of water is a problem for cultivation, or if we are interested in bad soil regions as a hindrance for cultivation, we can pose the following queries:

select region **from** weather **where** climate = "dry"
select region **from** soil **where** quality = "bad"

Note that the result of both queries is a set of vague regions.

If we want to find out about vague regions where cultivation is impossible due to a lack of water or bad soil quality, we ask for the union of two vague region sets. Thus, we first have to cast the sets into single *vregion* objects. We therefore use the built-in, overloaded aggregation function **sum** which, when applied to a set of vague regions, aggregates this set by repeated application of **union**. We can determine regions where cultivation is impossible by:

(select sum(region) **from** weather **where** climate = "dry")
union
(select sum(region) **from** soil **where** quality = "bad")

As a next example, we take the self-explaining relations pollution(type: *string*, region: *vregion*) and areas(use: *string*, region: *vregion*). Pollutions are nowadays a central ecological problem and cause an increasing number of environmental damages. Important examples are air pollution and oil soiling. Pollution control institutions, ecological researchers, and geographers, usually use maps for visualizing the expansion of pollution. We can ask, for example, for inhabitable areas which are air polluted (where the kernel part of an air pollution denotes heavily polluted areas and the conjecture part only gives slightly polluted regions) as follows:

select sum(pollution.region) **intersection sum**(areas.region)
from pollution, areas
where area.use = "inhabited" **and** pollution.type = "air"

Then the kernel part of the result consists of inhabited regions which are heavily polluted, and the conjecture part consists (a) of slightly polluted inhabited regions, (b) of heavily polluted regions which are only partially inhabited, and (c) of slightly polluted and partially inhabited regions.

If we want to reach all people who live in heavily polluted areas, we need the kernel part of the intersection together with conjecture part (b) of the intersection. How can we get this from the above query? The trick is to force boundary parts (a) and (c) to be empty by restricting pollution areas to their kernel region:

select kernel(sum(pollution.region)) **intersection sum**(areas.region)
from ...

A slightly different query is to find out all areas where people are definitely or possibly endangered by pollution. Of course, we have to use an intersection predicate. More precisely, we want to find those areas for which **intersects** either yields *true* or *maybe*. For this purpose we can prefix any predicate with **maybe** which causes the predicate to fail only if it returns *false*. Technically **maybe** turns a *maybe* value into *true*. So the query is:

select areas.name
from pollution, areas
where area.use = "inhabited" **and** pollution.region **maybe intersects** areas.region

This query is an example of a *vague spatial join*.

The following example is based on the the self-explaining relations resources(kind: *string*, region: *vregion*) and nature(type: *string*, region: *vregion*) and describes a situation which stresses the conflicting interests of economy and ecology. Assume on the one hand areas of animal species and plants that are worth being protected (nature reserves and national parks are the kernel parts) and on the other hand mineral resources the mining of which prospects high profits. An example for forming a difference of vague regions is a query which asks for mining areas that do not affect the living space of endangered species.

(**select sum**(region) **from** resources **where** kind = "mineral")
difference
(**select sum**(region) **from** nature **where** type = "endangered")

The kernel part of the result describes regions where mining should be allowed. The conjecture part consists (a) of regions where mineral resources are uncertain and (b) of resource kernels that lie in (non-kernel) regions hosting endangered species. Since national parks are generally protected by the government, it is especially regions (b) conservationists should carefully observe. We can determine these regions by:

(**select kernel(sum**(region)**)** **from** resources **where** kind = "mineral")
intersection
(**select conjecture(sum**(region)**)** **from** nature **where** type = "endangered")

The result is a vague region with an empty kernel part and a conjecture part that just consists of the intersection of the mineral resource kernel part and the endangered nature conjecture part.

Next, we consider an example from biology and assume living spaces of different animal species stored in a relation animals(name: *string*, region: *vregion*). The kernel part describes places where they normally live, and the conjecture part describes regions where they can be found occasionally(e.g., to hunt for food or to migrate from one kernel area to another through a corridor). We can search for pairs of species which share a common living space. This query asks for regions which have a non-empty intersection kernel:

select A.name, B.name
from animals **as** A, animals **as** B
where A.region **intersects** B.region

8   Conclusions and Future Work

We have defined a data model of points, lines, and regions that is capable of describing many different aspects of spatial vagueness. It is a canonical extension of determinate spatial data models, which facilitates the treatment of vague and exact objects in one model. Since our approach is based on exact spatial modeling concepts, it allows to build upon existing work and simplifies many definitions. In particular, we can leverage already existing implementations of crisp spatial type systems to realize vague spatial objects with only minimal effort by executable specifications.

Currently we are working on a comprehensive concept for *vague topological predicates* and also deal with *vague numerical operations*. Implementation tuning is another topic.

References

1. D. Altman. Fuzzy Set Theoretic Approaches for Handling Imprecision in Spatial Analysis. *Int. Journal of Geographical Information Systems*, 8(3):271–289, 1994.
2. P. A. Burrough and A. U. Frank, editors. *Geographic Objects with Indeterminate Boundaries*. GISDATA Series, vol. 2. Taylor & Francis, 1996.
3. E. Clementini and P. Di Felice. *An Algebraic Model for Spatial Objects with Indeterminate Boundaries*, pp. 153–169. In Burrough and Frank [2], 1996.
4. A. G. Cohn and N. M. Gotts. *The 'Egg-Yolk' Representation of Regions with Indeterminate Boundaries*, pp. 171–187. In Burrough and Frank [2], 1996.
5. M. J. Egenhofer, A. Frank, and J. P. Jackson. A Topological Data Model for Spatial Databases. *1st Int. Symp. on the Design and Implementation of Large Spatial Databases*, LNCS 409, pp. 271–286. Springer-Verlag, 1989.
6. M. Erwig and M. Schneider. Vague Regions. *5th Int. Symp. on Advances in Spatial Databases*, LNCS 1262, pp. 298–320. Springer-Verlag, 1997.
7. R. H. Güting and M. Schneider. Realm-Based Spatial Data Types: The ROSE Algebra. *VLDB Journal*, 4:100–143, 1995.
8. R.H. Güting, T. de Ridder, and M. Schneider. Implementation of the ROSE Algebra: Efficient Algorithms for Realm-Based Spatial Data Types. *Int. Symp. on Advances in Spatial Databases*, 1995.
9. OGC Abstract Specification. OpenGIS Consortium (OGC), 1999. URL: http://www.opengis.org/techno/specs.htm.
10. M. Schneider. *Modelling Spatial Objects with Undetermined Boundaries Using the Realm/ROSE Approach*, pp. 141–152. In Burrough and Frank [2], 1996.
11. M. Schneider. Uncertainty Management for Spatial Data in Databases: Fuzzy Spatial Data Types. *6th Int. Symp. on Advances in Spatial Databases*, LNCS 1651, pp. 330–351. Springer-Verlag, 1999.
12. M. Schneider. A Design of Topological Predicates for Complex Crisp and Fuzzy Regions. *Int. Conf. on Conceptual Modeling*, pp. 103–116, 2001.
13. M. Worboys. Computation with Imprecise Geospatial Data. *Computational, Environmental and Urban Systems*, 22(2):85–106, 1998.

Intelligent Multi-agent Based Database Hybrid Intrusion Prevention System

P. Ramasubramanian and A. Kannan

Department of Computer Science and Engineering
Anna University, Chennai 600025, India.
suryarams@cs.annauniv.edu, kannan@annauniv.edu

Abstract. This paper describes a framework for highly distributed real-time monitoring approach to database security using Intelligent Multi-Agents. The intrusion prevention system described in this paper uses a combination of both statistical anomaly prevention and rule based misuse prevention in order to detect a misuser. The statistical anomaly prediction system employs ensemble Quickprop neural networks forecasting model, which predicts unauthorized invasions of user based on previous observations and takes further action before intrusion occurs. The experimental study is performed using real data provided by a major Corporate Bank. A comparative evaluation of the two ensemble networks over the individual networks was carried out using mean absolute percentage error on a prediction data set and a better prediction accuracy has been observed. The Misuse Prevention system uses a set of rules that define typical illegal user behavior. A separate rule subsystem is designed for this misuse detection system and it is known as Temporal Authorization Rule Markup Language (TARML). In order to reduce single point of failures in centralized security system, a dynamic distributed system has been designed in which the security management task is distributed across the network using Intelligent Multi-Agents.

Keywords: Multi-Agents - Database Security - Quickprop Prediction Technique - Neural Networks.

1 Motivation

In information systems, the primary security threat comes from insider abuse and from intrusion. Security policies do not sufficiently guard data stored in a database system against "privileged users" [1]. Many intrusions into information systems manifest through the significantly increased or decreased intensity of transactions occurring in information systems. For example, intruders who have gained super-user privileges can perform malicious transactions and disable many resources in the information system, resulting in the abruptly decreased intensity of transactions [4]. This reinforces the point that intrusion detection systems should not only be employed at the network and hosts, but also at the database systems where the critical information assets lie [6]. Therefore, the

A. Benczúr, J. Demetrovics, G. Gottlob (Eds.): ADBIS 2004, LNCS 3255, pp. 393–408, 2004.

early detection of significant changes in the data object usage can help stop many intrusions early to protect information systems and assure reliability of information systems [2].

2   Related Works

The existing intrusion detection systems [1][6] operate in real time, capturing the intruder when or after intrusion occurs. From the existing methods of detecting the intrusion [1][6], we observed that all intrusion detection systems were lacking a vital component: that they take action, after the intrusion has been detected [9]. This serious weakness has led to the research on forecasting models. However, though the Intrusion Detection system is real-time, it can detect the intrusion after the action, but never before [2]. To address the problem of detecting intrusions after they take place, we utilize a Quickprop neural network(NN) ensemble prediction algorithm, which takes into account user behavior and generates a predicted profile to foresee the future user actions.

One of the most difficult problems for neural network modeling is selection of proper neural network structure. Usually single network fails to capture all the intricacy present in the data. Ensemble uses many neural network outputs to jointly solve a problem and at the same time improves the generalization ability of the network significantly [3]. Hence, prediction error of a combined network (ensemble) is less as compared to individual networks. Analysis was performed for different network architectures by varying number of hidden layers, hidden neurons and types of activation functions.

Existing works on Intrusion Detection has focused largely on network [9] and host intrusion [1]. Most of the research on database security revolve around access policies, roles, administration procedures, physical security, security models and data inference. Little amount of work is done on database IDSes. Although most emphasis in literature has been found for Network IDSes [6]. DIDAFIT [6] is a database intrusion detection system that identifies anomalous database accesses by matching SQL statements with a known set of legitimate database transaction fingerprints. Chung [1] work, a method was devised which generates profiles of the users and their roles in a relational database system. This method assumes that the legitimate users show some level of consistency in using the database system. If this assumption does not hold, or if the threshold for inconsistency is not set properly, the result will be a high level of false positives. It also faces the attribute selection problem like choosing a feature in building a work scope. To the best of the author's knowledge, there is no report on an intrusion prevention system for database. As far as the authors know, this is the only work using neural networks forecasting model and SQL transaction rules to prevent database intrusions.

2.1   User Audit Profile

Our Intrusion Detection system uses hybrid detection technique. Thus, the user profile is a collection of real-time negative authorization rules stated by database administrators and audit record. The rules include the access of database objects of the network computer system for which permission is not granted, data objects that users cannot use on their hosts, and even includes privileges that the database administrators feel that the users should not use.

2.2   Temporal Authorization Rule Markup Language

In our model, a negative authorization is specified as (time, auth), where time is a temporal attribute, and auth (s,o,p) is an authorization. Here, temporal represents either valid time or transaction time, during which auth is invalid. s represents the subject, o represents the database object and p, the privilege. These rules are represented by means of ETCA(Event-Time-Condition-Action) [5] rules. Stating the purpose of ETCA rules briefly, whenever the event takes place the negative authorization condition corresponding to it's checked and if the condition is satisfied then the defense action to be performed on a user when an attack signature is detected.

```
<?xml version="1.0" encoding="UTF-8"?>
<!DOCTYPE Rules[
<!ELEMENT Rules(Rule)*>
<!ELEMENT Rule(Rulename,Event,Condition,Action)>
<!ELEMENT Rulename(#PCDATA)>
<!ELEMENT Event(Eventname,DataEvent,TemporalEvent,
    OtherEvent)>
<!ELEMENT Eventname(#PCDATA)>
    <!Attlist Eventname Timestamp PCDATA #REQUIRED>
<!ELEMENT DataEvent(Create,Update,Delete,View)>
<!ELEMENT Create(Node)>
<!ELEMENT Update(Node)>
<!ELEMENT Delete(Node)>
<!ELEMENT View(Node)>
<!ELEMENT Node(#PCDATA)>
<!ELEMENT TemporalEvent(At,After,Before,Between,Every)>
<!ELEMENT At(Time)>
<!ELEMENT After(Time)>
<!ELEMENT Before(Time)>
<!ELEMENT Between(Time)>
<!ELEMENT Every(Time)>
<!ELEMENT OtherEvent(Data_too_Large,Division By Zero)>
<!ELEMENT Condition (User,Domain,Role,Priority,Context,
    XQUERY_stmt)>
<!ELEMENT Rule (User)+>
<!ELEMENT User (Domain)+>
<!ELEMENT Domain (Role)+>
<!ELEMENT Role (Object)+>
<!ELEMENT User (EMPTY)>
    <!ATTLIST User user_name CDATA#REQUIRED>
```

```
<!ELEMENT Domain (EMPTY)>
    <!ATTLIST Domain domain_name CDATA#REQUIRED>
<!ELEMENT Role (EMPTY)>
    <!ATTLIST Role role_name CDATA#REQUIRED>
<!ELEMENT Priority (EMPTY)>
    <!ATTLIST Priority pri_value CDATA#REQUIRED>
<!ELEMENT Context (EMPTY)>
    <!ATTLIST Context cont_value CDATA#REQUIRED>
<!ELEMENT XQUERY_stmt (#PCDATA)>
<!ELEMENT Action(SOAP_Header,SOAP_Envelope,SOAP_Body)>
<!ELEMENT Soap_Header(#PCDATA)>
<!ELEMENT Soap_Envelope(#PCDATA)>
<!ELEMENT Soap_Body(Oper)>
<!ELEMENT oper ("INVALID ACTION")>
    <!ATTLIST oper oper_name CDATA#REQUIRED>
```

The event part of the rule specifies the event responsible for rule triggering, which is enclosed into XML event tags. The time part of the rule defines the temporal events. XQuery [13] along with XPath [12] is used to specify the condition part of the rule. The action part of the Authorization Rule DTD is encapsulated using the Simple Object Access Protocol(SOAP) [7]. A SOAP message consists of three parts. The SOAP Envelope element is the root element of a SOAP message. It defines the XML document as a SOAP message. The optional SOAP Header element contains application specific information (like authentication, etc.,) about the SOAP message. If the Header element is present, it must be the first child element of the Envelope element. The SOAP Body contains the action data that is to be transmitted to the client.

2.3   Audit Record

Auditing is the monitoring and recording of selected user database actions. Auditing is used to investigate suspicious activity. There are three standard types of auditing to monitor the user behavior namely SQL statement-level, privilege-level and object-level auditing. Statement and privilege audit options are in effect at the time a database user connects to the database and remain in effect for the duration of the session. In contrast, changes to object audit options become effective for current sessions immediately [4]. So in this work, we have chosen object-level auditing to build profiles. The object-level auditing can be done by user on successful or non-successful attempts for session intervals. A session is the time between when a user connects to and disconnects from a database object. We need an utility to capture the submitted database transactions in order to compare them with those in the legitimate user profile. Oracle provides the sql_trace [6] utility that can be used to trace all database operations in a database session of an user. We make use of its capability to log SQL transactions executed by the database engine.

The following attributes are included in each audit trail record:

- User ID
- Group ID
- Process ID
- Session ID
- Host ID & IP address
- Object ID
- **Event:** It describes the type of transaction performed or attempted on a particular data object.
- **Completion:** It describes the result of an attempted operation. A successful operation returns the value zero, and unsuccessful operations returns the error code describing the reason for the failure.
- **Transaction Time:** The time at which the events or state changes are registered in the computer system. The total value of the user session is calculated based on this transaction time.
- **Valid Time:** It has two values namely start_time and end_time representing the interval during which the tuple in the audit record is valid. The prediction values that are generated by our 'statistical prediction engine', past observations and the on-line behavior of user are stipulated using valid time attribute.

The following metrics are considered to audit the user behavior:

- Audit the frequency of certain commands execution (Command Stroke Rate) by an user on an object in a session
- Audit Execution Denials or Access Violations on an object in a session
- Audit the Object utilization by an user for certain period
- Audit the overt requests for a data object in a session

3   Prediction Algorithm

Quickprop NN ensemble forecasting model makes periodic short-term forecasts, since long-term forecasts cannot accurately predict an intrusion [2]. In this we use a multivariate time series technique to forecast the hacker's behavior effectively. This algorithm consists of two phases: determination of the number of neurons in hidden layer(s) and construction of a Quickprop forecaster. The determined input patterns are then used to construct the Quickprop forecaster.

A rule of thumb, known as the Baum-Haussler rule, is used to determine the number of hidden neurons to be used:

$$N_{hidden} \leq \frac{N_{train} E_{tolerance}}{N_{pts} + N_{output}}$$

where N_{hidden} is the number of hidden neurons, N_{train} is the number of training examples, $E_{tolerance}$ is the error tolerance, N_{pts} is the number of data points per training example, and N_{output} is the number of output neurons.

Neural network ensemble is a learning paradigm where several neural networks are jointly used to solve the same problem. The networks with the highest accuracy was considered for the ensemble members. The purpose of the ensemble model is to reduce variance, or instability of the neural network. It is a weighted average combination of the individual NN outputs, which finds weight for each individual network output in order to minimize mean absolute percentage error(MAPE) of the ensemble. The ensemble weights are determined as a function of the relative error of each network determined in training. The generalized ensemble output is defined by:

$$GEM = \sum_{i=1}^{n} w_i f_i(x) \tag{1}$$

where w_i's ($\Sigma \, w_i = 1$) are chosen to minimize the MAPE with respect to the target function (estimated using the prediction set). The optimal weight for w_i is given by:

$$w_i = \sum_{i=1}^{n} C_{ij}^{-1} / \sum_{k=1}^{n} \sum_{j=1}^{n} C_{kj}^{-1} \tag{2}$$

where, C_{ij} is the correlation matrix = expected value of $[e_i(x)e_j(x)]$, $e_i(x)$ is the error of the network $f_i = f(x) - f_i(x)$, f(x) = true data. In practice, errors are often highly correlated. Thus rows of C is nearly linearly dependent, so that inverting C can lead to serious round off errors. To avoid this one could exclude the networks whose errors are highly correlated with each other. The total error of neural network training reflects partly the fitting to the regularities of the data and partly the fitting to the noise in the data. Ensemble averaging tends to filter the noise part as it varies amongst the ensemble members, and tends to retain the fitting to the regularities of the data, therefore, decreasing the overall error in the model.

In order to carry out a prediction, a d:n:n:1 four layer feed-forward Quickprop neural network(d input units, n hidden units, and a single unit) has been considered. For our study, Quickprop networks of the commercially available artificial neural network simulator JavaNNS 1.1 [10] was used.

4   Architecture

The general architectural framework for a Multi-Agent based database statistical anomaly prediction system is illustrated in Fig. 1. It has been implemented by using Aglets Software Development Kit(ASDK) [8], and API Java Aglet(J-AAPI) developed by IBM Tokyo Research Laboratory. In this architecture, two kinds of agents are considered: They are 1. Information Agent 2. Host Agent.

4.1   Information Agent

Information Agent(Static Agent) acts as a data processing unit, and as a data repository for the Host Agents. It is responsible for collecting and storing user

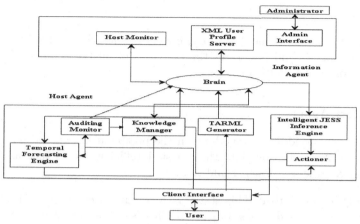

Fig. 1. Intelligent Multi-Agent based Database Statistical Anomaly Prediction System

profiles for all users from various agents in a timely fashion that has access to the data in the protected network. Also it provides the user profile to the Host Agent whenever it is requested. The Information Agent comprises of three main components namely 1. Host Monitor 2. XML Audit Profile Server 3. Admin Interface

- **Host Monitor(Mobile Agent):** In distributed environment, the performance of each host has to be monitored constantly so that performance drop or failure of any node can be detected. Based on that corrective measures can be taken to maintain the overall performance level of the network. When an Information Agent is created, it sends a monitor agent to every host in the network. The monitor agent then starts monitoring the performance as soon as it reaches the host at regular intervals and this interval can be programmed.

- **XML Audit Profile Server:** Audit records are written into the XML format and they are stored in XML Audit Profile Server. The generation and insertion of an audit trail record is independent of an user's transaction. Therefore, even if an user's transaction is rolled back, the audit trail record remains committed. The Profile Server must be able to provide the user behavior information about past, present and future and it must allow forecasting based on temporal logic. So, in this work we have chosen an audit record database, which maintains past, present and future data about users and is termed as a temporal database. Authorization rules are installed in the XML repository and these rules monitor the XML databases for the occurrence of events by the construction of event listeners on each node of the XML document.

- **Admin Interface:** Interface agent(Static Agent) provides friendly human-computer interface for system administrator and it can provide information for administrator in the form of GUI and receive control commands from the GUI.

4.2   Brain

Brain(Static Agent) is the central component of the agent and it initiates, controls, coordinates and integrates the activities of all the components of both Information Agent and Host Agent.

4.3   Host Agent

A Host Agent resides on every host on the protected distributed database environment. It can be split into three basic intelligent agents such as Auditing Monitor, Knowledge Manager and Actioner.

- **Auditing Monitor:** This static agent monitors every user who logs into the system. The database objects, privileges of the current users on the host machine are logged and send to the information agent.
- **Temporal Forecasting Engine:** It is responsible for processing the monitored data from the Host Agent and generates forecasting data for the next session of the specific user. We move the forecasting module from the Information Agent to the Host Agent and repeat the experiments to discover if there is any difference in the results, and to maximize the intrusion forbidden system performance, so the agents will be distributing not only the security, but also the workload of the processing requirements of the Information Agent.
- **Intelligent JESS Inference Engine:** When a transaction like insertion of element, deletion of element or updating of element happens at the XML file, the ETCA rule given in XML format is mapped to JESS authorization rule, which is predefined by database administrator. The events that occur are also converted to JESS facts. The JESS Inference engine constantly monitors the JESS rule and on the occurrence of a new fact, executes the JESS rule producing new JESS facts as the result. These JESS facts must later be converted into suitable action and it's transmitted to the client. It checks pre-defined rules in order to detect database anomalies caused by successful attacks. Users are then granted access privileges to only the system containing data, which they have been authorized via a JESS Rule Execution Engine. If the JESS Inference engine fires the rule that gets reflected in the database dynamically. This is happened dynamically when the client is still in the transaction.
- **Knowledge Manager:** This mobile agent gets the appropriate profile for the specific user, which is stored locally on the XML Audit Profile Server, and then it compares the user's historical profile with the information sent by the Host Monitor. The knowledge manager makes comparison constantly. If the current behavior profile does not match with the normal behavior pattern defined by the user historical profile, then the Knowledge Manager provides the following information to the Actioner: user identifier, session identifier, host identifier & IP address and the invalid privilege with the corresponding unauthorized object attempting to be accessed.

- **Actioner:** Actioner's(Static Agent) role is to take necessary actions when an intrusion is detected. It also uses the prediction data for a user, to take preemptive actions on the user behavior. When an attack is detected exactly, the Actioner does one of the following operations to terminate the attack: 1. Reject the user's attempt with the warning message 2. Terminate the specific operation on the particular database object 3. Lock the user's keyboard and prevent the user from consuming any further data resources 4. Reports an intrusion detected on a host to the system administrator via the Information Agent. In Actioner, the action element is put in the SOAP component. Then the SOAP header and SOAP envelope are constructed over it by putting the endpoint of where the data has to be sent. The output of this component is SOAP message, which is then appended to the action part of the rule. JAXM(Java API for XML Messaging) is a package that is used to send the SOAP message across different clients. The result should be presented in the user readable/understandable form. For example, XML documents can be presented as HTML pages with XSLT style sheets.

- **Profile Reader:** This mobile agent is responsible for fetching the on-line data from the auditing monitor and the predicted values from the temporal forecasting engine. Then it sends this information to the Information agent.

- **Rule Generator:** This static agent is assigned the task of rule creation based on the request from the client and it is responsible for the submission of the rules to the XML Server.

- **Intelligent JESS Inference Engine:** When a transaction like insertion of element, deletion of element or updating of element happens at the XML file, the ETCA rule given in XML format is mapped to JESS authorization rule, which is predefined by database administrator. The events that occur are also converted to JESS facts. The JESS Inference engine constantly monitors the JESS rule and on the occurrence of a new fact, executes the JESS rule producing new JESS facts as the result. These JESS facts must later be converted into suitable action and it's transmitted to the client. It checks pre-defined rules in order to detect database anomalies caused by successful attacks. Users are then granted access privileges to only the system containing data which they have been authorized via a JESS Rule Execution Engine. If the JESS Inference engine fires the rule that gets reflected in the database dynamically. This is happened dynamically when the client is still in the transaction.

- **Client Interface:** It is just an application dependent program that communicates with the Client to get the client's request and also provides the response to the client. In case of Stationary systems, the system needs to communicate via a network using standard HTTP format. In order to support mobile users, this component converts the XML data into WML(Wireless Markup Language) [11] data and a WAP(Wireless Application Protocol) [11] is used to transfer this WML data to the mobile devices.

5   Experimental Results

5.1   Model Development and Analysis of Data

This study obtains a collection of audit data for normal transactions from a major corporate bank, Chennai, India. The database objects considered are (1) Customer Deposit Accounts(CDAcc) and (2) Customer Loan Accounts(CLAcc) as well as (3) Ledger Reports related to each transactions on the Customer Accounts(LRep). The database objects are used by Tellers(Tlr), Customer Service Reps(CSR) and Loan Officers(LO) to perform various transactions. It is also used by Accountants(Acc), Accounting Managers(AccMr) and Internal Auditors(IntAud) to post, generate and verify accounting data. Branch Manager(BrM) has the ability to perform any of the functions of other roles in times of emergency and to view all transactions, account statuses and validation flags. Normal transactions are generated by simulating activities observed in a corporate bank information system in an usual operation condition. A number of intrusions are also simulated in our laboratory, including password guessing, to gain the root privilege, attempts to gain an unauthorized remote access, an overwhelming number of service requests can be sent to an information system over a short period of time to deplete the computational resource in the server and thus deny the server's ability to respond to user's service requests, etc., to create the audit data of intrusive activities [3].

5.2   Training and Testing Data

We obtain 8 weeks of the December 2003 & January 2004 audit dataset from the corporate bank in our study [4]. We use the first part of the audit data for normal activities as our training dataset, and use the remaining audit data for normal activities and attack activities as our testing dataset. The first half of the audit data, consisting of 16,413 audit transactions lasting four weeks, is used as the training data. In the testing dataset, the average session length is comparatively smaller in week-2 and week-3 than that in week-1 and week-4. In terms of sessions, almost one-fifth of the sessions in week-2 and one-fifteenth of the sessions in week-3 are intrusion sessions. Week-1 contains mostly normal sessions, week-4 also does not have too many intrusion sessions. Week-1 and week-2 contain 12 and 16 normal sessions, week-2 and week-3 contain 6 and 7 intrusion sessions. Hence, the testing data contains a total of 28,574 audit transactions with 3 segments of data in the sequence: 1. 7,320 normal events(the first half of the 14,640 normal events) 2. 13,934 intrusive events 3. 7,320 normal events (the second half of the 14,640 normal events).

5.3   Selection of NN Architecture

The topology of a network architecture is very crucial to its performance but there is no easy way to determine the optimum number of hidden layers and neurons without training several networks. For example, if there are too many neurons then it may result in a condition called "over-fitting" which means that the network will perform well on the training set but it won't generalize properly. In this case the network begins to learn the noise as well, whereas if there are relatively too few neurons then it may result in a condition termed as "under-fitting" that results in high training and generalization error [3]. In order to check the most appropriate parameters for prediction, we carried out a sweeping in the number of neurons of the hidden layer as an initial test. The learning rate value of 0.1 and the momentum factor value around 0.5 would produce the fastest learning for this problem. In this test, the weights were initialized for each of the networks with random values within the range [-0.5,0.5] and the number of iterations that were carried out was 15,000. Bounding the weights can help prevent the network from becoming saturated. The weights and unit outputs were being turned off hard during the early stages of the learning, and they were getting stuck in the zero state. We altered the sigmoid-prime function so that it does not go to zero for any output value. We simply added a constant 0.1 to the sigmoid prime value before using it to scale the error. This modification made a dramatic difference, cutting the learning time almost in half. In this way, various network architectures with different number of hidden layers and neurons in each layer was investigated. The network architectures used for this study are described in Table. 1.

Table 1. Ensemble members with different network architectures. HL:Number of Hidden Layer; HL 1:Number of Nodes, Activation function - Hidden Layer(1); HL 2: Number of Nodes, Activation function - Hidden Layer(2); TT: Training time

Model	HL	HL 1	HL 2	TT
I	1	10	-	748
II	1	20	-	1561
III	1	10,tanh	-	821
IV	2	12,tanh	10,tanh	1761
V	2	10,gaussian	12,gaussian	1899

It can be observed that the successive increase in the number of neurons in the hidden layer hardly diminishes the training error, and also that the validation error increases considerably. The training time it is approximately lineal and depends on the number of neurons of the hidden layer.

5.4 Experimental Topology

Fig. 2 shows a piece of the actual and predicted behavior curve for user Customer_Service_Reps(CSR), using Quickprop as a forecasting model. Fig. 2 shows the actual values for real observations and the associated single-step forecasts. The X-axis specifies the real observations with our forecasting results and the Y-axis defines the usage of an object for an hour. For example, 0.2 means that the user has used that particular object for 12 minutes, in a specific hour of the

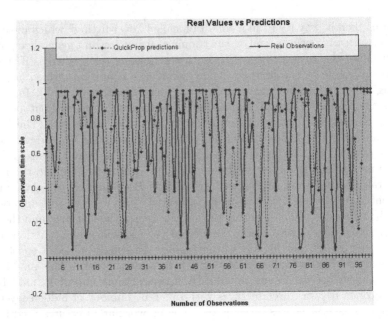

Fig. 2. Real values versus predicted values of the user

object usage. We present a comparative graph(Fig. 2) of the data resource consumption by CSR for 100 validation patterns, which gives the real values versus the predicted values.

5.5   Validating the Training

In this test we tried to analyze the effect of the number of iterations of the learning algorithm. A Quickprop neural network ensemble was used for this test.

Fig. 3 shows the learning epoch as well as the training and test errors. In Fig. 3 one can see the change of the MAPE error over time for the training of the network using 15,000 epochs. What is noticeable is the sharp decrease in both the errors for the first 1,200 epochs. Thereafter the errors decrease at a slower rate. We observed that the number of iterations has less influence on the obtained error than the number of neurons in the hidden layer. Since although the training error could be appreciably diminished when increasing the number of iterations, the same does not happen in the validation phase, in which the error remains more stable throughout the experiment.

5.6   Rule Processing Subsystem

A rule processing subsystem diagram for the two important process rule generation and transmission, rule triggering and action delivery are shown in Fig. 4 and Fig. 5 respectively.

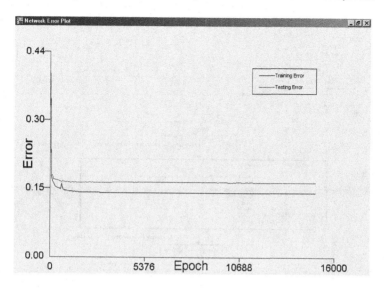

Fig. 3. Comparison of the errors associated with the Quickprop Neural Network Ensemble

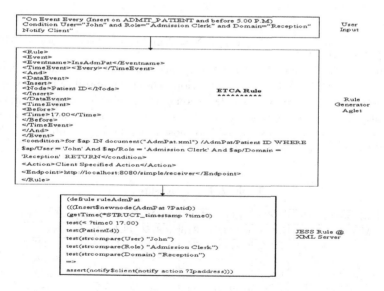

Fig. 4. Rule Generation

5.7   Performance Analysis Results and Discussion

In order to measure the error made by the neural network model, a widely accepted quantitative measure, such as Mean Absolute Percentage Error(MAPE) has been used. The performance analysis of the Quickprop forecaster was measured in terms of Mean Absolute Percentage Error (MAPE)=

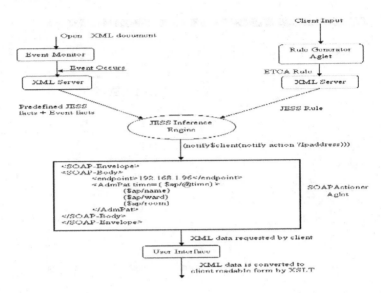

Fig. 5. Rule Triggering and Action Delivery

$$\frac{1}{N} \sum_{i=1}^{N} |\frac{Forecast_i - Target_i}{Target_i}|,$$ where N = Number of observations. MAPE will be employed in this paper as the performance criterion, for it's easy understanding and simple mathematical computation. The mean absolute percentage error determines the mean percentage deviation of the predicted outputs from the target outputs. This absolute deviation places greater emphasis on errors occurring with small target values as opposed to those of larger target values. The MAPE for all the above Quickprop network architectures is summarized in Table 2.

Table 2. Error Measurement

Models	Tlr	CSR	LO	Acc	AccMr	IntAud	Avg. of MAPE(%)
Model I	5.1448	7.6308	0.1392	7.8316	18.8750	48.4673	14.6814
Model II	1.9747	3.9965	0.0713	4.1780	9.1140	26.5326	7.64452
Model III	3.5841	5.0164	0.0912	5.5522	14.4856	37.2338	10.9939
Model IV	2.0667	4.9716	0.0873	5.2297	10.5408	30.3359	8.8720
Model V	4.2786	5.7335	0.1208	6.0443	15.5016	45.7680	12.9078

The generalized ensemble method(GEM) assigned weights to the individual models depending upon their relative performance which resulted in the reduction of the MAPE as shown in Table 2. If the MAPE between two models had been low, then one could use an ensemble of the two models to obtain an output that adequately represents the entire variability of the true data. In this study, the least MAPE for models II and IV. So when these two models were consid-

Table 3. Error Measurement

Model	Tlr	CSR	LO	Acc	AccMr	IntAud	Avg. of MAPE(%)
GEM(II,IV)	1.2812	2.59296	0.04626	2.71072	5.91323	17.2145	4.95982

ered as the ensemble members, and assigned the appropriate weights according to Equation. 2; it decreased the MAPE values(Table. 3). A slight degradation in the validation error for the proposed network can be observed.

The examination on the performance of the Quickprop ensemble technique with different combination of data sets leads to following findings:

- Users Tlr & CSR present a more uniform behavior. Because of this, all models achieve better performance with users Tlr & CSR as shown in Table. 2. This is specially noticeable for prediction models, because user CSR is much less affected by hour off's.
- With respect to the other users, it can be seen that prediction models achieve better accuracy for user LO. Though, he has a large amount of day off's and hour off's, the false alarm rate achieved by all prediction models is minimal due to the strong presence of weekly periodicity in that user.
- User Acc is an intermediate case. He has daily periodicity rated as high, but has large amount of day off's. This fact strongly penalizes the prediction models, that cannot achieve accuracy satisfactorily.
- Finally, it is worth adding that the error achieved by all prediction models is larger for AccMr, IntAud & BrM, because the mixed periodicities present in that users, but most important, they have a large amount of days off, that poses a difficulty for the models to find the relations between input and output variables. In fact, the least accurate predictions are obtained for this users, as shown in Table. 2.

6   Conclusions and Future Works

In this paper, an Intelligent Multi-Agent based distributed database intrusion prevention system has been presented to learn previously observed user behavior in order to prevent future intrusions in database systems. Quickprop NN is investigated as a tool to predict database intrusions and several NN architectures were explored by varying the parameters such as the number of neurons, number of hidden layers and activation functions. The ensemble method gave improved results i.e., decreased MAPE as compared to any individual NN model. The TARML has been designed in misuse prevention system and it can suit for any kind of real domain and any platform. For future expansion fuzzy rules can be extended with JESS, so that the intrusion prevention system can be made much more effective. Thus, the system is developed to demonstrate the use of intelligent agents for auditing the transactions within the organization, detecting potential risks, and avoiding uncontrollable transactions. Hence for the future we'll incorporate other NN models and ensemble techniques further to improve the predictability of database intrusion and reduce the rate of false negative alarms.

References

1. Chung, C.Y., Gertz, M., Levitt, K.: Misuse detection in database systems through user profiling. In Web Proceedings of the 2nd International Workshop on the Recent Advances in Intrusion Detection(RAID). (1999) 278.
2. Pikoulas, J., Buchanan, W.J., Manion, M., Triantafyllopoulos, K.: An intelligent agent intrusion system. In Proceedings of the 9th IEEE International Conference and Workshop on the Engineering of Computer Based Systems - ECBS, IEEE Comput. Soc., Luden, Sweden. (2002) 94–102.
3. Ramasubramanian, P., Kannan, A.: Quickprop Neural Network Short-Term Forecasting Framework for a Database Intrusion Prediction System. In Proceedings of the Seventh International Conference on Artificial Intelligence and Soft Computing (ICAISC 2004) June 7-11, 2004 at Zakopane, Poland, Lecture Notes in Computer Science, Vol. 3070, Springer-Verlag ISBN: 3-540-22123-9. (2004) 847–852.
4. Ramasubramanian, P., Kannan, A.: Multivariate Statistical Short-Term Hybrid Prediction Modeling for Database Anomaly Intrusion Prediction System. In Proceedings of the Second International Conference on Applied Cryptography and Network Security (ACNS 2004) June 8-11, 2004 at Yellow Mountain, China, Lecture Notes in Computer Science, Vol.3089, Springer-Verlag ISBN: 3-540-22217-0. (2004)
5. Ramasubramanian, P., Kannan, A.: An Active Rule Based Approach to Database Security in E-Commerce Systems using Temporal Constraints. In Proceedings of IEEE Tencon 2003, October 14-17, 2003 at Bangalore, India. 1148–1152.
6. Sin Yeung Lee, Wai Lup Low and Pei Yuen Wong.: Learning Fingerprints For A Database Intrusion Detection System. In Proceedings of the 7th European Symposium on Research in Computer Security, Zurich, Switzerland. (2002) 264–280.
7. Simple Object Access Protocol (SOAP) 1.1. Available at URL http://www.w3.org/TR/2000/SOAP (2004)
8. Java Aglet, IBM Tokyo Research Laboratory. Available at URL http://www.trl.ibm.co.jp/aglets (2004)
9. Triantafyllopoulos, K., Pikoulas, J.: Multivariate Bayesian regression applied to the problem of network security. Journal of Forecasting. 21 (2002) 579–594.
10. Java Neural Network Simulator 1.1. Available at URL http://www-ra.informatik.uni-tuebingen.de/downloads/JavaNNS (2004)
11. WAP specifications and WAP gateway. Available at URL http://www.wapforum.org, http://www.wapgateway.org (2004)
12. XML Path Language (XPath) 1.0. Available at URL http://www.w3.org/TR/XPATH (2004)
13. XQuery 1.0: An XML Query Language. Available at URL http://www.w3.org/TR/XQuery (2004)

Energy Efficient Transaction Processing in Mobile Broadcast Environments*

SangKeun Lee

Department of Computer Science and Engineering,
Korea University, Seoul, South Korea
yalphy@korea.ac.kr

Abstract. Broadcasting in wireless mobile computing environments is an effective technique to disseminate information to a massive number of clients equipped with powerful, battery operated devices. To conserve the usage of energy, which is scarce resource, the information to be broadcast must be organized so that the client can selectively tune in at the desired portion of the broadcast. In this paper, the energy efficient behavior of a predeclaration-based transaction processing in mobile broadcast environments is examined. The analytical studies have been performed to evaluate the effectiveness of our method. The analysis has shown that our predeclaration-based transaction processing with selective tuning ability can provide significant performance improvement of battery life, while retaining a low access time, in mobile broadcast environments.

1 Introduction

With the advent of third generation wireless infrastructure and the rapid growth of wireless communication technology such as Bluetooth and IEEE 802.11, mobile computing becomes possible. People with battery powered mobile devices can access various kinds of services at any time any place. However, existing wireless services are limited by the constraints of mobile environments such as narrow bandwidth, frequent disconnections, and limitations of the battery technology. Thus, mechanisms to efficiently transmit information from the server to a massive number of clients have received considerable attention [1], [2], [7].

Wireless broadcasting is an attractive approach for data dissemination in a mobile environment. Disseminating data through a broadcast channel allows simultaneous access by an arbitrary number of mobile users and thus allows efficient usage of scarce bandwidth. Due to this scalability feature, the wireless broadcast channel has been considered an alternative storage medium of the traditional hard disks [1], [7]. Such applications as using palmtops to access airline schedules, stock activities, traffic conditions, and weather information on the road are expected to become increasingly popular. It is noted, however, that

---

* This work was done as a part of Information & Communication Fundamental Technology Research Program, supported by Ministry of Information & Communication in Republic of Korea.

A. Benczúr, J. Demetrovics, G. Gottlob (Eds.): ADBIS 2004, LNCS 3255, pp. 409–422, 2004.
© Springer-Verlag Berlin Heidelberg 2004

several mobile computers, such as desktops and palmtops, use batteries of limited lifetime for their operations and are not directly connected to any power source. As a result, energy efficiency is a very important issue to resolve before we can anticipate an even wider acceptability for mobile computers [6], [11], [13].

Among others, one viable approach to energy efficiency is to use indexed data organization to broadcast data over wireless channels to mobile clients. Without any auxiliary information on the broadcast channel, a client may have to access all objects in a broadcast cycle in order to retrieve the desired data. This requires the client to listen to the broadcast channel all the time, which is power inefficient. *Air indexing* techniques address this issue by pre-computing some index information and interleaving it with the data on the broadcast channel, and many studies appear in the literature [4], [5], [7], [14]. By first accessing the broadcast index, the mobile client is able to predict the arrival time of the desired data. Thus, it can stay in the power saving mode most of the time, and tune into the broadcast channel only when the requested data arrives. The drawback of this solution is that broadcast cycles are lengthened due to additional index information. As such, there is a trade-off between access time and tuning time. In mobile broadcast environments, the following two parameters are of concern:

- *Access Time*: the period of time elapsed from the moment a mobile client issues a query to the moment when the requested data items are received by the client.
- *Tuning Time*: the period of time spent by a mobile client staying active in order to retrieve the requested data items.

While access time measures the overhead of an index structure and the efficiency of data and index organization on the broadcast channel, tuning time is frequently used to estimate the power consumption by a mobile client since sending/receiving data is power dominant in a mobile environment [8].

In this paper, we consider the issue of energy efficient transaction processing, where *multiple* data items are involved, in mobile broadcast environments. To the best of our knowledge, power conservation in the context of transaction processing has not been addressed before. In our previous work [9] a predeclaration-based query optimization was explored for efficient (in terms of access time) processing of wireless read-only transactions in mobile broadcast environments. There, clients are just tuning in broadcast channel and waiting for the data of interests. This paper extends our previous work to analyze the energy efficient behavior of predeclaration-based transaction processing in various types of indexed data organizations.

The remainder of this paper is organized as follows. Section 2 describes the background of our system model and indexed data organizations. Section 3 presents the proposed access method in the context of predeclaration-based transaction processing. Section 4 develops analytical models to examine the effectiveness of the proposed scheme, and Section 5 reports the access and tuning time of our transaction processing scheme in various indexed data organizations. The conclusion of the paper is in Section 6.

2   Preliminaries

2.1   Basics of Wireless Broadcasting

We here briefly describe the model of a mobile broadcast system, which is similar to the models in [1], [7]. The system consists of a data server and a number of mobile clients connected to the server through a low bandwidth wireless network. A server maintains the consistency of a database and reflects refreshment by update transactions being issued only on the server side. The correctness criterion in transaction processing adopted in this paper is *serializability* [3], which has been proven to be *not* expensive to achieve in the work [9]. The server broadcasts data items in the database periodically to a number of clients, on a communication channel which is assumed to have broadcasting capability. Clients will only receive the broadcast data and fetch individual items (identified by a key) from the broadcast channel. However, updates to the items are reflected only between successive broadcasts. Hence, the content of the current version of the broadcast is completely determined before the start of broadcast of that version.

In our model, filtering is by simple pattern matching of the primary key. Clients will remain in doze mode most of the time and tune in periodically to the broadcast channel, in order to download the required data. Selective tuning will require that the server, in addition to broadcasting the data, also broadcast index information that indicates the point of time in the broadcast channel when a particular data item is broadcast. The broadcast channel is the source of *all* information to the client including data as well as index.

Each version of the database items along with the associated index information will constitute a *bcast*, which will be organized as a sequence of *buckets*. A bucket is the smallest logical unit of a broadcast, and is a multiple of the size a packet. All buckets are of the same size. Both access time and tuning time will be measured in terms of number of data items with the assumption that, without loss of generality, the size of a data item is identical to the size of a bucket. Pointers to specific buckets within the bcast will be provided by specifying an *offset* from the bucket which holds pointer, to the bucket to which the pointer points to. The actual time of broadcast for such a bucket (from the current bucket) is the product of $(offset - 1)$ and the time necessary to broadcast a bucket.

It is assumed that each data item in the database appears once during one broadcast cycle, i.e. *uniform broadcast* [1]. We assume that the content of the broadcast at each cycle is guaranteed to be consistent. That is, the values of data items that are broadcast during each cycle correspond to the state of the database at the beginning of the cycle, i.e. the values produced by all transactions that have been committed by the beginning of the cycle.

2.2   Data Organization on the Broadcast Channel

In general, data organization techniques which seek optimum in two dimensional space of access and tuning time are of importance. Being interleaved with data, the index will provide a sequence of pointers which eventually lead to the required

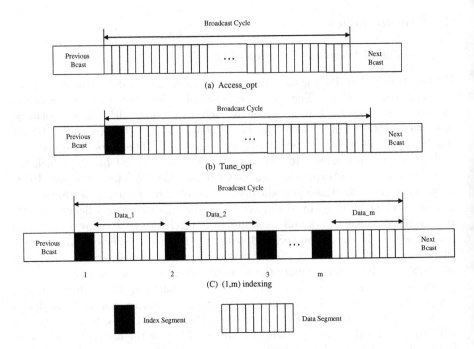

Fig. 1. Data and Index Organization

data. To interleave data and index on the wireless broadcast channel, *Access_opt*, *Tune_opt*, and $(1, m)$ *indexing* techniques [7] are considered in this paper, which are illustrated in Figure 1.

- *Access_opt*: This technique provides the best access time with a very large tuning time with respect to a single item. The best access time is obtained when no index is broadcast along with data items. The size of the entire broadcast is minimal in this way. Clients simply tune into the broadcast channel and filter all the data till the required data item is downloaded.
- *Tune_opt*: This technique provides the best tuning time with a large access time with respect to a single item. The server broadcasts the index at the beginning of each bcast. The client which needs the item with primary key K, tunes into the broadcast channel at the beginning of the next bcast to get the index. It then follows the index pointers to the item with the required primary key. This method has got the worst access time because, clients have to wait till the beginning of the next broadcast even if the required data is just in front of them.
- $(1, m)$ *indexing*: In this method, the index is broadcast m times during a single broadcast cycle. The whole index is broadcast preceding every $\frac{1}{m}$ fraction of the broadcast cycle. In order to reduce the tuning time, each index segment (i.e. the set of contiguous index buckets) and each data segment (i.e. the set of data buckets broadcast between successive index segments) contain a pointer pointing to the root of the next index.

In case of *Tune_opt* and $(1, m)$ *indexing*, selective tuning is accomplished by multiplexing an index with the data items in the broadcast. The clients are only required to operate in active mode when probing for the address of the index, traversing the index and downloading the required data, while spending the waiting time in doze mode. Each entry of the index contains the pair $(id, offset)$. Data bucket also has an offset that points to the next index.

3   Energy Efficient Predeclaration-Based Transaction Processing

In previous work [9], [10] we proposed three predeclaration-based transaction processing schemes in mobile broadcast environments, namely P (Predeclaration), PA (Predeclaration with Autoprefetching), and PA^2 (PA / Asynchronous). The analysis-based and simulation-based studies showed that they are able to greatly improve the access time of read-only transaction processing. The central idea was to deploy the predeclaration technique in order to minimize the number of different broadcast cycles from which transactions retrieve data.

In this work, method P is adopted as our basic transaction processing approach, and is extended to integrate selective tuning ability since, methods PA and PA^2 work with client caching technique which is orthogonal to the issue in the paper. Prior to proceeding, the usefulness of predeclaration-based transaction processing is explained briefly in the following to help understand the basic behavior of predeclaration-based transaction processing.

Predeclaration and its Usufulness: The uniform broadcast in *Access_opt* organization is illustrated in Figure 2, where the server broadcasts a set of data items $d0$ to $d6$ in one broadcast channel. Suppose that a client transaction program starts its execution: IF $(d2 \leq 3)$ THEN read($d0$) ELSE read($d1$). To show that the order in which a transaction reads data affects the access time of the transaction, consider the traditional client transaction processing in Figure 2-(a). Since both $d0$ and $d1$ precede $d2$ in the bcast with respect to the client and access to data is strictly sequential, the transaction has to read $d2$ first and wait to read the value of $d0$ or $d1$. Thus, the access time of the transaction is 11 in case $d2$ and $d0$ are accessed, or 12 in case $d2$ and $d1$ are accessed. If, however, all data items that will be accessed *potentially* by the transaction, i.e. $\{d0, d1, d2\}$, are predeclared in advance, a client can hold all necessary data items with a reduced response time of 6, which is illustrated in Figure 2-(b). Thus the use of predeclaration allows the necessary items to be retrieved in the order they are broadcast, rather than in the order the requests are issued.

Method P has been presented with *Access_opt* data organization in [9]. That is, without any form of index, the client has to tune to the channel all the time during the whole process of filtering. For realistic applications, however, this may be unacceptable as it requires the client to be active for a long time, thereby consuming scarce battery resource. In the paper, we would rather

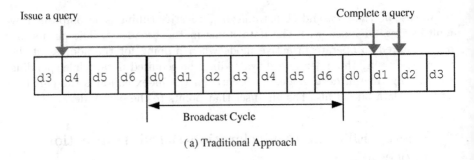

(a) Traditional Approach

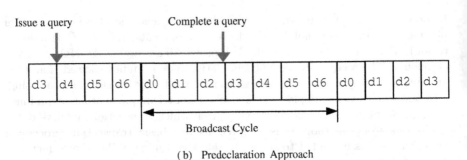

(b) Predeclaration Approach

Fig. 2. Usefulness of Predeclaration-based Transaction Processing

provide a selective tuning ability for P method, enabling the client to become active only when data of interest is being broadcast, in the context of *Tune_opt* and $(1, m)$ *indexing*. In general, the access protocol for *Tune_opt* and $(1, m)$ *indexing* involves the following steps:

- Initial probe: The client tunes into the broadcast channel and determines when the next nearest index will be broadcast. This is done by reading *offset* to determine the address of the next nearest index segment. It then tunes into the power saving mode until the next index arrives.
- Index search: The client searches the index. It follows a sequence of pointers (i.e. selectively tunes into the broadcast index) to locate the data of interest and find out when to tune into the broadcast channel to get the desired data. It waits for the arrival of the data in the power saving mode.
- Data retrieval: The client tunes into the channel when the desired data arrives and downloads the data.

3.1   Access Protocol for Multiple Data Items

We first need to elaborate the access protocol for searching and retrieving multiple data items effectively. In predeclaration-based transaction processing, all data items are predeclared prior to the actual processing and should be retrieved in the order they appear from the broadcast channel, the client is required to

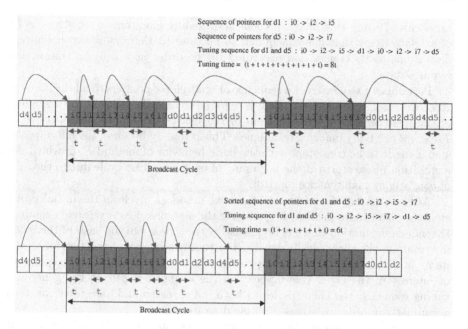

Fig. 3. Access Protocol for Multiple Data Items in *Tune_opt*

predict the arrival time of items by exploiting index information shown in the air. This can be done as follows: since the index provides a sequence of pointers which eventually lead to the single required item, with the index information the client is able to *sort* all the pointers, which constitute the index information for multiple data items of interest, in the order they appear on the channel. This would result in a long sequence of *multiplexed* pointers. This idea is illustrated at the bottom of Figure 3, where a client transaction requires two data items, $d1$ and $d5$, in the order with the current position $d4$. It is observed that some portion of index information, i.e. $i0$ and $i2$ in this specific example, needs to be visited only once to retrieve the two data items. This illustrates the reduction of tuning time which may be possible in our predeclaration-based transaction processing, compared to a straightforward approach where individual, separate initial probe and index search process are performed for each data item.

3.2 Method P with Selective Tuning

Now, we describe the behavior of method P to achieve improvement of tuning time, while retaining a low access time, with $Tune\_opt$ or $(1, m)$ *indexing* techniques in mind. Let us define the predeclared readset of a transaction T, denoted by $Pre\_RS(T)$, to be a set of data items that T reads *potentially*. Each client processes T in three phases: (1)*Preparation phase:* it gets $Pre\_RS(T)$ and constructs a sequence of *multiplexed* pointers to all the items in $Pre\_RS(T)$, (2)*Acquisition phase:* it acquires data items in $Pre\_RS(T)$ from the periodic broadcast. During this phase, a client additionally maintains a set $Acquire(T)$ of all data items that it has acquired so far, and (3)*Delivery phase:* it delivers data items to its transaction according to the order in which the transaction requires data.

Particularly, to construct a sequence of *multiplexed* pointers to all the items in $Pre\_RS(T)$, in this paper the client is required to read the index at the beginning of the next broadcast cycle, instead of the next nearest index, irrespective of $Tune\_opt$ or $(1, m)$ *indexing* techniques. This is mainly because, the initial probe step is made to be consistent with the basic behavior of method P, in which the acquisition phase starts at the beginning of next broadcast cycle due to the ease of consistency maintenance [9], [10].

After obtaining the address of the next broadcast cycle in the initial probe step, the client tunes in at the beginning of the next broadcast cycle and examines the index information which is broadcast by the server. On the basis of the index information, the client locally constructs a tuning sequence of pointers for all the items in $Pre\_RS(T)$. This tuning sequence is constructed by sorting pointers of interest in the order they appear on the channel. Based on the generated tuning sequence, the client performs both index search and data retrieval steps accordingly in order to access multiple data items.

With respect to consistency issue, since the content of the broadcast at each cycle is guaranteed to be consistent, the execution of each read-only transaction is clearly serializable if a client can fetch all data items within a single broadcast cycle. Now that all data items for its transaction are already identified and a sequence of *multiplexed* pointers to the data items is constructed, the client is able to complete the acquisition phase within a single broadcast cycle.

More specifically, a client processes its transaction T_i as follows:

1. On receiving $Begin(T_i)$ {
    get $Pre\_RS(T_i)$ by using preprocessor;
    $Acquire(T_i) = \emptyset$;
    tune into the current bucket on the broadcast channel;
    read the $offset$ to determine the address of the next broadcast cycle;
    go into *doze mode* and tune in at the beginning of the next broadcast cycle;
    from the index segment construct a sequence of *multiplexed* pointers
        by sorting a sequence of pointers to individual items in $Pre\_RS(T_i)$;
}
2. While $(Pre\_RS(T_i) \neq Acquire(T_i))$ {
    for d_j in $Pre\_RS(T_i)$ {
        according to the sequence of *multiplexed* pointers tune in when d_j is
            broadcast and download d_j;
        put d_j into local storage;
        $Acquire(T_i) \Leftarrow d_j$;
    }
}
3. Deliver data items to T_i according to the order in which T_i requires,
    and then commit T_i.

Table 1. Symbols and Their Meaning

Symbol	Meaning
D	num. of items in the database
I	the size of index in terms of buckets (i.e. items) in the index tree
n	num. of (primary-key plus pointer)s a bucket can hold
k	num. of levels in the index tree
m	num. of times the index is broadcast during a broadcast cycle
$access_s$	avg. access time for accessing a single item
$access_t$	avg. access time for accessing multiple items in a given transaction
$tune_s$	avg. tuning time for accessing a single item
$tune_t$	avg. tuning time for accessing multiple items in a given transaction
o_p	num. of items appearing on a transaction program

Theorem 1. *Method P generates serializable execution of read-only transactions if the server broadcasts only serializable data values in each broadcast cycle.*

Proof. It is straightforward from the fact that the data set read by each transaction is a subset of a single broadcast.

□

4   Analysis

In this section, we develop analytical models to examine average access time and tuning time of predeclaration-based transaction processing. We will derive the basic equation that describes the expected average access time and tuning time, which is measured in number of data items broadcast by the server. In the following analysis, we preclude the possibility of client's disconnections for the sake of simplicity. Note that, in wireless data broadcast, the performance of a single client read-only transaction for a given broadcast program is independent of the presence of other clients transactions. As a result, we will analyze the environment by considering only a single client. Furthermore, the performance of method P is totally *immune* to the update rate of data items in the database, since method P completes its acquisition phase within a single broadcast cycle without local caching technique. The symbols and their meaning used throughout the analysis are summarized in Table 1.

4.1   *Access_opt*

This organization provides the best access time with a very large tuning time.

Access Time : For a database of size D items (or buckets), $access_s$ will, on an average, be half the time between successive broadcasts of the data items, $access_s = \frac{D}{2}$. In method P, a transaction processing is divided into 3 phases: preparation, acquisition and delivery phase. If the time required by a client for each of three phases is expressed as PT, AT and DT respectively, the access time can be formulated by,

$$access_t = PT + AT + DT \tag{1}$$

PT will on average be half of one broadcast cycle and DT is trivial, thus Expression (1) can be reduced to

$$access_t = \frac{D}{2} + AT \tag{2}$$

AT involves retrieving all the items in the predeclared readset in the order they appear on broadcast channel. The retrieval time for the first item is $access_s$ itself. The retrieval time for the second item is half of the remaining bcast size, and the retrieval time for the next item is in turn half of the remaining bcast size, and so on. Thus, the expected AT for a transaction with o_p predeclared items is,

$$AT = \sum_{i=1}^{o_p} (\frac{1}{2})^i D \tag{3}$$

The expected average access time of method P is therefore computed as,

$$access_t = \frac{1}{2}D + \sum_{i=1}^{o_p} (\frac{1}{2})^i D \tag{4}$$

Tuning Time : The average tuning time is equal to access time. This is because, the client has to be in active mode throughout the period of access.

4.2   Tune_opt

This organization provides the best tuning time with a large access time with respect to a single item. The server broadcasts the index at the beginning of each bcast.

Access Time : *Probe wait*, i.e. the average duration for getting to the next index information, is $\frac{(D+I)}{2}$, which corresponds to PT in method P. With the similar reasoning to AT in *Access_opt*, *bcast wait*, i.e. the average duration from the point the index information relevant to the required transaction data items is encountered, to the point when the required items are downloaded, is $\sum_{i=1}^{o_p}(\frac{1}{2})^i(D+I)$, which again corresponds to AT in method P. Since the access time is the sum of *probe wait* (i.e. PT) and *bcast wait* (i.e. AT),

$$access_t = \frac{(D+I)}{2} + \sum_{i=1}^{o_p} (\frac{1}{2})^i (D+I) \tag{5}$$

Tuning Time : Average tuning time for accessing a single item, $tune_s$, is $k+1$, where k is the number of levels in the multi-leveled index tree, and 1 for the final probe to download the item. When the index tree is fully balanced, $k = \lceil \log_n(D) \rceil$ and $I = 1 + n + n^2 + \cdots + n^{k-1}$.

In a one-at-a-time access protocol fashion, average tuning time for accessing multiple items in a given transaction, $tune_t$, is $o_p(k+1)$. However, in our method, multiple data items are retrieved with the help of a sequence of *multiplexed* pointers. Therefore, in method P, $tune_t$, is $o_p(k+1)$ minus *num. of shared index buckets re-visits throughout the whole levels*. For example, the root level in the index tree needs to be visited only once for multiple items. Since the expected number of shared index buckets re-visits at level i is computed as $max(0, (o_p - (num.\ of\ index\ buckets\ at\ level\ i)))$, the expected total number of shared index buckets re-visits at whole levels are $\sum_{i=0}^{k-1} max(0, (o_p - n^i))$.

With the reasoning, the tuning time of method P is

$$tune_t = o_p(k+1) - \sum_{i=0}^{k-1} max(0, (o_p - n^i)) \tag{6}$$

4.3 $(1, m)$ *indexing*

In this organization, the index information is broadcast m times during the broadcast of the database.

Access Time : In general, the *probe wait* is $\frac{1}{2}(I + \frac{D}{m})$ when the client tunes in at the broadcast of the next nearest index segment. In method P, however, the client tunes in at the beginning of next broadcast cycle, and hence, the *probe wait* is $\frac{1}{2}(mI + D)$. With the similar reasoning to *Tune_opt*, the *bcast wait* is $\sum_{i=1}^{o_p}(\frac{1}{2})^i(mI + D)$. Since the access time is the sum of *probe wait* and *bcast wait*,

$$access_t = \frac{1}{2}(mI + D) + \sum_{i=1}^{o_p}(\frac{1}{2})^i(mI + D) \tag{7}$$

Tuning Time : The average tuning time is equal to that in *Tune_opt*. This is because, the client follows the same access protocol throughout the period of access.

5   Analytical Results and Practical Implications

In the following, we show some analytical results from scenarios [7]. Since we have reported in [9] the much better access time of method P than other transaction processing techniques such as *invalidation-based* or *multiversion-based* techniques [12] in pure-push broadcast environments, we concentrate on good power conservation, i.e. a low tuning time, while retaining a low access time in this paper.

Table 2. Access and Tuning Time Result

Symbol	Simple	Scenario 1	Scenario 2	Scenario 3
D	243	1000	10000	100000
I	121	111	1111	11111
n	3	10	10	10
k	5	3	4	5
m	2	3	3	3
o_p	3	6	6	6
$access_t$ in Access_opt	335	1485	14850	148500
$tune_t$ in Access_opt	335	1485	14850	148500
$access_t$ in Tune_opt	501	1650	16493	164931
$tune_t$ in Tune_opt	16	19	25	31
$access_t$ in (1,m)	667	1979	19792	197917
$tune_t$ in (1,m)	16	19	25	31

5.1   Some Scenarios and Results

Table 2 illustrates the access and tuning time required by three indexing techniques for various parameter settings, with the emphasis on Scenario 1 to 3 for $n = 10$. The second column, a simple scenario, is described to exemplify different variants of index distribution in a database consisting of 243 data buckets with $n = 3$. The bottom six rows denote the access and tuning time in *Access_opt*, *Tune_opt*, $(1, m)$ *indexing* respectively. As the table illustrates the tuning time in *Tune_opt*, $(1, m)$ *indexing* is the same. The tuning time in *Access_opt* is very large and very much higher than the other two. Both *Tune_opt* and $(1, m)$ *indexing* always perform better than *Access_opt* in terms of tuning time. The most interesting observation is that, P method with selective tuning ability shows the most desirable performance behavior in terms of access time and tuning time in *Tune_opt* indexing. This will be further explained in the following practical implications.

5.2   Practical Implications

Consider a broadcasting system that is similar to the *quotrex system* [7] where, a stock market information of size 16×10^4 Bytes is being broadcast. The broadcast channel has a bandwidth of 10 Kbps. Let the bucket length be 128 bytes. Thus, there are 1250 buckets of data. Let n, the number of *(primary-key plus pointer)*'s that can fit in a bucket, be 25. The index size is 53 buckets. It takes around 0.1 seconds to broadcast a single bucket and 125 seconds to broadcast the whole database (with no index). Let the clients be equipped with the Hobbit Chip (AT&T). The power consumption of the chip in doze mode is 50 μW and the consumption in active mode is 250 mW.

With *Access_opt*, the access time of transaction with size 6 predeclared items is 1856 buckets, i.e. 185.6 seconds. Tuning time is also 1856 buckets, i.e. the power consumption is 185.6 sec $\times$ 250 mW = 46.400 Joules.

With *Tune_opt*, the access time of transaction with size 6 predeclared items is 1935 buckets, i.e. 193.5 seconds. Tuning time is 15 buckets, i.e. the power consumption is 0.1 sec $\times$ $(15 \times 250 + 1920 \times 50 \times 10^{-3})$ mW = 0.385 Joules.

With $(1, m)$ *indexing*, optimum m can be computed to be 5 according to the equation in [7]. The access time of transaction with size 6 predeclared items is 2249 buckets, i.e. 224.9 seconds. The tuning time is 15 buckets, i.e. the power consumption is 0.1 sec $\times$ $(15 \times 250 + 2234 \times 50 \times 10^{-3})$ mW = 0.386 Joules.

To sum up, in *Tune_opt* case, the energy consumed *per transaction issue* is 120 times smaller than that of *Access_opt*. This is achieved by compromising on the access time which increases by just 4.25%, which is only marginal! Comparing with $(1, m)$ *indexing*, the power consumption is almost the same. However, the access time improves to 86% of the access time in $(1, m)$ *indexing*.

This practical implications are very interesting in that, if we want a low access time and also low power consumption then we can use *Tune_opt* indexing in the context of predeclaration-based transaction processing.

6 Conclusion

Energy efficiency is crucial to mobile computing. We have explored power-saving predeclaration-based transaction processing in mobile broadcast environments. In particular, we investigated an access protocol for multiple data items in *Tune_opt* and $(1, m)$ *indexing* techniques, and integrated it with predeclaration-based transaction processing. The preliminary analytical results demonstrated the advantages of this approach. Interestingly, the optimum solution for tuning time is well-suited to the predeclaration-based transaction processing. In the context of predeclaration-based transaction processing augmented with the proposed access protocol, *Tune_opt* shows better performance behavior than no index data organization and $(1, m)$ *indexing*. This is rather contradictory to the traditional belief that the optimum solution for tuning time is not practical since, it has (unacceptable) very large access time for a single item access.

As a future work, we are investigating the extension of the proposed access protocol for client caching techniques. A client may find data of interest in its local cache and thus needs to access the broadcast channel for a smaller number of times. Effective usage of this feature can provide more performance improvement in terms of power consumption.

References

1. S. Acharya, R. Alonso, M. Franklin, and S. Zdonik. Broadcast disks: Data management for asymmetric communication environments. In *Proceedings of the ACM SIGMOD Conference on Management of Data*, pages 199–210, 1995.
2. D. Barbara and T. Imielinski. Sleepers and workaholics: Caching in mobile environments. In *Proceedings of the ACM SIGMOD Conference on Management of Data*, pages 1–12, 1994.
3. P. A. Bernstein, V. Hadzilacos, and N. Goodman. *Concurrency Control and Recovery in Database Systems*. Addison Wesley, Massachusetts, 1987.

4. M.-S. Chen, P. S. Yu, and K. L. Wu. Optimizing index allocation for sequential data broadcasting in wireless mobile computing. *IEEE Transactions on Knowledge and Data Engineering*, 15(1):161–173, 2003.
5. Q. L. Hu, W.-C. Lee, and D. L. Lee. A hybrid index technique for power efficient data broadcast. *Distribtued and Parallel Databases*, 9(2):151–177, 2001.
6. T. Imielinski and R. Badrinath. Wireless mobile computing: Challenges in data management. *Communications of the ACM*, 37(10):18–28, 1994.
7. T. Imielinski, S. Viswanathan, and B. Badrinath. Data on air: Organization and access. *IEEE Transactions on Knowledge and Data Engineering*, 9(3):353–372, 1997.
8. R. Kravets and P. Krishnan. Power management techniques for mobile communication. In *Proceedings of ACM/IEEE International Conference on Mobile Computing and Networking*, pages 157–168, 1998.
9. S. Lee, C.-S. Hwang, and M. Kitsuregawa. Using predeclaration for efficient read-only transaction processing in wireless data broadcast. *IEEE Transactions on Knowledge and Data Engineering*, 15(6):1579–1583, 2003.
10. S. Lee and S. Kim. Performance evaluation of a predeclaration-based transaction processing in a hybrid data delivery. In *Proceedings of the 5th International Conference on Mobile Data Management*, pages 266–273, 2004.
11. J. R. Lorch and A. J. Smith. Software strategies for portable computer energy management. *IEEE Personal Communications*, 5(3):60–73, 1998.
12. E. Pitoura and P. Chrysanthis. Exploiting versions for handling updates in broadcast disks. In *Proceedings of the 25th International Conference on Very Large Data Bases*, pages 114–125, 1999.
13. S. Sheng, A. Chandrasekaran, and R. W. Broderson. A portable multimedia terminal. *IEEE Communications Magazine*, 30(12):64–75, December 1992.
14. K.-L. Tan and J. X. Yu. Energy efficient filtering of nonuniform broadcast. In *Proceedings of the 16th International Conference on Distributed Computing Systems*, pages 520–527, 1996.

Author Index

Lecture Notes in Computer Science

For information about Vols. 1–3119

please contact your bookseller or Springer